Social Science Research

A Cross Section of Journal Articles for Discussion and Evaluation

Fifth Edition

Turner C. Lomand

Editor

Pyrczak Publishing

P.O. Box 250430 • Glendale, CA 91225

"Pyrczak Publishing" is an imprint of Fred Pyrczak, Publisher, A California Corporation.

This edition was prepared in collaboration with Randall R. Bruce.

Although the editor and publisher have made every effort to ensure the accuracy and completeness of information contained in this book, we assume no responsibility for errors, inaccuracies, omissions, or any inconsistency herein. Any slights of people, places, or organizations are unintentional.

Project Director: Monica Lopez.

Editorial assistance provided by Cheryl Alcorn, Brenda Koplin, Jack Petit, Erica Simmons, and Sharon Young.

Cover design by Robert Kibler and Larry Nichols.

Printed in the United States of America by Malloy, Inc.

ISBN 1-884585-74-4

Contents

Continued ➔

Notes:

Introduction to the Fifth Edition

The research articles in this book will help students learn how to read and evaluate published research. The articles were selected because they are clearly written, employ straightforward research designs, deal with interesting topics, and, as a group, illustrate a variety of methodological techniques.

The articles represent a cross section of social science research. Although sociology, social work, social psychology, and criminal justice are most heavily represented, some works from other related disciplines are also included.

Learning How to Read Research

Social science students, instructors, researchers, and practitioners all read far more research than they conduct. The ability to comprehend research reports is clearly a useful skill, but it is not a skill most individuals acquire naturally. It needs to be learned. Like most learned skills, an individual gets better through instruction and practice. A classroom teacher can provide instruction, but learning to fully comprehend research reports also requires practice. Structured practice is exactly what this collection of articles and the associated questions provide.

Evaluating Research

All the research articles in this collection make a contribution to the advancement of knowledge in their fields. However, none of them are examples of perfect research. Perfect research eludes researchers for three primary reasons.

First, there is no perfect way to sample. Some groups, such as successful criminals, are difficult to locate. Even if they can be located, some of the people a researcher wants to include in a sample are unwilling or unable to participate. In addition, due to time and budgetary limitations, many researchers make do with samples of convenience such as the students in the classes they teach.

Second, there is no perfect way to measure the key variables of interest to social scientists. For example, if a researcher conducts interviews using a tape recorder, he or she can review the material as often as needed to obtain accurate transcripts and reliable interpretations. However, the presence of an audiotape recorder may influence what the respondents are willing to tell the researcher. Using alternatives such as taking notes or relying on the interviewer's memory are likely to lead to an incomplete record. In short, researchers often have to select among imperfect ways to measure the variables of interest.

Finally, interpreting and drawing implications from data involve subjectivity. Trained researchers may have honest differences of opinion on how to do this for a given set of data.

For the reasons stated above, important decisions in the social sciences should be based on the *body of relevant research*. Thus, before generalizing from the results of any given article in this book, students should examine the results of other published research on the same topic.

Reading Statistics

Most of the articles in this book employ relatively simple statistical procedures. There are exceptions, however. It is almost certain that every reader will encounter some statistical techniques with which he or she is not familiar. This happens not just to students but to professionals as well. Unless directed differently by an instructor, in these situations students should focus on the author's *interpretation* of the statistics in the narrative of the report.

The Appendix

For most students, primary instruction in reading research articles comes from a classroom instructor. Appendix A may help in that instruction. It contains an excellent article that explains the purpose of each part of a standard research article: heading, abstract, introduction, method, results, and discussion.

Factual and Discussion Questions

The *Factual Questions* at the end of each article address major points of the article, particularly methodological issues. These questions can be answered directly from the article itself. The lines in each article are numbered, which should help in documenting answers. These questions should help students recognize the types of information in research articles that are substantively important and should be noticed.

The *Questions for Discussion* draw attention to methodological issues on which there may be honest differences of opinion. There are no right or wrong answers to these questions. However, students should be prepared to provide reasons for their answers if they are discussed in class.

Evaluation Criteria

At the end of each article are 13 basic evaluation criteria that require quality ratings. These may also be used as the basis for classroom discussions. Depending upon the objectives for a research methods class, some instructors may require students to apply a more detailed set of criteria when evaluating the articles.

New to the Fifth Edition

Many of the articles from the Fourth Edition have been retained. The new articles that have been added to this edition are Articles 1, 2, 3, 5, 7, 10, 11, 12, 13, 14, 15, 16, 18, 19, 20, 21, 22, 23, 24, 25, 26, 27, 28, 29, 30, 33, 35, 36, 37, 38, 39, 40, 42, and 45.

Acknowledgment

Robert F. Szafran pioneered this reader in the social sciences. In his capacity as editor of the First Edition, he established many structural elements that guided the development of this edition. His contribution is greatly appreciated.

Feedback

I welcome your feedback on this collection and am especially interested in receiving suggestions for improving the next edition of this book. You can write to me care of the publisher using the address on the title page of this book or by e-mailing messages to me via Info@Pyrczak.com.

Turner C. Lomand
Editor

Article 1

A Survey of the Health, Sleep, and Development of Children Adopted from China

MICHAEL A. RETTIG
Washburn University

KELLY McCARTHY-RETTIG
Desoto School District

ABSTRACT. The health, development, and sleeping patterns of 240 children adopted from China were examined using a survey research approach. Eighty percent of the children were 18 months of age or younger when adopted, and 98% of the children were girls. Sixty-two percent of the children were reported to have been developmentally delayed at the time of adoption; of this number, 91% were reported to have had delays in motor development. Of the families, 52% reported that children experienced sleep problems, but only 9% of the total sample experienced significant sleep difficulties. Implications for social workers are also discussed.

From *Health & Social Work, 31*, 201–207. Copyright © 2006 by the National Association of Social Workers. Reprinted with permission.

International adoption is an increasingly popular method for parents seeking to increase the size of their families. For example, Arsonson (2003) reported that there were more than 15,000 international adoptions in 5 the United States in 1998. This was an increase of more than 2,000 from 1997. One of the main sources of international adoption is China. According to the National Adoption Information Clearinghouse (2003), there have been more than 32,000 visas issued for chil- 10 dren being adopted from China since 1995. Given the large number of children coming to this country from China and the general concerns about the psychological and behavioral impact of adoption, it is reasonable to investigate health and developmental outcomes after 15 the adoption.

Information on the postadoptive outcomes of children adopted from China is relevant to social workers, adoption agencies, and other professionals assisting families with international adoption. It is important that 20 these professionals be aware of any potential problems so that families can be prepared for possible child care issues. For example, Shapiro and colleagues (2001) indicated that studies of children of international adoption have shown potential problems with psychological 25 adjustment. These problems may be due to medical or nutritional deprivation, lack of a primary caregiver, or inconsistencies in caregivers. Howe (1997) noted that nearly 25% of adopted children will display some type of behavioral or mental health concern later in life, so it 30 is important to be aware of postadoptive outcomes.

Related Literature

We conducted a search for relevant literature using ERIC and Internet search engines. This search focused on studies relevant to children adopted from China and for reports investigating health, sleep, or developmen- 35 tal problems. Several reports relevant to this investigation were identified.

One potential area of concern regarding international adoptions involves medical concerns. Arsonson (2003), for example, identified and discussed 17 poten- 40 tial medical problems, including malnutrition, rickets, eczema, scabies, lead poisoning, bacterial intestinal infections, tuberculosis, hepatitis B and C, asthma, anemia, and visual or hearing problems. Despite the relatively large number of potential medical problems, 45 Arsonson noted that the children typically have limited long-term medical issues and that these are fairly easily addressed with diagnosis and proper treatment.

Another potential area of concern involves the fact that earlier research has indicated that it is typical for 50 children to present with developmental delays at the time of their adoption (Johnson & Traister, 1999; Miller & Hendrie, 2000; Miller, Kiernan, Mathers, & Klein-Gitelman, 1995). In the Miller and associates study, the mean age of children at arrival was 14 55 months, and they were seen within three months of arrival. These researchers found that approximately 74% of children showed delays in one or more areas of development at the time of their arrival in the United States. Miller and Hendrie assessed the health and de- 60 velopmental status of 452 children in two different groups. Of the 452 children, 98% were girls. They found that 75% of the children had significant developmental delays in at least one area and that the delays were related to length of time children spent in orphan- 65 ages. The longer the time spent in an orphanage, the greater the developmental delays. Delays in gross motor skills were most common (55%), followed by delays in language (43%), socioemotional (28%), and cognitive skills (32%). Miller and Hendrie also found 70 that a number of children had medical problems, including anemia (35%), elevated lead levels (14%), tu-

1

berculosis (3.5%), and hepatitis B surface antibody (22%). Each of these studies pointed to the need for continued long-term follow-up of the children.

75 A study conducted by Tessler and colleagues (1999) looked at intercountry adoption from a sociological perspective and examined the nature of families adopting children as well as some health and developmental outcomes. Children in this study were adopted

80 from China, Korea, Thailand, Peru, and the United States. Of the 361 families, 332 had adopted children from China. Similar to methods used in this study, the Tessler team set up a Web site and e-mail address through which families could complete questionnaires.

85 They received responses from 526 parents in 361 households in 38 states. Tessler and colleagues found that 97% of the children adopted were girls, and the mean age at adoption was two years. The children came from 15 different provinces across China. Sixty-

90 four percent of the adopted Chinese children were the only child in the family. A number of parents reported that the children lagged in development, especially in gross motor skills. However, they also reported that the children caught up quickly, learned English quickly,

95 adapted easily to new foods, and accepted their new families.

Shapiro and colleagues (2001) indicated that adoptive parents might be unprepared for a child's developmental problems or for possible problems with at-

100 tachment. Haugaard and colleagues (1999) pointed out that professionals and parents involved in the adoption process would benefit from knowing about specific child characteristics that can indicate which transracial children are at the greatest or least risk of short- or

105 long-term problems. Vonk and Angaran (2003) indicated that parents who adopt across race need training in cultural competence to be prepared for the demands of raising the child. They indicated in their survey of adoption agencies that only about half the agencies

110 provided training to facilitate transracial adoption.

Sleep Problems

A review of literature regarding the sleeping patterns of internationally adopted children revealed limited information. However, this also seems to be a potential area of concern given that approximately 25%

115 of children can experience sleep problems (Zuckerman, Stevenson, & Bailey, 1987) and that subpopulations of children, such as those with diagnosed disabilities or other developmental delays, may display greater difficulty with sleeping (Mindell, 1993). Zuckerman and

120 associates indicated that as many as 30% of children can have sleep problems during the first four years of life, with the highest incidence occurring from one to two years of age. They also found that many of these sleep problems do not disappear with age. In their

125 study, children who experienced sleeping problems at eight months of age also experienced sleep difficulties at three years of age.

According to the American Academy of Child and Adolescent Psychiatry (2000), children can experience

130 a variety of different sleep disorders. These can include nightmares, bedwetting, teeth grinding, or difficulty falling asleep. A subgroup of sleep disorders are referred to as parasomnias. These sleep disorders include sleep terrors, sleep talking, and sleepwalking. Para-

135 somnias usually occur during the first third of the night, and individuals have little memory of them.

Hopkins-Best (1998) indicated that sleep issues are among the most commonly reported problems of families of internationally adopted children. She noted that

140 sleeping alone, as is common in the United States, is different from many cultures that focus on a family bed. Although family beds may be more common in China than in the United States, it is uncertain what the sleeping conditions are for children in orphanages.

145 One study that addressed the sleep problems of internationally adopted children directly was conducted by Bishop (2001). This study examined the sleeping patterns of 17 internationally adopted girls (from China and Cambodia) compared with 15 children in nonadop-

150 tive families (seven boys and eight girls). The mean age of the adopted children was nine months; the mean age for the nonadopted children was 14 months. Bishop used a questionnaire to measure the children's sleeping patterns. The results indicated that there was only one

155 significant difference found in the sleep patterns of the two groups of children. The internationally adopted children had longer-duration night wakings than the nonadopted children. Overall, the hypothesis that the adopted children would display more sleep problems

160 than the nonadopted children was not supported.

Method

Participants

Participants in this survey were 240 families who had adopted children from China. Families responded from 35 states. All of the children were adopted between 1992 and 2001. Families responded by e-mail or

165 regular mail.

Procedures

A snowball sampling method was used. The national Families with Children from China (FCC) Web site (www.fwcc.org) was accessed to obtain member contact information. Families receiving the survey

170 were asked to forward it to other families with children adopted from China.

The survey questions were based in part on the interest regarding the health, development, and sleeping habits of children adopted from China and on the re-

175 search questions and format used by Tessler and colleagues (1999). A short introductory letter explaining the survey's purpose and providing contact information was included, as well as information on how to respond. The letter indicated that the results would be

180 made available through publication and that we would ask the FCC site to include this summary as a link.

A pilot test of the survey was sent electronically to 10 FCC families in the immediate geographic area. E-mail addresses for these families were obtained from the local FCC group. Feedback on the questions and methods being used was requested from these 10 families. Families who did not respond within three weeks were sent a follow-up survey. On the basis of this pilot test of the survey, three questions were revised and two additional questions were added to the survey, for a total of 23 questions.

Although not all families who have adopted children from China are members of FCC, it is the largest such organization, and we felt that a large number of families could be reached through it. A list of FCC contacts in several states was compiled, and e-mails were sent asking for permission to contact members. We asked, and hoped, that the contacts would forward the survey to local FCC members. Some of these contacts indicated either that they were not comfortable forwarding the survey or that some local FCC groups had policies about not forwarding e-mails. E-mails were sent to families across the country from April to July 2001.

An electronic database was set up to collect and summarize the information obtained from the surveys. E-mail addresses were used as a primary key to be sure that there were no duplicate survey returns. The surveys were examined using the database's sort capabilities, and reports were generated for each research question.

Results

Responses were obtained from 240 families by e-mail or regular mail, and all responses were obtained between April and August 2001. Responses came from 35 states, including 17 states east of the Mississippi River and 18 states west of the Mississippi River. Mothers responded to the survey in 89% of the returns; fathers, 11%. Children came from 22 different provinces: 19% were adopted from Guangdong, 17% from Hunan, and 14% from Jiangxi; fewer than 10% were adopted from each of the other provinces.

As indicated in Table 1, most of the children in this sample (69%) were adopted in their first year of life, and 80% were 18 months of age or younger when adopted. The vast majority of children adopted were girls (98%) (Table 1). Of the 240 responses, only three indicated that the adopted child was a boy.

The years in which these children were adopted ranged from 1992 to 2001; 38 children were adopted between 1992 and 1995, 90 between 1996 and 1998, and 112 between 1999 and 2001. Almost half the families in this survey reported having other children. Of these, 44% were biological children, 38% were adopted children, 15% were both biological and adopted children, and 3% were stepchildren (Table 2).

Table 1
Characteristics of Children Adopted from China

Survey questions	% Responses
Age of child when adopted	
0–1 year	68
1–2 years	20
2–3 years	5
3–4 years	3
4–5 years	1
> 5 years	1
Gender	
Male	2
Female	98
Length of stay in orphanage	
1–4 months	11
5–9 months	43
10–15 months	29
16–24 months	10
Developmental delays in children	
No	38
Yes	62
Domains of developmental delay	
Motor	91
Language	35
Social	35
2 of 3 areas	35
All 3 areas	18

Note. Rounding error accounts for totals less than 100%.

Table 2
Characteristics of Participants in Survey about Children Adopted from China

Survey questions	% Responses
Survey Respondents	
Mothers	89
Fathers	11
Time period of adoption	
1992–1995	16
1996–1998	38
1999–2001	46
Other children in the family	
No	52
Yes	48
If other children in family	
Biological children	44
Adopted children	38
Both biological and adopted	15
Stepchildren	3

As there have been reports raising concerns about the length of stay in orphanages, we included a question asking how long children had been in an orphanage before adoption. Most of the children in this study (43%) had been in an orphanage for five to nine months (Table 1). One child was reported to have been in an orphanage for 12 years.

Families were also asked whether they had visited the orphanage in China. Only 45% of families reported visiting the child's orphanage. Of these 109 families, 81 were families who adopted children in the age range of birth to one year. Only 24% of families reported that their children spent time living with a foster family before adoption.

Table 3
Problems with Sleep, Eating, Social Interactions, Bonding, or Acceptance Among Children Adopted from China

Area	% of families reporting problems	Extent of problems reported (%)		
		Minor	Some	Many
Sleep	52	68	14	17
Eating	19	60	28	11
Interacting with others	16	11	4	1
Bonding	13	10	2	1
Acceptance	9	7	2	—[a]

[a]Only two families (less than 1%) reported having many problems in this area.

250 Families were asked how much they had been told or knew about their children before adoption and whether this information was correct. Forty-five percent of families reported knowing something about their child, and 17% reported knowing nothing about 255 their child. Of the families who did get some prior information, 33% reported that this information was accurate, and 15% reported that the information was partly correct.

Families were asked whether the children were de-260 velopmentally delayed when adopted and if so, in what areas (language, social, motor, or any combination). Sixty-two percent of families reported that children were developmentally delayed at their arrival in the United States (Table 1). The families reporting devel-265 opmental delays indicated that motor delays were the most common.

Families were asked whether children had any serious medical conditions at the time of adoption. Thirty-two families, or 13% of the total sample, reported that 270 children had medical problems. Of these 32 children, 84% were 0 to two years old when adopted. Three children had positive tuberculosis tests, five tested positive for hepatitis B or C, three had hearing or ear problems, two had visual problems, two had seizures, 275 and two had asthma. Other problems mentioned included high lead levels, rickets, dental decay, dyspraxia, and scabies.

The survey asked whether there had been any problems with the children's sleeping or eating behaviors as 280 well as whether there had been any problems with social interactions, bonding, or acceptance. For each of these items, a scale including the following responses was used: "no problems (less than 25% of the time)," "minor problems (25% of the time)," "some problems 285 (50% of the time)," and "many problems (75% or more of the time)."

Nearly 52% of families reported that children had some degree of sleep problems and that most of these were minor (Table 3). Only 9% of the total sample 290 reported many sleep problems (75% of the time or more). A number of families included comments about their children's sleep patterns, stating that children did not want to sleep alone, that children had night terrors, or that the sleeping problems faded as the children got 295 older.

A relatively small number of families reported problems with diet or eating. The responses indicated that only 19% experienced problems in this area. The majority of children were eating dairy products, al-300 though a few families reported that children were lactose intolerant.

Families were asked whether there had been any problems with children interacting with others, bonding with family members, or being accepted by friends or 305 family. Survey responses indicated that 16% of the families reported problems with social interactions. Only 13% of the sample reported problems with bonding, and again most of these were minor. Very few problems were reported with acceptance of the child 310 (9%). Only two of the 240 families reported having many problems with the acceptance of their child by friends or family members.

Parents were also asked whether their children had been identified as gifted or in need of special education 315 services because of a disability. Seven percent of families reported that children had been identified as gifted; only 4% had been referred for special education services owing to disabilities. These figures need to be viewed with caution given that many of the children in 320 this survey were not yet of school age.

Discussion

What are the postadoptive outcomes of internationally adopted children and, specifically, of children adopted from China? This central question and related questions in this investigation were what we hoped to 325 address with this research. The answers to these questions are important to social workers helping children and families through the adoption process. They are also important for our society as a whole, given the thousands of children being adopted from all over the 330 world.

The focus of this investigation was to obtain information to help children, families, schools, and society to be prepared for possible postadoptive outcomes. These outcomes may often be very positive. Anecdotal 335 comments included in the completed surveys indicated that many of the children are healthy, happy, smart, and social. Given that the children are often adopted into good home environments with loving, well-educated, professional parents, one could easily assume

4

340 that the long-term outlook for these children is very good.

The results of this study are consistent with those obtained in other studies. First, the majority of children adopted from China are young girls 18 months of age

345 or younger, from a variety of provinces. Consistent with other studies, many of the children displayed developmental delays at the time of adoption. An important point of distinction in future studies is whether the determination of developmental delay was made

350 through an agency or clinic or based on the parents' opinion. In this survey, parents made this determination. None of the families reported a formal determination of developmental delay. However, it is possible that children will display some delays in development,

355 especially in motor skills, at the time of adoption. These delays will very likely be temporary and fade as children get older.

Only 13% of children in this survey were reported as having serious medical problems. As Arsonson

360 (2003) has noted, these medical conditions are usually easily diagnosed, and treatment can begin immediately with very few long-term effects.

Several children were reported to have problems with sleeping. Slightly more than half of the surveys

365 (125 families) reported children having some degree of sleeping problems. Most of these problems were minor, with only 9% of the total sample reporting serious sleep problems. The extent and nature of the sleeping problems was not examined as closely as in research

370 studies focusing specifically on this topic. However, a number of families reported children having a difficult time falling asleep, experiencing night terrors, or not wanting to sleep alone. A more detailed examination of children's sleep problems is warranted and must take

375 into consideration cultural differences between the United States and China. The length of stay in an orphanage or whether children lived in a foster family (and, if so, how long) may be variables to be examined in other studies investigating sleep disorders.

Limitations

380 The sampling technique and procedures used in this study were not effective. This contributed to the study's small sample size and makes generalization of the findings difficult. Given that thousands of children have been adopted from China in the past 10 years, the

385 total number of returns was far short of what we had hoped and represents approximately 1% of all children adopted from China. However, the research questions addressed in this survey are important, and an effective way to reach these families must be found. It is impor-

390 tant to the children, their families, and society that we know as much as possible about any potential problems both before and after the adoption.

Implications for Social Workers and Other Professionals

International adoption presents challenges to the

395 adoptive child, the adoptive parents, and the adoptive extended family. One of the most important things needed to assist in successful postadoptive outcome is information.

Issues that need to be addressed by social workers and families involve information on the child. Children

400 adopted from China may experience abandonment issues that may lead to sleep, bonding, or attachment problems. The children may feel a sense of loss that their native family and country could not take care of them. There may be attachment issues inasmuch as

405 children may have been cared for by several different caregivers in orphanages or foster families before coming to their homes in the United States. There may also be identity problems as children work to discover why they are in their new world. Some problems children

410 experience may be transitional ones that will fade over time, but others may not. Such problems may include sleep, eating, or behavioral problems. Social workers can help families understand that such problems may occur and that these problems may be expected in chil-

415 dren coming from institutional settings (Johnson & Dole, 1999).

The overall lack of information on children and their history is an issue for families. Adoptive families are unlikely to know anything about a child's medical

420 history or prior family background. Even a child's exact birth date may be in question. Parents may also be concerned about the child's developmental delays and what can be done about them as well as about problems that children may experience with diet or sleeping.

425 Social workers can help provide needed information.

A number of suggestions can be made to social workers and educational professionals who work with adoptive children and their families. These suggestions are consistent with those of Judge (1999). First, adop-

430 tive children should receive complete medical and developmental examinations soon after their arrival in the United States. For many children, this may simply be precautionary, but it is important that information be obtained so that when intervention is warranted, it can

435 begin as soon as possible. This examination should also include a follow-up on any information provided on immunizations. Such examinations would appear to be needed for all children adopted internationally.

Second, the children's emotional health should be

440 addressed. Children may experience a sense of loss or attachment issues, and they should be provided with considerable emotional support. It is important that parents provide a consistent, predictable, and well-structured environment (Judge, 1999). Although this is

445 a good suggestion for any family, it is very important for adopted children adapting to their new world. Parents should be encouraged to spend as much time as possible with the child, attend promptly to the child's needs, and provide a supportive, empathic home envi-

450 ronment. Social workers should be prepared to provide

families with resource information on sleep disorders or even thumb sucking as needed.

It is important to help families identify and locate local, state, and national resources and support groups
455 (Judge, 1999). This could include the FCC, which has many local chapters. It may also involve the use of more experienced parents who can discuss their adoption experiences and help new adoptive families learn what they can expect (Judge, 1999). For example, one
460 local community has an informal mothers' group that meets once a month. This group is made up only of mothers with internationally adopted children who can share their knowledge and experiences. The mothers and families have formed an important bond that also
465 allows the children an opportunity to get together on a regular basis.

In addition, families need to be encouraged to make an effort to learn about the child's native culture and to be prepared for the child's questions about Chinese
470 culture, language, and the adoption. Families should be encouraged to speak in an honest and matter-of-fact manner about the adoption, read books about adoption and China, and be prepared for the child's questions. Social workers could provide families with a list of
475 children's books that address adoption or Chinese culture. Parents should make an effort to learn about and celebrate Chinese holidays such as the Moon Festival or Chinese New Year, as this can be an important way for children to learn about their native country.

References

American Academy of Child and Adolescent Psychiatry. (2000). *Children's sleep problems.* Retrieved July 2004 from www.aacap.org/publications/factsfam/sleep.html

Arsonson, J. E. (2003). *An update on health issues in children adopted from China.* Retrieved May 1999 from www.orphandoctor.com/medical/regional/China/healthissues.html

Bishop, C. T. (2001). *Sleep habits of internationally adopted children.* Unpublished master's thesis, St. Joseph's University, Philadelphia.

Haugaard, J. J., Palmer, M., & Wojslawowicz, J. (1999). International adoption: Children primarily from Asia and South America. *Adoption Quarterly, 3*, 83–93.

Hopkins-Best, M. (1998). *Toddler adoption: The weaver's craft.* Indianapolis: Perspectives Press.

Howe, D. (1997). Parent-reported problems in 211 adopted children: Some risk and protective factors. *Journal of Child Psychology and Psychiatry and Allied Disciplines, 38*, 401–411.

Johnson, D. E., & Dole, K. (1999). International adoptions: Implications for early intervention. *Infants & Young Children, 11*, 34–45.

Johnson, D. E., & Traister, M. (1999). Micronutrient deficiencies, growth failure and developmental delays are more prevalent among infectious diseases in US adopted Chinese orphans. *Pediatric Research, 45*, 126A.

Judge, S. L. (1999). Eastern European adoptions: Current status and implications for intervention. *Topics in Early Childhood Special Education, 19*, 244–252.

Miller, L. C., Kiernan, M. T., Mathers, M. I., & Klein-Gitelman, M. (1995). Developmental and nutritional status of internationally adopted children. *Archives of Pediatrics & Adolescent Medicine, 149*, 40–44.

Miller, L. C, & Hendrie, N. W. (2000). Health of children adopted from China. *Pediatrics, 105*, E76.

Mindell, J. (1993). Sleep disorders in children. *Health Psychology, 12*, 151–162.

National Adoption Information Clearinghouse. (2003). *HealthFinder.* Retrieved April 2003 from http://www.calib.com/naic

Shapiro, V., Shapiro, J., & Paret, I. (2001). International adoption and the formation of new family attachment. *Smith College Studies in Social Work, 71*, 389–418.

Tessler, R., Gamache, G., & Liu, L. (1999). *West meets East: Americans adopt Chinese children.* Westport, CT: Bergin & Garvey.

Vonk, M. E., & Angaran, R. (2003). Training for transracial adoptive parents by public and private adoption agencies. *Adoption Quarterly, 6*, 53–62.

Zuckerman, B., Stevenson, J., & Bailey, V. (1987). Sleep problems in early childhood: Continuities, predictive factors, and behavioral correlates. *Pediatrics, 80*, 664–671.

Acknowledgments: Special thanks to Megan, Ryan, and Kate Li Rettig.

About the authors: *Michael A. Rettig,* Ph.D., is professor, Department of Education, Washburn University, 1700 SW College Avenue, Topeka, KS 66621 (E-mail: Michael.rettig@washburn.edu). *Kelly McCarthy-Rettig*, MS, is a teacher in the Desoto School District, Desoto, Kansas.

Exercise for Article 1

Factual Questions

1. Did the review of literature regarding the sleeping patterns of internationally adopted children reveal much information?

2. From how many states did families respond?

3. For what words does FCC stand?

4. Of the 240 responses, how many indicated that the adopted child was a boy?

5. According to the researchers, why should the findings regarding identification of children as gifted or in need of special education services be viewed with caution?

6. According to the researchers, were the findings of this study consistent with those obtained in other studies?

Questions for Discussion

7. The researchers state that they used "snowball sampling." What do you think this term means? (See lines 166–171.)

8. What is your opinion on defining "no problems" as being "less than 25% of the time"? (See lines 278–286.)

9. In your opinion, how important are the limitations discussed by the researchers? (See lines 380–392.)

10. In your opinion, to what extent are the implications directly based on the data generated by this survey? (See lines 393–479.)

11. In a future study, do you think it would be useful to include a comparison group such as children adopted from within the United States? Why? Why not?

12. If you were to conduct a survey on the same topic, what changes, if any, would you make in the research methodology?

Quality Ratings

Directions: Indicate your level of agreement with each of the following statements by circling a number from 5 for strongly agree (SA) to 1 for strongly disagree (SD). If you believe an item is not applicable to this research article, leave it blank. Be prepared to explain your ratings. When responding to criteria A and B below, keep in mind that brief titles and abstracts are conventional in published research.

A. The title of the article is appropriate.

SA   5   4   3   2   1   SD

B. The abstract provides an effective overview of the research article.

SA   5   4   3   2   1   SD

C. The introduction establishes the importance of the study.

SA   5   4   3   2   1   SD

D. The literature review establishes the context for the study.

SA   5   4   3   2   1   SD

E. The research purpose, question, or hypothesis is clearly stated.

SA   5   4   3   2   1   SD

F. The method of sampling is sound.

SA   5   4   3   2   1   SD

G. Relevant demographics (for example, age, gender, and ethnicity) are described.

SA   5   4   3   2   1   SD

H. Measurement procedures are adequate.

SA   5   4   3   2   1   SD

I. All procedures have been described in sufficient detail to permit a replication of the study.

SA   5   4   3   2   1   SD

J. The participants have been adequately protected from potential harm.

SA   5   4   3   2   1   SD

K. The results are clearly described.

SA   5   4   3   2   1   SD

L. The discussion/conclusion is appropriate.

SA   5   4   3   2   1   SD

M. Despite any flaws, the report is worthy of publication.

SA   5   4   3   2   1   SD

Article 2

Bullies Move Beyond the Schoolyard: A Preliminary Look at Cyberbullying

JUSTIN W. PATCHIN
University of Wisconsin, Eau Claire

SAMEER HINDUJA
Florida Atlantic University

ABSTRACT. Bullying in a school setting is an important social concern that has received increased scholarly attention in recent years. Specifically, its causes and effects have been under investigation by a number of researchers in the social and behavioral sciences. A new permutation of bullying, however, has recently arisen and become more common: Tech-savvy students are turning to cyberspace to harass their peers. This exploratory article discusses the nature of bullying and its transmutation to the electronic world and the negative repercussions that can befall both its victims and instigators. In addition, findings are reported from a pilot study designed to empirically assess the nature and extent of online bullying. The overall goal of the current work is to illuminate this novel form of deviance stemming from the intersection of communications and computers and to provide a foundational backdrop on which future empirical research can be conducted.

From *Youth Violence and Juvenile Justice*, 4, 148–169. Copyright © 2006 by Sage Publications, Inc. Reprinted with permission.

The home, neighborhood, and school are all recognized as important social and physical contexts within which adolescents develop. Bullying—an all too common form of youthful violence—has historically affected only children and teenagers while at school, while traveling to or from school, or in public places such as playgrounds and bus stops. Modern technology, however, has enabled would-be bullies to extend the reach of their aggression and threats beyond this physical setting through what can be termed *cyberbullying*, where tech-savvy students are able to harass others day and night using technological devices such as computer systems and cellular phones. Computers occupy a significant proportion of the homes in which children reside and are frequently used for social, entertainment, academic, and productivity needs (National Telecommunications and Information Administration [NTIA], 2002). Moreover, cellular phones are gaining widespread popularity and use among the younger age groups because they are perceived as a status symbol, allow for conversations with friends in different physical spaces, and provide a virtual tether of sorts for parents, allowing for supervision from afar.

Though they are intended to positively contribute to society, negative aspects invariably surface as byproducts of the development of new technologies such as these. The negative effects inherent in cyberbullying, though, are not slight or trivial and have the potential to inflict serious psychological, emotional, or social harm. When experienced among members of this highly impressionable and often volatile adolescent population, this harm can result in violence, injury, and even death (e.g., Meadows et al., 2005; Vossekuil, Fein, Reddy, Borum, & Modzeleski, 2002) and later criminality for both the initiator and recipient of bullying (e.g., Olweus, Limber, & Mihalic, 1999; Patchin, 2002). One particularly horrendous anecdotal account deserves mention. In May of 2001, viciously offensive messages denigrating and humiliating a high school sophomore girl who suffered from obesity and multiple sclerosis were posted anonymously to an online message board associated with a local high school in Dallas, Texas (Benfer, 2001). In time, the bullying crossed over to the physical world as the victim's car was vandalized, profanities were written on the sidewalk in front of her home, and a bottle filled with acid was thrown at her front door, which incidentally burned her mother. This example vividly depicts how bullying online can lead to physical harm offline.[1]

Little research to date has been conducted on cyberbullying. However, research on the correlates of traditional bullying can assist in comprehending the reality and growth of this new phenomenon. To begin, the desire to be and remain popular takes on almost lifelike proportions among kids and teenagers during certain stages of their life, and their self-esteem is largely defined by the way that others view them. Although it is unclear exactly when self-esteem increases or decreases during a child's life (Twenge & Campbell, 2001), it unquestionably shapes a child's development in profound ways. According to the social acceptance model, self-esteem stems from the perceptions that others have of the individual (Cooley, 1902). When individuals perceive themselves to be rejected or otherwise socially excluded, a number of ill effects can result (Leary, Schreindorfer, & Haupt, 1995). Much research has validated this theory (Leary & Downs,

1995; Leary, Haupt, Strausser, & Chokel, 1998; Leary, Tambor, Terdal, & Downs, 1995) and has pointed to the following potentially negative outcomes: depression (Quellet & Joshi, 1986; Smart & Walsh, 1993), substance abuse (Hull, 1981), and aggression (Coie & Dodge, 1988; French & Waas, 1987; Hymel, Rubin, Rowden, & LeMare, 1990; Paulson, Coombs, & Landsverk, 1990; Stewart, 1985). In addition, low self-esteem tends to be found among chronic victims of traditional bullying (Hoover & Hazler, 1991; Neary & Joseph, 1994; Rigby & Slee, 1993).[2] It is expected that cyberbullying can similarly cripple the self-esteem of a child or adolescent, and without a support system or prosocial outlets through which to resolve and mitigate the strain, the same dysphoric and maladaptive outcomes may result. Despite these solemn possibilities, there has been very little empirical attention to date devoted toward better understanding the electronic variant of this deviance (exceptions include Berson, Berson, & Ferron, 2002; Finn, 2004; Ybarra & Mitchell, 2004).

This research seeks to fill this gap by exploring cyberbullying and examining its potential to become as problematic as traditional bullying—particularly with society's increasing reliance on technology. Its goal is to illuminate this novel form of deviance stemming from the intersection of communications and computers and to provide a foundational backdrop on which future empirical research can be conducted. First, what is known about traditional bullying will be summarized to provide a comparative point of reference. Second, data collected from various media sources will be presented to describe the technology that facilitates electronic bullying and to portray its prevalence. Third, preliminary findings from a pilot study of adolescent Internet users will be presented, highlighting the characteristics of this group and their involvement (both as victims and offenders) in the activity. Finally, suggestions for future empirical research will be offered as guidance for additional exploration of this subject matter.

Traditional Bullying

Bullying Defined

A variety of scholars in the disciplines of child psychology, family and child ecology, sociology, and criminology have articulated definitions of bullying that generally cohere with each other. To begin, the first stages of bullying can be likened to the concept of harassment, which is a form of unprovoked aggression often directed repeatedly toward another individual or group of individuals (Manning, Heron, & Marshal, 1978). Bullying tends to become more insidious as it continues over time and is arguably better equated to violence rather than harassment. Accordingly, Roland (1989) states that bullying is "long-standing violence, physical or psychological, conducted by an individual or a group directed against an individual who is not

able to defend himself in the actual situation" (p. 21).[3] Stephenson and Smith (1989) contend that bullying is

> a form of social interaction in which a more dominant individual [the bully] exhibits aggressive behavior, which is intended to and does, in fact, cause distress to a less dominant individual [the victim]. The aggressive behavior may take the form of a direct physical and/or verbal attack or may be indirect as when the bully hides a possession that belongs to the victim or spreads false information about the victim. (p. 45)

Providing perhaps the most panoptic definition, Nansel et al. (2001) asserted that bullying is aggressive behavior or intentional "harm doing" by one person or a group, generally carried out repeatedly and over time and that involves a power differential. Many characteristics can imbue an offender with perceived or actual power over a victim and often provide a sophistic license to dominate and overbear. These include, but are not limited to, popularity, physical strength or stature, social competence, quick wit, extroversion, confidence, intelligence, age, sex, race, ethnicity, and socioeconomic status (Olweus, 1978, 1993, 1999; Rigby & Slee, 1993; Roland, 1980; Slee & Rigby, 1993). Nonetheless, research on the relevance of these differences between bullies and their victims has been inconclusive. For example, differences in physical appearance was not predictive of one's likelihood of being a bully or a victim (Olweus, 1978), but physical shortness (Voss & Mulligan, 2000) and weakness (Leff, 1999) were found to be relevant in other research.

Although the harassment associated with bullying can occur anywhere, the term *bullying* often denotes the behavior as it occurs among youth in school hallways and bathrooms, on the playground, or otherwise proximal or internal to the school setting. Bullies can also follow their prey to other venues such as malls, restaurants, or neighborhood hangouts to continue the harassment. In the past, interaction in a physical context was required for victimization to occur. This is no longer the case thanks to the increased prevalence of the Internet, personal computers, and cellular phones. Now, would-be bullies are afforded technology that provides additional mediums over which they can manifest their malice. The following sections outline the scope, breadth, and consequences of traditional bullying as a reference point from which cyberbullying can subsequently be viewed and understood.

Extent and Effects of Traditional Bullying

It is unclear exactly how many youth are bullied or bully others on any given day. In 1982, 49 fifth-grade teachers from Cleveland, Ohio, reported that almost one-fourth (23%) of their 1,078 students were either victims or bullies (Stephenson & Smith, 1989). More recently, a nationally representative study of 15,686 students in grades 6 through 10 identified that approximately 11% of respondents were victims of bullying, 13% were bullies, and 6% were both victims and bullies during a year (Nansel et al., 2001). Additional research conducted by the Family Work Institute substantiated these findings through interviews with 1,000 youth in grades 5 through 12. Their study found that 12% of youth were bullied five or more times during the previous month (Galinsky & Salmond, 2002). Finally, the Bureau of Justice Statistics reports that 8% of youth between the ages of 12 and 18 had been victims of bullying in the previous 6 months (Devoe et al., 2002). That said, conservative estimates maintain that at least 5% of those in primary and secondary schools (ages 7–16) are victimized by bullies each day (Björkqvist, Ekman, & Lagerspetz, 1982; Lagerspetz, Björkqvist, Berts, & King, 1982; Olweus, 1978; Roland, 1980).

Many young people are able to shrug off instances of being bullied, perhaps because of peer or familial support or higher self-efficacy. Nonetheless, others are not able to cope in a prosocial or normative manner or reconcile the pain experienced through more serious episodes or actions. Suicidal ideation, eating disorders, and chronic illness have beset many of those who have been tormented by bullies, whereas other victims run away from home (Borg, 1998; Kaltiala-Heino, Rimpelä, Marttunen, Rimpelä, & Rantanen, 1999; Striegel-Moore, Dohm, Pike, Wilfley, & Fairburn, 2002). In addition, depression has been a frequently cited consequence of bullying (e.g., Hawker & Boulton, 2000) and seems to perpetuate into adulthood, evidencing the potentially long-term implications of mistreatment during adolescence (Olweus, 1994). Finally, in extreme cases, victims have responded with extreme violence, such as physical assault, homicide, and suicide (Patchin, 2002; Vossekuil et al., 2002).

Following the fatal shootings at Columbine High School in Littleton, Colorado, in 1999, the educational system was challenged to address bullying because the two teenagers involved in the massacre were reported to have been ostracized by their classmates. Additional school violence research of 37 incidents involving 41 attackers from 1974 to 2000 found that 71% (29) of the attackers "felt bullied, persecuted, or injured by others prior to the attack" (Vossekuil et al., 2002, p. 21). It was also determined that the victimization played at least some role in their subsequent violent outburst. Other less serious but equally as negative outcomes can result from repeated bullying. For example, students who are constantly harassed may attempt to avoid the problems at school as much as possible, leading to tardiness or truancy (BBC News, 2001; Richardson, 2003; Rigby & Slee, 1999). Truancy has been identified as a significant antecedent to delinquency, dropout, and other undesirable outcomes in the juvenile justice literature (Farrington, 1980; Garry, 1996; Gavin, 1997; Nansel et al., 2001). Based on these findings, it is clear that victims of bullies are at risk to have a discontinuous developmental trajectory for many years.

The aggressors in the bullying dyad also appear to be more likely to engage in antisocial activities later in life (Tattum, 1989). For example, approximately 60% of those characterized as bullies in grades six through nine were convicted of at least one crime by the age of 24, compared to 23% who were not characterized as either bullies or victims (Olweus et al., 1999). Further underscoring the relationship between bullying and future criminality, Olweus and colleagues (1999) found that 40% of bullies had three or more convictions by the age of 24, compared to 10% of those who were neither instigators nor victims of bullying.

Based on this brief review, it is clear that both bully victims and offenders are at an increased risk for developmental problems that can continue into adulthood. As such, it is imperative that researchers seek to better understand the antecedents and consequences of bullying behavior, for practitioners to develop and implement antibullying programs in schools, and for societal institutions to better understand the ways in which bullying behaviors are carried out, both in traditional and nontraditional settings.

Cyberbullying

Because of the advent and continued growth of technological advances, the transmutation of bullying has occurred—from the physical to the virtual. Physical separation of the bully and the victim is no longer a limitation in the frequency, scope, and depth of harm experienced and doled out. As instances of bullying are no longer restricted to real-world settings, the problem has matured. Although a migration to the electronic realm is a seemingly logical extension for bullies, little is currently known regarding the nature and extent of the phenomenon. In short, we define *cyberbullying* as willful and repeated harm inflicted through the medium of electronic text. Based on the literature reviewed above, the constructs of malicious intent, violence, repetition, and power differential appear most salient when constructing a comprehensive definition of traditional bullying and are similarly appropriate when attempting to define this new permutation. To be sure, cyberbullies are malicious aggressors who seek implicit or explicit pleasure or profit through the mistreatment of other individuals. Violence is often associated with aggression and corresponds to actions intended to inflict injury (of any type). One instance of mistreatment, although potentially destructive, cannot accurately be equated to bullying, and so cyberbullying must also involve harmful behavior of a repetitive nature. Finally, because of the very nature of the behavior, cyberbullies have some perceived or actual power over their victims. Although power in traditional bullying might be physical (stature) or social (competency or popularity), online power may simply stem from proficiency. That is, youth who are able to navigate the electronic world and utilize technology in a way that allows them to harass others are in a position of power relative to a victim.

A brief editorial published in 2003 in *Journal of the American Academy of Child and Adolescent Psychiatry* pointed to the lack of academic references to this topic despite its anticipated proliferation (Jerome & Segal, 2003). Despite this call for research, very little scholarly attention has been devoted to the topic. In a notable exception, Ybarra and Mitchell (2004) conducted telephone surveys of 1,498 regular Internet users between the ages of 10 and 17, along with their parents, and found that 19% of youth respondents were either on the giving or receiving end of online aggression in the previous year. The vast majority of offenders (84%) knew their victim in person, whereas only 31 % of victims knew their harasser in person. This fact is noteworthy; it appears that power and dominance are exerted online through the ability to keep the offender's identity unknown (Ybarra & Mitchell, 2004). When comparing those who were only aggressors to those who had no involvement in online harassment, the former were significantly more likely to be the target of offline bullying, to display problematic behavior, to have low school commitment, and to engage in alcohol and cigarette use. When comparing those who had experience being both an offender and a victim with those who had no involvement in online harassment, the significant differences were the same as above—with the exception of low school involvement. It is interesting to note that real-world variables that play a contributive role in traditional forms of delinquency and crime—such as general deviance, low commitment to prosocial institutions such as school, and substance abuse—are also significantly related to bullying on the Internet.

There are two major electronic devices that young bullies can employ to harass their victims from afar. First, using a personal computer, a bully can send harassing e-mails or instant messages, post obscene, insulting, and slanderous messages to online bulletin boards, or develop Web sites to promote and disseminate defamatory content. Second, harassing text messages can be sent to the victim via cellular phones.

Personal Computers

Research by the U.S. Department of Commerce noted that almost 90% of youth between the ages of 12 and 17 use computers, and by age 10, youth are more likely than are adults to use the Internet (NTIA, 2002). Demonstrating the broad reach of instant messaging and chat programs, 20 million kids between the ages of 2 and 17 logged onto the Internet in July 2002, and 11.5 million used instant messaging programs (NetRatings, 2002). Similarly, according to a study of 1,081 Canadian parents conducted in March 2000, 86% stated that their kids used the Internet, 38% had their own e-mail address, 28% used ICQ (an instant messaging program short for "I seek you"), and 28% regularly spent time in chat rooms (Network, 2001). Indeed,

America Online (AOL, 2002, 2003)—the most popular Internet service provider, with more than 35 million users—states that members join in on more than 16,000 chat sessions and send more than 2.1 billion instant messages per day across their network. As a point of reference, 1.9 billion phone calls are made each day in the United States. Finally, the Internet relay channels provide a venue for many other users on a daily basis. For example, on the morning of an average Saturday in May 2005, there were more than 1 million users online in more than 800 chat rooms (Gelhausen, 2005).

Pew Internet and American Life Project (2001) conducted an extensive research endeavor in 2001 to ascertain demographic and behavioral characteristics of teenagers who use the Internet. A telephone survey was administered to 754 children between the ages of 12 and 17 in November and December of 2000. Though not generalizable to the population of online teenagers across the United States because of many methodological limitations, the study paints an interesting picture of the user population and their activities while connected to the Internet. About 17 million youth aged 12 to 17 regularly use the Internet. This figure represents approximately three-fourths (73%) of those in this age bracket.

According to the Pew Internet and American Life Project (2001), approximately 29% of youth younger than 12 regularly go online. Among teenagers, approximately 95% of girls and 89% of boys have sent or received e-mail, and 56% of girls and 55% of boys have visited a chat room. Almost three-fourths of teenagers (74%; 78% of girls and 71% of boys) in the study use instant messaging to communicate with their friends, with 69% using the technology several times a week. Almost half (46%) of respondents who report using instant messaging programs spend between 30 and 60 minutes per session doing so, whereas 21% state that they spend more than 1 hour in the activity in an average online session. Testifying to the benefits of textual communication over verbal communication, 37% used it to say something they would not have said in person. Underscoring the potential for harassment and negative treatment online, 57% have blocked messages from someone with whom they did not wish to communicate, and 64% had refused to answer messages from someone with whom they were angry.

Cellular Phones

In the United States, more than 150 million individuals, including half of the youth between 12 and 17 years of age, own cellular phones (Fattah, 2003). It is estimated that 74% of Americans between the ages of 13 and 24 will have a wireless device by 2006 (O'Leary, 2003). Cell phone usage is much higher among teenagers and young adults in Europe compared to the United States, 60% to 85% compared to 25% (O'Leary, 2003). Research estimates that by 2007 nearly 100 million individuals will use the text messaging service on their wireless device (Fattah, 2003). Statistics compiled in November 2001 by UPOC (2001)—a wireless communications firm in the United States—found that 43% of those who currently use text messaging are between the ages of 12 and 17. To note, the text messaging capabilities of cellular phones are being exploited to a greater degree in European and Asian countries. In 2002, approximately 90 billion text messages were sent through the two major telecommunication service providers in China, which equals approximately 246 million per day (CD, 2003). In Europe and Asia, more than 30 billion text messages are sent between individuals each month (Katz, 2002). It is predicted that 365 billion text messages will be sent across western Europe in 2006, up from 186 billion in 2002 (GSMBox, 2002).

Issues Specific to Cyberbullying

Gabriel Tarde's (1903) law of insertion suggests that new technologies will be applied to augment traditional activities and behaviors. Certain characteristics inherent in these technologies increase the likelihood that they will be exploited for deviant purposes. Cellular phones and personal computers offer several advantages to individuals inclined to harass others. First, electronic bullies can remain virtually anonymous. Temporary e-mail accounts and pseudonyms in chat rooms, instant messaging programs, and other Internet venues can make it very difficult for adolescents to determine the identity of aggressors. Individuals can hide behind some measure of anonymity when using their personal computer or cellular phone to bully another individual, which perhaps frees them from normative and social constraints on their behavior. Further, it seems that bullies might be emboldened when using electronic means to effectuate their antagonistic agenda because it takes less energy and fortitude to express hurtful comments using a keyboard or keypad than using one's voice.

Second, supervision is lacking in cyberspace. Although chat hosts regularly observe the dialog in some chat rooms in an effort to police conversations and evict offensive individuals, personal messages sent between users are viewable only by the sender and the recipient and are therefore outside regulatory reach. Furthermore, there are no individuals to monitor or censor offensive content in e-mail or text messages sent via computer or cellular phone. Another contributive element is the increasingly common presence of computers in the private environments of adolescent bedrooms. Indeed, teenagers often know more about computers and cellular phones than do their parents and are therefore able to operate the technologies without worry or concern that a probing parent will discover their participation in bullying (or even their victimization; NTIA, 2002).

In a similar vein, the inseparability of a cellular phone from its owner makes that person a perpetual target for victimization. Users often need to keep it turned on for legitimate uses, which provides the opportunity for those with malicious intentions to send threatening and insulting statements via the cellular phone's text messaging capabilities. There may truly be no rest for the weary as cyberbullying penetrates the walls of a home, traditionally a place where victims could seek refuge.

Finally, electronic devices allow individuals to contact others (both for prosocial and antisocial purposes) at all times and in almost all places. The fact that most adolescents (83%) connect to the Internet from home (Pew Internet and American Life Project, 2001) indicates that online bullying can be an invasive phenomenon that can hound a person even when not at or around school. Relatedly, the coordination of a bullying attack can occur with more ease because it is not constrained by the physical location of the bullies or victims. A veritable onslaught of mistreatment can quickly and effectively torment a victim through the use of these communications and connectivity tools.

Does Harm Occur?

Of course, cyberbullying is a problem only to the extent that it produces harm toward the victim. In the traditional sense, a victim is often under the immediate threat of violence and physical harm and also subject to humiliation and embarrassment in a public setting. These elements compound the already serious psychological, emotional, and social wounds inflicted through such mistreatment. One might argue that a victim of bullying in cyberspace—whether via e-mail, instant messaging, or cellular phone text messaging—can quickly escape from the harassment by deleting the e-mail, closing the instant message, and shutting off the cellular phone and is largely protected from overt acts of violence by the offender through geographic and spatial distance. Such an argument holds much truth; however, the fact remains that if social acceptance is crucially important to a youth's identity and self-esteem, cyberbullying can capably and perhaps more permanently wreak psychological, emotional, and social havoc.[4] It is not a stretch to say that physical harm, such as being beaten up, might even be preferred by some victims to the excruciating pain they experience from nonphysical harm because the former can heal quicker. Furthermore, it is yet to be determined if there is a causal pathway between cyberbullying and traditional bullying, and so physical harm might very well follow as a logical outcome of a continually increasing desire on the part of the offender to most severely hurt the victim. To be sure, this must be explored in future studies.

With regard to public embarrassment, life in cyberspace is often intertwined with life in the real world. For example, many kids and teenagers spend days with their friends in school and nights with those same friends online through instant message programs and

515 chat channels. That which occurs during the day at school is often discussed online at night, and that which occurs online at night is often discussed during the day at school. There is no clean separation between the two realms, and so specific instances of cyberbully-
520 ing—disrespect, name calling, threats, rumors, gossip—against a person make their way around the interested social circles like wildfire.

Does the mistreatment experienced through online bullying lead to the same feelings that result from tradi-
525 tional bullying, such as self-denigration, loss of confidence and self-esteem, depression, anger, frustration, public humiliation, and even physical harm? This remains to be clearly depicted through empirical research but seems plausible based on the linchpin role of self-
530 esteem among children and teenagers previously described and on anecdotal evidence specifically related to online aggression (BBC News, 2001; Benfer, 2001; Blair, 2003; Meadows et al., 2005; ÓhAnluain, 2002; Richardson, 2003).

535 Because of the widespread availability of electronic devices, there is no lack of participants using the technologies. Their ubiquity provides a seemingly endless pool of candidates who are susceptible to being bullied or to becoming a bully. Unfortunately, however, little
540 is known in terms of how often these technologies are mobilized for deviant purposes. One empirical study has been conducted to date: In 2002, the National Children's Home (NCH, 2002)—a charitable organization in London—surveyed 856 youth between the ages of
545 11 and 19 and found that 16% received threatening text messages via their cellular phone, 7% had been bullied in online chat rooms, and 4% had been harassed via e-mail. Following the victimization, 42% told a friend, 32% told a parent or guardian, and 29% did not reveal
550 the experience to anyone. Because more information is clearly warranted, a study was designed to explore the nature and extent of cyberbullying.

Current Study

Method

The current study involved an analysis of youthful Internet users in an effort to assess their perceptions of
555 and experiences with electronic bullying. It is difficult to individually observe the nature and extent of electronic bullying among adolescent Internet users because of the "private" nature of e-mails, cellular phone text messages, and instant messages and one-on-one
560 chat messages within online chat channels. To be sure, if the instances of cyberbullying occur in a public forum such as a popular chat channel and in the view of all chat room members, then direct observation and consequent analyses may be possible. Most of the time,
565 however, they occur through private (nonpublic), person-to-person communications. A survey methodology was therefore designed to collect data by requiring participants to recall and relate their cyberbullying practices and experiences via a questionnaire that was

570 linked from the official Web site of a popular music artist revered by the target age group. An electronic format was selected as it allows for efficiency in collecting data from a large number of participants (Couper, 2000; McCoy & Marks, 2001; Smith, 1997). The
575 survey was active between May 1, 2004, and May 31, 2004.

The context of the Internet must be considered when dealing with consent issues because forcing all online researchers to comply with traditional proce-
580 dures in this area is unduly onerous, particularly when possible harm is little to none. Because it is impossible to personally obtain informed consent from participants in much online survey research that solicits participants from postings on Web sites, implied consent has gener-
585 ally been accepted (Walther, 2002). This involves the presentation of informed consent information in electronic text (e.g., on a Web page), along with specific actions that must be performed prior to initiation of the survey. These actions often include the checking of a
590 check box (agreeing to participate) and clicking on a *submit* button to send the information to the server. From this, consent can be reasonably inferred (King, 1996). For the current study, researchers instructed participants who were younger than 18 to obtain per-
595 mission from their parent or guardian. Permission was demonstrated by the parent entering his or her initials in a specified box. Again, because of matters of anonymity associated with Internet research, it was impossible to actually verify that adolescents obtained proper
600 permission prior to completing the survey.

With survey research conducted over the Internet, questions also arise as to the reliability of the data (Cho & LaRose, 1999). Participants are self-selected, which introduces some bias as individuals are not randomly
605 chosen for inclusion in the study. Often, a convenience sample, where individuals are chosen because they are available (e.g., because they visit a particular Web site and see a solicitation for research participation), is employed. As a result, the sample obtained may not nec-
610 essarily be representative of all Internet users. Moreover, online demographic groups may not mirror those found in the real world (Witte, Amoroso, & Howard, 2000). Generalization to a larger population then becomes impossible with convenience sampling (Couper,
615 2000), but the technique has demonstrated utility for exploratory studies intended to probe a novel phenomenon. Researchers who seek to tap the resources of the World Wide Web will continue to face these challenging issues. Although these limitations are an unfor-
620 tunate cost of conducting Internet-based research, results from this preliminary study will help to inform a more methodologically rigorous investigation in the future.

The survey went through numerous iterations to op-
625 timize its design and presentation of questions. Prior research has determined that poor design can render dubious the quality of responses and may even affect

completion rate (Crawford, Couper, & Lamias, 2001; Krosnick, 1999; Preece, Rogers, & Sharp, 2002; Schwarz, 1999). Specifics to the survey design bear mentioning. Demographic data were solicited at the beginning of the survey, which has been shown to decrease rates of attrition because individuals are not surprised by more personal questions at the resolution of their participation (Frick, Bachtiger, & Reips, 2001). The survey in its entirety was presented to the respondent on one screen, which has also been shown to increase response rates (Crawford et al., 2001). Although our survey did consist of a vast number of questions, findings related to the relationship between survey length and response rate have been mixed and inconclusive (Brown, 1965; Bruvold & Comer, 1988; Eicherner & Habermehl, 1981; Jobber & Saunders, 1993; Mason, Dressel, & Bain, 1961; Sheehan, 2001; Witmer, Colman, & Katzman, 1999; Yammarino, Skinner, & Childers, 1991).

Incentives to participate in the form of cash or other prizes via a lottery have also been shown to increase response rate; human beings are motivated by the possibility of receiving something in return for their efforts, and this trait is manifested in survey participation as well (Cho & LaRose, 1999; Frick et al., 2001). As such, participants in the current study were entered into a random drawing to win one of three autographed photographs of the musical artist from whose fan Web site they reached the survey. We also specified that the institutional review board at the researchers' university had approved the project to verify its legitimacy and strengthen the trust relationship between the researchers and the potential participants (Cho & LaRose, 1999).

A final point bears mentioning. As the Internet protocol (IP) address and timestamp was recorded with each participant's responses, we were able to eliminate entries where all of the responses were completely the same. This might happen when a respondent fills out the questionnaire, clicks *submit*, goes back to the previous page where all of his or her responses are stored within the survey form, and then clicks *submit* again (and continues in this pattern). To note, there were survey entries from the same IP address but with completely different responses to the questions posed. This was because some Internet service providers route multiple users through one IP address when connecting from their internal network to the external Internet. To summarize, we browsed through all of the data and attempted to determine which entries were fraudulent and which were valid.

Findings

Because this was an Internet-based survey, anyone could participate. Even though the survey was associated with a teen-oriented Web site, individuals from all ages also frequent the site and therefore completed the survey. As noted in Table 1, out of the 571 total re-

spondents, 384 were younger than 18 (67.3%; henceforth referred to as the youth sample). In both groups, the vast majority of respondents were female. This finding is likely attributable to the nature of the Web site on which the survey was linked (a female pop music star). Similarly, the vast majority of respondents were Caucasian. There are several potential interpretations of this finding. First, individuals from different racial and ethnic backgrounds may be less interested in this particular entertainer than are others and may therefore be unlikely to visit the Web site to see the survey solicitation. Alternatively, the overrepresentation of Caucasian respondents could be evidence of the oft-mentioned digital divide, where some populations are not privy to the access and use of technology such as computers and the Internet. As expected, most respondents were between the ages of 12 and 20, and the average age of the youth sample was 14.1. Moreover, more than 70% of respondents from the complete sample were in grades 2 through 12. High school respondents (9th through 12th grade) represented the modal category of respondents for both groups. As might be expected, the vast majority of all respondents came from English-speaking countries (the Web site and survey were written in English), and about 60% of respondents in both groups reported living in the United States. It must be mentioned that because online identity is completely malleable (Hafner, 2001; Turkle, 1995), the demographic data obtained may not be completely accurate because of a lack of trust in our research project, mischief, or purposeful obfuscation. Research performed over the Internet cannot entirely preempt this problem—at least in its current stage of technological development—and so a caveat is justified.

The remainder of the findings discussed relate only to those respondents who were younger than 18 when they completed the survey (*n* = 384). Online bullying was specifically defined on the questionnaire for respondents as behavior that can include bothering someone online, teasing in a mean way, calling someone hurtful names, intentionally leaving persons out of things, threatening someone, and saying unwanted, sexually related things to someone. Table 2 presents the percentage of respondents who have been bullied ("Have you ever been bullied online?"), have bullied others ("Have you ever bullied others while online?"), or have witnessed bullying online ("Have you ever seen other kids bullied online?"). Almost 11% of youth reported bullying others while online, more than 29% reported being the victim of online bullying, and more than 47% have witnessed online bullying. Cyberbullying was most prevalent in chat rooms, followed by computer text messages and e-mail. Bullying using news groups or cellular phones was not as prominent for members of this sample. Indeed, although it is clear that all who responded to the survey have access to a

Table 1
Descriptive Statistics of Survey Respondents

	Complete sample[a]		Youth sample[b]	
	n	%	*n*	%
Sex				
Female	452	78.3	325	84.6
Male	115	19.9	55	14.3
Missing	10	1.7	4	1.0
Race				
Caucasian	429	74.4	289	75.3
Hispanic	43	7.5	32	8.3
Asian or Pacific Islander	43	7.5	28	7.3
African American	4	0.7	3	0.8
Indigenous or aboriginal	4	0.7	3	0.8
Multiracial	16	2.8	10	2.6
Other race	32	5.5	19	4.9
Missing	6	1.0	0	0.0
Age				
9–11	37	6.4	37	9.6
12–13	110	19.1	110	28.6
14–15	135	23.4	135	35.2
16–17	102	17.7	102	26.6
18–20	128	22.2	—	—
21–25	41	7.1	—	—
26 and older	18	3.1	—	—
Missing	6	1.0	—	—
Grade				
Grades 2–5	25	4.3	24	6.3
Grades 6–8	149	25.8	149	38.8
Grades 9–12	231	40.0	196	51.0
Community college	37	6.4	7	1.8
University	72	12.5	1	0.3
Do not attend school	52	9.0	4	1.0
Missing	11	1.9	3	0.8
Country				
United States	349	60.5	227	59.1
Canada	62	10.7	46	12.0
United Kingdom	53	9.2	35	9.1
Australia	29	5.0	23	6.0
Other or unknown	84	14.6	53	13.8

a. *N* = 571; b. *N* = 384.

computer, it is unknown what proportion of respondents have access to a cellular phone.

Table 2
Percentage of Youth Respondents Who Report Being a Bully, a Victim, or a Witness to Bullying

	Bully	Victim	Witness
Online	10.7	29.4	47.1
In a chat room	7.6	21.9	42.4
Via computer text message	5.2	13.5	15.1
Via e-mail	1.8	12.8	13.8
On a bulletin board	1.0	2.9	13.8
Via cell phone text message	0.8	2.1	6.3
In a newsgroup	0.5	1.6	3.6

Note. N = 384.

As previously described, youth were asked a general question regarding their involvement in online
745 bullying. In addition, youth were asked to relate whether they experienced a number of behaviors that may be associated with bullying. Table 3 presents in-

formation collected from these questions. Notably, 60.4% of respondents have been ignored by others
750 while online, 50.0% reported being disrespected by others, almost 30.0% have been called names, and 21.4% have been threatened by others. In addition, a significant proportion of youth were picked on by others (19.8%) or made fun of by others (19.3%) or had
755 rumors spread about them by others (18.8%).

Table 3
Types of Online Bullying

	Percentage victimized
Ignored by others	60.4
Disrespected by others	50.0
Called names by others	29.9
Been threatened by others	21.4
Picked on by others	19.8
Made fun of by others	19.3
Rumors spread by others	18.8

Note. N = 384.

15

Table 4
Average Number of Bullying Experiences During Previous 30 Days for Youth Who Reported Being a Victim or a Bully

	Bully			Victim		
	n	*M*	*Max*	*n*	*M*	*Max*
In a chat room	39	1.23	10	83	3.36	50
Via computer text message	30	1.20	6	68	4.65	76
Via e-mail	18	0.39	2	61	4.07	107
On a bulletin board	16	1.50	9	31	2.42	10
Via cell phone text message	9	3.22	23	19	3.37	23
In a newsgroup	2	0.00	0	6	1.67	6

Note. n reflects the number of youth who reported experience in that behavior; *M* is the average number of times the experience occurred in the previous 30 days, and *Max* is the highest number of times the experience was reported during the previous 30 days.

In addition to asking respondents whether they have experienced bullying online, researchers also asked youth how frequently the bullying occurred during the previous 30 days. Table 4 presents summary statistics
760 reflecting the number of youth who reported involvement in the bullying experience, the average number of times the bullying occurred, and the maximum number of times the bullying occurred. For example, 83 youth reported being victimized in a chat room an average of
765 3.36 times during the previous 30 days. One youth reported being bullied in a chat room 50 times during the previous 30 days. Bullying via computer text messaging and e-mail also occurred frequently during the previous 30 days.
770 Table 5 demonstrates the negative effects associated with online bullying on victims. For example, 42.5% of victims were frustrated, almost 40.0% felt angry, and more than 27.0% felt sad. Almost one-third (31.9%) reported that it affected them at school,
775 whereas 26.5% reported that it affected them at home. Only 22.1% were not bothered by the bullying they experienced, and less than 44.0% stated that the bullying did not affect them.

Table 5
Effects of Online Bullying

	Percentage yes
I felt frustrated	42.5
I felt angry	39.8
I felt sad	27.4
I was not bothered	22.1
It affected me at school	31.9
It affected me at home	26.5
It affected me with my friends	20.4
It did not affect me	43.4

Note. Responses for youth who reported being bullied online (*N* = 113).

Table 6 describes the response taken by victims of
780 online bullying. Notably, almost 20% of victims were forced to stay offline, whereas almost 32% had to remove themselves from the environment in some capacity or way. Victims also revealed a hesitation to tell authority figures about their experiences. Even though
785 most confided in an online friend (56.6%), fewer than 9.0% of victims informed an adult.

Additional analyses were conducted to attempt to uncover correlates of online bullying. There were no

790 statistically significant associations among age, race, or gender and who is likely to be a victim of online bullying. The lack of relationship among race or gender and victimization may be more a function of the homogeneous nature of the data than any substantive finding and must be further tested. In accordance with intui-
795 tion, youth who participate in more activities online (represented by a variety score of 13 different activities) were more likely to experience online bullying. Also not surprising, youth who bully others were more likely to be victims of online bullying. In all, 75% of
800 youth who have bullied others online have been victims of bullying, whereas fewer than 25% of youth bullies have never been on the other end of such malicious actions (χ^2 = 42.866; *p* < .001). Future research should seek to better understand what additional factors
805 are associated with online bullying.

Table 6
Response to Online Bullying

	Percentage yes
I tell the bully to stop	36.3
I get away	31.9
I do nothing	24.8
I stay offline	19.5
I bully others	2.7
I tell an online friend	56.6
I tell a friend	25.7
I tell nobody	23.0
I tell my mom and dad	19.5
I tell my brother or sister	16.8
I tell an adult	8.8

Note. Responses for youth who reported being bullied online (*N* = 113).

Discussion

The results of this study point to a number of key issues. First, bullying is occurring online and is impacting youth in many negative ways. Almost 30% of the adolescent respondents reported that they had been
810 victims of online bullying—operationalized as having been ignored, disrespected, called names, threatened, picked on or made fun of, or having had rumors spread by others. Admittedly, being ignored by another person may simply reflect obnoxious behavior that warranted
815 the outcome rather than actual and willful aggression. We were not able to parcel out the stimuli of instances when people were ignored but chose to include a

measure of it in the current analyses. This is because universal social acceptance is still largely desired by children and adolescents, even if as adults we understand that it is impossible to please everyone at all times. Being ignored would introduce dissonance and instability to the already tenuous relational and social equilibria sought by youths and may accordingly be considered a passive–aggressive form of bullying. Along similar lines, although some of this harassment may be characterized as trivial (e.g., being ignored by others or being disrespected), more than 20% reported being threatened by others. Anger and frustration was a commonly reported emotional response to the harassment. Finally, almost 60% of victims were affected by the online behaviors at school, at home, or with friends.

Several policy implications stem from the aforementioned findings. It is hoped that this harmful phenomena can be curtailed by proactively addressing the potentially negative uses of technology. Parents must regularly monitor the activities in which their children are engaged while online. Teachers, too, must take care to supervise students as they use computers in the classrooms. Police officers must investigate those instances of cyberbullying that are potentially injurious and hold responsible parties accountable. Unfortunately, there are no methods to discern which harassment involves simple jest and which has the potential to escalate into serious violence. Future research must analyze case studies and anecdotal stories of cyberbullying experiences to help determine when intervention by authority figures is most appropriate. Overall, parents, teachers, police officers, and other community leaders must keep up with technological advances so that they are equipped with the tools and knowledge to identify and address any problems when they arise.

Limitations of the Current Study

The most notable limitations of this study relate to its administration because data were collected exclusively online. With regard to sampling, it is unquestionable that Internet users are dissimilar from those who do not go online. However, Walther (2002, p. 209) argues that concerns related to the generalizability of data collected from the Internet to a target population assume that random samples of Internet users are sought in any study and that a sample obtained from the Internet is able to be generalized to other populations. We would have liked to obtain a random sample of all Internet users younger than 18 to ascertain the extent and prevalence of online bullying, but such a task is impossible as no reliable sampling frame of individuals in cyberspace exists. Thus, we carefully targeted certain Web sites presumably visited by at least some adolescents who have personal experience in the phenomenon. As it turned out, the sample was disproportionately Caucasian and female, and results therefore may be skewed toward these subgroups. As a result, any findings from the research should be very cautiously applied to the larger group of Internet-using youth.

Another issue related to online data collection concerns misrepresentation of age by participants in this research. Undoubtedly, we cannot guarantee that respondents honestly indicated their age during participation. Any qualms, though, can be overcome by considering the fallibility of traditional research methods, such as phone surveys or surveys distributed in highly populated settings (e.g., large college classes) or through the mail and even individual, face-to-face administration of questionnaires. A person can lie about his or her age in any of these contexts, and it is unreasonable to assume that a person would be more likely to do so in an online research setting (Walther, 2002).

Directions for Future Research

The current study provides the framework for future empirical inquiry on electronic bullying. Indeed, the authors are currently involved in a more comprehensive study that involves both Internet-based research and traditional paper-and-pencil surveys. As with any social scientific endeavor, replication is necessary to more fully understand the phenomena under consideration. There are several questions future research in this area must address. First, data must be collected to more accurately ascertain the scope, prevalence, and nuances of cyberbullying. For example, it is important to discover whether cyberbullies are simply traditional bullies who have embraced new technologies to accomplish their intentions or if they are youth who have never participated in traditional, school-based bullying. Moreover, do personal computers enable the stereotypical victims of bullies (i.e., those who are smart, physically small, and/or socially challenged) to retaliate using means that ensure their anonymity? It would also be important to determine whether commonly accepted stimuli for traditional bullying—the need to (a) exert power and dominate, (b) compensate for victimization in another area of one's life, (c) cope with one's insecurities, and (d) attract attention and popularity—are similarly predictive in cyberspace-based instances of the deviance.

Also of interest is the extent to which electronic bullying results in harm to adolescents in their physical environments (e.g., at school or in their neighborhoods). Are threats made in cyberspace followed through on the playground? Are victims of cyberbullying the same individuals who are also victims of traditional bullying, or are they distinct groups? What about offenders? One could hypothesize that the victims of traditional bullying may turn to the Internet to exact revenge on their schoolyard aggressors. That is, the victim becomes the offender by using his or her technological knowledge to inflict harm on the original bully.

In addition, it is useful to identify whether adults also participate in electronic harassment. Although they

930 may frequent chat rooms to a lesser degree than do children and adolescents, cellular phone use and even instant messaging programs are commonly utilized for both professional and personal purposes. Does electronic harassment occur to the same extent among 935 adults as compared to a population of adolescents? Does it occur in a more controlled and subtle manner or with the same degree of perceivably overt cruelty? Does it occur for fundamentally similar reasons across both groups, or are there factors endemic to youth or 940 adult life that condition and dictate bullying in an online context? These are just some of the important questions that need further examination.

Finally, future research efforts ought to more thoroughly examine the results of this preliminary investi- 945 gation using more rigorous methodology that ensures a more representative sample of responses. As indicated, the intent of this research is to generate scholarly interest in this unique form of adolescent harassment and therefore should be viewed simply as a small, but we 950 think significant, platform on which further research efforts should be built.

Conclusion

The preceding review provides a description of bullying in cyberspace for the purposes of introducing 5 it as a topic meriting academic inquiry and underscoring its 955 often inescapable pernicious nature. Indeed, 74% of the youth in this study reported that bullying occurs online, and almost 30% of the youth reported being victimized by others while online. Some may dismiss electronic bullying as normative behavior that does not physically 960 harm anyone. To be sure, some have this perception regarding traditional bullying, dismissing it as a rite of passage or an inevitable and even instructive element of growing up. Because of the familiarity and memorability of bullying as almost unavoidable in both the 965 schoolyard and neighborhood milieu during one's formative years, perhaps the reader may share those sentiments.

Because no consensus exists when considering whether cyberbullying merits increased attention be- 970 cause of society's continued progression into a wired world, perhaps it should just be considered another contemporary cultural challenge that kids often face when transitioning into adulthood. Conceivably there is no need to panic when introduced to the concept that 975 online bullying does and will continue to take place as children seek to carve out an identity for themselves and cope with various pressures associated with their development. Alternatively, perhaps there is a need for alarm as both those who bully and those who are bul- 980 lied might yield readily to other criminogenic influences and proceed down a path of deviance online, offline, or both. Regardless, cyberbullying is very real, and it is hoped that this work has highlighted its relevance for the purposes of inspiring additional interest 985 in its etiology and consequences.

End Notes

[1] The interested reader is encouraged to see Blair (2003) or ÓhAnluain (2002) for more examples.
[2] It should be mentioned that research has not identified a link between low self-esteem and the offenders of traditional bullying (Hoover & Hazler, 1991; Rigby & Slee, 1993).
[3] To be sure, females are also bullied to a substantive degree and must not be excluded from any analyses of the phenomenon.
[4] Cyberbullying repercussions have permanence because e-mails can be saved, instant messages and chat conversations can be logged, and Web pages can be archived for an offender, victim, or third party to read over in the future and thereby relive the experience.

References

America Online. (2002). *AOL facts—2002.* Retrieved September 2, 2003, from http://www.corp.aol.com/whoweare/Factbook_F.pdf

America Online. (2003). *Who we are: Fast facts.* Retrieved September 2, 2003, from http://www.corp.aol.com/whoweare/fastfacts.html

BBC News. (2001). *Girl tormented by phone bullies.* Retrieved January 16, 2001, from http://news.bbc.co.uk/1/hi/education/1120597.stm

Benfer, A. (2001). *Cyber slammed.* Retrieved July 7, 2001, from http://www.dir.salon.com/mwt/feature/2001/07/03/cyber_bullies/index.html

Berson, I. R., Berson, M. J., & Ferron, J. M. (2002). Emerging risks of violence in the digital age: Lessons for educators from an online study of adolescent girls in the United States. *Journal of School Violence, 1,* 51–71.

Björkqvist, K., Ekman, K., & Lagerspetz, K. (1982). Bullies and victims: Their ego picture, ideal ego picture, and normative ego picture. *Scandinavian Journal of Psychology, 23,* 307–313.

Blair, J. (2003). New breed of bullies torment their peers on the Internet. *Education Week.* Retrieved February 5, 2003, from http://www.edweek.org/ew/ewstory.cfm?slug=21cyberbully.h22

Borg, M. G. (1998). The emotional reaction of school bullies and their victims. *Educational Psychology, 18,* 433–444.

Brown, M. (1965). Use of a postcard query in mail surveys. *Public Opinion Quarterly, 29,* 635–637.

Bruvold, N. T., & Comer, J. M. (1988). A model for estimating the response rate to a mailed survey. *Journal of Business Research, 16,* 101–116.

CD. (2003). *Thumbs down on mobile messaging.* Retrieved July 22, 2003, from http://www.chinadaily.com.cn/en/doc/2003-07/22/content_247257.htm

Cho, H., & LaRose, R. (1999). Privacy issues in Internet surveys. *Social Science Computer Review, 14,* 421–434.

Coie, J. D., & Dodge, K. A. (1988). Multiple sources of data on social behavior and social status in the school: A cross-age comparison. *Child Development, 59,* 815–829.

Cooley, C. H. (1902). *Human nature and the social order.* New York: Scribner.

Couper, M. P. (2000). Web-based surveys: A review of issues and approaches. *Public Opinion Quarterly, 64,* 464–494.

Crawford, S., Couper, M. P., & Lamias, M. (2001). Web surveys: Perceptions of burden. *Social Science Computer Review, 19,* 146–162.

Devoe, J. F., Ruddy, S. A., Miller, A. K., Planty, M., Peter, K., Kaufman, P. et al. (2002). *Indicators of school crime and safety.* Washington, DC: U.S. Department of Education, National Center for Education Statistics, U.S. Department of Justice, Bureau of Justice Statistics.

Eicherner, K., & Habermehl, W. (1981). Predicting the response rates to mailed questionnaires (comment on Herberlien & Baumgartner). *American Sociological Review, 46,* 1–3.

Farrington, D. (1980). Truancy, delinquency, the home, and the school. In L. Hersov & I. Berg (Eds.), *Out of school: Modem perspectives in truancy and school refusal* (pp. 49–63). New York: John Wiley.

Fattah, H. (2003). *America untethered.* Retrieved September 1, 2003, from http://www.upoc.com/corp/news/UpocAmDem.pdf

Finn, J. (2004). A survey of online harassment at a university campus. *Journal of Interpersonal Violence, 19,* 468–483.

French, D. C., & Waas, G. A. (1987). Social–cognitive and behavioral characteristics of peer-rejected boys. *Professional School Psychology, 2,* 103–112.

Frick, A., Bachtiger, M. T., & Reips, U.-D. (2001). Financial incentives, personal information, and drop out in online studies. In U.-D. Reips & M. Bosnjak (Eds.), *Dimensions of Internet science* (pp. 209–219). Lengerich, Germany: Pabst Science.

Galinsky, E., & Salmond, K. (2002). *Youth and violence: Students speak out for a more civil society.* New York: Families and Work Institute.

Garry, E. M. (1996). *Truancy: First step to a lifetime of problems.* Washington, DC: U.S. Department of Justice, Office of Juvenile Justice and Delinquency Prevention.

Gavin, T. (1997). *Truancy: Not just kids' stuff anymore.* Washington, DC: Federal Bureau of Investigation.

Gelhausen, A. (2005). *Summary of IRC networks.* Retrieved May 7, 2005, from http://irc.netsplit.de/networks/

GSMBox. (2002). *Ten years of SMS messages.* Retrieved August 10, 2003, from http://uk.gsmbox.com/news/mobile_news/all/94480.gsmbox

Hafner, K. (2001). *The well: A story of love, death & real life in the seminal online community.* New York: Carrol and Graf.

Hawker, D. S. J., & Boulton, M. J. (2000). Twenty years' research on peer victimization and psychological maladjustment: A meta-analysis review of cross-sectional studies. *Journal of Child Psychology and Psychiatry, 41,* 441–445.

Hoover, J., & Hazler, R. (1991). Bullies and victims. *Elementary School Guidance and Counseling, 25,* 212–219.

Hull, J. G. (1981). A self-awareness model of the causes and effects of alcohol consumption. *Journal of Abnormal Psychology, 90,* 586–600.

Hymel, S., Rubin, K. H., Rowden, L., & LeMare, L. (1990). Children's peer relationships longitudinal prediction of internalizing and externalizing problems from middle to late childhood. *Child Development, 61,* 2004–2021.

Jerome, L., & Segal, A. (2003). Bullying by Internet—Editorial. *Journal of the American Academy of Child and Adolescent Psychiatry, 42,* 751.

Jobber, D., & Saunders, J. (1993). A note on the applicability of the Brurold-Comer model of mail survey response rates to commercial populations. *Journal of Business Research, 26,* 223–236.

Kaltiala-Heino, R., Rimpelä, M., Marttunen, M., Rimpelä, A., & Rantanen, P. (1999). Bullying, depression, and suicidal ideation in Finnish adolescents: School survey. *British Medical Journal, 319,* 348–351.

Katz, A. R. (2002). *Text messaging moves from cell to home.* Retrieved August 15, 2003, from http://www.iht.com/articles/51152.html

King, S. (1996). Researching Internet communities: Proposed ethical guidelines for the reporting of results. *The Information Society, 12,* 119–128.

Krosnick, J. A. (1999). Survey research. *Annual Review of Psychology, 50,* 537–567.

Lagerspetz, K. M. J., Björkqvist, K., Berts, M., & King, E. (1982). Group aggression among schoolchildren in three schools. *Scandinavian Journal of Psychology, 23,* 45–52.

Leary, M. R., & Downs, D. L. (1995). Interpersonal functions of the self-esteem motive: The self-esteem system as a sociometer. In M. H. Kernis (Ed.), *Efficacy, agency, and self-esteem* (pp. 123–144). New York: Plenum.

Leary, M. R., Haupt, A. L., Strausser, K. S., & Chokel, J. T. (1998). Calibrating the sociometer: The relationship between interpersonal appraisals and state self-esteem. *Journal of Personality and Social Psychology, 74,* 1290–1299.

Leary, M. R., Schreindorfer, L. S., & Haupt, A. L. (1995). The role of self-esteem in emotional and behavioral problems: Why is low self-esteem dysfunctional? *Journal of Social and Clinical Psychology, 14,* 297–314.

Leary, M. R., Tambor, E. S., Terdal, S. J., & Downs, D. L. (1995). Self-esteem as an interpersonal monitor: The sociometer hypothesis. *Journal of Personality and Social Psychology, 68,* 518–530.

Leff, S. (1999). Bullied children are picked on for their vulnerability. *British Medical Journal, 318,* 1076.

Manning, M., Heron, J., & Marshal, T. (1978). Style of hostility and social interactions at nursery school and at home: An extended study of children. In A. Lionel, M. B. Hersov, & D. Shaffer (Eds.), *Aggression and antisocial behavior in childhood and adolescence* (pp. 29–58). Oxford, UK: Pergamon.

Mason, W., Dressel, R., & Bain, R. (1961). An experimental study of factors affecting response to a mail survey of beginning teachers. *Public Opinion Quarterly, 25,* 296–299.

McCoy, S., & Marks, P. V., Jr. (2001, August). *Using electronic surveys to collect data: Experiences from the field.* Paper presented at the AMCIS Annual Conference, Boston.

Meadows, B., Bergal, J., Helling, S., Odell, J., Piligian, E., Howard, C. et al. (2005, March 21). The Web: The bully's new playground. *People,* pp. 152–155.

Nansel, T. R., Overpeck, M., Pilla, R. S., Ruan, W. J., Simons-Morton, B., & Scheidt, P. (2001). Bullying behaviors among US youth: Prevalence and association with psychosocial adjustment. *Journal of the American Medical Association, 285,* 2094–2100.

National Children's Home. (2002). *1 in 4 children are the victims of "on-line bullying" says children's charity.* Retrieved September 1, 2003, from http://www.nch.org.uk/news/news5.asp?auto=195

National Telecommunications and Information Administration. (2002). *A nation online: How Americans are expanding their use of the Internet.* Retrieved June 13, 2004, from http://www.ntia.doc.gov/ntiahome/dn/anationonline2.pdf

Neary, A., & Joseph, S. (1994). Peer victimization and its relationship to self concept and depression among schoolgirls. *Personality and Individual Differences, 16,* 183–186.

NetRatings, N. (2002). *IM programs draw US kids and teens online.* Retrieved July 30, 2003, from http://www.nua.com/surveys/index.cgi?f=VS&art_id=905358261&rel=true

Network, M. A. (2001). *Canada's children in a wired world: The parents' view—Final report.* Retrieved July 30, 2003, from http://www.media-

awareness.ca/english/resources/special_initiatives/survey_resources/parents_survey/loader.cfm?url=/commonspot/security/getfile.cfm&PageID=31576

ÓhAnluain, D. (2002). *When text messaging turns ugly.* Retrieved September 4, 2002, from http://www.wired.com/news/school/0,1383,54771,00.html

O'Leary, N. (2003). *Cell phone marketers tap teens as the next frontier.* Retrieved February 17, 2003, from http://www.adweek.com/aw/magazine/article_display.jsp?vnu_content_id=1818786

Olweus, D. (1978). *Aggression in the schools: Bullies and whipping boys.* Washington, DC: Hemisphere Press.

Olweus, D. (1993). *Bullying at school.* Oxford, UK: Blackwell.

Olweus, D. (Ed.). (1994). *Bullying at school: Long-term outcomes for victims and an effective school-based intervention program.* New York: Plenum.

Olweus, D. (1999). Norway. In P. K. Smith, Y. Morita, J. Junger-Tas, D. Olweus, R. Catalano, & P. Slee (Eds.), *Nature of school bullying: A cross-national perspective* (pp. 28–48). London: Routledge.

Olweus, D., Limber, S., & Mihalic, S. (1999). *Bullying prevention program.* Boulder, CO: Center for the Study and Prevention of Violence.

Patchin, J. (2002). Bullied youths lash out: Strain as an explanation of extreme school violence. *Caribbean Journal of Criminology and Social Psychology, 7,* 22–43.

Paulson, M. J., Coombs, R. H., & Landsverk, J. (1990). Youth who physically assault their parents. *Journal of Family Violence, 5,* 121–133.

Pew Internet and American Life Project. (2001). *Teenage life online: The rise of the instant-message generation and the Internet's impact on friendships and family relationships.* Retrieved July 13, 2004, from http://www.pewinternet.org/pdfs/PIP_Teens_Report.pdf

Preece, J., Rogers, Y., & Sharp, S. (2002). *Interaction design: Beyond human–computer interaction.* New York: John Wiley. .

Quellet, R., & Joshi, P. (1986). Loneliness in relation to depression and self-esteem. *Psychological Reports, 58,* 821–822.

Richardson, T. (2003). *Bullying by text message.* Retrieved February 20, 2003, from http://www.theadvertiser.news.com.au/common/story_page/0,5936,6012025%5E2682,00.html

Rigby, K., & Slee, P. T. (1993). Dimensions of interpersonal relating among Australian school children and their implications for psychological well-being. *The Journal of Social Psychology, 133,* 33–42.

Rigby, K., & Slee, P. T. (1999). Australia. In P. Smith, Y. Morita, J. Junger-Tas, D. Olweus, R. Catalano, & P. Slee (Eds.), *The nature of school bullying: A cross-national perspective* (pp. 324–339). London: Routledge.

Roland, E. (1980). *Terror i skolen* [Terrorism in school]. Stavanger, Norway: Rogaland Research Institute.

Roland, E. (1989). Bullying: The Scandinavian research tradition. In D. P. Tattum & D. A. Lane (Eds.), *Bullying in schools* (pp. 21–32). Stroke-on-Trent, UK: Trentham.

Schwarz, N. (1999). Self-reports: How the questions shape the answers. *American Psychologist, 54,* 93–105.

Sheehan, K. B. (2001). E-mail survey response rates: A review. *Journal of Computer Mediated Communication, 6.* Retrieved January 18, 2006, from http://jcmc.indiana.edu/vol6/issue2/sheehan.html

Slee, P. T., & Rigby, K. (1993). The relationship of Eysenck's personality factors and self-esteem to bully/victim behaviour in Australian school boys. *Personality and Individual Differences, 14,* 371–373.

Smart, R., & Walsh, G. (1993). Predictors of depression in street youth. *Adolescence, 28,* 41–53.

Smith, C. B. (1997). Casting the net: Surveying an Internet population. *Journal of Computer Mediated Communication, 3.* Retrieved January 18, 2006, from http://jcmc.indiana.edu/vol3/issue1/smith.html

Stephenson, P., & Smith, D. (1989). Bullying in junior school. In D. P. Tattum & D. A. Lane (Ed.), *Bullying in schools* (pp. 45–58). Stroke-on-Trent, UK: Trentham.

Stewart, M. A. (1985). Aggressive conduct disorder: A brief review. 6th Biennial Meeting of the International Society for Research on Aggression (1984, Turku, Finland). *Aggressive Behavior, 11,* 323–331.

Striegel-Moore, R. H., Dohm, F.-A., Pike, K. M., Wilfley, D. E., & Fairburn, C. G. (2002). Abuse, bullying, and discrimination as risk factors for binge eating disorder. *The American Journal of Psychiatry, 159,* 1902–1907.

Tarde, G. (Ed.). (1903). *Gabriel Tarde's laws of imitation.* New York: Henry Holt.

Tattum, D. P. (1989). Violence and aggression in schools. In D. P. Tattum & D. A. Lane (Eds.), *Bullying in schools* (pp. 7–19). Stroke-on-Trent, UK: Trentham.

Turkle, S. (1995). *Life on the screen: Identity in the age of the Internet.* New York: Simon & Schuster.

Twenge, J. M., & Campbell, W. K. (2001). Age and birth cohort differences in self-esteem: A cross-temporal meta-analysis. *Personality and Social Psychology Review, 5,* 321–344.

UPOC. (2001). *Wireless stats.* Retrieved September 1, 2003, from http://www.genwireless.com/stats.html

Voss, L. D., & Mulligan, J. (2000). Bullying in school: Are short pupils at risk? Questionnaire study in a cohort. *British Medical Journal, 320,* 612–613.

Vossekuil, B., Fein, R. A., Reddy, M., Borum, R., & Modzeleski, W. (2002). *The final report and findings of the Safe School Initiative: Implications for* the prevention of school attacks in the United States. Retrieved August 29, 2003, from http://www.secretservice.gov/ntac/ssi_final_report.pdf

Walther, J. B. (2002). Research ethics in Internet enabled research: Human subjects issues and methodological myopia. Ethics and Information Technology, 4, 205.

Witmer, D. F., Colman, R. W., & Katzman, S. L. (1999). From paper-and-pencil to screen-and-keyboard. In S. Jones (Ed.), Doing Internet research: Critical issues and methods for examining the Net (pp. 145–161). Thousand Oaks, CA: Sage.

Witte, J. C., Amoroso, L. M., & Howard, P. E. N. (2000). Research methodology—Method and representation in Internet-based survey tools—Mobility, community, and cultural identity in Survey 2000. Social Science Computer Review, 18, 179–195.

Yammarino, F. J., Skinner, S., & Childers, T. L. (1991). Understanding mail survey response behavior. Public Opinion Quarterly, 55, 613–639.

Ybarra, M. L., & Mitchell, J. K. (2004). Online aggressor/targets, aggressors and targets: A comparison of associated youth characteristics. Journal of Child Psychology and Psychiatry, 45, 1308–1316.

Acknowledgments: We would like to thank the anonymous reviewers for helpful comments on an earlier draft.

Address correspondence to: Justin W. Patchin, Department of Political Science, University of Wisconsin, Eau Claire, 105 Garfield Avenue, Eau Claire, WI 54702-4004. E-mail: patchinj@uwec.edu

About the authors: Justin W. Patchin is an assistant professor of criminal justice at the University of Wisconsin, Eau Claire. His research areas focus on policy and program evaluation, juvenile delinquency prevention, and school violence. Sameer Hinduja is an assistant professor in the Department of Criminology and Criminal Justice at Florida Atlantic University. His research largely involves the integration of social science and computer science perspectives.

Exercise for Article 2

Factual Questions

1. The questionnaire was linked from what?

2. Did the researchers solicit demographic data at the "beginning" or at the "end" of the survey?

3. Were the majority of the respondents "male" or "female"?

4. Which ethnic/racial group constituted the vast majority of the respondents?

5. Are the results presented in Tables 2 through 6 based on the responses of "all respondents" or "only respondents younger than 18"?

6. What was the most frequent response to online bullying?

Questions for Discussion

7. The introduction and literature review in lines 1–552 are longer than most others in this book. In your opinion, is this lengthy review an important part of this research report? Would the report have been as effective with a shorter review?

8. What is your opinion on the importance of the researchers' inability to verify if participants under 18 years of age actually obtained permission from their parents and guardians? (See lines 593–600 and 876–888.)

9. The researchers used an incentive to encourage participation in the survey. What is your opinion on the particular incentive used in this research? (See lines 647–656.)

10. The researchers make a number of suggestions for future research in lines 889–951. In your opinion, are some of the suggestions more important than others? Are some more interesting than others? Explain.

11. The researchers conclude by stating that they hope this research will inspire additional interest in the etiology and consequences of cyberbullying. Do you think that it will? Explain. (See lines 982–985.)

Quality Ratings

Directions: Indicate your level of agreement with each of the following statements by circling a number from 5 for strongly agree (SA) to 1 for strongly disagree (SD). If you believe an item is not applicable to this research article, leave it blank. Be prepared to explain your ratings. When responding to criteria A and B below, keep in mind that brief titles and abstracts are conventional in published research.

A. The title of the article is appropriate.

SA   5   4   3   2   1   SD

B. The abstract provides an effective overview of the research article.

SA   5   4   3   2   1   SD

C. The introduction establishes the importance of the study.

SA   5   4   3   2   1   SD

D. The literature review establishes the context for the study.

SA   5   4   3   2   1   SD

E. The research purpose, question, or hypothesis is clearly stated.

SA   5   4   3   2   1   SD

F. The method of sampling is sound.

SA   5   4   3   2   1   SD

G. Relevant demographics (for example, age, gender, and ethnicity) are described.

SA   5   4   3   2   1   SD

H. Measurement procedures are adequate.

SA   5   4   3   2   1   SD

I. All procedures have been described in sufficient detail to permit a replication of the study.

SA   5   4   3   2   1   SD

J. The participants have been adequately protected from potential harm.

SA   5   4   3   2   1   SD

K. The results are clearly described.

SA   5   4   3   2   1   SD

L. The discussion/conclusion is appropriate.

SA   5   4   3   2   1   SD

M. Despite any flaws, the report is worthy of publication.

SA   5   4   3   2   1   SD

Article 3

"I Missed the Bus": School Grade Transition, the Wilmington Truancy Center, and Reasons Youth Don't Go to School

ARTHUR H. GARRISON
Delaware Criminal Justice Planning Council

ABSTRACT. Data from a 3-year truancy reduction program operating in Wilmington, Delaware, are analyzed to assess the association of truancy and reasons for truancy with school grade transition points from elementary to middle school and from middle school to high school. Data showed that there was a 95% increase in the number of truants between fifth and sixth grade and a 76% increase in the number of truants between eighth and ninth grade. There was an 87% increase in truancy among youth between 10 and 11 years old and 68% increase in truancy among youth 13 and 14 years old. The study includes analysis of truancy by various demographic variables and makes policy suggestions on how truancy can be reduced by focusing on the two key school transition points, the fifth and eighth grades.

From *Youth Violence and Juvenile Justice*, 4, 204–212. Copyright © 2006 by Sage Publications. Reprinted with permission.

Data from a truancy reduction center in Wilmington, Delaware, are used in this study to assess the association of truancy and reasons for truancy at school grade transition points. This research seeks to add to
5 the literature on the relationship between the reasons youth give for why they are truant and school grade transition. Research that has been conducted on why youth are truant generally includes poor school performance, lack of interest in school, or that youth do
10 not see any purpose or benefit in going to school (Ames & Archer, 1988; L. Anderman, Maehr, & Midfley, 1999; Chung, Elias, & Schneider, 1998).

One aspect of the newer research on truancy is how transition from one level of education to another (Akos,
15 2002; Alspaugh, 1998a, 1998b, 2000; Alspaugh & Harting, 1995; Arowosafe & Irvin, 1992; Mizelle & Mullins, 1997) can influence school performance and lead to truancy. School transition research has also examined the relationship between school grade transi-
20 tions and various protective factors (Entwisle & Alexander, 1993; Gutman & Midgley, 2000; Newman, Myers, Newman, Lohman, & Smith, 2000). School level transition has also been used to explain why both dropout and truancy patterns increase when youth

25 move from elementary to middle school and from middle school to high school (Alspaugh, 1998a, 1998b). Researchers have noted "potential dropouts from high school can be differentiated from graduates with 75% accuracy as early as third grade" (Phelan, 1992, p. 33;
30 see also Lloyd, 1978). Robins and Ratcliff (1980) found that youth truants in elementary school were 3 times more truant in high school than were youth who were not truant in elementary school. Research presented shows that patterns of truancy start as early as 6
35 years old in the second grade.

Part of the difficulty students have transitioning from elementary to middle school is in the change in the learning environment they encounter. In elementary school, the educational environment is one of task-goal
40 orientation in that students "engage in academic work in order to improve their competency or the intrinsic satisfaction that comes from learning" (E. Anderman & Midgley, 1997, p. 270). In addition to the change in the number of children in a class and the presence of mul-
45 tiple teachers for multiple subjects, middle schools have a performance-goal orientation learning environment. In a performance-goal orientation learning environment, students "engage in academic work to demonstrate or prove their competency, or to avoid the ap-
50 pearance of lack of ability relative to others" (E. Anderman & Midgley, 1997, p. 270).

In addition to the change in the educational environment, factors of puberty (Fenzel, 1989) and the students' perceptions about the transition and of being
55 able to fit in (Hertzog & Morgan, 1999; Pintrich & Schunk, 1996) play a role in the ability of students to adapt to the new school environment. Other factors affecting the transition include increased peer pressure, cliquishness among students, fear of bullying, being the
60 youngest in the new school, the need to fit in, and finding the right bus to go home (Akos, 2002; Schumacher, 1998). School transition research has shown that when youth transfer between school levels, a shift occurs in how the youth perceive and measure themselves. Far-
65 rington (1980) found that teacher labeling of elemen-

tary youth as "troublesome" was the best predictor of truancy in middle school.

The buildup of self-doubt or anxiety can develop while the youth is in the prior school transition grade (fifth grade—elementary before sixth grade—middle school) and continue into the school transition grade. Chung et al. (1998) concluded, "Students showing high levels of psychological distress prior to transition represent early adolescents at a greater risk than their peers for a continued stressful school transition" (p. 98). As the research by Midgley and Urban (1992) explained, after the "transition many students feel less positively about their academic potential and the value of schooling, they give up more quickly and put forth less effort, and their grades decline" (p. 5). Phelan (1992) concluded this alienation from school occurs when students "rightly or wrongly feel harassed or ignored by teachers [and] see no connection between school and their futures" (p. 33), and for "these children, this is the beginning of a downward trajectory that leads to school failure and school leaving" (Midgley & Urban, 1992, p. 5).

Method

In an effort to reduce truancy in the city of Wilmington, a truancy reduction center was established in a local community center, West End Neighborhood House, to provide services to youth who were found truant by the Wilmington Police Department. Wilmington police officers brought youth who were found not in school during school hours to the West End Neighborhood House. Truant youth were turned over to a police officer who was assigned to the program at the community center (to maintain legal custody of the youth and release the patrol officer) and were interviewed by a social worker also assigned to the truancy center. Truant youth were interviewed, parents were contacted, and the schools they attended were also contacted to determine why the youth were not in school and to establish plans to address the reasons for the truancy.

This study involves a nonrandomized group of 756 youth who were truant and brought to the truancy reduction center by the Wilmington Police Department during the 3-school-year period of the program operation (1999–2002). The majority of youth were black (79.5%) and between 12 and 16 years old. The majority of the youth were enrolled in school (66.5%). The majority of the truant youth were not on probation (56.3%) or suspension (62.4%). The majority of the truant youth were not attending alternative schools (57.4%).

Information was collected from each youth as he or she was brought to the truancy reduction center by staff of the truancy center. The social worker interviewing each truant used a one page questionnaire in which the date and time a truant was brought to the center was recorded, and demographic, home school assignment, age, race, sex, home address, the address where the youth was found truant, grade level, school district, whether the youth was suspended from school, and the stated reason the youth was truant were collected from each truant youth. Additional information including the number of days absent prior to being taken to the truancy center and whether the youth was on probation through the Delaware Family Court was collected through school contacts. This study provides results of cross-tabulation of age, race, sex, grade, and the reasons given for truancy.

Finding

Although the majority of youth were in the early pubescent through teenage years, truancy showed a progressive pattern even at the younger ages. As shown in Figure 1, from the ages of 7 to 15, each year showed a progressive increase in the number of youth who were truant. There was an 87% increase in truancy among youth between 10 and 11 years old and a 68% increase in truancy among youth 13 and 14 years old.

The same pattern of progressive truancy was demonstrated when viewing truancy by grade progression. As shown in Figure 2, the number of truant youth increased with each grade progression up until the 9th grade. After youth reached the 10th grade, the number of truant youth decreased. The majority of truant youth, 76%, were in the middle school grades (6th through 8th) and the first year of high school (9th grade). Truancy between 5th grade and 6th grade (transition from elementary to middle school) increased by 95% and by 76% between 8th and 9th grade (transition from middle school to high school).

As shown in Table 1, the reasons "missed the bus" and "didn't feel like going" accounted for the majority (53.0%) of explanations given when asked about not being in school. Whether the youth were on probation, enrolled in school, or enrolled in an alternative school, these two reasons dominated. A third of the males (31.3%) and 26.7% of the females claimed they missed the bus. Less than a quarter (23.6%) of the males and 21.4% of the females stated they did not feel like going to school. Of the youth who were on school behavior probation (n = 103), 27.2% stated that they did not feel like going, whereas 26.2% of them stated that they missed the bus. Of those enrolled in school (n = 503), 32.8% stated that they missed the bus, and 25.0% stated that they did not feel like going. The majority of youth attending alternative schools provided the same two explanations but differed from other youth in that the main excuse was that they did not feel like going. Although 16.3% of the youth stated that they missed the bus, 24% stated that they did not feel like going to school.

The reasons of "missed the bus" and "didn't feel like going" accounted for the greatest number among youth between 9 and 15 years old. Use of the excuse "missed the bus" increased each year with youth be-

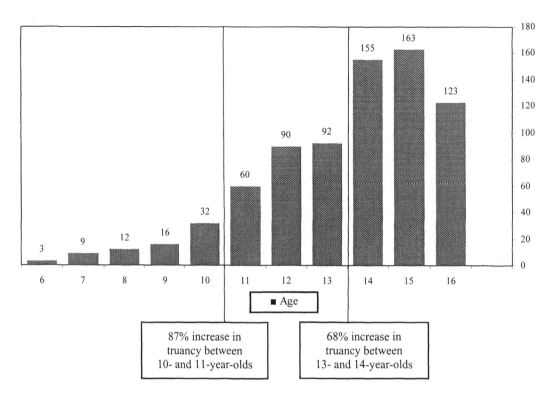

Figure 1. Number of youth truant by age.

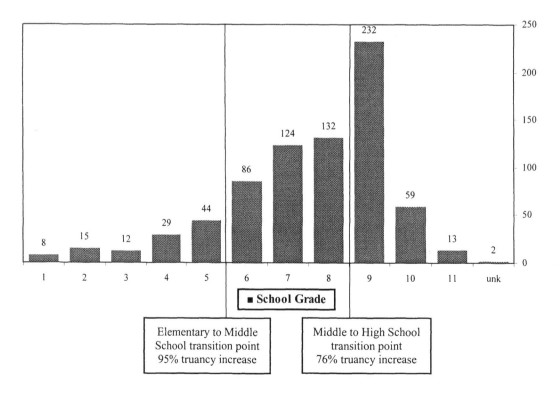

Figure 2. Number of youth truant by grade.

tween 9 and 14, after which use of the excuse decreased. The excuse "didn't feel like going" culminated with youth between 10 and 15, after which the excuse was used less often. The ages 9 through 15 and 10 through 15 are closely related to transition from elementary to middle school and from middle school to high school, respectively. As shown in Table 2, the two greatest increases in truancy are in the transfer grades (fifth to sixth and eighth to ninth).

The majority of youth who were truant were black (79.5%) and Hispanic (13.0%). Both Hispanic and black youth stated either to have "missed the bus" or that they "didn't feel like going" to school as explanations for truancy. Although 33.3% of Hispanic males stated they "didn't feel like going," only 22.0% of black males stated not wanting to go to school as an excuse. Overall, 53.0% of black youth stated that they either "missed the bus" or "didn't feel like going," and 54.0% of Hispanic youth provided the same two excuses. A greater majority of white youth (65.0%) provided the same two excuses.

The results of this study show that the majority of truant youth were in the transitional grades. The reason "didn't feel like going" increased consistently between the fifth and ninth grades. There was a 186% increase in the "didn't feel like going" explanation between the fifth and sixth grades and a 42% increase of the same excuse between the eighth and ninth grades. The number of youth truant increased by 95% between the fifth and sixth grades and 76% between the eighth and ninth grades. Use of the excuse "didn't feel like going" increased consistently between the fifth and ninth grades. Truancy occurred more with males than with females, and the age most vulnerable to truancy was between 11 and 15 years old. The most vulnerable grade to truancy was between the sixth and ninth grades.

The majority of truant youth were not "problem" youth (youth on school probation or attending alternative schools). In contrast to some research (Kee, 2001; McGiboney, 2001), youth have many reasons other than boredom and fear of other youth for not attending school. Only 2.8% of the youth stated they did not like school, and fear of other students was not reported as a reason for truancy.

A 186% increase in the "didn't feel like going" explanation between the fifth and sixth grade and a 42% increase of the same excuse between the eighth and ninth grade, as well as a 183% increase in the "missed the bus" explanation between the fifth and sixth grade and a 57% increase of the same excuse between the eighth and ninth grade, reflect the difficulty of school transition points. The use of the "missed the bus" explanation by elementary school youth (42%) and youth between 6 and 9 years old (50%) also demonstrates the problem of youth at very young ages being responsible for their own preparation and transportation to school. The use of the excuse "missed the bus" presupposes that they were responsible for catching the bus.

Policy Implications and Conclusion

Truancy is one of the early risk factors to future academic failure and one of the first delinquent behaviors that leads to more serious delinquent and criminal behaviors. As shown by this study, truancy increased 95% between fifth and sixth grade and increased 87% among youth between 10 and 11 years old. Antitruancy programs should be designed for youth who begin fifth grade and continue through the sixth grade. Such programs should focus on the fears of youth who are about to enter middle school and should acclimate them to life in middle school. Programs such as visiting the middle school and spending time with teachers and other students in middle school could help alleviate the fears and anxieties that youth feel about the transfer. Similar programs should be established for youth starting their eighth year through the start of the ninth year. Research has shown that "students showing a high level of psychological distress during transition tended to have more adaptive difficulties in middle school," and youth who show "high levels of psychological distress prior to transition represent early adolescents at a greater risk...for continued stressful school transition" (Chung et al., 1998, p. 98). This study found that truancy begins at a very early age and has a progressive development through the early life and grade development of youth through to the middle of high school. Research has shown that there are various reasons for youth disengagement from school; thus, antitruancy programs should be progressively both age and grade appropriate when designed and developed.

Research on school transition suggests that some students develop self-esteem problems after transition. The reduction in self-esteem and not fitting in can lead to other adjustment problems including declined academic achievement, difficulties in peer relationships (Chung et al., 1998), alienation from teachers, and negative views on the utility of school. Such negative views can lead to truancy and dropping out. Programs designed to match youth who are at risk of maladjustment to school after transition with one teacher throughout the first year of transition and with one upperclassman could be a solution. Together, the teacher and the upperclassman could shepherd the youth through the first year. The teacher would focus on keeping the youth on task with school and help deal with any problems the student may have with other teachers. The upperclassman could guide a desperate youth through some of the social pitfalls that await a youth who is not fitting in.

To conclude, it is proposed that truancy can be explained, in part, by the transition from one school level to another. This study found that truancy increases at the two main transfer points in a youth's education, between elementary and middle school and between middle school and high school. Programs designed to address the stress of these two points can have an effect on reducing truancy as a whole.

Table 1
Reasons Given for Not Going to School

Reason	*n*	%
Missed the bus	227	30.0
Didn't feel like going	174	23.0
Suspended	91	12.0
Not enrolled	67	8.9
No reason	46	6.1
Left early	29	3.8
Sick	28	3.7
Overslept	21	2.8
Doesn't like school	21	2.8
Medical appointment	17	2.2
Problems with other students	14	1.9
Court appointment	9	1.2
No transportation	6	0.8
Meeting parents	4	0.5
Lunch	2	0.3
Total	756	100.0

Table 2
Reason for Not Going to School, Cross-Tabulation to Grade of Truant

	Elementary					Middle			High			Unknown	Total
	1	2	3	4	5	6	7	8	9	10	11		
Missed the bus	4	6	6	11	12	34	42	37	58	14	3		227
Didn't feel like going	2	4		7	7	20	25	36	51	18	4		174
Suspended			2	3	5	14	17	15	30	4	1		91
Not enrolled	1			1	3	2	5	14	32	7	1	1	67
No reason	1	1	2	3	4	6	9	5	12	2	1		46
Left early					2		2	4	17	3	1		29
Sick		1		1	4	2	6	2	8	4	1		28
Overslept		1			4	2	5	5	3			1	21
Doesn't like school		1					4	4	8	4			21
Medical appointment		1		1			3	3	7	1			17
Problems with other students				1	1	2	1	3	3	2	1		14
Court appointment						2	2	3	2				9
No transportation			1	1	1		2		1				6
Meeting parents			1		1		1	1					4
Lunch						2							2
Total	8	15	12	29	44	86	124	132	232	59	13	2	756

References

Akos, P. (2002). Student perceptions of the transition from elementary to middle school. *Professional School Counseling Journal, 5*, 339–345.

Alspaugh, J. (1998a). Achievement loss associated with the transition to middle school and high school. *The Journal of Educational Research, 92*, 20–25.

Alspaugh, J. (1998b). The relationship of school-to-school transitions and school size to high school dropout rates. *The High School Journal, 81*, 154–160.

Alspaugh, J. (2000). The effect of transition grade to high school, gender, and grade level upon dropout rates. *American Secondary Education, 29*, 2–9.

Alspaugh, J., & Harting, R. (1995). Transition effects of school grade-level organization on student achievement. *Journal of Research and Development in Education, 28*, 145–149.

Ames, C., & Archer, J. (1988). Achievement goals in the classroom: Students' learning strategies and motivation process. *Journal of Educational Psychology, 80*, 260–270.

Anderman, E., & Midgley, C. (1997). Changes in achievement goal orientations, perceived academic competence, and grades across the transition to middle-level schools. *Contemporary Educational Psychology, 22*, 269–298.

Anderman, L., Maehr, M., & Midgley, C. (1999). Declining motivation after the transition to middle school: Schools can make a difference. *Journal of Research and Development in Education, 32*, 131–147.

Arowosafe, D., & Irvin, J. (1992). Transition to a middle level school: What kids say. *Middle School Journal, 24*, 15–19.

Chung, H., Elias, M., Schneider, K. (1998). Patterns of individual adjustment changes during middle school transition. *Journal of School Psychology, 36*, 83–101.

Entwisle, D., & Alexander, K. (1993). Entry into school: The beginning school transition and educational stratification in the United States. *Annual Review of Sociology, 19*, 401–423.

Farrington, D. (1980). Truancy, delinquency, the home and the school. In L. Hersov & I. Berg (Eds.), *Out of school: Modern perspectives in truancy and school refusal* (pp. 49–63). Chichester, UK: Wiley.

Fenzel, L. (1989). Role strains and the transition to middle school: Longitudinal trends and sex differences. *Journal of Early Adolescence, 9*, 211–226.

Gutman, L., & Midgley, C. (2000). The role of protective factors in supporting the academic achievement of poor African American students during the middle school transition. *Journal of Youth and Adolescence, 29*, 223–248.

Hertzog, C., & Morgan, P. (1999). Making the transition from middle level to high school. *High School Magazine, 6*, 26–30.

Kee, T. (2001). Attribution style and school truancy. *Early Child Development and Care, 169*, 21–38.

Lloyd, D. (1978). Prediction of school failure from third-grade data. *Educational and Psychological Measurement, 38*, 1193–1200.

McGiboney, G. (2001). Truants welcome here: An alternative school designed specially for truants is boosting student attendance. *American School Board Journal, 188*, 43–45.

Midgley, C., & Urban, T. (1992). The transition to middle level schools: Making it a good experience for all students. *Middle School Journal, 24*, 5–14.

Mizelle, N., & Mullins, E. (1997). Transition into and out of middle school. In J. Irvin (Ed.), *What current research says to the middle level practitioner* (pp. 303–313). Columbus, OH: National Middle School Association.

Newman, B., Myers, M., Newman, P., Lohman, B., & Smith, V. (2000). The transition to high school for academically promising, urban, low-income African American youth. *Adolescence, 35*, 45–66.

Phelan, W. (1992). Building bonds to high school graduation: Dropout intervention with seventh and eighth graders. *Middle School Journal, 24*, 33–35.

Pintrich, P., & Schunk, D. (1996). Motivation in education: Theory, research and applications. Englewood Cliffs, NJ: Prentice Hall.

Robins, L., & Ratcliff, K. (1980). The long-term outcome of truancy. In L. Hersov & I. Berg (Eds.), *Out of school: Modern perspectives in truancy and school refusal* (pp. 65–83). Chichester, UK: Wiley.

Schumacher, D. (1998). *The transition to middle school.* Retrieved February 24, 2004, from http://www.ericfacility.net/ericdigests/ed422119.html

About the author: Arthur H. Garrison, MS, is the director of criminal justice planning and senior researcher for the Delaware Criminal Justice Planning Council. He is also the project director for the Wilmington Hope Commission, which is a citywide initiative to design a strategy to reduce juvenile and adult violence in Wilmington, Delaware. He has written more than 20 program evaluations and has published more than 15 articles on a variety of juvenile and criminal justice issues. He has a master of science (1995) in criminal justice from West Chester University of Pennsylvania and a BA (1990) from Kutztown University of Pennsylvania.

Exercise for Article 3

Factual Questions

1. The youth were brought to the Neighborhood House by whom?

2. Who conducted the interviews?

3. Between what two ages was there the largest percentage increase in truancy?

4. What was the main excuse for truancy among students attending alternative schools?

5. How many of the truants were in fifth grade?

6. For all participants, how many indicated that they missed the bus?

Questions for Discussion

7. The researcher states that the participants were a "nonrandomized group." What is your understanding of the meaning of this term? (See lines 105–109.)

8. Only truants who were caught by police participated in this survey. Could valuable information also be obtained by questioning a sample of all students about their truancy behavior? Explain.

9. Are you surprised at the dramatic drop in truancy after grade 9? Explain. (See Figure 2.)

10. The findings of this survey focus on (a) reasons given for being truant and (b) patterns of truancy across grade and age levels. Do you regard one of these types of findings as more important than the other? Explain.

11. This survey was conducted at one program. In your opinion, does this limit the generalizability of the results? Explain.

12. In your opinion, how important are the implications of this study? (See lines 236–292.)

13. If you were to conduct a survey on the same topic, what changes in the research methodology, if any, would you make?

Quality Ratings

Directions: Indicate your level of agreement with each of the following statements by circling a number from 5 for strongly agree (SA) to 1 for strongly disagree (SD). If you believe an item is not applicable to this research article, leave it blank. Be prepared to explain your ratings. When responding to criteria A and B below, keep in mind that brief titles and abstracts are conventional in published research.

A. The title of the article is appropriate.

SA   5   4   3   2   1   SD

B. The abstract provides an effective overview of the research article.

SA   5   4   3   2   1   SD

C. The introduction establishes the importance of the study.

SA   5   4   3   2   1   SD

D. The literature review establishes the context for the study.

SA   5   4   3   2   1   SD

E. The research purpose, question, or hypothesis is clearly stated.

SA   5   4   3   2   1   SD

F. The method of sampling is sound.

SA   5   4   3   2   1   SD

G. Relevant demographics (for example, age, gender, and ethnicity) are described.

SA   5   4   3   2   1   SD

H. Measurement procedures are adequate.

SA   5   4   3   2   1   SD

I. All procedures have been described in sufficient detail to permit a replication of the study.

SA   5   4   3   2   1   SD

J. The participants have been adequately protected from potential harm.

SA   5   4   3   2   1   SD

K. The results are clearly described.

SA   5   4   3   2   1   SD

L. The discussion/conclusion is appropriate.

SA   5   4   3   2   1   SD

M. Despite any flaws, the report is worthy of publication.

SA   5   4   3   2   1   SD

Article 4

Homelessness in a Small Southern City

LINDA A. MOONEY
East Carolina University

KEVIN R. OUSLEY
East Carolina University

ABSTRACT. With recent predictions of the increase in the numbers of homeless, there has been a renewed interest in estimating homeless populations in a variety of locations. While a considerable amount of research has been conducted on homelessness in urban areas, less research has been directed toward estimating and describing the numbers of homeless in rural or nonurban areas. Further, several methodological issues surrounding the definitions of urban, nonurban, and rural (Toomey, First, Greenlee, & Cummins, 1993) have made comparisons between these locations difficult. Despite methodological confusion and the consensus that few comprehensive studies of nonurban and rural homelessness exist (Lawrence, 1995; Toomey et al., 1993; NCH, 1997a; Fitchen, 1992), researchers have been quick to conclude that rural and nonurban homelessness are demographically different from urban homelessness. The present research fills the gap in the homeless literature by collecting data on the homeless in a nonurban location, and comparing the results to representative urban and rural samples. A discussion of homelessness within the context of recent welfare reform follows the presentation of results.

From *Electronic Journal of Sociology*, *5*, May 2000. Copyright © by Linda A. Mooney and Kevin R. Ousley. Reprinted with permission.

Introduction

The study of homelessness has become "old hat" (Hopper, 1998; Wright, Rubin, & Devine, 1998; Hambrick & Johnson, 1998). Once the target of a flurry of research activity, by the early 1990s the significance of homelessness as a major social problem had considerably diminished. For example, in 1985, 32 separate bills relating to homelessness were introduced in the U.S. Congress; by 1992, politicians were all but silent on the topic—a topic soon to be dubbed as "last decade's issue" (Wright et al., 1998:2). Further evidence is gleaned from the news media's coverage of "the homeless problem." In the fall of 1988, the *New York Times* carried over 50 articles on homelessness; in the fall of 1992, 25; and by the fall of 1998, 10 (Hsiao, 1999).

Of the many reasons homelessness has faded from the public's consciousness, one stands out—the tendency to view the problem as temporary (Hambrick & Johnson, 1998; Wright et al., 1998). Such a belief led to quick fixes in which the day-to-day needs of the homeless became the focus of attention (e.g., food,

shelter) rather than addressing structural constraints (e.g., lack of affordable housing) or individual deficiencies (e.g., alcoholism) (*Priority Home!*, 1994; Wright et al., 1998; *America*, 1999).[1] Thus, few significant changes in the causes of homelessness have been initiated and, with the signing of the 1996 welfare reform bill, the numbers of homeless are likely to increase dramatically over the next several years (NCH, 1997; Willis, 1997a; Applewhite, 1997; Stanfield, 1997; U.S. Conference of Mayors, 1998; Wright et al., 1998).

Such predictions have led to a renewed interest in homelessness and a return to empirical documentation of the numbers and characteristics of the homeless to better develop policy directives. Estimates of the numbers of homeless and their characteristics have significantly changed over the years. Much of the variation in estimates is a result of definitional problems, that is, what constitutes homelessness (cf. Toomey et al., 1993). Estimates also vary with the political persuasion of those involved—activist, for example, versus government official. It is not surprising that calculations vary considerably, from a low of 300,000 to a high of several million (Barak, 1991; National Law Center on Homelessness and Poverty, 1996; NCH, 1998; Wright et al., 1998).

While there is little agreement over the number of homeless, there is some consensus that they are a heterogeneous population, at least in urban areas where the bulk of research has been conducted (Rossi, 1989; Barak, 1991; Snow & Anderson, 1993; Jencks, 1994; NAEH, 1998; Reganick, 1997; NCH, 1999). There is also evidence that the rural homeless are different from their urban counterparts, more often female, intact families, White, and currently working. They also have lower rates of chronic substance abuse and mental illness, and are disproportionately Native Americans and migrant workers (First, Rife & Toomey, 1994; NCH, 1999; NRHA, 1996; Vissing, 1996; U.S. Department of Agriculture, 1996; Butler, 1997).

Considering the relatively few studies on rural homelessness, there is a remarkable lack of agreement as to what constitutes a "rural area" (Hewitt, 1989; Toomey et al., 1993). Despite the implied dichotomy of a rural–urban designation, "the distribution of people and the density and form of living arrangements exist on a continuum" (Toomey et al., 1998:25). The U.S. Census Bureau defines rural areas as incorporated locations that have a population of less than 2,500 residents, and unincorporated less densely populated areas. Urbanized areas are places with a population greater than 50,000. Any area with a population between 2,500 and 50,000 is simply considered a nonurban location (Hewitt, 1989; Toomey et al., 1993; *Statistical Abstract of The United States*, 1998).

Despite these relatively unambiguous definitions, in studies of rural homelessness the distinctions have become muddied. Butler defines small towns as *cities* which are "not incorporated...but have populations of more than 2,500" (1997:430); Vissing speaks of "urbanized rural areas" (1996:10); Segal investigates "two contiguous small towns" (1989:28); and Fitchen refers to "small towns and the open countryside" (1992:173).

Of even greater concern, many investigators appear willing to draw definitive conclusions about the differences between these ill-defined, inadequately researched areas. For example, Lawrence (1995:298) states that "...homelessness in the countryside is qualitatively different from homelessness in the city." Similarly, Vissing (1996:12) concludes that "[H]omeless people in small towns are much more like those in rural areas than those in cities...." Alternatively, Dahl, Harris, and Gladden comment that comparisons of rural data from North Dakota to several urban samples suggest that "...the origin of homelessness, demographics, and medical problems of urban and rural homeless are quite similar" (1992:2).

The present research thus fills a gap in the homeless literature by: 1) providing a picture of homelessness in a clearly defined nonurban location, and 2) comparing the results to both urban and rural samples of homeless. The two studies selected for comparison have each been hailed as the leading research in their respective locations. First, Toomey and Rice's (1990) *Homelessness in Rural Ohio* has been called the "largest and most comprehensive study of homelessness in rural America" (Dahl et al., 1992). Although almost a decade old, the results of this study still serve as the foundation for present-day discussions on rural homelessness (cf. Wright et al., 1998:182–184).

Similarly, Burt and Cohen's (1989, 1990) investigation of homelessness in a national sample of 20 urban areas with populations over 100,000, has been described as the "most comprehensive study of its kind" (Jencks, 1994:10) as well as the "most methodologically sound" (Toomey et al., 1993:23). As recently as 1998, the Urban Institute described this data set as the "most recent nationwide study of the urban homeless" available (Urban Institute, 1999).[2]

Methodological variations in sampling techniques, however, should be noted. Burt and Cohen's (1989, 1990) respondents were from homeless shelters and/or soup kitchens, while the rural data included people staying in shelters, inexpensive hotels and motels, or other unique transient locations (First et al., 1990, 1994). The use of nonshelter sources of the homeless is common in rural areas where there are fewer shelters and thus fewer visible homeless (Aron & Fitchen, 1996; NCH, 1997; Wright et al., 1998; NCH, 1998).

The present investigation uses shelter residences only—the common denominator between the two other data sets.[3] Although the rural data's inclusion of nonshelter residents may make data comparisons more difficult, Shlay and Rossi (1992) state that the majority of studies on the homeless use shelter residents as a criteria for inclusion, and Jencks (1993:13) concludes that "...the rate of shelter use is about the same in smaller communities as in big cities." Further, respondents were asked if they knew other homeless people who did not stay at the shelter. Ninety-seven percent of the respondents said no. Nonetheless, estimates of the homeless from shelter populations may *underestimate* the numbers of the homeless and, thus, skew the resulting demographics.

Methodology

Situated on the coastal plains of North Carolina,[4] Southern City had a population of 46,000 and a land area of 18.1 square miles at the time the survey was conducted. Serving as the regional center for commerce, health care, and education, Southern City is surrounded by several smaller communities with populations ranging from just over 5,000 to just less than 500. Dominated by agriculture in general, and tobacco and cotton production in particular, Southern City is the county seat—the county having a population of 108,000 with an unemployment rate of 5.5% in 1992.

Southern City's homeless shelter was established in 1988 as a response to citizen complaints of a number of people "hanging around in the streets." The shelter operates as a nonprofit organization, supported by a variety of church-affiliated groups and volunteers from the community. Although small grants through the Federal Emergency Management Agency and United Way provide the bulk of the over $100,000 operating budget, much of the food provided to the residents comes from contributions by the U.S. Department of Agriculture and donations from local churches, restaurants, and private individuals. Nonfood items such as bedding and clothes are exchanged with other facilities such as the County Family Violence Shelter.

The shelter is located in an abandoned elementary school, built in the 1950s and located in an inner-city Black residential neighborhood. The "gymtorium" serves as the center of the facility. It is here that residents sleep in a barracks-like setting with access to bathrooms and showers, and limited access to a cafeteria. There are no admitting restrictions, although "troublemakers" are required to leave the shelter for the night.[5] Facilities are sex-segregated with women and children sleeping on the stage behind a cloth barrier. The facility also contains an office and sleeping quar-

Table 1
Characteristics of Homeless by Location

	URBAN Burt and Cohen	SOUTHERN CITY	RURAL First et al.
Year of study:	1987	1992	1990
Age			
Percent 18–30	30	34	52 (18–29)
Percent 31–50	51	57	40 (30–49)
Percent 51–65	16	9	5 (50–59)
Percent over 65	3	0	3 (60+)
Mean age	n/a	36	32
Marital status			
Percent never married	55	44	32
Percent married/living together	10	15	28
Percent divorced/separated/widowed	34	41	39
Education			
Percent 0–11 years	48	40	43
Percent H.S. graduate or equivalent	32	29	57 (H.S.+)
Percent some post H.S.	14	25	
Percent college graduate or more	6	6	
Percent H.S. graduate or more	52	60	57
Sex			
Percent male	81	75	49
Percent female	19	25	51
Race			
Percent Black	41	54	10
Percent White	46	29	85
Percent Hispanic	10	17	2
Percent Other	3	0	2
Percent non-White	54	71	14

Note. Numbers do not necessarily sum to 100 due to rounding error and/or missing data.

ters for the full-time director and two part-time assistants. The shelter is open from 6:00 p.m. to 6:00 a.m.

Interviews of shelter residents took place in February and March of 1992, and were conducted by senior
185 and graduate sociology students who had undergone several hours of faculty-led sessions on interviewing techniques. All interviews were conducted at the shelter between 7:00 and 10:00 in the evening and were, with the participants' permission, tape recorded. Each
190 of the seven students was assigned ten of the seventy beds (although not necessarily occupied) located in the shelter and were responsible for interviewing residents in those beds over the course of a six-week period. The days on which the interviews were conducted were
195 determined by shelter activities (i.e., no interviews took place on, for example, "clinic night" or "church night"). Hispanic residents were interviewed with the help of an interpreter. Forty-one residents were interviewed in total.
200 In addition to asking homeless-specific questions, standard demographic data were recorded (sex, race, age, number of children, marital status, education, and employment). Following Wright (1986: 228–229), percentage differences of ten or more were considered
205 meaningful.

Results

Table 1 reports demographic data from Southern City, as well as from the rural and urban samples. As in previous studies of the homeless, the majority of shelter residents were male—75%. The percentage of
210 males and females is significantly different from that of the rural sample, but varies little from the urban data.

Females have traditionally made up a larger proportion of the shelter population than other homeless populations, for example, the soup kitchen population.
215 Most research suggests that the overrepresentation of women in shelters is due to their need to care for dependent children (Vissing, 1996; Burt & Cohen, 1989, 1990; Butler, 1997). While just over half the respondents reported having children (57.1%), females
220 (77.8%) compared to males (52.0%) were more likely to report so and to have their children with them at the shelter.

Southern City homeless shelter residents were predominantly non-White (71%), a number significantly
225 higher than the percentage of non-Whites in the urban or rural samples. While approximately 34% of the county population is non-White, the disproportionately high rate of non-Whites in the Southern City sample may be an artifact of the time of year in which the in-

Table 2
Characteristics of Homeless by Location

Year of data collection:		URBAN Burt and Cohen 1987	SOUTHERN CITY 1992	RURAL First et al. 1990
Time homeless?[a]				
Percent < 3 months		21	52	50 (49 days or less)
Percent 4–12 months		33	33	89 (1 year or less)
Percent over 1 year		46	15	6 (2 years or more)
Mean days		1170	141	221
Work for pay previous month?		25	34	31
Income maintenance				
Percent yes (any form)		20	48	n/a
Percent mentioning:				
SSI		4	13	11
GA		5	27	38
AFDC		12	n/a	n/a
SS/Pension		n/a	7	3
Causes of homelessness (self-report)?[b]				
Economics	75	(unemployed)	43	55
Chronic disability	13	(poor health)	21	7
Personal crisis	33	(alcohol/drugs)	26	36
	21	(suicide attempt)		
	43	(psychologically distressed)		
	66	(institutionalized)		
N =		1,704	41	919

[a] The urban and Southern City homeless were asked, "How long have you been homeless?" First et al. (1994) asked, "When was the last time you had a home or a permanent place to stay?"
[b] Burt and Cohen (1989) asked respondents a series of questions about: 1) employment for pay in the last month, 2) self-reported health as excellent, very good, good, fair, or poor, 3) suicide attempts: "Was there ever a time in your life when you felt so bad that you tried to kill yourself?" 4) alcohol and drug involvement, 5) psychological distress as measured by a score of 16 or above on the CES-D scale, and 6) whether or not respondents had ever been institutionalized in a prison/jail, detoxification center, or mental hospital. Answers to these questions, although not dealing directly with the causes of homelessness, are conditions that could "impair their ability to become self-sufficient" (Burt & Cohen, 1990, p. 31).

230 terviews were conducted—in the winter months. Of the 71% non-White residents, 54% were African American and 17% Hispanics. Hispanics were more likely than any other racial/ethnic group to report being "farm laborers" (83%). Farm labor, like construction, the sec-
235 ond most frequently reported work category, is seasonal and may have been responsible for the inflated number.

Consistent with both the urban and rural samples, the average age of shelter respondents was 36, with a
240 median value of 34. As Rossi (1990:957) states, "...today's homeless are surprisingly young; virtually all recent studies of the homeless report median ages in the low to middle 30s." Somewhat surprisingly, however, younger respondents were not more likely to re-
245 port being first-time shelter residents.

Southern City shelter residents were less likely to never be married (44%) than their urban counterparts (55%), but more likely than rural respondents (32%). As Barak (1991:36) notes, the percentage of married
250 people among the urban homeless is lower than that among the rural homeless. However, Southern City and

urban data in other marital categories are comparable. Respectively, Southern City and the urban data indicate that 15% and 10% of the respondents were married or
255 living together, and 41% and 34% of the respondents were divorced, separated, or widowed.

Over half the Southern City respondents reported graduating from high school or higher levels of education (60%), which is similar to the urban and rural
260 samples. Educational levels varied little by sex, but were substantively interesting by race/ethnicity. Forty percent of the non-White respondents reported having less than a high school degree compared to 67% of the White respondents. Thus, in the present sample, minor-
265 ity shelter residents were better educated than their White counterparts.

Of the variables of interest, length of time homeless was the most difficult to compare across samples given differences in measurement intervals. Some respon-
270 dents initially explained being unsure how long they had been homeless, reporting moving in and out of relatives' and friends' homes and abandoned houses. When asked how long he had been homeless, one 39-

year-old White male responded, "Off and on. I would
275 say approximately, you know, maybe a year and a
half...two years...maybe three." (#7)

Table 2 continues the analysis of characteristics of
urban, nonurban, and rural respondents. Southern City
residents most often reported being homeless three
280 months or less (52%), followed by 4 to 12 months
(33%), and more than 12 months (15%). Burt and
Cohen's (1989; 1990) research found that the modal
interval was over a year (46%) while 89% of the rural
respondents report being homeless for a year or less.
285 Mean days homeless indicate that time homeless is
significantly greater in urban areas (1,170 days), followed by rural (221 days) and nonurban areas (141
days).

Respondents in the rural and Southern City samples
290 were asked whether they had worked for pay in the
previous month. While rural and Southern City respondents varied little in the percent responding yes, 31%
and 34%, respectively, urban homeless respondents
reported that 25% were "presently working."

295 Income maintenance was measured by whether or
not a respondent, at the time of the survey, was receiving Aid to Families with Dependent Children (AFDC),
General Assistance (GA), Supplemental Security Income (SSI), or Social Security (SS)/pension. A slightly
300 higher than might be expected proportion of Southern
City shelter residents received income maintenance
benefits—48%—over twice the number receiving such
benefits in the urban sample. However, when asked the
type of benefit received, respondents in the nonurban
305 and rural samples were most likely to mention General
Assistance over any other type of benefit.

Finally, respondents were asked, "What do you
think caused your homelessness?"[6] Categories included
chronic disability (mental and physical illness, sub-
310 stance abuse, institutionalization); *personal crisis* (divorce, runaway/throwaway, family conflicts, death of
spouse); and *economic conditions* (loss of employment,
lack of sufficient funds, eviction, and/or no transportation). Consistent with other research (cf. Momeni,
315 1990:79), the modal category for the nonurban and
rural samples is economic conditions (43% and 55%,
respectively). As one 30-year-old Black female responded (#15):

> The reason I'm in this place is because I do not have a
320 > job. It is simply that. You have to have money to pay for
> those things and most people are staying here because
> they don't have a job. If you had a job you could stay and
> save up money. No one wants to stay. The only people
> who have to stay here, some of the people like, have al-
325 > cohol problems or something like that, and they can't
> work but I don't have any of those problems. There is no
> reason why I should not be able to work and get out of
> this shelter—none.

Chronic disability variables were the least likely to
330 be mentioned in both the nonurban and rural samples.
However, an examination of responses from the urban

sample indicates that a fairly high proportion of respondents reported being in poor health (13%) and
receiving some form of institutionalized treatment at
335 least once in their life (66%).

Discussion

The results, although reaffirming the heterogeneity
of the homeless population and the need for consistent
measurement techniques, also suggest that, contrary to
Vissing (1996), Lawrence (1995) and Dahl et al.
340 (1992), the characteristics of the nonurban homeless
reflect those of both comparison samples. The homeless in Southern City were predominantly non-White
males, with an average age of 36. Most were never
married; almost half did not graduate from high school
345 and, on the average, had been homeless for four to five
months. A third had worked for pay in the month prior
to the survey, and almost half were receiving some
kind of income maintenance.

The above portrait bears a remarkable similarity to
350 Burt and Cohen's (1989:36) description of urban respondents:

> ...homeless persons in cities with a population of 100,000
> over...are male...the majority are non-White...between 30
> and 51 years of age...[A]lmost half have not graduated
355 > from high school....

Southern City homeless were also disproportionately Black, young, single males. However, similarities
between Southern City homeless and First et al.'s
(1990, 1994) rural sample also exist. Nonurban and
360 rural homeless were less likely to be homeless for over
a year, the mean days for rural and Southern City samples being 141 and 221 respectively. The mean number
of days of homelessness for the urban sample was
1,170.

365 Further, the distribution of income maintenance between the rural and Southern City samples are similar—General Assistance being the most common form
of aid in both samples. While comparisons of self-
reported causes of homelessness are difficult given
370 differences in the interview formats, educational levels
appear analogous for all three groups with a range of
only 52% to 60% completing high school and/or with
some post-high school experience.

It is possible, however, that the variations in the
375 characteristics of the homeless may, in part, be an artifact of variations in the three sampling designs. For
example, Southern City homeless were exclusively
from shelters. Some research suggests that women are
more likely to seek refuge in shelters and, thus, the
380 Southern City estimates of the number of homeless
females may be exaggerated (Toomey et al., 1993). On
the other hand, Vissing (1996) and First et al. (1994)
suggest that homeless rural families, the highest proportion of which are headed by females, are more
385 likely to stay with friends and family than in shelters,
which would suggest that the Southern City sample
underestimated the number of homeless females. Given

that 75% of the sample were men, the second interpretation appears more likely.

390   Additionally, as noted earlier, the proportion of non-Whites was considerably higher than that in the urban or rural samples. It was suggested that the months in which the interviews took place—February and March—may have impacted the number of African

395   Americans and Hispanics who were disproportionately migrant workers. State statistics support this contention. North Carolina farm worker service providers estimate that between 15% and 50% of all migrant workers spend at least some time in a shelter, most

400   frequently in the winter months (North Carolina Consolidated Plan, 1996). Further, the number of the homeless in Southern City could be overestimated and/or "urbanized" as the homeless migrate south from the harsh winters of the northern states (Jencks, 1994:1).

405   The shelter has grown considerably since the data were collected. As if in preparation for what lies ahead, the staff has more than doubled. Consistent with national trends, there have been rumblings of funding cutbacks and moving the shelter to a different (i.e., less

410   visible) location. The National Law Center on Homelessness and Poverty recently published a report, *Out of Sight, Out of Mind?*, which documents similar efforts to conceal the homeless through the relocation of shelters, nightly "sweeps," and forcible removal from high

415   visibility areas (Nieves, 1998; Hsiao, 1998; *America*, 1999).

Such trends reflect a general movement toward what Hooper (1998) calls "remoralizing" the poor and, by extension, the homeless. The implication that the

420   poor and homeless are somehow accomplices in their own circumstances, that poverty is symptomatic of individual deficiency, is implicit in the Personal Responsibility and Work Opportunity Reconciliation Act of 1996, which subordinates need to merit. Ironically,

425   many of the same people who have been denied welfare assistance are now homeless and, once again, are being penalized for their poverty. For example, New York City officials have declared that shelters are a form of public assistance and, therefore, shelter resi-

430   dents must meet the requirements of all public assistance recipients including workfare (Bernstein, 1999:1).

The effects of welfare reform are, and will continue to be, disproportionately felt in rural areas where

435   homelessness is most closely linked to poverty and there are fewer shelters and other services to compensate for the loss of welfare benefits (Aron & Fitchen, 1996; Butler, 1997; NCH, 1998; Wright et al., 1998). In Wisconsin, a largely rural state, a 75% reduction in

440   welfare recipients has resulted in a three-fold increase in the homeless population (DeParle, 1999; Willis, 1997a; Stanfield, 1997); and in Maine, a five-year limit on welfare benefits has increased homelessness in a state "where welfare has kept many [of the respon-

445   dents] one step away from life on the streets" (Butler, 1997:432).

Thus, while government officials, as indicated by the policies they initiate, pursue the path of least resistance by blaming the victim, homeless advocates con-

450   tinue to call for structural alterations, most notably the reduction of poverty and an adequate supply of low-income housing (Wright et al., 1998:210). Ultimately, homelessness is a problem of poverty and in areas where poverty rates are the highest, often nonurban

455   areas, homelessness will continue to increase, particularly with the removal of the safety net of public assistance. The need to count and classify, describe and define, hence remains paramount in identifying the causes of homelessness in the hopes of developing

460   public policies that work.

References

America. 1999. "More Homeless, More Hungry." *America* 180 (3): 3.

Applewhite, Steven Lozano. 1997. "Homeless Veterans: Perspectives on Social Services Use." *Social Work* 42 (1): 19–31.

Aron, Laudan Y. and Janet M. Fitchen. 1996. "Rural Homelessness: A Synopsis" in *Homelessness in America* 1996. National Coalition for the Homeless. Washington, DC: Oryx Press.

Barak, Gregg. 1991. *Gimme Shelter*. NY: Praeger.

Bernstein, Nina. 1998. "New York City Plans to Extend Workfare to Homeless Shelters." *New York Times* (February 20): 1.

Burt, Martha and Barbara E. Cohen. 1989. *America's Homeless: Numbers, Characteristics, and Programs That Serve Them*. Washington, DC: The Urban Institute Press.

Burt, Martha and Barbara E. Cohen. 1990. "A Sociodemographic Profile of the Service-Using Homeless: Findings from a National Survey." Pp. 17–38 in *Homelessness in the United States—Data and Issues*, edited by Jamshid Momeni. NY: Praeger.

Butler, Sandra Sue. 1997. "Homelessness Among AFDC Families in a Rural State: It Is Bound to Get Worse." *Affilia* 12 (4): 427–441.

Dahl, Sherlyn, Helen Harris, and Joanne Gladden. 1992. "Homelessness: A Rural Perspective." *Prairie Rose* (August):1–6.

DeParle, Jason. 1999. "Wisconsin Welfare Overhaul Justifies Hope and Some Fear." *New York Times* (January 15): A1.

Department of Health and Human Services. 1998. "National Survey of Homeless Assistance Providers and Clients." HHS Homepage. http://www.dhhs.gov

First, Richard, John Rife, and Beverly Toomey. 1994. "Homelessness in Rural Areas: Causes, Patterns and Trends." *Social Work* 39 (1): 97–108.

First, Richard, Beverly Toomey, and J. Rife. 1990. *Homelessness in Rural Ohio*. Columbus, OH: Ohio State University.

Fitchen, Janet M. 1991. "On the Edge of Homelessness: Rural Poverty and Housing Insecurity." *Rural Sociology* 57 (2): 173–193.

Hambrick, Ralph S. and Gary Johnson. 1998. "The Future of Homelessness." *Society* 35 (6): 28–38.

Hewitt, M. 1989. "Defining 'Rural' Areas: Impact on Health Care Policy and Research." Washington, DC: Community for Creative Nonviolence.

Hopper, Kim. 1998. "Housing the Homeless." *Social Policy* 28 (3): 64–67.

Hsiao, Andrew. 1998. "The Disappeared." *The Village Voice* 43 (49): 32–33.

Jencks, Christopher. 1994. *The Homeless*. Cambridge, MA: Harvard University Press.

Lawrence, Mark. 1995. "Rural Homelessness: A Geography without a Geography." *Journal of Rural Studies* 11 (3): 297–301.

Momeni, Jamshid. 1990. "No Place to Go: A National Picture of Homelessness in America." Pp. 165–183 in *Homelessness in the United States—Data and Issues*, edited by Jamshid Momeni. NY: Praeger.

NAEH (National Alliance to End Homelessness). 1998. "Facts about Homelessness." National Alliance to End Homelessness, 1518 K Street, NW, Washington, DC, 20005 <http://www.naeh.org>

NCH (National Coalition for the Homeless). 1999. "Who is Homeless?: Fact Sheet No. 3." February. 1012 14th Street, NW. Suite 600. Washington, DC 20005. 202/73775-6444.

_____. 1998. "How Many Homeless: Fact Sheet No. 2." May. 1012 14th Street NW. Suite 600. Washington, DC. 20005. 202/73775-6444.

_____. 1997a. "Rural Homelessness: Fact Sheet Number 13." October. 1012 14th Street, NW. Suite 600. Washington, DC. 20005. 202/73775-6444.

_____. 1997b. "Homelessness in America: Unabated and Increasing." 1012 14th Street, NW. Suite 600. Washington, DC. 20005. 202/73775-6444.

National Law Center on Homelessness and Poverty. 1996. "Mean Sweeps: A Report on Anti-Homeless Laws, Litigation and Alternatives in 50 United

States Cities." National Law Center on Homelessness and Poverty. 918 F Street, NW, Washington, DC 20004. 202/638-2535.

National Rural Health Association. 1996. "The Rural Homeless: America's Lost Population." Kansas City: NRHA #PU0896-42.

Nieves, Evelyn. 1998. "Homelessness Tests San Francisco's Ideals." *New York Times* (November 13): A1.

North Carolina Consolidated Plan. 1996. "Housing Needs Assessment: Homeless Needs, Facilities and Services." November. Washington, DC: U.S. Department of Housing and Urban Development. Office of Community Planning and Development. <http:www.state.nc.us/commerce/commasst/plan>

Oreskes, Michael and Robin Toner. 1989. "The Homeless at the Heart of Poverty and Policy." *New York Times* (January 29).

Priority Home! 1994. "The Federal Plan to Break the Cycle of Homelessness." Interagency Council on the Homeless. Washington, DC: Government Printing Office.

Reganick, Karol A. 1997. "Prognosis for Homeless Children and Adolescents." *Childhood Education* 73 (3): 133–136.

Rossi, Peter H. 1989. *Down and Out in America: The Origins of Homelessness.* Chicago, Il.: University of Chicago Press.

Shinn, Marybeth. 1997. "Family Homelessness: State or Trait?" *American Journal of Community Psychology* 25(6): 755–770.

Shlay, Anne B. and Peter Rossi. 1992. "Social Science Research and Contemporary Studies on Homelessness." *Annual Review of Sociology* 18: 129–160.

Snow, David and Leon Anderson. 1993. *Down on Their Luck: A Study of Homeless Street People.* Berkeley: California University Press.

Snow, David, Susan Baker, Leon Anderson, and Michael Martin. 1986. "The Myth of Pervasive Mental Illness Among the Homeless." *Social Problems* 33 (5): 407–423.

Sosin, Michael. 1992. "Homeless and Vulnerable Meal Program Users: A Comparison Study." *Social Problems* 39 (2): 170–188.

Stanfield, Rochelle. 1997. "HUD Choice May Face Old Problems." *National Journal* 28 (3): 120–122.

Statistical Abstract of the United States, 118th edition. 1998. Washington, DC: Government Printing Office.

Toomey, Beverly, Richard First, Richard Greenlee, and Linda Cummings. 1993. "Counting the Rural Homeless Population: Methodological Dilemmas." *Social Work Research and Abstracts* 29 (4): 23–27.

U.S. Conference of Mayors. 1998. "A Status Report on Hunger and Homelessness in American Cities." U.S. Conference of Mayors. <http://www.usmayors.org/uscm/>

U.S. Department of Agriculture, Rural Economic and Community Development. 1996. "Rural Homelessness: Focusing on the Needs of the Rural Homeless." U. S. Department of Agriculture, Rural Housing Service, Rural Economic and Community Development, 14th St. and Independence Ave. SW. Washington, DC 20250-1533.

Urban Institute. 1998. "Homelessness: Ten Basic Questions Answered." <http://www.urban.org/news/ factsheet/homelessFS.html>

Vissing, Yvonne M. 1996. *Out of Sight, Out of Mind.* Lexington: University of Kentucky Press.

Willis, Laurie. 1997a. "Grim Forecast for Needy." *News and Observer.* December 5: B1.

Willis, Laurie. 1997b. "Conference to Focus on Homeless." *News and Observer.* December 4: B7.

Wright, James D., Beth A. Rubin, and Joel A. Devine. 1998. *Beside the Golden Door.* New York: Aldine.

Wright, S. E. 1986. *Social Science Statistics.* Newton, MA: Allyn and Bacon, Inc.

Note: This paper was presented at the annual meetings of the Southern Sociological Society in Chattanooga, TN, on April 2, 1993.

Acknowledgments: The authors gratefully acknowledge the valuable assistance of Jon Beckert, Brian Crisp, Michael Dalecki, Donna Evans, Bonnie Haswell, Michelle Hilhorst, Sarah Poulos, Christine Ransdell, Lisa Tripp, and Amy Whitcher.

Address correspondence to: Linda A. Mooney, Department of Sociology, East Carolina University, Greenville, NC 27858. E-mail: mooneyl@mail.ecu.edu

Endnotes

[1]Obviously, any given individual's homelessness has multiple causes. Nonetheless, the debate over causality most often has been framed as one between structural versus individualistic variables or what Shinn (1997) calls "states versus traits." Wright et al. (1998) proposes an intermediate and theoretically sound position: "defects and dislocations of structure…create a population at risk of homelessness; defects of persons determine who within the at-risk population actually becomes homeless" (p. 9).

[2]A more recent survey, the 1996 National Survey of Homeless Assistance Providers and Clients, was modeled after the Burt and Cohen (1989) study. Its emphasis, however, unlike its predecessor, is

on the providers of homeless assistance and the clients they serve (Department of Health and Human Services, 1998).

[3]Southern City does not have a soup kitchen or any other assisting services, with the exception of the Salvation Army, which, if called by the police, accompany the homeless person to the shelter.

[4]According to the North Carolina Consolidated Plan (1996), homelessness in the state varies by geographical region. The most populated area of the state, the Piedmont, has the highest rate of homeless, followed by the coastal plains and the mountains. Statistics from 1994, those that most closely approximate the study date, indicate that North Carolina had 187 emergency shelters with a sleeping capacity of 4,271 in 64 of the state's 100 counties. As in other states, homelessness in North Carolina is predicted to grow with a 1997 estimate of over 500,000 North Carolinians on the verge of homelessness (Willis, 1997b).

[5]Several city police were interviewed, as was the police attorney, in reference to police policy concerning the homeless. Police indicated that on any given night, the shelter was the location of an estimated 90 to 100 percent of the homeless in the city limits. Police, when coming upon a homeless person, drive the person to the shelter if so desired, or simply make sure that the person "moves along" since there is a policy of "no sleeping" in public parks at night, or in alleys, streets, or sidewalks. Additionally, the shelter director and staff members were interviewed concerning shelter policy and history.

[6]Burt and Cohen did not ask for self-reported causes of homelessness. They did, however, ask about employment, health concerns, institutionalization (prison/jail, mental hospital, drug/alcohol treatment facility), psychological distress, and attempted suicide.

Exercise for Article 4

Factual Questions

1. Estimates of the number of homeless nationally vary from a low of 300,000 to a high of how many?

2. Who conducted the interviews?

3. Were the interviews conducted in the shelter?

4. In Southern City, what percentage of the homeless were males?

5. According to the researchers, of the variables of interest, which one was the most difficult to compare across samples?

6. Did a higher percentage of Southern City *or* urban respondents receive income maintenance benefits?

Questions for Discussion

7. In your opinion, is it reasonably valid to compare the results of a study in which only respondents in shelters/soup kitchens were interviewed with results of a study in which other groups were also included, such as respondents in inexpensive motels? Explain. (See lines 120–144.)

8. Would it be interesting to know why Southern City and not some other city was chosen as the site for the survey?

9. If you had been conducting this study, are there any other questions you would have asked the homeless? Explain.

10. The researchers are critical of "government officials." In your opinion, is it acceptable for researchers to voice such opinions? Explain. (See lines 447–460.)

11. In light of the information in this article, do you believe that more research on the homeless is needed?

Quality Ratings

Directions: Indicate your level of agreement with each of the following statements by circling a number from 5 for strongly agree (SA) to 1 for strongly disagree (SD). If you believe an item is not applicable to this research article, leave it blank. Be prepared to explain your ratings. When responding to criteria A and B below, keep in mind that brief titles and abstracts are conventional in published research.

A. The title of the article is appropriate.

SA 5 4 3 2 1 SD

B. The abstract provides an effective overview of the research article.

SA 5 4 3 2 1 SD

C. The introduction establishes the importance of the study.

SA 5 4 3 2 1 SD

D. The literature review establishes the context for the study.

SA 5 4 3 2 1 SD

E. The research purpose, question, or hypothesis is clearly stated.

SA 5 4 3 2 1 SD

F. The method of sampling is sound.

SA 5 4 3 2 1 SD

G. Relevant demographics (for example, age, gender, and ethnicity) are described.

SA 5 4 3 2 1 SD

H. Measurement procedures are adequate.

SA 5 4 3 2 1 SD

I. All procedures have been described in sufficient detail to permit a replication of the study.

SA 5 4 3 2 1 SD

J. The participants have been adequately protected from potential harm.

SA 5 4 3 2 1 SD

K. The results are clearly described.

SA 5 4 3 2 1 SD

L. The discussion/conclusion is appropriate.

SA 5 4 3 2 1 SD

M. Despite any flaws, the report is worthy of publication.

SA 5 4 3 2 1 SD

Article 5

Latino Students in North Carolina: Acculturation, Perceptions of School Environment, and Academic Aspirations

ELVIA Y. VALENCIA
Rutgers, The State University of New Jersey

VALERIE JOHNSON
Rutgers, The State University of New Jersey

ABSTRACT. This study describes results from an investigation of Latino students attending a Hispanic Education Summit (HES) in North Carolina. Findings from data gleaned from 275 middle and high school students' perceptions are presented. Self-report data assessed level of acculturation, as well as students' perceptions with regard to a variety of issues, including school programs, barriers to participation in programs, problems in the school environment, and academic aspirations. Results revealed that students reported few perceived barriers to school and aspirations. However, there was a significant relationship between acculturation level and the frequency with which students reported selected barriers and future life goals. Gender differences were found with regard to acculturation level, perception of barriers, and academic aspirations. Directions for further research are discussed.

From *Hispanic Journal of Behavioral Sciences*, 28, 350–367. Copyright © 2006 by Sage Publications. Reprinted with permission.

During adolescence, youth encounter normative physical, cognitive, emotional, social, and environmental life changes that are unique, challenging, and often stressful (Blechman & Culhane, 1993; Rice, 5 Herman, & Peterson, 1993). In addition to the normative stress of adolescence, immigrant youth face multiple stressors and adversities. Ethnic minority status has been associated with psychosocial distress for Hispanic adolescents (Padilla & Ruiz, 1973). Also, impression-10 istic and clinical reports (e.g., Vargas-Willis & Cervantes, 1987) have identified problems associated with linguistic differences, changing personal and familial values, changing role expectations, lowered socioeconomic conditions, immigrant status, and per-15 ceived discrimination as stressful events (Cervantes, Padilla, & Salgado de Snyder, 1991). These factors, in turn, have been linked to a host of negative outcomes, including school dropout, substance use problems, delinquency, and poor overall psychological adjustment 20 (Blechman & Culhane, 1993; Nelson & Pearson, 1994; Walton, Blow, Bingham, & Chermack, 2003).

Latinos have quickly become the largest minority group enrolled in public schools throughout the United States. According to the U.S. Department of Educa-25 tion's National Center on Education Statistics (NCES, 2003), today one in every six children who attend public school in the United States is of Latino origin. Furthermore, recent figures released by the U.S. Census Bureau (2000) indicate that in four southern states—30 Arkansas, Georgia, North Carolina, and Tennessee—the Latino school-aged population has grown by more than 250% since 1990. Among these states, North Carolina, with a 397% growth, represents the state with the largest increase in the number of Latino school-35 aged children.

Latino youth, especially Mexican-origin youth, are especially at risk of academic underachievement and school dropout (Alva, 1995; Okagaki & Frensch, 1998). Glennie and Steams (2002), for example, re-40 ported that in North Carolina, the latest statistics of 9th- and 10th-grade dropouts show that Latino adolescents have the highest school dropout rate (7.9%) compared with Native Americans (5.8%), African Americans (4.5%), and Whites (3.1%). The Department of 45 Public Instruction (DPI, 2002) also reported that the total number of Hispanic dropouts in North Carolina increased from the 2000–2001 academic year to the following academic year. Among the main reasons reported for Hispanic students dropping out was poor 50 attendance. These reports offer limited information with regard to these students' perceptions of their school experience, problems they face at school, and the factors that contribute to their decision to drop out.

Acculturation is one of the most studied concepts 55 thought to influence academic achievement and aspirations in Latino adolescents. Nonetheless, studies examining the effect of acculturation have yielded inconsistent results. Some studies have found that those students who are more acculturated tend to fare better 60 academically (Martinez, DeGarmo, & Eddy, 2004; Plunkett & Bamaca-Gomez, 2003; Rogler, Cortes, & Malgady, 1991), whereas others have presented findings to the contrary (Amaro, 1990; Burnam, Hough, Kamo, Escobar, & Telles, 1987; Moscicki, Locke, Rae, 65 & Boyd, 1989). Research has found that acculturation produces a differential effect on outcomes of interest depending on factors such as country of origin (Gil, Vega, & Dimas, 1994; Guilamo-Ramos, Jaccard, Johansson, & Tunisi, 2004; Rogler et al., 1991; Slavin & Calderon, 2001), English (as well as native language) proficiency (Riggs & Greenberg, 2004; Slavin & Calderon, 2001), family socioeconomic status and education level (Jimenez, 2002; Riggs & Greenberg, 2004; Ruiz, 2002; Slavin & Calderon, 2001), family pride (Rogler et al., 1991), perceptions of academic and social mobility (Jimenez, 2002), and gender (Jimenez, 2002; Plunkett & Bamaca-Gomez, 2003; T. D. Rodriguez, 2003; Ruiz, 2002).

Adding to the difficulty in assessing the effect of acculturation is the fact that there has been considerable debate with regard to the selection of salient constructs in measuring acculturation (Escobar & Vega, 2000). This debate not only encompasses the challenge of identifying the necessary and sufficient dimensions of culture important to what is termed cultural orientation but, as Berry (2003) indicates, at the heart of the acculturation debate are two core issues: (a) whether acculturation affects all groups in contact (dominant and nondominant) and hence is a mutual process and (b) whether acculturation is essentially unidimensional (and unidirectional) or whether it is multidimensional, with complex variations taking place. As Escobar and Vega (2000) point out, culture is one of the most complex words in the human vocabulary, making the measurement of acculturation a very difficult process. These researchers propose that simple historical indicators, such as preferred language, place of birth, and years in the United States, have consistently demonstrated predictive ability for drug use or psychiatric disorders. Furthermore, they suggest that when multidimensional acculturation scales are used in multivariate models to predict health outcomes, language and place of birth are routinely found to be far stronger predictors than other cultural factors nested within these scales.

For the purposes of this study, acculturation is defined as the bidirectional and multidimensional process of adapting to a culture as a result of changes in cultural attitudes, values, and behaviors that come from being in contact with two or more distinct cultures (Berry, 2003). This is to be distinguished from the process commonly referred to as *assimilation* or a definition of acculturation as a unidirectional process in which the immigrant is expected to gradually relinquish his or her cultural mores and to adopt those of the country of residence (Berry, 2003). Examination of the latter process is beyond the scope of this study.

Aside from cultural variables, research has demonstrated the importance of other factors salient to academic achievement, including the sense of connection to the school (Brown & Evans, 2002), perceived support (E. J. Lopez, Ehly, & Garcia-Vasquez, 2002; Prelow & Loukas, 2003), perceived barriers (Martinez et al., 2004; Taylor, 2002), and parenting variables including support/warmth, monitoring, involvement, as well as educational attainment (Arellano & Padilla, 1996; Gutman & Midgley, 2000; Hubbard, 1999; Newman, Lohman, Newman, Myers, & Smith, 2000; Newman, Myers, Newman, Lohman, & Smith, 2000; O'Connor, 1997; Smokowski, Reynolds, & Bezruczko, 1999; Werner, 1993; Werner & Smith, 1992).

In summary, immigrant adolescents face unique challenges in adapting to a new country, culture, language, and educational system. Whereas many, if not most, immigrant adolescents have to cope with issues of adjustment, Latino adolescents must also cope with negative stereotypes about their academic abilities and the perception that Latino culture does not value educational attainment. These negative stereotypes can often lead to isolation from the school environment. These unique challenges and stereotypes are thought to affect each child differently as a function of both acculturation level and gender. It is important to understand Latino students' perceptions of their school environment and how these perceptions might affect their academic aspirations. Furthermore, the development of culturally sensitive programs that aim to meet the unique needs of this population should not merely aspire to enhance their levels of academic achievement but should also seek to address their perceptions of culturally related barriers and expectations.

The purpose of this article is to describe students' perceptions with regard to the barriers and problems they face at school, as well as their perceived level of adult support, attachment to school and community, and academic aspirations. These constructs were examined by acculturation level and gender.

Method

Sample

The sample for this study was a convenience sample generated by those students who participated in the 2004 annual Hispanic Education Summit (HES). Data were collected from 277 7th- through 12th-grade students from 10 counties in North Carolina.

Design and Procedure

The HES is an annual conference organized by the North Carolina Society of Hispanic Professionals (NCSHP), whose primary objective is to promote and disseminate information on the benefits of formal and higher education among the Latino youth of North Carolina. The NCSHP sent invitation letters to all limited English proficiency (LEP) coordinators in the state of North Carolina. LEP coordinators in turn sent out invitation letters to all middle and high school teachers in their corresponding counties encouraging them to invite all of their Latino students to attend the NCSHP-HES. Prior to attending the HES, the NCSHP Student Questionnaire was administered to students. Questionnaires were sent to teachers who had registered students for participation in the HES and were asked to

have their students complete the questionnaire prior to their arrival at the HES. Teachers were asked to inform
180 their students about the nature of the questionnaire and that participation was voluntary and anonymous. Participating teachers were entered into a raffle for a personal computer for having their students complete and return the survey questionnaires. Students were in-
185 formed that they would have a chance to win one of five portable CD players for completing the questionnaire.

Measures

NCSHP Student Questionnaire. Students were assessed using the NCSHP Student Questionnaire, a self-
190 report, open-ended questionnaire designed by the NCSHP to obtain information with regard to students' perceptions of their school environment as well as their future goals and academic aspirations. The NCSHP Student Questionnaire contained 22 questions and took
195 approximately 30 minutes to complete. This survey included demographic information, perceptions of needs and barriers, level of school involvement, level of perceived support, as well as future life goals and academic aspirations.
200   The open-ended responses on questionnaires were coded based on categories derived through qualitative data analysis of prior data obtained in the 2003 NCSHP-HES using grounded theory and constant comparisons methods (Strauss & Corbin, 1990). These
205 categories were used to create a coding template for quantitative analysis of the present (2004) HES questionnaires. Outcome variables were numerically coded as follows:

Perceptions of school environment: Students were
210 asked three two-part questions about barriers, dangers, and problems faced at school. Barriers, dangers, and problems were coded as 1 if the student cited it in his or her response and as 0 if there was no specific mention of this item in the response.

215 *Perceived level of engagement/support:* Five items on the survey asked students about their perceived engagement with their school and community as well as their perceived level of support from teachers and parents. Responses to these questions were coded on
220 a scale from 1 (*no involvement*) to 3 (*high level of involvement or support*).

Academic aspirations: Students were asked, "What are your goals for the future?" The majority of students answered this question by providing a specific
225 career aspiration. Based on these responses, three categories were created: professional (e.g., doctor), assigned a value of 3; semiprofessional (e.g., schoolteacher), assigned a value of 2; and nonprofessional (e.g., soccer player, singer), assigned a value of 1.
230 Some students answered this question by indicating a particular life goal (and not a specific career). These life goal responses included the following themes: (a)

do well in school; (b) attend a college/university; (c) be successful; (d) finish high school; and (e) have a
235 career (nonspecified). Each future life goal was coded as 1 if the student mentioned it in his or her response and 0 if there was no specific mention of this category in his or her response.

Acculturation

For the purposes of this study, acculturation was
240 measured by combining language preference and years of residence in the United States. Each questionnaire contained questions presented in both English and Spanish. If a student completed the entire questionnaire in Spanish, the language preference was coded as
245 Spanish; likewise, if the student answered the entire questionnaire in English, the language preference was coded as English. Finally, if the student completed the questionnaire using both languages, the language preference was coded as bilingual. Years of residence was
250 taken directly from the student's response of the question "How long have you been in the United States?" The length of time measure was dichotomized into two groups—those who reported being in the United States for 5 years or less and those who reported being in the
255 United States for more than 5 years. Previous studies have found significant differences in outcomes such as level of distress (Rotenberg, Kutsay, & Venger, 2000) and immersion in a host society (Bowen, 2004) as well as immigrants' identity and acculturation experience
260 (Onishi & Murphy-Shigematsu, 2003) between those immigrants who have resided in the United States for 5 years or less and those who have been here longer. Students who lived in the United States for fewer than 5 years and chose to complete the questionnaire solely
265 in Spanish were categorized as low in acculturation. Those who resided in the United States for more than 5 years and chose to complete the questionnaire solely in English were categorized as high in acculturation. Finally, all students who completed the questionnaire in
270 both languages as well as those who did not fit into the low or high acculturation groups because the length of time and language were inconsistent (i.e., they were either in this country for more than 5 years [including those who were born in the United States] but still
275 chose Spanish or lived in this country fewer than 5 years but chose English) were categorized as mixed in acculturation level. Nine students were omitted due to missing data.

Analyses

Chi-square tests were used to assess the relationship
280 between acculturation level (a three-level categorical variable) and the frequencies with which students reported about barriers, support, school engagement, community engagement, and academic aspirations. Chi-square analyses were also used to examine gender
285 differences with regard to the different outcome variables.

39

Results

The demographic characteristics of the sample were as follows: Their ages ranged from 11 to 20 years old (median age = 15). (Two students were not included as
290 they listed their age as being 7 and 8 years old.) Most were high school students (69%) and reported Mexico as their place of birth (71%). A large percentage (68%) reported having lived in the United States for fewer than 5 years. Length of time in the United States
295 ranged from 2 months to 18 years (median = 3 years). Most participants chose to answer the questionnaire in English (49%), followed by Spanish (40%), and both languages (11%). Females represented 54% of the sample.
300 Results of students' perceptions of their school environment revealed overall low percentages of reported barriers. Among those barriers reported, discrimination (8%) was the most frequently mentioned barrier to school involvement, no time (8%) was the most fre-
305 quently mentioned barrier to after-school program attendance, and lack of time (8%) was the most frequently reported barrier to parental involvement in school. Language difficulties and time were approximately equally reported as barriers to community in-
310 volvement (5% and 4%, respectively). The most frequently reported danger/problem was violence/fights (19%), followed by drugs/alcohol (17%), and discrimination (11%). Fifty-eight percent of students expressed a desire to be professionals (e.g., doctor, lawyer) and
315 28% reported a desire to go to college/university as academic aspirations. The distribution of students' perceptions of involvement and support revealed that whereas most students perceived having high involvement with their school (60%), less than a third (30%)
320 reported a high level of involvement in their community. The majority of students reported a high level of teacher (74%) and parent (92%) support, but less than a third of the students (32%) reported high levels of parental involvement in school.
325 Significant results of chi-square analyses examining the relationship between school perceptions, future life goals, level of support/engagement, and acculturation are presented in Table 1. The results show that there were significant relationships between acculturation
330 level and discrimination and language problems as students' barriers to school involvement. Students who were rated as low in acculturation reported discrimination as a barrier to school involvement more frequently (14%), compared with those who were rated high (3%)
335 or those who were categorized as mixed (inconsistent; 5%) in acculturation level. Similarly, those students who were rated as low in acculturation also reported language problems more often, as well as a lack of time as a barrier to parental involvement. With regard to
340 barriers to community involvement, students rated as low in acculturation again reported language difficulties more frequently (8%) than others. Similar results were obtained with time as a barrier to community in-

345 volvement. Acculturation level was also significant with regard to no interest as a barrier to after-school program attendance. In this instance, students who were rated as high and mixed in acculturation reported no interest as a barrier to after-school program atten-
350 dance more frequently than those who were rated as low in acculturation. There were no statistically significant differences between acculturation level and any of the dangers/problems mentioned by students.

Results of analyses examining the relationship between acculturation level and distribution of students'
355 perceptions of support and engagement indicate that those students categorized as high in acculturation reported "none" more frequently (55%) with regard to parental involvement in school as compared with those categorized as low in acculturation (35%). In contrast,
360 those students who were rated as mixed in acculturation reported "none" for community involvement more frequently (57%) than those rated as low (50%) or high (37%) in acculturation level. No significant relationship was found with regard to acculturation level and
365 perceived level of teacher support, parent support, or students' perceived level of involvement in school.

There were no significant differences in the reported specific future career goals by students' level of acculturation. However, results (see Table 1) indicate
370 that there was a significant relationship between acculturation level and the frequency with which students indicated a variety of life goals. Those students rated as low in acculturation reported a desire to do well in school more often (32%) than those in the high (15%)
375 or mixed (20%) acculturation groups. Similarly, those rated as low (18%) and mixed (15%) in acculturation reported a desire to have a (nonspecified) career more often compared with students rated as high in acculturation (5%). In contrast, the students rated as high
380 (39%) and mixed (37%) in acculturation reported a desire to go to college or university more often than those in the low-acculturation group (17%).

Chi-square analysis examining gender differences (see Table 2) with regard to acculturation level, distri-
385 bution of school perceptions, as well as perceptions of support and engagement indicated that females were rated as low in acculturation more frequently (48%) than males (34%). Females were more likely to report language problems (11%) and discrimination (11%) as
390 barriers to school involvement than males (1% and 3%, respectively). Males reported that they did not attend after-school programs due to no interest more frequently than did females. No statistically significant gender differences were found in terms of reported
395 dangers/problems faced at school, perceptions of support, or perceptions of level of engagement.

Gender differences were found in the distribution of expressed future life goals (see Table 2). Females reported a desire to do well in school (29%) and a desire
400 to be successful (29%) more frequently than males (17% and 19%, respectively). Similarly, females re-

Table 1

Percentage of Students Reporting School Perceptions, Support/Engagement, and Future Life Goals by Acculturation Level

	Acculturation level			
	% Low (*n* = 109)	% High (*n* = 78)	% Mixed (*n* = 79)	*p* value
School perceptions				
Barriers to school involvement				
Discrimination	14	3	5	.01
Language problems	14	0	3	< .001
Barriers to parental involvement				
Lack of time	13	4	4	.04
Barriers to student involvement in community				
Language difficulties	8	0	1	.005
Time	6	4	0	.05
Barriers to after-school program attendance				
No interest	1	8	6	.05
Level of support/engagement				
Parental involvement in school				.03
High	33	23	39	
Some	31	22	18	
None	35	55	43	
Students' community involvement				.01
High	24	45	24	
Some	26	18	19	
None	50	37	57	
Future life goals				
Do well in school	32	15	20	.02
Have a (nonspecified) career	18	5	15	.03
Go to college or university	17	39	37	< .001

Table 2

Significant Gender Differences by Acculturation Level, Perceptions, and Aspirations

	Gender		
	% Female (*n* = 142)	% Male (*n* = 121)	*p* value
Acculturation level			.04
High	24	37	
Low	48	34	
Other	28	30	
Perceptions			
Barrier to school involvement			
Language problems	11	1	.001
Discrimination	11	3	.02
Barrier to program attendance			
No interest	2	7	.04
Future life goals			
Do well in school	29	17	.02
Be successful	29	19	.04
Specific career			.01
Professional	86	69	
Semiprofessional	7	13	
Nonprofessional	7	18	
Combined aspirations			.01
High	67	56	
Medium	27	27	
Low	6	18	

Note. For specific career, female *n* = 106, male *n* = 93. For combined aspirations, female *n* = 139, male *n* = 117.

ported professional career aspirations more frequently (85%) than males (69%). To obtain a better picture of the relationship between gender and academic aspirations, and assuming that higher values equate with higher academic aspirations, a combined variable was created made up of the sum of expressed future career goals and a classification of life goals into three categories (high = 3, mixed = 2, low = 1). Life goals were classified as high if they indicated a clear sense of a future career (i.e., go to college or university or have a career) and low if the expressed life goal was totally unrelated to academic aspirations (i.e., have a family, help community). Again, females reported high combined aspirations more frequently (67%) than did males (56%).

Discussion

The purpose of this study was to provide a descriptive analysis of how Latino junior high and high school students perceive their school environment, including barriers, problems, engagement, and support. In addition, this study aimed to examine if these factors varied by acculturation level and gender. Although it is important to keep in mind that the sample overall reported few barriers and problems, discrimination was the most frequently mentioned barrier to school involvement. This finding lends support to previous studies in which perceptions of school climate are strongly and consistently related to perceptions of discrimination (Stone & Han, 2005). Furthermore, findings indicating a lack of time and language problems as barriers to parental involvement lend support to previous research showing this lack of time as a barrier to parental involvement in poor working populations (Galarza-Hernandez, 1996; Heymann & Earle, 2000). Note, however, that no information is available with regard to socioeconomic status of the participants. It is noteworthy that the most frequently cited dangers perceived by this group of students are violence, fights, drugs, and alcohol. Although there are very few studies examining recent immigrant students' perceptions of dangers/problems at school, these results are consistent with general findings of dangers and problems faced by many school systems in the United States (Braaten, 2004; Smokowski, Mann, Reynolds, & Fraser, 2004).

Acculturation Differences

As anticipated, results of this study indicated that low-acculturated students more often reported language-related problems as barriers to school involvement. Also reported by those students in the low-acculturation group were perceived discrimination, parental lack of time as a barrier, and low or no community involvement. Note that the association of language as a barrier with acculturation is expected given that language preference was used to construct the acculturation measure. Nonetheless, these results indicate that high acculturation provides some students with a greater sense of belonging to their community and

fewer barriers, including perceived discrimination. In addition, it is important to note that the majority of the students in this sample (92%) report high parental support. Even so, students who were rated as low or inconsistent in acculturation were more likely to perceive high levels of parental involvement with the school. Although no direct parental reports were obtained, students' perceptions support previous research that indicates that, contrary to popular belief, Latino parents are either highly involved (L. C. Lopez, Sanchez, & Hamilton, 2000; R. F. Rodriguez & Lopez, 2003) or have a desire to be involved in their children's school but are unable to do so because of significant barriers (Ramirez, 2003).

These findings are equivocal with regard to academic aspirations. Most of the students who reported aspiring to a specific career chose a professional career. Upon examining the relationship between specific career aspirations and acculturation, these results indicated that there were no differences in terms of specific careers mentioned by students depending on their acculturation level. Nevertheless, results indicated that the higher acculturated students expressed a desire to go to college more frequently when compared with the low-acculturated students, whereas the less acculturated students reported a desire to be successful, do well in school, and have a career more frequently than those students rated as high in acculturation. One possible explanation for these results is that all of the students in this sample have generally higher academic aspirations, but the difference lies in their expression of academic goals and of their knowledge as to the specific steps to obtain those goals. It may be possible to speculate that the higher acculturated students, due to their comprehension of the language and the fact that they have been in the United States for an extended time, have a greater appreciation that to obtain a career one would need to attend college or a university, whereas the less acculturated students might not view this as a necessary path to success and therefore state their goals and objectives in a more abstract fashion (i.e., be successful, do well in school, have a career). These results suggest that the relationship between acculturation and academic achievement is not a simple one and might provide some clarification on the apparently contradictory findings in other studies.

Gender Differences

Findings with regard to gender reveal very interesting results. With the exception of lack of interest, females reported more barriers than males and were rated as low in acculturation more frequently than males. Nonetheless, females also reported higher levels of academic aspirations, desires to do well in school, and a desire to be successful more frequently than males. It is clear that being female promotes resiliency with regard to academic aspirations for Latino/as. These results lend support to previous research studies such as

that of T. D. Rodriguez (2003), who found that females' higher value of academic achievement was re-
515 lated to the fact that they were less acculturated or less
vulnerable to assimilation of adversarial attitudes and
behaviors responsible for academic failure.

Limitations and Further Research Recommendations

Whereas this study represents a first look at a convenience sample of students in North Carolina, it may
520 not be possible to generalize these findings to students
in other regions of the United States. Measures were
devised using self-report data and so there is no information for matching these students to their actual academic performance. In addition, because the data were
525 collected from students enrolled in school, there is no
information on students who have already decided to
drop out of school. However, we have taken advantage
of a large gathering of high school students from a state
reporting a relatively new influx of Latino immigrants
530 to obtain important information concerning their school
experiences and aspirations. Although the Latino population is growing in states such as North Carolina, relatively little is known about diversity among them because, until recently, only a few states were frontrun-
535 ners in focusing inquiry on Latinos within the public
education system.

Finally, whereas these variables have been widely
used as measures of acculturation in previous literature,
they may not reflect the complex dynamics inherent in
540 adjustment to a new culture. Note that whereas less-
acculturated students report lack of time as a barrier for
parents' involvement in school much more often than
high-acculturated students, it is also the low-
acculturated students who more frequently report that
545 their parents are highly involved with their school
compared with the high-acculturated student. It is possible that students' perception of parental involvement
could be related to other variables (such as family values or family cohesion). In the same vein, it is impor-
550 tant to keep in mind that this is the students' self-
reported perception of their parents' involvement, as no
direct measure was obtained from parents. Finally,
classification of students into high- and low-
acculturation categories based on language and years in
555 the United States leaves a percentage of students in the
mixed or inconsistent categories. This classification
does not take into consideration the special dynamics
or processes that may be contributing to those students
who have been in this country for fewer than 5 years
560 and still chose English to complete the questionnaire or
those students who have been here for more than 5
years and still chose Spanish as their preferred way of
communicating.

These findings indicate that there may be no linear
565 relationship between acculturation and academic aspirations but, rather, this relationship may be mediated
by a variety of factors, including students' beliefs and

attitudes, family cohesion, parental monitoring, parental attitudes concerning education, cultural identity,
570 perceived stereotypes, and discrimination. Further studies examining acculturation would benefit from a
framework that clearly captures the complex dynamics
of acculturation and how this phenomenon affects academic achievement and the overall adjustment of La-
575 tino immigrant students into their environment.

References

Alva, S. A. (1995). Academic invulnerability among Mexican American students: The importance of protective resources and appraisals. In A. M.
Padilla (Ed.), *Hispanic psychology: Critical issues in theory and research*
(pp. 288–302). Thousand Oaks, CA: Sage.

Amaro, H. (1990). Acculturation and marijuana and cocaine use: Findings
from the HANES 82–84. *American Journal of Public Health, 80,* 54.

Arellano, A. R., & Padilla, A. M. (1996). Academic invulnerability among a
select group of Latino university students. *Hispanic Journal of Behavioral
Sciences, 18,* 485–507.

Berry, J. W. (2003). Conceptual approaches to acculturation. In K. M. Chun, P.
Balls Organista, & G. Marin (Eds.), *Acculturation advances in theory,
measurement, and applied research* (pp. 17–37). Washington, DC: American Psychological Association.

Blechman, E. A., & Culhane, S. E. (1993). Aggressive, depressive, and prosocial coping with affective challenges in early adolescence. *Journal of Early
Adolescence, 13,* 361–382.

Bowen, N. A. (2004). Satisfaction with life of refugees and immigrants. *Dissertation Abstracts International, 64*(7-B), 3515.

Braaten, S. (2004). Creating safe schools: A principal's perspective. In J. C.
Conoley & A. P. Goldstein (Eds.), *School violence intervention: A practical
handbook* (2nd ed., pp. 54–67). New York: Guilford Press.

Brown, R., & Evans, W. P. (2002). Extracurricular activity and ethnicity creating greater school connection among diverse student populations. *Urban
Education, 37,* 41–58.

Burnam, M. A., Hough, R. L., Kamo, M., Escobar, J. I., & Telles, C. A. (1987).
Acculturation and lifetime prevalence of psychiatric disorders among Mexican Americans in Los Angeles. *Journal of Health and Social Behavior, 28,*
89–102.

Cervantes, R. C., Padilla, A. M., & Salgado de Snyder, N. (1991). The Hispanic Stress Inventory: A culturally relevant approach to psychosocial assessment. *Psychological Assessment, 3,* 438–447.

Department of Public Instruction. (2002). *2001–02 dropout data report.* Retrieved from http://www.ncpublicschools.org/school improvement/effective/
dropout/downloads/2001–2002.pdf

Escobar, J. I., & Vega, W. A. (2000). Mental health and immigration's AAAs:
Where are we and where do we go from here? *Journal of Nervous and Mental Disease, 188,* 736–740.

Galarza-Hernandez, A. (1996). An exploration of Mexican-American parents'
construction of parent involvement and the role of acculturation in parental
involvement in children's education. *Dissertation Abstracts International,
56*(9-A), 3533.

Gil, A. G., Vega, W. A., & Dimas, J. M. (1994). Acculturative stress and
personal adjustment among Hispanic adolescent boys. *Journal of Community Psychology, 22,* 43–54.

Glennie, E., & Steams, E. (2002). Why Hispanic students drop out of high
school early: Data from North Carolina. *Education Reform, 2,* 1–4.

Guilamo-Ramos, V., Jaccard, J., Johansson, M., & Tunisi, R. (2004). Binge
drinking among Latino youth: Role of acculturation-related variables. *Psychology of Addictive Behaviors, 18,* 135–142.

Gutman, L. M., & Midgley, C. (2000). The role of protective factors in supporting the academic achievement of poor African American students during
the middle school transition. *Journal of Youth & Adolescence, 29,* 223–248.

Heymann, S., & Earle, A. (2000). Low-income parents: How do working
conditions affect their opportunity to help school-age children at risk?
American Educational Research Journal, 37, 833–848.

Hubbard, L. (1999). College aspirations among low-income African American
high school students: Gendered strategies for success. *Anthropology & Education Quarterly, 30,* 363–383.

Jimenez, N. V. (2002). Quien va a sobresalir? (Who will come out ahead?):
Exploring academic achievement among low-income adolescents of Mexican descent across different generations. *Dissertation Abstracts International, 63*(6-A), 2095.

Lopez, E. J., Ehly, S., & Garcia-Vasquez, E. (2002). Acculturation, social
support and academic achievement of Mexican and Mexican American high
school students: An exploratory study. *Psychology in the Schools, 39,* 245–
257.

Lopez, L. C., Sanchez, V. V., & Hamilton, M. (2000). Immigrant and native-
born Mexican-American parents' involvement in a public school: A preliminary study. *Psychological Reports, 86,* 521–525.

Martinez, C. R., Jr., DeGarmo, D. S., & Eddy, J. M. (2004). Promoting academic success among Latino youths. *Hispanic Journal of Behavioral Sciences, 26,* 128–151.

Moscicki, E. B., Locke, B., Rae, D., & Boyd, J. (1989). Depressive symptoms among Mexican Americans: The Hispanic Health and Nutrition Examination Survey. *American Journal of Epidemiology, 130,* 348–360.

National Center on Education Statistics. (2003). *Public high school dropouts and completers from the common core of data: School year 2000–01.* Retrieved from http://nces.ed.gov/pubsearch/pubsinfo.asp?pubid=2004310

Nelson, C. M., & Pearson, C.A. (1994). Juvenile delinquency in the context of culture and community. In R. L. Peterson & S. Ishii-Jordan (Eds.), *Multicultural issues in the education of students with behavioral disorders* (pp. 78–90). Cambridge, MA: Brookline.

Newman, B. M., Lohman, B. J., Newman, P. R., Myers, C., & Smith, V. L. (2000). Experiences of urban youth navigating the transition to ninth grade. *Youth & Society, 31,* 387–416.

Newman, B. M., Myers, M. C., Newman, P. R., Lohman, B. J., & Smith, V. L. (2000). The transition to high school for academically promising, urban, low-income African American youth. *Adolescence, 35,* 45–66.

O'Connor, C. (1997). Dispositions toward (collective) struggle and educational resilience in the inner city: A case analysis of six African-American high school students. *American Educational Research Journal, 34,* 593–629.

Okagaki, L., & Frensch, P. A. (1998). Parental support for Mexican-American children's school achievement. In H. I. McCubbin & E. A. Thompson (Eds.), *Resiliency in Native American and immigrant families: Vol. 2. Resiliency in families series* (pp. 325–342). Thousand Oaks, CA: Sage.

Onishi, A., & Murphy-Shigematsu, S. (2003). Identity narratives of Muslim foreign workers in Japan. *Journal of Community & Applied Social Psychology, 13,* 224–239.

Padilla, A. M., & Ruiz, R. A. (1973). *Latino mental health: A review of literature.* Washington, DC: Government Printing Office.

Plunkett, S. W., & Bamaca-Gomez, M. Y. (2003). The relationship between parenting, acculturation, and adolescent academics in Mexican-origin immigrant families in Los Angeles. *Hispanic Journal of Behavioral Sciences, 25,* 222–239.

Prelow, H. M., & Loukas, A. (2003). The role of resource, protective, and risk factors on academic achievement-related outcomes of economically disadvantaged Latino youth. *Journal of Community Psychology, 31,* 513–529.

Ramirez, A. (2003). Dismay and disappointment: Parental involvement of Latino immigrant parents. *Urban Review, 35,* 93–110.

Rice, K. G., Herman, M. A., & Peterson, A. C. (1993). Coping with challenge in adolescence: A conceptual model and psycho-educational intervention. *Journal of Adolescence, 16,* 235–251.

Riggs, N. R., & Greenberg, M. T. (2004). Moderators in the academic development of migrant Latino children attending after-school programs. *Journal of Applied Developmental Psychology, 25,* 349–367.

Rodriguez, R. F., & Lopez, L. C. (2003). Mexican-American parental involvement with a Texas elementary school. *Psychological Reports, 92,* 791–792.

Rodriguez, T. D. (2003). School social context effects on gender differences in academic achievement among second-generation Latinos. *Journal of Hispanic Higher Education, 2,* 30–45.

Rogler, L. H., Cortes, D. E., & Malgady, R. G. (1991). Acculturation and mental health status among Hispanics. *American Psychologist, 46,* 585–597.

Rotenberg, V., Kutsay, S., & Venger, A. (2000). The subjective estimation of integration into a new society and the level of distress. *Stress Medicine, 16,* 117–123.

Ruiz, Y. (2002). Predictors of academic resiliency for Latino middle school students. *Dissertation Abstracts International, 63*(2-B), 1067.

Slavin, R. E., & Calderon, M. (Eds.). (2001). *Effective programs for Latino students.* Mahwah, NJ: Lawrence Erlbaum.

Smokowski, P. R., Mann, E. A., Reynolds, A. J., & Fraser, M. W. (2004). Childhood risk and protective factors and late adolescent adjustment in inner city minority youth. *Children & Youth Services Review, 26,* 63–91.

Smokowski, P. R., Reynolds, A. J., & Bezruczko, N. (1999). Resilience and protective factors in adolescence: An autobiographical perspective from disadvantaged youth. *Journal of School Psychology, 37,* 425–448.

Stone, S., & Han, M. (2005). Perceived school environments, perceived discrimination, and school performance among children of Mexican immigrants. *Children & Youth Services Review, 27,* 51–66.

Strauss, A., & Corbin, J. M. (1990). *Basics of qualitative research: Grounded theory procedures and techniques.* Thousand Oaks, CA: Sage.

Taylor, A. Z. (2002). Writing off ambition: A developmental study of gender, ethnicity, and achievement values. *Dissertation Abstracts International, 63*(3-A), 863.

U.S. Census Bureau. (2000). *The population profile of the United States: 2000 (Internet release).* Retrieved from http://www.census.gov/population/www/pop-profile/profile2000.html

Vargas-Willis, G., & Cervantes, R. C. (1987). Consideration of psychosocial stress in the treatment of the Latina immigrant. *Hispanic Journal of Behavioral Sciences, 9,* 315–329.

Walton, M. A., Blow, F. C., Bingham, C. R., & Chermack, S. T. (2003). Individual and social-environmental predictors of alcohol and drug use 2 years following substance abuse treatment. *Addictive Behaviors, 28,* 627–642.

Werner, E. E. (1993). Risk and resilience in individuals with learning disabilities: Lessons learned from the Kauai Longitudinal Study. *Learning Disabilities Research & Practice, 8,* 28–34.

Werner, E. E., & Smith, R. S. (1992). *Overcoming the odds: High risk children from birth to adulthood.* Ithaca, NY: Cornell University Press.

Acknowledgments: The development, distribution, and administration of the student surveys at the Hispanic Educational Summit 2003 and 2004 were fully organized and funded by the North Carolina Society of Hispanic Professionals (NCSHP). This article would not have been possible without the help of many of the NCSHP members, including Marco A. Zárate, president; Luz M. Frye; Susan D. Zárate; Jorge Fernández; Ricardo Perez; Jennifer Reed; and the volunteer work of Mohammed Taheri, an undergraduate student at UNC-CH. Special thanks to David C. Steffens, M.D. (director of the PREMIER program at Duke University Medical Center); Bercedis Peterson, Ph.D.; Stephanie Coard, Ph.D. (faculty of the Duke Clinical Research Training Program); and the Latino/a students who completed the survey. The authors would also like to thank the anonymous reviewers for helpful comments. Work on this study was made possible by the support of NIDA grant DA 017552.

About the authors: *Elvia Y. Valencia* obtained her doctorate in clinical psychology (PsyD) at the Chicago School of Professional Psychology and her master's degree in health sciences in clinical research (MHS) at Duke University School of Medicine. She is currently a research associate with the Rutgers University Center of Alcohol Studies. Her research interests focus on understanding and employing protective factors in the development of substance abuse and school desertion prevention interventions for Latinos and other minorities in the United States. She also provides clinical services through the University of Medicine and Dentistry's Employee Assistance Program. In her free time, she enjoys dancing and learning from other cultures through reading and traveling. *Valerie Johnson* received her Ph.D. in sociology from Rutgers, The State University of New Jersey. She is currently an associate research professor at the Rutgers University Center of Alcohol Studies. Her research interests include the study of children from alcoholic and dysfunctional families, the documentation of long-term outcomes of diverse drug-using patterns in community and high-risk samples, and the evaluation of prevention/intervention programs. When free time permits, she stays active by skiing, gardening, and playing golf.

Exercise for Article 5

Factual Questions

1. According to the researchers, have the previous studies on the influence of acculturation on academic achievement produced consistent results?

2. According to the researchers, are the terms "acculturation" and "assimilation" synonymous?

3. What three categories were used for classifying the specific career aspirations of the respondents?

4. How many students were omitted due to missing data?

5. Was there a significant relationship between acculturation and discrimination?

6. Do the researchers characterize the sample as a "convenience sample"?

Questions for Discussion

7. What is your opinion on the procedure used to recruit participants? Is it likely to produce a representative sample? Explain. (See lines 163–187.)

8. How important is it to know that participation was voluntary and anonymous? Explain. (See lines 179–181.)

9. If you had conducted this study, would you have used open-ended questions *or* closed-ended questions (e.g., questions with choices)? Explain. (See lines 188–208.)

10. What is your opinion on defining acculturation as a combination of language preference and years of residence? (See lines 239–278.)

11. All of the values of *p* in Tables 1 and 2 are .05 or less. What does this indicate to you?

12. The researchers note that this survey does not include data on students who have already dropped out of school. In your opinion, is this an important limitation of this study? Explain. (See lines 524–527.)

Quality Ratings

Directions: Indicate your level of agreement with each of the following statements by circling a number from 5 for strongly agree (SA) to 1 for strongly disagree (SD). If you believe an item is not applicable to this research article, leave it blank. Be prepared to explain your ratings. When responding to criteria A and B below, keep in mind that brief titles and abstracts are conventional in published research.

A. The title of the article is appropriate.

  SA 5 4 3 2 1 SD

B. The abstract provides an effective overview of the research article.

  SA 5 4 3 2 1 SD

C. The introduction establishes the importance of the study.

  SA 5 4 3 2 1 SD

D. The literature review establishes the context for the study.

  SA 5 4 3 2 1 SD

E. The research purpose, question, or hypothesis is clearly stated.

  SA 5 4 3 2 1 SD

F. The method of sampling is sound.

  SA 5 4 3 2 1 SD

G. Relevant demographics (for example, age, gender, and ethnicity) are described.

  SA 5 4 3 2 1 SD

H. Measurement procedures are adequate.

  SA 5 4 3 2 1 SD

I. All procedures have been described in sufficient detail to permit a replication of the study.

  SA 5 4 3 2 1 SD

J. The participants have been adequately protected from potential harm.

  SA 5 4 3 2 1 SD

K. The results are clearly described.

  SA 5 4 3 2 1 SD

L. The discussion/conclusion is appropriate.

  SA 5 4 3 2 1 SD

M. Despite any flaws, the report is worthy of publication.

  SA 5 4 3 2 1 SD

Article 6

Most Working Women Deny Gender Discrimination in Their Pay

LYDIA SAAD
The Gallup Poll

EDITOR'S NOTE: The material in lines 1 through 56 appears at the beginning of each issue of *The Gallup Poll Monthly*. It describes general issues in the conduct and interpretation of the telephone surveys reported in the journal. The report on the survey on working women's views on pay discrimination begins with line 57.

From *The Gallup Poll Monthly* (Number 413: February 2000), 35–36. Copyright © 2000 by The Gallup Poll. Reprinted with permission. All rights reserved.

The Gallup Poll gathers public opinion data primarily through surveys conducted by telephone, which are designed to provide representative samples of adults living in the continental United States.

5 The standard methods used to conduct telephone surveys and the sampling tolerances for interpreting results collected by telephone are detailed below.

Design of the Sample for Telephone Surveys

The samples of telephone numbers used in telephone interview surveys are based on a random digit

10 stratified probability design. The sampling procedure involves stratifying the continental U.S. into 4 time zones and 3 city size strata within each time zone to yield a total of 12 unique strata.

In order to avoid possible bias if only listed tele-

15 phone numbers are used, the Gallup Poll uses a random digit procedure designed to provide representation of both listed and unlisted (including not-yet-listed) numbers. Samples are drawn within each stratum only from "active blocks," where an "active block" is defined as

20 100 contiguous telephone numbers containing three or more residential telephone listings. By eliminating nonworking blocks of numbers from the sample, the likelihood that any sampled telephone number will be associated with a residence increases from only 20%

25 (where numbers are sampled from all banks) to approximately 55%. Since most banks of telephone numbers are either substantially filled (i.e., assigned) or empty, this practical efficiency is purchased at a negligible cost in terms of possible coverage bias.

30 The sample of telephone numbers drawn by this method is designed to produce, with proper adjustments for differential sampling rates, an unbiased random sample of telephone households in the continental United States.

35 The standard size for national Gallup Poll telephone surveys is 1,000 interviews. More interviews are conducted in specific instances where greater survey accuracy is desired. Fewer interviews are conducted in specific instances where speed in collecting data and re-

40 porting the results is required.

Telephone Survey Weighting Procedures

After the survey data have been collected and processed, each respondent is assigned a weight so that the demographic characteristics of the total weighted sample of respondents matches the latest U.S. Census Bu-

45 reau estimates of the demographic characteristics of the adult population living in households with access to a telephone.

The procedures described above are designed to produce samples approximating the adult civilian

50 population (18 and older) living in private households (i.e., excluding those in prisons, hospitals, hotels, religious and educational institutions, and those living on reservations or military bases), with access to a telephone. Survey percentages may be applied to Census

55 estimates of the size of these populations to project percentages into numbers of people.

The Report on Pay Discrimination

A new Gallup Poll finds that 30% of working women in the U.S. believe they are paid less than they would be if they were a man, while more than two in

60 three, 70%, do not. On the other hand, with just 13% saying women at their workplace get paid less than men who perform the same job, working men are even less likely to perceive that women are victims of gender discrimination in their pay.

65 "Pay equity," a longtime goal of the feminist movement, resurfaced in the news a few weeks ago when President Clinton proposed increased federal funding for programs aimed at closing the wage gap between working men and women in this country. Clinton did

70 so touting statistics showing that the average salary for full-time working women is only 75 cents on the dollar of what full-time working men earn.

The Gallup survey, conducted January 25–26, asked respondents about their employment status. Roughly two-thirds of men and just under half of women indicated they are employed full time. Among these groups, only slight differences in attitudes about women's pay were found along age, educational status, income, and other dimensions. The largest difference among full-time employed women is seen by education. Those with a college degree are less likely to feel discriminated against in this way than are women with less formal education, by a 22% to 35% margin.

Clinton's Plan

Critics of President Clinton's initiative say that the "75 cents" indicator is misleading, and cite other statistics showing that men and women of equal educational and work experience are actually virtually equal when it comes to pay. Nevertheless, Gallup finds the American people widely supportive of Clinton's proposal to spend $27 million on additional pay equity efforts. Seventy-nine percent favor the proposed spending, including 70% of men and 86% of women. Just 18% are opposed to the plan.

Table 1
Question: As you may know, President Clinton has proposed that Congress allocate $27 million to increase enforcement of equal pay laws relating to women in the workplace. Do you favor or oppose this proposal?

	Favor	Oppose	No opinion
2000 Jan 25–26	79%	18%	3%

Table 2
Question: Which of the following best describes your current situation—employed full time, employed part time, retired, a homemaker, a student, unemployed but looking for work, or unemployed and not looking for work?

	Men	Women
Employed full time	65%	45%
Employed part time	5%	12%
Retired	19%	20%
Homemaker	0%	15%
Student	5%	4%
Unemployed, looking for work	3%	2%
Unemployed, not looking for work	1%	2%
Disabled (vol.)	2%	*
No answer	*	*
* Less than 0.5%		

Methodology

The results are based on telephone interviews with a randomly selected national sample of 1,044 adults, 18 years and older, conducted January 25–26, 2000. For results based on this sample, one can say with 95% confidence that the maximum error attributable to sampling and other random effects is plus or minus 3 per-centage points. In addition to sampling error, question wording and practical difficulties in conducting surveys can introduce error or bias into the findings of public opinion polls.

Table 3
[Based on – 265 – Women employed full time; ± 7 Pct Pts]
Question: Do you personally feel that because you are a woman, you get paid less than a man would in your same job, or is this not the case?

	Yes, get paid less	No, not the case	No opinion
2000 Jan 25–26	30%	70%	0%

Table 4
[Based on – 331 – Men employed full time; ± 6 Pct Pts]
Question: From what you know or just your impression —do women at your workplace get paid less than men who do the same job, or is this not the case?

	Yes, get paid less	No, not the case	No opinion
2000 Jan 25–26	13%	78%	9%

Exercise for Article 6

Factual Questions

1. The 12 strata are based on which two variables?

2. What is done to avoid a possible bias if only listed telephone numbers are used?

3. What is the standard sample size for Gallup telephone surveys?

4. What is the purpose of assigning "weights" to the respondents?

5. For the full sample of 1,044 respondents used in this poll, how many percentage points should be allowed for sampling and other random effects (based on 95% confidence)?

6. What percentage of the women were homemakers?

7. A separate question was asked of men who were employed full time. What percentage of these men had no opinion on the question?

Questions for Discussion

8. This poll was conducted via telephone. In your opinion, are there advantages to polling via telephone over polling via direct face-to-face interviews? Explain.

9. This poll was conducted via telephone. In your opinion, are there disadvantages to polling via telephone over polling via direct face-to-face interviews? Explain.

10. The researcher uses procedures to approximate the adult civilian population, excluding certain groups. Do you think that the exclusions affect the validity of the poll? (See lines 48–56.)

11. The researcher notes that question wording can introduce error or bias into the findings of public opinion polls. Do you think that the wording of the four questions used in this poll is adequate? Explain. (See lines 100–103 and Tables 1–4.)

Quality Ratings

Directions: Indicate your level of agreement with each of the following statements by circling a number from 5 for strongly agree (SA) to 1 for strongly disagree (SD). If you believe an item is not applicable to this research article, leave it blank. Be prepared to explain your ratings. When responding to criteria A and B below, keep in mind that brief titles and abstracts are conventional in published research.

A. The title of the article is appropriate.

    SA   5   4   3   2   1   SD

B. The abstract provides an effective overview of the research article.

    SA   5   4   3   2   1   SD

C. The introduction establishes the importance of the study.

    SA   5   4   3   2   1   SD

D. The literature review establishes the context for the study.

    SA   5   4   3   2   1   SD

E. The research purpose, question, or hypothesis is clearly stated.

    SA   5   4   3   2   1   SD

F. The method of sampling is sound.

    SA   5   4   3   2   1   SD

G. Relevant demographics (for example, age, gender, and ethnicity) are described.

    SA   5   4   3   2   1   SD

H. Measurement procedures are adequate.

    SA   5   4   3   2   1   SD

I. All procedures have been described in sufficient detail to permit a replication of the study.

    SA   5   4   3   2   1   SD

J. The participants have been adequately protected from potential harm.

    SA   5   4   3   2   1   SD

K. The results are clearly described.

    SA   5   4   3   2   1   SD

L. The discussion/conclusion is appropriate.

    SA   5   4   3   2   1   SD

M. Despite any flaws, the report is worthy of publication.

    SA   5   4   3   2   1   SD

Article 7

Does Therapist Experience Influence
Interruptions of Women Clients?

RONALD JAY WERNER-WILSON
Iowa State University

MEGAN J. MURPHY
Iowa State University

JENNIFER LYNN FITZHARRIS
Iowa State University

ABSTRACT. The feminist critique of marriage and family therapy and studies of interruptions in conversation influenced the topic of the present study. We replicated methodology from a study (Werner-Wilson, Price, Zimmerman, & Murphy, 1997) in which the researchers reported that student therapists interrupted women clients more frequently than male clients. Those results may have been related to therapist inexperience—since the therapists were students. In the present study, we compared interruptions from student therapists to those identified as "master" therapists who had extensive clinical experience. Analysis of Variance was used to compare videotaped sessions of therapists in marriage and family therapy training sessions to therapists from the American Association for Marriage and Family Therapy (AAMFT) Masters series. Results suggest that there is no statistically significant difference between the rate of interruptions used by students versus experienced therapists. Both groups interrupted women clients more often than men clients, a finding that replicates the earlier study by Werner-Wilson and colleagues (1997), which increases the generalizability about this pattern in marriage and family therapy.

From *Journal of Feminist Family Therapy*, 16, 39–49. Copyright © 2004 by The Haworth Press, Inc. Reprinted with permission.

One of the first empirical quantitative analyses of power in marriage and family therapy investigated interruptions, which were viewed as a sign of conversational power. That study reported that women clients

5 were interrupted three times more often than men clients regardless of therapist gender (Werner-Wilson et al., 1997). The study published in 1997 included only student therapists so the findings could have been the result of limited professional training because therapist

10 inexperience seems to be associated with a more directive interviewing style (Auerbach & Johnson, 1978). The present study represents a replication of the 1997 study with a sample of therapists that includes some who have significantly more experience so interrup-

15 tions could be compared between student therapists and those identified by the American Association for Marriage and Family Therapy as "master" therapists. This present study was influenced by two themes: language and therapeutic discourse as well as the feminist cri-

20 tique of marriage and family therapy.

Relevant Literature

The Feminist Critique

Feminists have brought to the forefront the importance of attending to social and political issues within the therapeutic context, such as examining the effects of race/ethnicity on client problems, openly discussing

25 power and privilege one may or may not have within the context of a relationship, and making gender a central component of case conceptualization and intervention (Silverstein, 2003). Embedded within these suggestions is a central issue of power: How does power

30 play out in relationships? Do therapists recognize power differences in the couples and families they treat? How do therapists attend to these power differences in the therapeutic context, that is, both between members of a couple and between themselves and their

35 clients? Although feminists have long called for therapists to examine power in relationships, only recently have concrete suggestions been given regarding how therapists can address abstract concepts like power in therapy (Blanton & Vandergriff-Avery, 2001; Had-

40 dock, Zimmerman, & MacPhee, 2000).

In addition to offering ways of conceptualizing and intervening in family therapy, feminists have highlighted the differential treatment of men and women in therapy by their therapists. One of the themes of the

45 feminist critique is associated with therapeutic process: women's voices are to be encouraged, heard, and validated in therapy. Feminist therapists actively encourage equal participation from women and men in therapy and in relationships (Cantor, 1990). From a feminist

50 perspective, therapists should attend to gender issues rather than ignore gender hierarchies in relationships. If "therapeutic talk is, of course, all about the politics of influence" (Goldner, 1989, p. 58), then how well do therapists negotiate power in therapy? Are therapists

55 replicating or challenging existing power inequalities in therapy? Furthermore, are therapists aware of their own stereotypes regarding gender and communication? One frequently heard stereotype is that women talk more than men (O'Donohue, 1996). Do therapists con-

60 sciously mitigate their own gender-related biases? These questions seem relevant in light of recent studies that show a negative relationship between marital satis-

faction and power inequality (Gray-Little, Baucom, & Hamby, 1996; Whisman & Jacobson, 1990).

65 Recent research seems to provide empirical support for this feminist critique of therapy. For example, Haddock and Lyness (2002) reported that male therapists frequently and negatively challenged female clients. The same pattern was not found for male clients. Other
70 research suggests that therapists scored low on taking a stance against client behaviors intended to control another (Haddock, MacPhee, & Zimmerman, 2001). Even though therapists may be aware of the importance of attention to power and gender issues in therapy, it
75 appears that they may not follow through in terms of how they communicate and/or intervene regarding conversational power. It could be argued that therapists have an ethical responsibility to challenge the hierarchies inherent in couples' relationships. Failure to do
80 so would be maintaining the status quo. Therefore, therapists' use of self seems particularly important given the power they have in relation to their clients to shape, end, or shift conversation (Avis, 1991).

Language and Therapeutic Discourse

Given that therapists are responsible for monitoring
85 and perhaps intervening in the relational and communicational therapeutic context, it seems important to pay attention to interruptions—especially those employed by therapists—in therapeutic conversation. The language and communication literature is helpful in this
90 regard. In their pioneering investigation of interruptions as a power tactic in conversation, Zimmerman and West (1975) reported that males more frequently interrupt females in cross-sex pairs, whereas interruptions occur in equal numbers between same-sex con-
95 versational partners. Some studies have not found support for males interrupting more, regardless of partner sex (Hannah & Murachver, 1999; Turner, Dindia, & Pearson, 1995). Explanations of mixed results in studies of interruptions may result from different defini-
100 tions of "interruption," situational context, and whether activities are structured (Anderson & Leaper, 1998). In their meta-analysis of studies of interruption, Anderson and Leaper (1998) suggested that definitions of interruption may moderate gender differences, gender dif-
105 ferences are larger in unstructured activities, and situational factors may influence interruptions more than gender.

In the language theory literature, two theories have been used to explain gender miscommunication: *two-*
110 *cultures theory* and *dominance theory*. The *two-cultures theory* of gender-linked language differences suggest that boys and girls grow up in different gender cultures, in which they learn different ways of communicating (Mulac, Erlandson, Farrar, Hallett, Molloy, &
115 Prescott, 1998). Boys use questions, for example, to control conversation, whereas girls use questions to sustain conversation. These cultural differences produce miscommunication when children grow up to be

120 adults, when they are interacting more with others from "different cultures." From this position, men do not view interruptions as a display of power; rather, men and women use language differently based on their previous experiences in their cultural sub-groups.

125 The *dominance theory* of gender-linked language differences suggests that men's domination of conversations via interruption and topic introduction is reflective of the power they hold in larger society. From this perspective, men use questions, interruptions, and other means of communication as a way to dominate conver-
130 sation and to keep women in a subordinate position. The result is that women speak less and men talk more, again isomorphic to patterns at a larger, societal level in which men have more power than women.

Proponents of both theories seem to suggest that
135 there are communication differences between men and women, yet the theories posit different explanations for why these differences exist. Given that there have been few empirical investigations of interruptions in therapy, the first step should be to first examine whether there
140 are differences between rates of interruption in the therapeutic context. If gender differences related to interruption are discovered, then therapists may be compelled to address these differences, particularly if these differences impact power within the couple rela-
145 tionship.

In recent years, researchers have begun to explore interruptions within the context of therapy. Although there are differences in results about the influence of therapist gender on use of interruptions, two different
150 studies (Stratford, 1988; Werner-Wilson et al., 1997) reported that women clients were much more likely than men clients to be interrupted by therapists. Stratford (1998) found that male therapists were more likely than female therapists to interrupt clients; Stratford also
155 reported that female clients were more likely than male clients to be interrupted. Werner-Wilson and his colleagues (1997) also reported that women clients were more likely than men clients to be interrupted in therapy but did not find a difference between women and
160 men therapists. Stratford (1988)—noting that therapist inexperience is associated with a more directive interviewing style (Auerbach & Johnson, 1978)—suggested that the difference in findings about therapist gender and interruptions might be due to differences in thera-
165 pist experience: her study included experienced therapists while the Werner-Wilson et al. (1997) study included student therapists who have less experience. If Stratford's (1998) speculation is true, we might expect differences in interruption rates based on therapist ex-
170 perience level. The purpose of the present study is to investigate two related research questions:

1. Are women clients interrupted more than men clients?

2. Do student therapists interrupt women clients more than experienced therapists?
175

Method

Participants

The sample for the present study included clients and therapists from two sources: (a) doctoral student therapists and clients at a nonprofit marriage and family therapy clinic at a major southern university that was accredited by the American Association for Marriage and Family Therapy, and (b) "master" therapists from the Master Series video collection distributed by the American Association for Marriage and Family Therapy. "The Master Series presents the world's most respected marriage and family therapists conducting live, unedited therapy sessions at AAMFT annual conferences" (AAMFT Catalog, 1993, p. 4). Including these master therapists provides an opportunity to compare therapy process between two levels of clinical experience: doctoral students versus master therapists. In each case, the session was the initial consultation with either the student therapist or the master therapist and it featured both an adult woman client and an adult man client who were romantic partners. Table 1 provides descriptive information about cases included in the study.

Procedures

We replicated the approach used by Werner-Wilson and colleagues (1997) to investigate interruptions in therapy process. We examined the first therapy session to control for treatment duration. Therapy sessions have predictable stages (e.g., social, engagement, information collection, intervention, closure), so we examined multiple time points in the session. Three five-minute segments were coded for every client from early, middle, and later stages in the session: (a) 10:00 to 15:00 minute segment; (b) 25:00 to 30:00 minute segment; and (c) 40:00 to 45:00 minute segment. Two senior-level undergraduate students, who were unaware of the purpose of this research, coded videotapes from the first therapy session.

Table 1
Descriptive Information about Videotapes

	Student Therapists	Master Therapists	Total
Therapist gender			
Men	52	14	66
Women	22	14	36
Total	74	28	102
Modality			
Marital	60	16	76
Family	14	12	26
Total	74	28	102

Coder training. Coders learned the coding scheme by practicing on tapes not featured in the sample until they achieved 80 percent agreement. A graduate student, who was also unaware of the purpose of the present study, coded every sixth session; these tapes were used to calculate interrater reliability. The coders maintained an acceptable level of interrater reliability throughout the coding process: intraclass correlations were .68.

Coding scheme. The transcripts were arranged with codes adjacent to each spoken turn to promote reliability by eliminating the need for coders to memorize codes: The coders viewed the video with the transcript and circled the appropriate code as they occurred during each speaking turn. A distinct set of codes was printed next to each speaker (e.g., therapist, woman client, man client) but each set of codes featured the same possible codes. For example, the therapist could interrupt either the woman or man client. Similarly, each client could interrupt either her/his partner or the therapist. In addition to enhancing reliability, this coding arrangement disguised the nature of the research project because coders identified conversational strategies used by each speaker, not just the therapist.

Dependent Measures

Interruptions. Interruptions—defined as a violation of a speaking turn, and operationalized as an overlap of speech that is disruptive or intrusive (West & Zimmerman, 1983; West & Zimmerman, 1977; Zimmerman & West, 1975)—were distinguished from other forms of overlap such as supportive statements that represent active listening skills. Statements that tailed off in tone or volume were not coded as interruptions because they represented invitations for reply. It is possible that people who talk more are interrupted more, so, following the procedure used by Werner-Wilson and colleagues (1997), we controlled for amount of client participation: A variable was constructed from the ratio of interruptions made by the therapist to number of speaking turns taken by the client. These ratios provided standardized measures to examine therapist interruptions.

Results

Based on our review of the literature, it seemed important to consider the influence of client gender, therapist gender, modality, and client experience since each variable has been found to have an influence on some dimension of therapy process. Analysis of Variance (ANOVA) was conducted to examine the following main effects on the dependent variable (ratio of therapist interruptions to number of client speaking turns): client gender (man, woman), therapist gender (man, woman), modality (couple, family), and therapist experience (student, AAMFT master therapist). Based on our review of the literature, it also seemed important to investigate the following interaction effects:

- Client gender × Therapist gender (Stratford, 1998; Werner-Wilson, Zimmerman, & Price, 1999);
- Client gender × Modality (Werner-Wilson, 1997; Werner-Wilson et al., 1999);

51

270
- Therapist gender × Modality (Werner-Wilson et al., 1999); Therapist gender × Therapist experience (Stratford, 1998); Client gender × Therapist gender × Modality (Werner-Wilson et al., 1999);
- Client gender × Therapist gender × Modality × Therapist experience (Stratford, 1998).

275 There was a statistically significant difference for gender of client on the dependent variable (see Table 2). Neither therapist gender, modality, therapist experience, nor the interaction of any variables was significant (see Table 2). On average, therapists in the present

280 study interrupted women clients ($M = 0.064$) almost two times more often than men clients ($M = 0.037$).

Table 2

Analysis of Variance for Therapist Behaviors: Interruption

Source	MS	F
Client Gender	0.014	4.780*
Therapist Gender	0.007	2.497
Modality	0.001	0.259
Therapist Experience	0.009	3.312
Client Gender × Therapist Gender	0.004	1.370
Client Gender × Modality	0.000	0.046
Therapist Gender × Modality	0.006	2.189
Therapist Gender × Therapist Experience	0.003	0.923
Client Gender × Therapist Gender × Modality	0.005	0.189
Client Gender × Therapist Gender × Modality × Therapist Experience	0.002	0.869

*$p < .05$, $n = 102$

Discussion

Gender as a Process Issue

285 Results from the present study continue to suggest that women clients are interrupted more often than men clients in conjoint couple and family therapy, although the rate was slightly lower in the present study than in the original study published in 1997. For some aspects

290 of therapy process (e.g., therapy alliance, goal setting), there seems to be an interaction effect between client gender and therapy modality (Werner-Wilson et al., 1997; Werner-Wilson, Zimmerman, & Price, 1999) but this effect was not demonstrated in the present study.

295 Results from the present study also suggest that therapist experience—which was not measured in the 1997 study—does not significantly influence the number of interruptions directed toward women clients. In fact, master therapists interrupted women clients at a higher

300 rate than student therapists, although it was not statistically significant.

Our findings contribute to the literature in providing evidence that women clients are interrupted more frequently than men clients, regardless of therapist

305 gender or experience. Although the design of the current study could not directly test the validity of the two-cultures theory or the dominance theory (explain-

ing differences for men and women in language use),
310 we tentatively suggest that these theories are too simplistic to adequately capture the complexity of interactions and power dynamics at play in relationships. Both theories, for example, posit that women may be more likely to be interrupted than men, *and* suggest that men use language in a way that is different from how
315 women use language. One might hypothesize, from either theory of language use, that men therapists would be somehow different from women therapists in how often they interrupt clients, yet results from the current study do not support this view. Simply put, a
320 more comprehensive theory that incorporates therapist and client markers of social standing may be more helpful for future researchers seeking to expand on the repeated finding in the therapy literature that women clients are more frequently interrupted than men cli-
325 ents.

Findings from the present study suggest an ongoing need to consider the influence of gender as a process variable in marriage and family therapy. Most therapists would agree to the notion that men and women
330 should have relatively equal participation in therapy; it is likely that therapists are unaware that they tend to interrupt women far more frequently than men in therapy. The first step is for therapists to be aware of these patterns in therapy; the second step is for therapists to
335 use their positional power to assist men and women to equitably share the therapeutic floor.

References

Anderson, K. J., & Leaper, C. (1998). Meta-analyses of gender effects on conversational interruption: Who, what, when, where, and how. *Sex Roles, 39*, 225–252.

Auerbach, A., & Johnson, M. (1978). Research on therapists' level of experience. In A. Gorman & A. Razin (Eds.), *The therapists' contribution to effective psychotherapy: An empirical assessment.* New York: Pergamon Press.

Avis, J, M. (1991). Power politics in therapy with women. In T. J. Goodrich (Ed.), *Women and power: Perspectives for family therapy* (pp. 183–200). New York: Norton.

Blanton, P. W., & Vandergriff-Avery, M. (2001). Marital therapy and marital power: Constructing narratives of sharing relational and positional power. *Contemporary Family Therapy, 23*, 295–308.

Cantor, D. W. (1990). Women as therapists: What we already know. In D. W. Cantor (Ed.), *Women as therapists: A multitheoretical casebook* (pp. 3–19). Northvale, NJ: Aronson.

Goldner, V. (1989). Generation and gender: Normative and covert hierarchies. In M. McGoldrick, C. M. Anderson, & F. Walsh (Eds.), *Women in families: A framework for family therapy* (pp. 42–60). New York: Norton.

Gray-Little., B., Baucom, D. H., & Hamby, S. L. (1996). Marital power, marital adjustment, and therapy outcome. *Journal of Family Psychology, 10*, 292–303.

Haddock, S., A., & Lyness, K. P. (2002). Three aspects of the therapeutic conversation in couples therapy: Does gender make a difference? *Journal of Couple & Relationship Therapy, 1*, 5–23.

Haddock, S. A., MacPhee, D., & Zimmerman, T. S. (2001). AAMFT Master Series Tapes: An analysis of the inclusion of feminist principles into family therapy practice. *Journal of Marital and Family Therapy, 27*, 487–500.

Haddock, S. A., Zimmerman, T. S., & MacPhee, D. (2000). The Power Equity Guide: Attending to gender in family therapy. *Journal of Marital and Family Therapy, 26*, 153–170.

Hannah, A., & Murachver, T. (1999). Gender and conversational style as predictors of conversational behavior. *Journal of Language and Social Psychology, 18*, 153–174.

Mulac, A., Erlandson, K. T., Farrar, W. J., Hallett, .T. S., Molloy, J. L., & Prescott, M. E. (1998). "Uh-huh. What's that all about?" Differing interpretations of conversational backchannels and questions as sources of miscommunication across gender boundaries. *Communication Research, 25*, 642–668.

O'Donohue, W. (1996). Marital therapy and gender-linked factors in communication. *Journal of Marital and Family Therapy, 22*, 87–101.

Silverstein, L. B. (2003). Classic texts and early critiques. In L. B. Silverstein & T. J. Goodrich (Eds.), *Feminist family therapy: Empowerment in social context* (pp. 17–35). Washington, DC: APA.

Stratford, J. (1998). Women and men in conversation: A consideration of therapists' interruptions in therapeutic discourse. *Journal of Family Therapy, 20*, 393–394.

Turner, L. H., Dindia, K., & Pearson, J. C. (1995). An investigation of female/male verbal behaviors in same-sex and mixed-sex conversations. *Communication Reports, 8*, 86–96.

Werner-Wilson, R. J. (1997). Is therapeutic alliance influenced by gender in marriage and family therapy? *Journal of Feminist Family Therapy, 9*, 3–16.

Werner-Wilson, R. J., Price, S. J., Zimmerman, T. S., & Murphy, M. J. (1997). Client gender as a process variable in marriage and family therapy: Are women clients interrupted more than men clients? *Journal of Family Psychology, 11*, 373–377.

Werner-Wilson, R. J., Zimmerman, T. S., & Price, S. J. (1999). Are goals and topics influenced by gender and modality in the initial marriage and family therapy session? *Journal of Marital and Family Therapy, 25*, 253–262.

West, C., & Zimmerman, D. H. (1977). Women's place in everyday talk: Reflections on parent-child interaction. *Social Problems, 24*, 521–529.

West, C. & Zimmerman, D. H. (1983). Small insults: A study of interruptions in cross-sex conversations between unacquainted persons. In B. Thorne, C. Kramarae, & N. Henley (Eds.), *Language, gender and society* (pp. 103–117). Rowley, MA: Newbury House.

Whisman, M. A., & Jacobson, N. S. (1990). Power, marital satisfaction, and response to marital therapy. *Journal of Family Psychology, 4*, 202–212.

Zimmerman, D. H., & West, C. (1975). Sex roles, interruptions, and silences in conversation. In B. Thorne & N. Henley (Eds.), *Language & sex: Difference & dominance* (pp. 105–129). Rowley, MA: Newbury House.

About the authors: *Ronald Jay Werner-Wilson*, PhD, associate professor and Marriage and Family Therapy Program and Clinic director; *Megan J. Murphy*, PhD, assistant professor, and *Jennifer Lynn Fitzharris*, MS, are all affiliated with the Department of Human Development and Family Studies, Iowa State University, Ames, IA.

Address correspondence to: Ronald Jay Werner-Wilson, PhD, Department of Human Development and Family Studies, 4380 Palmer Building, Suite 1321, Iowa State University, Ames, IA 50011-4380. E-mail: rwwilson@iastate.edu

Exercise for Article 7

Factual Questions

1. The researchers state that recent studies show what type of relationship between marital satisfaction and power inequality?

2. Dominance theory suggests that men use questions, interruptions, and other means of communication as a way to do what?

3. Coding for interruptions in each therapy session was done for three segments. How long was each segment?

4. The researchers defined "interruptions" as a violation of a speaking turn. How was "interruptions" operationalized?

5. Was the difference between women clients and men clients being interrupted statistically significant? If yes, at what probability level?

6. Was the difference between men therapists and women therapists statistically significant? If yes, at what probability level?

Questions for Discussion

7. The researchers discuss theories relating to their research in lines 108–145 and lines 302–325. In your opinion, is this discussion an important strength of this research report? Explain.

8. This study examined interruptions in only the initial consultation with a therapist. Would you be willing to generalize the results to subsequent sessions? Explain. (See lines 191–192.)

9. The researchers state that the undergraduate students who coded the videotapes were unaware of the purpose of this research. Speculate on why the researchers did not make them aware of the purpose. (See lines 207–210.)

10. In your opinion, is the "coder training" described in lines 211–219 an important part of this study? Explain.

11. The current study does not support the view that men therapists are different from women therapists in how often they interrupt clients. Does this result surprise you? Explain. (See lines 315–319.)

12. In your opinion, does this study make an important contribution to understanding how clients' gender *influences* therapists' behavior? Explain.

Quality Ratings

Directions: Indicate your level of agreement with each of the following statements by circling a number from 5 for strongly agree (SA) to 1 for strongly disagree (SD). If you believe an item is not applicable to this research article, leave it blank. Be prepared to explain your ratings. When responding to criteria A and B below, keep in mind that brief titles and abstracts are conventional in published research.

A. The title of the article is appropriate.

SA   5   4   3   2   1   SD

B. The abstract provides an effective overview of the research article.

SA   5   4   3   2   1   SD

C. The introduction establishes the importance of the study.

SA   5   4   3   2   1   SD

D. The literature review establishes the context for the study.

SA   5   4   3   2   1   SD

E. The research purpose, question, or hypothesis is clearly stated.

SA   5   4   3   2   1   SD

F. The method of sampling is sound.

SA   5   4   3   2   1   SD

G. Relevant demographics (for example, age, gender, and ethnicity) are described.

SA   5   4   3   2   1   SD

H. Measurement procedures are adequate.

SA   5   4   3   2   1   SD

I. All procedures have been described in sufficient detail to permit a replication of the study.

SA   5   4   3   2   1   SD

J. The participants have been adequately protected from potential harm.

SA   5   4   3   2   1   SD

K. The results are clearly described.

SA   5   4   3   2   1   SD

L. The discussion/conclusion is appropriate.

SA   5   4   3   2   1   SD

M. Despite any flaws, the report is worthy of publication.

SA   5   4   3   2   1   SD

Article 8

An Unobtrusive Measure of Racial Behavior in a University Cafeteria

STEWART PAGE
University of Windsor
Windsor, Ontario, Canada

ABSTRACT. Observational data were gathered from a large university cafeteria for a period of 22 days, in l-hour periods per day, over one semester. Observations were made of the frequency with which Black and White cashiers were selected. Chi-square analyses showed a significant association between a cashier's being Black and increased likelihood that she would not be selected. Some comments and comparisons are made with other research using similar measures.

Reprinted with permission from *Journal of Applied Social Psychology*, Vol. 27, No. 24, 2172–2176. Copyright © 1997 V. H. Winston & Son, Inc., 360 South Ocean Boulevard, Palm Beach, FL 33480. All rights reserved.

The study of interracial behavior has long-standing familiarity to social and community psychologists, as well described in the classic writings of Kenneth Clark, Gordon Allport, Thomas Pettigrew, and others. Allport's (1958) *The Nature of Prejudice,* for example, remains one of the most frequently cited books on the issue, both within and without the discipline of psychology (Pettigrew, 1988). The dramatic effects of race as a variable in research have been demonstrated, for example, in a variety of situations assessing social influence and stigmatization. Many such studies have used some form of Bogardus' (1931, 1959) notion of *social distance* (social intimacy) measures of racial acceptance.

Observational and experimental studies of race have undoubtedly declined somewhat in recent times, while more pragmatic and biopolitical aspects such as equal opportunity, affirmative action, ethnic and cultural diversity, and so on have become more prominent. These issues are important, yet many aspects of interracial behavior remain incompletely understood.

One such aspect involves behavior in open situations; that is, those without racial demand characteristics or obligations (Orne, 1962). Moreover, the factor of race may also function differently at varying levels of awareness and in accordance with the extent of reactivity in measures used to observe it (e.g., Webb, Campbell, Schwartz, & Sechrest, 1966). For example, in a study which has now become a classic, Weitz (1972) administered a questionnaire assessing White–Black racial attitudes to a university population. For many of her subjects who had expressed egalitarian attitudes, Weitz nevertheless found that these same individuals showed subtly, rejecting nonverbal behaviors when later placed in a laboratory situation requiring cooperative work alongside a Black individual. From a psychoanalytic perspective, Weitz referred to these results as supporting a *repressed-affect model* of racial behavior. In this view, racial behavior assessed reactively, such as with questionnaires or interviews, is typically egalitarian, yet may show "leakage," that is, negative aspects, when assessed nonreactively and unobtrusively. Similarly, in a series of studies (e.g., Page, 1995; Page & Day, 1990), we have found frequently that publicly advertised rental accommodation is likely to be described privately (thus, unobservably) as "already rented" when landlords receive telephone inquiries from persons alleging to have some type of stigmatizing characteristic.

Although their study was not concerned directly with race, Hechtman and Rosenthal (1991) found, as another example of such leakage, that teachers showed more nonverbal warmth toward pupils for whom the teaching task was stereotypically gender appropriate (e.g., vocabulary items for girls; mechanical items for boys), as compared to when they taught a task which was gender inappropriate. Lott (1987), also in a nonracial context, similarly found that men did not show unfavorable attitudes toward women on paper-and-pencil measures. They did, however, in unobtrusively observed work situations, show subtle avoidance behaviors, more negative statements, and increased social distance specifically toward female coworkers. In a racial context, Taylor (1979) found that teachers' nonverbal behaviors varied subtly according to the race (White vs. Black) of their pupils in an unobtrusively observed teaching situation.

A long-standing difficulty in many studies remains that of generalization from laboratory-based research. The present study examined some aspects of racial behavior using a nonlaboratory (cafeteria) setting, whose essential functions are those of dining and socialization. Such settings generally carry no outward prescriptions or expectations regarding race, based on the tacit assumption that this factor indeed "does not exist." The cafeteria setting is also one in which many behaviors, performed with little awareness or at low levels of intensity, may be unobtrusively observed. The speculative hypothesis was explored that a predominantly White population of customers, consisting mostly of undergraduate students, might select a White cashier more frequently than a Black cashier.

Method

Participants

During a recent semester, observations were made of a university population in a large public cafeteria at the University of Windsor over a period of 22 (nonconsecutive) weekdays, excluding Fridays. A daily 1-hour observation period, from approximately noon until approximately 1:00 p.m. each day, was used.

Procedure

The spatial arrangement of the cafeteria was such that once food items are collected and before entering the main eating area, customers must select a cashier from (usually) three choices during peak lunchtime hours throughout the academic year. Cashiers for the current period of observation were three females, located at the end of three separate pathways, one of which must be selected by exiting customers. Distances to each cashier, from locations occupied by customers after selecting all food items, are approximately equal. In the eating area directly beyond the cashiers is a counter area, containing a straight row of individual seats. A vertical partition attached to the front edge of the counter partially obscures the occupants of these seats from view. From one end of the counter, the activities of each cashier can be observed reliably and unobtrusively.

Throughout the above time period, one of the three cashiers was Black; the remaining two were White. On the campus, as typical of Ontario universities generally, Black students form a distinct and visible minority group. A daily record was kept of the number of (non-Black) customers paying for food at each cashier. For consistency, observations were made only when three cashiers, at separate locations, were on duty. Individual cashiers varied nonsystematically in their location from day to day. Cases in which a single person paid for one or more companions' food were counted as representing only a single customer. Cases where individuals only requested change or approached a cashier for reasons other than paying for food were excluded. In general, therefore, a "unit" of observation was recorded and signaled, in most cases, when a cashier was observed extending her hand to return change. No subjective judgments or ratings were thus required; data (Table 1) were gathered solely in the form of frequency counts.

Results and Discussion

Results, in terms of frequency of cashier selection, are shown in Table 1. A goodness-of-fit (χ^2) analysis of the frequency data showed a significant tendency for customers to select less frequently a cashier who was Black, $\chi^2(2, N = 9,713) = 6.57, p < .038$.

Table 1
Frequency of Cashier Selection by Race

Cashier	Frequency of selection
1 (White cashier)	3,320
2 (White cashier)	3,271
3 (Black cashier)	3,122
Cashier selection: Three White cashiers	
1	2,659
2	2,622
3	2,734

In order to evaluate further the possibility that a directional or spatial bias played some role in cashier selection, some additional data (covering 19 days; non-Fridays) were gathered, during a different semester. For these data, all three cashiers were White. There was no significant location preference in selection, $\chi^2(2, N = 8,015) = 2.44, p < .296$.

In interpreting such results, one must exercise caution in view of certain limitations. One cannot know precisely what percentage of customers might have been included more than once over the total time period, nor does one have complete information about other factors in a university population which are germane to the issue of race. Moreover, populations such as the one observed in the present study consider themselves (and are considered) highly accepting, aware, and sensitive to matters concerning race, as congruent with commonly prevailing values and norms within a North American university campus.

Yet there remain other, more abstract issues, still largely unresolved by social and community psychologists. One concerns Kelman's (1958) early distinctions between levels of attitude internalization, and between the emotional, evaluative, and behavioral components of attitudes. Another concerns the unreliable, indeed sometimes disturbing, relationship between racial attitudes and racial behavior (Pettigrew, 1988). Another concerns the related issue of congruence between behaviors elicited under reactive conditions, in which they may be detected, and those which may be observed nonreactively and which may be performed at low levels of awareness. In this light, one is reminded of recent videotaped demonstrations on the ABC network program *Prime Time Live,* in which Black "pseudoclients" were given false information about job availability, higher prices for used cars, and less accommodating service in stores. One is also reminded of LaPiere's (1934) classic study in which restaurateurs indicated by telephone that Chinese couples would not

170 be served, yet most such couples were served when they actually entered the restaurants.

Again, while the factor of race may become a conspicuous factor in research situations where reactive measures or manipulations are used, its presence and
175 effects in other situations may remain more insidious and ill-defined. Indeed, the present data reflect only frequency counts; that is, simple observations of human behavior. They seem sufficient, however, to illustrate the myth that race is irrelevant or does not exist in
180 the context of everyday acts and social routines. Further research on the repressed affect model of racial behavior therefore seems clearly warranted.

References

Allport, G. (1958). *The nature of prejudice.* Garden City, NY: Doubleday Anchor Books.

Bogardus, E. (1931). *Fundamentals of social psychology.* New York, NY: Century Press.

Bogardus, E. (1959). *Social distance.* Yellow Springs, OH: Antioch.

Hechtman, S., & Rosenthal, R. (1991). Teacher gender and nonverbal behavior in the teaching of gender-stereotyped materials. *Journal of Applied Social Psychology, 21,* 446–459.

Kelman, H. (1958). Compliance, identification, and internalization: Three processes of attitude change. *Journal of Conflict Resolution, 2,* 51–60.

LaPiere, R. (1934). Attitudes versus actions. *Social Forces, 13,* 230–237.

Lott, B. (1987). Sexist discrimination as distancing behavior: A laboratory demonstration. *Psychology of Women Quarterly, 11,* 47–59.

Orne, M. (1962). On the social psychology of the psychological experiment: With particular reference to demand characteristics and their implications. *American Psychologist, 17,* 776–783.

Page, S. (1995). Effects of the mental illness label in 1993: Acceptance and rejection in the community. *Journal of Health and Social Behavior, 7,* 61–69.

Page, S., & Day, D. (1990). Acceptance of the "mentally ill" in Canadian society: Reality and illusion. *Canadian Journal of Community Mental Health, 9,* 51–61.

Pettigrew, T. (1988). The ultimate attribution error. In E. Aronson (Ed.), *The social animal* (pp. 325–344). New York, NY: W. H. Freeman.

Taylor, M. (1979). Race, sex, and the expression of self-fulfilling prophecies in a laboratory teaching situation. *Journal of Personality and Social Psychology, 37,* 897–912.

Webb, E., Campbell, D., Schwartz, R., & Sechrest, L. (1966). *Unobtrusive measures.* New York, NY: Rand-McNally.

Weitz, S. (1972). Attitude, voice, and behavior: A repressed affect model of interracial interaction. *Journal of Personality and Social Psychology, 24,* 14–21.

Address correspondence to: Stewart Page, Department of Psychology, University of Windsor, 401 Sunset, Windsor, Ontario N9B 3P4, Canada.

Exercise for Article 8

Factual Questions

1. What is the "speculative hypothesis" that was explored in this study?

2. The observations were made during which hour of the day?

3. Did the individual cashiers work in the same station (location) every day?

4. What was the "unit" of observation?

5. The Number 1 White cashier was selected how many more times than the Black cashier?

6. Was the first chi-square test statistically significant at the .05 level (i.e., with a probability of .05 *or less*)? Explain.

7. What is the first limitation mentioned by the researcher?

Questions for Discussion

8. The researcher suggests that questionnaires and interviews assess racial behavior *reactively*. What do you think this term means? Is it a good idea to use questionnaires and interviews for this purpose? Explain. (See lines 39–43.)

9. The researcher points out that this is a *nonlaboratory* study. In your opinion, is this important? Explain. (See lines 70–78.)

10. Would it be informative to have a larger number of White and Black cashiers in a future study on this topic? Explain.

11. In your opinion, does this study *prove* that there is racial discrimination? Explain.

Quality Ratings

Directions: Indicate your level of agreement with each of the following statements by circling a number from 5 for strongly agree (SA) to 1 for strongly disagree (SD). If you believe an item is not applicable to this research article, leave it blank. Be prepared to explain your ratings. When responding to criteria A and B below, keep in mind that brief titles and abstracts are conventional in published research.

A. The title of the article is appropriate.

SA   5   4   3   2   1   SD

B. The abstract provides an effective overview of the research article.

SA   5   4   3   2   1   SD

C. The introduction establishes the importance of the study.

SA   5   4   3   2   1   SD

D. The literature review establishes the context for the study.

SA   5   4   3   2   1   SD

E. The research purpose, question, or hypothesis is clearly stated.

SA   5   4   3   2   1   SD

F. The method of sampling is sound.

    SA   5   4   3   2   1   SD

G. Relevant demographics (for example, age, gender, and ethnicity) are described.

    SA   5   4   3   2   1   SD

H. Measurement procedures are adequate.

    SA   5   4   3   2   1   SD

I. All procedures have been described in sufficient detail to permit a replication of the study.

    SA   5   4   3   2   1   SD

J. The participants have been adequately protected from potential harm.

    SA   5   4   3   2   1   SD

K. The results are clearly described.

    SA   5   4   3   2   1   SD

L. The discussion/conclusion is appropriate.

    SA   5   4   3   2   1   SD

M. Despite any flaws, the report is worthy of publication.

    SA   5   4   3   2   1   SD

Article 9

Shopping Center Fire Zone Parking Violators:
An Informal Look

JOHN TRINKAUS
Baruch College (CUNY)

SUMMARY. Data for 33 1-hr. observations at a shopping center in a suburban location showed about 700 violations of a traffic regulation prohibiting parking in a fire zone. Women driving vans were the least compliant—accounting for approximately 35% of the total.

From *Perceptual and Motor Skills*, *95*, 1215–1216. Copyright © 2002 by Perceptual and Motor Skills. Reprinted with permission.

To glean some information about the profile of motorists who fail to comply with rules on parking in designated fire zones in shopping centers (5), an informal enquiry was conducted, June through August of 2001, 5 at a shopping center located in a suburb of a large city in New York State. The center housed a bank, a large grocery food supermarket, three sit-down restaurants, and an assortment of 12 other shops and stores. The center was arranged in the form of a "U." The busi- 10 nesses—with sidewalks in front—lined the periphery, with parking (for about 450 vehicles) in the central area. Painted on the pavement in front of the establishments was a 6-ft.-wide continuous yellow zebra-striping, which, along with sign postings, delineated a 15 no-parking fire zone.

Three shops were located in one corner of the center—a dry cleaner, a bakery, and a laundromat—all of which opened early in the morning and appeared to do a brisk business seemingly with folks on their way to 20 work: people dropping off or picking up dry cleaning, those buying rolls, pastry, and coffee, and people leaving laundry to be done. It was the parking behavior of these people that was observed; in particular, those who pulled up in front of one of the three shops and 25 parked their vehicles in the fire zone.

Convenience sampling of the number of parkers, the type of vehicles driven (car or van), and the gender of the driver was conducted. Hour-long observations were made on weekdays, between the hours of 0700 30 and 0900: none during inclement weather. No note was made of commercial vehicles or those in which the driver remained behind the wheel while a passenger exited the vehicle and entered the shop to conduct business. As counting was done early in the day, there 35 were always many "legal" parking spaces available

(but necessitated walking approximately 75 to 150 feet further).

Thirty-three 1-hr. observations were made. A total of 916 parkings were noted: 693 (76%) in the fire zone 40 and 223 (24%) in designated lot spaces. Of the fire zone parkings, 396 (57%) were cars and 297 (43%) vans. Women were driving 222 (56%) of the cars, and men 174 (44%). Two hundred forty-one (81%) of the vans were driven by women, 56 (19%) by men. For 45 every three motorists who parked in the fire zone, there was approximately one motorist who parked in a designated lot space.

Recognizing such methodological limitations as the use of a relatively small sample of convenience, the 50 possibility of double counting, the lack of factoring for the intrinsic moral code of conduct of individual drivers, and the problem of verifiable replication of this enquiry, it seems that compliance with rules on parking in fire zones may leave something to be desired. As to 55 the finding that women driving vans appeared to be the least compliant with the parking regulation, it should be cautiously interpreted. For example, it may well be that the pattern observed could simply reflect a sample of the population of drivers and their vehicle types in 60 the geographical area or those normally frequenting the shopping center during the observation period. However, it does appear to track four other prior related informal enquiries by Trinkaus. Those who exceeded school zone limits (1), those who failed to observe stop 65 signs (2), those who delayed moving out at left-turning traffic signals (3), and those who blocked road intersections (4) all tended to be women driving vans.

Epilogue: To assess whether the parking behavior of drivers frequenting this shopping center might have 70 changed following the World Trade Center incident of September 11—more law abiding—five additional observations were made in late September. No note was made of vehicle type nor driver gender, but note was made of whether or not vehicles were adorned 75 with American flags or other patriotic trappings. A total of 129 parkings were observed: 94 (73%) in the fire zone and 35 (27%) in designated lot spaces. Of those that were parked in the fire zone, 22 (23%) were

80 decorated, while in designated lot spaces there were 3 (9%).

References

1. Trinkaus, J. School-zone speed-limit dissenters: An informal look. *Perceptual and Motor Skills*, 1999, *88*, 1057–1058.
2. Trinkaus, J. Stop-sign dissenters: An informal look. *Perceptual and Motor Skills*, 1999, *89*, 193–194.
3. Trinkaus, J. Left-turning traffic procrastinators: An informal look. *Perceptual and Motor Skills*, 2000, *90*, 961–962.
4. Trinkaus, J. Blocking the box: An informal look. *Psychological Reports*, 2001, *89*, 315–316.
5. *Vehicle and traffic law.* (2000–2001) New York State, Stopping, standing, and parking. Article 32, Basic rules, Section 1200.

Address correspondence to: J. Trinkaus, One Linden Street, New Hyde Park, NY 11040.

Exercise for Article 9

Factual Questions

1. The observations were made in front of what types of shops?

2. How many one-hour observations were made?

3. What percentage of the fire zone parkings were made by individuals in vans?

4. The researcher mentions several "methodological limitations." What is the first one that is mentioned?

5. Five additional observations were made to assess what?

Questions for Discussion

6. In your opinion, how important is it to know that the observations were made between 7 AM and 9 AM (i.e., between 0700 and 0900)? (See lines 28–30.)

7. Speculate on why the researcher did not make observations during inclement weather. (See lines 28–30.)

8. Do any of the findings surprise you? Do you find any especially interesting? Explain.

9. If you were conducting a study on the same topic, what changes in the research methodology, if any, would you make?

Quality Ratings

Directions: Indicate your level of agreement with each of the following statements by circling a number from 5 for strongly agree (SA) to 1 for strongly disagree (SD). If you believe an item is not applicable to this research article, leave it blank. Be prepared to explain your ratings. When responding to criteria A and B below, keep in mind that brief titles and abstracts are conventional in published research.

A. The title of the article is appropriate.

   SA   5   4   3   2   1   SD

B. The abstract provides an effective overview of the research article.

   SA   5   4   3   2   1   SD

C. The introduction establishes the importance of the study.

   SA   5   4   3   2   1   SD

D. The literature review establishes the context for the study.

   SA   5   4   3   2   1   SD

E. The research purpose, question, or hypothesis is clearly stated.

   SA   5   4   3   2   1   SD

F. The method of sampling is sound.

   SA   5   4   3   2   1   SD

G. Relevant demographics (for example, age, gender, and ethnicity) are described.

   SA   5   4   3   2   1   SD

H. Measurement procedures are adequate.

   SA   5   4   3   2   1   SD

I. All procedures have been described in sufficient detail to permit a replication of the study.

   SA   5   4   3   2   1   SD

J. The participants have been adequately protected from potential harm.

   SA   5   4   3   2   1   SD

K. The results are clearly described.

   SA   5   4   3   2   1   SD

L. The discussion/conclusion is appropriate.

   SA   5   4   3   2   1   SD

M. Despite any flaws, the report is worthy of publication.

   SA   5   4   3   2   1   SD

Article 10

Students' Ratings of Teaching Effectiveness: A Laughing Matter?

GARY ADAMSON
University of Ulster at Magee College

DAMIAN O'KANE
University of Ulster at Magee College

MARK SHEVLIN
University of Ulster at Magee College

ABSTRACT. Gump in 2004 identified a positive significant relationship between awareness of daily class objectives and ratings of the instructor's overall teaching effectiveness. The idea that rating of teaching effectiveness can be related to other nonteaching related attributes of the lecturer was further examined. Correlations based on ratings of teaching effectiveness from 453 undergraduate students ($M = 21$ yr., $SD = 5.5$; 73% women) showed that another nonteaching related variable, namely, how funny the instructor was perceived, was significantly related to indicators of teaching effectiveness.

From *Psychological Reports*, *96*, 225–226. Copyright © 2005 by Psychological Reports. Reprinted with permission.

The practice of having students evaluate teaching in universities is widespread in the UK and the USA, and the information from such surveys can be a useful guide for potential changes in course material and
5 method of delivery (QAA, 1997). For students' evaluation of teaching questionnaires to be used, there should be clear evidence that such measures are producing valid scores, that is, that such questionnaires are actually measuring teaching effectiveness.
10 Research suggests that ratings of teaching effectiveness are positively related to teaching and student-related variables such as awareness of daily class objectives (Gump, 2004), expected grades (Feldman, 1976; Marsh, 1987), the students' prior interest in the
15 topic (Marsh & Roche, 1997), and grading leniency (Greenwald & Gillmore, 1997). More alarmingly Shevlin, Banyard, Davies, and Griffiths (2000) tested a model that specified ratings of the lecturers' charisma, measured by a single item, as a predictor of teaching
20 effectiveness, in particular "lecturer ability" and "module attributes." Using structural equation modeling, they found that the charisma ratings accounted for 69% of the variation of the lecturer ability factor and 37% of the module attributes factor.
25 The idea that ratings of teaching effectiveness can be related to other nonteaching related attributes of the lecturer was further examined. An additional item, "The lecturer was funny," was included in a larger questionnaire designed to measure teaching effective-
30 ness. All items used a 5-point Likert response format

with anchors of 1 (Strongly Disagree) and 5 (Strongly Agree). This questionnaire was administered at a UK university to a sample of 453 undergraduate students who were enrolled in full-time courses within a de-
35 partment of social sciences (M age = 21 yr., $SD = 5.5$; 73% women). In total, six lecturers were rated (four men and two women) in this study.

Analysis showed items designed to reflect aspects of effective teaching were positively correlated with
40 rating how funny the lecturer was. Scores on the item "The lecturer was funny" were positively correlated with scores on the items "The lecturer helped me to develop an interest in the subject matter" ($r = .60$, $p < .01$), "I wanted to learn more about the topic" ($r = .49$,
45 $p < .01$), "The lectures were well organised ($r = .40$, $p < .01$), and "The lecturer is successful in encouraging students to do supplementary reading on the subject matter of the module" ($r = .38$, $p < .01$).

The results suggest that students' perceptions of
50 funniness were moderately and significantly associated with ratings of teaching-related activity.

Whereas previous research has focused mainly on the dimensionality of measures of teaching effectiveness (Abrami, d'Apollonia, & Rosenfield, 1997), it is
55 suggested here that the validity of scores derived from any measure of teaching effectiveness ought to be ascertained prior to use of the measure.

References

Abrami, P. C., d'Apollonia, S., & Rosenfield, S. (1997). The dimensionality of student ratings of instruction: What we know and what we do not. In R. P. Perry & J. C. Smart (Eds.), *Effective teaching in higher education: Research and practice*. New York: Agathon Press. pp. 321–367.

Feldman, K. A. (1976). Grades and college students' evaluations of their courses and teachers. *Research in Higher Education*, *18*, 3–124.

Greenwald, A. G., & Gillmore, G. M. (1997). Grading leniency is a removable contaminant of student ratings. *American Psychologist*, *52*, 1209–1217.

Gump, S. E. (2004). Daily class objectives and instructor's effectiveness as perceived by students. *Psychological Reports*, *94*, 1250–1252.

Marsh, H. W. (1987). Students' evaluations of university teaching: Research findings, methodological issues, and directions for future research. *International Journal of Educational Research*, *11*, 253–388.

Marsh, H. W., & Roche, L. A. (1997). Making students' evaluations of teaching effectiveness effective. *American Psychologist*, *52*, 1187–1197.

Quality Assurance Agency for Higher Education. (1997). *Subject review handbook: October 1998 to September 2000*. (QAA 1/97) London: Quality Assurance Agency for Higher Education.

Shevlin, M., Banyard, P., Davies, M. D., & Griffiths, M. (2000). The validity of student evaluation of teaching in higher education: Love me, love my lectures? *Assessment and Evaluation in Higher Education*, *25*, 397–405.

Address correspondence to: Dr. Mark Shevlin, School of Psychology, University of Ulster at Magee Campus, Londonderry, BT48 7JL, UK.

Exercise for Article 10

Factual Questions

1. What were the anchors for the statement, "The lecturer was funny"?

2. How many students participated in this study?

3. What was the average age of the students in this study?

4. What is the value of the correlation coefficient for the relationship between "The lecturer was funny" and "I wanted to learn more about the topic"?

5. The strongest correlation was between the lecturer being funny and what other item?

6. Do all the correlation coefficients reported in this study indicate direct (positive) relationships?

Questions for Discussion

7. The researchers characterize being funny as a "nonteaching related" attribute. Do you agree with this characterization (i.e., that being funny is not a teaching attribute)? (See lines 25–30.)

8. Six lecturers were rated by the students. Would you recommend using a larger number of lecturers in a future study on this topic? Explain. (See lines 36–37.)

9. After each correlation coefficient, this information appears: $p < .01$. What does this tell you about the correlation coefficients? (See lines 43–48.)

10. Would you characterize any of the correlation coefficients in lines 43–48 as representing very strong relationships?

11. The relationships reported in this study are positive. If you had planned this study, would you have anticipated finding any inverse (negative) relationships among the variables studied? Explain.

12. Do you think that this study shows a *causal* relationship between being funny and perceptions of other teaching attributes (i.e., does it provide evidence that being funny causes higher ratings on other items)? Explain.

13. This research report is shorter than others in this book. In your opinion, is its brevity a defect of the report? A strength of the report? Explain.

Quality Ratings

Directions: Indicate your level of agreement with each of the following statements by circling a number from 5 for strongly agree (SA) to 1 for strongly disagree (SD). If you believe an item is not applicable to this research article, leave it blank. Be prepared to explain your ratings. When responding to criteria A and B below, keep in mind that brief titles and abstracts are conventional in published research.

A. The title of the article is appropriate.

   SA   5   4   3   2   1   SD

B. The abstract provides an effective overview of the research article.

   SA   5   4   3   2   1   SD

C. The introduction establishes the importance of the study.

   SA   5   4   3   2   1   SD

D. The literature review establishes the context for the study.

   SA   5   4   3   2   1   SD

E. The research purpose, question, or hypothesis is clearly stated.

   SA   5   4   3   2   1   SD

F. The method of sampling is sound.

   SA   5   4   3   2   1   SD

G. Relevant demographics (for example, age, gender, and ethnicity) are described.

   SA   5   4   3   2   1   SD

H. Measurement procedures are adequate.

   SA   5   4   3   2   1   SD

I. All procedures have been described in sufficient detail to permit a replication of the study.

   SA   5   4   3   2   1   SD

J. The participants have been adequately protected from potential harm.

   SA   5   4   3   2   1   SD

K. The results are clearly described.

   SA   5   4   3   2   1   SD

L. The discussion/conclusion is appropriate.

        SA   5   4   3   2   1   SD

M. Despite any flaws, the report is worthy of publication.

        SA   5   4   3   2   1   SD

Article 11

Relationships of Assertiveness, Depression, and Social Support Among Older Nursing Home Residents

DANIEL L. SEGAL

University of Colorado at Colorado Springs

ABSTRACT. This study assessed the relationships of assertiveness, depression, and social support among nursing home residents. The sample included 50 older nursing home residents (mean age = 75 years; 75% female; 92% Caucasian). There was a significant correlation between assertiveness and depression ($r = -.33$), but the correlations between social support and depression ($r = -.15$) and between social support and assertiveness ($r = -.03$) were small and nonsignificant. The correlation between overall physical health (a subjective self-rating) and depression was strong and negative ($r = -.50$), with lower levels of health associated with higher depression. An implication of this study is that an intervention for depression among nursing home residents that is targeted at increasing assertiveness and bolstering health status may be more effective than the one that solely targets social support.

From *Behavior Modification*, 29, 689–695. Copyright © 2005 by Sage Publications. Reprinted with permission.

Most older adults prefer and are successful at "aging in place"—that is, maintaining their independence in their own home. For the frailest and most debilitated older adults, however, nursing home placement is of-
5 tentimes necessary. About 5% of older adults live in a nursing home at any point in time, a figure that has remained stable since the early 1970s (National Center for Health Statistics, 2002). Depression is one of the most prevalent and serious psychological problems
10 among nursing home residents: About 15% to 50% of residents suffer from diagnosable depression (see review by Streim & Katz, 1996).

Social support is also an important factor in mental health among nursing home residents, and psychosocial
15 interventions often seek to bolster the resident's level of supportive relationships.

Assertiveness training plays an important role in traditional behavioral therapy with adults, and it has been recommended as a treatment component among
20 older adults with diverse psychological problems as well (Gambrill, 1986). Assertiveness may be defined as the ability to express one's thoughts, feelings, beliefs, and rights in an open, honest, and appropriate way. A

key component of assertiveness is that the communica-
25 tion does not violate the rights of others, as is the case in aggressive communications. It is logical that nursing home residents with good assertiveness skills would more often get what they want and need. Having basic needs met is a natural goal of all people, and failure to
30 do so could lead to depression or other psychological problems. Personal control has long been noted to improve mental health among nursing home residents (see Langer & Rodin, 1976), and assertiveness training would likely help residents express more clearly their
35 desires and needs.

Two studies have examined links between assertiveness, depression, and social support among older adult groups. Among 69 community-dwelling older adults, Kogan, Van Hasselt, Hersen, and Kabacoff
40 (1995) found that those who are less assertive and have less social support are at increased risk for depression. Among 100 visually impaired older adults, Hersen et al. (1995) reported that higher levels of social support and assertiveness were associated with lower levels of
45 depression. Assertiveness may rightly be an important skill among nursing home residents because workers at the institutional setting may not be as attuned to the emotional needs of a passive resident and the workers may respond poorly to the aggressive and acting-out
50 resident. However, little is known about the nature and impact of assertiveness in long-term care settings. The purpose of this study, therefore, was to assess relationships of assertiveness, social support, and depression among nursing home residents, thus extending the lit-
55 erature to a unique population.

Method

Participants were recruited at several local nursing homes. Staff identified potential volunteers who were ostensibly free of cognitive impairment. Participants completed anonymously the following self-report
60 measures: Wolpe-Lazarus Assertiveness Scale (WLAS) (Wolpe & Lazarus, 1966), Geriatric Depression Scale (GDS) (Yesavage et al., 1983), and the Social Support List of Interactions (SSL 12-I) (Kempen & van Eijk, 1995). The WLAS consists of 30 yes/no

65 items and measures levels of assertive behavior. Scores can range from 0 to 30, with higher scores reflecting higher levels of assertiveness. The GDS includes 30 yes/no items and evaluates depressive symptoms specifically among older adults. Scores can range from 0
70 to 30, with higher scores indicating higher levels of depression. The SSL12-I is a 12-item measure of re-ceived social support that has good psychometric prop-erties among community-dwelling older adults. Re-spondents indicate on a 4-point scale the extent to
75 which they received a specific type of support from a member of their primary social network (1 = seldom or never, 2 = now and then, 3 = regularly, 4 = very often). Scores can range from 12 to 48 with higher scores cor-responding to higher levels of support. The sample
80 included 50 older adult residents (mean age = 74.9 years, SD = 11.9, age range = 50–96 years; 75% fe-male; 92% Caucasian).

Results and Discussion

The mean WLAS was 18.1 (SD = 4.1), the mean GDS was 9.0 (SD = 5.5), and the mean SSL12-I was
85 29.2 (SD = 7.3). The correlation between the WLAS and GDS was moderate and negative ($r = -.33$, $p < .05$), with lower levels of assertiveness associated with higher depression. The correlation between the SSL12-I and GDS was small and nonsignificant ($r = -.15$, ns),
90 indicating a slight negative relationship between over-all support and depression. Similarly, the correlation between the SSL12-I and WLAS was small and non-significant ($r = -.03$, ns), indicating almost no relation-ship between overall support and assertiveness. Next,
95 correlations between a subjective self-rating of overall physical health status (0–100 scale, higher scores indi-cating better health) and the WLAS, GDS, and SSL12-I were calculated. As expected, the correlation between physical health and GDS was strong and negative
100 ($r = -.50$, $p < .01$), with poorer health associated with higher depression. The correlation between health and WLAS was positive in direction but small and nonsig-nificant ($r = .17$, ns), indicating little relationship be-tween health and assertiveness. Similarly, the correla-
105 tion between health and SSL12-I was also small and nonsignificant ($r = -.02$, ns), indicating no relationship between health and overall support. The slight relation-ship between health and assertiveness is an encourag-ing sign because it suggests that assertiveness (which is
110 primarily achieved through effective verbalizations) is not limited to only the least physically impaired nurs-ing home residents. Finally, gender differences on all dependent measures were examined (independent t tests) and no significant differences were found (all ps
115 > .05).

Notably, the mean assertion and depression scores among nursing home residents are consistent with means on identical measures in community-dwelling older adults (assertion M = 19.1; depression M = 7.9;
120 Kogan et al., 1995) and visually impaired older adults (assertion M = 18.3; depression M = 10.4; Hersen et al., 1995), suggesting that the higher functioning group of nursing home residents are no more depressed and no less assertive than other samples of older persons.
125 Regarding social support, our nursing home sample appeared to show somewhat higher levels of overall support than community older adults in the normative sample (N = 5,279, M = 25.5) in the SSL12-I valida-tion study (Kempen & van Eijk, 1995). This may pos-
130 sibly be due to the nature of institutional living and the large numbers of support staff and health care person-nel.

The correlational results regarding the moderate negative association between assertion and depression
135 are consistent with data from community-dwelling older adults ($r = -.36$; Kogan et al., 1995) and visually impaired older adults ($r = -.29$; Hersen et al., 1995), suggesting a pervasive relationship among the vari-ables in diverse older adult samples and extending the
140 findings to nursing home residents. Contrary to the literature, the relationship between social support and depression among nursing home residents was weaker than the one reported in community-dwelling older adults ($r = -.50$; Kogan et al., 1995) and visually im-
145 paired older adults ($r = -.48$; Hersen et al., 1995). The relationship between assertiveness and overall support in this study was almost nonexistent, also contrary to earlier reports in which the relationship was moderate and positive in direction. Our results are consistent
150 with prior research showing no gender differences among older adults in assertiveness, depression, and social support using similar assessment tools (Hersen et al., 1995; Kogan et al., 1995). This study also suggests a strong negative relationship between health status and
155 depression among nursing home residents. An implica-tion of this study is that an intervention for depression among nursing home residents that is targeted at in-creasing assertiveness and bolstering health status may be more effective than the one that solely targets social
160 support.

Several limitations are offered concerning this study. First, the sample size was modest and the sample was almost exclusively Caucasian. Future studies with more diverse nursing home residents would add to the
165 knowledge base in this area. All measures were self-report, and future studies with structured interviews and behavioral assessments would be stronger. We are also concerned somewhat about the extent to which the WLAS is content valid for older adults. Notably, a
170 measure of assertive behavior competence has been developed specifically for use with community-dwelling older adults (Northrop & Edelstein, 1998), and this measure appears to be a good choice for future research in the area. A final limitation was that partici-
175 pants were likely the highest functioning of residents because they were required to be able to complete the measures independently and were selected out if there was any overt cognitive impairment (although no for-

mal screening for cognitive impairment was done),
180 thus limiting generalizability to more frail nursing home residents. Cognitive screening should be done in future studies. Nonetheless, results of this study suggest a potentially important relationship between assertiveness and depression among nursing home residents.
185 Finally, it is imperative to highlight that there are many types of interventions to combat depression among nursing home residents: behavioral interventions to increase exercise, participation in social activities, and other pleasurable activities; cognitive inter-
190 ventions to reduce depressogenic thoughts; and pharmacotherapy, to name a few. (The interested reader is referred to Molinari, 2000, for a comprehensive description of psychological issues and interventions unique to long-term care settings.) The present data
195 suggest that training in assertiveness may be yet one additional option for psychosocial intervention in nursing homes. A controlled outcome study is warranted in which intensive assertiveness training is compared to a control group of nursing home residents who do not
200 receive such training. Only with such a study can cause-and-effect statements be made about the role that assertiveness skills training may play in the reduction of depressive symptoms among nursing home residents.

References

Gambrill, E. B. (1986). Social skills training with the elderly. In C. R. Hollin & P. Trower (Eds.), *Handbook of social skills training: Applications across the lifespan* (pp. 211–238). New York: Pergamon.

Hersen, M., Kabacoff, R. L, Van Hasselt, V B., Null, J. A., Ryan, C. F., Melton, M. A., et al. (1995). Assertiveness, depression, and social support in older visually impaired adults. *Journal of Visual Impairment and Blindness, 7*, 524–530.

Kempen, G. I. J. M., & van Eijk, L. M. (1995). The psychometric properties of the SSL12-I, a short scale for measuring social support in the elderly. *Social Indicators Research, 35*, 303–312.

Kogan, S. E., Van Hasselt, B. V., Hersen, M., & Kabacoff, I. R. (1995). Relationship of depression, assertiveness, and social support in community-dwelling older adults. *Journal of Clinical Geropsychology, 1*, 157–163.

Langer, E. J., & Rodin, J. (1976). The effects of choice and enhanced personal responsibility for the aged: A field experiment in an institutional setting. *Journal of Personality and Social Psychology, 34*, 191–198.

Molinari, V. (Ed.). (2000). *Professional psychology in long-term care: A comprehensive guide.* New York: Hatherleigh.

National Center for Health Statistics. (2002). *Health, United States, 2002.* Hyattsville, MD: Author.

Northrop, L. M. E., & Edelstein, B. A. (1998). An assertive-behavior competence inventory for older adults. *Journal of Clinical Geropsychology, 4*, 315–331.

Streim, J. E., & Katz, I. R. (1996). Clinical psychiatry in the nursing home. In E. W. Busse & D. G. Blazer (Eds.), *Textbook of geriatric psychiatry* (2nd ed., pp. 413–432). Washington, DC: American Psychiatric Press.

Wolpe, J., & Lazarus, A. A. (1966). *Behavior therapy techniques.* New York: Pergamon.

Yesavage, J. A., Brink, T. L., Rose, T. L., Lum, O., Huang, V, Adey, M., et al. (1983). Development and validation of a geriatric depression screening scale: A preliminary report. *Journal of Psychiatric Research, 17*, 314–317.

Acknowledgment: The author thanks Jessica Corcoran, M.A., for assistance with data collection and data entry.

About the author: Daniel L. Segal received his Ph.D. in clinical psychology from the University of Miami in 1992. He is an associate professor in the Department of Psychology at the University of Colorado at Colorado Springs. His research interests include diagnostic and assessment issues in geropsychology, suicide prevention and aging, bereavement, and personality disorders across the lifespan.

Exercise for Article 11

Factual Questions

1. Were the participants cognitively impaired?

2. Was the mean score for the participants on the GDS near the highest possible score on this instrument? Explain.

3. What is the value of the correlation coefficient for the relationship between the WLAS and the GDS?

4. Was the relationship between SSL12-I and GDS strong?

5. Was the correlation coefficient for the relationship between SSL12-I and GDS statistically significant?

6. Was the relationship between physical health and GDS a direct relationship *or* an inverse relationship?

Questions for Discussion

7. The researcher obtained participants from "several" nursing homes. Is this better than obtaining them from a single nursing home? Explain. (See lines 56–57.)

8. The researcher characterizes the *r* of −.33 in line 86 as "moderate." Do you agree with this characterization? Explain.

9. In lines 85–107, the researcher reports the values of six correlation coefficients. Which one of these indicates the strongest relationship? Explain the basis for your choice.

10. In lines 85–107, the researcher reports the values of six correlation coefficients. Which one of these indicates the weakest relationship? Explain the basis for your choice.

11. For the *r* of −.50 in line 100, the researcher indicates that "*p* < .01." What is your understanding of the meaning of the symbol "*p*"? What is your understanding of ".01"?

12. Do you agree with the researcher that a different type of study is needed in order to determine the role of assertiveness skills training in the reduction of depressive symptoms? Explain. (See lines 197–204.)

Quality Ratings

Directions: Indicate your level of agreement with each of the following statements by circling a number from 5 for strongly agree (SA) to 1 for strongly disagree (SD). If you believe an item is not applicable to this research article, leave it blank. Be prepared to explain your ratings. When responding to criteria A and B below, keep in mind that brief titles and abstracts are conventional in published research.

A. The title of the article is appropriate.

    SA   5   4   3   2   1   SD

B. The abstract provides an effective overview of the research article.

    SA   5   4   3   2   1   SD

C. The introduction establishes the importance of the study.

    SA   5   4   3   2   1   SD

D. The literature review establishes the context for the study.

    SA   5   4   3   2   1   SD

E. The research purpose, question, or hypothesis is clearly stated.

    SA   5   4   3   2   1   SD

F. The method of sampling is sound.

    SA   5   4   3   2   1   SD

G. Relevant demographics (for example, age, gender, and ethnicity) are described.

    SA   5   4   3   2   1   SD

H. Measurement procedures are adequate.

    SA   5   4   3   2   1   SD

I. All procedures have been described in sufficient detail to permit a replication of the study.

    SA   5   4   3   2   1   SD

J. The participants have been adequately protected from potential harm.

    SA   5   4   3   2   1   SD

K. The results are clearly described.

    SA   5   4   3   2   1   SD

L. The discussion/conclusion is appropriate.

    SA   5   4   3   2   1   SD

M. Despite any flaws, the report is worthy of publication.

    SA   5   4   3   2   1   SD

Article 12

Correlations Between Humor
Styles and Loneliness

WILLIAM P. HAMPES
Black Hawk College

ABSTRACT. In a previous study, a significant negative correlation between shyness with affiliative humor and a significant positive one with self-defeating humor were reported. Since shyness and loneliness share many of the same characteristics, poor social skills and negative affect, for example, significant negative correlations of loneliness with affiliative and self-enhancing humor and a significant positive one with self-defeating humor were hypothesized. 106 community college students (34 men, 72 women) ranging in age from 17 to 52 years ($M = 23.5$, $SD = 7.7$) were tested. The hypotheses were supported. Interrelationships among humor, shyness, and loneliness should be examined within one study.

From *Psychological Reports*, *96*, 747–750. Copyright © 2005 by Psychological Reports. Reprinted with permission.

Various studies, using self-report and rating scales, have yielded correlations of .40 or more between shyness and loneliness (Cheek & Busch, 1981; Jones, Freeman, & Goswick, 1981; Moore & Schultz, 1983; Anderson & Arnoult, 1985). Research studies have shown that those high in both variables tend to have poor social skills (Zahaki & Duran, 1982; Moore & Schultz, 1983; Wittenberg & Reis, 1986; Miller, 1995; Carducci, 2000; Segrin & Flora, 2000), poor interpersonal relationships (Jones, 1981; Jones, Rose, & Russell, 1990; Carducci, 2000), and low self-esteem (Jones et al., 1981; Olmstead, Guy, O'Malley, & Bentler, 1991; Kamath & Kanekar, 1993; Schmidt & Fox, 1995).

Hampes (in press) reported shyness negatively correlated with affiliative humor and positively correlated with self-defeating humor. Affiliative humor is an interpersonal form of humor that involves use of humor (telling jokes, saying funny things, or witty banter, for example), to put others at ease, amuse others, and to improve relationships (Martin, Puhlik-Doris, Larsen, Gray, & Weir, 2003). Since those high on affiliative humor tend to score high on extraversion and intimacy (Martin et al., 2003), and lonely people, like shy people, have poor social skills and relationships, it was hypothesized that loneliness would be negatively correlated with affiliative humor.

Self-defeating humor "involves excessively self-disparaging humor, attempts to amuse others by doing or saying funny things at one's expense as a means of ingratiating oneself or gaining approval, allowing oneself to be the 'butt' of others' humor, and laughing along with others when being ridiculed or disparaged" (Martin et al., 2003, p. 54). Since both lonely and shy people tend to have low self-esteem, and those high in self-defeating humor tend to score low on self-esteem (Martin et al., 2003), it was hypothesized that loneliness and self-defeating humor would be positively correlated.

Hampes (in press) did not find a significant correlation for his total group of 174 subjects between scores on shyness and self-enhancing humor, an adaptive intrapersonal dimension of humor that "involves a generally humorous outlook on life, a tendency to be frequently amused by the incongruities of life, and to maintain a humorous perspective even in the face of stress or of adversity" (Martin et al., 2003, p. 53). However, Martin et al. reported self-enhancing humor scores were positively correlated with those on self-esteem, social intimacy, and social support, just the opposite of the relationships between loneliness and self-esteem, social intimacy, and social support. Therefore, it was hypothesized that loneliness and self-enhancing humor would be negatively correlated.

Hampes (in press) did not find a significant correlation for his total group between scores on shyness and aggressive humor (a maladaptive interpersonal type of humor, involving sarcasm, teasing, ridicule, derision, hostility, or disparagement humor) for the total group. Therefore, it was hypothesized that there would be a nonsignificant correlation between loneliness and aggressive humor.

Method

The subjects were 106 students (34 men, 72 women) at a community college in the midwestern United States. These students ranged in age from 17 to 52 years ($M = 23.5$, $SD = 7.7$). Students in four psychology classes were asked to participate, and those who volunteered were included in the sample.

The UCLA Loneliness Scale (Version 3) measures loneliness as a unidimensional emotional response to a

difference between desired and achieved social contact. It contains 20 items, each of which has four response options in a Likert-type format, anchored by 1 = Never and 4 = Always (e.g., "How often do you feel isolated
75 from others?"). Coefficients alpha for the scale ranged from .89 to .94 (Russell & Cutrona, 1988). Russell, Kao, and Cutrona (1987) reported a 1-yr. test–retest correlation of .73 and estimated discriminant validity through significant negative correlations between
80 scores on loneliness with those on social support and measures of positive mental health status.

In the Humor Styles Questionnaire, each of four scales has eight items. Each item has seven response options in a Likert-type format, anchored by 1 = To-
85 tally Disagree and 7 = Totally Agree. The Cronbach alpha for the four scales ranged from .77 to .81. The convergent validity for the Affiliative Humor Scale was indicated by significant correlations with scores on the Miller Social Intimacy Scale and Extraversion on
90 the NEO PI–R. Discriminant validity for the Self-enhancing Humor Scale was estimated by a significant negative correlation with scores on Neuroticism of the NEO PI–R, and convergent validity was estimated with significant positive correlations with the Coping Hu-
95 mor Scale and the Humor Coping subscale of the Coping Orientations to Problems Experienced Scale. Convergent validity for the Aggressive Scale was supported by a significant correlation with scores on the Cook-Medley Hostility Scale. Discriminant validity for
100 the Self-defeating Scale was based on significant negative correlations with ratings on the Rosenberg Self-esteem Scale and on the Index of Self-esteem (Martin et al., 2003).

Results and Discussion

Four Pearson product-moment correlations were
105 computed for the scores on the UCLA Loneliness Scale-Version 3 ($M = 41.1$, $SD = 10.7$) and those on each of four humor scales: Affiliative ($M = 45.5$, $SD = 7.3$), Self-enhancing ($M = 37.4$, $SD = 8.4$), Aggressive ($M = 25.8$, $SD = 7.4$), and Self-defeating ($M = 26.0$, SD
110 $= 8.9$). In each case, the hypotheses were supported, as correlations were significant for scores in Loneliness with Affiliative Humor ($r = -.47$, $p < .001$, $CI_{95} = -.28$ to $-.66$), Self-enhancing Humor ($r = -.39$, $p < .001$, $CI_{95} = -.20$ to $-.58$), and Self-defeating Humor ($r = .32$,
115 $p < .001$, $CI_{95} = .13$ to $.51$). The correlation between scores on Loneliness and Aggressive Humor was not significant ($r = -.04$, $p > .05$, $CI_{95} = -.23$ to $.15$).

Dill and Anderson (1999) posited that shyness precedes loneliness. Given their social anxiety, shy people
120 tend to be unsuccessful in social situations, and so they try to avoid these. Even if they do not avoid social relationships, they tend not to have satisfying personal relationships. As a result, they may report being lonely. The idea that shyness precedes loneliness is supported
125 by the developmental research of Kagan (1994), who stated that shyness has a strong genetic component and

is manifested early in infancy, and Cheek and Busch (1981), who found shyness influenced loneliness reported by students in an introductory psychology
130 course. If shyness does precede loneliness, it could be in part because shy individuals do not use affiliative humor and self-enhancing humor to help them be more successful in social situations and score high in self-defeating humor, which other people might not find
135 appealing. Further studies are needed to evaluate the causal relationships among shyness, loneliness, and styles of humor.

References

Anderson, C. A., & Arnoult, L. H. (1985). Attributional style and everyday problems in living: Depression, loneliness, and shyness. *Social Cognition, 3*, 16–35.

Carducci, B. (2000). *Shyness: a bold new approach.* New York: Perennial.

Cheek, J. M., & Busch, C. M. (1981). The influence of shyness on loneliness in a new situation. *Personality and Social Psychology Bulletin, 7*, 572–577.

Dill, J. C., & Anderson, C. A. (1999). Loneliness, shyness, and depression: the etiology and interrelationships of everyday problems in living. In T. Joiner & J. C. Coyne (Eds.), *The interactional nature of depression* (pp. 93–125) Washington, DC: American Psychological Association.

Hampes, W. P. (in press). The relation between humor styles and shyness. *Humor: The International Journal of Humor Research.*

Jones, W. H. (1981) Loneliness and social contact. *Journal of Social Psychology, 113*, 295–296.

Jones, W. H., Freeman, J. A., & Goswick, R. A. (1981). The persistence of loneliness: Self and other determinants. *Journal of Personality, 49*, 27–48.

Jones, W. H., Rose, J., & Russell, D. (1990). Loneliness and social anxiety. In H. Leitenberg (Ed.), *Handbook of social evaluation anxiety* (pp. 247–266) New York: Plenum.

Kagan, J. (1994). *Galen's prophecy: Temperament in human nature.* New York: Basic Books.

Kamath, M., & Kanekar, S. (1993). Loneliness, shyness, self-esteem, and extraversion. *The Journal of Social Psychology, 133*, 855–857.

Martin, R. A., Puhlik-Doris, P., Larsen, G., Gray, J., & Weir, K. (2003). Individual differences in uses of humor and their relation to psychological well-being: Development of the Humor Styles Questionnaire. *Journal of Research in Personality, 37*, 48–75.

Miller, R. S. (1995). On the nature of embarassability, shyness, social evaluation, and social skill. *The Journal of Psychology, 63*, 315–339.

Moore, D., & Schultz, N. R. (1983). Loneliness at adolescence: Correlates, attributions and coping. *Journal of Youth and Adolescence, 12*, 95–100.

Olmstead, R. E., Guy, S. M., O'Malley, P. M., & Bentler, P. M. (1991). Longitudinal assessment of the relationship between self-esteem, fatalism, loneliness, and substance abuse. *Journal of Social Behavior and Personality, 6*, 749–770.

Russell, D. W., & Cutrona, C. E. (1988). Development and evolution of the UCLA Loneliness Scale. (Unpublished manuscript, Center for Health Services Research, College of Medicine, University of Iowa)

Russell, D. W., Kao, C., & Cutrona, C. E. (1987). Loneliness and social support: Same or different constructs? Paper presented at the Iowa Conference on Personal Relationships, Iowa City.

Schmidt, L. A., & Fox, N. A. (1995). Individual differences in young adults' shyness and sociability: Personality and health correlates. *Personality and Individual Differences, 19*, 455–462.

Segrin, C., & Flora, J. (2000). Poor social skills are a vulnerability factor in the development of psychosocial problems. *Human Communication Research, 26*, 489–514.

Wittenberg, M. T., & Reis, H. T. (1986). Loneliness, social skills, and social perception. *Personality and Social Psychology Bulletin, 12*, 121–130.

Zahaki, W R., & Duran, R. L. (1982). All the lonely people: The relationship among loneliness, communicative competence, and communication anxiety. *Communication Quarterly, 30*, 202–209.

Address correspondence to: William Hampes, Department of Social, Behavioral, and Educational Studies, Black Hawk College, 6600 34th Avenue, Moline, IL 61265. E-mail: hampesw@bhc.edu

Exercise for Article 12

Factual Questions

1. In the introduction to the research article, the researcher hypothesizes a positive correlation between which two variables?

2. What was the mean age of the students in this study?

3. The correlation coefficient for the relationship between Loneliness and Affiliative Humor was −.47. This indicates that those who had high loneliness scores tended to have

   A. low Affiliative Humor scores.
   B. high Affiliative Humor scores.

4. In lines 111–117, the researcher reports four correlation coefficients. Which correlation coefficient indicates the strongest relationship?

5. Is the correlation coefficient for the relationship between Loneliness and Self-enhancing Humor statistically significant? If yes, at what probability level?

6. Is the correlation coefficient for the relationship between Loneliness and Aggressive Humor statistically significant? If yes, at what probability level?

Questions for Discussion

7. In your opinion, does the use of volunteers affect the quality of this study? (See lines 63–68.)

8. The correlation coefficient between Loneliness and Affiliative Humor equals −.47. The researcher also reports the 95% confidence interval (CI_{95}) for this correlation coefficient. What is your understanding of the meaning of the confidence interval? (See lines 111–113.)

9. Would you characterize any of the correlation coefficients reported in lines 111–117 as representing a "very strong" relationship? Explain.

10. Would you characterize any of the correlation coefficients reported in lines 111–117 as representing a "very weak" relationship? Explain.

11. The researcher mentions "causal relationships" in line 136. In your opinion, do the results of this study offer evidence regarding causal relationships? Explain.

Quality Ratings

Directions: Indicate your level of agreement with each of the following statements by circling a number from 5 for strongly agree (SA) to 1 for strongly disagree (SD). If you believe an item is not applicable to this research article, leave it blank. Be prepared to explain your ratings. When responding to criteria A and B below, keep in mind that brief titles and abstracts are conventional in published research.

A. The title of the article is appropriate.

   SA   5   4   3   2   1   SD

B. The abstract provides an effective overview of the research article.

   SA   5   4   3   2   1   SD

C. The introduction establishes the importance of the study.

   SA   5   4   3   2   1   SD

D. The literature review establishes the context for the study.

   SA   5   4   3   2   1   SD

E. The research purpose, question, or hypothesis is clearly stated.

   SA   5   4   3   2   1   SD

F. The method of sampling is sound.

   SA   5   4   3   2   1   SD

G. Relevant demographics (for example, age, gender, and ethnicity) are described.

   SA   5   4   3   2   1   SD

H. Measurement procedures are adequate.

   SA   5   4   3   2   1   SD

I. All procedures have been described in sufficient detail to permit a replication of the study.

   SA   5   4   3   2   1   SD

J. The participants have been adequately protected from potential harm.

   SA   5   4   3   2   1   SD

K. The results are clearly described.

   SA   5   4   3   2   1   SD

L. The discussion/conclusion is appropriate.

   SA   5   4   3   2   1   SD

M. Despite any flaws, the report is worthy of publication.

   SA   5   4   3   2   1   SD

Article 13

Effects of Participants' Sex and Targets' Perceived Need on Supermarket Helping Behavior

PAMELA C. REGAN
California State University, Los Angeles

DELIA M. GUTIERREZ
California State University, Los Angeles

ABSTRACT. A field experiment was focused on whether participants' sex and targets' perceived need influenced helping behavior. Confederates approached 332 (166 women, 166 men) same-sex participants in a supermarket and asked for 25 cents to help purchase one of three randomly assigned food items: milk, which was defined as a high-need item; frozen cookie dough, which served as a low-need item; or alcohol, which was a low-need item with negative social connotations. The dependent variable was whether a participant provided help. Participants' sex was not associated with helping behavior as equal proportions of men and women provided assistance to the confederate; however, perceived need strongly influenced whether the confederate received help. Specifically, the high-need item produced more helping behavior than did either of the low-need items, and the socially acceptable low-need item of cookie dough produced more helping behavior than the socially unacceptable low-need item of alcohol. This may be interpreted as showing that what one buys and how deserving of help one appears to be influence whether one is helped by others.

From *Perceptual and Motor Skills*, *101*, 617–620. Copyright © 2005 by Perceptual and Motor Skills. Reprinted with permission.

Social psychologists have extensively documented the variables associated with prosocial or helping behavior (Batson, 1998). Much of this research has focused upon characteristics of the person in need. Physically attractive individuals, for example, are more likely to receive help than are their less attractive peers (Wilson, 1978; Regan & Llamas, 2002). Another perhaps equally important variable in helping behavior is the target's perceived need; that is, how deserving of assistance the person appears to be. In general, targets in greater need of assistance tend to elicit more helping behavior from others (Enzle & Harvey, 1978; Sinha & Jain, 1986). For example, an early classic field experiment conducted by Bickman and Kamzan (1973) indicated women shoppers were more likely to help a female confederate who asked for 10 cents when she was attempting to buy a high-need food item like milk, and thereby presumably appeared more deserving of help, than when she was purchasing a low-need food item such as frozen cookie dough. The present field experiment was designed to replicate and extend this earlier work by investigating the extent to which two variables, participants' sex and targets' perceived need, would influence helping behavior. Perceived need was manipulated by using three different food items: milk (a high-need item), frozen cookie dough (a low-need item), and alcohol (a low-need item with negative social connotations). Based upon earlier research, the high-need item was predicted to elicit greater helping behavior than either of the low-need items. Because previous research exploring the association between participants' sex and helping behavior has yielded inconsistent results (Eagly & Crowley, 1986), there were no *a priori* predictions concerning this variable.

Methods

Participants

Participants were 332 adult (166 women, 166 men; estimated M age = 26 yr., SD = 4 yr.), shoppers at three large supermarkets located in Southern California. Participants were selected for inclusion in the experiment if they were the same sex as the confederate, appeared to be over 21 years of age, were shopping alone as defined by being unaccompanied by friends or family members, and appeared to be somewhat relaxed and not in a hurry to find a particular item or finish their shopping.

Confederates were four university students, two men and two women, whose ages ranged from 24 to 31 years (M age = 27 yr., SD = 2.5 yr.). Each dressed in clean, informal attire (pants with a shirt or blouse). Two confederates were present for each experimental session; one acted as an observer while the other approached the participant. Prior to entering the supermarket, each confederate team randomly selected the item they would use when soliciting help: a quart of milk, which served as a high-need item; a roll of frozen cookie dough, which was defined as low need; or a large bottle of beer, which represented a low-need item with negative social connotations.

Procedure

Upon entering the store, Confederate 1 picked up the assigned food item and proceeded down the next adjacent aisle. Confederate 2, masquerading as a shopper with a cart, followed at a discreet distance to observe the interaction, record the participant's response, and estimate the participant's age. The first shopper in the aisle who fulfilled the selection criteria was approached. Specifically, Confederate 1 approached the participant with two dollar bills and some change crumpled in one hand and with the selected food item held in the other. The confederate's statement was "Hi. I'm a little embarrassed, but I'm short 25 cents for this [carton of milk/package of cookie dough/bottle of beer]. Can you spare a quarter?" If the participant questioned the confederate, he or she replied, "I thought I had enough money with me."

The participant's response of help or no help served as the dependent variable. If the participant responded negatively to the confederate's request, the confederate said, "No problem, I understand" and proceeded to exit the aisle. If the participant responded affirmatively to the request and gave the confederate a quarter, the confederate accepted the quarter, thanked the participant, began to walk away, and then suddenly "found" a quarter in his or her own pocket. He or she immediately returned the participant's quarter, thanked the participant, and exited the aisle. Note that 23 participants insisted that the confederate keep the quarter.

Results and Discussion

In Table 1 are the number and percentage of participants who provided help in each of the three conditions. There was no sex difference in rates of helping behavior; across conditions, roughly equal percentages of men (51.2%) and women (56.6%) gave a quarter to the confederate when asked ($z = 0.99$, ns); however, perceived need clearly influenced helping behavior. As hypothesized, the high-need item produced greater helping behavior than both of the low-need items. Specifically, a series of z tests for proportions indicated that significantly more participants gave assistance to the confederate when he or she was trying to purchase milk than when he or she was trying to purchase frozen cookie dough (70.1 % vs 52.6%; $z = 2.85$, $p < .005$) or alcohol (70.1% vs 29.3%; $z = 5.86$, $p < .0001$). Similarly, cookie dough, a low-need but nonetheless socially acceptable item, produced greater helping behavior than did alcohol, a low-need item with questionable social desirability (52.6% vs 29.3%; $z = 3.27$, $p < .001$). In addition and in keeping with the lack of an overall sex difference in helping rates, the same result pattern was obtained when the responses of the men and women were examined separately.

These findings indicate that people in general are fairly helpful. Over half of the participants and equal numbers of men and women gave assistance to the confederate when asked. They did not help indiscrimi-

nately, however, but based their decision to provide assistance, at least in part, on how deserving of help the confederate appeared to be. Although other researchers also have found high rates of helping behavior (North, Tarrant, & Hargreaves, 2003), it is important to recognize that the scenario created here to elicit helping behavior from participants involved little risk of personal endangerment and low involvement with the target. It is possible that rates of helping behavior would be significantly lower in situations requiring greater personal involvement or risk.

Table 1
Helping Behavior As a Function of Targets' Perceived Need

Group		Milk	Cookie dough	Alcohol
Women	Total *N*	68	58	40
	Participants who helped			
	n	49	32	13
	%	72.0	55.2	32.5
Men	Total *N*	66	58	42
	Participants who helped			
	n	45	29	11
	%	68.2	50.0	26.2
Total	Total *N*	134	116	82
	Participants who helped			
	n	94	61	24
	%	70.1[ab]	52.6[ac]	29.3[bc]

Note. Percentages that share a superscript are significantly different. Z and *p* values are given in the text. Response patterns for men and women separately are identical with that of the total sample.

References

Batson, C. D. (1998). Altruism and prosocial behavior. In D. T. Gilbert, S. T. Fiske, & G. Lindzey (Eds.), *The handbook of social psychology.* (4th ed.) Vol. 2. Boston, MA: McGraw-Hill. Pp. 282–316.

Bickman, L., & Kamzan, M. (1973). The effect of race and need on helping behavior. *Journal of Social Psychology, 89,* 73–77.

Eagly, A. H., & Crowley, M. (1986). Gender and helping behavior: A meta-analytic review of the social psychological literature. *Psychological Bulletin, 100,* 283–308.

Enzle, M. E., & Harvey, M. D. (1978). Recipient vs. third-party requests, recipient need, and helping behavior. *Personality and Social Psychology Bulletin, 4,* 620–623.

North, A. C., Tarrant, M., & Hargreaves, D. J. (2003). The effects of music on helping behavior: A field study. *Environment and Behavior, 36,* 266–275.

Regan, P. C., & Llamas, V. (2002). Customer service as a function of shopper's attire. *Psychological Reports, 90,* 203–204.

Sinha, A. K., & Jain, A. (1986). The effects of benefactor and beneficiary characteristics on helping behavior. *Journal of Social Psychology, 126,* 361–368.

Wilson, D. W. (1978). Helping behavior and physical attractiveness. *Journal of Social Psychology, 104,* 313–314.

Acknowledgment: This research was supported in part by NIH MBRS-RISE Grant R25 GM61331.

Address correspondence to: Pamela Regan, Ph.D., Department of Psychology, California State University, 5151 State University Drive, Los Angeles, CA 90032-8227. E-mail: pregan@calstatela.edu

Exercise for Article 13

Factual Questions

1. According to the literature review, have high-need and low-need items been examined in an earlier experiment?

2. Confederate 2 masqueraded as what?

3. According to the researchers, what is the "dependent variable" in this experiment?

4. Was there a statistically significant sex difference in rates of helping behavior?

5. For the total sample, did cookie dough produce significantly greater helping behavior than alcohol?

6. Of the 66 men who were asked to help purchase milk, how many helped?

Questions for Discussion

7. This article is classified as an example of an experiment in the Contents of this book. In your opinion, is this classification correct? If yes, what feature of this study makes it an experiment?

8. In your opinion, are the criteria for inclusion of participants in this study reasonable? Explain. (See lines 37–44.)

9. Is the procedure in lines 58–85 sufficiently detailed so that you could conduct a replication of this study? Explain.

10. Do you agree with the researchers' concluding comment in lines 115–123? Explain.

11. This research article is shorter than most others in this book. In your opinion, is the article informative despite its brevity? Does it provide important results? Explain.

12. If you were on a funding board (e.g., on the board of a foundation that sponsors research), would you recommend funding for additional studies on this topic? Explain.

Quality Ratings

Directions: Indicate your level of agreement with each of the following statements by circling a number from 5 for strongly agree (SA) to 1 for strongly disagree (SD). If you believe an item is not applicable to this research article, leave it blank. Be prepared to explain your ratings. When responding to criteria A and B below, keep in mind that brief titles and abstracts are conventional in published research.

A. The title of the article is appropriate.

   SA   5   4   3   2   1   SD

B. The abstract provides an effective overview of the research article.

   SA   5   4   3   2   1   SD

C. The introduction establishes the importance of the study.

   SA   5   4   3   2   1   SD

D. The literature review establishes the context for the study.

   SA   5   4   3   2   1   SD

E. The research purpose, question, or hypothesis is clearly stated.

   SA   5   4   3   2   1   SD

F. The method of sampling is sound.

   SA   5   4   3   2   1   SD

G. Relevant demographics (for example, age, gender, and ethnicity) are described.

   SA   5   4   3   2   1   SD

H. Measurement procedures are adequate.

   SA   5   4   3   2   1   SD

I. All procedures have been described in sufficient detail to permit a replication of the study.

   SA   5   4   3   2   1   SD

J. The participants have been adequately protected from potential harm.

   SA   5   4   3   2   1   SD

K. The results are clearly described.

   SA   5   4   3   2   1   SD

L. The discussion/conclusion is appropriate.

   SA   5   4   3   2   1   SD

M. Despite any flaws, the report is worthy of publication.

   SA   5   4   3   2   1   SD

Article 14

Baby Think It Over: Evaluation of an Infant Simulation Intervention for Adolescent Pregnancy Prevention

DIANE de ANDA
University of California

ABSTRACT. In an intervention aimed at showing students the amount of responsibility involved in caring for an infant, 353 predominantly ninth-grade and Latino students carried the Baby Think It Over simulation doll in an intervention and completed matched pre- and posttest measures. Statistically significant gains were found on the total score and the impact of having a baby on academics, social life, and other family members; emotional risks; understanding and handling an infant's crying; and apprehension of the amount of responsibility involved in infant care. On a posttest-only measure, 108 participants reported statistically significant differences before and after carrying the doll with regard to the age at which they wished to have a child, their career and education plans, and the perceived interference of an infant with those education and career plans and their social life.

From *Health & Social Work, 31*, 26–35. Copyright © 2006 by the National Association of Social Workers. Reprinted with permission.

To alter adolescents' perception of the effort involved in caring for a baby and successfully increase their intent to avoid pregnancy in adolescence, students at a Los Angeles County high school participated in an
5 intervention using a life-size infant simulation doll known as "Baby Think It Over" (BTIO). The participating high school is in one of the 10 poorest cities in the nation (United Way of Greater Los Angeles, 1998–1999) and has been designated one of the adolescent
10 pregnancy "hot spots" in California because of its high rates of adolescent pregnancy (California Department of Health Services, 2001). The intervention places the tangible consequences of pregnancy before adolescent participants rather than offering only the abstract mes-
15 sages about pregnancy risks often presented in other programs.

Adolescent Pregnancy in the United States

The steady rise in adolescent pregnancy rates became a significant concern among social service and health professionals, legislators, and the general public
20 during the 1970s and 1980s. The rates increased from 95.1 per 1,000 for 15- to 19-year-olds and 62.4 per 1,000 for 15- to 17-year-olds in 1972 to an all-time high of 117.1 (in 1990) and 74.4 (in 1989), respectively. Following a variety of intervention efforts, a
25 slow decline in the rates was noted in the first half of the 1990s, followed by a more rapid decrease to below the 1972 rate by 1997: 93.0 for 15- to 19-year-olds and 57.7 for 15- to 17-year-olds (Alan Guttmacher Institute, 1999a). This period included a 20% drop in the
30 pregnancy rate among African American adolescents and a 16% reduction among white adolescents. The pregnancy rate for Latina adolescents, however, increased between 1990 and 1992 and by 1996 decreased by only 6% (Alan Guttmacher Institute, 1999b), result-
35 ing in the birth rate of 149.2 per 1,000 for Latino adolescents—the highest among the total adolescent population (National Center for Health Statistics, 2000). Inasmuch as 54.1% of Latino high school youths report they have had sexual intercourse, and only slightly
40 more than half of those who are sexually active report using protection or birth control, Latino adolescents represent a population at high pregnancy risk (Kann et al., 2000).

As early as 1967, Elkind (1967) posited the impor-
45 tance of cognitive development in understanding adolescent risk-taking behavior, including pregnancy risks. Based on empirical research, the author and colleagues also proposed that adolescent pregnancy resulting from the risk taking of unprotected sexual intercourse might
50 be significantly related to cognitive development. Specifically, this behavior might reflect a lack of full attainment of formal operations and "the sense of invulnerability—described by Elkind as the 'personal fable'" (Becerra, Sabagh, & de Anda, 1986, p.136). For-
55 mal operations refer to the individual's ability to engage in abstract and hypothetical–deductive thinking (Piaget, 1972; Piaget & Inhelder, 1958) and, in this case, project the potential for pregnancy and ultimately becoming a parent. Adolescence typically includes a
60 period of transition from concrete to formal operations, at the beginning of which recognizing oneself as a sexual being is relatively easy because it is in the present and very concrete. By contrast, considering oneself

fertile can be a rather abstract concept for a young adolescent, and the consequences of fertility can be distant and hypothetical. Others have offered similar explanatory frameworks with regard to risk taking and adolescent pregnancy (e.g., Gordon, 1990; Kralweski & Stevens-Simon, 2000; Out & Lefreniere, 2001).

Interventions have been developed to accommodate these cognitive factors by creating simulated parenting experiences to provide a concrete learning situation that will make the hypothetical risks and consequences of adolescent pregnancy more real to the adolescent participants. Some past interventions have involved caregiving situations not directly analogous to caring for an infant, involving, for example, carrying a sack of flour or an egg. More recent interventions have used a simulation more directly analogous to caring for an infant—a computerized infant simulation doll that requires attention to its demands in the form of intermittent periods of crying.

BTIO: The Intervention

BTIO is an intervention using a computerized infant simulation doll to offer adolescents experiences similar to those involved in attending to an infant. The doll is programmed to cry at random intervals and to stop crying only when the adolescent "attends" to the doll by inserting a key into a slot in the doll's back until it stops crying. An examination of participant logs indicated that most crying periods ranged between 10 and 15 minutes, and the frequency between eight and 12 times in 24 hours (including the early A. M. hours). The key is attached to a hospital-style bracelet, which is worn by the participant 24 hours a day to ensure that the adolescent provides the caregiving responsibilities during an entire two-and-a-half-day study period. The bracelets are designed so that an attempt to remove the bracelet is detectable. "Babysitting" of the doll by another student with a key or by the health class teacher who has extra keys is permitted only in certain situations—to take an examination, for example. The doll records data, including the amount of time the adolescent takes to "attend" to the infant (insert the key) and any form of "rough handling," such as dropping or hitting the doll. The term "rough handling" is used rather than abuse because there is no way to determine intentionality. Students whose records indicate neglect and rough handling receive a private counseling session with the health class teacher and have mandatory participation in a parenting class.

The purpose of carrying the infant simulation doll is to provide the students with an understanding of the amount of time and effort involved in the care of an infant and how an infant's needs might affect their daily lives and the lives of their family and significant others. This experience is augmented by presentations and group discussions led by staff from a local social services agency, covering such topics as the high incidence of adolescent pregnancy in the community, the factors that increase risk of adolescent pregnancy, and the costs of adolescent pregnancy and parenthood, with particular emphasis on the limitation of education and career opportunities and achievement. The health class teacher also offers a pregnancy prevention education program in preparation for carrying the doll and a debriefing discussion period after everyone in the class has carried the doll.

BTIO in Previous Research

A relatively small amount of research has been conducted on the effectiveness of BTIO. A literature search produced eight published research articles evaluating BTIO interventions aimed at modifying attitudes, perceptions, and behaviors related to pregnancy risk. Six studies examined whether the program affected the adolescents' view of parenthood and child-rearing responsibilities: two found their objectives met in this respect, but four determined no change in perception. In a study conducted by Divine and Cobbs (2001) with 236 eighth-grade students in nine Catholic schools in a midwestern city, a greater number of BTIO students than control group students ($p < .05$) indicated a change on two of seven items: the amount of effort and cost involved in infant care, and the feeling that they have enough knowledge about what taking care of a baby entails. The majority (63% of the male adolescents, 75.5% of female adolescents) felt carrying the doll was effective in "helping me know the challenges of infant care" (p. 599). In Out and Lafreniere's (2001) sample of 114 Canadian students in the 11th grade, BTIO participants reported significantly ($p < .01$) more examples of child-rearing consequences and responsibilities than did control group students.

In contrast to these limited positive findings, Kralewski and Stevens-Simon's (2000) sample of 68 sixth-grade and 41 eighth-grade female Hispanic students from a middle school in a lower socioeconomic status Colorado neighborhood revealed no significant differences between anticipated difficulty and the actual difficulty in caring for the BTIO doll. In addition, BTIO did little to change the girls' desire to have a baby during adolescence, with 13 expressing this intent before BTIO and 16 after carrying the doll. Somers and Fahlman (2001) used a quasi-experimental design with a predominantly white, middle-class sample drawn from three high schools in the Midwest; MANCOVA performed on the posttest scores using the pretest scores as the covariate found no differences between the 151 students in the experiment group and 62 students in the control group on perceptions regarding childcare responsibilities. Somers, Gleason, Johnson, and Fahlman's (2001) study in two Midwest high schools found no change in participants' understanding of the responsibilities involved in child rearing. Strachan and Gorey (1997) did not find a change on their Parenting Attitude Scale measuring "realistic par-

175 enting expectations" (p. 175) in their sample of 48 African American and white youths ages 16 to 18.

Only one of the studies found any significant difference or change in attitudes or behavior related to sexuality. Out and Lafreniere (2001) found that "ado-
180 lescents in the intervention group...rated themselves as being significantly more susceptible to an unplanned pregnancy compared with adolescents in the comparison group" (p. 577). However, they found no differences between the groups in attitudes toward absti-
185 nence and contraceptive use. In studies conducted by Somers and Fahlman (2001) and Somers et al. (2001), no significant change from pretest to posttest in attitudes and behaviors related to sexual behavior, contraception, and pregnancy was detected. Out and La-
190 freniere found no changes from pretest to posttest in attitudes toward abstinence and contraceptive use. Finally, Divine and Cobbs (2001) found no differences between experimental and control groups in attitudes regarding contraception, abstinence, and sexuality.

195 Although no differences were found between their 245 BTIO participants and 186 control group participants, Tingle (2002) found the majority of parents reported that the intervention had increased both their children's perceptions of the difficulties involved in
200 caring for an infant and parent–child communication regarding sexuality and parenting. Moreover, the great majority (92%) indicated they would recommend the program to a friend; 82% for use in middle schools and 97% for use in high schools. Similarly, the majority of
205 the 89 parents in a rural Ohio sample felt that the program was successful in teaching their children that a baby was a considerable responsibility (85%), time consuming (79%), and a barrier to achieving their life goals (71%), and 90% indicated they would recom-
210 mend the BTIO program to friends (Price, Robinson, Thompson, & Schmalzried, 2000).

Of the 22 teachers in Tingle's (2002) study, 59% evaluated BTIO as "somewhat effective" in preventing pregnancies and 45% said it was effective in initiating
215 communication between parent and child. In Somers and colleagues' (2001) study, few of the 57 teachers felt that BTIO reduced sexual intercourse (5%) or the number of sexual partners (7%). However, the majority (91%) believed that students learned about the respon-
220 sibilities of parenthood and recommended that BTIO be continued in the school (86%) and be adopted in other schools (84%).

There were serious methodological limitations and flaws in the preceding studies. Many of the samples
225 were small and not random, thereby limiting generalizability. In addition, volunteers were also used in a number of the studies; for example, Out and Lafreniere's (2001) intervention group consisted of students from elective courses on parenting and the con-
230 trol group from geography and physical education classes at the same schools. Additional research with larger samples, greater control of confounds (especially

selection bias), and more rigorous research designs and methodology are needed, preferably with replication,
235 before any conclusions can be drawn regarding the effectiveness of this intervention as a model for reducing the risk of adolescent pregnancy.

Objectives

The present Baby Think It Over intervention had seven major objectives. The first four posited an in-
240 crease in the degree to which the adolescent recognized: (1) that caring for a baby affects an adolescent's academic and social life; (2) that other family members are affected by having an adolescent with a baby in the family; (3) that there are emotional risks for each par-
245 ent in having a baby during adolescence; and (4) that there are family and cultural values related to having a baby during adolescence. The remaining three proposed an increase in the number planning to postpone parenthood: (5) until a later age (for the majority until
250 graduation from high school); (6) until education and career goals were met; or (7) until marriage.

Research Design and Method

Program objectives and additional constructs were measured with two main instruments: BTIO-1 and BTIO-2. A repeated-measures design was used, with
255 the BTIO-1 measure as the pretest and posttest. To increase validity, participants were used as their own controls through paired pretest-posttest comparisons, with all data entered anonymously. Moreover, confounds related to history and maturation were elimi-
260 nated because the intervention was conducted sequentially and continuously across the academic year with multiple individuals as their own controls. A posttest-only evaluation measure (BTIO-2) also was used to obtain self-report data on the impact of the program.

Measures

265 *BTIO-1.* The four main program objectives were measured using a 25-item, closed-ended instrument with a four-point Likert-type scale, ranging from 4 = strongly agree to 1 = strongly disagree. Total score and scores for each of the first four objectives were created
270 by summing the scores of the relevant items. Two separate scores were also calculated for items pertaining to understanding and dealing with a crying infant and those related to overall infant care. A higher score indicated a higher level of agreement consonant with
275 the program objectives and greater accuracy in their evaluation of the statements. The measure demonstrated good internal consistency ($\alpha = .84$).

In addition, the youths were asked to indicate *when* they would "like to have children": (1) never, (2) right
280 now, (3) when I finish junior high school, (4) when I'm in high school, or (5) after I graduate from high school. Students also checked items they would like to do "before having a baby": (1) have a good paying job, (2) go to college, (3) graduate from a junior college, (4)
285 graduate from a four-year college, (5) go to a trade or

76

technical school, (6) get married, (7) have a career, and (8) "other" write-in responses. Multiple responses were possible.

BTIO-2. The Baby Think It Over-2 measure is a post hoc, self-report measure indicating whether the experience changed what participants thought it would be like to have a baby; when they thought they would like to have a baby in terms of age and educational and career achievements; beliefs regarding the use of birth control or protection; and how much time and work are involved in taking care of a baby. Perceptions before and after carrying the BTIO doll were indicated along Likert-type scales for use of birth control or protection, amount of effort involved in caring for a baby, and the interference of infant caregiving with education goals, career goals, and social life.

Data Analysis

Paired *t* tests were performed on the summated scores for the total number of items on the Likert-type scale, the summated scores for each of the first four objectives, and the scores for crying and overall care. ANCOVAs, using the pretest as the covariate, were also conducted to determine whether there were differences in responses based on gender. Chi-square analyses were performed on the nominal data for the last three objectives on postponing pregnancy and parenthood.

Findings

Demographic Data

A total of 353 of the students who carried the infant simulation doll completed matched pre- and posttest measures: 140 male participants and 204 female participants. Nine students did not report gender. The overwhelming majority (94.3%, *n* = 333) of the participants were in the ninth grade, with the remaining five (1.4%) in the 10th and three (.9%) in the 11th grade; 12 students (3.4%) did not indicate grade level. Correspondingly, most of the participants were 14 (48.2%, *n* = 170) to 15 (47.9%, *n* = 169) years old. Reflecting the demographics of the community, 92.9% of the participants in the sample were Latino (70.8% Mexican American, *n* = 250; 5.1% Central American, *n* = 18; 17.0% other Latino, *n* = 60). The remaining participants included one African American, five American Indian, three Asian/Pacific Islander, nine white, and two multiethnic youths; five students did not provide this information.

BTIO-1

On the BTIO-1 measure, statistically significant gains from pretest to posttest were found on all but one of the paired analyses (Table 1). The statistically significant increase in the means from pretest to posttest indicates that objective 1 was met: a greater recognition of the impact of caring for a baby on academic and social life. The posttest mean approached 20, equivalent to "agree" and edging closer to the "strongly agree" point on the scale. When items related to the students' academic and social life were summed separately, the gains were also found to be statistically significant: academics [$t(352) = 7.893$, $p < .001$]; social life [$t(352) = 9.862$, $p < .001$].

The gain from pretest to posttest for objective 2 was also statistically significant, indicating a greater recognition of the effect of adolescent parenthood on other family members. However, the gain was modest (from 10.8 to 11.24 in a range of possible scores from four to 16), and the mean at posttest did not quite reach the point of "agree" (12.0) on the scale. An examination of the responses to the various items provides clarification. Most participants "agreed" or "strongly agreed" on items that recognize how adolescent parenthood affects the adolescent's family: 93.8% that an infant's crying or illness might disturb other family members' sleep and 70.8% that a baby's needs would reduce money available for the needs of others in the family. The mean was reduced by the 25% to 30% who disagreed on two items that indicated that other family members would share care and responsibility for the baby.

On objective 3, a statistically significant increase in the recognition of emotional risks accompanying adolescent parenthood was found, with the posttest mean corresponding to "agree."

Objective 4—regarding cultural and family values on adolescent parenthood—was not met. The increase was minimal (.14); however, the mean of 8 (in a range of possible scores of three to 12) is equivalent to "agree" on the four-point scale. High pretest scores may have resulted in a ceiling effect, and it is likely that cultural and family values are relatively stable.

Responses to items related to understanding why a baby cries and what actions should be taken in response were calculated into a summated score. The gain from pretest (*M* = 14.18) to posttest (*M* = 15.98) achieved statistical significance [$t(352) = 12.266$, $p < .001$], moving the mean beyond a score of 15 (range five to 20) or "agree" on the scale. The individual items clearly reflect aspects of the experience of carrying the BTIO doll: 92.6% (*n* = 327) disagreed or strongly disagreed that it was "easy to ignore a fussy, crying baby"; 86.1% (*n* = 304) disagreed or strongly disagreed that babies would not cry if they were loved and loved the parent in return. Moreover, the majority appeared to understand why infants cry and refrained from making inaccurate and judgmental appraisals of both infant and parent behavior: 85.3% (*n* = 301) did not view a baby who "cries a lot" as "spoiled," 65.7% (*n* = 232) did not attribute the crying to insufficient care by parents, and 94.6% (*n* = 334) saw crying as a form of communication (trying "to tell you something").

Three questions ascertained the participants' views regarding overall care of an infant. The increase in the mean (from 9.24 to 10.28) was statistically significant [$t(352) = -9.471$, $p < .001$], indicating an increase in

Table 1
Paired t Test Results on Objectives 1 to 4 of the Baby Think It Over Program (N = 353)

	M	SD	df	t
Objective 1: Academic and social			252	−10.633***
Pretest	18.08	3.52		
Posttest	19.99	2.48		
Objective 2: Impact on family members			352	−3.935***
Pretest	10.80	1.65		
Posttest	11.24	1.59		
Objective 3: Emotional risks			352	−6.951***
Pretest	14.50	2.25		
Posttest	15.46	2.11		
Objective 4: Family and cultural values			352	−1.593***
Pretest	8.44	1.40		
Posttest	8.58	1.36		

***$p \leq .001$.

the recognition of the substantial time and effort involved in caring for an infant. A high percentage concurred regarding the 24-hour caregiving required for the BTIO doll: 89.8% ($n = 317$) agreed or strongly agreed that, for adolescent parents, taking care of a baby might be "too much for them to handle"; 88.7% ($n = 313$) disagreed or strongly disagreed that taking care of a baby was "fun and easy"; and 96.1% ($n = 339$) agreed or strongly agreed that "taking care of a baby takes a lot of time and hard work."

The difference between the pretest ($M = 72.2$) and posttest ($M = 78.27$) means for the total score on the 25 items was statistically significant [$t(352) = −12.655$, $p < .001$], demonstrating an increase in agreement with the objectives of the program. With a range of 25 to 100, the posttest mean is equivalent to beyond "agree" (75.0) on the four-point scale.

To determine whether there were any differences in outcomes based on gender, ANCOVA was conducted using the pretest as the covariate. Female participants demonstrated greater gains on the total score [$F(1, 352) = 6.446$, $p < .012$]; objective 1 (academic and social life) [$F(1, 352) = 4.411$, $p < .05$]; objective 3 (emotional risks) [$F(1, 352) = 10.619$, $p < .001$]; and crying [$F(1, 352) = 9.290$, $p < .01$]. Male participants showed greater gains on objective 4 (family and cultural values) [$F(1, 352) = 4.679$, $p < .05$], with gains negligible for both (males: 8.44 to 8.79; females: 8.42 to 8.43).

Objective 5 posited an increase in the length of time the adolescents planned to postpone parenthood. There was only a 1.4% increase (72.5% to 73.9%) in the number of those intending to wait until after graduating from high school to have children. However, the number of those wanting children before graduating from high school decreased dramatically, from 8.7% ($n = 31$) to 1.5% ($n = 5$). Perhaps the BTIO experience was extremely negative for some participants, as the number never wanting children increased from 15.9% ($n = 56$) to 23.8% ($n = 84$).

Objective 6 was met with a statistically significant increase on every item related to postponing pregnancy

to achieve academic and career goals (Table 2). Financial stability was the highest priority, as job and career had the highest frequency at both pretest and posttest. For the majority of the youths, college aspirations took precedence over having a child. Although there was minimal increase in those who desired parenthood within a marital relationship after the BTIO experience—an additional 12 adolescents—the majority of the youths (71%; $n = 251$) had already indicated this preference at pretest.

BTIO-2

The BTIO-2 measure was completed by 108 participants, 60 female and 48 male, with most ages 14 to 15 (94.4%, $n = 102$), in the ninth grade (99.1%, $n = 107$), and Latino (92.6%, $n = 100$).

To obtain the adolescents' own view of the changes they experienced in perceptions and behavior as a result of carrying the BTIO doll, they were asked to indicate their thoughts, desires, or behavior "before BTIO" and "after BTIO/Now." Paired t test analyses found statistically significant differences in the desired direction on all items (Table 3).

Students reported that carrying the BTIO doll delayed the age at which they desired to have a child, from a mean of 23 to 25 years. A dramatic drop occurred in those indicating an age of 24 years or less (67% to 32.3%). Moreover, the majority (58.3%, $n = 63$) responded "yes," that carrying the BTIO doll had helped them change their mind regarding the age to have a child.

More than three-quarters of the BTIO-2 respondents indicated that they wanted to complete college and have a job or career before becoming parents. The already high "before" rate of 72.2% ($n = 78$) increased to 77.8% ($n = 84$) "after." There was an increase in those indicating that having a baby would interfere with their education (from 65.7%, $n = 71$ to 83.3%, $n = 90$); getting a good job or career (from 54.6%, $n = 59$ to 77.8%, $n = 84$); and their social life (from 58.3%, $n = 63$ to 73.1%, $n = 79$).

Table 2
Frequency of Response Selected by Participants in the Baby Think It Over Program

| | Pretest | | Posttest | | |
Factor	f	%	f	%	χ^2 ($df = 1$)
Good paying job	298	84.4	318	89.2	65.62***
Go to college	270	76.5	296	83.9	71.02***
Graduate from junior college	108	30.6	106	30.0	80.33***
Graduate from four-year college	173	49.0	183	51.8	89.17***
Technical school	102	28.9	112	31.7	59.75***
Career	288	81.6	303	85.8	92.95***
Married	251	71.1	263	74.5	61.02***

***$p < .001$.

Table 3
t Test Results BTIO-2: Before and After BTIO

	N	M	SD	df	t
Age want to have first baby				86	−7.210***
Before	87	23.16	3.55		
After	87	25.36	3.49		
School/job prior to having baby				91	−4.061***
Before	92	5.11	1.21		
After	92	5.51	1.08		
Amount of time it takes to care for baby				96	−5.821***
Before	97	3.24	.998		
After	97	3.78	.616		
How much baby interferes with education				102	−3.966***
Before	103	4.43	.986		
After	103	4.77	.675		
How much baby interferes with job/career				103	−4.984***
Before	104	4.16	1.18		
After	104	4.63	.827		
How much baby interferes with social life				100	−3.287***
Before	101	4.29	1.061		
After	101	4.60	.873		

Note. BTIO = Baby Think It Over
***$p \leq .001$.

More than half of the respondents (55.6%, $n = 60$) answered affirmatively that BTIO changed their perceptions of what having a baby would be like. In the open-ended questions, the most frequently cited reason was that it was much harder work to care for a baby than they had previously thought (39.8%, $n = 43$). Many students chose not to respond to the open-ended questions.

Nearly two-thirds (58.3%) reported that BTIO helped change their minds about using birth control or protection to prevent unwanted pregnancies. Reported use of birth control or protection increased from 22.2% ($n = 24$) to 28.7% ($n = 31$). Few "never" used protection, and the number dropped slightly from 13.9% ($n = 15$) to 11.1% ($n = 12$). The remaining either indicated that they had never had sexual intercourse or left it blank, as the item was supposed to be skipped if not applicable.

Among the varied responses to the open-ended question regarding what they thought of the program in general, a few appeared with greater frequency including comments describing the program as "good" or "effective" (61.1%, $n = 66$), and that BTIO helped them learn how hard taking care of a baby actually was and that they did not want a child at this time (39.9 %, $n = 43$).

Discussion

The Baby Think It Over program appears to be a well-designed intervention that has multiple educational components, a well-controlled simulation experience, debriefing procedures, a stable position in the school's curriculum, support from the school faculty and administration, and a working collaboration with the staff from a local social services agency that funds the program through a state grant. Both the results of the data analyses and the adolescents' own evaluation confirm the effectiveness of the Baby Think It Over intervention in changing perceptions regarding the time and effort involved in caring for an infant and in recognizing the significant effect having a baby has on all major aspects of one's life. Participants increased their awareness of how caring for an infant would interfere with future plans and goals with regard to both education and career. The majority aspired to a college education, and the BTIO experience intensified this desire to further their education. Pregnancy prevention was increasingly recognized as important to ensure their future. Furthermore, the adolescents began to have a more realistic understanding of the demands of adolescent parenthood, acknowledging the loss to their social life along with loss of sleep and the freedom to use their time as they desired. The effect on other family members was also noted as well as the emotional stress created by the responsibility for an infant.

Most of the youths were surprised by how labor-intensive taking care of the BTIO doll was, by the frequency with which they had to attend to the doll's needs (crying), and the disruption this caused in their lives. For most, this ended their romanticized view of having a baby—for a few, to the point of never wanting to have a baby. In general, the youths appeared to be more realistic about how much time and work is involved in caring for a baby. The majority responded by adjusting the timeframe within which they desired to have a child, opting for parenthood at a later age and after important educational and career achievements. In summary, the program appears to have been eminently successful in achieving its immediate objectives.

It should be noted, however, that these are all changes in perceptions and intention rather than longitudinal measures of actual behavior. Nevertheless, perceptions and intentions are important antecedents of behavior. From a social learning theory perspective, perception and intention increase or decrease the probability that a behavior will occur. Moreover, the perceived consequences of behavior and one's perceived self-efficacy in determining the outcome of the behavior affect the likelihood that the behavior will occur (Bandura, 1995). In this case, the students appeared to have made a strong connection between unprotected sexual intercourse and what they now evaluate as a negative outcome: having to care for a demanding infant and the subsequent social, emotional, and academic costs. Most of the respondents wished to have financial stability, an established career, and a marital relationship before parenthood.

The quantitative analyses as well as the students' own comments testify to the importance of the "hands on," simulated experience. Given that most of these youths were 14 and 15 years old, still making the transition from concrete to formal operations, the use of a concrete mechanism that offers direct experiential learning appears to be extremely appropriate.

The program appears to be successful in changing perceptions and intentions; however, to increase the likelihood of its effectiveness in preventing adolescent pregnancy in the long term, an intervention that also provides the adolescents with methods for dealing with situations that involve pregnancy risk is needed. A comprehensive program that covers methods from abstinence to birth control methods and access would provide adolescents with the knowledge and skills needed to actualize their intentions and the opportunity for choice in the means to accomplish this.

Finally, a number of strengths in the design of the program should also be noted. First, the intervention was offered to both male and female adolescents. Second, the mechanism (BTIO) ensured that all participants received the same intervention experience. Third, the process was a mandatory part of a required class, so that all students participated, thereby eliminating selection bias within the school sample. Fourth, the intervention was used sequentially throughout the school year with different participants each time used as their own controls so that there was control of confounds, particularly related to history and maturation. Fifth, the program was not simply a two-day intervention, as the simulation is part of a complex educational program that involves both preparation for the experience, group and individual discussion of the experience, and additional intervention for those students who experienced difficulty during the simulation.

It would be ideal to assess the long-term effects of the program by obtaining data on the pregnancy rates of the participants over the subsequent three years. However, an accurate count is questionable as pregnancies are not necessarily reported to the school, and adolescents who become pregnant may drop out of school, transfer, or have a miscarriage or abortion without the school ever knowing they were pregnant. Moreover, because all students in a single grade receive the experience, no long-term control group will be available.

In the short term, students in the educational planning course, which runs parallel with the health course, can be used as controls to improve the validity of the evaluation because assignment to the courses is on a relatively random basis; that is, determined by fit within the student's schedule. Because the students switch classes the second semester, the controls will then also receive the intervention, thus eliminating any ethical questions regarding the withholding of the intervention. Furthermore, to ascertain the effects of the BTIO doll alone, a comparison group who receives all the educational components except the doll could be used.

The findings offer a number of implications for social work practice with adolescents, particularly regarding pregnancy prevention. It appears that an intensive, realistic experience can effect a rapid and significant amount of attitude change about sexual behavior and adolescent parenthood in a relatively short amount of time. Therefore, even if funds are limited, because the

experience is only two-and-a-half days long, a small number of the simulation dolls might suffice to bring
630   about a change. However, it is important to note that the experiential intervention was supported by an educational component that included didactic instruction and peer discussion. It cannot be assumed that merely allowing an adolescent to carry the doll for a couple of
635   days will have the same effect. It is also possible that the memory of the experience may decrease in intensity over time, so that a repeated experience in the later grades might be necessary to reinforce and maintain the long-term effects of the intervention. Moreover, the
640   social worker needs to make sure that the experience is a balanced one, so that infants are not seen primarily as a source of annoyance and frustration. Finally, the findings suggest that an experiential learning component can alter perspectives and behavior, so that simulation,
645   because it makes the situation very concrete, might be a powerful intervention tool in general with youths who are transitioning to formal operations.

References

Alan Guttmacher Institute. (1999a). *Teenage pregnancy: Overall trends and state-by-state information*. New York: Author.

Alan Guttmacher Institute. (1999b). *U.S. teenage pregnancy statistics: With comparative statistics for women aged 20–24*. New York: Author.

Bandura, A. (Ed.) (1995). *Self-efficacy in changing societies*. New York: Cambridge University Press.

Becerra, R., Sabagh, G., & de Anda, D. (1986). *Sex and pregnancy among Mexican American adolescents: Final report to the Office of Adolescent Pregnancy Programs, Department of Health and Human Services*. Washington, DC: U.S. Department of Health and Human Services.

California Department of Health Services, Maternal and Child Health Branch, Epidemiology and Evaluation Section. (2001). *Teen birth rate hot spots in California, 1999–2000: A resource developed using a geographic information systems approach*. Sacramento: Author.

Divine, J. H., & Cobbs, G. (2001). The effects of infant simulators on early adolescents. *Adolescence, 36*, 593–600.

Elkind, D. (1967). Egocentrism in adolescence. *Child Development, 38*, 1025–1034.

Gordon, D. E. (1990). Formal operational thinking: The role of cognitive-developmental processes in adolescent decision-making about pregnancy and contraception. *American Journal of Orthopsychiatry, 60*, 346–356.

Kann, L., Kinchen, S. A., Williams, B. I., Ross, J. G., Lowry, R., Grunbaum, J., & Kolbe, L. J. (2000). Youth risk behavior surveillance—United States, 1999. *Morbidity and Mortality Weekly Report Surveillance Summaries, 49*, 1–96.

Kralewski, J., & Stevens-Simon, C. (2000). Does mothering a doll change teens' thoughts about pregnancy? [electronic edition], *Pediatrics, 105*, e. 30.

National Center for Health Statistics. (2000). *Health, United States, 2000*. Hyattsville, MD: Author.

Out, J. W., & Lafreniere, K. D. (2001). Baby Think It Over: Using role-play to prevent teen pregnancy. *Adolescence, 36*, 571–582.

Piaget, J. (1972). Intellectual evolution from adolescence to adulthood. *Human Development, 15*, 1–12.

Piaget, J., & Inhelder, B. (1958). *The growth of logical thinking from childhood to adolescence* (A. Parsons & S. Seagrin, Trans.). New York: Basic Books.

Price, J. H., Robinson, L. K., Thompson, C., & Schmalzried, H. (2000). Rural parents' perceptions of the Baby Think It Over Program—A pilot study. *American Journal of Health Studies, 16*, 34–40.

Somers, C. L., & Fahlman, M. M. (2001). Effectiveness of the "Baby Think It Over" teen pregnancy prevention program. *Journal of School Health, 71*, 188–195.

Somers, C. L., Gleason, J. H., Johnson, S.A., Fahlman, M. M. (2001). Adolescents and teachers' perceptions of a teen pregnancy prevention program. *American Secondary Education, 29*, 51–66.

Strachan, W., & Gorey, K. (1997). Infant simulator lifespan intervention: Pilot investigation of an adolescent pregnancy prevention program. *Child Adolescent Social Work Journal, 14*, 1–5.

Tingle, L. R. (2002). Evaluation of North Carolina "Baby Think It Over" project. *Journal of School Health, 72*, 178–183.

United Way of Greater Los Angeles. (1998–1999). *State of the county report, 1999–1999*. Los Angeles: Author.

About the author: Diane de Anda, Ph.D., is associate professor, Department of Social Welfare, School of Public Affairs, University of California, 3250 Public Policy Building, Box 951656, Los Angeles, CA 90095. E-mail: ddeanda@ucla.edu

Exercise for Article 14

Factual Questions

1. According to the researcher, is the previous research on the effectiveness of the BTIO intervention extensive?

2. According to the researcher, do the previous studies have serious methodological limitations and flaws?

3. Was the BTIO-2 measure administered as both a pretest *and* as a posttest?

4. According to the researcher, was the gain from pretest to posttest for objective 2 very large?

5. For objective 3, was the increase from pretest to posttest statistically significant? If yes, at what probability level?

6. On the pretest, what percentage of the participants desired parenthood within a marital relationship? On the posttest, what percentage desired it?

Questions for Discussion

7. In your opinion, is the experimental intervention described in sufficient detail? Explain. (See lines 83–127.)

8. Is it important to know that the participants responded anonymously? Explain. (See line 258.)

9. In a future study of the intervention, would you recommend a longitudinal follow-up? Explain. (See lines 543–549 and 597–604.)

10. Is it important to know that participation was a mandatory part of a required class? Explain. (See lines 583–586.)

11. In a future experiment on this topic, would you recommend the use of a control group? Explain. (See lines 605–620.)

12. Based on this experiment, do you regard the intervention as promising? Would you recommend funding to extend the program to additional schools? Explain.

Quality Ratings

Directions: Indicate your level of agreement with each of the following statements by circling a number from 5 for strongly agree (SA) to 1 for strongly disagree (SD). If you believe an item is not applicable to this research article, leave it blank. Be prepared to explain your ratings. When responding to criteria A and B below, keep in mind that brief titles and abstracts are conventional in published research.

A.   The title of the article is appropriate.

SA   5   4   3   2   1   SD

B.   The abstract provides an effective overview of the research article.

SA   5   4   3   2   1   SD

C.   The introduction establishes the importance of the study.

SA   5   4   3   2   1   SD

D.   The literature review establishes the context for the study.

SA   5   4   3   2   1   SD

E.   The research purpose, question, or hypothesis is clearly stated.

SA   5   4   3   2   1   SD

F.   The method of sampling is sound.

SA   5   4   3   2   1   SD

G.   Relevant demographics (for example, age, gender, and ethnicity) are described.

SA   5   4   3   2   1   SD

H.   Measurement procedures are adequate.

SA   5   4   3   2   1   SD

I.   All procedures have been described in sufficient detail to permit a replication of the study.

SA   5   4   3   2   1   SD

J.   The participants have been adequately protected from potential harm.

SA   5   4   3   2   1   SD

K.   The results are clearly described.

SA   5   4   3   2   1   SD

L.   The discussion/conclusion is appropriate.

SA   5   4   3   2   1   SD

M.   Despite any flaws, the report is worthy of publication.

SA   5   4   3   2   1   SD

Article 15

Project Trust: Breaking Down Barriers Between Middle School Children

MARY ELLEN BATIUK
Wilmington College

JAMES A. BOLAND
Wilmington College

NORMA WILCOX
Wright State University

ABSTRACT. This paper analyzes the success of a camp retreat weekend called Project Trust involving middle school students and teachers. The goal of the camp is to break down barriers between cliques identified as active in the school. The camp focuses on building team relationships across clique membership and incorporates elements of peace education and conflict resolution. A treatment group (campers) and comparison group (noncampers) were administered an adaptation of the Bogardus Social Distance Test and the Piers-Harris Children's Self-Concept Scale before and after the camp. Attendance was found to lower social distance scores for nine of the ten groups/cliques. Campers also had higher self-concept scores after the retreat.

From *Adolescence*, *39*, 531–538. Copyright © 2004 by Libra Publishers, Inc. Reprinted with permission.

The *Final Report and Findings of the Safe School Initiative* indicates that from 1993 to 1997, the "odds that a child in grades 9–12 would be threatened or injured with a weapon in school were 8 percent, or 1 in 13 or 14; the odds of getting into a physical fight at school were 15 percent, or 1 in 7" (Vossekuil, Fein, Reddy, Borum, & Modzeleski, 2002, p. 12). Such widespread experiences of school violence have led to what McLaren, Leonardo, and Allen (2000) call a "bunker mentality" on many school campuses. As Tompkins (2000) points out, "increased levels of security suggest to students and teachers that they learn and teach in a violent environment where students cannot be trusted and are under suspicion" (p. 65). This is doubly unfortunate, not only because positive school climates promote learning, but that they have been found to be strong predictors of the absence of school violence (Welsh, 2000).

Further, one of the ten key findings of the analysis of the Safe School Initiative is that "many attackers felt bullied, persecuted or injured by others prior to the attack" (Vossekuil et al., 2002, p. 18). In a word, attackers felt excluded. Kramer (2000) has established that patterns of individual exclusion in school settings contribute to violence among students because exclusion separates them from the informal social control networks provided by parents, schools, and communities. This lack of informal social control has been linked to diminishing social and cultural capital (Hagen, 1985) and ultimately delinquency (Cullen, 1994; Currie, 1998; Sampson & Laub, 1993). Exclusion also preempts the kind of dialogue that can resolve conflicts (Aronowitz, 2003).

As a result, many educators have called for curricular changes incorporating programs in peace education (Caulfield, 2000; Harris, 1996; Pepinsky, 2000) and conflict resolution (Bretherton, 1996; Children's Defense Fund, 1998). For example, 10 years ago, Wilmington College collaborated with a local middle school to provide programming aimed at eliminating patterns of mistrust and exclusion fostered by student cliques. The collaboration was a natural one since Wilmington College offers extensive teacher education programs and maintains a strong tradition of conflict resolution and peacemaking tied to its Quaker heritage.

The training emphasized a mutual and reflexive process of problem solving and conflict resolution in which involved parties actively frame the understanding of both the problem and its solution. Teachers and students at the middle school overwhelmingly pointed to the ongoing problem of conflicts arising from student cliques. As a response, teachers and students designed activities that would help break down barriers among the cliques. From this collaboration emerged Project Trust—a weekend camp retreat in which student opinion/clique leaders engaged in discussions, role-playing, and noncompetitive risk-taking tasks.

The present paper focuses on a program for middle school children that incorporates principles of peace education and conflict resolution techniques to address the pervasive sources of these conflicts within networks of student cliques. It was hypothesized that by engaging student leaders in activities focused on cooperation and breaking down barriers, these same students would become more receptive to interacting with members of other cliques. It was also hypothesized that participation in the retreat weekend would lead to increased self-esteem in the participants.

Method

Project Trust

In the fall of 1990, middle school teachers and stu-

70 dents were asked to brainstorm about the kinds of cliques that were active in the school. A list of 24 groups, active within the school, emerged from these initial brainstorming sessions. Discussions with both students and teachers allowed project managers to hone

75 the list to eight, and these groups became the focal point for Project Trust. The groups included: (1) preps—smart and well dressed, well to do or at least giving the perception that they are, doing what they are told to do; (2) alternatives—baggy clothes, various

80 colors of hair, might be skaters, long hair; (3) jocks— athletes or individuals whose lives are dominated by sports interests, wearing NBA and NFL jerseys; (4) hoods/gangsters/thugs—rule-breakers, tough, like to fight, might be in a gang, wearing black; (5) dorks—

85 geeks, socially awkward, nonathletic; (6) cheerleaders—attractive and active girls; (7) hicks/hillbillies— rural kids, possibly live in trailer parks, like country music; and (8) dirties—poor kids, dirty and cannot help it, poor hygiene.

90   The names of the cliques came directly from the students and teachers. Ethnic groups were not mentioned by the students but were added by the project managers after discussions with the teachers (i.e., whites and African Americans).

Treatment and Comparison Groups

95   Project Trust camp retreats include student opinion/clique leaders who are identified by teachers and invited to spend the weekend at a local camp that regularly provides team-building exercises to local civic groups and businesses. Middle school teachers receive

100 training from Wilmington College project managers in group process and team building. Both teachers and Wilmington College professors lead the retreats. Once at the camp, students and teachers are placed into Family Groups of 8–10 members designed to cut across

105 clique memberships. Students are encouraged to take ownership of the weekend agenda by developing contracts with retreat leaders. Contracting processes involve eliciting from students what they hope to "get" from the weekend (everything from food to fun activi-

110 ties) and what they are willing to "give" to get those things. During the course of the weekend (Friday evening through Sunday afternoon), student family groups take part in discussions, cooperative tasks, and team building and survival exercises.

115   One team-building activity, titled Toxic Waste, involves blindfolded team members "dumping" a cupful of sludge into another cup inside of a 4 × 4 square. Unsighted family team members cannot cross into the square, have access only to 4 bungee cords, the cup of

120 sludge and a rubber band, and are given directions by their sighted team members. Another activity, called Plane Crash, involves the completion of various tasks by team members who have received several handicaps (broken bones, loss of sight) and limited supplies

125 (food, water, blankets). Also included in the retreat are an extended outdoor trust walk and a structured discussion about the harmful effects of put-downs and techniques for resolving conflicts around them. Students and teachers discuss the case study of a young girl who

130 committed suicide, leaving a note explaining the exclusion she felt because of being called a "fat hog" by her classmates.

Family groups are brought together regularly to assess how the retreat is progressing. Plenty of snacks,

135 pizza, and pop are provided to foster an environment of fun and relaxation during the time that students and teachers spend together.

In addition to this treatment group, fellow students who did not attend the camp were selected on the basis

140 of availability and assessed using the same instrument, for the purposes of comparison. Treatment group students were identified by teachers on the basis of being "opinion leaders."

Assessments

Assessment of Project Trust weekends relies pri-

145 marily on an adaptation of the Bogardus (1933) Social Distance Scale to measure the social distances between the students and identified groups before and after the camp experience. The scale was chosen because of its ease of scoring and high reliability (Miller, 1991;

150 Owen et al., 1981). In addition, the scale has also been successfully and widely adapted for use with school-age children (Cover, 2001; Lee, Sapp, & Ray, 1996; Mielenz, 1979; Payne, 1976; Williams, 1992). On this modified scale, students were asked to rate all ten

155 groups on a scale of 0–7, with 7 representing the greatest degree of social distance: 0–be best friends with; 1–invite over to my house; 3–choose to eat lunch with; 4–say "hi" to only; 5–as a member of my homeroom only; 6–as a member of my school only; 7–exclude

160 them from my school. Both treatment and comparison groups completed this scale immediately before the retreat weekend and within one month after the camp.

In addition, treatment and nontreatment groups completed the Piers-Harris Children's Self-Concept

165 Scale (Piers, 1984). This self-report scale measures self-concept using 80 yes/no questions and is intended for use with youths aged 8–18. The scale was administered to the treatment group before and after the camp experience, and to the comparison group before the

170 camp experience.

Results

Camps have been held from 1998 through 2002 in both the fall and spring. An independent-samples t test (equal variances not assumed) comparing the pretest mean scores of the treatment group ($n = 298$) and com-

175 parison group ($n = 215$) found significant differences between only two groups: preps ($t = 5.058$, $df = 405$, $p < .01$) and jocks ($t = 2.654$, $df = 378$, $p < .01$). In both cases, the means of the treatment group social distance scores were lower than for the comparison group: preps

180 ($M = 2.28$, $SD = 2.06$, for campers, vs. $M = 3.34$, $SD =$

2.24, for noncampers), jocks (*M* = 2.07, *SD* = 2.14, for campers, vs. *M* = 2.66, *SD* = 2.43, for noncampers). Thus, treatment and comparison students were roughly equivalent in their perceptions of social distance from
185 their classmates with the exception of the preps and the jocks. In these two instances, the campers reported statistically significant lower social distance scores when compared to noncampers.

A paired-samples *t* test was calculated for both the
190 treatment group (*n* = 216) and comparison group (*n* = 80). Table 1 reports the results for the treatment group. For all eight cliques, attendance at the camp significantly reduced perceptions of social distance. In addition, perceptions of social distance were significantly
195 reduced for African Americans but not whites. Mean scores for whites were already low (pretest *M* = .54, *SD* = 1.00) and did fall (posttest *M* = .47, *SD* = .86), though not to a statistically significant degree. The greatest change for campers was in their perceptions of
200 dirties, moving an average of 1.55 points on the 7-point scale (pretest *M* = 5.55, *SD* = 1.40; posttest *M* = 4.00, *SD* = 1.71); dorks, moving an average of 1.37 points (pretest *M* = 4.60, *SD* = 2.10; posttest *M* = 3.23, *SD* = 1.65); and hicks, moving an average of 1.23 points
205 (pretest *M* = 4.38, *SD* = 2.07; posttest *M* = 3.15, *SD* = 1.96).

Table 1

Paired-Samples Two-Tailed t Test for the Treatment Group (n = 216)

Campers	*t*	*df*	*p*
Preps	6.816	212	.000
Alternatives	5.254	196	.000
Jocks	6.532	207	.000
Hoods	6.709	205	.000
Dorks	10.810	206	.000
Cheerleaders	3.282	213	.001
Hicks	8.608	203	.000
Dirties	11.751	204	.000
African Americans	2.500	208	.013
Whites	1.141	206	.255

Table 2 reports the results for the comparison group (noncampers). The only statistically significant shift was for preps (pretest *M* = 3.18, *SD* = 2.23; posttest *M*
210 = 2.74, *SD* = 2.37). In all other instances, there were no statistically significant changes. However, there were two instances, for dorks and African Americans, in which social distance scores actually regressed.

On the Piers-Harris Children's Self-Concept Scale,
215 self-concept scores also shifted for the treatment (camper) group. The mean score on the pretest was 61.37 (*SD* = 12.6) and the mean on the posttest was 66.13 (*SD* = 11.32). The difference was statistically significant (*p* < .01).

Conclusions

220 The results suggest that educational programs for middle school children that incorporate peace education and conflict resolution hold potential for reducing divisive student cliques built around difference, mistrust, and exclusion, that often result in the violence
225 found in schools today. While this is only one study in a rural area of a mid-Atlantic state with a unique subculture, it does offer hope of greater validity and reliability with its longitudinal character. Obviously, the study needs to be replicated in a variety of cultural and
230 institutional contexts and across different age groups. However, there is much to be gained by such replication in a society struggling to understand the attitudes of the "other."

Table 2

Paired-Samples Two-Tailed t Test for the Comparison Group (n = 80)

Noncampers	*t*	*df*	*p*
Preps	2.035	72	.046
Alternatives	0.967	63	.337
Jocks	0.150	65	.881
Hoods	0.567	61	.573
Dorks	−0.068	68	.946
Cheerleaders	0.935	72	.353
Hicks	2.264	72	.353
Dirties	1.589	67	.117
African Americans	−0.271	74	.787
Whites	0.090	206	.928

References

Aronowitz, S. (2003). Essay on violence. In *Smoke and mirrors: The hidden context of violence in schools and society* (pp. 211–227). New York: Rowman and Littlefield.

Bogardus, E. S. (1933). A social distance scale. *Sociology and Social Research, 17*, 265–271.

Bretherton, D. (1996). Nonviolent conflict resolution in children. *Peabody Journal of Education, 71*, 111–127.

Caulfield, S. L. (2000). Creating peaceable schools. *ANNALS: The American Academy of Political and Social Science, 567*, 170–185.

Children's Defense Fund. (1998). *Keeping children safe in schools: A resource for states.* Available: http://www.childrensdefense.org.

Cover, J. D. (1995). The effects of social contact on prejudice. *The Journal of Social Psychology, 135*, 403–405.

Cullen, F. T. (1994). Social support as an organizing concept for criminology: Presidential address to the Academy of Criminal Justice Sciences. *Justice Quarterly, 11*, 527–559.

Currie, E. (1998). *Crime and punishment in America.* New York: Metropolitan Books.

Hagen, J. (1985). *Modern criminology: Crime, criminal behavior and its control.* New York: McGraw-Hill.

Harris, I. M. (1996). Peace education in an urban school district in the United States. *Peabody Journal of Education, 71*, 63–83.

Kramer, R. (2000). Poverty, inequality, and youth violence. *ANNALS: The American Academy of Political and Social Science, 567*, 123–139.

Lee, M. Y., Sapp, S. G., & Ray, M. C. (1996). The Reverse Social Distance Scale. *The Journal of Social Psychology, 136*, 17–24.

McLaren, P., Leonardo, Z., & Allen, R. L. (2000). Rated "cv" for cool violence. In S. U. Spina (Ed.), *Smoke and mirrors: The hidden context of violence in schools and society* (pp. 67–92). New York: Rowman and Littlefield.

Mielenz, C. C. (1979). Non-prejudiced Caucasian parents and attitudes of their children toward Negroes. *The Journal of Negro Education, 1979*, 12–21.

Miller, D. (1991). *Handbook of research design and social measurement.* Newbury Park, CA: Sage Publications.

Owen, C. A., Eisner, H. C., & McFaul, T. R. (1981). A half century of social distance research: National replication of the Bogardus studies. *Sociology and Social Research, 66*, 80–98.

Payne, W. J. (1976). Social class and social differentiation: A case for multidimensionality of social distance. *Sociology and Social Research, 61*, 54–67.

Pepinsky, H. (2000). Educating for peace. *ANNALS: The American Academy of Political and Social Science, 567,* 157–169.

Piers, E. V. (1984). *Piers-Harris Children's Self-Concept Scale revised manual 1984.* Los Angeles: Western Psychological Services.

Sampson, R. J., & Laub, J. H. (1993). *Crime in the making: Pathways and turning points through life.* Cambridge, MA: Harvard University Press.

Tompkins, D. E. (2000). School violence: Gangs and a culture of fear. *ANNALS: The American Academy of Political and Social Science, 567,* 54–71.

Vossekuil, B., Fein, R A., Reddy, M., Borum, R., & Modzeleski, W. (2002). *The final report and findings of the Safe School Initiative: Implications for the prevention of school attacks in the United States.* Washington, DC: U.S. Secret Service and U.S. Department of Education.

Welsh, W. N. (2000). The effects of school climate on school disorder. *ANNALS: The American Academy of Political and Social Science, 567,* 88–107.

Williams, C. (1992). The relationship between the affective and cognitive dimensions of prejudice. *College Student Journal, 26,* 50–54.

About the authors: *Mary Ellen Batiuk,* Department of Social and Political Studies, Wilmington College. *James A. Boland,* Department of Education, Wilmington College. *Norma Wilcox,* Department of Sociology, Wright State University.

Address correspondence to: Mary Ellen Batiuk, Department of Social and Political Studies, Wilmington College, Wilmington, OH 45177. E-mail: mebatiuk@wilmington.edu

Exercise for Article 15

Factual Questions

1. What resulted from the brainstorming sessions?

2. On the Social Distance Scale, what does a rating of "3" represent?

3. On the Social Distance Scale, does a high rating (e.g., "7") represent the greatest degree of social distance *or* does it represent the least degree of social distance?

4. In terms of social distance, the greatest change for campers from pretest to posttest was in their perceptions of what group?

5. In Table 1, all differences are statistically significant except for one group. Which group?

6. Was the treatment group's pretest to posttest difference on self-concept statistically significant? If yes, at what probability level?

Questions for Discussion

7. Keeping in mind that this is a research report and not an instructional guide, is the description of the treatment in lines 95–137 sufficiently detailed so that you have a clear picture of it? Explain.

8. For the comparison group, fellow students who did not attend the camp were selected on the basis of availability. How much stronger would this experiment have been if students had been randomly assigned to the treatment and comparison groups? Explain. (See lines 138–143.)

9. In your opinion, is the Piers-Harris Children's Self-Concept Scale described in sufficient detail? Explain. (See lines 163–170.)

10. The researchers state that "the study needs to be replicated in a variety of cultural and institutional contexts and across different age groups." (See lines 228–230.) In your opinion, are the results of this study sufficiently promising to warrant such replications? Explain.

11. What changes, if any, would you suggest making in the research methodology used in this study?

Quality Ratings

Directions: Indicate your level of agreement with each of the following statements by circling a number from 5 for strongly agree (SA) to 1 for strongly disagree (SD). If you believe an item is not applicable to this research article, leave it blank. Be prepared to explain your ratings. When responding to criteria A and B below, keep in mind that brief titles and abstracts are conventional in published research.

A. The title of the article is appropriate.

    SA   5   4   3   2   1   SD

B. The abstract provides an effective overview of the research article.

    SA   5   4   3   2   1   SD

C. The introduction establishes the importance of the study.

    SA   5   4   3   2   1   SD

D. The literature review establishes the context for the study.

    SA   5   4   3   2   1   SD

E. The research purpose, question, or hypothesis is clearly stated.

    SA   5   4   3   2   1   SD

F. The method of sampling is sound.

    SA   5   4   3   2   1   SD

G. Relevant demographics (for example, age, gender, and ethnicity) are described.

    SA   5   4   3   2   1   SD

H. Measurement procedures are adequate.

    SA   5   4   3   2   1   SD

I. All procedures have been described in sufficient detail to permit a replication of the study.

    SA   5   4   3   2   1   SD

J. The participants have been adequately protected from potential harm.

    SA   5   4   3   2   1   SD

K. The results are clearly described.

    SA   5   4   3   2   1   SD

L. The discussion/conclusion is appropriate.

    SA   5   4   3   2   1   SD

M. Despite any flaws, the report is worthy of publication.

    SA   5   4   3   2   1   SD

Article 16

Effect of Petting a Dog on Immune System Function

CARL J. CHARNETSKI
Wilkes University

SANDRA RIGGERS
Marywood University

FRANCIS X. BRENNAN
VA Medical Center, Philadelphia

ABSTRACT. The present study assessed the effect of petting a dog on secretory immunoglobulin A (IgA) levels. 55 college students were randomly assigned to either an experimental group or one of two control groups. Group 1 ($n = 19$) petted a live dog; Group 2 ($n = 17$) petted a stuffed dog, while Group 3 ($n = 19$) simply sat comfortably on a couch. Each participant was exposed to one of the three conditions for 18 min. Pre- and posttreatment saliva samples yielded a significant increase in IgA for Group 1 only. Participants were also asked to complete the Pet Attitude Scale of Templer, Salter, Dickey, Baldwin and Veleber (1981). Scores on this scale correlated with IgA increases only for participants in Group 2 (petting a stuffed animal). Results are discussed in terms of the beneficial effects of pets on health in general, and immunity in particular.

From *Psychological Reports*, 95, 1087–1091. Copyright © 2004 by Psychological Reports. Reprinted with permission.

A number of influences on immune system function have been documented during the past several decades (see Cohen & Herbert, 1996, for a review). The effects of stress and negative psychological states have been extensively studied (e.g., McLelland, Ross, & Patel, 1985). Far fewer studies have documented immuno-enhancing effects. We have published several studies in which increases in Immunoglobulin A (IgA) were noted (see Charnetski & Brennan, 2001, for a review). This protein is by far the most prevalent of the immunoglobulins in the body and is present in virtually all mucosal linings of the body as well as the bloodstream (Ogra, 1985). This underscores its importance as a first line of defense in the prevention of a wide variety of pathologies. IgA may increase after listening to music (e.g., Charnetski, Brennan, & Harrison, 1998), relaxing for 20 min. (Green & Green, 1987), or watching a humorous videotape (Dillon, Minchoff, & Baker, 1986).

In separate literature, a number of studies have indicated the positive influence of pets on physical health in general (see Serpell, 1991). Prior research has shown that pets can positively influence physiological variables such as heart rate (e.g., Lynch, Thomas, Pastwity, Katcher, & Weir, 1977), blood pressure (e.g., Vormbrock & Grossberg, 1988), and even cholesterol and triglycerides (Anderson, Reid, & Jennings, 1992). The use of pets as therapeutic agents has become a common activity in many hospitals and long-term care facilities (Thomas, 1996). Studies of the effect of tactile contact on the heart and respiratory rates of dogs and horses have suggested that petting, as a form of touch, may be associated with physiological changes in humans (Baun, Bergstrom, Langston, & Thomas, 1984). Jenkins (1986) examined the physiological effects (i.e., heart rate and blood pressure) of pet owners petting their own dogs. Even the mere presence of a companion animal was beneficial as autonomic reactivity of women as defined by pulse rate, blood pressure, and skin conductance changed during a standard experimental stress task as compared to the presence of a human friend or no companion (Allen, Blascovich, Tomaka, & Kelsey, 1991).

Of all the studies of animals on human health-related issues, by far the most common animal studied is the dog. Consequently, we chose a Shelti for our study and hypothesized that petting the dog would have a positive effect on IgA. While no other such studies with animals could be located, we know from manipulation of other variables (e.g., music) that influence of IgA can occur in a relatively brief period of time.

Method

Participants

We recruited 59 college students for the current study and randomly assigned them to one of three conditions. The first group ($n = 19$) sat individually on a couch with the Shelti right next to them. They were instructed to pet the dog for 18 min. We specifically instructed the participants to control individual variation of interaction with the dog. A second group ($n = 19$) sat comfortably on the couch for 18 min. Finally, to control for the effect of tactile stimulation, we utilized a stuffed replica similar in size, shape, and texture to the dog to which our third group was exposed ($n = 17$). This group sat on the couch and spent 18 min. stroking the stuffed dog.

Materials

All participants were given the Pet Attitude Scale (Templer, Salter, Dickey, Baldwin, & Veleber, 1981) prior to participation. In addition, unstimulated saliva samples were collected from each participant immediately before and after exposure to the conditions. The saliva samples were immediately frozen for later analysis. IgA levels were determined via a single radial immunodiffusion technique (Mancini, Carbonara, & Heremens, 1965) that yielded IgA concentration data for pre- vs. postexposure comparisons.

A small, 10-yr.-old, 20-lb. female Shelti/mixed breed dog, documented to be in good health by a veterinarian, was utilized in Group 1. A replica of the same size, colors, and proportions was utilized in Group 3.

Procedure

All participants were individually exposed to the experimental conditions in a room with two chairs, a table, a desk, and a couch. After completing the Pet Attitude Scale in an adjacent room, participants were seated on the couch and were given a small cup and lid. They were then instructed to deposit a saliva sample. All participants were then instructed to sit quietly until the experimenter indicated that time was up. To ensure that the dog remained on the couch with the participants, the experimenter remained in the room seated at one end of the couch for all three groups while the participants sat at the other end. For Group 1, the experimenter (S.R.) brought the dog in from an adjacent room and placed the dog next to the participant on the couch. As mentioned earlier, Group 2 simply sat comfortably on the couch for 18 min. For Group 3, the experimenter brought in the stuffed replica of the dog. After the completion of the experimental manipulation, participants produced another saliva sample and were debriefed.

IgA Analysis

IgA analysis was performed after samples were thawed at room temperature for 60 min. Twenty microliter aliquots of whole saliva were diluted 1:2 with albumin for each sample. Ten microliters of the diluted saliva were then pipetted into wells on agarose gel plates. The gel on the plates contained antihuman monospecific IgA antibodies. After a 96-hr. incubation period, diffusion ring diameters were measured in millimeters and converted from a calibration curve into milligrams per liter. Technicians performing the assay were blind to experimental conditions.

Results

Analyses

The IgA of most of the subjects appeared to increase from pre- to the postexposure. The raw data are presented in Table 1. The two-factor (group × time), repeated-measures analysis of variance on IgA levels yielded a significant main effect of time ($F_{1,52} = 8.58$, $p < .005$). Neither the main effect of group ($F_{2,52}$. 1.78, $p > .05$) nor the interaction ($F_{2,52} = 1.53$, $p > .05$) were significant. Post hoc tests yielded no significant change

in either the stuffed dog-petting group ($t = 2.43$, $p > .05$) or the control group ($t = 1.95$, $p > .05$). However, significant pre- vs. postexposure differences were noted in IgA levels of the dog-petting group ($t = 3.28$, $p < .02$; Table 2). Further analyses included Pearson product-moment correlations between IgA changes, as ascertained by pre- vs. postexposure difference scores, and scores on the Pet Attitude Scale. There was no significant overall correlation ($r = .23$, $p > .05$). Correlations for each group were not significant for the dog-petting group ($r = -.10$, $p > .05$) or the control group ($r = .13$, $p > .05$), but were for the stuffed dog group ($r = .62$, $p < .001$).

Table 1
IgA Means and Standard Errors of Mean for Three Groups Pre- and Post-manipulation

Group	n	Pre-manipulation M	Pre-manipulation SE	Post-manipulation M	Post-manipulation SE
Dog Group	19	712.6	60.5	947.4	92.3
Stuffed Dog Group	17	957.2	92.5	980.0	64.3
Control Group	19	705.8	60.2	910.3	91.5

Table 2
Difference Scores for Three Groups

Group	n	M	SD
Dog Group	19	235.2*	71.6
Stuffed Dog Group	17	34.6	97.1
Control Group	19	204.5	104.8

*$p < .05$

Comment

A significant increase in IgA levels occurred after petting a dog. The lack of significant correlation between IgA change and the Pet Attitude Scale scores in the dog-petting group indicates that one's attitude toward pets is not relevant to benefit from this interaction. These results complement some of the general health benefits of animals that have been documented elsewhere in the literature. Examples on higher levels of IgA show relation to less frequent illness (e.g., Yodfat & Silvian, 1977) and less susceptibility to upper respiratory infection (Martin, Guthrie, & Pitts, 1993). Apparently, interactions with animals have many beneficial effects on humans, as other physiological measures have been positively influenced by the presence of or interaction with animals. These results may have been associated with relaxation (Green, Green, & Santoro, 1988), which has been shown to have an enhancing effect on the immune system. However, the control group who sat comfortably should also have experienced significant effects were relaxation the primary factor. However, we did not record an independent measure of relaxation.

The correlation between Pet Attitude Scale scores and IgA level change for the stuffed animal group may
155 indicate that those who have a more positive attitude toward pets may benefit, perhaps by way of Pavlovian conditioning, from interaction with even a stuffed animal. Alternative explanations also clearly exist. It seems entirely possible that subjects found the situation
160 humorous, and the correlation simply reflects that. Further research should be designed to ascertain whether the high correlation observed in this group was spurious.

Ader and Cohen (1975) found evidence for Pav-
165 lovian conditioning of immunosuppression; perhaps the opposite effect may be found as well. Perhaps persons with a more positive attitude toward pets have had more life experiences with pets. The act of petting an animal may then have more positive effects on them
170 than on someone with less of an affinity toward animals. Perhaps further investigation into each participant's experience with animals (i.e., do they have a pet, how long, etc.) as well as their attitudes toward animals, would be helpful to clarify this.

References

Ader, R., & Cohen, N. (1975). Behaviorally conditioned immunosuppression. *Psychosomatic Medicine, 37*, 333–340.

Allen, K. M., Blascovich, J., Tomaka, J., & Kelsey, R. M. (1991). Presence of human friends and pet dogs as moderators of autonomic responses to stress in women. *Journal of Personality and Social Psychology, 61*, 582–589.

Anderson, W. P., Reid, C. M., & Jennings, G. L. (1992). Pet ownership and risk factors for cardiovascular disease. *Medical Journal of Australia, 157*, 298–301.

Baun, M. M., Bergstrom, N., Langston, N. F., & Thomas, L. (1984). Physiological effects of human/companion animal bonding. *Nursing Research, 33*, 126–129.

Charnetski, C. J., & Brennan, F. X. (2001). *Feeling good is good for you: How pleasure can boost your immune system and lengthen your life.* Emmaus, PA: Rodale Press.

Charnetski, C. J., Brennan, F. X., & Harrison, J. F. (1998). Effect of music and auditory stimuli on secretory immunoglobulin A (IgA). *Perceptual and Motor Skills, 87*, 1169–1170.

Cohen, S., & Herbert, T. B. (1996). Health psychology: Psychological factors and physical disease from the perspective of human psychoneuroimmunology. *Annual Review of Psychology, 47*, 113–142.

Dillon, K. M., Minchoff, B., & Baker, K. H. (1986). Positive emotional states and enhancement of the immune system. *International Journal of Psychiatry in Medicine, 15*, 13–18.

Green, M. L., Green, R. G., & Santoro, W. (1988). Daily relaxation modifies serum and salivary immunoglobulins and psychophysiologic symptom severity. *Biofeedback and Self-Regulation, 13*, 187–199.

Green, R. G., & Green, M. L. (1987). Relaxation increases salivary immunoglobulin A. *Psychological Reports, 61*, 623–629.

Jenkins, J. L. (1986). Physiological effects of petting a companion animal. *Psychological Reports, 51*, 21–22.

Lynch, J. J., Thomas, S. A., Pastwity, D. A., Katcher, A. H., & Weir, L. O. (1977). Human contact and cardiac arrhythmia in a coronary care unit. *Psychosomatic Medicine, 39*, 188–192.

Mancini, G., Carbonara, A. O., & Heremens, J. F. (1965). Immunochemical quantification of antigens by single radial immunodiffusion. *Immunochemistry, 2*, 235–254.

Martin, R. B., Guthrie, C. A., & Pitts, C. G. (1993). Emotional crying, depressed mood and secretory immunoglobulin A. *Behavioral Medicine, 9*, 111–114.

McLelland, D. C., Ross, G., & Patel, V. (1985). The effect of an examination on salivary norepinephrine and immunoglobulin levels. *Journal of Human Stress, 11*, 52–59.

Ogra, P. L. (1985). Local immune responses. *British Medical Bulletin, 41*, 28.

Serpell, J. A. (1991). Beneficial effects of pet ownership on some aspects of human health and behavior. *Journal of the Royal Society of Medicine, 84*, 717–720.

Templer, D., Salter, C. A., Dickey, S., Baldwin, R., & Veleber, D. M. (1981). The construction of a pet attitude scale. *The Psychological Record, 31*, 343–348.

Thomas, W. H. (1996). *Life worth living.* Acton, MA: VanderWyk & Burnham.

Vormbrock, J. K., & Grossberg, J. M. (1988). Cardiovascular effects of human-pet dog interactions. *Journal of Behavioral Medicine, 11*, 509–517.

Yodfat, Y., & Silvian, H. (1977). A prospective study of acute respiratory infections among children in kibbutz. *Journal of Infectious Disease, 135*, 26–30.

Address correspondence to: Carl J. Charnetski, Ph.D., Department of Psychology, Wilkes University, Wilkes-Barre, PA 18766. E-mail: charnets@wilkes.edu

Exercise for Article 16

Factual Questions

1. What is the researchers' stated hypothesis?

2. What was the basis for assigning the students to the three conditions?

3. The researchers used a stuffed replica of a dog in order to control for the effect of what?

4. For the dog-petting group, the researchers found a significant difference from pre- to posttest. What significance test was used to test for the significance of this difference?

5. What is the value of the correlation coefficient for the relationship between the difference scores and the scores on the Pet Attitude Scale for the stuffed dog group?

6. What was the mean IgA score for the control group on the pretest? What was it on the posttest?

Questions for Discussion

7. This study is classified as an example of true experimental research in the Contents of this book. If you are familiar with how to classify experiments, explain why this study is a true experiment.

8. The researchers indicate that after the experiment they "debriefed" the participants. What is your understanding of the meaning of this term? (See lines 96–98.)

9. The researchers state that the analysis of variance revealed a "significant main effect of time." What is your understanding of the meaning of this statement? (See lines 110–115.)

10. The researchers speculate that the stuffed animal group might have found the situation humorous and the humor could have affected the results. In a future study, do you think that it would be advis-

able to question such a group on how humorous they found the task? Explain. (See lines 158–163.)

11. Has this study convinced you that petting a dog increases immune system function? Explain.

12. Do you think that this topic deserves further investigation? Explain. (See lines 171–174.)

Quality Ratings

Directions: Indicate your level of agreement with each of the following statements by circling a number from 5 for strongly agree (SA) to 1 for strongly disagree (SD). If you believe an item is not applicable to this research article, leave it blank. Be prepared to explain your ratings. When responding to criteria A and B below, keep in mind that brief titles and abstracts are conventional in published research.

A.   The title of the article is appropriate.

   SA   5   4   3   2   1   SD

B.   The abstract provides an effective overview of the research article.

   SA   5   4   3   2   1   SD

C.   The introduction establishes the importance of the study.

   SA   5   4   3   2   1   SD

D.   The literature review establishes the context for the study.

   SA   5   4   3   2   1   SD

E.   The research purpose, question, or hypothesis is clearly stated.

   SA   5   4   3   2   1   SD

F.   The method of sampling is sound.

   SA   5   4   3   2   1   SD

G.   Relevant demographics (for example, age, gender, and ethnicity) are described.

   SA   5   4   3   2   1   SD

H.   Measurement procedures are adequate.

   SA   5   4   3   2   1   SD

I.   All procedures have been described in sufficient detail to permit a replication of the study.

   SA   5   4   3   2   1   SD

J.   The participants have been adequately protected from potential harm.

   SA   5   4   3   2   1   SD

K.   The results are clearly described.

   SA   5   4   3   2   1   SD

L.   The discussion/conclusion is appropriate.

   SA   5   4   3   2   1   SD

M.   Despite any flaws, the report is worthy of publication.

   SA   5   4   3   2   1   SD

Article 17

Evaluation of a Brief Intervention for Increasing Seat Belt Use on a College Campus

LUIGI PASTÒ
Defence and Civil Institute of Environmental Medicine

ANDREW G. BAKER
McGill University

ABSTRACT. The authors evaluated a brief intervention for increasing seat belt use among the front seat occupants of cars at a junior college in a jurisdiction with a mandatory belt use law. The intervention included public posting of performance feedback and distribution of an informational flyer to cars in a target parking lot. Feedback was the display of the proportion of drivers observed wearing seat belts on the previous observation day. Seat belt use among drivers increased from 64% during the baseline phase to 71% during the intervention phase. Seat belt use among front passengers increased from 49% during the baseline phase to 67% during the intervention phase. In both cases, seat belt use at follow-up was comparable to seat belt use during the intervention phase, although a trend toward decreasing belt use was noted. Also found was higher seat belt use among females as compared with males irrespective of their front seat occupant status (driver or passenger). Effects of the intervention are discussed in the context of increasing seat belt use in a hardcore nonuser population of predominantly young adults.

From *Behavior Modification*, 25, 471–486. Copyright © 2001 by Sage Publications. Reprinted with permission.

A large proportion of car occupants does not use seat belts, despite their proven effectiveness in reducing the likelihood of injury and death in traffic accidents (Conn, Chorba, Peterson, Rhodes, & Annest, 1993; Smith-Seemiller, Lovell, Franzen, Smith, & Townsend, 1997) and the enforcement of mandatory belt use laws (Dee, 1998; Thyer & Geller, 1990). There is evidence that resistance to mandatory belt use laws reflects a hardcore nonuser population also characterized by a greater frequency of other risk behaviors (Foss, Beirness, & Sprattler, 1994; Hunter, Stutts, Stewart, & Rodgman, 1990). Among this presumably hardcore nonuser population are young adults who are both least likely to wear seat belts (Clark, 1993; Reinfurt, Williams, Wells, & Rodgman, 1996; Wilson, 1990) and more likely than older adults to be involved in traffic accidents (Hunter et al., 1990; Miller, Lestina, & Spicer, 1998). In this article, we evaluate the effectiveness of a brief intervention to increase seat belt use among predominantly young adults above that achieved with a mandatory belt use law.

Behavioral interventions for increasing seat belt use may include extrinsic or intrinsic incentives. Extrinsic incentives emphasize external, tangible inducements and include stepped-up enforcement of mandatory belt use laws or monetary incentives (Hagenzieker, Buleveld, & Davidse, 1997; Johnston, Hendricks, & Fike, 1994). Monetary incentives may involve immediate rewards, such as cash, and delayed rewards, such as sport tickets or chances to win a lottery (Hagenzieker et al., 1997). Interventions for increasing seat belt use that include extrinsic incentives are effective across a broad range of populations and contexts (Hagenzieker et al., 1997; Johnston et al., 1994). Interventions that promote the acquisition of internal justifications for performing a target behavior are typically characterized as involving intrinsic incentives (Thyer & Geller, 1990). Examples of interventions with primarily internal incentives are participative goal setting (e.g., Ludwig & Geller, 1997), awareness and consensus building sessions (e.g., Kelo, Geller, Rice, & Bryant, 1988; Ludwig & Geller, 1991), public information and education (e.g., Hunter, Stewart, Stutts, & Marchetti, 1993), and posting of group performance feedback (e.g., Malenfant, Wells, Van Houten, & Williams, 1996). These interventions differ from those involving primarily extrinsic incentives as behavior change is presumed to occur as a consequence of the internalization of behavior-consistent attitudes and standards of conduct. For example, group performance feedback may invoke social comparison processes through which behavior-consistent attitudes and standards of conduct are internalized and consequently modify behavior. Conformity pressure in the direction of seat belt use emerges from the social comparison process itself rather than from any external incentive such as a threat of punishment or a monetary reward.

Despite the effectiveness of interventions with extrinsic incentives, there are reasons why researchers and policy makers alike may wish to focus on intrinsically based programs. First, in a review of seat belt promotion programs, Geller, Rudd, Kalsher, Streff, and Lehman (1987) reported that interventions with and without extrinsic incentives have similar immediate impacts on seat belt use but that the maintenance of behavior change appears to be greater following interventions without extrinsic incentives (Cope, Grossnickle, & Geller, 1986). Second, interventions for increasing driving-related safety behaviors with intrinsic incentives often result in the generalization of behavior changes to other driving-related behaviors (e.g., Ludwig & Geller, 1991; Streff, Kalsher, & Geller, 1993). For example, Ludwig and Geller (1997) reported that a participative goal setting intervention for car stops increased the target behavior, as well as turn signal and seat belt use. Finally, those who are at a relatively high risk of car accidents, such as younger drivers, appear to be more responsive to interventions with intrinsic incentives as compared to interventions with extrinsic incentives. For example, mandatory belt use laws appear to be least effective among younger drivers (Dee, 1998; Tipton, Camp, & Hsu, 1990). Ludwig and Geller (1991) assessed the effectiveness of an intervention that consisted of the participation in a seat belt awareness session, as well as the signing of a buckle-up promise card. Postintervention seat belt use among drivers younger than 25 years of age increased by about 50% as compared to baseline use. In contrast, seat belt use among drivers older than 25 years of age was unaffected by the intervention (Ludwig & Geller, 1991).

Intervention and Rationale

The objective of this report is to evaluate the effectiveness of a two-component intervention for increasing seat belt use among front seat occupants of cars using one target parking lot on the campus of a junior college. The intervention included both the public posting of performance feedback and the distribution of an informational flyer among a sample of predominantly young adults and adolescents. Although the separate and combined effects of performance feedback and public information on seat belt use have been evaluated in previous reports, their effect on the seat belt use of younger car occupants is unknown.

Public posting of performance feedback typically includes display of the proportion of drivers observed performing a target behavior in a previous observation period (e.g., Van Houten & Nau, 1981). Performance feedback has been shown to promote a number of safety behaviors including the following: seat belt use (Grant, Jonah, Wilde, & Ackersville-Monte, 1983), slower driving (Van Houten & Nau, 1981; Van Houten, Nau, & Marini, 1980), and greater compliance with workplace safety guidelines (Sulzer-Azaroff & De Santamaria, 1980). Malenfant et al. (1996) assessed the effect of a roadside sign providing belt use rates to car occupants in two cities where a belt use law was in force. Seat belt use in both cities increased reliably above an already high baseline use rate of more than 70%. Grant (1990) evaluated a seat belt promotion program that included both feedback and education components in a jurisdiction with a belt use law. Seat belt use at the intervention site increased by 26% for drivers and by 65% for passengers as compared to the seat belt use at a control site (Grant, 1990). The effect of performance feedback on seat belt use appears to be greatest in jurisdictions with a mandatory belt use law and where the majority of car occupants wear seat belts (Grant et al., 1983).

It remains unclear if public posting can increase belt use among younger adults above that achieved with a mandatory belt use law. Previous reports on the effect of performance feedback on seat belt use have been conducted among predominantly older drivers. For example, in the report by Grant (1990), 95% of the participants targeted by the public posting intervention were older than 25 years of age. As younger car occupants are more likely to be involved in traffic accidents and less likely to wear seat belts as compared to older occupants (Miller et al., 1998; Reinfurt et al., 1996), evaluating the effect of seat belt promotion interventions among this presumably hardcore nonuser population is desirable. Accordingly, the current intervention occurred among participants who were predominantly younger than 25 years of age.

The performance feedback component of the intervention was supplemented by the distribution of an informational flyer to cars in the target parking lot. The flyer informed car occupants about the nature and goal of the investigation under way and also provided feedback on the change in seat belt use that occurred between the baseline and the intervention phases. Although information is typically considered to be insufficient on its own to motivate behavior change, it may be a necessary prerequisite (Grant et al., 1983). Consequently, providing information is often one of several components of a seat belt promotion program that also includes incentives or enhanced enforcement of mandatory belt use laws (e.g., Decina, Temple, & Dorer, 1994; Hunter et al., 1993; Kay, Sapolsky, & Montgomery, 1995; Williams, Hall, Tolbert, & Wells, 1994).

Information approaches to reducing risk behaviors are predicated on the assumption that people will behave in a fashion to increase the likelihood of personal safety if provided with the appropriate information and behavioral options (Thyer & Geller, 1990). When assessed independently of incentives or enforcement, public information interventions result in only very modest increases in seat belt use (Johnston et al., 1994). The effectiveness of public information appears related to the frequency of exposure to the informational sources. For example, the modest effects of mass media campaigns on the frequency of risk behaviors is often attributed to limited exposure (Gantz, Fitzmaurice, & Yoo, 1990). To maximize any direct behavioral response, the informational flyer was distributed to every car in the target parking lot three times during a 5-day intervention phase, each time during peak hours of parking lot use.

Table 1

Number and Percentage of Observations by Occupant Status (Driver, Front Passenger), Gender, and Estimated Age

	< 25		24–45		> 45		Total	
	#	%	#	%	#	%	#	%
Driver								
Female	817	36	153	7	59	3	1029	45
Male	915	40	209	9	132	6	1256	55
Total	1732	76	362	16	191	8	2285	100
Front passenger								
Female	309	47	24	4	8	1	341	51
Male	289	44	18	3	12	2	319	49
Total	598	91	42	6	20	3	660	100

Note. Percentages are calculated relative to front seat occupant status. Percentage totals may not sum accurately due to rounding.

Method

Participants and Setting

The participants in this study included drivers and front passengers of cars that used one parking lot on the campus of Vanier College in Montreal during a 4-week period of the winter academic term. The parking lot could accommodate approximately 300 cars and had only one access point. An attendant was stationed in a booth at the entrance of the parking lot during business hours, and cars entering or exiting the lot first came to a full stop at the attendant's booth before proceeding. At the time of this study, a belt use law was in effect in the province of Quebec, with a $25 fine for violators. No comparable seat belt promotion program was ever attempted at the college.

The front seat occupants of 2,285 cars were observed during the course of the study, resulting in 2,285 observations of driver belt use and 660 observations of front passenger belt use. Consistent with previous reports (Williams et al., 1994), the age of front seat occupants was estimated according to broad criteria to minimize error (i.e., < 25, 25–45, > 45). Table 1 lists the number and percentage of participants by occupant status (driver, front passenger), gender, and estimated age. The age distribution of participants is consistent with the status of Vanier as a junior college, which provides preuniversity degrees as well as professional diplomas primarily to recent high school graduates.

Observation Procedures and Data Collection

One observer recorded shoulder belt use, gender, and estimated age of front seat occupants on a portable tape recorder from within the parking lot attendant's booth. A pilot study demonstrated that data obtained with this procedure are reliable, which also ensured unobtrusive observations.

Eighteen observation sessions were conducted during the 4-week duration of the study. Cars were observed exiting the parking lot from 15:30 to 17:30 during each day of the study. These observation times represented the period of greatest traffic flow from the parking lot. In addition, probe observation sessions were conducted of cars entering the parking lot from 07:00 to 09:00 on two occasions: one on the last day of the first week and the other on the last day of the second week of the study. These sessions were to ensure that the seat belt use observed between 15:30 and 17:30 accurately represented the use rate of people using the parking lot throughout the day. Observations during the probe sessions were obtained at an intersection of a public street and the private road leading to the target parking lot. The entrance of the parking lot and the feedback sign were not visible from this location. Observations were not taken on weekends.

Weather and road conditions were noted throughout the 4-week duration of the study. The pavement was wet, due to a light drizzle, on 4 of the 6 observation periods during the first week of the study (i.e., baseline phase). Wet road conditions, without precipitation, were noted on 2 of 12 observation periods conducted from the 2nd to the 4th week of the study, one in each of the intervention and follow-up phases.

Experimental Phases

Baseline. During baseline, shoulder belt use, gender, and estimated age of the front seat occupants of cars were recorded during the observation sessions for 5 consecutive days (i.e., Monday to Friday) according to the procedure outlined above. Five daily observation sessions were conducted from 15:30 to 17:30, and a probe observation session was conducted from 07:00 to 09:00 on the Friday of this week. Only administrative personnel, who granted permission to conduct this study, and the parking lot attendant were aware of the data collection under way.

Intervention. During the intervention, the sampling of shoulder belt use, gender, and estimated age of front seat occupants proceeded as during baseline for 5 consecutive days of the 2nd week of the study (i.e., Monday to Friday). During this period, two different intervention components were implemented simultaneously: a) public posting of the seat belt use rate of drivers using the lot on the previous observation day, and

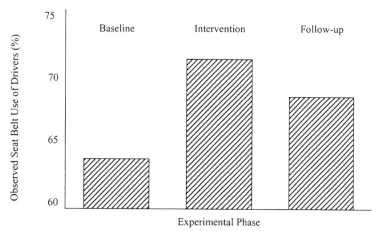

Figure 1. Rate of driver belt use in each of the three experimental phases (number of observations: Baseline = 739, Intervention = 869, Follow-up = 677).

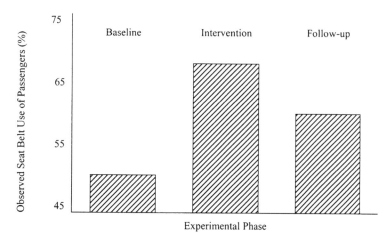

Figure 2. Rate of front passenger belt use in each of the three experimental phases (number of observations: Baseline = 222, Intervention = 236, Follow-up = 202).

b) distribution of an informational flyer to all the cars within the parking lot at prescribed times.

A feedback sign, placed adjacent to the entrance of the parking lot, indicated the percentage of drivers wearing a seat belt on the previous observation day. Cars entering the parking lot came to a full stop at the attendant's booth approximately 6 meters away from the sign. The sign measured 46 cm wide and 91 cm high, and was fastened to a stand approximately 2 meters above the ground. The reflective lettering on the sign measured approximately 6 cm wide and 9 cm high, and the message read "DRIVERS WEARING SEAT BELTS YESTERDAY, XX%." The actual rate indicated on the sign was changed daily to reflect the percentage of drivers observed to be wearing seat belts on the previous observation day. The sign was erected on the 2nd day of the intervention phase and remained there for 4 consecutive days until the end of this phase.

Flyers were distributed to all cars in the parking lot on the 1st, 3rd, and 5th days of the intervention phase (Monday, Wednesday, and Friday). A total of 284 flyers was distributed on Monday, 102 flyers on Wednes-

day, and 261 flyers on Friday. The distribution occurred at 11:30 on each of the 3 days, when the parking lot contained the greatest number of cars. Flyers were placed under the driver's side windshield wiper of the cars, ensuring both visibility and accessibility by the driver.

The flyer was divided into four different content areas. The first area presented a message in bold print stating "SEAT BELTS SAVE LIVES. BUCKLE UP PLEASE." The second area presented fatality and injury rates due to car accidents in Quebec and a statement of the effectiveness of seat belts in reducing fatalities and injuries in car accidents. The third content area contained the message "Whether or not you wear a seat belt may be your own business, but tell that to the family and friends of someone who has been injured in a car accident." The content of the fourth area of the flyer was changed between the first 2 days of distribution and the 3rd day. During the first 2 distribution days, the fourth content area advised the reader that the safety belt use of people using the parking lot was being monitored and explained the purpose of the feed-

300 back sign. On the 3rd day of distribution, the fourth content area provided feedback on the actual change in seat belt use that occurred between the baseline phase and the intervention phase.

Follow-up. During this phase, the sampling of
305 shoulder belt use, gender, and estimated age of front seat occupants proceeded as before on the 3rd and 4th weeks of the study, with the exception that a probe observation session was not conducted. Observations during this phase were interrupted by school holidays.
310 Consequently, observations for the follow-up phase were conducted on the first 2 days of the 3rd week of the study (Monday and Tuesday) and the last 4 days of the 4th week (Tuesday, Wednesday, Thursday, and Friday). During this phase, the feedback sign was not
315 present and no flyers were distributed.

Results

On the 2 days that included probe sessions, observations were made from 07:00 to 09:00 and from 15:30 to 17:30. Belt use during these two different observation periods was equivalent. Consequently, data for
320 these two observation periods were pooled for the subsequent discussion.

Results from the seat belt observations are considered separately for the data that included all the cars (n = 2,285) and for the subset of the data that included
325 cars with both a driver and a front passenger (n = 660).

Driver Belt Use

The overall rate of seat belt use among drivers across experimental phases was 68%, and more female drivers wore seat belts than did male drivers (female drivers' belt use = 75%, male drivers' belt use = 63%).
330 Figure 1 displays the rate of driver belt use in each of the three experimental phases. Inspection of this figure reveals that driver belt use was higher during the intervention phase of the experiment (71%) relative to driver belt use during the baseline phase (64%), repre-
335 senting a relative increase in seat belt use of about 11%. Although driver belt use remained higher during the follow-up phase (68%) relative to the baseline phase, there appeared a tendency for driver belt use to decline between intervention and follow-up phases.

Front Passenger Belt Use

340 The overall rate of seat belt use among front passengers across experimental phases was 59%, and more female front passengers wore seat belts than did male front passengers (female passengers' belt use = 66%, male passengers' belt use = 52%). Figure 2 displays the
345 rate of front passenger belt use in each of the three experimental phases. Inspection of this figure reveals a similar pattern of observed seat belt use as described above for drivers. Passenger belt use was higher during the intervention phase of the experiment (67%) relative
350 to passenger belt use during the baseline phase (49%), representing a relative increase of about 37%. Passenger belt use during the follow-up phase (61%) was lower than passenger belt use during the intervention phase, but remained about 25% higher relative to the
355 baseline phase.

Discussion

In this article, we evaluated a brief intervention for increasing seat belt use among front seat occupants of cars on the campus of a junior college. The combination of public posting of performance feedback and the
360 distribution of an informational flyer effectively increased the seat belt use both of drivers and of front passengers. The belt use rate of drivers increased by about 11% following the intervention phase, whereas the belt use of front passengers increased by about
365 37%, relative to the baseline phase. In both cases, belt use at follow-up was comparable to belt use during the intervention phase, although a trend toward decreasing belt use was noted.

These findings are important in light of two predominant considerations. First, the observed increases
370 in seat belt use were obtained among participants who were not previously complying with a mandatory belt use law. The minority of car occupants who do not comply with belt use laws are thought to be part of a
375 hardcore nonuser population also characterized by other risk behaviors. For example, nonuse of seat belts is related with poorer driving records, larger consumption of alcohol, and increased likelihood of having an arrest record (Dee, 1998; Foss et al., 1994; Hunter et
380 al., 1993; Hunter et al., 1990; Reinfurt et al., 1996; Wilson, 1990). Second, the participants in this study were predominantly young adults who are among the least likely to wear seat belts (Clark, 1993; Schootman, Fuortes, Zwerling, Albanese, & Watson, 1993; Wilson,
385 1990). It was estimated that 76% of drivers and 91% of front passengers observed in this study were younger than 25 years of age. Consequently, increases in seat belt use observed with the current intervention occurred among predominantly younger drivers and front
390 passengers whose behavior is most resistant to change (Dee, 1998; Reinfurt et al., 1996).

The positive effects of the intervention, however, are tempered by one other finding. The seat belt use of drivers during the follow-up phase (68%) was between
395 their belt use rate during the intervention (71%) and baseline (64%) phases. Gains in seat belt use were clearly maintained at follow-up relative to the baseline phase only among front passengers. However, this finding may be more striking because of a much lower
400 baseline belt use among front passengers as compared to drivers. Driver belt use at baseline was already 64%. In comparison, belt use among front passengers was only 49% during the baseline phase. In general, significantly less baseline belt use among passengers than
405 drivers is consistent with previous reports (e.g., Grant, 1990; Malenfant et al., 1996).

Also consistent with previous reports is that seat belt use was greater among females than among males irrespective of their front seat occupant status. Among drivers, seat belt use for females was 75% as compared with 63% for males. Among passengers, 66% of females and only 52% of males wore seat belts. Females are typically reported to have higher belt use rates than males during both baseline and follow-up phases of intervention programs (Johnston et al., 1994). As this intervention occurred in a jurisdiction with a mandatory belt use law, this finding is also consistent with reports that males are less responsive to belt use laws than are females (Dee, 1998; Hunter et al., 1990; Tipton et al., 1990).

The effect of performance feedback on seat belt use may have been mediated by at least two separate processes (Grant et al., 1983). As already considered in the introduction to this article, performance feedback may present car occupants with a group standard against which their own behavior is compared. According to social comparison theory (Festinger, 1954), people tend to compare themselves with their peers and to bring their behavior more in line with the group standard or norm. In the face of evidence that a majority of drivers use seat belts, nonusers may change their behavior to conform with the majority. In the current report, driver belt use was consistently higher than 60%, and any conformity pressure was in the direction of belt use from the outset of the intervention phase. The effect of the performance feedback on seat belt use may also be extrinsically motivated. The mere presence of performance feedback implies that individual behavior is monitored. Implied surveillance may motivate seat belt use particularly in a jurisdiction with a belt use law, where police officers are the most likely surveillants. Car occupants, then, may wear seat belts to avoid receiving a traffic fine. Consequently, the context in which the current intervention was implemented provided the two conditions that are most favorable to the effective use of performance feedback: (a) initial belt use rate greater than 50%, and (b) enforced mandatory belt use law. In this context, both social comparison and implied surveillance may have contributed to increasing the observed seat belt use.

The effect of the current intervention among participants estimated to be predominantly younger than 25 years of age is consistent with evidence that feedback of seat belt use may be selectively effective among younger drivers. Grant et al. (1983, Experiment 1) reported that a feedback sign increased seat belt use only among younger drivers (i.e., younger than 25 years of age). However, as seat belt use among the participants in Grant et al.'s experiment was consistently less than 50%, the extent to which social comparison mediated the effect of their intervention is unclear. More generally, age differences in the effect of performance feedback may be consistent with the notion that social comparison is implicated. This is because younger persons may be more likely to conform than older persons when faced with conformity pressure

(e.g., Pasupathi, 1999), and the use of social comparison itself may decline with age (Gibbons & Gerrard, 1997). To the extent that the effect of performance feedback is at least partly mediated by social comparison, this intervention may be selectively targeted at younger drivers who have the greatest to benefit from increased seat belt use.

Although the current findings suggest that posting of performance feedback is an effective method of increasing seat belt use among younger adults, these findings must be considered in light of a major methodological consideration. The two components of the intervention described in this article (i.e., posting of performance feedback, and distribution of an informational flyer) were implemented simultaneously. Consequently, the differential effect of each component on the observed seat belt use could not be assessed. The assumption in the previous discussion is that the posting of performance feedback was the primary active component in the intervention package. This assumption is based on the finding that public information interventions result in only very modest increases in seat belt use when assessed independently of other treatment components (Johnston et al., 1994). As the resources and effort required to implement each of the two components of the current intervention package differed greatly, future investigations could be designed to directly assess their relative effectiveness.

In sum, an intervention with performance feedback increased seat belt use among predominantly young adults (i.e., younger than 25 years of age), who are both less likely to wear seat belts and more likely to be involved in traffic accidents as compared to older adults (Dee, 1998; Miller et al., 1998). Although the absolute increase in driver seat belt use following the intervention was modest, it occurred in a presumably hardcore nonuser population who would benefit most from increased seat belt use. Brief interventions with performance feedback may be a cost-effective method for promoting seat belt use in institutional settings and with younger persons whose behavior is refractory to mandatory belt use laws and who are at greater risk of traffic accidents.

References

Clark, M. J. (1993). Seat belt use on a university campus. *College Health, 41*, 169–171.

Conn, J. M., Chorba, T. L., Peterson, T. D., Rhodes, P., & Annest, J. L. (1993). Effectiveness of safety-belt use: A study using hospital-based data for nonfatal motor-vehicle crashes. *Journal of Safety Research, 24*, 223–232.

Cope, J. G., Grossnickle, W. F., & Geller, E. S. (1986). An evaluation of three corporate strategies for safety belt use promotion. *Accident Analysis and Prevention, 18*, 243–251.

Decina, L. E., Temple, M. G., & Dorer, H. S. (1994). Increasing child safety-seat use and proper use among toddlers. *Accident Analysis and Prevention, 26*, 667–673.

Dee, T. S. (1998). Reconsidering the effects of seat belt laws and their enforcement status. *Accident Analysis and Prevention, 30*, 1–10.

Festinger, L. (1954). A theory of social comparison processes. *Human Relations, 7*, 117–140.

Foss, R. D., Beirness, D. J., & Sprattler, K. (1994). Seat belt use among drinking drivers in Minnesota. *American Journal of Public Health, 84*, 1732–1737.

Gantz, W., Fitzmaurice, M., & Yoo, E. (1990). Seat belt campaigns and buckling up: Do the media make a difference? *Health Communication, 2*, 1–12.

Geller, E. S., Rudd, J. R., Kalsher, M. J., Streff, F. M., & Lehman, G. R. (1987). Employer-based programs to motivate safety belt use: A review of short- and long-term effects. *Journal of Safety Research, 18*, 1–17.

Gibbons, F. X., & Gerrard, M. (1997). Health images and their effects on health behavior. In B. P. Buunk & F. X. Gibbons (Eds.), *Health, coping, and well-being: Perspectives from social comparison theory* (pp. 63–94). Mahwah, NJ: Erlbaum.

Grant, B. A. (1990). Effectiveness of feedback and education in an employment based seat belt program. *Health Education Research: Theory and Practice, 5*, 197–205.

Grant, B. A., Jonah, B. A., Wilde, G. J. S., & Ackersville-Monte, M. (1983). *The use of feedback to encourage seat belt wearing* (TMRU 8301). Road Safety and Motor Vehicle Regulation Directorate, Transport Canada, Ottawa, Canada.

Hagenzieker, M. P., Buleveld, F. D., & Davidse, R. J. (1997). Effects of incentive programs to stimulate safety-belt use: A meta-analysis. *Accident Analysis and Prevention, 29*, 759–777.

Hunter, W. W., Stewart, J. R., Stutts, J. C., & Marchetti, L. M. (1993). Nonsanction seat belt law enforcement: A modern day tale of two cities. *Accident Analysis and Prevention, 25*, 511–520.

Hunter, W. W., Stutts, J. C., Stewart, J. R., & Rodgman, E. A. (1990). Characteristics of seat belt users and nonusers in a state with a mandatory belt use law. *Health Education Research: Theory and Practice, 5*, 161–173.

Johnston, J. J., Hendricks, S. A., & Fike, J. M. (1994). Effectiveness of behavioral safety belt interventions. *Accident Analysis and Prevention, 26*, 315–323.

Kay, B. K., Sapolsky, B. S., & Montgomery, D. J. (1995). Increasing seat belt use through PI & E and enforcement: The thumbs up campaign. *Journal of Safety Research, 26*, 235–245.

Kelo, J. E., Geller, E. S., Rice, J. C., & Bryant, S. L. (1988). Motivating auto safety belt wearing in industrial settings: From awareness to behavior change. *Journal of Organizational Behavior Management, 9*, 7–21.

Ludwig, T. D., & Geller, E. S. (1991). Improving the driving practices of pizza deliverers: Response generalization and moderating effects of driving history. *Journal of Applied Behavior Analysis, 24*, 31–44.

Ludwig, T. D., & Geller, E. S. (1997). Assigned versus participative goal setting and response generalization: Managing injury control among professional pizza deliverers. *Journal of Applied Psychology, 82*, 253–261.

Malenfant, L., Wells, J. K., Van Houten, R., & Williams, A. F. (1996). The use of feedback signs to increase daytime seat belt use in two cities in North Carolina. *Accident Analysis and Prevention, 28*, 771–777.

Miller, T. R., Lestina, D. C., & Spicer, R. S. (1998). Highway crash costs in the United States by driver age, blood alcohol level, victim age, and restraint use. *Accident Analysis and Prevention, 30*, 137–150.

Pasupathi, M. (1999). Age differences in response to conformity pressure for emotional and nonemotional material. *Psychology and Aging, 14*, 170–174.

Reinfurt, D., Williams, A., Wells, J., & Rodgman, E. (1996). Characteristics of drivers not using seat belts in a high belt use state. *Journal of Safety Research, 27*, 209–215.

Schootman, M., Fuortes, L. J., Zwerling, C., Albanese, M. A., & Watson, C. A. (1993). Safety behavior among Iowa junior high and high school students. *American Journal of Public Health, 83*, 1628–1630.

Smith-Seemiller, L., Lovell, M. R., Franzen, M. D., Smith, S. S., & Townsend, R. N. (1997). Neuropsychological function in restrained versus unrestrained motor vehicle occupants who suffer closed head injury. *Brain Injury, 11*, 735–742.

Streff, F. M., Kalsher, M. J., & Geller, E. S. (1993). Developing efficient workplace safety programs: Observations of response covariation. *Journal of Organizational Behavior Management, 13*, 3–14.

Sulzer-Azaroff, B., & De Santamaria, M. (1980). Industrial safety hazard reduction through performance feedback. *Journal of Applied Behavior Analysis, 13*, 287–295.

Thyer, B. A., & Geller, E. S. (1990). Behavior analysis in the promotion of safety belt use: A review. In M. Hersen, R. M. Eisler, & P. Miller (Eds.), *Progress in behavior modification* (vol. 26, pp. 150–172). Newbury Park, CA: Sage.

Tipton, R. M., Camp, C. C., & Hsu, K. (1990). The effects of mandatory seat belt legislation on self-reported seat belt use among male and female college students. *Accident Analysis and Prevention, 22*, 543–548.

Van Houten, R., & Nau, P. A. (1981). A comparison of the effects of posted feedback and increased police surveillance on highway speeding. *Journal of Applied Behavior Analysis, 14*, 261–271.

Van Houten, R., Nau, P. A., & Marini, Z. (1980). An analysis of public posting in reducing speeding behavior on an urban highway. *Journal of Applied Behavior Analysis, 13*, 383–395.

Williams, A. F., Hall, W. L., Tolbert, W. G., & Wells, J. K. (1994). Development and evaluation of pilot programs to increase seat belt use in North Carolina. *Journal of Safety Research, 25*, 167–175.

Wilson, R. J. (1990). The relationship of seat belt nonuse to personality, lifestyle and driving record. *Health Education Research: Theory and Practice, 5*, 175–185.

About the authors: Luigi Pastò is an experimental psychologist at the Defence and Civil Institute of Environmental Medicine in Toronto, Canada. He received a B.A. and an M.A. in psychology from McGill University and a Ph.D. in clinical psychology from the University of Ottawa. His research interests include large-scale modification of health-related behaviors, stress management, and judgment and decision-making processes. Andrew G. Baker is a professor in the Department of Psychology at McGill University.

Note: This project was partially supported by scholarships from the Fonds pour la Formations de Chercheurs et l' aide à la Recherché du Québec and the Ontario Graduate Scholarships Program to Luigi Pastò.

Acknowledgments: We thank the students, faculty, and staff of Vanier College in Montreal, Canada, for their participation. We also thank Megan Thompson, Valérie Gil, Pierre Mercier, Ross Pigeau, Joe Baranski, and two anonymous reviewers for helpful comments on earlier drafts of this article.

Address correspondence to: Luigi Pastò, Defence and Civil Institute of Environmental Medicine, 1133 Sheppard Avenue West, P.O. Box 2000, Toronto, Ontario, Canada, M3M 3B9. E-mail: lpasto@dciem.dnd.ca

Exercise for Article 17

Factual Questions

1. According to the literature review, are those who are at high risk of car accidents more likely to be responsive to interventions with intrinsic incentives *or* are they more likely to be responsive to interventions with extrinsic incentives?

2. Across all age groups combined (i.e., total group) of front passengers, what percentage was female?

3. The baseline period lasted how many consecutive days?

4. Where was the feedback sign placed?

5. Were flyers distributed during the follow-up phase?

6. According to the researchers, was there a "similar pattern" of observed seat belt use for drivers and passengers?

7. The researchers refer to a theory discussed by Festinger (1954), which suggests that people tend to compare themselves with their peers and to bring their behavior more in line with the group standard or norm. What is the name of the theory?

Questions for Discussion

8. The informational flyers were distributed only during peak hours of parking lot use. Is this an important consideration? Is it a limitation of the study? Explain. (See lines 174–178 and lines 274–276.)

9. The researchers used only three age categories. Was this a good idea? Explain. (See lines 195–198.)

10. The researchers report on weather and road conditions. Is this important information? Explain. (See lines 229–236.)

11. Posting performance feedback and distribution of the informational flyers were done at the same time (i.e., during the intervention phase). Hence, they cannot isolate the effects of each of these interventions separately. Do you think it would be a good idea to present the interventions separately in a future study? Why? Why not? (See lines 478–494.)

12. To what populations, if any, would you be willing to generalize the results of this study?

Quality Ratings

Directions: Indicate your level of agreement with each of the following statements by circling a number from 5 for strongly agree (SA) to 1 for strongly disagree (SD). If you believe an item is not applicable to this research article, leave it blank. Be prepared to explain your ratings. When responding to criteria A and B below, keep in mind that brief titles and abstracts are conventional in published research.

A. The title of the article is appropriate.

SA 5 4 3 2 1 SD

B. The abstract provides an effective overview of the research article.

SA 5 4 3 2 1 SD

C. The introduction establishes the importance of the study.

SA 5 4 3 2 1 SD

D. The literature review establishes the context for the study.

SA 5 4 3 2 1 SD

E. The research purpose, question, or hypothesis is clearly stated.

SA 5 4 3 2 1 SD

F. The method of sampling is sound.

SA 5 4 3 2 1 SD

G. Relevant demographics (for example, age, gender, and ethnicity) are described.

SA 5 4 3 2 1 SD

H. Measurement procedures are adequate.

SA 5 4 3 2 1 SD

I. All procedures have been described in sufficient detail to permit a replication of the study.

SA 5 4 3 2 1 SD

J. The participants have been adequately protected from potential harm.

SA 5 4 3 2 1 SD

K. The results are clearly described.

SA 5 4 3 2 1 SD

L. The discussion/conclusion is appropriate.

SA 5 4 3 2 1 SD

M. Despite any flaws, the report is worthy of publication.

SA 5 4 3 2 1 SD

Article 18

Sex Differences on a Measure of Conformity in Automated Teller Machine Lines

STEPHEN REYSEN
California State University Fresno

MATTHEW B. REYSEN
Purdue University

ABSTRACT. Sex differences in conformity were examined as participants approached two ATMs, one of which was occupied by three confederates and the other immediately available. The number of men and women in the line in front of one of the ATMs was manipulated (3 men or 3 women), and an unobtrusive observer recorded the sex of each participant. The results indicated that women were more likely than men to wait in line to use the ATM regardless of the makeup of the line. Thus, the present study provides evidence in favor of the idea that sex differences in conformity are evident on a common task performed in a natural setting.

From *Psychological Reports, 95,* 443–446. Copyright © 2004 by Psychological Reports. Reprinted with permission.

In a highly influential series of experiments conducted in the 1950s, Solomon Asch (1952, 1955, 1956) examined conformity pressure in a group situation. Asch's classic conformity studies involved individuals
5 making line-length judgments in the presence of others also making judgments about the same stimuli. Asch found that participants often agreed with incorrect confederate responses even though, presumably, they could easily discern which of three presented lines
10 matched a target line. Based on Asch's results, it is clear that the behavior of others can influence an individual's own behavior.

Since Asch's experiments (1952, 1955, 1956), a great many studies have examined conformity in be-
15 havior (see McIlveen & Gross, 1999; Wren, 1999, for reviews). One important area of this research concerns whether women are more likely to conform than men. Sistrunk and McDavid (1971) reported that women conform more often than men on judgment tasks com-
20 pleted in the laboratory. They determined that the nature of the task plays a large role in contributing to sex differences in conformity and that a cultural role explanation is inadequate to explain the effect. A number of other studies have also demonstrated that women
25 tend to conform more than men in laboratory situations (e.g., Krech, Crutchfield, & Ballachey, 1962; Aronson, 1972; Worchel & Cooper, 1976).

Based on the results of a meta-analysis, Eagly (1978) concluded that women may be conditioned to
30 yield to men under certain circumstances. Eagly suggested that this tendency was the primary explanation for why women tend to conform more often than men. The current study was designed to analyze sex differences in conformity on a common task in a real world
35 setting. Examining a situation in which participants complete a common task in their natural environment provides a much-needed test of the external validity of more artificial laboratory paradigms. A sex-neutral task was chosen in which men and women are likely to be
40 equally competent.

In the present experiment, a line of two confederates was created behind another confederate using one of two adjacent ATMs. The three confederates were either all men or all women. The primary purpose of
45 the study was to assess whether women would conform to the group more often than men. Conformity was operationally defined by number of times a participant stood in line behind the confederates for at least 5 sec. instead of using the vacant ATM. A participant who
50 waited in line was assumed to accept implicitly the confederates' judgment that the available ATM was nonfunctional.

Method

Participants

Two hundred ATM users were observed at an outdoor shopping area in a small coastal town in Califor-
55 nia. This sample included 106 men and 94 women.

Design and Procedure

The purpose of the present experiment was to observe individuals' behavior while they used a public automated teller machine. To accomplish this, we located two ATMs at a local shopping area that met sev-
60 eral specifications. The ATMs were less than 1 ft. apart and were not separated by a divider. There were no overt signs that either of the machines was nonfunctional. In fact, both of the machines were in perfect working order. The procedure used was straightfor-
65 ward. Two confederates stood behind another confederate using one of the two ATMs. On half of the trials, the left ATM was used and on the other half of the trials the right ATM was used. Thus, on every trial, the participant approached two ATMs, one vacant and the

70 other in use with two people waiting in line. In half of the trials, two men stood in line behind a man, while in the other half of the trials two women stood in line behind a woman.

A trial began when an individual approached the
75 two ATMs. To constitute a usable trial, the person had to be alone and easily identifiable as being in line. An observer, sitting unobtrusively at a nearby table, recorded the sex of the participant and whether the participant stood in line or used the vacant ATM. "Wait-
80 ing in line" was operationally defined as standing in line behind the confederates for a period of at least 5 sec. Two hundred trials were recorded on weekday afternoons over the course of two weeks. Approximately 25 trials were recorded each day that observa-
85 tions were made.

Results and Discussion

The primary purpose of the present experiment was to examine whether men and women showed differential conformity on this common task. Our hypothesis, based on previous laboratory observations, was that
90 women would tend to conform more often than men. The data appear to support our hypothesis. The 89 women did, in fact, tend to wait in line more often than the 78 men (74%) for a period of at least 5 sec. This difference in distribution gave a statistically significant
95 chi-square (χ_1^2 ($N = 200$) = 16.09, $p < .001$).

Interestingly, the sex makeup of the line seemed to play little role in influencing the participants' behavior. Women tended to wait in line more often than men regardless of the sex of the confederates. With two
100 male confederates in line, 43 (91%) of the women waited in line, while only 35 (66%) of the men did so. This difference was statistically significant (χ_1^2 ($N = 100$) = 9.40, $p < .01$). In addition, when female confederates were in line, 46 (98%) of the women stood in
105 line, while only 43 (81%) of the men waited in line. This difference was also statistically significant (χ_1^2 ($N = 100$) = 7.13, $p < .01$). Thus, even when the sex composition of the line was manipulated, women were still more likely than men to wait in line.
110 The sex-role socialization explanation has been proposed to account for sex differences in conformity (Crutchfield, 1955; Tuddenham, 1958; Eagly, 1978). This account suggests that sex differences in conformity are a result of socialization. According to this
115 idea, women adopt a sex role that includes traits such as submissiveness and a tendency to rely on others. This idea could potentially explain why the women in our study may have been reluctant to challenge the judgment of others and instead chose to wait in line
120 rather than trying the vacant ATM. Whereas the present results seem to support the sex-role socialization theory, they are not consistent with several other prominent explanations for sex differences in conformity, namely, the information-deficit explanation (see
125 Allen, 1965; Endler, Wiesenthal, Coward, Edwards, &

Geller, 1975), the verbal processing account (Eagly & Warren, 1976), and status allocation differences (Eagly, Wood, & Fishbaugh, 1981; Santee & Maslach, 1982; Eagly, 1987).
130 One limitation that must be considered with respect to the present results is the location in which the trials took place. The experiment was conducted in a small coastal town in California. It is unclear whether the results would remain consistent in a different setting. In
135 fact, this realization suggests other possible questions. For example, it would be interesting to evaluate whether manipulating the race, age, or status of the confederates would affect the outcome. It would also be informative to include a condition in which a line of
140 persons of mixed sex was used. In sum, the present data suggest that women conform more often than men when conducting a common task in a real world setting. This observation suggests that results obtained in laboratory paradigms using similar methods may not be
145 limited with respect to external validity.

References

Allen, V L. (1965). Situational factors in conformity. In L. Berkowitz (Ed.), *Advances in experimental social psychology*. Vol. 2. (pp. 133–176). New York: Academic Press.

Aronson, E. (1972). *The social animal*. (2nd ed.) Oxford, UK: Freeman.

Asch, S. E. (1952). *Social psychology*. Englewood Cliffs, NJ: Prentice-Hall.

Asch, S. E. (1955). Opinions and social pressure. *Scientific American, 193*, 31–35.

Asch, S. E. (1956). Studies of independence and conformity: a minority of one against a unanimous majority. *Psychological Monographs, 70*, Whole No. 416.

Crutchfield, R. S. (1955). Conformity and character. *American Psychologist, 10*, 191–198.

Eagly, A. H. (1978). Sex differences in influenceability. *Psychological Bulletin, 85*, 86–116.

Eagly, A. H. (1987). *Sex differences in social behavior: a social-role interpretation*. Hillsdale, NJ: Erlbaum.

Eagly, A. H., & Warren, R. (1976). Intelligence, comprehension, and opinion change. *Journal of Personality, 44*, 226–242.

Eagly, A. H., Wood, W, & Fishbaugh, L. (1981). Sex differences in conformity: surveillance by the group as a determinant of male nonconformity. *Journal of Personality and Social Psychology, 40*, 384–394.

Endler, N. S., Wiesenthal, D. L., Coward, T., Edwards, J., & Geller, S. H. (1975). Generalization of relative competence mediating conformity across differing tasks. *European Journal of Social Psychology, 5*, 281–287.

Krech, D., Crutchfield, R. S., & Ballachey, E. L. (1962). Individual in society: a textbook of social psychology. New York: McGraw-Hill.

McIlveen, R., & Gross, R. (1999). *Social influence*. London: Hodder & Stoughton.

Santee, R. T., & Maslach, C. (1982). To agree or not to agree: personal dissent amid social pressure to conform. *Journal of Personality and Social Psychology, 42*, 690–700.

Sistrunk, F., & McDavid, J. (1971). Sex variable in conforming behavior. *Journal of Personality and Social Psychology, 17*, 200–207.

Tuddenham, R. D. (1958). The influences of a distorted group norm upon individual judgment. *Journal of Psychology, 46*, 227–241.

Worschel, S., & Cooper, J. (1976). *Understanding social psychology*. Oxford, UK: Dorsey.

Wren, K. (1999). *Social influences*. Florence, KY: Taylor & Francis/Routledge.

Acknowledgments: Thanks to Faye Crosby, Robert Levine, and Ellen Ganz for their helpful comments on previous versions of this article.

Address correspondence to: Stephen Reysen, Department of Psychology, California State University Fresno, Fresno, CA 93740-8019. E-mail: sreysen@jasnh.com

Matthew Reysen is now at University of Mississippi.

Exercise for Article 18

Factual Questions

1. How did the researchers operationally define "conformity"?

2. In half the trials, two men stood behind another man. Who stood in line in the other half?

3. With two male confederates in line, what percentage of the women waited in line? What percentage of the men did so?

4. Was the difference between the men and women in Question 3 above statistically significant? If yes, at what probability level?

5. When two female confederates were in line, what percentage of the men waited in line?

6. What is the limitation of the study that the researchers briefly discuss?

Questions for Discussion

7. This research report begins with a literature review with references to studies conducted in the 1950s. In your opinion, is it appropriate to cite older literature? Explain.

8. The researchers suggest that studying the variables of interest in their "natural environment" is needed. In your opinion, is this important? Explain. (See lines 33–38.)

9. Because the study was conducted in a natural environment, the researchers could not assign the individuals who approached the ATMs at random to the experimental conditions. In your opinion, is this an important issue? Explain.

10. In your opinion, is it important that the observer was unobtrusive? Explain. (See lines 76–79.)

11. Has this study convinced you that there are gender differences in conformity? Explain.

12. Do you agree with the researchers that it would be interesting to evaluate whether manipulating the race, age, or status of the confederates would affect the outcome? Explain. (See lines 136–138.)

Quality Ratings

Directions: Indicate your level of agreement with each of the following statements by circling a number from 5 for strongly agree (SA) to 1 for strongly disagree (SD). If you believe an item is not applicable to this research article, leave it blank. Be prepared to explain your ratings. When responding to criteria A and B below, keep in mind that brief titles and abstracts are conventional in published research.

A. The title of the article is appropriate.
   SA   5   4   3   2   1   SD

B. The abstract provides an effective overview of the research article.
   SA   5   4   3   2   1   SD

C. The introduction establishes the importance of the study.
   SA   5   4   3   2   1   SD

D. The literature review establishes the context for the study.
   SA   5   4   3   2   1   SD

E. The research purpose, question, or hypothesis is clearly stated.
   SA   5   4   3   2   1   SD

F. The method of sampling is sound.
   SA   5   4   3   2   1   SD

G. Relevant demographics (for example, age, gender, and ethnicity) are described.
   SA   5   4   3   2   1   SD

H. Measurement procedures are adequate.
   SA   5   4   3   2   1   SD

I. All procedures have been described in sufficient detail to permit a replication of the study.
   SA   5   4   3   2   1   SD

J. The participants have been adequately protected from potential harm.
   SA   5   4   3   2   1   SD

K. The results are clearly described.
   SA   5   4   3   2   1   SD

L. The discussion/conclusion is appropriate.
   SA   5   4   3   2   1   SD

M. Despite any flaws, the report is worthy of publication.
   SA   5   4   3   2   1   SD

Article 19

Benefits to Police Officers of Having a Spouse or Partner in the Profession of Police Officer

RONALD J. BURKE
York University

ASLAUG MIKKELSEN
Stavanger University College

ABSTRACT. This exploratory study of police officers examined potential effects of having a spouse or partner who is also in police work on levels of work–family conflict and spouse or partner concerns. Data were collected from 776 police officers in Norway using anonymously completed questionnaires. Police officers having spouses or partners also in police work reported significantly lower spouse or partner concerns but the same levels of work–family conflict. Possible explanations for these findings are offered.

From *Psychological Reports*, 95, 514–516. Copyright © 2004 by Psychological Reports. Reprinted with permission.

It has been observed that individuals sometimes follow the same occupation or profession as their parents and that individuals sometimes have a spouse or partner in the same occupation and profession (Hall, 1976).
5 It is not clear, however, how common this is, why this happens, and whether some professions are more likely to have couples working in them. In an earlier study of men and women in policing, it became clear that police officers' children often became police officers and the
10 possible benefits of this association were examined (Burke, 1997). In that research, we found that police officers with family in policing reported fewer job stressors, but the two groups were similar on measures of work outcomes and psychological health.

15 In the present study, the possible benefits are considered of having one's spouse or partner in the same profession: policing. Policing is seen as a demanding, highly stressful occupation, which may have potential negative effects on the psychological well-being and
20 physical health of police officers (Abdollahi, 2002). There is no doubt that police officers sometimes face high-risk, violent, and threatening situations. But police officers most often face the same demands as members of most other occupations, and there is no compelling
25 evidence that policing is in fact more stressful than other occupations (Abdollahi, 2002).

It is likely that having a spouse or partner in the same profession would increase the shared understanding of the experiences and challenges of that profes-
30 sion. The focus of this study is on the effect of the police officer's job on the family and, given the assump-

tion that policing can be dangerous and threatening, on the spouse's or partner's perceived concerns about the officers' safety. It was hypothesized that police officers
35 whose spouse or partner was also in policing would report lower work–family conflict and spouse's or partner's concerns about the respondent officer's safety and security.

Data were collected from a random sample of po-
40 lice officers in Norway ($N = 766$) using anonymous questionnaires that were mailed to respondents by the Police Union and returned to an independent research institute. The response rate was 62%. Most respondents were male (84%), married (82%), had children (88%),
45 held constable positions (62%), worked in urban areas (73%), worked in large departments (100 or more, 36%), worked between 36–39 hours per week (85%), worked 5 or fewer hours of overtime per week (75%), held fairly long police tenure (21 years or more, 39%),
50 and were born in 1960 or before (42%). A total of 623 police officers were married or partnered (538 men and 85 women). Ten percent of male officers and 44% of female officers had a spouse or partner in policing.

The two dependent variables, work–family conflict
55 and spousal concerns, were measured as did Torgen, Stenlund, Ahlberg, and Marklund (2001). Work–Family Conflict was measured by five items ($\alpha = .83$). One item was "My work has a negative impact on my family." Spousal Concerns was also measured by five
60 items ($\alpha = .81$); for example, "My spouse or partner worries about the health effects of my work." Respondents rated how frequently they experienced each item on a 5-point scale (1 = never, 5 = always).

Table 1 shows the comparisons of responses to the
65 Work–Family Conflict and Spouse Concerns scales, separating males' and females' spouses or partners in police work and those whose spouses or partners were not employed in police work. Mean values were compared using one-way analysis of variance. In the latter
70 group, some spouses or partners were employed in other jobs, while others were not employed outside the home for pay.

Both male and female officers reported the same mean values on Work–Family Conflict (nonsignificant
75 difference) whether the spouse or partner was em-

Table 1
Work–Family Conflict and Spouse Concerns by Sex of Respondent and Whether or Not Spouse or Partner Works in Policing

	Spouse/partner in policing			Spouse/partner not in policing			*p*
	M	*SD*	*n*	*M*	*SD*	*n*	
Male officers							
Work–family conflict	12.7	3.90	55	12.8	3.93	475	ns
Spouse concerns	9.6	4.07	48	11.0	3.76	419	.01
Female officers							
Work–family conflict	12.6	4.36	37	12.6	3.79	48	ns
Spouse concerns	9.2	3.62	37	11.1	3.79	48	.05

ployed in police work or not. But both male and female police officers reported lower scores on Spousal Concerns if the spouse or partner was also in policing than if they were not.

80   There are several possible reasons why having a spouse or partner in the law enforcement profession may have benefits. Such spouses or partners understand the realities of the job—the challenges, demands, rewards, and frustrations. They may share common
85 experiences and be better able to appreciate the experiences of their spouses or partners. They may also share more common attitudes, values, and aspects of personality. These common factors may diminish unrealistic thoughts on the realities of policing and the nature of
90 their spouse's or partner's job experiences.

It is not clear the extent to which these findings generalize to police officers in other countries or to other occupations. It should also be noted that all data were collected from police officers and not their
95 spouses. It would be informative to collect data from spouses or partners of police officers directly.

References

Abdollahi, M. K. (2002). Understanding police stress research. *Journal of Forensic Psychology Practice, 2*, 1–24.

Burke, R. J. (1997). On "inheriting" a career. *Psychological Reports, 80*, 1233–1234.

Hall, D. T. (1976). *Careers in organizations.* Pacific Palisades, CA: Goodyear.

Torgen, M., Stenlund, C., Ahlberg, G., & Marklund, S. (2001). *Ett hallbart arbetsliv foralla aldrar.* Stockholm: Arbetslivsinstitutet.

Acknowledgments: Preparation of this manuscript was supported in part by the Rogaland Institute, Stavanger, Norway, and the School of Business, York University. We acknowledge the support of the Police Union in conducting the study and collecting the data. Lisa Fiksenbaum assisted with data analysis.

Address correspondence to: R. J. Burke, Department of Organizational Behaviour, Schulich School of Business, York University, 4700 Keele Street, North York, ON, Canada M3J IP3. E-mail: rburke@schulich.yorku.ca

Exercise for Article 19

Factual Questions

1. What did the researchers hypothesize?

2. What percentage of the respondents were male?

3. For the female officers, was the difference between the means on Work–Family Conflict statistically significant?

4. What was the mean on Spouse Concerns for male officers who had a spouse/partner in policing?

5. What was the mean on Spouse Concerns for male officers who had a spouse/partner *not* in policing?

6. Was the difference between the two means in the answers to Questions 4 and 5 statistically significant?

Questions for Discussion

7. Is it important to know that the researchers used a random sample? Explain. (See lines 39–40.)

8. In your opinion, was the response rate satisfactory? Explain. (See line 43.)

9. The researchers indicate that there were two "dependent variables." What is your understanding of the meaning of this term? (See lines 54–55.)

10. Speculate on the meaning of "ns" in Table 1.

11. Do you think it would be important in future studies to collect information directly from the spouses (instead of from the police officers)? Why? Why not? (See lines 93–96.)

12. Does this article convince you that being married to a police officer *causes* less spousal concern? Explain.

13. This research article is shorter than most of the others in this book. Do you think that this article provides valuable information despite its shortness? Explain.

Quality Ratings

Directions: Indicate your level of agreement with each of the following statements by circling a number from 5 for strongly agree (SA) to 1 for strongly disagree (SD). If you believe an item is not applicable to this research article, leave it blank. Be prepared to explain your ratings. When responding to criteria A and B below, keep in mind that brief titles and abstracts are conventional in published research.

A.   The title of the article is appropriate.

SA   5   4   3   2   1   SD

B.   The abstract provides an effective overview of the research article.

SA   5   4   3   2   1   SD

C.   The introduction establishes the importance of the study.

SA   5   4   3   2   1   SD

D.   The literature review establishes the context for the study.

SA   5   4   3   2   1   SD

E.   The research purpose, question, or hypothesis is clearly stated.

SA   5   4   3   2   1   SD

F.   The method of sampling is sound.

SA   5   4   3   2   1   SD

G.   Relevant demographics (for example, age, gender, and ethnicity) are described.

SA   5   4   3   2   1   SD

H.   Measurement procedures are adequate.

SA   5   4   3   2   1   SD

I.   All procedures have been described in sufficient detail to permit a replication of the study.

SA   5   4   3   2   1   SD

J.   The participants have been adequately protected from potential harm.

SA   5   4   3   2   1   SD

K.   The results are clearly described.

SA   5   4   3   2   1   SD

L.   The discussion/conclusion is appropriate.

SA   5   4   3   2   1   SD

M.   Despite any flaws, the report is worthy of publication.

SA   5   4   3   2   1   SD

Article 20

Relationship of Personalized Jerseys and Aggression in Women's Ice Hockey

JAMIE BLOME
University of Northern Iowa

JENNIFER J. WALDRON
University of Northern Iowa

MICK G. MACK
University of Northern Iowa

SUMMARY. The present study examined the relationship between aggression and players' names on uniforms in collegiate women's ice hockey. Aggression was defined as mean penalty minutes per game. Information (i.e., win/loss record, penalties, and names on uniforms) about the 2002–2003 season women's ice hockey team was obtained via e-mail from 53 of 72 (74% return rate) sports information directors (Division I = 23, Division II = 2, Division III = 28). Analysis indicated that teams with personalized jerseys had significantly more penalty minutes per game than teams without personalized jerseys. However, as the majority of the teams with personalized jerseys were Division I teams and the majority of the teams without personalized jerseys were Division III teams, it is unclear whether results were due to personalized jersey or competition level of play.

From *Perceptual and Motor Skills, 101,* 499–504. Copyright © 2005 by Perceptual and Motor Skills. Reprinted with permission.

Aggression has become a frequent topic of investigation in sport psychology, and several factors have been examined. For example, researchers have investigated the relationship between aggression and location
5   of games (Lefebvre & Passer, 1974), crowd size (Russell & Drewry, 1976), possible lunar influences (Russell & Dua, 1983), outcome of game (Worrell & Harris, 1986), frequency of competition (Widmeyer & McGuire, 1997), personality (Bushman & Wells,
10   1998), level of competition (Coulomb & Pfister, 1998), wearing personalized jerseys (Wann & Porcher, 1998), and type of sport (Huang, Cherek, & Lane, 1999). Because ice hockey offers a unique field setting in which aggression is tolerated and often encouraged, many
15   studies have focused on this sport. Not surprisingly, however, they have only examined male hockey teams.

Sex is one potential moderator of aggressive behaviors. For example, women are more likely to use indirect types of aggression (i.e., backbiting, spreading of
20   false rumors, gossiping, etc.), while men are more likely to engage in violence or acts of physical behavior (Bjorkqvist, Osterman, & Kaukiainen, 1992). Most of the previous studies examining sport aggression, however, have been conducted with male athletes so it
25   is not clear whether this relationship would occur in sports with women. With the substantial increase in the number of women participants in contact sports such as soccer, ice hockey, and football (Theberge, 1997), it is now possible to examine physical aggression during
30   women's athletic competitions.

Aggression in sports can be defined as a nonaccidental act that has the potential to cause psychological or physiological harm to another individual (Kirker, Tennebaum, & Mattson, 2000). Because penalty min-
35   utes are "acts of interpersonal aggression judged by highly trained and experienced referees to be in violation of the rules of competition" (Russell & Dua, 1983, p. 42), they are often used to measure aggression operationally in men's ice hockey (Russell & Dua, 1983;
40   Widmeyer & Birch, 1984; Widmeyer & McGuire, 1997; Bushman & Wells, 1998; Wann & Porcher, 1998). The use of penalty records has been a valid indicator of aggression in sports (Vokey & Russell, 1992), as more aggressive infractions require longer
45   periods of time of being restricted from participation. The same is true in women's ice hockey. However, it should be noted that there are slight differences in rules between the men's and women's games. The National Collegiate Athletic Association (NCAA) rules for
50   women's ice hockey do not allow body checking but do permit body contact (National Collegiate Athletic Association, 2002[1]). In other words, women's ice hockey has "rules that limit but by no means eliminate body contact" (Theberge, 1997, p. 71). Interestingly,
55   some of the women in Theberge's study believed that not permitting body checking actually caused more illegal contact during competition.

Understanding the triggers for aggression in sports is an important area of investigation and has been stud-
60   ied primarily in relation to men's sporting behaviors. The current study extends Wann and Porcher's study of men's ice hockey (1998) to women's ice hockey teams. Based on 86 Division I, II, and III ice hockey programs, Wann and Porcher found that the teams with
65   personalized jerseys showed more aggression, measured using penalties, than teams with identification on

---

[1] Men's and women's ice hockey rules and interpretations. Retrieved November 6, 2003, from http://www.ncaa.org/library/rules/2003/ice_hockey_rules.pdf

their jerseys and explained the findings using self-presentation theory.

Self-presentation theory predicts that individuals attempt to present themselves in a positive manner to others (Schlenker, 1980). For many male athletes, portraying a positive image to others requires them to be tough. Thus, especially in a sport such as ice hockey, which is known for its aggressive nature, participants may desire to present themselves as being aggressive (Wann & Porcher, 1998). Having one's name appear on the uniform would ensure that personal identity as an aggressor is known and would serve to enhance the "positive" image to their teammates, opponents, and fans.

Because self-presentation is a socially based concept, research examining sport aggression in women may yield different results. For example, researchers have reported that collegiate female athletes from a variety of sports were less violent on the playing field than their male counterparts (Tucker & Parks, 2001). Perhaps, as suggested by Bjorkqvist et al. (1992), women, following traditional norms of femininity, may desire to present themselves in a more socially desirable nonaggressive manner, which suggests that they would be more likely to engage in indirect acts of aggression that "mask" their behavior. This explanation would predict that wearing a jersey with one's name on the back would result in fewer acts of aggression for female athletes than for male athletes. Thus, it was hypothesized that there would be no significant difference between aggression of women's collegiate ice hockey teams, as measured by number of penalty minutes, with and without personalized names on their jerseys.

Method

A list of all colleges with women's ice hockey in Divisions I, II, and III was obtained from the NCAA Web site. E-mail addresses were obtained, and the sports information directors from each school were then contacted via e-mail. In the two cases where no sport information director was listed, the head coach was contacted. Two weeks following the initial e-mail, a follow-up was sent through e-mail to those who had not yet responded. The sports information directors or coaches of all NCAA women's ice hockey teams ($N = 72$) were contacted and 53 responded (Division I = 23, Division II = 2, Division III = 28). Therefore, the present sample represented approximately 74% of all NCAA women's hockey programs from the 2002–2003 season.

Each e-mail began with an introduction of the researchers' affiliation and an explanation of the research. This was followed by a request for the following information concerning the 2002–2003 women's ice hockey season: (1) What was your win/loss record? (2) What was the total number of penalty minutes? (3) Did your team have personalized names on their jerseys for home games? (4) Did your team have personalized names on their jerseys for away games? One of the sports information directors responded by telephone, while the rest of the directors replied using e-mail.

Aggression was operationally defined as the mean number of penalty minutes per game. This measure was calculated by dividing the total number of penalty minutes for the season by the total number of games. Because penalties for more aggression require more minutes in the penalty box (i.e., 2 min. for a minor penalty versus 5 min. for a major penalty), a larger number indicates more aggression.

Results

Of the 53 women's hockey teams for which responses were received, 21 had personalized names on both home and away jerseys (Division I = 19, Division II = 1, Division III = 1), 23 teams did not have personalized names on either home or away jerseys (Division I = 2, Division II = 1, Division III = 20), and 9 teams had names on either home or away jerseys, but not both (Division I = 2, Division III = 7). The mean number of penalties per game was 4.5 ($SD = 1.2$), and the mean for penalty minutes per game was 9.5 ($SD = 2.6$).

An independent-samples t test was used to compare penalty minutes per game between teams with and without personalized names on their jerseys. Teams whose jerseys had names for either their home or away games were not included in this analysis. Analysis indicated that the teams with personalized jerseys had significantly more penalty minutes per game ($M = 10.7$, $SD = 2.4$) than teams without personalized jerseys ($M = 8.4$, $SD = 2.2$; $t_{42} = 3.19$, $p < .01$, $d = 1.0$). Because the vast majority of teams having personalized jerseys were Division I ice hockey programs (90.5%), while most teams not having personalized jerseys were Division III programs (87.0%), an additional independent samples t test was performed to examine potential differences between the two divisions. Since data were received from only two Division II ice hockey programs, they were not included in this analysis. The analysis indicated that Division I teams had significantly more penalty minutes per game ($M = 10.7$, $SD = 2.3$) than Division III ($M = 8.2$, $SD = 2.3$; $t_{49} = 3.86$, $p < .01$, $d = 1.1$). For both of the independent samples t tests, the effect size (d) was large (Cohen, 1988). In other words, the magnitude or meaningfulness of the difference between the two groups was substantial.

Discussion

Contrary to what was predicted, results of the present study are similar to Wann and Porcher's findings (1998). The combined results from these two studies indicate that both samples of men's and women's ice hockey teams with personalized jerseys had more penalty minutes and thus more aggression than teams without personalized jerseys. The self-presentation explanation of desiring to be perceived as an aggres-

sive player might be appropriate for both men and women. Both male and female ice hockey players may
180 want an aggressive self-presentation to intimidate opponents, keep their position on the team, or maintain their self-identity (Widmeyer, Bray, Dorsch, & McGuire, 2002).

However, closer scrutiny of the demographic back-
185 ground of the teams involved raises doubts about the potential effectiveness of wearing personalized jerseys. When examining the data in the current study, it was noted that only one team in Division III had personalized jerseys, whereas only two teams in Division I did
190 not have names on their jerseys. Follow-up analyses comparing aggression between the divisions found that Division I teams had significantly higher aggression measured as penalties (min.) than Division III teams. A cursory examination of the demographic data provided
195 by Wann and Porcher (1998) raises similar questions. In their study, 95% of Division I teams had personalized jerseys, while 85% of Division III teams did not have personalized jerseys.

Wann and Porcher's attempt to provide evidence
200 that increased aggression could be attributed to personalized jerseys rather than competition level was also suspect. As noted in their results, small sample sizes precluded statistical analysis at the Division I level. Their analysis at the Division III level could similarly
205 be questioned given the unequal sample sizes (i.e., personalized jerseys = 28 and no personalized jerseys = 5). Unfortunately, the current study's design showed the same limitations, so additional *t* tests within each division could not be conducted given the small number of
210 teams without personalized jerseys in Division I and teams with personalized jerseys in Division III. Having only nine teams whose names were on jerseys worn during either their home or away games but not both was insufficient data on which to conduct statistical
215 analyses between the groups. Therefore, it is unclear whether differences in aggression were related to wearing personalized jerseys or to competition level.

In summary, research on the possible association of wearing personalized jerseys on aggression in men and
220 women's collegiate ice hockey appears inconclusive given the confounding variable of competition level. Significant differences in penalty minutes may have been a function of the competition level rather than wearing a personalized jersey. Researchers must fur-
225 ther delineate the various factors that may be associated with expression of aggression by both male and female participants in ice hockey and other sports.

References

Bjorkqvist, K., Osterman, K., & Kaukiainen, A. (1992). The development of direct and indirect aggressive strategies in males and females. In K. Bjorkqvist & P. Niemela (Eds.), *Of mice and women: aspects of female aggression.* San Diego, CA: Academic Press. Pp. 51–64.

Bushman, B. J., & Wells, G. L. (1998). Trait aggressiveness and hockey penalties: Predicting hot tempers on the ice. *Journal of Applied Psychology, 83,* 969–974.

Cohen, J. (1998). *Statistical power analysis for the behavioral sciences.* (2nd ed.) Hillsdale, NJ: Erlbaum.

Coulomb, G., & Pfister, R. (1998). Aggressive behaviors in soccer as a function of competition level and time: A field study. *Journal of Sport Behavior, 21,* 222–231.

Huang, D. B., Cherek, D. R., & Lane, D. (1999). Laboratory measurement of aggression in high school age athletes: Provocation in a nonsporting context. *Psychological Reports, 85,* 1251–1262.

Kirker, B., Tennebaum, G., & Mattson, J. (2000). An investigation of the dynamics of aggression: Direct observations in ice hockey and basketball. *Research Quarterly for Exercise and Sport, 71,* 373–386.

Lefebvre, L., & Passer, M. W. (1974). The effects of game location and importance on aggression in team sport. *International Journal of Sport Psychology, 5,* 102–110.

Russell, G. W., & Drewry, B. R. (1976). Crowd size and competitive aspects of aggression in ice hockey: An archival study. *Human Relations, 29,* 723–735.

Russell, G. W., & Dua, M. (1983). Lunar influences on human aggression. *Social Behavior and Personality, 11,* 41–44.

Schlenker, B. R. (1980). *Impression management: The self-concept, social identity, and interpersonal relations.* Monterey, CA: Brooks/Cole.

Theberge, N. (1997). "It's a part of the game": Physicality and the production of gender in women's hockey. *Gender and Society, 11,* 69–87.

Tucker, L. W, & Parks, J. B. (2001). Effects of gender and sport types on intercollegiate athletes' perceptions of the legitimacy of aggressive behaviors in sport. *Sociology of Sport Journal, 18,* 403–413.

Vokey, J. R., & Russell, G. W. (1992). On penalties in sport as measures of aggression. *Social Behavior and Personality, 20,* 219–225.

Wann, D. L., & Porcher, B. J. (1998). The relationship between players' names on uniforms and athlete aggression. *International Sport Journal, 2,* 28–35.

Widmeyer, W. N., & Birch, J. S. (1984). Aggression in professional ice hockey: A strategy for success or a reaction to failure? *Journal of Psychology, 117,* 77–84.

Widmeyer, W. N., Bray, J. S., Dorsch, K. D., & McGuire, E. J. (2002). Explanations for the occurrence of aggression: Theories and research. In J. M. Silva & D. E. Stevens (Eds.), *Psychological foundations of sport.* Boston, MA: Allyn & Bacon. Pp. 352–379.

Widmeyer, W. N., & McGuire, E. J. (1997). Frequency of competition and aggression in professional ice hockey. *International Journal of Sport Psychology, 28,* 57–66.

Worrell, L. L., & Harris, D. V. (1986). The relationship of perceived and observed aggression of ice hockey players. *International Journal of Sport Psychology, 17,* 34–40.

Address correspondence to: Jennifer J. Waldron, Ph.D., School of Health, Physical Education, and Leisure Services, 203 Wellness/Recreation Center, Cedar Falls, IA 50614-0241. E-mail: jennifer.waldron@uni.edu

Exercise for Article 20

Factual Questions

1. Near the beginning of the article, the researchers provide a conceptual definition of "aggression." (See lines 31–33.) Later in the article, they provide an operational definition. What is the operational definition?

2. How were the participants contacted for this study?

3. Was there a significant difference between teams with personalized jerseys and teams without personalized jerseys? If yes, at what probability level was it significant?

4. What is the name of the significance test used in this research?

5. According to the researchers, were both effect sizes (*d*) "large"?

6. Are the results of this study consistent with what was predicted (i.e., consistent with the hypothesis)?

Questions for Discussion

7. Out of the 72 potential participants, 53 responded. In your opinion, does this affect the validity of the study? Explain.

8. If you had planned this study, would you have hypothesized that there would be no significant difference? Explain. (See lines 95–100.)

9. Do you agree with the researchers' statement that "…it is unclear whether differences in aggression were related to wearing personalized jerseys or to competition level."? (See lines 215–217.)

10. In your opinion, would a true experiment in which some women are randomly assigned to wear personalized jerseys while the remaining ones are not provide better information on this potential cause of aggression? Explain.

Quality Ratings

Directions: Indicate your level of agreement with each of the following statements by circling a number from 5 for strongly agree (SA) to 1 for strongly disagree (SD). If you believe an item is not applicable to this research article, leave it blank. Be prepared to explain your ratings. When responding to criteria A and B below, keep in mind that brief titles and abstracts are conventional in published research.

A. The title of the article is appropriate.

SA   5   4   3   2   1   SD

B. The abstract provides an effective overview of the research article.

SA   5   4   3   2   1   SD

C. The introduction establishes the importance of the study.

SA   5   4   3   2   1   SD

D. The literature review establishes the context for the study.

SA   5   4   3   2   1   SD

E. The research purpose, question, or hypothesis is clearly stated.

SA   5   4   3   2   1   SD

F. The method of sampling is sound.

SA   5   4   3   2   1   SD

G. Relevant demographics (for example, age, gender, and ethnicity) are described.

SA   5   4   3   2   1   SD

H. Measurement procedures are adequate.

SA   5   4   3   2   1   SD

I. All procedures have been described in sufficient detail to permit a replication of the study.

SA   5   4   3   2   1   SD

J. The participants have been adequately protected from potential harm.

SA   5   4   3   2   1   SD

K. The results are clearly described.

SA   5   4   3   2   1   SD

L. The discussion/conclusion is appropriate.

SA   5   4   3   2   1   SD

M. Despite any flaws, the report is worthy of publication.

SA   5   4   3   2   1   SD

Article 21

Significance of Gender and Age in African American Children's Response to Parental Victimization

CATHERINE N. DULMUS
University at Buffalo

CAROLYN HILARSKI
Buffalo State College

ABSTRACT. This study examined gender and age differences in children's psychological response to parental victimization in a convenience sample of African American children. Thirty youths, ages 6 to 12, whose parents had been victims of community violence (i.e., gunshot or stabbing), and a control group of 30 children matched on variables of race, age, gender, and neighborhood served as the sample for this study. Parents completed a demographics sheet and the Child Behavior Checklist. Data were collected within six weeks of parental victimization. No significant difference was found in male and female youths' internalizing and externalizing behavior at ages 6 to 8. However, beginning at age 9 there was a significant difference in behavior. Youths exposed to parental victimization internalized and externalized to a greater degree than those children who were not exposed. Males externalized more than females, and females internalized more than males. Thus, the perceived trauma response may vary as a function of the child's gender and developmental level or age. These findings suggest that gender-specific response related to trauma exposure may begin as early as age 9.

From *Health & Social Work*, 31, 181–188. Copyright © 2006 by National Association of Social Workers. Reprinted with permission.

The United States is a violent country (Trickett & Schellenbach, 1998), and our children's exposure to this violence is a national public health issue (Glodich, 1998). Violence exposure, as either a witness or victim, is rampant among inner-city youths (Hien & Bukszpan, 1999). Although violence has decreased in recent years, youths in poor urban areas continue to be disproportionately exposed (Gorman-Smith & Tolan, 1998; Gorman-Smith, Tolan, & Henry, 1999). Children exposed to violence (either directly or indirectly) are vulnerable to serious long-term consequences, such as posttraumatic stress (Kilpatrick & Williams, 1997; McCloskey & Walker, 2000), delinquency (Farrell & Bruce, 1997; Gorman-Smith & Tolan, 1998; Miller, Wasserman, Neugebauer, Gorman-Smith, & Kamboukos, 1999), depression (Gorman-Smith et al., 1999;

Kliewer, Lepore, Oskin, & Johnson, 1998), and impaired attention (Ford, Racusin, Ellis, & Daviss, 2000).

Trauma and post-trauma reactions have far-reaching effects beyond the individual victim. Trauma can touch the victim's entire system (e.g., partner, professional helper, family members, and friends) (Figley, 1995a). In fact, the greater the degree of crisis (i.e., type of trauma event and length of stress reaction), the greater the system stress (Peebles-Kleiger & Kleiger, 1994). Concern must be extended beyond the direct victims of violence to include those indirectly affected. Indirect victims include those children who have heard about violence occurring to members of their immediate and extended family or acquaintances. Indirect victims are also those children who fear for their safety and that of their family and friends (Figley, 1995b).

Simply being in the presence of violence is harmful to children (Osofsky, 1995). Safety is an important concept in childhood (Cicchetti & Aber, 1998). Learning to trust others, exploring the environment, developing confidence in oneself, and expanding social contacts outside of the family are important childhood challenges (Cicchetti & Aber, 1998; Dahlberg & Potter, 2001). In a predictable, safe, and secure environment, children are more likely to explore their surroundings to learn about themselves, their relationships with others, and the world (Cicchetti & Aber, 1998; Garbarino, 1995a). Violence exposure undermines feelings of safety and restricts the range of experiences necessary for healthy development (Calvert, 1999).

Exposure to community violence affects children of all ages (Berman, Kurtines, Silverman, & Serafini, 1996; Ensink, Robertson, Zissis, & Leger, 1997; Glodich & Allen, 1998; Gorman-Smith & Tolan, 1998). The response to a perceived violent event may actually overwhelm very young children. For example, they may become obsessed with the details of the event. They may re-enact violent themes in play and unconsciously in dreams (Eth, 2001). Younger children are also more likely to engage in bedwetting, thumb sucking, somatic complaints, social withdrawal, and high anxiety during caregiver separation (Eth, 2000).

School-age children exposed to violence display externalizing and internalizing behaviors and show declines in concentration, school performance, and overall functioning (Eth, 2001; Garbarino, 1993; Osofsky, 1999). These children have difficulty regulating their emotions, showing empathy, and integrating cognitions (Cicchetti & Rogosch, 1997). Such behaviors can interfere with the developmental challenges of adapting to the school environment and establishing positive peer relations. For example, traumatized children are often hypervigilant of their environment as a protective mechanism against additional traumatic events. This behavior can lead to environmental misinterpretations of hostile intent by others, thus, interfering with constructive social interactions (Dodge, Lochman, Harnish, Bates, & Pettit, 1997).

The effects of exposure to violence may differ from child to child. Following a similar exposure, children who internalize behave differently from those who externalize (Keane & Kaloupek, 1997; Keane, Taylor, & Penk, 1997). Moreover, there is an indication that gender influences traumatic response (Berton & Stabb, 1996; Miller et al., 1999; Singer, Anglin, Song, & Lunghofer, 1995). A study that examined the rates of depression and anxiety among bereaved children found that boys reported fewer depressive symptoms than girls did up to 18 months after the death of a parent (Raveis, Siegel, & Karus, 1999). Leadbeater, Kuperminc, Blatt, and Hertzog (1999) reported gender differences in the internalizing and externalizing of problems relative to stressful life events: Boys were at risk of externalizing their problems, and girls tended to internalize (Dulmus, Ely, & Wodarski, 2003). This study examined the effects of age and gender independently and conjointly on reactions to trauma.

Theoretical Model

The adverse effects of trauma on people other than the direct victim have been observed and documented (Terr, 1979, 1981). The actual manner of symptom transfer is not definitively established by empirical research. However, one explanation for externalizing behavior trauma response is the social interactional model of development in which children come to view what they are exposed to as normative and model these behaviors (Lorion & Saltzman, 1993). The cognitive processing theory attempts to explain internalizing response to trauma, suggesting that making sense of community violence can be distressing as it may conflict with the child's beliefs that home and neighborhood are safe (Finkelhor, 1997; Garbarino, 1995a; Marans & Adelman, 1997). The idea that the environment is not safe can challenge the child's basic need to trust and be part of a secure attachment, which is a fundamental developmental process for future health (Cicchetti & Rogosch, 1997; Pynoos et al., 1993). The struggle to cognitively assimilate violent events may lead to unwanted and uncontrolled thoughts resulting in

anxiety and depressive symptomatology (Cicchetti & Toth, 1998). Violation of essential developmental processes can lead to internal dissonance and defensive behavioral and cognitive responses that are reminiscent of posttraumatic symptoms (Pynoos et al., 1993; Pynoos, Nader, Frederick, Gonda, & Stuber, 1987). Clinical observations and developmental research indicate that children's distress responses to trauma may manifest as a range of impaired symptomatology (Garbarino, 1995b).

From a developmental perspective, age-relevant achievements in cognition, social relationships, and emotional development provide children with specific vulnerabilities and unique strengths to interpret traumatic events and master violence-related stress and arousal (Apfel, 1996). Internal and external factors, therefore, interact to establish resiliency or risk. Trauma exposure may lead to traumatization or distress when fear, anger, or stress overwhelms the child's internal attributes and protective mechanisms (Finkelhor & Asdigian, 1996). A particular concern is that traumatic stress reactions may prevent young children from resolving stage-salient developmental challenges, which may then present as psychopathology (Cicchetti & Toth, 1998).

In sum, the primary victims of violence are not the only sufferers. Having a personal relationship with someone who has been a victim of violence can have long-term negative consequences. An understanding of the developmental circumstance (i.e., age) and gender-related response of children residing in a family where a parent has been victimized is vital to prevention and treatment efforts. Only by understanding the developmental effects of such exposure can we advance our remedial efforts.

Current Study

Internal Review Board (IRB) approval was obtained from the State University of New York at Buffalo before study implementation. Initial analysis of the data set used in this study reported that children in the exposure group were experiencing symptoms in the borderline clinical range (total score of 67–70) as indicated by scores on the Child Behavior Checklist (CBCL) (Achenbach, 1991), and children in the control group fell below this range (Dulmus & Wodarski, 2000). Direct and indirect exposure to community violence can negatively affect children (Dulmus & Wodarski, 2000), often resulting in children showing their distress by engaging in internalizing or externalizing behavior. However, research is unclear regarding the age-related influences of the trauma response, as only a few studies have examined the link between community violence exposure and negative outcomes in children younger than age 10. One study suggested that younger children engage in internalizing behavior more than older children (Schwab-Stone et al., 1999). Fitzpatrick and Boldizar (1993) suggested that younger children indirectly exposed to violence are less likely to engage in internalizing behavior. Hence, there is no real understanding of how age may influence community violence exposure for young children.

175 Another factor that requires consideration is gender. Research has suggested that gender influences the behavioral outcome of violence exposure (Schwab-Stone et al., 1999; Song, Singer, & Anglin, 1998). Our research question thus was: Do children behaviorally 180 respond to perceived trauma differently according to age and gender?

Method

Sample and Procedures

A convenience sample of 30 children (exposure group), ages 6 to 12 years, whose parents had been admitted to Erie County Medical Center (ECMC) 185 trauma unit (December 1997 through May 1998) in Buffalo, New York, for treatment of injuries sustained as a result of community violence, were recruited for this study. The principal investigator daily reviewed the surgery list for those individuals who had surgery 190 because of a gunshot or stabbing wound. Such individuals were then approached to determine whether injuries had been sustained as a result of community violence. If so, they were asked whether they had a child between the ages of 6 and 12 who could partici- 195 pate in this study. One hundred percent of parents approached who met the criteria for the study and who had a child between the ages of 6 and 12 provided contact information on how to access their child's primary caregiver for study recruitment purposes. All primary 200 caregivers contacted agreed to allow themselves and their child to participate in this study. Mothers, who were the dominant primary caregivers in the exposure group, offered names of other parents in their neighborhood with a child of the same gender, race, and age as 205 their own child, but who had not had a parent who was a victim of community violence, to compose the control group. An exposure group (n = 30) and control group (n = 30) were matched on age, race, gender, and neighborhood. The sample size was adequate for a 210 large effect size, a .80 level of power, and an alpha of .05 (Cohen, 1992). Inclusion criteria for the exposure group were: (1) The child participant had to be the biological child of the victimized person admitted to the Buffalo trauma unit; (2) The victimized person had to 215 be a victim of community violence (thus, victims of domestic violence and self-inflicted wounds were excluded); (3) The victimized person had to be admitted to a medical floor for at least one night; (4) The child was not a witness to the parent's victimization; (5) The 220 child was not receiving mental health services; (6) The child had no documented history of mental retardation; and (7) Only one child per family could participate.

The exposure and control groups' female caregivers voluntarily provided, through interview and self- 225 administered instruments, demographic and behavioral descriptions of their child during a one-hour appointment with the principal investigator two to eight weeks following the parent's hospitalization. Confidentiality was discussed and ensured. Each parent received $20, 230 and each child $5, in addition to transportation, if needed.

Measures

A form was developed requesting social and demographic data. In addition, the parent with whom the child resided completed the CBCL. The CBCL can be 235 self-administered or administered by an interviewer and is designed to record in standardized format children's (ages 4 to 18) competencies and problems as reported by their parents or caregiver. The 118-item checklist allows parents to evaluate the behavior of 240 their children and provides a total score, as well as scores for internalizing and externalizing behaviors. It asks questions regarding a wide variety of symptoms and behaviors that children may have experienced in the past six months and asks parents to respond to each 245 question with three possible answers: "not true," "somewhat true or sometimes true," or "very or often true." The CBCL is widely used and accepted with good reliability ($r = .87$) and validity (Achenbach, 1991).

Results

Sample Characteristics

250 All children were African American, with 47% being females, and a mean age of nine years. Half of the sample was age 6 through 8. One child lived with an aunt, and the remaining children lived with their mother. The mean number of siblings in the home was 255 three, and the mean family gross income per month was $985. More than three-quarters of the victimized parents were men. Of those, 77% were shot and 23% had been stabbed. The average hospital stay was nine days, with a range of one to 24 nights. More than half 260 of the youths had visited their parent in the hospital. Sixty-one percent of the youths were in daily contact with their parent before the victimizing event. The remaining youths had a minimum of monthly contact.

Statistical Analysis of CBCL Internalizing and Externalizing Scores

Internalizing Scores. A 2 (gender: male and female) 265 × 2 (group: control or exposure) × 2 (agecode: 1 = 6 to 8 years, and 2 = 9 to 12 years) analysis of variance (ANOVA) was conducted on internalizing CBCL scores. There was a significant main effect for group, $F(1,52) = 9.27$, $p = .004$ and agecode, $F(1,52) = 5.6$, $p =$ 270 .022. The control group had lower internalizing CBCL scores ($M = 9.24$, $SE = 1.17$) than the exposure group ($M = 14.24$, $SE = 1.16$). The youths age 9 to 12 had higher internalizing CBCL scores ($M = 13.68$, $SE = 1.16$) than the 6- to 8-year-olds ($M = 9.8$, $SE = 1.16$).

Externalizing Scores. A 2 (gender: male and fe- 275 male) × 2 (group: control or exposure) × 2 (agecode)

112

ANOVA was conducted on externalizing CBCL scores. There was a significant main effect for group, $F(1,52) = 12.73$, $p = .001$ and gender, $F(1,52) = 12.75$, $p = .001$. The control group had lower externalizing CBCL scores ($M = 6.27$, $SE = 1.31$) than the exposure group ($M = 12.86$, $SE = 1.30$). Males had higher externalizing CBCL scores ($M = 12.87$, $SE = 1.31$) than females ($M = 6.27$, $SE = 1.31$).

Younger Age Group. Male and female youths ages 6 to 8 years in the exposure group did not differ on their internalizing $t(13) = 1.550$, $p = .145$ and externalizing $t(13) = -0.186$, $p = .855$ CBCL scores according to independent t tests. Similarly, the independent t test was not significant for those 6- to 8-year-old male and female youths not exposed to parental victimization on internalizing $t(13) = .856$, $p = .408$ and externalizing $t(13) = 1.12$, $p = .284$ CBCL scores (see Table 1).

Older Age Group. The independent t test was significant for males and females ages 9 to 12 years in the exposure group on externalizing $t(13) = -2.57$, $p = .023$ and internalizing $t(13) = 5.09$, $p = .000$ CBCL scores. Youths ages 9 to 12 years in the control group showed no difference between male and female internalizing $t(13) = -.688$, $p = .503$ and externalizing $t(13) = .012$, $p = .990$ scores (see Table 1).

Table 1
Mean CBCL Internalizing and Externalizing Scores for Control and Exposure Groups, by Age and Gender

	6–8 year olds' internal/external mean scores	9–12 year olds' internal/external mean scores
Control		
Male	8.25/5.75	10.50/7.83
Female	6.00/3.71	12.22/7.78
Exposure		
Male	12.13/14.88	11.13/23.00
Female	12.86/8.00	20.86/5.57

Note. CBCL = Child Behavior Checklist

Discussion and Implications for Practice

Initial analysis of these data reported that children in the exposure group were experiencing symptoms in the borderline clinical range, and children in the control group fell below this range (Dulmus & Wodarski, 2000). The current analysis reports additional supportive findings in regard to gender and age-specific differences. No significant difference in male and female youths' internalizing and externalizing behavior at ages 6 to 8 in either the control or the exposure groups was found. In other words, male and female youths in early childhood engage in both internalizing and externalizing behavior. However, youths exposed to parental victimization internalized and externalized to a greater degree, according to caregiver report, than those children who were not exposed. At age 9, there was a significant difference in behavior. In the exposure group, males externalized more than females, and females internalized more than males. In the control group,

there was no significant difference in the internalizing and externalizing behavior of the male and female youths. Thus, the perceived trauma response may vary as a function of the child's gender and developmental level or age.

Research is beginning to suggest that internalizing and externalizing behavior is reciprocal (Hodges & Perry, 1999). For example, youths who engage in externalizing behaviors tend to be socially rejected, which can lead to internalizing behaviors (e.g., withdrawal). Conversely, youths who internalize can be perceived by parents and teachers as passive aggressive and noncooperative (e.g., externalizing) (Shaw et al., 1998). This internalizing and externalizing behavior is the child's defensive coping and is influenced by gender (Carter & Levy, 1991; Dubowitz et al., 2001). Indeed, females can be more reflective or passive, and males more antagonistic (Cramer, 1979; Erikson, 1964; Freud, 1933; Levit, 1991). Support for this premise was found in this study as well. However, the significance here is that both males and females internalize similarly in response to trauma according to age. This is pertinent information regarding assessment of an externalizing male. He may be externalizing because of internalizing a trauma exposure.

Young children respond to trauma by attempting to explain it. The cognitive level or age of the child influences the explanation. For example, a child in the preoperational stage of cognitive development (two to seven years) (Piaget, 1973) is said to view the world egocentrically. Thus, the self is at the root of the explanation for the trauma event. A child in the concrete operations stage of cognitive development (7 to 11 years) is able to produce several explanations for the trauma event, such as blaming others, the self, or both. These distorted or dysfunctional schemas are born from stages of development not equipped to integrate traumatic circumstances. Moreover, the beliefs and attitudes formed during these stages are relatively stable and are the foundations for internalizing and externalizing behavior (Finkelhor, 1995), depending on gender (Levit, 1991). The traumagenic dynamic cites powerlessness as the fundamental dysfunctional cognition stemming from a trauma exposure (Finkelhor, 1997). Helplessness is a core belief for such disorders as anxiety, the need for control, and identification of self as either aggressor or victim, and is linked to depressive and aggressive behavior (Finkelhor, 1997).

Such knowledge has implications for practice as gender-specific assessment and intervention approaches must be used at younger ages than previously presumed. Moreover, feeling unsafe because of trauma exposure can lead to cognitive perceptions of chronic threat and feelings of powerlessness, which is associated with symptoms of psychological distress and maladaptive means of coping, including internalizing or externalizing behavior depending on gender. Failure to identify and intervene with children exposed to violence may result in a lifetime of social, emotional, and vocational difficulties. There is now a beginning understanding that gender and age are important influencing variables regarding a youth's behavioral response to trauma.

Limitations

This descriptive study of CBCL scores in a group of children recently exposed to parental trauma versus a similar group of children not recently exposed to parental trauma had a number of limitations. First, the design lacked random assignment and the small sample limits the findings. Second, all participants in the study lived in the same area, which increased the risk of confounding variables and decreased generalizability. Third, all findings were based on self-reported data from primary caregivers (mothers); it is therefore possible that certain events and experiences were overestimated, underestimated or otherwise distorted through recall or gender influences. Also, the study did not take into account the amount of contact the child had with the parent before the victimization, which may have affected study results. Another limitation is that the sociodemographics of the sample limit the generalizability of the findings because all children in this sample were African American. Finally, there is no historical information regarding the child's primary trauma exposure.

Future Research

Additional research needs to be conducted in other locales, with a larger sample size, greater age range, and other racial backgrounds for results to be more conclusive. Studies need to be developed to examine the long-term effects of this type of perceived trauma and children. Although this study did control for the specific trauma of parental victimization, future research may want to focus on children's responses in relation to the gender of the parent who is victimized, as well as the type of the parents' victimizations (i.e., beating, gunshot, stabbing) and circumstances surrounding the incidents as to the impact on children. Last, the development of empirically based gender-sensitive assessment instruments and interventions that respond to individual gender differences in the expression of symptoms related to trauma are essential (Feiring, Taska, & Lewis, 1999).

References

Achenbach, T. M. (1991). *Manual for the Child Behavior Checklist/4–18 and 1991.* Burlington: University of Vermont.

Apfel, R. J. (1996). "With a little help from my friends I get by": Self-help books and psychotherapy [Essay review]. *Psychiatry, 59,* 309–322.

Berman, S. L., Kurtines, W. M., Silverman, W. K., & Serafini, L. T. (1996). The impact of exposure to crime and violence on urban youth. *American Journal of Orthopsychiatry, 66,* 329–336.

Berton, M. W., & Stabb, S. D. (1996). Exposure to violence and post-traumatic stress disorder in urban adolescents. *Adolescence, 31,* 489–498.

Calvert, W. J. (1999). Integrated literature review on effects of exposure to violence upon adolescents. *ABNF Journal, 10,* 84–96.

Carter, D. B., & Levy, G. D. (1991). Gender schemas and the salience of gender: Individual differences in nonreversal discrimination learning. *Sex Roles, 25,* 555–567.

Cicchetti, D., & Aber, J. L. (1998). Contextualism and developmental psychopathology [Editorial]. *Development and Psychopathology, 10,* 137–141.

Cicchetti, D., & Rogosch, F. A. (1997). The role of self-organization in the promotion of resilience in maltreated children. *Development and Psychopathology, 9,* 797–815.

Cicchetti, D., & Toth, S. L. (1998). The development of depression in children and adolescents. *American Psychologist, 53,* 221–241.

Cohen, J. (1992). A power primer. *Psychological Bulletin, 112,* 155–159.

Cramer, P. (1979). Defense mechanisms in adolescence. *Developmental Psychology, 15,* 477–478.

Dahlberg, L. L., & Potter, L. B. (2001). Youth violence: Developmental pathways and prevention challenges. *American Journal of Preventive Medicine, 20* (Suppl. 1), 3–14.

Dodge, K. A., Lochman, J. E., Harnish, J. D., Bates, J. E., & Pettit, G. S. (1997). Reactive and proactive aggression in school children and psychiatrically impaired chronically assaultive youth. *Journal of Abnormal Psychology, 106,* 37–51.

Dubowitz, H., Black, M. M., Kerr, M. A., Hussey, J. M., Morrel, T. M., Everson, M. D., & Starr, R. H., Jr. (2001). Type and timing of mothers' victimization: Effects on mothers and children. *Pediatrics, 107,* 728–735.

Dulmus, C. N., Ely, G. E., & Wodarski, J. S. (2003). Children's psychological response to parental victimization: How do girls and boys differ? *Journal of Human Behavior in the Social Environment, 7,* 23–36.

Dulmus, C. N., & Wodarski, J. S. (2000). Trauma-related symptomatology among children of parents victimized by urban community violence. *American Journal of Orthopsychiatry, 70,* 272–277.

Ensink, K., Robertson, B. A., Zissis, C., & Leger, P. (1997). Post-traumatic stress disorder in children exposed to violence. *South African Medical Journal, 87,* 1526–1530.

Erikson, E. (Ed.). (1964). *Inner and outer space: Reflections on womanhood.* Boston: Beacon Press.

Eth, S. (2001). *PTSD in children and adolescents: A developmental-interactional model of child abuse.* Washington, DC: American Psychiatric Association.

Farrell, A. D., & Bruce, S. E. (1997). Impact of exposure to community violence on violent behavior and emotional distress among urban adolescents. *Journal of Clinical Child Psychology, 26,* 2–14.

Feiring, C., Taska, L., & Lewis, M. (1999). Age and gender differences in children's and adolescents' adaptation to sexual abuse. *Child Abuse & Neglect, 23,* 115–128.

Figley, C. R. (1995a). Compassion fatigue as secondary traumatic stress disorder: An overview. In R. E. Charles (Ed.), *Compassion fatigue: Coping with secondary traumatic stress disorder in those who treat the traumatized* (pp. 1–20). New York: Brunner/Mazel.

Figley, C. R. (Ed.). (1995b). *Compassion fatigue: Coping with secondary traumatic stress disorder in those who treat the traumatized.* New York: Brunner/Mazel.

Finkelhor, D. (1995). The victimization of children: A developmental perspective. *America Journal of Orthopsychiatry, 65,* 177–193.

Finkelhor, D. (Ed.). (1997). *The victimization of children and youth: Developmental victimology* (Vol. 2). Thousand Oaks, CA: Sage Publications.

Finkelhor, D., & Asdigian, N. L. (1996). Risk factors for youth victimization: Beyond a lifestyles/routine activities theory approach. *Violence Victims, 11,* 3–19.

Fitzpatrick, K. M., & Boldizar, J. P. (1993). The prevalence and consequences of exposure to violence among African-American youth. *Journal of the American Academy of Child & Adolescent Psychiatry, 32,* 424–430.

Ford, J. D., Racusin, R., Ellis, C. G., & Daviss, W. B. (2000). Child maltreatment, other trauma exposure, and posttraumatic symptomatology among children with oppositional defiant and attention deficit hyperactivity disorders. *Child Maltreatment, 5,* 205–217.

Freud, S. (1933). *The psychology of women* (J. Strachey, Trans. Vol. 22). London: Hogarth Press.

Garbarino, J. (1993). Children's response to community violence: What do we know? Irving Harris Symposium on Prevention and Intervention: The effects of violence on infants and young children: International perspectives on prevention (1992, Chicago, Illinois). *Infant Mental Health Journal, 14,* 103–115.

Garbarino, J. (1995a). The American war zone: What children can tell us about living with violence. *Journal of Developmental & Behavioral Pediatrics, 16,* 431–435.

Garbarino, J. (1995b). Growing up in a socially toxic environment: Life for children and families in the 1990s. In B. M. Gary (Ed.), *The individual, the family, and social good: Personal fulfillment in times of change. Nebraska Symposium on Motivation, Vol. 42* (pp. 1–20). Lincoln: University of Nebraska Press.

Glodich, A. (1998). Traumatic exposure to violence: A comprehensive review of the child and adolescent literature. *Smith College Studies in Social Work, 68,* 321–345.

Glodich, A., & Allen, J. G. (1998). Adolescents exposed to violence and abuse: A review of the group therapy literature with an emphasis on preventing trauma reenactment. *Journal of Child & Adolescent Group Therapy, 8,* 135–154.

Gorman-Smith, D., & Tolan, P. (1998). The role of exposure to community violence and development problems among inner-city youth. *Development and Psychopathology, 10,* 101–116.

Gorman-Smith, D., Tolan, P. H., & Henry, D. (1999). The relation of community and family to risk among urban-poor adolescents. In P. Cohen, L. Robins, & C. Slomkowski (Eds.), *Where and when: Influence of historical time and place on aspects of psychopathology* (pp. 349–367). Hillsdale, NJ: Lawrence Erlbaum Associates.

Hien, D., & Bukszpan, C. (1999). Interpersonal violence in a "normal" low-income control group. *Women & Health, 29,* 1–16.

Hodges, E. V., & Perry, D. G. (1999). Personal and interpersonal antecedents and consequences of victimization by peers. *Journal of Personality and Social Psychology, 76,* 677–685.

Keane, T. M., & Kaloupek, D. G. (1997). Comorbid psychiatric disorders in PTSD. Implications for research. *Annals of the New York Academy of Sciences, 821,* 24–34.

Keane, T. M., Taylor, K. L., & Penk, W. E. (1997). Differentiating post-traumatic stress disorder (PTSD) from major depression (MDD) and generalized anxiety disorder (GAD). *Journal of Anxiety Disorders, 11,* 317–328.

Kilpatrick, K. L., & Williams, L. M. (1997). Post-traumatic stress disorder in child witnesses to domestic violence. *American Journal of Orthopsychiatry, 67,* 639–644.

Kliewer, W., Lepore, S. J., Oskin, D., & Johnson, P. D. (1998). The role of social and cognitive processes in children's adjustment to community violence. *Journal of Consulting and Clinical Psychology, 66,* 199–209.

Leadbeater, B. J., Kuperminc, G. P., Blatt, S. J., & Hertzog, C. (1999). A multivariate model of gender differences in adolescents' internalizing and externalizing problems. *Developmental Psychology, 35,* 1268–1282.

Levit, D. B. (1991). Gender differences in ego defenses in adolescence: Sex roles as one way to understand the differences. *Journal of Personality and Social Psychology, 61,* 992–999.

Lorion, R. P., & Saltzman, W. (1993). Children's exposure to community violence: Following a path from concern to research to action. *Psychiatry, 56,* 55–65.

Marans, S., & Adelman, A. (Eds.). (1997). *Experiencing violence in a developmental context.* New York: Guilford Press.

McCloskey, L. A., & Walker, M. (2000). Posttraumatic stress in children exposed to family violence and single-event trauma. *Journal of the American Academy of Child & Adolescent Psychiatry, 39,* 108–115.

Miller, L. S., Wasserman, G. A., Neugebauer, R., Gorman-Smith, D., & Kamboukos, D. (1999). Witnessed community violence and antisocial behavior in high-risk, urban boys. *Journal of Clinical Child Psychology, 28,* 2–11.

Osofsky, J. D. (1995). The effect of exposure to violence on young children. *American Psychologist, 50,* 782–788.

Osofsky, J. D. (1999). The impact of violence on children. *Future of Children, 9,* 33–49.

Peebles-Kleiger, M. J., & Kleiger, J. H. (1994). Reintegration stress for Desert Storm families: Wartime deployments and family trauma. *Journal of Traumatic Stress, 7,* 173–194.

Piaget, J. (1973). The affective unconscious and the cognitive unconscious. *Journal of the American Psychoanalytic Association, 21,* 249–261.

Pynoos, R. S., Goenjian, A., Tashjian, M., Karakashian, M., Manjikian, R., Manoukian, G., Steinberg, A. M., & Fairbanks, L. A. (1993). Post-traumatic stress reactions in children after the 1988 Armenian earthquake. *British Journal of Psychiatry, 163,* 239–247.

Pynoos, R. S., Nader, K., Frederick, C., Gonda, L., & Stuber, M. (1987). Grief reactions in school-age children following a sniper attack at school. *Israel Journal of Psychiatry and Related Sciences, 24,* 53–63.

Raveis, V. H., Siegel, K., & Karus, D. (1999). Children's psychological distress following the death of a parent. *Journal of Youth and Adolescence, 28,* 165–180.

Schwab-Stone, M., Chen, C., Greenberger, E., Silver, D., Lichtman, J., & Voyce, C. (1999). No safe haven. II: The effects of violence exposure on urban youth. *Journal of the American Academy of Child & Adolescent Psychiatry, 38,* 359–367.

Shaw, D. S., Winslow, E. B., Owens, E. B., Vondra, J. I., Cohn, J. F., & Bell, R. Q. (1998). The development of early externalizing problems among children from low-income families: A transformational perspective. *Journal of Abnormal Child Psychology, 26,* 95–107.

Singer, M. I., Anglin, T. M., Song, L. Y., & Lunghofer, L. (1995). Adolescents' exposure to violence and associated symptoms of psychological trauma. *JAMA, 273,* 477–482.

Song, L. Y., Singer, M. I., & Anglin, T. M. (1998). Violence exposure and emotional trauma as contributors to adolescents' violent behaviors. *Archive of Pediatric & Adolescent Medicine, 152,* 531–536.

Terr, L. C. (1979). Children of Chowchilla: A study of psychic trauma. *Psychoanalytical Study of Children, 34,* 547–623.

Terr, L. C. (1981). Psychic trauma in children: Observations following the Chowchilla school-bus kidnapping. *American Journal of Psychiatry, 138,* 14–19.

Trickett, P. K., & Schellenbach, C. J. (1998). *Violence against children in the family and the community.* Washington, DC: American Psychological Association.

About the authors: *Catherine N. Dulmus,* Ph.D., LCSW, ACSW, is associate professor and director, Buffalo Center for Social Research, University at Buffalo, 221 Parker Hall, Buffalo, NY 14214 (E-mail: cdulmus@buffalo.edu). *Carolyn Hilarski,* PhD, LCSW, ACSW, is associate professor, Social Work Department, Buffalo State College, New York.

Exercise for Article 21

Factual Questions

1. What is the explicitly stated research question?

2. What percentage of the parents approached who met the criteria provided contact information?

3. Who offered names of children who might serve in the control group?

4. Did the children in the exposure group witness the parents' victimization?

5. Were all the children in daily contact with their parents before the victimizing event?

6. Did the "9- to 12-year olds" *or* the "6- to 8-year olds" have higher internalizing scores on the CBCL?

Questions for Discussion

7. Is it important to know that review board approval to conduct this research was obtained? Explain. (See lines 150–152.)

8. The researchers state that they used a "convenience sample." Is it important to know this? Explain. (See lines 182–195.)

9. What is your opinion on the advisability of paying individuals for participation in research? (See lines 229–231.)

10. In your opinion, do the researchers make the meanings of the term "internalizing" and "externalizing" behavior clear? (See lines 238–241 and 264–284.)

11. In your opinion, does the use of a control group make this study an "experiment"? Explain.

12. The researchers state this limitation: "…the study did not take into account the amount of contact the child had with the parent before the victimization, which may have affected study results." How important is this limitation? (See lines 395–398.)

Quality Ratings

Directions: Indicate your level of agreement with each of the following statements by circling a number from 5 for strongly agree (SA) to 1 for strongly disagree (SD). If you believe an item is not applicable to this research article, leave it blank. Be prepared to explain your ratings. When responding to criteria A and B below, keep in mind that brief titles and abstracts are conventional in published research.

A. The title of the article is appropriate.

SA   5   4   3   2   1   SD

B. The abstract provides an effective overview of the research article.

SA   5   4   3   2   1   SD

C. The introduction establishes the importance of the study.

SA   5   4   3   2   1   SD

D. The literature review establishes the context for the study.

SA   5   4   3   2   1   SD

E. The research purpose, question, or hypothesis is clearly stated.

SA   5   4   3   2   1   SD

F. The method of sampling is sound.

SA   5   4   3   2   1   SD

G. Relevant demographics (for example, age, gender, and ethnicity) are described.

SA   5   4   3   2   1   SD

H. Measurement procedures are adequate.

SA   5   4   3   2   1   SD

I. All procedures have been described in sufficient detail to permit a replication of the study.

SA   5   4   3   2   1   SD

J. The participants have been adequately protected from potential harm.

SA   5   4   3   2   1   SD

K. The results are clearly described.

SA   5   4   3   2   1   SD

L. The discussion/conclusion is appropriate.

SA   5   4   3   2   1   SD

M. Despite any flaws, the report is worthy of publication.

SA   5   4   3   2   1   SD

Article 22

Drug Use Patterns Among High School Athletes and Nonathletes

ADAM H. NAYLOR
Boston University

DOUG GARDNER
ThinkSport® Consulting Services

LEN ZAICHKOWSKY
Boston University

ABSTRACT. This study examined drug use patterns and perceptions of drug intervention programs among adolescent interscholastic athletes and nonathletes. In particular, it explored the issue of whether participation in high school athletics is related to a healthier lifestyle and decreased use of recreational drugs and ergogenic aids. One thousand five hundred fifteen Massachusetts high school students completed a 150-item survey that assessed illicit and nonillicit substance use. Chi-square analyses revealed that athletes were significantly less likely to use cocaine and psychedelics, and were less likely to smoke cigarettes, compared with nonathletes. Conversely, nonathletes were less likely to use creatine than were athletes. There was no difference in the use of anabolic steroids and androstenedione between athletes and nonathletes. Descriptive analyses appear to indicate that drug interventions for athletes are falling short of their objectives. This study suggests that athletes have a healthier lifestyle and that the efficacy of intervention programs must be further examined.

From *Adolescence, 36*, 627–639. Copyright © 2001 by Libra Publishers, Inc. Reprinted with permission.

Drug use by athletes has made newspaper headlines, sport governing body rulebooks, and doctors' waiting rooms on a regular basis. Despite this, the relationship between drug use and participation in athletics
5 is not yet a clear one. On one hand, it has been suggested that participation in athletics leads to a healthier lifestyle and wiser decisions about substance use (Anderson, Albrecht, McKeag, Hough, & McGrew, 1991; Shephard, 2000; Shields, 1995). Conversely,
10 others have suggested that drug use is inherent in sports and its culture (Dyment, 1987; Wadler & Hainline, 1989). In between these two perspectives, one is left wondering if there is any difference in the substance use patterns of athletes and the general public (Adams,
15 1992; Anshel, 1998).

One way to begin clarifying this issue is to differentiate between recreational substances and ergogenic aids. Recreational substances are typically used for intrinsic motivates, such as to achieve altered affective
20 states. Examples of such drugs are alcohol, tobacco, marijuana, psychedelics, and cocaine. Ergogenic substances are used to augment performance in a given domain. In sports, such drugs are typically used to assist athletes in performing with more speed and
25 strength, and to endure more pain than normal. Examples of ergogenic aids are creatine, androstenedione, anabolic steroids, major pain medication, barbiturates, and amphetamines. The categorization of specific substances is debatable in some cases (Adams, 1992). For
30 instance, although marijuana is traditionally viewed as a recreational substance, it recently has been banned by the International Olympic Committee for its performance-enhancing potential (i.e., lowering of physiological arousal) (H. Davis, personal communication, Octo-
35 ber 4, 1999). Similarly, amphetamines have been used for recreational purposes. Nevertheless, the attempt to label substances as either recreational or ergogenic assists in clarifying differences between athletes and nonathletes in their drug use patterns.

Recreational Drugs

40 It has been traditionally believed that participation in athletics leads to a healthier lifestyle and less use of recreational drugs. Increased physical activity not only creates a physically healthier person, but also may lead to changes in overall lifestyle, highlighted by "a pru-
45 dent diet and abstinence from cigarette smoking" (Shephard, 2000). Some research has supported the popular notion that substance use is negatively correlated with healthful activities. In the university setting, athletes have self-reported less alcohol and drug use
50 than their peers (Anderson et al., 1991), providing further evidence that the high-level physical and mental demands of sports are incompatible with recreational drug use. Shields (1995) indicated that high school athletic directors perceived that students who partici-
55 pated in athletics were less likely to smoke cigarettes, consume alcohol, chew tobacco, and smoke marijuana than were students who did not participate in extracurricular athletic activities. These findings, while encouraging, ought to be verified through confidential self-
60 reports of high school students themselves. Nonetheless, these findings offer support for the notion that participation in sports promotes health and wellness.

Conversely, Wadler and Hainline (1989) have suggested that athletes may be more likely to experiment
65 with recreational and ergogenic aids than individuals

not participating in athletics. Physically, athletes might use recreational drugs to cope with the pain of injury rehabilitation. Mentally, stress (arising from the competitive demands of sports) and low self-confidence are issues that might lead athletes to recreational drug use. Furthermore, the "culture" of the particular sport might socialize athletes into drug use (e.g., baseball and smokeless tobacco) (Anshel, 1998). However, there is little evidence to suggest that recreational drug use is higher for athletes than nonathletes.

Ergogenic Aids

Unlike recreational substances, use of ergogenic aids is more likely in competitive athletic settings (Dyment, 1987). Wadler and Hainline (1989) have pointed out five instances that might lead athletes to utilize performance-enhancing pharmacological aids: (1) athletes who are at risk for not making a team or achieving the level of performance they desire; (2) athletes who are approaching the end of their career and are striving to continue to compete in their sport; (3) athletes who have weight problems and are seeking a means to increase or decrease weight; (4) athletes who are battling injuries and are trying to find ways to heal quicker; and (5) athletes who feel external pressure, such as from teammates, coaches, and parents, to use performance-enhancing drugs. Little research has contradicted the notion that those participating in sports are more disposed to use ergogenic aids. However, the findings of Anderson and colleagues (1991) did not support the notion that there is an anabolic steroid epidemic in collegiate athletics. Although their study did not examine whether athletes more frequently use anabolic steroids than do nonathletes, Anderson et al. concluded that steroid use by intercollegiate athletes did not increase over a four-year span. However, the prevalence of ergogenic aids a decade later has multiplied, with the advent of over-the-counter supplements (Hendrickson & Burton, 2000).

Educational Interventions

While the relationship between drug use and participation in organized athletics is still unclear, few disagree that early identification of, and education about, drug use is necessary. Andrews and Duncan (1998) have noted that cigarette smoking that begins during adolescence proceeds to more frequent use in the two years following high school. Furthermore, onset of drug use has been found to be a major determinant of adolescent morbidity and failure to perform age-related social roles (Grant & Dawson, 1998). In light of these facts, identification of substance use patterns during the high school years is important for preventing and curbing at-risk behaviors that might arise later in an individual's life.

Sports organizations have made it their mission to deter substance use by athletes. In 1986, the National Collegiate Athletic Association implemented a national drug education and drug-testing program for its member institutions (Anderson et al., 1991). Other organizations at various levels of sports have also adopted programs to monitor and police drug use behaviors in athletes (Shields, 1995). The Massachusetts Interscholastic Athletic Association (MIAA) has initiated one such program for high school athletic programs in the state (Massachusetts Interscholastic Athletic Association, 1999). The cornerstone of this intervention is the MIAA Chemical Health Eligibility Rule.

During the season of practice or play, a student shall not, regardless of the quantity, use or consume, possess, buy/sell or give away any beverage containing alcohol; any tobacco product; marijuana; steroids; or any controlled substance.... The penalty for the first violation is that a student shall lose eligibility for the next two (2) consecutive interscholastic events or two (2) weeks of a season in which the student is a participant, whichever is greater. If a second or subsequent violation occurs, the student shall lose eligibility for the next twelve (12) consecutive interscholastic events or twelve (12) consecutive weeks, whichever is greater, in which the student is a participant.

It is the desire of the MIAA that this rule will not only be effective during the athletic season, but lead to an overall healthier lifestyle. High school coaches and athletic directors are responsible for implementing this rule and levying punishments as infractions occur. Adams (1992) found that students favored the eligibility rule and would like to see it strictly enforced. Furthermore, student athletes supported the notion of mandatory/random drug testing in high school athletics. Although drug intervention programs have been supported by both administrators and athletes, their efficacy must still be determined.

Purpose of the Present Study

The purpose of this study was to examine the incidence of drug use by interscholastic high school athletes, and to see if participation in interscholastic athletics is related to a healthier lifestyle, and specifically decreased use of recreational drugs and ergogenic aids year-round. Exploring possible differences in drug use patterns between athletes and nonathletes was a central element. This study sought to replicate previous high school drug use and abuse surveys conducted in the state of Massachusetts (Adams, 1992; Gardner & Zaichkowsky, 1995).

Besides the desire to update the findings on substance use habits since 1991, two other issues motivated this research. First, drug use by athletes has received a great deal of media attention. For example, the supplement androstenedione came to wide public attention during the baseball season in which Mark McGwire broke the home run record. Second, the governing bodies of state high school athletics have instituted wellness programs, drug education, and specific rules to prevent drug use. This study examined descriptive data relating to the effectiveness of these rules and programs.

Method

Participants

One thousand five hundred fifteen students, representing 15 high schools within the state of Massachusetts, were surveyed. Male students represented 51% of the sample ($n = 773$), while female students accounted for 49% ($n = 742$). Thirty-five percent were freshmen, 24.6% were sophomores, 23.4% were juniors, and 17% were in their senior year of high school. Seventy-four percent reported they had participated in one or more formally sanctioned interscholastic sports within the past 12 months.

The 150-item questionnaire used in this study was based on previous studies that have examined drug use patterns among high school students and student athletes (Adams, 1992; Anderson & McKeag, 1985; Johnston, O'Malley, & Bachman, 1999; Gardner & Zaichkowsky, 1995; Zaichkowsky, 1987). It included questions about students' drug use within the past 12 months, and made "nonuse" as stringent a classification as possible. Consistent with previous studies, both recreational and ergogenic substance use was self-reported. Recreational substances included alcohol, cigarettes, smokeless tobacco, marijuana, cocaine, and psychedelic drugs. Ergogenic aids included major pain medications, anabolic steroids, barbiturates, amphetamines, androstenedione, and creatine. A final section of the questionnaire asked students to address the effectiveness of the Massachusetts Interscholastic Athletic Association's substance use rules and educational interventions.

Table 1
Drug Use Patterns Among High School Athletes and Nonathletes

	Athletes (%)	Nonathletes (%)	Total (%)
Alcohol	68.8	68.4	68.7
Cigarettes**	36.1	44.0	38.4
Smokeless tobacco	8.0	7.7	7.9
Marijuana	37.5	42.9	39.1
Cocaine**	3.1	7.2	4.3
Psychedelics***	9.8	18.1	12.3
Creatine**	10.4	4.4	8.6
Androstenedione	2.3	2.1	2.2
Anabolic steroids	2.5	3.4	2.8
Pain medication	29.3	31.9	30.1
Barbiturates	3.7	6.1	4.4
Amphetamines	6.8	9.6	7.6

**Significant difference between athletes and nonathletes at the .01 level.
***Significant difference between athletes and nonathletes at the .001 level.

Procedure

Permission to conduct the study was obtained from the principals of 15 randomly selected public high schools in Massachusetts. Each principal agreed to allow between 100 and 180 students to participate in the study, and assigned a school athletic director or wellness coordinator to be the primary contact person for the researchers.

Each contact person was asked to select students who were representative of the school's gender, ethnic, and athletic demographics to participate in the study. Students were categorized as athletes if they participated on any state-sanctioned interscholastic athletic team. Upon creating the sample, the principal investigator and each school's contact person selected a class period and date in which to administer the questionnaire.

The principal investigator and two research assistants visited the 15 schools over a period of a month and a half. Students were administered the questionnaire in the school auditorium or cafeteria. They were assured that they would remain anonymous, that their responses would be viewed only by researchers, and that all information would be kept confidential. The questionnaire took approximately 30 minutes to complete.

Data Analysis

The frequencies of all variables were calculated. Descriptive statistics and chi-square analyses were conducted using the Statistical Package for the Social Sciences (SPSS).

Results

Athlete/Nonathlete Differences

Chi-square analyses indicated statistically significant differences between athletes and nonathletes in reported use of 4 of the 12 substances (see Table 1). In terms of recreational drugs, significantly more nonathletes than interscholastic athletes have smoked cigarettes, $\chi^2(1, N = 520) = 7.455, p < .01$. Nonathletes also reported using cocaine, $\chi^2(1, N = 59) = 11.491, p < .01$, and psychedelics, $\chi^2(1, N = 171) = 18.382, p < .001$, with greater frequency. One ergogenic aid, creatine, was used significantly more by athletes than nonathletes, $\chi^2(1, N = 115) = 7.455, p < .01$. Athletes were less likely to use marijuana, amphetamines, and barbiturates than were nonathletes, although the differences fell just short of being statistically significant.

Interscholastic Drug Intervention Feedback

The Massachusetts Interscholastic Athletic Association's Chemical Health Eligibility Rule seeks to discourage the use of recreational and ergogenic substances by high school athletes. Sixty-eight percent of the student athletes were aware of this rule (see Table 2). Thirty-eight percent reported having violated the rule; only 12% of these student athletes reported having been punished by school officials. Thirteen percent of those caught breaking the rule said they had not been punished. Seventy-one percent believed that some of their teammates had violated the Chemical Health Eligibility Rule.

Not only does the MIAA set drug use rules for student athletes, but it also seeks to implement intervention programs. Fifty-seven percent of the athletes stated that their coaches further this mission by discussing the issue of drug use and abuse. Thirty-one percent of the athletes expressed interest in drug education programs provided by the athletic department, while 48% stated that they would submit to random drug testing.

Table 2
Interscholastic Athletes' Perceptions of Drug Intervention Effectiveness

Topic	Yes	No
Do you know the Chemical Health Eligibility Rule?	68%	32%
Have you violated this rule during the season?	38%	62%
Have you received a penalty if you violated this rule?	12%	88%
Have you been caught and not been penalized?	13%	87%
Have any of your teammates violated this rule?	71%	29%
Does your coach discuss the issue of drugs?	57%	43%
Would you submit to voluntary random drug testing?	48%	52%
Are you interested in drug prevention programs from the athletic department?	31%	69%

Discussion

270   The results of this study appear to reflect current trends in substance use by high school students when compared with national averages (see Johnston et al., 1999). One encouraging finding was that cigarette smoking in Massachusetts was lower than national
275 averages. Roughly 38% of the students surveyed here reported smoking at least one cigarette as compared with the lowest estimate of 51% of the adolescents surveyed by the National Institute on Drug Abuse (Johnston et al., 1999). Massachusetts has engaged in
280 an aggressive anti-tobacco campaign over the last decade, which might account for this finding.

Previous research suggests three possible reasons for adolescent drug use: experimentation, social learning, and body image concerns (Anshel, 1998; Collins,
285 2000). Experimentation with drugs has been associated with boredom and is often supported by adolescents' belief that they are impervious to the harmful side effects of dangerous substances. Social learning theory states that individuals will take their drug use cues
290 from others in the environment. Modeling of parents' and friends' behavior is a prime example of social learning. Last, individuals have been found to use certain drugs to improve their appearance.

Recreational Substances

It has been suggested that recreational drug use
295 does not differ for athletes and nonathletes (Adams, 1992; Anshel, 1998; Dyment, 1987; Wadler & Hainline, 1989). The results of the present study were mixed in regard to student athlete and nonathlete substance use differences. There were no significant dif-

300 ferences for three of the six recreational drugs: alcohol, marijuana, and smokeless tobacco.

It is clear that alcohol use is socially accepted (Bailey & Rachal, 1993; Bush & Iannotti, 1992; Reifman et al., 1998), which might explain the high percentage of
305 students who consumed alcohol and the lack of difference in alcohol use between athletes and nonathletes. Further, the media provide opportunities for high school students to model the drinking behaviors of their professional and collegiate counterparts (Collins,
310 2000). Although the peer group influences the use of most substances, the culture of sports has also promoted alcohol use.

Slightly over 37% of the athletes reported smoking marijuana in the last year as opposed to about 43% of
315 the nonathletes. This is similar to the pattern for cigarette smoking, although the difference between athletes and nonathletes for marijuana was not significant ($p <$ .052). Even though marijuana and cigarettes are two different types of drugs, it seems that the athletes were
320 more aware of the negative impact smoking any kind of substance has on athletic performance.

Conversely, the lack of conclusive difference in marijuana use may reflect the availability of marijuana, the rising social acceptability of the drug, and the de-
325 sire to experiment (Johnston et al., 1999). In addition, athletes might not perceive marijuana as being as harmful as cocaine or psychedelics, and therefore may be more inclined to try the perceived lesser of two evils.

330   Marijuana has often been labeled a "gateway" drug to more addictive substances (Bush & Iannotti, 1992), yet the present study does not support this contention. Perhaps participation in athletics acts as a barrier to the use of more addictive substances. The significantly
335 lower use of cocaine and psychedelics by athletes can possibly be explained by the commitment necessary to participate in high school athletics. Seasons are year-round for some athletes, and others may be multisports athletes. After-school practices and weekend competi-
340 tions leave student athletes with less time for drug use/experimentation and less time to recover. Thus, organized athletics might reduce the desire of youth to indulge in more addictive and socially unacceptable drugs.

Ergogenic Aids

345   There was no significant difference between athletes and nonathletes for most ergogenic aids (anabolic steroids, androstenedione, pain medication, barbiturates, and amphetamines), which is a positive finding. This suggests that the culture of high school athletics in
350 Massachusetts does not encourage widespread use of these illicit substances. However, it should be noted that the lack of differences might reflect body image issues, specifically in regard to nonathletes who take steroids. Steroids increase an individual's muscle mass,
355 thus increasing self-confidence (Anshel, 1998). Addi-

tionally, muscle-building substances provide the opportunity for individuals to live up to societal standards for physical appearance. Similarly, amphetamines may be used to lose weight and help an individual achieve the 360 "ideal" figure. These substances may not necessarily be utilized to improve athletic performance, but rather to help students improve their body image (Anshel, 1998).

The lack of differences for most of the ergogenic 365 aids might further be explained by the skill level of the typical high school athlete. Wadler and Hainline (1989) have pointed out that few adolescents compete at "elite" levels. In light of this fact, there is little need for illicit performance-enhancing substances in the average 370 high school athlete's competitive endeavors. As the competitive demands get greater and the opposition tougher, one might expect the usage levels of ergogenic aids to increase (Wadler & Hainline, 1989).

The sole difference in the use of ergogenic aids by 375 athletes and nonathletes was for creatine, a nutritional supplement. High school athletes were more than twice as likely to use creatine than were nonathletes. The legality and availability of creatine are perhaps the greatest reasons for the higher level of use among ath-380 letes, who are likely trying to gain a competitive edge (Dyment, 1987).

Intervention

Can the differences in illicit drug use behaviors between student athletes and nonathletes be explained by interscholastic chemical health programs? While it 385 would appear that the eligibility rule has helped in policing the substance use of interscholastic athletes, many are still unaware of this rule or ignore it. Seventy-one percent of the athletes reported that teammates have violated the Chemical Health Eligibility 390 Rule. Furthermore, almost 40% of the athletes admitted to having broken this rule, with 13% having not been penalized after being caught. These figures bring the effectiveness of the rule and its enforcement into question. Only 57% reported that their coaches addressed 395 the issue of substance use and abuse, which indicates that this is an educational opportunity that needs to be strengthened.

Educating this population is not an easy feat. A majority of the students were not interested in any further 400 drug interventions. Over half said they would not submit to voluntary random drug testing, and 69% were not interested in drug prevention programs provided by their athletic departments. These findings indicate a change in student attitudes over the last decade. Adams 405 (1992) found that a majority of student athletes were receptive to the idea of random drug testing and additional substance abuse programming through their athletic departments. One reason for the change might be that students have been saturated with drug education. 410 Alternatively, the fact that athletes generally used fewer illicit substances than nonathletes might suggest

that athletes felt they had already acquired healthful behaviors. Furthermore, recent studies have suggested that drug education programming needs to begin early 415 (Faigenbaum, Zaichkowsky, Gardner, & Micheli, 1998), and interventions aimed at high school athletes might be too late for high success rates.

Conclusion

Despite this study's large sample size, one must be cautious regarding generalization of the findings. The 420 high school and sports cultures examined here might only be representative of Massachusetts or the northeastern United States. Because the social circumstances of adolescents and their athletic participation greatly influence their substance use behaviors, more must be 425 done to understand the social climate of high school athletics.

Nevertheless, the present study suggests that participation in athletics is related to a healthier lifestyle. It also reveals that marijuana and alcohol are the two 430 primary substances where more education and intervention are necessary. Furthermore, this study suggests that coaches and administrators must assess the efficacy of their drug prevention programs and their efforts to enforce rules and regulations.

435 Athletic activities provide many opportunities to promote healthful behaviors. Therefore, sports organizations ought to assess the needs of their athletes and provide effective interventions in a timely manner.

References

Adams, C. L. (1992). *Substance use of Massachusetts high school student athletes.* Unpublished doctoral dissertation, Boston University.

Anderson, W. A., Albrecht, R. R., McKeag, D. B., Hough, D. O., & McGrew, C. A. (1991). A national survey of alcohol and drug use by college athletes. *The Physician and Sportsmedicine, 19,* 91–104.

Anderson, W. A., & McKeag, D. B. (1985). *The substance use and abuse habits of college student athletes* (Report No. 2). Mission, KS: The National Collegiate Athletic Association.

Andrews, J. A., & Duncan, S. C. (1998). The effect of attitude on the development of adolescent cigarette use. *Journal of Substance Abuse, 10,* 1–7.

Anshel, M. H. (1998). Drug abuse in sports: Causes and cures. In J. M. Williams (Ed.), *Applied sport psychology: Personal growth to peak performance* (pp. 372–387). Mountain View, CA: Mayfield Publishing Company.

Bailey, S. L., & Rachal, J. V. (1993). Dimensions of adolescent problem drinking. *Journal of Studies on Alcohol, 54,* 555–565.

Bush, P. J., & Iannotti, R. J. (1992). Elementary schoolchildren's use of alcohol, cigarettes, and marijuana and classmates' attribution of socialization. *Drug and Alcohol Dependence, 30,* 275–287.

Collins, G. B. (2000). Substance abuse and athletes. In D. Begel & R. W. Burton: (Eds.), *Sport psychiatry.* New York: W. W. Norton & Company.

Dyment, P. G. (1987). The adolescent athlete and ergogenic aids. *Journal of Adolescent Health Care, 8,* 68–73.

Faigenbaum, A. D., Zaichkowsky, L. D., Gardner, D. E., & Micheli, L. J. (1998). Anabolic steroid use by male and female middle school students. *Pediatrics, 101,* p. e6.

Gardner, D. E., & Zaichkowsky, L. (1995). *Substance use patterns in Massachusetts high school athletes and nonathletes.* Unpublished manuscript.

Grant, B. F., & Dawson, D. A. (1998). Age of onset of drug use and its association with DSM-IV drug abuse and dependence: Results from the National Longitudinal Alcohol Epidemiologic Survey. *Journal of Substance Abuse, 10,* 163–173.

Hendrickson, T. P., & Burton, R. W. (2000). Athletes' use of performance-enhancing drugs. In D. Begel & R. W. Burton (Eds.), *Sport psychiatry.* New York: W. W. Norton & Company.

Johnston, L. D., O'Malley, P. M., & Bachman, J. G. (1999). *National survey results on drug use from the Monitoring the Future study, 1975–1998: Volume I. Secondary school students* (NIH Publication No. 99–4660). Rockville, MD: National Institute on Drug Abuse.

Massachusetts Interscholastic Athletic Association. (1999). *Massachusetts Interscholastic Athletic Association wellness manual.* Milford, Massachusetts.

Mayer, R. R., Forster, J. L., Murray, D. M., & Wagenaar, A. C. (1998). Social settings and situations of underage drinking. *Journal of Studies on Alcohol, 59,* 207–215.

Nurco, D. N. (1985). A discussion of validity. In B. A. Rouse, N. J. Kozel, & L. G. Richards (Eds.), *Self-report methods of estimating drug use: Meeting current challenges to validity* (NIDA Research Monograph No. 57, DHHS Publication No. ADM 85–1402). Washington, DC: U.S. Government Printing Office.

Reifman, A., Barnes, G. M., Dintscheff, B. A., Farrell, M. P., & Uhteg, L. (1998). Parental and peer influences on the onset of heavier drinking among adolescents. *Journal of Studies on Alcohol, 59,* 311–317.

Shephard, R. J. (2000). Importance of sport and exercise to quality of life and longevity. In L. Zaichkowsky & D. Mostofsky (Eds.), *Medical and psychological aspects of sport and exercise.* Morgantown, WV: FIT.

Shields, E. W., Jr. (1995). Sociodemographic analysis of drug use among adolescent athletes: Observations–perceptions of athletic directors–coaches. *Adolescence, 30,* 849–861.

Wadler, G. I., & Hainline, B. (1989). *Drugs and the athlete.* Philadelphia: F. A. Davis Company.

Zaichkowsky, L. (1987). *Drug use patterns in Massachusetts high school athletes and nonathletes.* Unpublished manuscript.

Acknowledgments: The researchers would like to thank the Massachusetts Governor's Committee on Physical Fitness and Sports for the grant that supported this study, and Bill Gaine and the Massachusetts Interscholastic Athletic Association for their assistance and support.

Address correspondence to: Adam H. Naylor, School of Education, Boston University, 605 Commonwealth Avenue, Boston, Massachusetts 02215. E-mail: adamnaylor@juno.com

Exercise for Article 22

Factual Questions

1. Barbiturates are classified as
   A. a recreational drug.   B. an ergogenic drug.

2. According to a study reported in the literature review, do student athletes support the notion of mandatory/random drug testing in high school athletics?

3. Male students represented what percentage of the sample?

4. Permission to conduct the study was obtained from whom?

5. What percentage of the athletes reported using cocaine? What percentage of nonathletes reported using cocaine?

6. Was the difference between the two percentages in your answer to question 5 statistically significant? If yes, at what probability level?

7. What percentage of the student athletes reported that their coaches discussed the issue of drugs?

8. Which drug often has been labeled a "gateway" drug?

Questions for Discussion

9. In this study, a relatively large number of schools (15) was represented. To what extent does this increase your confidence in the results? Explain. (See lines 178–180.)

10. The students were asked to report on their drug use during the past 12 months. Do you think that this is an appropriate time interval? Explain. (See lines 193–195.)

11. The contact person at each school was asked to select students who were representative of the school's gender, ethnic, and athletic demographics to participate in the study. In your opinion, was this a good way to select the sample? (See lines 214–216.)

12. The students were assured that they would remain anonymous, that their responses would be viewed only by researchers, and that all information would be kept confidential. In your opinion, how important were these assurances? Do you think that some students might still deny their illicit drug use even though they were given these assurances? Explain. (See lines 226–229.)

13. The researchers mention the northeastern United States as an area to which these results "might only be representative." Do you agree? Explain. (See lines 419–422.)

14. The researchers state that "the present study suggests that participation in athletics is related to a healthier lifestyle." Do you agree? Do you also think that this study provides evidence that participation in athletics *causes* a reduction in students' substance use? Explain. (See lines 427–428.)

Quality Ratings

Directions: Indicate your level of agreement with each of the following statements by circling a number from 5 for strongly agree (SA) to 1 for strongly disagree (SD). If you believe an item is not applicable to this research article, leave it blank. Be prepared to explain your ratings. When responding to criteria A and B below, keep in mind that brief titles and abstracts are conventional in published research.

A.   The title of the article is appropriate.
            SA   5   4   3   2   1   SD

B. The abstract provides an effective overview of the research article.

    SA   5   4   3   2   1   SD

C. The introduction establishes the importance of the study.

    SA   5   4   3   2   1   SD

D. The literature review establishes the context for the study.

    SA   5   4   3   2   1   SD

E. The research purpose, question, or hypothesis is clearly stated.

    SA   5   4   3   2   1   SD

F. The method of sampling is sound.

    SA   5   4   3   2   1   SD

G. Relevant demographics (for example, age, gender, and ethnicity) are described.

    SA   5   4   3   2   1   SD

H. Measurement procedures are adequate.

    SA   5   4   3   2   1   SD

I. All procedures have been described in sufficient detail to permit a replication of the study.

    SA   5   4   3   2   1   SD

J. The participants have been adequately protected from potential harm.

    SA   5   4   3   2   1   SD

K. The results are clearly described.

    SA   5   4   3   2   1   SD

L. The discussion/conclusion is appropriate.

    SA   5   4   3   2   1   SD

M. Despite any flaws, the report is worthy of publication.

    SA   5   4   3   2   1   SD

Article 23

Age Effects in Earwitness Recall of a Novel Conversation

JONATHAN LING
University of Teesside, UK

ALLISON COOMBE
University of Teesside, UK

ABSTRACT. Recall of conversation is an important part of memory for events. Previous studies have focused predominantly on adults. In the present study, 195 participants ages 11 to 63 years listened to a novel audiotaped conversation. They were not informed they would later have to recall elements of this conversation. Recall was a week later. There were no age-related differences in the recall of children ages 11, 13, and 15; however, there was a difference between retention over 7 days of children and adults, with adults recalling more information correctly. No sex differences were observed. These results are evaluated in the context of research on eye and earwitness recall and suggestions for research are given.

From *Perceptual and Motor Skills*, *100*, 774–776. Copyright © 2005 by Perceptual and Motor Skills. Reprinted with permission.

Most investigations of earwitness testimony have focused on identification (Roebuck & Wilding, 1993) rather than recall, although recall of conversation does appear to be a particularly poor aspect of memory
5 (Huss & Weaver, 1996). Researchers have yet to clarify whether there is a relationship between age and earwitness performance, as there may be confounds with other variables like knowledge (Chi, 1983). In a study of children ages 8, 11, and 15 yr., Saywitz (1987)
10 found few differences between 11- and 15-year-olds, which may be indicative of a plateau in auditory recall from mid to late childhood. It is unclear whether this plateau persists into adulthood.

The aim of this investigation was to compare the
15 recall of children and adults for a conversation heard as bystanders. No direct comparison has been made, so it is unclear how or whether earwitness recall changes across age groups. To control for knowledge, we presented information to participants about which they
20 would have little knowledge, daily life in rural Angola.

Method

Participants

A sample of 195 participants, including 95 females, was recruited. There were 93 children ages 11 to 16 years. Thirty-five were ages 11 to 12 ($M = 11.5$), 32 ages from 13 to 14 ($M = 13.4$), and 26 ages from 15 to
25 16 ($M = 15.6$). There were 98 adults ages 20 to 63 years. Adults were divided into four age groups: 20–29 yr. (45 participants; $M = 23.6$), 30–39 yr. (18 participants; $M = 34.5$), 40–49 (17 participants; $M = 44.7$), and 50–59 (18 participants; $M = 54.8$). Children came
30 from one school; adults were recruited from social clubs.

Materials

A 12-min. audiotape of a conversation between two females was produced. This contained information about one female's experiences in Angola, including
35 information about the weather, the guerilla war, and everyday life in the country.

Recall was assessed by questionnaire, which was checked by teachers from the participating school to ensure comprehension. The questionnaire had 17 ques-
40 tions that related to characteristics of Angola (e.g., "What was a katanger?").

Procedure

Children listened to the tape in class; adults listened in quiet areas of the clubs. Participants were not informed they had to recall the conversation; as a cover,
45 adults rated the age-appropriateness of the conversation. A week later, they were read a set of instructions before completion of a questionnaire. There was no time limit. Participants were thanked and fully debriefed.

Results and Discussion

50 No age group had a high mean, and no group scored higher than 10 out of a maximum of 17. Analysis of variance ($F_{6,190} = 47.01$, $p < .001$) indicated an age effect. Post hoc tests indicated that children of all ages differed from all age groups of adults (Tukey
55 HSD, all $p < .01$), with children performing more poorly (see Table 1).

There was no sex difference ($F_{1,190} = .330$, $p > .05$) or interaction between sex and age ($F_{6,190} = .665$, $p > .05$).

60 Overall, recall of conversation after a 1-wk. delay was poor, with no group exceeding 60% correct. Although recall was generally inaccurate, adults showed no age group differences in performance, unlike those in recognition observed by Bull and Clifford (1984).
65 The findings that children did not show good recall for

124

Table 1
Mean Proportion Correct and Raw Scores

Age (yr.)	n	Proportion correct	M	SD
11	35	.23	3.94	2.22
13	32	.24	4.00	2.22
15	26	.22	3.68	1.74
20–29	45	.51	8.69	2.05
30–39	18	.55	9.39	1.65
40–49	17	.51	8.59	1.87
50+	18	.53	9.06	2.04
Overall	191	.38	6.39	3.20

the content of the conversation and the absence of age differences in recall by children of different ages replicate those of other researchers. Such results indicate children and adults appear to have particular difficulty
70 in remembering conversations.

This study highlights that children's recall of conversation may be less reliable than adults', at least when recall occurs some time after the event. However, the reported age differences may be related to the way
75 children were questioned—with a questionnaire—unlike the more supportive methods employed by police and social workers. Although other research using interviews has also shown that children do not have good recall for conversations (Saywitz, 1987), re-
80 searchers should explore whether such supportive methods may reduce age differences.

References

Bull, R., & Clifford, B. R. (1984). Earwitness testimony. *Medicine, Science, and the Law, 39*, 120–127.

Chi, M. T. H. (Ed.) (1983). *Trends in memory development*. Basel: Karger.

Huss, M. T., & Weaver, K. A. (1996). Effect of modality in earwitness identification: Memory for verbal and nonverbal auditory stimuli presented in two contexts. *The Journal of General Psychology, 123*, 277–287.

Roebuck, R., & Wilding, J. (1993). Effects of vowel variety and sample length on identification of a speaker in a line-up. *Applied Cognitive Psychology, 7*, 475–481.

Saywitz, K. J. (1987). Children's testimony: Age-related patterns of memory errors. In S. J. Ceci, M. P. Toglia, & D. F. Ross (Eds.), *Children's eyewitness memory*. New York: Springer-Verlag. Pp. 36–52.

Address correspondence to: Dr. Jonathan Ling, School of Psychology, Keele University, Keele, Staffs ST5 5BG, UK. E-mail: j.r.ling@psy.keele.ac.uk

Exercise for Article 23

Factual Questions

1. The children who participated came from how many schools?

2. The adults were recruited from what?

3. Was the analysis of variance for the age effect statistically significant? Explain.

4. Was there a statistically significant sex difference? Explain.

5. Did the researchers regard the recall of the conversation after one week to be "good"?

6. Table 1 shows the proportion correct for various age groups. Proportions can be converted to percentages by multiplying by 100. What is the correct *percentage* for the 11-year-old group?

Questions for Discussion

7. The researchers state that to control for knowledge, they presented information to participants about which they would have little knowledge. In your opinion, is this important? Explain. (See lines 18–20.)

8. The questionnaire was checked by teachers to ensure comprehension. Was this a good idea? Explain. (See lines 37–39.)

9. The conversation used in this study concerned daily life in rural Angola. In your opinion, might a conversation on a different topic produce differences in recall? Explain. (See lines 18–20.)

10. Do you think that this study shows that increasing age *causes* increased earwitness recall? Explain. (See lines 71–73.)

11. Do you agree with the researchers that measuring recall with a questionnaire might produce different results than more supportive methods (e.g., individual interviews) used by police and social workers? (See lines 73–77.)

Quality Ratings

Directions: Indicate your level of agreement with each of the following statements by circling a number from 5 for strongly agree (SA) to 1 for strongly disagree (SD). If you believe an item is not applicable to this research article, leave it blank. Be prepared to explain your ratings. When responding to criteria A and B below, keep in mind that brief titles and abstracts are conventional in published research.

A.   The title of the article is appropriate.

  SA   5   4   3   2   1   SD

B.   The abstract provides an effective overview of the research article.

  SA   5   4   3   2   1   SD

C.   The introduction establishes the importance of the study.

  SA   5   4   3   2   1   SD

D.   The literature review establishes the context for the study.

  SA   5   4   3   2   1   SD

E.   The research purpose, question, or hypothesis is clearly stated.

  SA   5   4   3   2   1   SD

F.   The method of sampling is sound.

  SA   5   4   3   2   1   SD

G.   Relevant demographics (for example, age, gender, and ethnicity) are described.

  SA   5   4   3   2   1   SD

H.   Measurement procedures are adequate.

  SA   5   4   3   2   1   SD

I.   All procedures have been described in sufficient detail to permit a replication of the study.

  SA   5   4   3   2   1   SD

J.   The participants have been adequately protected from potential harm.

  SA   5   4   3   2   1   SD

K.   The results are clearly described.

  SA   5   4   3   2   1   SD

L.   The discussion/conclusion is appropriate.

  SA   5   4   3   2   1   SD

M.   Despite any flaws, the report is worthy of publication.

  SA   5   4   3   2   1   SD

Article 24

Reducing Adolescent Substance Abuse and Delinquency: Pilot Research of a Family-Oriented Psychoeducation Curriculum

THOMAS EDWARD SMITH
Florida State University

JEFFREY RODMAN
Here-4-You Consulting

SCOTT P. SELLS
Savannah Family Institute

LISA RENE REYNOLDS
Nova Southeastern University

ABSTRACT. Ninety-three parents and 102 adolescents were referred by juvenile court and treated for substance abuse and a co-morbid diagnosis of either oppositional defiant or conduct disorder using a parent education program over a six-week period. The goals of this study were to assess whether or not active parent involvement and the concurrent treatment of severe behavior problems would reduce teen substance as measured by the adolescent SASSI scale. In addition, if the SASSI scale indicated a significant reduction in substance abuse, would these changes be maintained after a 12-month follow-up period as measured by re-arrest rates through juvenile court records? The results indicated that parents' participation in their teen's treatment of substance abuse and other severe behavioral problems did have a major positive impact. Even though the adolescent's attitudes and defensiveness toward drugs or alcohol did not significantly change, their substance abuse did. This was demonstrated by both the statistically significant changes on the adolescent's SASSI scores and the fact that 85% did not relapse over the course of an entire year after treatment was completed.

From *Journal of Child & Adolescent Substance Abuse*, *15*, 105–115. Copyright © 2006 by The Haworth Press, Inc. Reprinted with permission.

Introduction

There is a growing concern in our society about the dramatic increase of adolescent drug and alcohol abuse and dependence. There is no shortage of reports de-
5 scribing these alarming trends (e.g., Muck, Zempolich, Titus, Fishman, Godley et al., 2001; Rowe & Liddle, 2003). Overall, drug abuse by teenagers has risen dramatically since 1996 while the overall use among adults has stayed the same or dropped (Department of Health and Human Services, 2002).
10 Increases in teen substance use have led to a greater need for theoretically based and empirically supported treatments (*The Brown University Digest*, 1999). Indeed the number of studies devoted to substance abuse and treatment in youth is continually growing (e.g.,
15 Coatsworth, Santisteran, McBride, & Szapocznik,

2001; Latimer & Newcomb, 2000; Liddle, Dakof, Parker, Diamond, Barrett et al., 2001). However, many agree that a gap still exists between research on adolescent substance abuse and the treatments currently being
20 provided (Liddle, Rowe, Quille, Mills et al., 2002; Robbins, Bachrach, & Szapocznik, 2002; Rowe & Liddle, 2003).

Recent studies have pointed to three critical gaps in adolescent substance-abuse research and treatment.
25 First, there is a growing body of evidence that links adolescent substance abuse to dysfunctional family dynamics (e.g., Carr, 1998; Friedman, Terras, & Glassman, 2000; Liddle & Schwartz, 2002; McGillicuddy, Rychtarik, Duquette, & Morsheimer, 2001; Public Health Reports, 1997; Tuttle, 1995). Brown, Monti,
30 Myers, Waldron, and Wagner (1999) reported that "family support" was often cited by teens as being most helpful in quitting drugs and maintaining sobriety. Despite the growing support for the incorporation
35 of family therapy into adolescent substance abuse treatment (e.g., Berlin, 2002; Lambie & Rokutani, 2002; Rowe, Parker-Sloat, Schwartz, & Liddle, 2003; Wallace & Estroff, 2001), many programs still do not involve the family as an intricate part of their ap-
40 proaches. Instead, the primary emphasis is still on the individual teen through traditional treatment approaches (e.g., Alcoholics Anonymous [AA] or Narcotics Anonymous [NA]), which are often designed for adults without taking into consideration the unique
45 needs of adolescents (Berlin, 2002). Deas and Thomas (2001) agree that many tenets of twelve-step programs may be overly abstract and distasteful for developing adolescents (p. 187).

Second, the majority of substance-abusing teens in
50 treatment also exhibits other problems such as truancy, fighting, and defiance (Fisher & Harrison, 2000), running away (Slesnick, Myers, Meade, & Segelken, 2000), or other problem behaviors (Schmidt, Liddle, & Dakof, 1996). In these cases, family-based treatments
55 were found to be highly effective not only in reducing

substance use, but also in alleviating associated symptomatic behaviors. In 1999, the National Assembly on Drug and Alcohol Abuse and the Criminal Offenders concluded that addressing "adolescent drug addiction 60 or substance abuse without also treating, for example, behavioral problems such as truancy, running away, or threats of violence reduced the likelihood of success" (p. 2). Yet researchers at the National Assembly cited the failure of most treatment programs to address both 65 substance abuse and severe behavioral problems concurrently.

Finally, researchers have found the psychoeducational component of family substance-abuse treatment to be successful in reducing the teen's drug use as well 70 as heightening parents' functioning. Studies have highlighted the utility of psychoeducation in adolescent substance abuse treatment, including parent training (Bamberg et al., 2001; Schmidt et al., 1996) and skills training (McGillicuddy et al., 2001; Wagner, Brown, 75 Monty, & Waldron, 1999). One problem with traditional parenting groups, however, is the significant dropout rate of parents and teens. Parents are often resistant to acceptability for their children's substance abuse. Not surprisingly, they state that adolescents are 80 responsible for their own difficulties. Thus, they resent coming to a parent education group to learn new skills because their teen "got caught" abusing drugs or alcohol. As a result, parents are resistant to helping their teen overcome their substance abuse. However, a sys-85 temic approach to teen substance abuse treatment has been shown to result in a higher level of engagement in treatment and to lower dropout rates than other routine procedures (Cormack & Carr, 2000).

To address these deficits, a parent education pro-90 gram was used to treat teens that were diagnosed with substance abuse as well as oppositional defiant or conduct disorders (*DSM-IV*; American Psychiatric Association [APA], 1994) and the teens' parents. Ninety-three parents and 102 adolescents were referred by 95 juvenile court and treated using the parent education program over a six-week period. Research studies have shown that teen substance abuse and conduct disorder relapse rates are typically extremely high with some as high as 75% (Long, 1999; Sholevar & Schwoeri, 100 2003).

The goals of this study were to assess whether or not active parent involvement and the concurrent treatment of severe behavior problems would reduce teen substance as measured by the adolescent SASSI 105 scale and if these changes would be maintained over a 12-month period after treatment ended.

Research Questions

Three questions were examined in this study. First, would active parent involvement and the concurrent treatment of severe behavior problems reduce teen sub-110 stance abuse as measured by the adolescent SASSI subscales? Second, would reductions in substance

abuse behavior as measured by the SASSI subscales be maintained at the 12-month follow-up? Third, would adolescents relapse within a 12-month period as meas-115 ured by re-arrest rates through juvenile court records?

Methods

The sample consisted of 102 adolescents and 93 parents who together attended a six-week *Parenting with Love and Limits*™ substance-abuse prevention program. The adolescents ranged in age from 9 to 18, 120 with the average participant being 15 years old. Each participant was diagnosed with substance abuse and a co-morbid diagnosis of either oppositional defiant or conduct disorder. The study was conducted within an opportunistic window of opportunity. This required 125 that the study be nonreactive in terms of measurement. As a result, we were unable to track demographic variables such as socioeconomic data and severity of offense.

The majority of the adolescents were white 130 (82.4%). The remaining participants were African American (11.8%) and Mexican American (1.0%). Both males and females were present in the sample, with males accounting for the majority of the participants (56.9%). These adolescents committed a wide 135 variety of offenses, with the most commonly occurring offense being shoplifting (22.5%). The next most frequent offense was possession of marijuana (14.7%). Each participant was court-ordered into treatment by the judge at juvenile court. Once those cases that were 140 missing data related to the SASSI subscales were deleted, 93 adolescents remained in the sample.

Parenting with Love and Limits™

The six-week *Parenting with Love and Limits*™ psychoeducational program was developed from a three-year process-outcome research study (Sells, 145 1998; Sells, 2000; Sells, Smith, & Sprenkle, 1995) and integrated the best principles of a structural family therapy approach. Structural Family Therapy was rated a Model Program in the United States Department of Education's *Applying Effective Strategies to Prevent or 150 Reduce Substance Abuse, Violence, and Disruptive Behavior Among Youth* (Scattergood, Dash, Epstein, & Adler, 1998). Programs using the framework of structural family therapy have consistently demonstrated success in reducing or eliminating substance abuse in 155 adolescents (Lambie & Rokutani, 2002; Springer & Orsbon, 2002; Rowe, Parker-Sloat, Schwartz, & Liddle, 2003).

Two group facilitators led a small group of parents, caregivers, and their teenagers (no more than 4–6 fami-160 lies with no more than 15 people total in the group) in six classes, each two hours long. Two co-facilitators were needed because breakout groups were an essential piece of the program. Parents and teens met together collectively as a group but there were times in which 165 each group met separately in breakout groups. The rationale for these breakouts was that oftentimes both parents and teens need to meet separately to address issues that collectively they cannot.

The *Parenting with Love and Limits*™ program provides parents with a detailed six-module treatment manual on curtailing their teenagers' substance abuse and other behavior problems. To assist in intervention delivery, workbooks were available for parents, their children, and group facilitators. In addition, a final workbook was available on how to train group facilitators to implement the program.

In the first module, parents learned reasons why teens engage in substance abuse, disrespect, running away, or violence as a form of "parent abuse." Presumably, parents are faced with adolescents whose normal rebellious stance is compounded by self-injurious behaviors such as substance abuse, extreme disrespectful behaviors, and so on. At the end of this module, parents and teens form respective breakout groups to vent their feelings and frustrations.

In the second module, presentations are made on how adolescents engage in provocative behavior (e.g., swearing, argumentative discussions). Presentations are also made on how parents engage in activities that are ineffective (e.g., lecturing, criticizing, acrimonious comments about past conflict).

In the third module, effective behavioral contracting methods are presented. Parents are taught to critique their contingency management contracts to ensure that adolescents will be apprised on the consequences of violating provisions of a behavioral contract. Parents and adolescents retire into separate breakout groups to critique and write new contracts.

In the fourth module, presentations are made on how adolescents creatively circumvent seemingly well-designed behavioral contracts.

In the fifth module, parents choose from a recipe menu of creative consequences to respond to adolescents' provocative behaviors. Such behaviors include skipping school, drug/alcohol abuse, sexual promiscuity, violence, and threats of suicide.

In the sixth module, parents and children are taught about the necessity to recreate a positive climate within a household and specific methods of doing so.

The rationale behind the use of this program is twofold. First, *Parenting with Love and Limits*™ is one of the first parent education programs of its kind to specifically address both substance abuse and oppositional and conduct disorder behaviors concurrently. Traditional psychoeducation group programs are not based on a lengthy period of process and qualitative research with adolescents and their families. Further, they are not designed to address a range of extreme behavior problems in adolescents. Finally, teens are not typically active participants in the parenting group process. Traditional groups are either for the parents only or the teens as passive observers and not active participants.

The high completion rate (i.e., 85% completion rate by adolescents and a 94% completion rate by parents of

all six weeks of the *Parenting with Love and Limits*™ program) ensured that the study was a credible investigation into the programmatic effects.

Measures

The Adolescent SASSI questionnaire was administered to the 93 adolescents before they began the first *Parenting with Love and Limits*™ class and again after the last parenting class was completed. It has five subscales: The FVA subscale measured self-perception of alcohol abuse. The FVOD subscale measured self-perception of other drug abuse (e.g., marijuana). The OAT (overt measure of attitudes toward drug use) and SAT (subtle measure of attitudes toward drug use) together measured adolescents' overt and covert willingness to admit that they have personality characteristics that are commonly and stereotypically associated with substance abusers (e.g., impatience, low frustration tolerance, grandiosity, etc). The fifth subscale was the DEF, which measured defensiveness toward drug use.

The Adolescent SASSI has a high reliability coefficient of .91 and high face validity for each of its five subscales (SASSI Manual, 2000). To assess for change following program participation, paired sample t tests were conducted for each subscale of the SASSI.

Recidivism or relapse rates for all 93 adolescents who completed the program were measured through juvenile court records for each adolescent. Re-arrest records for substance abuse or conduct related problems, such as shoplifting, were obtained for all 93 adolescents six months after the completion of the parenting program, and then again after twelve months of completing the program.

Results

Table 1 indicates both the FVA and FVOD subscale scores were significantly lower following their participation in the *Parenting with Love and Limits*™ six-week program. The pretest mean for the FVA was 2.06, whereas the posttest mean was .73. The pretest mean for the FVOD was 2.83, whereas the posttest mean was .95.

The adolescent's attitudes about their drug or alcohol use were measured through the OAT and SAT. On the OAT subscale, the average respondent changed only slightly. The pretest mean for the OAT subscale was 6.19, whereas the posttest mean was 5.85. A similar pattern is seen in the SAT subscale, with the exception of direction. The average respondent had a pretest SAT score of 1.90 and a posttest SAT score of 2.08. The difference between these scores was not statistically significant.

The last subscale (DEF) measured defensiveness concerning substance use. The primary purpose of the DEF scale is to identify defensive clients who are trying to conceal evidence of personal problems and limitations. Whether it is due to life events or to personality characteristics, excessive defensiveness can be prob-

Table 1
Paired Sample t-Test Results for the SASSI Subscales

Subscale	Pretest mean (standard deviation)	Posttest mean (standard deviation)	t-score	p-value
FVA	2.06 (2.79)	.73 (1.41)	4.532	< .001
FVOD	2.83 (4.94)	.95 (2.05)	3.732	< .001
OAT	6.19 (3.23)	5.85 (3.65)	1.176	.243
SAT	1.90 (1.76)	2.08 (1.80)	−1.038	.302
DEF	6.60 (2.46)	7.05 (2.90)	−1.830	.070

lematic and it must be taken into account in treatment planning.

On this subscale, the average respondent's score increased slightly (6.60–7.05). This indicates that the average program participant increased slightly in defensiveness. However, this change was very small and did not reach statistical significance. In addition, the average respondent was in the normal range at the time of pretest, so high levels of change were not expected on this subscale.

Only six (15%) of the 93 adolescents who completed the *Parenting with Love and Limits*™ program relapsed or re-offended over a 12-month period as indicated by juvenile court arrest records that tracked each of the 93 adolescents. Re-offenses included both substance abuse behaviors (e.g., illegal possession of alcohol or drugs like marijuana) and conduct disorders behaviors (e.g., shoplifting, violence, running away, etc.).

Discussion

The results indicate that parents' participation in adolescents' treatment of substance abuse and severe behavioral problems can have a major positive impact on program effectiveness. One key indicator was adolescents' self-reported substance use dropped significantly. This finding was juxtaposed by the finding that adolescents' attitudes and defensiveness toward drugs or alcohol did not significantly change. The significant change in subscales on perceived alcohol and drug use showed that adolescents believed that they misused these substances. This was demonstrated by both the statistically significant changes on the adolescent's SASSI scores and the fact that 85% did not relapse over the course of an entire year after treatment ended.

The low OAT and SAT scores among adolescents were not unexpected because while they may judge themselves as misusing or using drugs or alcohol, they do not see themselves as having a drug or alcohol problem. That is, adolescents often do not see themselves as chemically dependent or having personality characteristics that are associated with society's stereotypical alcoholic or drug abuser on skid row (SASSI Manual, 2000). Thus, a high score and level of change on these subscales was not wholly unexpected.

This evidence suggests that a group-oriented, family therapy informed psychoeducation is effective in helping parents reassert their authority and reduce, if not curtail, their teen's severe behavior problems and substance abuse. Additionally, attitudes toward alcohol and drug abuse may well change following behavioral changes. Notwithstanding this optimistic viewpoint, there are potential problems with the lack of congruence between attitudes and behavior. Without understanding why adolescents changed their behavior, the possibility of recidivism is elevated. The lack of recidivism in this study suggests that this process needs to be further studied.

One key ingredient in the current study may be parental involvement and providing them with the proper skills to address their adolescents' behavioral problems. The parental involvement may explain the 94% completion rate by parents and the 84% completion rate by adolescents of all six two-hour parenting classes. One intuitive explanation for adolescents' high rate of attendance was that they were ordered into treatment. However, that does not explain why parents' involvement was so elevated. High parent attendance in this six-week course contradicts research findings that this population of parents is resistant to treatment and shows a lack of participation in the overall therapeutic process. Therefore, the 94% completion rate shows promise that programs with the right curriculum can engage a population of parents who are traditionally highly resistant to participation.

Future studies that use qualitative research methods are needed to discover what particular concepts or techniques within the *Parenting with Love and Limits*™ program are reducing parental resistance and increasing their readiness to change. The identified key concepts can then be refined and modified to increase both parent and teen participation and readiness to change.

References

Bamberg, J., Toumbourou, J. W., Blyth, A., & Forer, D. (2001). Change for the BEST: Family changes for parents coping with youth substance abuse. *Australian and New Zealand Journal of Family Therapy, 22*, 189–198.

Berlin, M. (2002). Adolescent substance abuse treatment: A unified model. *Dissertation Abstracts International: Section B: The Sciences & Engineering, 63*, 2999.

Brown, S.A., Monti, P. M., Myers, M. G., Waldron, H. B., & Wagner, E.F. (1999). More resources, treatment needed for adolescent substance abuse. *The Brown University Digest of Addiction Theory and Application, 18*, 6–7.

Carr, A. (1998). The inclusion of fathers in family therapy: A research based perspective. *Contemporary Family Therapy, 20*, 371–383.

Coatsworth, J. D., Dsanisteban, D. A., McBride, C. K., & Szapocznik, J. (2001). Brief strategic family therapy versus community control: Engagement, retention, and an exploration of the moderating role of adolescent symptom severity. *Family Process, 40*, 313–333.

Cormack, C., & Carr, A. (2000). Drug abuse. In A. Carr (Ed.), *What works with children and adolescents? A critical review of psychological interventions with children, adolescents, and their families.*

Deas, D., & Thomas, S. E. (2001). An overview of controlled studies of adolescent substance abuse treatment. *The American Journal on Addictions, 10,* 178–189.

Fisher, G. L., & Harrison, T. C. (2000). *Substance abuse: Information for school counselors, social workers, therapists, and counselors.* Needham Heights, MA: Allyn & Bacon.

Friedman, A. S., Terras, A., & Glassman, K. (2000). Family structure versus family relationships for predicting to substance use/abuse and illegal behavior. *Journal of Child & Adolescent Substance Abuse, 10,* 1–16.

Lambie, G. W., & Rokutani, J. (2002). A systems approach to substance abuse identification and intervention for school counselors. *Professional School Counseling, 5,* 353–360.

Latimer, W. W., & Newcomb, M. (2000). Adolescent substance abuse treatment outcome: The role of substance abuse problem severity. *Journal of Consulting and Clinical Psychology, 68,* 684–697.

Liddle, H. A., Dakof, G. A., Parker, K., Diamond, G. S., Barrett, K., & Tejeda, M. (2001). Multidimensional family therapy for adolescent drug abuse: Results of a randomized clinical trial. *American Journal of Drug and Alcohol Abuse, 27,* 651–688.

Liddle, H. A., Rowe, C. L., Quille, T. J., Dakof, G. A., Mills, D. S., Sakran, E., & Biaggi, H. (2002). Transporting a research-based adolescent drug treatment into practice. *Journal of Substance Abuse Treatment, 22,* 231–243.

Liddle, H. A., & Schwartz, S. J. (2002). Attachment and family therapy: The clinical utility of adolescent-family attachment research. *Family Process, 41,* 455–476.

Long, W. C. (1999). The dilemma of addiction and recovery during adolescence. *Dissertation Abstracts International Section A: Humanities and Social Sciences, 59,* 2440.

McGillicuddy, N. B., Rychtarik, R. G., Duquette, J. A., & Morsheimer, E. T. (2001). Development of a skill training program for parents of substance-abusing adolescents. *Journal of Substance Abuse Treatment, 20,* 59–68.

Muck, R., Zempolich, K. A., Titus, J. A., Fishman, M., Godley, M. D., & Schwebel, R. (2001). An overview of the effectiveness of adolescent substance abuse treatment models. *Youth and Society, 33,* 143–168.

Public Health Reports. (1997). Adolescent substance abuse tied to family structure. *Public Health Reports, 112,* 4–6.

Robbins, M. S., Bachrach, K., & Szapocznik, J. (2002). Bridging the research-practice gap in adolescent substance abuse treatment: The case of brief strategic family therapy. *Journal of Substance Abuse Treatment, 23,* 123–132.

Rowe, C. L., & Liddle, H. A. (2003). Substance abuse. *Journal of Marital and Family Therapy, 29,* 97–120.

Rowe, C. L., Parker-Sloat, E., Schwartz, S., & Liddle, H. (2003). Family therapy for early adolescent substance abuse. In S. J. Stevens & A. R. Morral (Eds.), *Adolescent substance abuse treatment in the United States: Exemplary models from a national evaluation study* (pp. 105–132). New York: The Haworth Press, Inc.

Schmidt, S. E., Liddle, H. A., & Dakof, G. A. (1996). Changes in parenting practices and adolescent drug abuse during multidimensional family therapy. *Journal of Family Psychology, 10,* 12–27.

Sholevar, G. P., & Schwoeri, L. D. (2003). Alcoholic and substance-abusing families. In G.P. Sholevar (Ed.), *Textbook of family and couples therapy: Clinical applications* (pp. 671–694). Washington, DC: American Psychiatric Publishing, Inc.

Slesnick, N., Meyers, R. J., Meade, M., & Segelken, D. H. (2000). Bleak and hopeless no more: Engagement of reluctant substance-abusing runaway youth and their families. *Journal of Substance Abuse Treatment, 19,* 215–222.

Springer, D. W., & Orsbon, S. H. (2002). Families helping families: Implementing a multifamily therapy group with substance-abusing adolescents. *Health and Social Work, 27,* 204–208.

Tuttle, J. (1995). Family support, adolescent individuation, and drug and alcohol involvement. *Journal of Family Nursing, 1,* 303–327.

Wagner, E. F., & Waldron, H. B. (1999). Innovations in adolescent substance abuse intervention. *Alcoholism: Clinical and Experimental Research, 23,* 236–249.

Wallace, S., & Estroff, T. W. (2001). Family treatment. In T. W. Estroff (Ed.), *Manual of adolescent substance abuse treatment* (pp. 235–252). Washington, DC: American Psychiatric Publishing, Inc.

About the authors: *Thomas Edward Smith*, PhD, is professor, Florida State University, School of Social Work, Tallahassee, FL (E-mail: tsmith@mailer.fsu.edu). *Scott P. Sells*, PhD, is director of the Savannah Family Institute, Savannah, GA (E-mail: spsells@difficult.net). *Jeffrey Rodman*, MA, is executive director, Here-4-You Consulting, LLC (E-mail: Jeffter46@hotmail.com). *Lisa Rene Reynolds*, PhD, is affiliated with the Nova Southeastern University (E-mail: lreynolds@norwalkreds.com).

Address correspondence to: Thomas Edward Smith, PhD, Florida State University, School of Social Work. Tallahassee, FL 32306. E-mail: tsmith@mailer.fsu.edu

Exercise for Article 24

Factual Questions

1. According to the researchers, there are how many "critical gaps" in adolescent substance abuse research and treatment?

2. The adolescents in this study committed a wide variety of offenses. What was the most commonly occurring offense?

3. The initial sample consisted of 102 adolescents. The researchers had complete data for how many?

4. What did the FVA subscale measure?

5. Was the "pretest mean" *or* the "posttest mean" on the FVA subscale higher?

6. Using .05 as the cutoff level for statistical significance, was the difference between the pretest and posttest means on the FVA subscale statistically significant? Explain.

Questions for Discussion

7. In your opinion, how important is the fact that a follow-up was conducted? Is 12 months an appropriate amount of follow-up for an evaluation of this type? (See the research questions in lines 107–115.)

8. How important is it to know that each participant was court-ordered into treatment by a judge? Would you be willing to generalize the results of this study to adolescents who volunteered to participate? (See lines 138–139 and 341–343.)

9. In your opinion, is the program that was evaluated in this study described in sufficient detail, keeping in mind that journal articles tend to be relatively short? Explain. (See lines 142–227.)

10. The researchers report a 15% relapse rate. Would it have been informative to have determined the relapse rate for a control group that did not receive the program? Explain. (See lines 289–297.)

11. In your opinion, might it be informative to ask the parents for their personal reactions to the program in a future evaluation of the program? Explain. Note that the completion rate for parents was 94%. (See lines 223–227 and 338–341.)

12. Do the data in this research article convince you that the *Parenting with Love and Limits*™ program is effective? Explain.

Quality Ratings

Directions: Indicate your level of agreement with each of the following statements by circling a number from 5 for strongly agree (SA) to 1 for strongly disagree (SD). If you believe an item is not applicable to this research article, leave it blank. Be prepared to explain your ratings. When responding to criteria A and B below, keep in mind that brief titles and abstracts are conventional in published research.

A. The title of the article is appropriate.

SA   5   4   3   2   1   SD

B. The abstract provides an effective overview of the research article.

SA   5   4   3   2   1   SD

C. The introduction establishes the importance of the study.

SA   5   4   3   2   1   SD

D. The literature review establishes the context for the study.

SA   5   4   3   2   1   SD

E. The research purpose, question, or hypothesis is clearly stated.

SA   5   4   3   2   1   SD

F. The method of sampling is sound.

SA   5   4   3   2   1   SD

G. Relevant demographics (for example, age, gender, and ethnicity) are described.

SA   5   4   3   2   1   SD

H. Measurement procedures are adequate.

SA   5   4   3   2   1   SD

I. All procedures have been described in sufficient detail to permit a replication of the study.

SA   5   4   3   2   1   SD

J. The participants have been adequately protected from potential harm.

SA   5   4   3   2   1   SD

K. The results are clearly described.

SA   5   4   3   2   1   SD

L. The discussion/conclusion is appropriate.

SA   5   4   3   2   1   SD

M. Despite any flaws, the report is worthy of publication.

SA   5   4   3   2   1   SD

Article 25

Living with Mental Illness—What Families and Friends Must Know: Evaluation of a One-Day Psychoeducation Workshop

DAVID E. POLLIO
Washington University

CAROL S. NORTH
University of Texas Southwestern
Medical Center

DONNA L. REID
Independence Center

MICHELLE M. MILETIC
Special School District of St. Louis County

JENNIFER R. McCLENDON
Washington University

ABSTRACT. One-day "family survival" psychoeducation workshops are a promising, convenient method of disseminating basic information to families with a relative who is diagnosed with a serious mental illness such as schizophrenia, major depression, or other affective disorders. At five separate psychoeducation workshops, 83 participating families completed the self-report North-Sachar Family Life Questionnaire and open-ended "problem lists" of issues facing the families both before and after the workshops. Outcomes consistently demonstrated positive change pre- to post-workshop. Issues reported by workshop participants included desire for education about illness, identification of resources, coping with the illness, and family relationships. The workshop model demonstrated consistent achievement of the outcomes measured, meeting short-term goals. Although models such as the family responsive approach reported in this article are not designed to create long-term gains for the family, they appear to benefit families and may help connect families with more intensive services to facilitate long-term change.

From *Social Work, 51,* 31–38. Copyright © 2006 by the National Association of Social Workers. Reprinted with permission.

Deinstitutionalization has shifted responsibility of care into community settings for even individuals with the most serious mental illnesses. Simultaneously, recent government policies have cut funding for intensive
5 psychosocial stabilization services in the community. As a result of these changes, overburdened families are finding themselves increasingly responsible for care of a family member with a serious mental illness. These families often struggle with this role because of their
10 lack of special training, knowledge, and sufficient professional support (McFarlane, 1991; North et al., 1998; Pollio, North, Osborne, Kap, & Foster, 2001; Solomon, 1996).

The stress of managing a family member's mental
15 illness can have a serious impact on families (Dixon & Lehman, 1995). The effects include not only problems interacting with the family member and the grief associated with the illness (Atkinson, 1994; Miller, Dworkin, Ward, & Barone, 1990), but also difficulties
20 in obtaining appropriate care and communicating effectively with service providers. Hanson (1993) found that families of people with mental illness were confused by their roles and felt helpless as these roles shifted over the course of treatment. Family stress can be asso-
25 ciated with physical and psychological problems in caregivers (Oldrige & Hughes, 1992; Vaddadi, 1996).

Families have critical needs for novel approaches to train them to assume their new responsibilities for care of their ill loved one. Psychoeducation models have
30 been developed to help families learn how to help their mentally ill member. Psychoeducation combines elements of education, support, and problem solving, generally within a standardized model (Pollio, Brower, & Galinsky, 2000). Psychoeducational goals for families
35 include obtaining relevant information, developing support within the group, learning to cope with the emotional aspects of care giving, recognizing the need for self-care, improving relationships with the care recipients and other family members, and using avail-
40 able formal services (Pollio et al., 2000; Smith, Majeski, & McClenny, 1996).

Multifamily psychoeducation group research for families coping with mental illness consistently demonstrates improved outcomes for the member with a
45 mental illness and the family. For the member with a mental illness, participation in psychoeducation and family treatment is associated with significantly decreased relapse rates (Anderson, Reiss, & Hogarty, 1986; Falloon et al., 1982; Leff, 1989; McFarlane,
50 Lukens, Link, & Dushay, 1995; North et al., 1998; Tarrier, Barrowclough, Vaughn, & Bamrah, 1989), reduced psychiatric symptoms (Leff; Leff, Kuipers, Berkowitz, Eberlein-Vries, & Sturgeon, 1982; Leff, Kuipers, Berkowitz, & Sturgeon, 1985; Tarrier et al.,
55 1988), and improved social adjustment (Anderson et

133

al., 1986; Leff et al., 1985; Falloon et al., 1985; Falloon, McGill, Boyd, & Pederson, 1987; Tarrier et al., 1988, 1989). Psychoeducation helps the caregiver by increasing social and family adjustment (Leff, 1989;
60   Leff et al., 1982, 1985; Levene, Newman, & Jeffries, 1989; McFarlane, Dunne, Lukens, & Newmark, 1993; McFarlane et al., 1995), coping and well-being (Doane, Goldstein, Miklowitz, & Falloon, 1986; Zastowny, Lehman, Cole, & Kane, 1992), and by decreasing fam-
65   ily burden and time spent worrying (Lam, 1991; McFarlane et al., 1995; Pollio, North, & Osborne, 2002; Solomon, 1996; Solomon & Draine, 1995; Solomon, Draine, Mannion, & Meisel, 1996, 1997).

A limitation of psychoeducation is its intensive
70   time commitment for families participating in the groups (Smith & Birchwood, 1990). The chaos families experience trying to cope with mental illness in the family, along with multiple other factors (e.g., work and family commitments, difficulties gaining access to
75   services), may make them reluctant to commit to long-term interventions.

Because of the substantial time commitment required by groups, brief psychoeducation workshops (Anderson et al., 1986) have become a popular forum.
80   Few studies, however, have evaluated the outcomes of educational workshops for family members of individuals with mental illness. Reilly and colleagues (1988) examined the effects of a day-long workshop for families immediately before state hospital discharge
85   and found no reduction in recidivism or engagement of families. It can be argued, however, that it may be unrealistic to expect long-term effects from this brief intervention. It is more appropriate to conceptualize such brief interventions as portals to more intensive ser-
90   vices, providing hope and support, and offering ideas for coping with family concerns and problems related to the illness. Thus, an appropriate evaluation would focus on whether the family's perceived needs were met and skills or knowledge were acquired as part of
95   the evaluation process. Establishing the effectiveness of a replicable model that meets these simple goals would contribute an important piece to the arsenal of systems of care seeking to support people with mental illness and their families.
100   The purpose of this study, therefore, was to measure the effectiveness of the "family survival" workshop, a one-day program developed collaboratively by researchers at Washington University and the National Alliance for the Mentally Ill (NAMI) of St. Louis. Its
105   effectiveness was measured by answering the following three questions: (1) Did families report gains in family members' perceived ability to manage the illness and related crises, knowledge about the illness, feelings of control, guilt feelings, and knowledge of
110   resources? (2) Which characteristics of families (age, race, gender, relationship to member with illness) and members with illness (primary diagnosis, length, and recent severity of illness) are associated with increased

likelihood of benefiting from the workshop? and (3)
115   Did the topics presented match the reported needs of the participant families? We addressed these questions by comparing the families' responses to five questions before and after the workshop, modeling predictors of improvement in outcome variables, and qualitatively
120   examining the families' responses to an open-ended question about their goals for attending the workshop.

Method

Setting

Five one-day "family survival" workshops in St. Louis provided the sources of data for this study between October 1999 and May 2001. Notices of the
125   workshops were mailed to mental health services providers on a NAMI mailing list requesting them to disseminate information to their patients and clients, and to families on a NAMI mailing list. Staff at inpatient and outpatient mental health agencies in the St. Louis
130   area were asked to post program announcements in their waiting areas. Workshop participants were also recruited directly through local newspaper and television announcements of the program. Family members paid $15 for the day per member (with scholarships
135   available on request).

Workshop Format and Structure

The workshops were developed to serve families with a member suffering from a serious mental illness, primarily schizophrenia, bipolar disorder, major depression, and other affective disorders. The model is
140   based on the authors' "family responsive" approach to services for these families (North et al., 1998; Pollio et al., 2002). This approach views family members (including the one with the illness) as capable partners in the intervention process. The philosophy of interven-
145   tion includes a willingness to create services based on identifying and responding directly to family needs (rather than providing clinician or research-initiated information). In creating the workshop format, this philosophy influenced the workshop development
150   process, choice of material presented, and structure of the program. For the workshop development process, the planning committee included family members and professionals working together. As part of the planning process, the team decided to present information to
155   families at the same level of complexity as might be used for a professional audience. Anecdotally, this led to attendance by a number of students and professionals at these workshops (although this evaluation does not include data by this group). Finally, along with
160   inclusion of rigorously developed materials produced for the workshops, material identified by participants uniquely for each workshop was included.

The workshops' programs included three opening plenary addresses: (1) "Mental Illness: What It Is and
165   Is Not," which provided descriptive and diagnostic information on schizophrenia and mood disorders; (2) "The Brain," which described the biological basis of

mental illness, including neurochemistry and genetics; and (3) "Treatment of Mental Disorders," which reviewed medication and other forms of treatment. These sessions were standardized across all workshops, with PowerPoint presentations and accompanying handouts created by the second author. All lecturers were recruited by at least one of the authors to speak in their area of expertise, and all presentations were monitored to ensure that the general material was presented.

Before the initial plenary address, families were asked to list problems they faced with having mental illness in their family. During the workshops, these lists were analyzed to identify issues of interest unique to each group of attending families. The topics created from these lists were used to organize informal discussion groups at a midday luncheon titled "Your Issues." Placards announcing the topics created from the workshop problem lists were placed on luncheon tables seating eight to 12 participants each. Program participants and staff were asked to sit at the table of the topic in which they had the greatest interest. The topic generated a starting place for their lunchtime discussions. Issues chosen were those that appeared on the participants' lists but were not specifically included in the presentations.

The afternoon's program consisted of two sets of hour-long breakout sessions. These sessions, chaired by professionals with special expertise on the topic, consisted of brief didactic presentations followed by audience discussion. Although the content of these sessions varied somewhat among the different workshops, the sessions generally included area resources; success stories from families and their member with a mental illness; "Ask the Doc," an informal question and answer session with a psychiatrist; religion and religious resources; and legal rights. As a part of these workshops, families were asked permission to be contacted to participate in a randomized clinical trial testing a year-long family-responsive psychoeducation group model developed by the authors (North et al., 1998; Pollio et al., 2002).

Data Collection

At the start of the program, one member from each family was asked to complete the North-Sachar Family Life Questionnaire (FLQ), consisting of 11 questions that elicit information about family members' perceived ability to manage the illness and related crises, knowledge about the illness, disruptions to family life, communication with the ill member, success with behavioral expectations, guilt feelings, and hospitalization history (number of hospital days and episodes) (for more details on this instrument, see North et al., 1998). Workshop participants also completed a basic demographic form providing characteristics of both respondents and members with illness. Finally, families completed the list of "problems faced" to help provide the content of sessions in response to their specific concerns (Pollio, North, & Foster, 1998; Pollio et al., 2001). Where more than one family member was present, we did not stipulate which family member completed the form, only requesting that the same family member complete all forms and that family members discuss responses where possible. At the workshop's conclusion, one participant from each family completed a satisfaction questionnaire about the workshop. This questionnaire, developed for the workshops, was piloted and used in earlier research by this research team (North et al., 1998; Pollio et al., 2002). Five questions provided postworkshop information using North-Sachar FLQ items. The five items selected measured separate concepts identified in earlier research, and through workshop development procedures, as of interest to the workshop organizers. Of the 160 participating families, 83 (52%) completed both pre- and posttests and 77 (48%) completed only the pretest.

Variables in the Analysis

The outcome variables analyzed in the current report included the five items from the North-Sachar FLQ completed both pre- and postworkshop: (1) family members' perceived ability to manage the illness and related crises, (2) knowledge about the illness, (3) feelings of control, (4) guilt feelings, and (5) knowledge of resources. Each item was scored on a scale ranging from 1 to 5, with higher scores being more positive. To assess change, scores from the pretest were subtracted from those from the posttest for each item. Demographic variables used in the analysis included respondents' age, race (white/not white), gender, and relationship to the person with a mental illness (parent, sibling, or friend); primary diagnosis of the member with a mental illness coded into three dichotomous variables for schizophrenia, bipolar disorder, and depression (all other diagnoses being the excluded categories); length in years since first episode; number of days hospitalized; and number of hospital episodes for the previous year. Scoring of the remaining items from the North-Sachar FLQ collected only at baseline was similar to that described previously.

Data Analysis

Quantitative data analyses were performed to identify systematic biases of posttest noncompletion for variables of gender, race, age of respondent, primary reported diagnosis, number of inpatient days and episodes, and all items in the pretest North-Sachar FLQ, using chi-square and t test analyses; to determine change (research question 1), using t tests to compare pre- and posttest scores for the five paired variables; and to identify predictors of change ($n = 83$: research question 2). For this final analysis, we used simple regression models to examine correlations between single predictors and change scores for each outcome variable. Once significant associations were identified in simple regressions, multiple regressions were performed with all significant variables identified in simple models included in final regressions. For clarity, we report only significant results from these final models.

Qualitative data analysis was used to describe reasons for attending the workshop. Although these data did not provide information on outcomes, reasons identified by families provide evidence of the fit (or lack thereof) between the family issues and the workshop content (research question 3). These analyses followed procedures we used previously to categorize data from the "problem lists." All items in the analysis were examined by at least two authors who created categories by consensus and placed items into categories. Earlier use of this methodology yielded interrater reliabilities of 85% to 91% for the categories (Pollio et al., 1998; Pollio et al., 2000).

Results

Respondents

Participants completing both pre- and posttest were female (78%) and predominantly white (97%). A majority of the family members were parents of the person with illness (68%), with a mean age of 54 years (SD = 13). Families listed their member with illness' primary diagnoses as bipolar disorder (51%), schizophrenia (22%), major depression (6%), and other (22%). The person with illness averaged 25 (SD = 57) inpatient days in the previous year, and 47% had at least a single episode of illness exacerbation (mean episodes = 1.0, SD = 1.4). Families were experienced in care of their ill members, who had been affected an average of 12.8 years (SD = 11.1). Finally, a majority of the families attending the workshop (61%) agreed to consider an invitation to participate in a multifamily psychoeducation clinical trial.

Across the entire sample, more than one-half (56%, n = 90) of families attending the workshop reported serious effects of the illness on other family members for that item. Most families (63%, n = 101) reported at least occasional yelling or violent episodes with their ill member, and many of these families felt the violence was frequent or constant (27% overall, n = 43). Families reported difficulties in behavioral expectations, with only 28% (n = 45) reporting being "usually" or "always" successful at setting expectations and 25% (n = 40) reporting the member as usually or always successful at meeting expectations. Only a minority of families (33%, n = 53) felt they communicated well with their member with illness. However, respondents generally reported that their family member with illness was usually or always medication compliant (74%, n = 120).

No significant differences were found between completers of pretest only and completers of both pre- and posttest in any analysis.

Outcomes

All five questions asked in the North-Sachar FLQ reflected significant improvements from workshop start to finish. Paired responses indicated that families felt more in control of their daily lives, more effective in crisis situations, more knowledgeable in obtaining community resources, more knowledgeable about mental illness and treatment, and decreased feelings of guilt after the one-day psychoeducation workshop. Pre- and posttest scores, t tests, and probabilities are displayed in Table 1.

Multivariate Analyses. For the five variables reflecting change, three had significant predictors in a final model, with two models as a whole providing statistical significance. For prediction of change in knowledge of community resources, although the equation as a whole was not significant, number of days hospitalized for the ill member was negatively associated with change ($ß$ = –.01, SE = .005, t = –2.02, p = .05). Number of hospital episodes was significantly predicted in the simple regression model, but not in the multiple regression. The equation for prediction of guilt feelings was significant [$F(4,58)$ = 4.6, p < .01], with the diagnosis of major depression significantly negatively associated with guilt reduction ($ß$ = –.97, SE = .36, t = –2.68, p = .01), and higher pretest ratings of the member with a mental illness meeting behavioral expectations were associated with reduction in guilt ($ß$ = .26, SE = .12, t = 2.13, p = .04). Two other variables, medication compliance and number of episodes, were not significantly associated with guilt reduction in simple regressions in this final model. The overall model predicting families' ability to cope with crisis was statistically significant [$F(1,72)$ = 6.94, p = .01]. In it, poor medication compliance was associated with increased feelings of ability to respond to crises ($ß$ = –.19, SE = .07, t = –2.63, p = .01).

Qualitative Analysis. A total of 360 items were tallied from the families' problem lists, with 4.4 items per family on average (range = 1 to 14). Five categories identified by the analysis included 93% of the individual items (Table 2). The remaining 7% were either unique or included in categories containing fewer than nine items.

Discussion

Results from the workshop evaluation were overwhelmingly positive. Families consistently reported significant gains from pre- to postworkshop. Limited findings from multivariate analysis suggest the general appropriateness of the model to accommodate the range of families attending the workshop. Despite the study's important limitations, all indications point to the ability of the model to achieve its goals. The Family Skills Workshop not only appears to address identified needs of families coping with this significant challenge, but also may serve as a portal to more intensive services.

The answer to the first research question (Did families report gains after the workshop?) appears to be resoundingly positive. All items generated positive change. Families reported gains in all areas specified

Table 1

Pre- and Posttest Scores on the North Sachar FLQ for Families with a Member with a Mental Illness

Variable	Pre-score	Post-score	*t* test	*p*	*N*
Feelings of control	2.31	2.46	2.0	.05	80
Crisis intervention	2.47	2.70	3.2	.002	81
Knowledge of resources	2.27	2.62	3.5	.001	82
Knowledge of illness	2.53	2.79	3.1	.003	77
Feelings of guilt	3.86	4.17	3.3	.002	78

Notes. FLQ = Family Life Questionnaire. Higher scores indicate improvement. All items range from 1 to 5.

Table 2

Categories and Percentages from the Qualitative Problem List Analysis for Families with a Member with a Mental Illness

Category	% of items
Education about illness, including new information and advice on specific illnesses	36
Coping strategies, including problem solving and support skills and increasing personal effectiveness	21
Resources, including local and national information on getting help and legal resources	17
Social support and communication with the family member with illness, including the future for the person with illness, increasing communication and social support, and improving relationships	13
Increasing support from others in the community, including agency and informal support networks	4

Note. All items were placed in unique categories. Rounding errors and items not categorized caused differences in percentages.

for this research question. It may be the case that this response reflects a general positive appraisal of the workshop, rather than independent gains in each area. In either case, whether a generic positive response or a specific response to the items, it is clear that families reported an immediate positive experience to the workshop. Although the large percentage of families volunteering to be recruited for the longer-term intervention study suggests otherwise (and argues for the clinical impact of the findings), in making this interpretation, we would be remiss if we did not at least raise the possibility that this finding may represent a measurement artifact.

The paucity of findings from the second research question (Which characteristics of family and member with illness increased likelihood of benefiting from the workshop?) suggests that family and member-with-illness characteristics had little consistent association with gains. Higher functioning in the family member with a mental illness may allow family members to concentrate less on immediate needs and crises and more on acquiring new ways of coping. In addition, findings suggest that problems with medication compliance may encourage families to attend workshops in search of specific solutions, leading to greater gains when their needs are met. However, the few significant findings indicate need for a cautious approach to these speculations, as the potential for spurious significant "false positive" associations (Type II errors) may account for some or all of the apparent associations.

The third research question (Did the topics presented match the reported needs of the participant families?) is potentially confounded by the structure of the workshop. The "Your Issues" luncheon ensured

that each workshop was tailored to the audience's specific needs. However, examination of the categories emerging from the analysis and their relative emphasis with the structure described provides compelling evidence that the general structure of the workshops addressed the participants' expressed issues with some precision. The most frequently addressed category provided by preworkshop questionnaire data, desire for education about the illness, paralleled the focus of the plenary sessions of the morning's program. Thus, the material most frequently identified as family issues in qualitative analysis was provided to all participants. Similarly, content of the three next frequently identified categories was provided in the afternoon breakout sessions when families had opportunities to participate in two self-selected sessions. Finally, the smallest category, need for informal support, was addressed within the structure of the "Your Issues" luncheon.

Study Limitations

As an exploratory study, this research was not without significant limitations. The sample was neither random nor representative of all families affected by mental illness; therefore, the results may not be generalizable to families not participating in family psychoeducation workshops. This sampling bias also may limit the general applicability of success of the workshop to other settings. However, biases associated with self-selection to participate in educational workshops are inherent to these programs, as these programs are not for everyone. The sample also was demographically nonrepresentative, with low representation of African American and other racial and ethnic minority groups. Other researchers have identified the impor-

455 tance of racial differences in the experience of having a family member with a mental illness (Stueve, Vine, & Struening, 1997). Future research should focus on issues of generalizability and should include comparison groups and more racial and ethnic diversity. In addi-
460 tion, although the statistical analyses did not indicate any significant bias based on completers of both pre- and posttest versus those completing pretest only, the high attrition rates represent a limitation of the data and an area for potential untested biases. Finally, the meth-
465 odology of a pre- and post-model does not strictly allow for assignment of causality.

Service Implications

Although this study had obvious limitations, the results clearly provide service implications. The ability to conduct multiple workshops and recruit participants
470 from them for more intensive services suggests the potential not only for the workshops, but also for this model as a means to attract service-willing families to services. The positive gains identified for the workshop participants, combined with the willingness of families
475 to be contacted about potential participation in future programs, suggest that these kinds of time-limited services have utility as a portal to more intensive and powerful family interventions. Families willing to pay for and commit to day-long attendance demonstrate
480 their readiness for more intensive services.

The results also provide directions for tailoring services for these families across locations. Although the educational content is highly valued, it is clear that families desire information relevant to finding and ef-
485 fectively using services within their specific communities. Agencies wishing to create a similar workshop model would need to include presentations specific to available treatment options and local systems of care. Furthermore, workshops can be modified to focus on
490 more specific subpopulations. For example, workshops might be developed to serve families whose member with a mental illness has higher levels of functioning, with greater attention paid to independence issues.

The promising evidence for the workshop presented
495 here also indicates the potential for this family responsive approach to creating and adapting interventions for a range of families coping with a variety of mental illnesses. Multifamily psychoeducation groups already have a broad history of generalizability to other popu-
500 lations (Pollio et al., 2000). Findings from the family responsive workshop presented here suggest the utility of models aimed at addressing, in a single setting, families coping with multiple diagnoses and complex challenges, rather than aiming interventions at specific
505 diagnostic groups or issues.

References

Anderson, C. M., Reiss, D. J., & Hogarty, G. E. (1986). *Schizophrenia and the family: A practitioner's guide to psychoeducation and management.* New York: Guilford Press.

Atkinson, S. D. (1994). Grieving and loss in parents with a schizophrenic child. *American Journal of Psychiatry, 151,* 1137–1139.

Dixon, L. B., & Lehman, A. F. (1995). Family interventions for schizophrenia. *Schizophrenia Bulletin, 21,* 631–643.

Doane, J. A., Goldstein, M. J., Miklowitz, D. J., & Falloon, I. R. (1986). The impact of individual and family treatment on the affective climate of families of schizophrenics. *British Journal of Psychiatry, 148,* 279–287.

Falloon, I. R., Boyd, J. L., McGill, C. W., Razani, J., Moss, H. B., & Gilderman, A. M. (1982). Family management in the prevention of exacerbations of schizophrenia: A controlled study. *New England Journal of Medicine, 306,* 1437–1440.

Falloon, I. R., Boyd, J. L., McGill, C. W, Williamson, M., Razani, J., Moss, H. B., Gilderman, A. M., & Simpson, G. M. (1985). Family management in the prevention of morbidity of schizophrenia: Clinical outcome of a two-year longitudinal study. *Archives of General Psychiatry, 42,* 887–896.

Falloon I. R., McGill, C. W., Boyd, J. L., & Pederson, J. (1987). Family management in the prevention of morbidity of schizophrenia: Social Outcome of a two-year longitudinal study. *Psychological Medicine, 17,* 59–66.

Hanson, J. G. (1993). Families of people with a severe mental illness: Role conflict, ambiguity, and family burden. *Journal of Sociology & Social Welfare, 20,* 105–118.

Lam, D. H. (1991). Psychosocial family intervention in schizophrenia: A review of empirical studies. *Psychological Medicine, 21,* 423–441.

Leff, J. (1989). Family factors in schizophrenia. *Psychiatric Annals, 19,* 542–547.

Leff, J., Kuipers, L., Berkowitz, R., Eberlein-Vries, R., & Sturgeon, D. (1982). A controlled trial of social intervention in the families of schizophrenic patients. *British Journal of Psychiatry, 141,* 121–134.

Leff, J., Kuipers, L., Berkowitz, R., & Sturgeon, D. (1985). A controlled trial of social intervention in the families of schizophrenic patients: Two-year follow-up. *British Journal of Psychiatry, 146,* 594–600.

Levene, J. E., Newman, F., & Jeffries, J. J. (1989). Focal family therapy outcome study I: Patient and family functioning. *Canadian Journal of Psychiatry, 34,* 641–647.

McFarlane, W. R. (1991). Family psychoeducational treatment. In A. S. Gurman, & D. P. Kniskern (Eds.), *Handbook of Family Therapy* (Vol. 2, pp. 363–395). Philadelphia: Brunner/Mazel.

McFarlane, W. R., Dunne, E., Lukens, E., & Newmark, M. (1993). From research to clinical practice: Dissemination of New York State's family psychoeducation project. *Hospital and Community Psychiatry, 44,* 265–270.

McFarlane, W R., Lukens, E., Link, B., & Dushay, R. (1995). Multiple-family groups and psychoeducation in the treatment of schizophrenia. *Archives of General Psychiatry, 52,* 679–687.

Miller, F., Dworkin, J., Ward, M., & Barone, D. (1990). A preliminary study of unresolved grief in families of seriously mentally ill patients. *Hospital and Community Psychiatry, 41,* 1321–1325.

North, C. S., Pollio, D. E., Sachar, B., Hong, B., Isenberg, K., & Bufe, G. (1998). The family as caregiver for schizophrenia: A group psychoeducation model. *American Journal of Orthopsychiatry, 68,* 39–47.

Oldrige, M., & Hughes, I. (1992). Psychological well-being in families with a member suffering from schizophrenia. *British Journal of Psychiatry, 161,* 249–251.

Pollio, D. E., Brower, A., & Galinsky, M. J. (2000). Change in groups. In C. Garvin & P. Allen-Meares (Eds.), *Handbook of Social Work Direct Practice* (pp. 281–301). Thousand Oaks, CA: Sage Publications.

Pollio, D. E., North, C. S., & Foster, D. E. (1998). Content and curriculum in multifamily psychoeducation. *Psychiatric Services, 49,* 816–822.

Pollio, D. E., North C. S., & Osborne, V. (2002). Family-responsive psychoeducation groups for families with an adult member with mental illness: Pilot results. *Community Mental Health Journal, 38,* 413–421.

Pollio, D. E., North, C. S., Osborne, V., Kap, N., & Foster, D.A. (2001). The impact of psychiatric diagnosis and family system relationship on problems identified by families coping with a mentally ill member. *Family Process, 40,* 199–210.

Reilly, J. W, Rohrbaugh, M., & Lackner, J. M. (1988). A controlled evaluation of psychoeducation workshops for relatives of state hospital patients. *Journal of Marital & Family Therapy, 14,* 429–432.

Smith, J., & Birchwood, M. (1990). Relatives and patients as partners in the management of schizophrenia: The development of a service model. *British Journal of Psychiatry, 156,* 654–660.

Smith, G., Majeski, R. A., & McClenny, B. (1996). Psychoeducational support groups for aging parents: Development and preliminary outcomes. *Mental Retardation, 34,* 172–181.

Solomon, P. (1996). Moving from psychoeducation to family education for families of adults with serious mental illness. *Psychiatric Services, 47,* 1364–1370.

Solomon, P., & Draine, J. (1995). Subjective burden among family members of mentally ill adults: Relation to stress, coping, and adaptation. *American Journal of Orthopsychiatry, 65,* 419–427.

Solomon, P., Draine, J., Mannion, E., & Meisel, M. (1996). Impact of brief family therapy on self-efficacy. *Schizophrenia Bulletin, 22,* 41–50.

Solomon, P., Draine, J., Mannion, E., & Meisel, M. (1997). Effectiveness of two models of brief family education: Retention of gains by family members of adults with severe mental illness. *American Journal of Orthopsychiatry, 67,* 177–187.

Stueve, A., Vine, P., & Struening, E. L. (1997). Perceived burden among caregivers of adults with serious mental illness: Comparison of black, Hispanic, and white families. *American Journal of Orthopsychiatry, 67*, 199–209.

Tarrier, N., Barrowclough, C., Vaughn, C., & Bamrah, J. S., Porceddu, K., Watts, S., & Freeman, H. (1988). The community management of schizophrenia: A controlled trial of a behavioral intervention with families to reduce relapse. *British Journal of Psychiatry, 153*, 532–542.

Tarrier, N., Barrowclough, C., Vaughn, C., & Bamrah, J. S., Porceddu, K., Watts, S., & Freeman, H. (1989). Community management of schizophrenia: A two-year follow-up of a behavioural intervention with families. *British Journal of Psychiatry, 154*, 625–628.

Vaddadi, K. (1996). Stress of caregiving for the chronically mentally ill. *Psychiatric Annals, 26*, 766–771.

Zastowny, T. R., Lehman, A. F., Cole, R. E., & Kane, C. (1992). Family management of schizophrenia: A comparison of behavioral and supportive family treatment. *Psychiatric Quarterly, 63*, 159–186.

About the authors: *David E. Pollio*, Ph.D., LCSW; is associate professor, George Warren Brown School of Social Work, Washington University. *Carol S. North*, MD, is Ron & Nancy Hunt Professor of Psychiatry at University of Texas Southwestern Medical Center, Dallas. *Donna L. Reid*, MSW, is evaluation specialist, Independence Center, St. Louis. *Michelle M. Miletic*, MSW, is school social worker, Special School District of St. Louis County. *Jennifer R. McClendon*, MSW, is a doctoral student, George Warren Brown School of Social Work, Washington University, St. Louis.

Address correspondence to: David E. Pollio, George Warren Brown School of Social Work, Washington University, Campus Box 1196, One Brookings Drive, St. Louis, MO 63130-4899. E-mail: depollio@wustl.edu

Acknowledgments: The authors wish to thank staff and volunteers for the Family Survival Project and the National Alliance for the Mentally Ill of St. Louis, and Richard D. Stevenson and Marge Parrish for their participation in the research project. The project was funded by the National Institute of Mental Health, grant no. 22-1620-51320.

Exercise for Article 25

Factual Questions

1. Did the researchers recruit participants from a single source?

2. There were how many participating families?

3. What percentage of the families had a member with major depression?

4. What was the pretest mean for "knowledge of illness"? What was the posttest mean?

5. What is the value of p for the difference between the two means in Question 4?

6. What percentage of the responses to the open-ended question referred to "coping strategies"?

Questions for Discussion

7. Participants were paid to participate in the program. Is this important? Why? Why not? (See lines 133–135.)

8. Keeping in mind that journal articles tend to be relatively short, is the workshop described in sufficient detail? (See lines 163–208.)

9. Is it important to know that only 52% of the participants completed both the pre- and posttests? Explain. (See lines 239–241, 327–329, and 459–466.)

10. Do you agree that it would be desirable to have comparison groups in future evaluations of this program? Explain. (See lines 457–459.)

11. Do you believe that the program caused the changes from pretest to posttest? Explain. (See lines 464–466.)

12. Based on this evaluation, do you believe that the workshop deserves further investigation in the future? Explain.

Quality Ratings

Directions: Indicate your level of agreement with each of the following statements by circling a number from 5 for strongly agree (SA) to 1 for strongly disagree (SD). If you believe an item is not applicable to this research article, leave it blank. Be prepared to explain your ratings. When responding to criteria A and B below, keep in mind that brief titles and abstracts are conventional in published research.

A. The title of the article is appropriate.

    SA   5   4   3   2   1   SD

B. The abstract provides an effective overview of the research article.

    SA   5   4   3   2   1   SD

C. The introduction establishes the importance of the study.

    SA   5   4   3   2   1   SD

D. The literature review establishes the context for the study.

    SA   5   4   3   2   1   SD

E. The research purpose, question, or hypothesis is clearly stated.

    SA   5   4   3   2   1   SD

F. The method of sampling is sound.

    SA   5   4   3   2   1   SD

G. Relevant demographics (for example, age, gender, and ethnicity) are described.

    SA   5   4   3   2   1   SD

H. Measurement procedures are adequate.

    SA   5   4   3   2   1   SD

I. All procedures have been described in sufficient detail to permit a replication of the study.

    SA   5   4   3   2   1   SD

J. The participants have been adequately protected from potential harm.

    SA   5   4   3   2   1   SD

K. The results are clearly described.

    SA   5   4   3   2   1   SD

L. The discussion/conclusion is appropriate.

    SA   5   4   3   2   1   SD

M. Despite any flaws, the report is worthy of publication.

    SA   5   4   3   2   1   SD

Article 26

Evaluation of a Program Designed to Reduce Relational Aggression in Middle School Girls

CHERYL DELLASEGA
Penn State College of Medicine

PAMELA ADAMSHICK
Moravian College

ABSTRACT. Physical and verbal aggression is an increasing problem in both middle and high schools across the United States. While physical forms of aggression are targeted in traditional "bullying" programs, relational aggression (RA), or the use of relationships to hurt another, is often not detected or addressed. For girls in the stage of identity formation, RA can impact negatively on self-concept, peer relationships, school performance, and mental and physical health. An innovative program designed specifically to help middle school girls confront and cope with issues related to RA was developed, implemented, and evaluated in two school systems. Attitudes and self-reported behaviors were measured before and after the program. Results show an improvement in relationship skills after participation in the program. Most noticeable improvements were in a girl's stated willingness to become involved when witnessing another girl being hurt and girls benefiting from the mentoring they received from high school juniors and seniors.

From *Journal of School Violence*, 4, 63–76. Copyright © 2005 by The Haworth Press, Inc. Reprinted with permission.

Introduction

Aggression in Youth

Since Columbine, the issue of aggression in youth has been at the forefront of the nation's consciousness. Across the country, administrators, guidance counselors, school nurses, and teachers witness violence be-
5 tween young people in the classroom, often on a daily basis. In a recent survey of high school students, more than one-third of respondents reported being in a physical fight in the past twelve months (CDC, 2002). A report commissioned by former President Clinton
10 showed that 30 to 40 percent of male youths and 15 to 30 percent of female youths admit to having committed a serious violent offense by age 17. The violent offenses included in this group are homicides, robberies, aggravated assaults, and forcible rapes (U.S. Depart-
15 ment of Health and Human Services, 2001).

Statistics on adolescent female violence show that the self-reported rate of violent acts by female adolescents is closing the gender gap. In 1998, the prevalence rates for male and female violence were similar to
20 1993, but the incidence rate for violent acts by females

rose (U.S. Department of Health and Human Services, 2001). In addition, the arrest of girls for assault and weapon charges has increased and now exceeds that for boys (Smith & Thomas, 2000). According to U.S. De-
25 partment of Justice statistics from 1991, 54% of reported violent crimes against 12–15 year old girls were committed by other girls or women (Whitaker & Bastian, 1991). In response to these troubling data, one of the national goals designated in *Healthy People 2010* is
30 to decrease physical fighting among adolescents (U.S. Department of Health and Human Services, 2000).

Bullying and School Violence

Bullying is a form of violence that may include behaviors that are verbally and/or physically aggressive. While many different definitions of bullying are used,
35 consensus has been reached on these characteristics: the bully's intent to inflict harm, his or her perceived or real power over the victim, repeated nature of the aggression, nonprovoking behavior by the victim, and the occurrence of the bullying within familiar social groups
40 (Griffin & Gross, in press; Olweus, 1994; Greene, 2000).

The bullying dynamic is a complex inter-relational process that relies on and is fueled by behaviors and responses of more than one participant. Typical roles
45 are the aggressor, the victim, and bystanders (also referred to as "witnesses" or "in-betweeners"). Victims may or may not provoke their aggressors, and many victims become retaliatory aggressors. As observers or passive participants, bystanders can deliberately or
50 inadvertently facilitate bullying (Hazler, 1996).

Relational Aggression

In studies on styles of aggression, interesting gender-specific findings have emerged. Researchers Lagerspetz, Bjorkqvist, and Peltonen (1988) studied 167 children aged 11–12 years and found that girls
55 engaged in more indirect aggression, a circuitous type of attack on another that amounted to social manipulation. Boys tended to use direct means of aggression. The term "social aggression" is sometimes applied to these behaviors because they occur within the context
60 of groups and because the participants have some de-

gree of relationship with one another (Underwood, Galen, & Paquette, 2001).

Some behaviors that can be involved in this type of nonphysical aggression can be found in Figure 1.

Gossip
Manipulation
Intimidation
Exclusion
Gestures
Ridicule
Saying something mean then pretending you were "joking"
Name calling
Teasing
Cliques
Campaigns
"On again–off again" friendships
Betrayal of confidence
Sending hurtful messages via cell phone or computer
Other subtle or not-so-subtle forms of harassment

Figure 1. Examples of Relational Aggression.

65   Crick and Grotpeter (1995) also found that girls were significantly more relationally aggressive than boys. They chose the term "relational aggression" rather than "indirect aggression" to describe the type of aggression displayed by females because the behaviors
70   they found were aimed at harming others through purposeful manipulation and damage of peer relationships. Their research, done with 491 third- through sixth-grade children in a Midwestern town in the United States, included children of varying ethnic backgrounds
75   (60% European American), thus supporting cross-cultural validity of gender differences in style of aggression. Their study added greater refinement to terms by using an instrument that did not confound relational aggression with nonverbal aggression.

80   The notion that girls can be bullies too is a phenomenon of great interest, as demonstrated by the recent movie *Mean Girls*. While physical aggression is an obvious cause for concern and intervention, the types of social aggression portrayed in the movie and
85   played out in classrooms, sports, and online every day are harder to detect and measure. These behaviors are sometimes dismissed as a female rite of passage, perhaps because RA seems to be most problematic in adolescent girls in middle and secondary school (Ahmad &
90   Smith, 1994).

RA may be more threatening to girls than physical forms of violence. In an online survey of over 2,000 girls ages 8–17, 41% of preteen girls and 22% of teen girls listed being teased or made fun of as their top
95   safety concern, remarkable when choices such as "terrorism" and "kidnapping" were other alternatives offered (Girl Scout Research Institute, 2003).

The developmental needs of adolescent girls who are struggling with identity formation through forging
100   connections with others may explain many RA behaviors (Gilligan, 1982). For example, exclusionary tactics

whereby a girl distances herself from peers she identifies as being "not like me," allows her to perceive a sense of status and being part of a select group (Hazler,
105   1996). There is also evidence that RA occurs within a girl's friendship circle, whereas males tend to aggress outside their circle of friends (Dellasega & Nixon, 2003). Relational aggression can impair normal development in that girls who consistently use RA behaviors
110   to interact with others begin to believe that their indirect bullying is not only acceptable, but also normal (Dellasega & Nixon, 2003).

Research by Galen and Underwood (1997) added another dimension to understanding nonphysical ag-
115   gression in youth. They defined social aggression to include not only verbal rejection or social exclusion, but also negative facial expressions or body movements. Their use of vignette measures that included nonverbal examples of social aggression had high in-
120   ternal consistency. The importance of nonverbals in aggression was further supported in a study by Paquette and Underwood (1999) with pre-adolescents. Findings showed that nonverbal forms of social aggression are experienced most frequently in that age group.

125   Cillessen and Mayeux (2004) followed a group of 905 students from fifth to ninth grade and examined the interplay between popularity and aggression during this developmental period. They found that as participants moved from middle childhood into early adolescence
130   relational aggression increasingly predicted high popularity, but low levels of liking. However, the concept of popularity itself changed during this span of time. "Popular" evolved from being well liked as a fifth grader to being influential and powerful in the ninth
135   grade. The researchers conclude that adolescents use relational aggression to maintain their dominant, influential position in the peer group. The results suggest that intervention studies to reduce bullying should take into account the status enhancing and rewarding quali-
140   ties of relationally aggressive behaviors for this developmental period.

While the old adage of "names will never hurt you" (as opposed to sticks and stones, which will break bones) is often cited, the reality is that RA can have
145   serious outcomes for both aggressors and victims (Crick & Grotpeter, 1995; Dellasega & Nixon, 2003; Nansel et al. 2001; Paquette & Underwood, 1999). These include risk for substance abuse, bulimic behaviors, delinquency, and development of low self-esteem
150   and adjustment problems in victims (Crick, Casas, & Nelson, 2002). In one tragic case, repeated RA led a Canadian girl to suicide, and others have observed that in girls, RA often precedes physical forms of violence (Dellasega, in preparation). Some negative impacts
155   specifically reported by aggressors include a sense of loneliness and depression (Tomada & Schneider, 1997). Crick and Grotpeter (1995) found that relationally aggressive youth were significantly more rejected than their nonrelationally aggressive peers and reported

160 higher levels of isolation, depression, and loneliness. Young women often replicate these roles into adulthood, adopting a "victim" or "bully" stance in their relationships with men (Dellasega, in press).

Risk for relationally victimized females is sup-
165 ported by the research of Crick and Grotpeter (1995), which showed females had a stronger relationship between relational aggression and social–psychological maladjustment than males. Paquette and Underwood's (1999) study of gender differences in the experience of
170 peer victimization found that girls were more distressed by social aggression than boys were. Their findings showed that frequency of social aggression was more strongly related to girls' self-concepts than to boys'.

Studies on factors that motivate young females to
175 use relational aggression in their relationships have also been conducted. One qualitative study using focus groups was completed with adolescent females in Australia to determine their perspectives on the causes of relational aggression. Some explanations for the behav-
180 ior included boredom and desire for excitement (Owens, Shute, & Slee, 2000). Further studies are needed to determine factors that underlie relational aggression in girls of nonwhite cultures and disadvantaged economic groups. By illuminating the experience
185 of peer-to-peer aggression in diverse groups of adolescent females, a more comprehensive view of etiological factors in relational aggression will emerge.

Interventions

Empirical studies of antibullying interventions in general suggest that school-based interventions
190 (Olweus, 1994), strategies aimed at peer involvement ("befriending") (Menesini, Codecasa, Benelli, & Cowie, 2003) and peer support processes (Stevens, De Bourdeaudhuij, & van Oost, 2000) may be effective. The most efficacious treatments for bullying appear to
195 be those that utilize the peer group in a supportive way to assist the bully or victims.

Few interventions to specifically address RA have been developed, and often teachers admit they feel ill-prepared to handle these behaviors (Smith, personal
200 communication, 2003). While empirical studies are lacking, innovative approaches to mediate relational aggression seem to be achieving success. Camp Ophelia™ and Club Ophelia™ are two initiatives that function in a preventive mode for middle school girls.
205 These programs are designed to create safe environments for middle school girls to learn positive relational skills. The programs use an arts-based curriculum and mentoring by high school girls in an ERI model: educate, relate, and integrate. Girls first are
210 taught about RA and how it hurts others. They then relate RA to their everyday lives, and develop alternative behaviors. Finally, they integrate the new healthy relationship behaviors they have identified as feasible for them into their everyday life. For example, not
215 every girl who is a bystander or witness of RA is brave enough to speak out. One realistic alternative some girls felt they could use was to move away from the aggression and stand next to the victim.

The Study

This study involved a program evaluation of Club
220 Ophelia™, which was offered at two middle schools serving a diverse population of girls during the 2003–2004 academic year. Each program lasted throughout a semester (twelve weeks) and utilized the same ERI model.

Methods

225 In both locations, the director of Club Ophelia (CD) implemented the program with a school faculty as co-director. Middle school girls could self-select or be referred into the program. Junior and senior girls from the same school system served as mentors for the mid-
230 dle school girls with a 1:5 ratio. Each session of the program was supervised by the director and at least one other adult director with counseling skills.

Evaluation

A basic demographic sheet, which also measured relationship-oriented behaviors, was the first part of the
235 evaluation. These questions asked girls what they thought their "RA role" was, and how often they suffered from the consequences of RA in a week's time.

To assess the impact of the program on relationship skills of the participants, The Girls Relationship Scale
240 (GRS) was administered. This scale was developed using a previous evaluation tool from camp and club as well as input from participants. It contains 20 items in a four-point Likert-type format that measures Knowledge About Relationships (4 items), Beliefs About Self (4
245 items) and Beliefs About Relationships with Others (10 items). A higher score represents better relational skills. To prevent response-set bias, some items are reverse coded. After establishing content validity, to assess the reliability of the scale, a test–retest Pearson's
250 correlation coefficient was calculated and revealed a coefficient of .74.

Procedures

Forty-two girls (*M* age 13.2 yrs.) participated in the program. In addition to a face sheet that collected demographic and relationship information, the GRS
255 was given before beginning and upon completion of the program. Girls responded anonymously by using birth date rather than name so confidentiality was preserved. In the closing session, girls were also given the opportunity to share what, if anything, they had learned
260 during the program in small and large group discussions.

Analysis

Data were coded and entered using Minitab, Release 14 (2003). Summary statistics on demographic data at baseline were performed first. Although re-
265 sponses were matched from pre- to post-program for

143

those girls who completed two evaluation forms, only 26 girls (62%) did so. The data here, therefore, use group averages to estimate changes in behavior.

Characteristics of participants are presented in Table 1. Due to the preliminary nature of the program evaluation, details such as self-referral vs. referral by others, history of delinquency, and other variables which would be relevant in an empirical study were not collected.

Table 1
Demographic Characteristics of Participants

Variable	N	(%)
Ethnicity		
Caucasian	16	(66)
Black	3	(3)
Bi- or Multiracial	5	(20)
No response	18	
Your role in RA in the last week		
Bully	1	(2)
Bystander	10	(23)
Victim	9	(21)
All three	12	(28)
None	10	(23)
Difficulty concentrating in school because of RA		
Very often	4	(10)
Often	5	(12)
Not sure	19	(45)
Not often	3	(7)
Never	11	(26)
Think of staying home from school due to RA		
Very often	4	(10)
Often	5	(12)
Not sure	19	(45)
Not often	6	(23)
Never	3	(12)

The next series of analyses focused on RA behaviors. First, girls were asked to identify how many times in the previous week relationships with other girls had influenced their behavior. A separate series of *t*-tests were used to compare before and after program responses. These results are in Table 2.

Table 2
RA Behaviors

Variable	Pre	Post
# of times hurt by RA	5.2	3.04
# of times seen others hurt by RA	6.3	4.8
# of times girl used RA	2.4	2.4
# of times RA message sent via computer	1.1	.76
# of times felt physically sick or depressed because of RA	.90	.88

Note. All questions within context of week immediately before.

Next, the subscales and total scores of the GRS were compared using *t*-test and ANOVA to check for significant differences (Table 3).

Table 3
Means for Responses on the Girls Relationship Scale

Item	Time one	Time two	Change	p
Feelings about self	2.8	2.9	+.1	NS
Believe girls are nice	2.1	2.4	+.3	NS
Trust other girls	1.2	1.5	+.3	NS
Want more friends	2.0	2.0		NS
Okay to be mean back	1.5	1.4	−.1	NS
Enjoy being with girls	2.2	2.1	−.1	NS
Girls in my school are nicer	1.2	1.2		NS
I know what RA is	1.4	1.6	+.2	NS
Okay to defend physically	2.3	2.0	−.3	NS
Want to change behavior	1.7	1.9	+.2	NS
Relationships make me afraid to come to school	3.1	3.0	−.1	NS
I know where to get help	2.8	2.8		NS
I know what to do when hurt	2.7	2.8	+.1	NS
Feel confident of friend-ability	2.7	2.9	+.2	NS
Mentoring helps	2.2	2.7	+.5	NS
Feeling safe is important	2.4	2.3	−.1	NS
Ability to communicate	2.4	2.5	+.1	NS
Okay to hurt back	1.8	1.9	−.1	NS
Don't get involved when other girl hurt	1.8	2.4	+.6	NS
Total score	45.2	47.1	+1.9	NS

Results

Nearly a quarter of this diverse group of middle school girls experienced an impact of RA on their behavior, either in thinking of staying home from school, being unable to concentrate, or actually feeling physically sick or depressed because of relationship issues with girls. Girls recognized that they could play all three RA roles at some time or another in an average week.

Actual behaviors were reported to change in a favorable direction, although, again not statistically significant. Girls were hurt less by RA, did not see others hurt by RA as much (perhaps because they intervened), and sent fewer hurtful messages on the computer. Although none of the change scores on the GRS or the total score reached significance, relationship skills improved in the expected dimension for all items except: "Feeling safe with other girls is important to me," which girls indicated was slightly less important. The most noticeable improvement (but still nonsignificant) in relationship skills was demonstrated for two items that related to getting involved when you saw another girl being hurt and benefiting from mentoring.

Limitations of the Study

Obviously, this was a very preliminary study with a small sample and new evaluation tool. Since the two middle schools used were very different in demographic and ethnic composition, specific comparisons across sites with a larger sample would enhance the findings of the study. Since the evaluation was focused on the program, more sophisticated data collection which could assess variables connected with RA did not occur.

Discussion

315 This study shows that the everyday life of many middle school girls is profoundly influenced by the negative consequences of RA, whether it arrives face-to-face or online. The degree to which girls could not concentrate in school or thought of staying home from

320 school because of relationship issues with other girls suggests that verbal aggression is as intimidating and distressing as physical forms of violence. However, after completing a program specifically targeted at RA, girls developed a sense of confidence about them-

325 selves, their friend-ability, and what to do when hurt and where to go for help.

Implications for Practice

Although many excellent programs exist for addressing overt physical bullying, this study suggests that strategies for overcoming relational aggression are

330 equally important. Perhaps more significant than the statistics contained here is the observation of a guidance counselor in one of the participating schools that the frequency of certain girls' visits to her office decreased during the program. One administrator calcu-

335 lated (roughly) that delinquent episodes decreased 33% in girls participating in the program.

Girls in middle school need to feel safe in relationships. Initiatives such as Club Ophelia™ address the core safety issues in girls' relationships through a plat-

340 form of mentoring that allows girls to experience a positive and safe relationship with an older peer. Research on bullying has confirmed that processes using befriending and peer support are the most efficacious (Menesini, Codecasa, Benelli, & Cowie, 2003; Stevens,

345 De Bourdeaudhuij, & van Oost, 2000).

Teachers, school nurses, administrators, guidance counselors, and school social workers are in a front line position to facilitate use of the ERI model to educate, relate, and integrate principles of RA for girls. The

350 addition of the arts-based curriculum and mentoring from senior girls as occurs in Club Ophelia™ can enhance effectiveness of this intervention.

Girls in this study responded that they have awareness of where and how to get help when hurt in their

355 relationships, which is another important strategy that can be promoted by school personnel. Asking each girl to identify a "safe place, safe person" empowers her to have a response ready when RA occurs.

School personnel need to be alert to aggressive sub-

360 tleties that are the hallmark of relational aggression. Early and appropriate recognition of these behaviors as well as an understanding of the damage they can inflict is a key first step in combating RA. Ground rules for classroom RA behaviors and student-generated conse-

365 quences for infringement can be a powerful experiential activity that accomplishes both of these purposes. To address RA on a school-wide basis, one middle school administrator chose to have all girls participate in a brief intervention which used the ERI model.

370 Middle school is the learning laboratory for relationship skills that can last a lifetime. In this study, an intervention with concrete skills for "helping rather than hurting" demonstrated that girls really do want to be kind.

References

Centers for Disease Control. (2002). Youth risk behavior surveillance—United States, 2001. *MMWR, 51* (SS-04) 1–64.

Cillessen, A. H. N., & Mayeux, L. (2004). From censure to reinforcement: Developmental changes in the association between aggression and social status. *Child Development, 75*.

Club Ophelia a safe place for girls. (n.d.). *What's Club Ophelia? You are!* Retrieved March 8, 2004, from http://www.clubophelia.com/index.htm

Crick, N. R., Casas, J. F., & Nelson, D. A. (2002). Toward a more comprehensive understanding of peer maltreatment: Studies of relational victimization. *Current Directions in Psychological Science, 11*, 98–101.

Crick, N. R., & Grotpeter, J. (1995). Relational aggression, gender, and social-psychological adjustment. *Child Development, 66*, 710–722.

Dellasega, C. (In preparation). *The impact of mentoring.*

Dellasega, C. (In press). *Two faced: Adult women who aggress.* John Wiley: 2005.

Dellasega, C., & Nixon, C. (2003). *Girl wars: Twelve strategies that will end female bullying.* New York: Fireside.

Galen, B. R., & Underwood, M. K. (1997). A developmental investigation of social aggression among children. *Developmental Psychology, 33*, 589–600.

Gilligan, C. (1982). *In a different voice: Psychological theory and women's development.* Cambridge, MA: Harvard University Press.

Girl Scout Research Institute. (2003). *Feeling safe: What girls say.* New York: Girl Scouts of the USA.

Greene, M. B. (2000). Bullying and harassment in schools. In R. S. Moser, & C. E. Franz (Eds.), *Shocking violence: Youth perpetrators and victims—A multi-disciplinary perspective* (pp. 72–101). Springfield, IL: Charles C. Thomas.

Griffin, R. S. & Gross, A. M. (in press). Childhood bullying: Current empirical findings and future directions for research. *Aggression and Violent Behavior.*

Hazler, R. J. (1996). *Breaking the cycle of violence: Interventions for bullying and victimization.* Washington, DC: Taylor & Francis.

Lagerspetz, K. M., Bjorkqvist, K., & Peltonen, T. (1988). Is indirect aggression typical of females? Gender differences in aggressiveness in 11 to 12 year old children. *Aggressive Behavior, 14*, 403–414.

Menesini, E., Codecasa, E., Benelli, B., & Cowie, H. (2003). Enhancing children's responsibility to take action against bullying: Evaluation of a befriending intervention in Italian middle schools. *Aggressive Behavior, 29*, 1–14.

Nansel, T. R., Overpeck, M., Ramani, S. P., Pilla, R. S., Ruan, W. J., Simons-Morton, B. et al. (2001). Bullying behaviors among U.S. youth: Prevalence and association with psychosocial adjustment. *Journal of the American Medical Association, 285*, 2094–2100.

Olweus, D. (1994). Annotation: Bullying at school: Basic facts and effects of a school-based intervention program. *Journal of Child Psychology and Psychiatry, 35*, 1171–1190.

Owens, L., Shute, R., & Slee, P. (2000). "I'm in and you're out...." Explanations for teenage girls' indirect aggression. *Psychology, Revolution, and Gender, 2.1*, 19–46.

Paquette, J. A., & Underwood, M. K. (1999). Gender differences in young adolescents' experiences of peer victimization: Social and physical aggression. *Merrill-Palmer Quarterly, 45*, 242–266.

Smith, H., & Thomas, S. P. (2000). Violent and nonviolent girls: Contrasting perceptions of anger experiences, school, and relationships. *Issues in Mental Health Nursing, 21*, 547–575.

Stevens, V., De Bourdeaudhuij, I., & van Oost, P. (2000). Bullying in Flemish schools: An evaluation of anti-bullying intervention in primary and secondary schools. *British Journal of Educational Psychology, 70*, 195–210.

Tomada, G., & Schneider, B. H. (1997). Relational aggression, gender, and peer acceptance: Invariance across culture, stability over time, and concordance among informants. *Developmental Psychology, 33*, 601–609.

Underwood, M. K., Galen, B. R., & Paquette, J. A. (2001). Top ten challenges for understanding gender and aggression in children: Why can't we all just get along? *Social Development, 10*, 248–266.

U.S. Department of Health and Human Services. (2000). *Healthy people 2010.* (Conference Edition, in Two Volumes). Washington, DC: U.S. Government Printing Office.

U.S. Department of Health and Human Services. (2001). *Youth violence: A report of the surgeon general.* Washington, DC: U.S. Government Printing Office.

Whitaker, C., & Bastian, L. (1991). *Teenage victims: A national crime survey report*. Washington, DC: U.S. Department of Justice, Bureau of Justice Statistics.

About the authors: *Cheryl Dellasega* is professor, Penn State College of Medicine, Hershey, PA. *Pamela Adamshick* is assistant professor of nursing, Moravian College, 1200 Main Street, Bethlehem, PA 18018.

Address correspondence to: Dr. Dellasega, Department of Humanities, H134, 500 University Drive, P.O. Box 850, Hershey, PA 17033-0850. E-mail: cdellasega@psu.edu

Exercise for Article 26

Factual Questions

1. For the GRS, what is the value of the test–retest Pearson correlation coefficient?

2. Did the girls respond anonymously?

3. What percentage of the girls completed two evaluation forms (pre and post)?

4. What was the mean total score at time one on the GRS?

5. Was the difference between the time one and time two means on the GRS statistically significant?

Questions for Discussion

6. In your opinion, is the program described in sufficient detail? (See lines 197–232.)

7. This evaluation used a one-group, pretest-posttest design. In future studies, would you recommend using a control group? Explain.

8. The researchers describe the limitations of the evaluation in lines 306–314. In your opinion, are there any additional limitations that are not mentioned here?

9. Do you agree with the statement in the last sentence of the article? (See lines 371–374.)

10. Based on this evaluation, would you recommend funding for widespread implementation of this program? Would you want to see the results of additional evaluations before making such a recommendation? Explain.

Quality Ratings

Directions: Indicate your level of agreement with each of the following statements by circling a number from 5 for strongly agree (SA) to 1 for strongly disagree (SD). If you believe an item is not applicable to this research article, leave it blank. Be prepared to explain your ratings. When responding to criteria A and B below, keep in mind that brief titles and abstracts are conventional in published research.

A. The title of the article is appropriate.

SA   5   4   3   2   1   SD

B. The abstract provides an effective overview of the research article.

SA   5   4   3   2   1   SD

C. The introduction establishes the importance of the study.

SA   5   4   3   2   1   SD

D. The literature review establishes the context for the study.

SA   5   4   3   2   1   SD

E. The research purpose, question, or hypothesis is clearly stated.

SA   5   4   3   2   1   SD

F. The method of sampling is sound.

SA   5   4   3   2   1   SD

G. Relevant demographics (for example, age, gender, and ethnicity) are described.

SA   5   4   3   2   1   SD

H. Measurement procedures are adequate.

SA   5   4   3   2   1   SD

I. All procedures have been described in sufficient detail to permit a replication of the study.

SA   5   4   3   2   1   SD

J. The participants have been adequately protected from potential harm.

SA   5   4   3   2   1   SD

K. The results are clearly described.

SA   5   4   3   2   1   SD

L. The discussion/conclusion is appropriate.

SA   5   4   3   2   1   SD

M. Despite any flaws, the report is worthy of publication.

SA   5   4   3   2   1   SD

Article 27

An Application of Fear Appeal Messages to Enhance the Benefits of a Jail Encounter Program for Youthful Offenders

JAMES O. WINDELL
Oakland County Circuit Court
Family Division Psychological Clinic

J. SCOTT ALLEN, JR.
Oakland County Circuit Court
Family Division Psychological Clinic

ABSTRACT. Research has consistently shown that so-called Scared Straight types of jail encounter programs do not have positive benefits for youthful offenders. However, few, if any, inmate–youth encounter programs have utilized the results of fear appeals message research. Results of the present study suggest that an inmate–youth encounter program may lead to attitude change in youthful offenders if components of successful fear appeals are incorporated into the program.

From *Youth Violence and Juvenile Justice*, 3, 388–394. Copyright
© 2005 by Sage Publications, Inc. Reprinted with permission.

After almost 20 years of researching and studying aversion programs for juveniles, Finckenauer and other criminologists have concluded that Scared Straight and similar programs are failures (Finckenauer, Gavin, Hovland, & Storvoll, 1999; Sherman et al., 1998). Nonetheless, such programs persist, usually with public and governmental approval. The underlying theory of all such programs is criminal deterrence. Program advocates believe that the realistic depiction of adult prison will deter juvenile delinquents or children at risk from becoming delinquent and from further involvement with crime (Finckenauer, 1982; Szymanski & Fleming, 1971).

However, no matter how often researchers review programs that provide juveniles with scary messages about crime and delinquency, the results are at best disheartening. Most recently, Petrosino, Turpin-Petrosino, and Finckenauer (2000) reviewed nine randomized evaluations of Scared Straight prison programs conducted between 1967 and 1992. Data from this review indicate that such programs likely have harmful effects leading to increased crime and delinquency. The authors concluded that given the harmful effects of these kinds of interventions, governments have an ethical responsibility to rigorously evaluate the policies, practices, and programs they implement (Petrosino et al., 2000).

Although Scared Straight types of programs have a dubious theoretical and research history, there is a considerable body of research related to persuasive messages that arouse fears. The psychology of using fear to influence people has been studied during the past 50 years, but this research has not been applied to Scared Straight types of programs. Because the purpose of jail tours and youth–inmate confrontations is to evoke fear of consequences, the psychology of fear appeals is particularly relevant. Witte and Allen (2000) indicate that the nearly 5 decades of research on fear appeals show that certain fear appeals are successful. Recent research (Witte & Allen, 2000) suggests that the stronger the fear appeal, the greater the potential influence over attitudes toward relevant behaviors, intentions to change, and actual behavior changes.

Witte (1992) proposed a model known as the extended parallel process model (EPPM) that postulates that threat and corresponding fear motivates a response and that the efficacy of the threat determines the nature of that response. The possible responses to the perceived threat include either danger-control or fear-control actions. In this model, if the perceived threat is low, then the individual does no further cognitive processing of the fear because of a lack of motivation. If the perceived threat is high and there is also a high perception of one's ability (efficacy) to perform the recommended action (for instance, avoid further criminal behavior), the individual will be more inclined to follow the danger control recommendations. On the other hand, if the threat is high but the individual's perceived ability to deal with the danger is low or the individual believes the recommended action might not work (e.g., an individual might believe that he or she has no power to avoid criminal behavior), then the individual will be more likely to take some action to control his or her fear. A possible way of dealing with the fear is to become defensive or deny that the threat is real or that it applies to him or her.

Pratkanis and Aronson (1991) claim that a fear appeal is most effective when (a) it genuinely scares people, (b) it offers a specific recommendation for overcoming the fear-aroused threat, (c) the recommended

action is perceived as effective for reducing the threat, and (d) the message recipient believes he or she can perform the recommended action. These four criteria for an effective fear appeal may help explain why pre-
75   vious research on Scared Straight types of programs shows negative results.

It is suggested that the EPPM theoretical model is useful for understanding adolescent juvenile offenders who participate in any fear-arousing jail tour program
80   or any modified Scared Straight type of program. The Jail Tour Program (JTP) in the present study involved scheduling a group of adolescent offenders to go to an adult jail, view the facilities, hear lectures from police officers, and have a series of face-to-face confronta-
85   tions and encounters with inmates. Inaugurated in 1992 and run continuously since then, the program has had several hundred adolescent participants. To date, there has been no evaluation or assessment of its effective-ness, even though it continues to be included as a stan-
90   dard part of the probation requirements for many young people in the juvenile court selected for this study.

Most fear-inducing inmate–youth encounter pro-grams do not couple the induced fear with either an
95   underlying theoretical approach or specific components that have been found to bring about effective results in the fear appeals literature. In comparing the JTP of the present study to previous Scared Straight types of pro-grams, it was the addition of a segment incorporating
100   support for positive choices and recommendations to avoid future delinquency that differentiated it from others. The authors recognized that this fit with a fear appeals model and suggested the approach may hold greater potential for success than those previously stud-
105   ied. The program herein studied was unique in that it does use components that lead to more efficacious fear appeals.

The jail exposure program in the present study in-corporated fear, followed by useful recommendations
110   and efforts to heighten participants' efficacy—all com-ponents outlined by the EPPM model. Therefore, it was hypothesized that adolescent offenders participating in the program would report less favorable attitudes to-ward jail following the jail tour. Second, research has
115   shown that fear appeals do not affect males and fe-males in a differential manner. Therefore, it was hy-pothesized that adolescent offenders in the present study would develop less favorable attitudes toward jail regardless of their gender.

Method

JTP Description

120   The data collection for the present study took place in the county jail of a suburb of a large midwestern city. Corrections officers in the county jail developed a program for juvenile offenders, referred to as the JTP. The 2-hour JTP, in brief, utilizes a fear appeal coupled
125   with encouragement and recommendations for avoid-

ing future criminal activity. The evening JTP begins shortly after juveniles, who were court-ordered to par-ticipate, arrive with their parents. Three deputies (often three males but sometimes two males and one female)
130   experienced in running this program start by treating the adolescents as if they are new inmates of the jail. They are asked to store coats, hats, and belts in a locker and to stand in a line. They are led into the jail (without their parents, as parents are discouraged from going on
135   the tour) and in the succeeding hour and a half are in-troduced to how adult inmates are expected to adhere to a concrete, limited behavioral repertoire. In addition, the juveniles are given harsh messages about the mag-nitude of reduced individuality and restrictions on free-
140   dom in jails and the likelihood of experiencing un-pleasantness or harm. Vivid and personal language is used by the officers to emphasize the similarities be-tween the participants and the adult inmates. Messages, commands, and remarks that heighten the seriousness
145   of incarceration and even the likelihood that the juve-niles are highly susceptible to being incarcerated are repeated. The juveniles are allowed to see various sec-tions of the jail and to get a firsthand view of how in-mates are housed. Along the way they are given infor-
150   mation about recidivism, jailhouse management, and typical treatment of prisoners. When they reach group cells housing several prisoners, they are told to stand outside of these cells and ask any questions of the in-mates they choose. There is a give-and-take with in-
155   mates, with some inmates trying to intimidate the juve-niles. Some inmates reiterate the themes that were de-livered by the corrections officers, whereas others offer useful and well-intentioned advice.

In the last half hour of the JTP, the tone of the tour
160   changes, and the corrections officers soften their ap-proach. They ask more questions and try to relate more with the juveniles. The officers focus more on efficacy messages (e.g., "You can make the choice to avoid high-risk situations") and offer recommendations.
165   Based on Witte and Allen (2000), how individuals think about the threat and their assessment of their own power in dealing with that threat leads to adaptive or maladaptive attitudes and behaviors. The juveniles are finally taken to a cafeteria where they are encouraged
170   to talk about their goals and aspirations along with how they can avoid becoming jail inmates in the future. The officers give encouragement about how the juveniles will be able to implement their goals, stay in school, and avoid troublesome peers. The officers provide rein-
175   forcing statements that suggest they believe the juve-niles have it within their abilities to avoid further criminal behavior.

Participants

Juvenile Court hearing officers routinely order ado-lescents between the ages of 16 and 17 who have been
180   adjudicated for a criminal offense to go through the JTP. Overall, 327 adolescents participated in this study.

Table 1

Means and Standard Deviations for Scores on a Measure of Impressions of Jail for Juvenile Offenders

Group	Pretest		Posttest	
	M	SD	M	SD
Male	25.7	6.17	20.1	3.03
Female	25.6	5.69	19.9	6.19
Violent	27.8	5.32	22.3	5.07
Nonviolent	25.2	5.90	20.0	6.61

Note. The maximum possible score was 65, and the minimum possible score was 13.

Of these, 282 were males and 45 were females. A planned exploratory analysis necessitated identifying the nature of the offenses committed by the females in the sample. Of the females, 32 had committed nonviolent crimes, whereas 13 had been convicted of violent offenses.

Instrument

An instrument, termed the Jail Tour Adolescent Questionnaire (JTAQ), was developed for use in the present study. The JTAQ was constructed with the assistance of psychologists who work with adolescent offenders, and it was reviewed by juvenile probation officers and corrections officers. The JTAQ has 13 self-report items with a 5-point Likert-type scale (the points include strongly disagree, disagree, not sure, agree, and strongly agree). Each question asks the respondent to evaluate certain behaviors that occur in jail. The JTAQ items address favorable or unfavorable attitudes toward incarceration held by the respondent. Examples of items include, "Prisoners these days are treated very nicely by prison staff," "While in prison, prisoners get along and support each other," and "I think living in jail would be fun sometimes." The instrument was completed just prior to the program and again following the JTP.

Results

This study looked at the overall effect of the JTP on participants' responses on a self-report questionnaire. A one-way analysis of variance was used to assess the degree to which there were changes in adolescent offenders' scores on a questionnaire designed to reflect favorable and unfavorable evaluations of certain behaviors in jail. It was anticipated that participants would report a less favorable impression of jail after the JTP relative to their reported attitude before the JTP. A significant time effect was found, $F(1, 327) = 139.9$, $p < .001$, indicating that significant changes on the measure of attitude were associated with the JTP. Means for the pre-JTP versus post-JTP groups were 25.7 ($SD = 6.11$) and 20.1 ($SD = 6.06$), respectively.

This study also examined if significant differences existed between male and female participants on the instrument before and after the program. Previous research found no differential effect of fear appeals on boys and girls. No studies have examined the differential effect of a Scared Straight type of program on boys' and girls' evaluations of jail. Therefore, a subsequent focus of the current project was to identify if the sex of the participant mattered in whether or not they responded to the JTP as measured by changes in their attitudes as measured by the JTAQ. It was expected that male and female participants would develop a more critical attitude toward incarceration.

Based on these predictions, the data were analyzed using two-tailed paired samples t tests with a 95% confidence interval computed for the true differences between each pair of group means. All assumptions were met to allow for a parametric test. First, boys' pre-JTP and post-JTP mean standard scores on the JTAQ were compared. The boys' perspectives decreased significantly from pre-JTP to post-JTP: $t(281) = 14.6$, $p < .001$. Second, girls' mean pre-JTP and post-JTP standard scores on the JTAQ were compared using a paired t test. The girls' perspectives also decreased significantly from pre-JTP to post-JTP: $t(44) = 14.6$, $p < .001$. Both boys and girls were influenced by the JTP as reflected in the changes on the JTAQ (see Table 1 for means and standard deviations).

Discussion

The present study integrated fear appeal theory (the EPPM in particular) with a naturalistic inmate–juvenile encounter program. It was hypothesized that participants would report differences in their attitudes and impressions of jail after the JTP and that there would be no difference between the attitude of boys and the attitude of girls.

Consistent with the first hypothesis, it was found that participants did report a less favorable impression of jail after experiencing the JTP. Boys and girls were analyzed separately, and it was found that both groups had less favorable impressions of jail.

Although other studies found no difference or a negative influence from Scared Straight and juvenile–inmate encounter programs, this study found, on a questionnaire administered both before and after the encounter, that there was a significant and positive difference. One reason for this finding may be that this study used a pre-JTP and post-JTP self-report survey that was designed to measure attitudes toward jail and incarceration. Other research projects have used recidivism and various other indicators of attitude change as a measurement (Finckenauer, 1982; Petrosino, Turpin-Petrosino, & Buehler, 2003). The JTAQ was developed for this research project to gauge adolescent respon-

dents' attitudes toward jail. However, no psychometric properties were established for the JTAQ. Neverthe-
275 less, the results from the use of the JTAQ suggest that going through the JTP may have had a significant effect on the participants' impressions of jail. In particular, their attitudes toward being incarcerated became less favorable following the JTP.

280   Although the theory underlying the JTP is criminal deterrence, the mechanism for change in this type of intervention is through fear appeal. Because the purpose of jail tours and youth–inmate confrontations is to invoke fear, the psychology of fear appeals is particu-
285 larly relevant. That is, the JTP offers solutions that may be viewed by the juveniles as within their ability. In the EPPM explanation of fear appeals, messages that fail to offer solutions that the participants believe they can implement are less likely to lead to attitude and behav-
290 ior change. This theory suggests that for any jail tour program to be effective, it should incorporate the elements necessary for a fear appeals program to be successful. It should not only deliver a strong and scary message, but it should also tell adolescents very clearly
295 how they can avoid the scary outcome (going to jail). Then, participants need to come away convinced that they can apply the strategy successfully in their own life. The JTP may satisfy the conditions of a successful fear appeal.

300   A strength of this study is that it was conducted in a naturalistic setting. Most previous research into the effectiveness of fear appeals has studied participants in artificial settings (Witte & Allen, 2000). However, a limitation of this study is that multiple independent t
305 tests were conducted with no correction for chance significant findings. At least one significant finding may be because of chance. Furthermore, the questionnaire used in this study may not be a measurement of attitude but a measure of fear or some other construct.
310 Therefore, normed and standardized instruments need to be employed to better understand the effectiveness of the JTP. Also, this study did not have a follow-up phase, nor did it take into account recidivism or post-JTP behavior.

315   Finally, this research needs to be extended with the addition of other measures (such as recidivism) to determine effectiveness. A future direction for research could include development of an instrument that is based on the EPPM model to determine more precisely
320 if this model does explain positive changes. Determining this can help in the development of a paradigm for Scared Straight types of programs with a greater potential for bringing about the expected results.

References

Finckenauer, J. O. (1982). *Scared straight! And the panacea phenomenon.* Englewood Cliffs, NJ: Prentice Hall.

Finckenauer, J. O., Gavin, P. W., Hovland, A., & Storvoll, E. (1999). *Scared straight: The panacea phenomenon revisited.* Prospect Heights, IL: Waveland Press.

Petrosino, A., Turpin-Petrosino, C., & Buehler, J. (2003). Scared straight and other juvenile awareness programs for preventing juvenile delinquency: A systematic review of the randomized experimental evidence. The *Annals of the American Academy of Political and Social Science, 589,* 41–62.

Petrosino, A., Turpin-Petrosino, C., & Finckenauer, J. O. (2000). Well-meaning programs can have harmful effects! Lessons from experiments of such programs as scared straight. *Crime & Delinquency, 46,* 354–379.

Pratkanis, A., & Aronson, E. (1991). *Age of propaganda.* New York: Freeman.

Sherman, L. W., Gottfredson, D. C., MacKenzie, D. L., Eck, J., Reuter, P., & Bushway, S. D. (1998). *Preventing crime: What works, what doesn't, what's promising* (NCJ 171676). Rockville, MD: National Institute of Justice, U.S. Department of Justice.

Szymanski, L., & Fleming, A. (1971). Juvenile delinquency and an adult prisoner—A therapeutic encounter? *Journal of the American Academy of Child Psychiatry, 10,* 308–320.

Witte, K. (1992). Putting the fear back into fear appeals: The extended parallel process model. *Communication Monographs, 59,* 329–349.

Witte, K., & Allen, M. (2000). A meta-analysis of fear appeals: Implications for effective public health campaigns. *Health Education & Behavior, 27,* 591–615.

About the authors: *James O. Windell*, M.A., is a court psychologist at the Oakland County Court Clinic, where he runs adolescent treatment groups and conducts high-conflict, postdivorce treatment groups. He is also an instructor in the Criminal Justice Department of Wayne State University. His major interests include parenting, juvenile delinquency, social skills training of adolescents, and treatment of high-conflict divorces. *J. Scott Allen Jr.*, Ph.D., works as a senior psychologist at the Oakland County Court Clinic, where he primarily conducts court-ordered psychological evaluations for children, adolescents, and adults and supervises doctoral candidate students. His private practice focuses on family issues (e.g., child behavior management, challenges of adolescence) and mood and anxiety disorders.

Exercise for Article 27

Factual Questions

1. The letters "JTP" stand for what three words?

2. The researchers state two hypotheses. What is the first one that they state?

3. How many of the females had committed nonviolent crimes?

4. What was the mean pretest score for the females? What was the mean posttest score for the females?

5. Was the difference between the two means in your answer to Question 4 statistically significant? If yes, at what probability level?

6. According to the researchers, what is cited as a "strength" of this study?

Questions for Discussion

7. In your opinion, is the program described in sufficient detail? Explain. (See lines 120–177.)

8. The researchers provide examples of the items in lines 200–203. To what extent do these examples help you understand what the instrument measures?

9. In this evaluation, the researchers used a self-report instrument. An alternative is to use recidivism as an outcome measure for judging the effectiveness of such a program. In your opinion, is self-report or recidivism a better measure? Are they equal? (See lines 265–271 and 312–314.)

10. For a future study on the effectiveness of this program, would you recommend using a control group? Why? Why not?

11. If you were on a panel considering the possibility of major funding to permit widespread use of the JTP, what recommendation would you make? Would you recommend major funding? Limited funding until additional evaluations are made? No funding? Explain.

Quality Ratings

Directions: Indicate your level of agreement with each of the following statements by circling a number from 5 for strongly agree (SA) to 1 for strongly disagree (SD). If you believe an item is not applicable to this research article, leave it blank. Be prepared to explain your ratings. When responding to criteria A and B below, keep in mind that brief titles and abstracts are conventional in published research.

A. The title of the article is appropriate.

    SA   5   4   3   2   1   SD

B. The abstract provides an effective overview of the research article.

    SA   5   4   3   2   1   SD

C. The introduction establishes the importance of the study.

    SA   5   4   3   2   1   SD

D. The literature review establishes the context for the study.

    SA   5   4   3   2   1   SD

E. The research purpose, question, or hypothesis is clearly stated.

    SA   5   4   3   2   1   SD

F. The method of sampling is sound.

    SA   5   4   3   2   1   SD

G. Relevant demographics (for example, age, gender, and ethnicity) are described.

    SA   5   4   3   2   1   SD

H. Measurement procedures are adequate.

    SA   5   4   3   2   1   SD

I. All procedures have been described in sufficient detail to permit a replication of the study.

    SA   5   4   3   2   1   SD

J. The participants have been adequately protected from potential harm.

    SA   5   4   3   2   1   SD

K. The results are clearly described.

    SA   5   4   3   2   1   SD

L. The discussion/conclusion is appropriate.

    SA   5   4   3   2   1   SD

M. Despite any flaws, the report is worthy of publication.

    SA   5   4   3   2   1   SD

Article 28

Examining Delinquent Nongang Members and Delinquent Gang Members: A Comparison of Juvenile Probationers at Intake and Outcomes

PAMELA J. SCHRAM
California State University, San Bernardino

LARRY K. GAINES
California State University, San Bernardino

ABSTRACT. This study examines differences between juvenile gang and nongang members participating in a juvenile probation program designed to identify and intervene with youth considered to be high risk for subsequent criminal and delinquent activity. After participating in the Multidisciplinary Team Program, both gang and nongang members significantly improved their grade point average, lowered the number of classes missed, and reduced the number of suspensions. Both groups also improved on family functioning and a decrease in reported alcohol and substance abuse. There were also improvements for gang and nongang members concerning subsequent delinquent activity. The results suggest that at some levels, gang affiliation is not an impediment to treatment programming. A limitation to the study was that gang membership was based on self-report and law enforcement identification, which results in false positive and false negative designations. Additionally, the nongang group may have included youths who escaped being identified as gang members.

From *Youth Violence and Juvenile Justice*, *3*, 99–115. Copyright © 2005 by Sage Publications. Reprinted with permission.

Youth or juvenile gangs have become a significant criminal justice problem in recent years. Although they have existed in this country for many decades, they became more problematic with the emergence of the

5 crack problem in the 1980s. A number of established cultural gangs evolved into entrepreneurial gangs, and new entrepreneurial gangs developed as a result of the largesse of profits from crack dealing (Skolnick, Correl, Navarro, & Rabb, 1997). This shift resulted in in-

10 creased levels of criminality. Moreover, it seems that juvenile gang members commit a disproportionate amount of crime (Huff, 2004; Thornberry & Burch, 1997).

Nationally, the number of gangs and gang members

15 has increased exponentially over the last several years, which is owed in large part to gangs' increased involvement in drug trafficking. Egley and Arjunan (2002) report that the 2000 National Youth Gang Survey estimated that there were more than 24,500 gangs

20 and 772,500 gang members in more than 3,330 jurisdictions in the United States. As the gang problem increased in severity, so did efforts to deal with it and the crime problems associated with gangs. Reaves and Hickman (2002) report that 84% of large police de-

25 partments now have gang units.

Essentially, the response to the gang problem has taken three broad directions: suppression, prevention, and treatment. In terms of suppression, police departments implemented a number of gang suppression units

30 and operations (Archbold & Meyer, 1991; Bureau of Justice Assistance, 1997; Fritsch, Caeti, & Taylor, 1999), a number of legislative bodies passed stiffer gang penalties (Klein, 1996), and jurisdictions have used civil injunctions to intervene in gang activities

35 (Maxson, Hennigan, & Sloane, 2003). Preventative efforts also increased. Probation departments organized special units to more closely supervise gang members and other high-risk juveniles (Shelden, Tracy, & Brown, 2004), and a number of agencies across the

40 country implemented GREAT, a school-based prevention program similar to DARE (Esbensen, Osgood, & Taylor, 2001; Winfree, Lynskey, & Maupin, 1999). New treatment or rehabilitation programs evolved. Most of these programs have been cognitive behavioral

45 programs that target antisocial attitudes and values that delinquent juveniles possess (Latessa & Allen, 2003). All of these programs operate under the assumption that gang members are more difficult to treat or are involved in more heinous crimes than nongang delin-

50 quents.

The purpose of this study is to examine a juvenile treatment program that includes gang members and nongang juvenile offenders. There is evidence that gangs commit a disproportionately high volume of

55 crime (Huff, 2004; Thornberry & Burch, 1997), and Hill, Howell, Hawkins, and Battin-Pearson (1999) and Esbensen, Huizinga, and Weiher (1993) found that gang members often are exposed to a host of risk factors prior to joining a gang. This high-risk environment

60 may result in gang members being more difficult to treat or rehabilitate. There is a paucity of research examining differences between these two groups once they have been apprehended and processed through the court system. This study focuses on a juvenile proba-
65 tion program operated in San Bernardino County, California. It is a unique program in that it consists of a multidisciplinary team that attempts to provide a wide spectrum of services to both the juvenile and the family. The study consists of a truncated sample of juve-
70 niles. On one hand, they have been apprehended for crimes that warrant some form of supervision pointing to serious criminality. At the other end of the spectrum, their violations are not serious enough for them to be sentenced to the California Youth Authority or some
75 other form of out-of-home placement.

Defining Gangs and Gang Membership

One difficulty in examining the differences among delinquents and gang member delinquents is determining who is a member of a gang. First and foremost, there is substantial debate over what constitutes a gang,
80 with a number of definitions found throughout the literature (Bursik & Grasmick, 1993). Thrasher (1927) was the first to define gangs, and subsequently a number of other researchers have developed definitions with varying degrees of gradation of differences
85 (Klein, 1971; Miller, 1980; Spergel & Curry, 1990) or critiqued or expounded on definitional issues (Hagedorn, 1988; Klein & Maxson, 1989; Morash, 1983). This complicates gang-related research, particularly sampling and the generalization of results, because
90 there may be substantial differences among the various research populations based on the definition used to define the research population. For example, Los Angeles consistently has reported proportionately more gangs and gang membership than Chicago because of a
95 more liberal definition of what constitutes a gang (Maxson & Klein, 1990).

Definitional issues certainly are a factor affecting any gang-related research. In many cases, research involving gangs uses samples drawn from populations
100 identified by the police or another criminal justice agency or based on self-report. Esbensen, Winfree, He, and Taylor (2004) report that self-reporting is the most accurate method of identifying gang membership, whereas Curry (2000) found substantial overlap or con-
105 sistency in self-reported gang membership and criminal justice reports of gang membership. Thus, it appears that these two methods are the most promising methods of identifying gang membership.

Even though these methods are used to identify
110 gang membership, they do little to discern the level of gang involvement. There are gradations of gang involvement, usually noted by terms such as *wannabe*, *associate*, *hardcore*, and *O.G.* or *original gangster*. Winfree, Fuller, Backstrom, and Mays (1992), in a
115 self-report study, found that admissions of gang in-

volvement yielded an equal number of wannabes, former gang members, and current gang members. Even though a youth may be identified as a gang member, the designation does not shed light on the extent of
120 involvement, which is an inherent problem in gang research.

In this study, as others, we relied on official records to determine if a youth was a member of a gang. These official reports were generated as a result of law en-
125 forcement identification or admissions of gang membership. Law enforcement potentially labels juveniles as gang members when there is a history of gang membership, involvement in the commission of a gang-related crime, the presence of gang-related tattoos, or
130 associating with known gang members. Law enforcement determination of gang involvement and juvenile self-reports often leads to false positive and false negative identification, and they fail to identify level of involvement. Regardless of error and debate over the
135 definition of gangs, the officially identified gang members are used in this study.

This study examines the effectiveness of a comprehensive juvenile treatment program on gang members using nongang delinquents as a control group. The pur-
140 pose of the study is to determine if gang members are more difficult to treat relative to nongang delinquents. The following section provides a description of the program and its operation.

The Multidisciplinary Team (MDT) Home Run Program

The Home Run Program was designed to identify
145 and provide immediate consequences for first-offender behavior. The purpose of the Home Run Program was to reach those youth the probation department had identified as being at a high risk of becoming involved in serious crime. Determination of high risk was based
150 on the seriousness of the offense committed by the juvenile and the results of a risk assessment survey that examined the juvenile's social functioning, which includes factors such as crime at an early age, disrupted families, school failure, drug and alcohol abuse, and
155 association with other delinquent youth. The risk assessment used for the current study was based on findings from a previous study that assessed its validity in Orange County, California (Schumacher & Kurz, 2000). The program was developed to create positive
160 behavior among high-risk youth and give them the potential for a "home run" in life endeavors.

Although the probation department designated the juveniles in this study as high risk, it should be noted that their crimes included misdemeanors and low-level
165 felonies; otherwise, they would have been adjudicated to the California Youth Authority. The high-risk designation came from their risk assessment scores, which, for the most part, predicted future involvement in criminal behavior. Even though these juveniles were
170 identified as high risk, they essentially have been

minimally involved in criminal behavior, but they possess a number of social functioning problems. For the most part, the gravity of their social functioning out-weighs the crimes they have committed and is indica-
175 tive of future, more severe criminality (Schumacher & Kurz, 2000). Research indicates that gang membership, social function problems, and criminal activity, especially at an early age, places youths on a trajectory toward more severe criminal involvement and greater
180 gang participation (Huff, 2004).

The Home Run Program attempted to identify the chronic repeat offender early, even widening the net of current intake and assessment processes and maximizing the effectiveness of intervention to deter these indi-
185 viduals from further delinquency. Interventions included the efforts of a coordinated team of professionals from social services, mental health, public health, probation, and the community. The MDTs first attempted to holistically diagnose a juvenile's problems
190 and then provided intensive treatment to juveniles and their families. Interventions included elements of restorative justice, such as victim restitution and community services as well as traditional treatment modalities such as counseling and group therapy.

195 For example, the public health nurse may recommend that the juvenile receive some dental services; the clinical therapist may recommend that a family member receive some type of treatment for adult substance abuse; and the social services practitioner may
200 recommend that the family receive some type of programming to enhance parenting skills. By having a public health nurse, a clinical therapist, and a social service practitioner, in addition to a probation officer, all of the juvenile's problems could be addressed in a
205 holistic manner. This approach then paves the way to reducing the juvenile's involvement in subsequent delinquent and criminal behavior.

The major objectives of these MDTs included significantly reducing subsequent criminal behavior in
210 high-risk youth, strengthening families, improving school attendance and achievement, and strengthening communities. These goals demonstrated the comprehensiveness of the program and how it differed from more traditional programming.

Program Components

215 The MDT Program consisted of five teams located throughout San Bernardino County. The program was implemented in an effort to allow access to any youth in the county. Each team had a probation officer, a public health nurse, a licensed clinical therapist, and a
220 social services practitioner, as well as volunteers and others as dictated by client need. The teams implemented a case management protocol where high-risk juvenile probationers received extensive diagnosis and were exposed to a comprehensive individualized treat-
225 ment plan. The teams provided direct services and service referrals relevant to each team member's profes-

sional expertise. The teams were supervised by a supervising probation officer. Table 1 is a summary of various types of treatment interventions and supervi-
230 sory or justice interventions available for program participants.[1]

Table 1
Summary of Intervention Options

Treatment interventions	Supervisory or justice interventions
Tutoring	Home visits–probation officer
Mentoring	Home visits–other provider
Peer counseling	School visits–probation officer
Vocational training	School visits–other provider
Family counseling	Family visits–probation officer
Family conferencing	Family visits–other provider
Alcohol abuse counseling	Intensive probation supervision
Alcohol abuse treatment	Community service
Drug abuse counseling	Financial restitution
Drug abuse treatment	Interface with victim
Antitobacco use	Victim mediation
Life skills	Teen court
Mental health	Outside placement (not institution)
Parent training	Institutional commitment
Medical services	Work programs
Health education	Electronic monitoring
Physical therapy	Voice tracking
Conflict resolution	Day reporting center
Anger management	Neighborhood accountability board
Financial support	Police
ESL instruction	Judge
Crisis intervention or shelter care	Juvenile hall counselor
Speech therapy	
Youth leadership training	
After-school recreation	
Special-school-based programs	
Referral to child protective services	
Youth leadership program	
Social worker	
Doctor or nurse	
Big brothers or sisters	
School counselor	
Community service officer	
Child protective service worker	
Minister or religious counselor	

Note. ESL = English as a second language.

The philosophy of the MDT approach was that most agencies often provide services to these clients but do not usually share information or do not imple-
235 ment joint service planning. Thus, the MDT approach was an alternative style of resource sharing with the intent of providing a more comprehensive and collaborative treatment experience. This service delivery system came to be called *wrap-around* or *one-stop* service
240 where all of a juvenile's needs could be met in one comprehensive program. Furthermore, the case management approach attempted to ensure that each client received the treatment services that he or she required.

Program Implementation

The San Bernardino County MDT Program tar-
245 geted high-risk juvenile offenders. High risk was defined as offenders who were at a greater risk to chronically reoffend based primarily on their risk assessment scores. The criteria for identification of appropriate juvenile offenders were based on the following: (a) age
250 (17.5 years old or younger), (b) residency (San Bernardino County resident), (c) first-time offender status,

and (d) high-risk status based on the risk assessment instrument.

Referral process. The San Bernardino County Probation Department identified various points of intake for juveniles participating in the MDT Program including the following: (a) juvenile hall intake officers for in-custody juveniles, (b) community-service team officers located in most law enforcement agencies throughout the County who serve as out-of-custody intake officers, and (c) school probation officers who also served as out-of-custody intake officers on matters referred to them or matters initiated by them. Once a juvenile was placed on probation, and he or she met the above-listed criteria, a risk assessment was administered. This risk assessment was a modified version of the assessment administered in the Orange County 8% Factor Risk Assessment Worksheet (Schumacher & Kurz, 2000). It included such risk factors as family issues, school problems, delinquency factors, and substance abuse, which is consistent with the risk factors identified in either research (Huff, 2004).

If the juvenile met the criteria and was designated a high-risk youth, the intake officer contacted either the clerk or a supervising probation officer who entered the information into the MDT database, which verified that the juvenile met the program qualifications. Subsequently, the youth was randomly designated into the treatment or comparison group for the evaluation portion of the MDT program. For the present study, we have focused only on those juveniles who participated in the MDT program.

Assessment procedures. Following the referral process, those juveniles who were randomly designated into the MDT Program continued to the assessment process. This assessment included not only the juvenile but also his or her immediate family, as well as those significant friends and relatives who were a major influence in the youth's life. Part of the MDT philosophy was to treat the whole family because the juvenile affected family functionality, and the family had an impact on the juvenile's amenability to treatment (see Kakar, 1998). In addition, the risk assessment tool was also used (a) to ensure interrater reliability, (b) to verify that the juvenile was high risk, and (c) to provide data for the research portion of this program. The assessment process also included determining family functioning. The purpose of this procedure was to provide the team with necessary information about the family and possibly build a treatment program for family members who were having an influence on the youth.

An essential aspect to the assessment process was the initial contact made between the juvenile, his or her family, and the MDT members. Although team members made contact with the families independently, they often made contact as a team. During the initial contacts, the team members incorporated their unique ideology, training, and experience to develop an assessment relative to their function on the team. For instance, the clinical therapists would assess the juvenile and his or her family on psychological well-being and functioning. The public health representative attempted to address any health issues in the family. After all the assessments were completed, a meeting was held among the team members to share and to disseminate information. Subsequently, a treatment plan was developed.

The treatment plan. The treatment plan was conceptualized after the initial assessment and finalized through team consensus. At the beginning of the program, team members were invited to attend "wrap around training," which strengthened the importance of group decision making in terms of meeting client needs. It also emphasized a holistic approach to problem solving. The treatment planning process incorporated not only the specific client needs but also family, school, and other relevant aspects of the client's life. The treatment plan was developed by focusing on specific problems, possible solutions, strengths of the juvenile and the family, and goals to be met during the treatment phase.

On completion of the plan, the treatment period began for purposes of the MDT Program as well as for the research study. This was an essential distinction because the treatment assessment was a time-consuming activity. If the assessment was considered part of the treatment period, the juvenile would not obtain the necessary services for a 6-month time period. During the following 6 months, interventions were provided to this youth and his or her family based on those factors identified in the planning process. Throughout the treatment phase, the treatment plan could be modified based on the youth's success of meeting the specific goals as outlined in the plan.

The exit process. The exit of a juvenile from the MDT Program occurred exactly 6 months after the youth entered the treatment period. The exit process included completing a risk assessment, administering measures of family functioning, and collecting additional information.

Method

This research is based on a larger evaluation study that implemented an experimental research design that randomly designated juveniles into a treatment or control group (Campbell & Stanley, 1966; Lempert & Visher, 1988).

Sample

Juveniles were selected for the MDT Program during intake. Entry into the program was based on their meeting the program requirements listed above. Minors who had been previously under the supervision of the San Bernardino County Probation Department and those currently under supervision were excluded from the program. After a juvenile had been identified, and he or she met the above-listed criteria, a risk assess-

365 ment was administered. It included risk factors in four critical areas: (a) family issues, (b) school, (c) substance abuse, and (d) delinquency.

The sample for this study was selected from only those juveniles who participated in the MDT Program, 370 and the study attempted to discern any differences between the gang-affiliated and nongang juveniles in terms of their progress as a result of the program intervention.[2]

Data Collection

The data collection for the evaluation of the MDT 375 Program involved numerous individuals responsible for obtaining the necessary information throughout various points of the program and research time period. This process involved collecting data required by the California Board of Corrections as well as county-level 380 data specifically for San Bernardino. Data collection was initiated during intake with the risk assessment instrument.

The MDT members were provided with training on how the relevant data were to be collected and coded. 385 The training was repeated several times during the program to ensure quality control. The members were responsible for (a) obtaining data on those youth they were servicing and (b) completing the required intake and exit data forms. These data forms were then for- 390 warded to the researchers. The researchers also collected additional follow-up information on subsequent criminal and delinquent behavior by examining official records for any new offenses.[3] School records were examined to collect data on suspensions and unexcused 395 absences.

There were numerous measures implemented in this evaluation study. The data were collected from various sources (i.e., interviews with the juvenile, interviews with the juvenile's family members, San Ber- 400 nardino County Probation database, school officials) and included many individuals involved with the MDT Program. To ensure consistency in data collection from these various individuals, the data were coded on standardized data sheets and subsequently entered into the 405 data system file by the researchers.

Results

The initial analysis examines the background information of both gang and nongang members. Next, we examine the various types of treatment and supervisory interventions that each group received, as well as 410 their respective family members. Subsequent analyses explore whether there are any significant differences between these two groups on various risk factors such as school, alcohol and drug abuse, family, and criminal or delinquent behavior.

Background Information

415 There were 145 juveniles identified as gang members, and 137 juveniles identified as nongang members. Table 2 summarizes various background information

pertaining to these two groups. The average age for the juveniles in each group was slightly more than 15 years 420 old. There was no significant gender difference between each group. There was a significant racial or ethnic difference between both groups ($\chi^2 = 47.91$, $p < .001$). More than 70% of the juveniles in the gang member group were Hispanic (71.1%), followed by 425 African American (14.8%) and white (14.1%). Almost half of the juveniles in the nongang member group were white (52.9%), followed by Hispanic (36.8%) and African American (10.3%). The difference in racial composition of the two groups raises a limiting validity 430 issue in the research design, but as noted below, the two groups were virtually equivalent in terms of risk. It is not known if race or ethnicity plays a significant role at this point in the crime–gang projectory.

In reference to family factors, juveniles in both 435 groups reported similar trends with their primary care provider. There was a significant difference between these two groups and the number of siblings living at home ($t = 2.00$, $p < .05$); the gang member group reported an average of 2.04 siblings compared to the 440 nongang member group reporting 1.66. There was no significant group difference in self-reported or documented abuse or neglect.

For all three variables measuring school performance, there were no significant differences between the 445 gang member and nongang member groups. There were no significant differences between these two groups on various measures of criminal or delinquent background.

Program Interventions

Both groups reported similar trends concerning the 450 most frequent types of treatment interventions assigned and completed: family conferencing (gang member, $n = 112$; nongang member, $n = 133$); family counseling (gang member, $n = 110$; nongang member, $n = 117$); and mental health (gang member, $n = 100$; nongang 455 member, $n = 117$).

The most frequent type of supervisory or justice interventions assigned and completed among the gang member group was home visits–other provider ($n = 121$) followed by home visits–probation officer ($n = 460$ 95) and school visits–probation officer ($n = 93$). The nongang member group also reported a similar pattern regarding supervisory or justice interventions assigned and completed: home visits–other provider ($n = 161$), family visits–other provider ($n = 127$), and home vis- 465 its–probation officer ($n = 105$). When comparing the total number of interventions between these two groups, there was no significant difference ($t = 1.41$, $p = .160$).

When the gang and nongang groups were compared 470 as to whether they differed on overall program completion, there were no significant differences ($\chi^2 = 2.37$, $p = .307$). Specifically, 74 gang members completed the program requirements, whereas 59 failed to complete

Table 2
Summary of Background Information

	Gang member (n = 145)			Nongang member (n = 137)			Significance	
	$\overline{X}$	SD	%	$\overline{X}$	SD	%	t	χ^2
Age	15.34	1.38		15.8	1.94		0.85	
Gender								2.97
Male			69.0			59.1		
Female			31.0			40.9		
Race or ethnicity								47.91**
African American			14.8			10.3		
Hispanic			71.1			36.8		
White			14.1			52.9		
Primary care provider								2.34
Natural parents			69.7			76.3		
Natural parent and stepparent			15.5			14.5		
Relative(s)			14.8			9.2		
Number of siblings living with juveniles	2.04	1.70		1.66	1.38		2.00*	
Changes in residence in last year	0.54	0.79		0.67	0.98		1.20	
Reported abuse or neglect								1.55
Yes			34.5			38.7		
No			57.9			56.9		
Unknown			7.6			4.4		
Currently at grade level								0.13
Yes			10.6			11.9		
No			89.4			88.1		
School attendance problem								0.38
Yes			85.5			82.8		
No			14.5			17.2		
Any suspensions or expulsions in past year								5.00
Yes			83.9			72.7		
No			16.1			27.3		
Severity of current offense								2.06
Felony			20.1			20.6		
Misdemeanor			38.2			45.6		
Incorrigibility, truancy, runaway			2.8			2.2		
Does not apply			39.9			31.6		
Institutional commitments for now or in the past								1.09
Yes			25.7			20.4		
No			74.3			79.6		

*p < .05. **p < .001.

these requirements and an additional 7 youth dropped out of the program. In reference to nongang members, 79 completed the program requirements, 44 failed to complete the requirements, and 9 dropped out of the program.

The MDT Program also provided services beyond the juvenile offender to include his or her family members. Both the gang member and nongang member groups reported similar patterns in service delivery to family members. For both groups, mothers were the family member most likely to receive some type of service (gang member, *n* = 78; nongang member, *n* = 94), followed by siblings.

School Risk Factors

We examined various school factors between the gang member and nongang member groups at the beginning and the end of the treatment period (see Table 3). There were no significant differences in mean grade point average between these two groups at either the beginning or the end of the treatment period. We also examined additional school factors including class periods missed, classes enrolled, credits earned, and number of suspensions. Among these various factors, there was only one significant difference between these two groups: number of suspensions at the beginning of the treatment period. The gang member group had 2.49 suspensions, whereas the nongang member group had 1.65 suspensions (*t* = 2.22, *p* < .05). During the 6-month treatment period, there was no significant difference between these two groups and the number of suspensions and expulsions (*t* = 1.27, *p* = .206).

When comparing pretest and posttest measures within the gang member and nongang member groups, there were significant improvements on various school factors. For the gang member group, there were significant improvements in grade point average (*t* =

157

Table 3
School Risk Factors

	Gang member		Nongang member		
	$\overline{X}$	SD	$\overline{X}$	SD	t Test
GPA–Beginning of treatment	0.99	0.94	1.02	1.00	−0.24
GPA–End of treatment	1.61	1.07	1.59	1.16	−0.13
Class periods missed–Beginning of treatment	163.34	190.92	148.41	227.31	0.51
Class periods missed–End of treatment	61.41	76.96	57.88	68.18	0.35
Classes enrolled–Beginning of treatment	5.18	1.81	5.19	2.05	−0.40
Classes enrolled–End of treatment	5.66	4.08	5.56	2.57	0.21
Credits earned–Beginning of treatment	16.14	23.23	19.50	23.95	−1.02
Credits earned–End of treatment	18.61	22.92	22.93	28.94	−1.18
Number of suspensions–Beginning of treatment	2.48	3.29	1.65	2.21	2.22*
Number of suspensions–End of treatment	0.81	1.42	0.85	1.88	−0.19

*$p < .05$.

−5.03, $p = .000$), a reduction in the number of classes missed ($t = 2.80$, $p = .006$), and a decrease in the number of suspensions ($t = 4.35$, $p = .000$). The nongang member group also revealed the same areas of improvement: grade point average ($t = -3.53$, $p = .001$), number of classes missed ($t = -3.06$; $p = .003$), and number of suspensions ($t = 2.74$, $p = .007$).

Family Functioning

The Global Assessment of Relational Functioning (GARF) was administered to measure family functioning. The GARF is located in Appendix B of the *Diagnostic and Statistical Manual of Mental Disorders* (4th ed.; American Psychiatric Association, 1994). The GARF scale is a 100-point scale that measures interpersonal functioning of a relational unit on three dimensions: problem solving, organization, and emotional climate. The anchor points range from *very poor relational functioning* (low scores) to *satisfactory relational functioning* (high scores; Ross & Doherty, 2001, pp. 244–245). The GARF scale was administered to three groups: (a) the juveniles, (b) the parents or guardians of the juveniles, and (c) the MDT members who used the form to obtain their assessment of the juvenile. For each group, analyses were conducted to determine if there were any significant differences between the gang member and nongang member groups for both the pretests and posttests. The results revealed no significant differences between these two groups among the juveniles, parents or guardians, and MDT members (see Table 4).

When comparing pretest and posttest measures within the gang member and nongang member groups, there were significant improvements among the juveniles, parents or guardians, and MDT members' assessments. For the gang member group, there were significant improvements in perceptions of family functioning among the parents or guardians ($t = 4.61$, $p = .000$) and the MDT members ($t = 2.40$, $p = .019$). The nongang member group revealed significant improvements among the juveniles ($t = 3.40$, $p = .001$), the parents or guardians ($t = 5.17$, $p = .000$), and the MDT members ($t = 5.02$, $p = .000$).

Alcohol and Drug Problem

Pretest and posttest measures asked juveniles whether they had an alcohol or drug problem. Pretest data were collected at the time of the assessment, whereas posttest data were collected during a program exit interview. Juveniles were simply asked if they used either alcohol or drugs. If the juvenile responded in the affirmative, it was noted as a problem. This self-reporting obviously is suspect and is a limitation in the study.[4] However, it was believed that both groups would generate approximately similar error rates. There were no significant group differences in either the pretest or posttest measure regarding a drug problem (see Table 5), which was surprising because most research has found that gang members have a greater propensity toward drug and alcohol abuse (Jenson & Howard, 1998; Santman, Myner, & Cappelletty, 1997). There were, however, significant group differences in both these measures pertaining to an alcohol problem. In both tests, juveniles in the gang member group reported having more alcohol problems than juveniles in the nongang member group (pretest: $\chi^2 = 18.28$, $p < .01$; posttest: $\chi^2 = 10.19$, $p < .01$).

When examining within group differences, both the gang and nongang member groups demonstrated improvements. At the beginning of the program, 84.1% of the gang members reported a drug problem. At the end of the treatment period, this number dropped to 57.1%. In reference to an alcohol problem, 56.9% of the gang members reported having an alcohol problem. At the end of the program, 31.7% stated they had an alcohol problem. The nongang members also reported a similar pattern. More than 80% reported having a drug problem at the beginning of the program, whereas 42.9% stated they had a drug problem at the end of the program. At the beginning of the program, 38% had an alcohol program, whereas 15.3% stated they had an alcohol problem at the end of the program.[5]

Criminal or Delinquent Behavior

This portion of the analyses examines whether there were significant differences between the gang member

Table 4
Family Functioning

Instrument	Gang member		Nongang member		*t* Test
	$\overline{X}$	SD	$\overline{X}$	SD	
Juvenile GARF Scale					
Pretest	58.28	29.05	59.73	29.86	0.40
Posttest	64.16	28.00	67.33	27.00	0.83
Parent or Guardian GARF Scale					
Pretest	53.77	27.64	53.79	29.12	0.08
Posttest	66.40	29.86	68.83	26.02	0.63
Team GARF Scale					
Pretest	29.45	20.11	30.94	18.65	0.62
Posttest	38.27	24.23	43.23	26.56	1.47

Note. GARF = Global Assessment of Relational Functioning.

Table 5
Drug and Alcohol Problem

	Gang member	Nongang member	χ^2
Drug problem–Beginning of treatment			
Yes	122	114	1.44
No	9	13	
Unknown	14	10	
Alcohol problem–Beginning of treatment			
Yes	82	52	18.28*
No	36	68	
Unknown	26	17	
Drug problem–End of treatment			
Yes	56	42	2.25
No	68	75	
Unknown	11	12	
Alcohol problem–End of treatment			
Yes	44	20	10.19*
No	80	91	
Unknown	15	20	

*p < .01.

and nongang member group on criminal behavior.
590 Various indicators of subsequent criminal behavior
were tested for two time periods—during the program
and 6-month follow-up.[6] These indicators include the
mean number of arrests, any sustained petitions,[7] completion of probation, and completion of restitution. The
595 only significant difference between these two groups
and these various measures was the mean number of
arrests during the program; the juveniles in the gang
member group had a slightly higher number of mean
arrests ($\overline{X}$ = .55) than the juveniles in the nongang
600 member group ($\overline{X}$ = .37; see Table 6).

Discussion

Youngsters who experience problems in school,
with their families and peers, and face dangers or potential dangers to their health and development have
been described as at-risk youth (Huff, 2004). These at-
605 risk youth can endure such negative consequences as
delinquency, school failure, poor physical health, and
substance abuse. Policies attempting to address juvenile crime need to recognize the various environmental

factors that affect juveniles' propensities toward delin-
610 quent behavior.

One county in Southern California recognized that
a major gap in the continuum of services available to
juveniles and their families was to identify and intervene with youth considered to be high risk for subse-
615 quent criminal and delinquent activity. The Home Run
Program attempted to address this need by identifying
potentially chronic offenders early in an effort to
maximize the effectiveness of interventions to deter
these individuals from further delinquency. Interven-
620 tions included the efforts of a coordinated team of professionals from social services, mental health, public
health, probation, and the community. These coordinated teams were designated as MDTs. The major objectives of the MDT Program included significantly
625 reducing subsequent criminal behavior among high-
risk youth, strengthening families, improving school
attendance and achievement, and strengthening communities.

The overwhelming positive aspect of the MDT
630 Program was the number of interventions that both the

159

Table 6
Rearrests

	Gang member	Nongang member	Test statistic
Mean number of arrests during program	$\overline{X} = 0.55, SD = 0.72$	$\overline{X} = 0.37, SD = 0.62$	$t = 2.18*$
Mean number of arrests during 6-month follow-up	$\overline{X} = 0.20, SD = 0.42$	$\overline{X} = 0.19, SD = 0.39$	$t = 0.18$
Petition sustained for criminal offense during program			$\chi^2 = 0.91$
Yes	32	24	
No	108	108	
Petition sustained for criminal offense during 6-month follow-up			$\chi^2 = 0.53$
Yes	18	13	
No	99	95	
Completion of probation during program			$\chi^2 = 1.64$
Yes	24	32	
No	103	93	
Completion of probation during 6-month follow-up			$\chi^2 = .001$
Yes	32	28	
No	67	58	
Completion of restitution program			$\chi^2 = 1.64$
Yes	23	24	
No	61	51	
Completion of restitution program during 6-month follow-up			$\chi^2 = 0.24$
Yes	18	13	
No	66	58	

*$p < .05$.

juveniles and their families received while participating in the program. Another positive aspect to the MDTs and their service delivery was that the scope of their services went beyond the juvenile offender to include his or her family. Furthermore, these interventions were administered within a framework that encouraged teamwork and coordination from various professions rather than in a haphazard and uncoordinated approach.

This study wanted to further explore juveniles' participation in this MDT Program by examining whether there were any differences between youth who were involved in some type of gang activity with youth who were not involved with gangs. The results revealed few gang member and nongang member differences prior to and after participating in the program. Specifically, after participating in the MDT Program, both gang and nongang members revealed significant improvements on such school factors as increased grade point average, lower number of classes missed, and reduced number of suspensions. Both groups also improved on family functioning, as well as a decrease in reported alcohol and substance abuse. There were also improvements for gang and nongang members concerning subsequent delinquent activity. Thus, this study revealed that some juveniles benefited from participating in the MDT Program, regardless of their involvement in or identification with gang activities.

However, these results are tentative because of (a) validity problems associated with identifying gang-related participants in the study and because (b) program participants may not have had extensive gang affiliation. Even though self-identification and law enforcement designation are accepted methods of identifying gang members (Esbensen et al., 2004; Curry,

2000), the two groups in this study may have been contaminated as a result of errors in differentiating gang and nongang juveniles. Another validity problem is that there were no data detailing the extent of gang involvement by the designated gang group. Such limitations exist in gang research, especially in post hoc evaluation research.

Given this, however, these results suggest that at some levels, gang affiliation may not be an impediment to treatment programming. Those youth who are not yet seriously enmeshed in and strongly identified with the gang lifestyle may benefit from the same type of programming for those youth who have no gang affiliation. Intervention programs may be able to disrupt the gang culture trajectory.

Those youth more seriously involved in gang activities, however, may require some type of specialized treatment that recognizes gang membership as an impediment to programming efforts. On the other hand, gang affiliation at any level may not be an impediment to rehabilitation programming. Future research should concentrate on the levels of gang involvement and treatment modality. Because gang members who are seriously enmeshed in the gang culture tend to commit larger numbers of severe crimes, it would be fruitful to pursue more effective treatment strategies, especially early in the gang member's career.

Notes

1. These treatment and supervisory interventions, for the most part, are also available to juveniles placed on traditional probation. However, the primary purpose of the MDT Program was to coordinate the efforts of the various service providers (e.g., proba-

tion, public health, mental health, and social services) to develop a holistic treatment plan for the juveniles in the MDT Program to avoid any overlap, or oversight, when providing these interventions.

2. The current research study is from a larger evaluation study that compared youth who received treatment (i.e., MDT Program) and youth who received traditional probation services. The sample for the current study is based only on those juveniles who participated in the MDT Program.

3. Although this study used official arrest statistics as a measure of criminal or delinquent behavior, the researchers recognize the limitations of these data. First, official statistics usually underestimate the amount of criminal activity; specifically, these data only include criminal activity that has come to the attention of law enforcement. Second, the official statistics used for this study included only incidents in San Bernardino County. Thus, although a juvenile may not have any arrests in San Bernardino County, he or she may have been arrested in an adjacent county; but the researchers did not have access to that database.

4. It is noteworthy, however, that researchers have shown that self-report delinquency study results are quite reliable when checked against official records, reports of family and friends, and polygraph tests (Empey, 1978; Farrington, Loeber, Stouthamer-Loeber, Van Kammen, & Schmidt, 1996).

5. Tests of significance (χ^2) could not be conducted on these data because of more than 20% of the cells having an expected count less than 5.

6. Although it would have been useful to extend the follow-up period to 12 months, the California Board of Corrections, which funded and monitored this program, initially required a 6-month follow-up period.

7. A sustained petition has been filed by the district attorney's office and has been found true by the juvenile court.

References

American Psychiatric Association. (1994). *Diagnostic and statistical manual of mental disorders* (4th ed.). Washington, DC: Author.

Archbold, C., & Meyer, M. (1991). Anatomy of a gang suppression unit: The social construction of an organizational response to gang problems. *Police Quarterly, 2*, 201–224.

Bureau of Justice Assistance. (1997). Urban street gang enforcement. In *Gang suppression operations and tactics* (pp. 49–72). Washington, DC: Bureau of Justice Assistance.

Bursik, R. J., & Grasmick, H. G. (1993). *Neighborhoods and crime: The dimensions of effective community control.* New York: Lexington Books.

Campbell, D. T., & Stanley, J. (1966). *Experimental and quasi-experimental designs for research.* Chicago: Rand McNally.

Curry, G. D. (2000). Self-reported gang involvement and officially recorded delinquency. *Criminology, 38*, 1253–1274.

Egley, A., & Arjunan, M. (2002). Highlights of the 2000 National Youth Gang Survey. In *OJJDP Fact Sheet* (pp. 1–5). Washington, DC: U.S. Department of Justice.

Empey, L. T. (1978). *American delinquency: Its meaning and construction.* Homewood, IL: Dorsey.

Esbensen, F., Huizinga, D., & Weiher, A. W. (1993). Gang and nongang youth: Differences in explanatory variables. *Journal of Contemporary Criminal Justice, 9*, 94–116.

Esbensen, F., Osgood, D., & Taylor, T. (2001). How great is GREAT? Results from a longitudinal quasi-experimental design. *Criminology and Public Policy, 1*, 87–118.

Esbensen, F., Winfree, L., He, N., & Taylor, T. (2004). Youth gangs and definitional issues: When is a gang a gang and why does it matter? In F. Esbensen, S. Tibbetts, & L. Gaines (Eds.), *American youth gangs at the millennium* (pp. 52–90). Long Grove, IL: Waveland.

Farrington, D. P., Loeber, R., Stouthamer-Loeber, M., Van Kammen, W. B., & Schmidt, L. (1996). Self-reported delinquency and a combined delinquency seriousness scale based on boys, mothers, and teachers: Concurrent and predictive validity for African-Americans and Caucasians. *Criminology, 34*, 493–514.

Fritsch, E. J., Caeti, T. J., & Taylor, R. W. (1999). Gang suppression through saturation patrol, aggressive curfew, and truancy enforcement: A quasi-experimental test of the Dallas anti-gang initiative. *Crime & Delinquency, 45*, 122–139.

Hagedorn, J. M. (1988). *People and folks: Gangs, crime, and the underclass in a rustbelt city.* Chicago: Lakeview Press.

Hill, K. G., Howell, J. C., Hawkins, J. D., & Battin-Pearson, S. R. (1999). Childhood risk factors for adolescent gang membership: Results from the Seattle social development project. *Journal of Research in Crime and Delinquency, 36*, 300–322.

Huff, R. (2004). Comparing the criminal behavior of youth gangs and at-risk youths. In F. Esbensen, S. Tibbetts, & L. Gaines (Eds.), *American youth gangs at the millennium* (pp. 77–89). Long Grove, IL: Waveland.

Jenson, J., & Howard, M. (1998). Correlates of gang involvement among juvenile probationers. *Journal of Gang Research, 5*, 7–15.

Kakar, S. (1998). Youth gangs and their families: Effect of gang membership on family's subjective well-being. *Journal of Crime and Justice, 21*, 157–172.

Klein, M. W. (1971). *Street gangs and street workers.* Englewood Cliffs, NJ: Prentice-Hall.

Klein, M. W. (1996). Street gangs and deterrence legislation. In D. Shichor & D. Sechrest (Eds.), *Three strikes you're out* (pp. 203–232). Thousand Oaks, CA: Sage.

Klein, M. W., & Maxson, C. L. (1989). Street gang violence. In N. A. Weiner & M. E. Wolfgang (Eds.), *Violent crime, violent criminals* (pp. 198–234). Newbury Park, CA: Sage.

Latessa, E., & Allen, H. (2003). *Corrections in the community.* Cincinnati, OH: Anderson.

Lempert, R. O., & Visher, C. A. (1988). *Randomized field experiments in criminal justice agencies.* Washington, DC: U.S. Department of Justice, Office of Justice Programs, National Institute of Justice.

Maxson, C. L., Hennigan, K., & Sloane, D. (2003). For the sake of the neighborhood? Civil gang injunctions as a gang intervention tool in Southern California. In S. H. Decker (Ed.), *Policing gangs and youth violence* (pp. 239–266). Belmont, CA: Wadsworth.

Maxson, C. L., & Klein, M. W. (1990). Street gang violence. In C.R. Huff (Ed.), *Gangs in America* (pp. 71–100). Newbury Park, CA: Sage.

Miller, W. B. (1980). Gangs, groups, and serious youth crime. In D. Shichor & D. H. Kelly (Eds.), *Critical issues in juvenile delinquency* (pp. 115–138). Lexington, MA: D.C. Heath.

Morash, M. (1983). Gangs, groups, and delinquency. *British Journal of Criminology, 23*, 309–335.

Reaves, B. A., & Hickman, M. J. (2002). *Police departments in large cities, 1990–2000.* Washington, DC: U.S. Department of Justice.

Ross, N. M., & Doherty, W. J. (2001). Validity of the Global Assessment of Relational Functioning (GARF) when used by community-based therapists. *American Journal of Family Therapy, 29*, 239–253.

Santman, J., Myner, J., & Cappelletty, G. (1997). California juvenile gang members: An analysis of case records. *Journal of Gang Research, 5*, 45–53.

Schumacher, M., & Kurz, G. A. (2000). *The 8% Solution: Preventing serious, repeat juvenile crime.* Thousand Oaks, CA: Sage.

Shelden, G., Tracy, S., & Brown, W. (2004). *Youth gangs in American society.* Belmont, CA: Wadsworth.

Skolnick, J., Correl, T., Navarro, E., & Rabb, R. (1997). The social structure of street drug gangs. In L. Gaines & P. Kraska (Eds.), *Drugs, crime, and justice* (pp. 159–192). Prospect Heights, IL: Waveland Press.

Spergel, I. A., & Curry, G. D. (1990). Strategies and perceived agency effectiveness in dealing with the youth gang problem. In C. R. Huff (Ed.), *Gangs in America* (pp. 288–317). Newbury Park, CA: Sage.

Thornberry, T., & Burch, J. (1997). Gang members and delinquent behavior. In *OJJDP Juvenile Justice Bulletin* (pp. 1–5). Washington, DC: Department of Justice.

Thrasher, F. M. (1927). *The gang.* Chicago: University of Chicago Press.

Winfree, T., Fuller, K., Backstrom, T., & Mays, G. (1992). The definition and measurement of "gang status": Policy implications for juvenile justice. *Juvenile and Family Court Journal, 43*, 20–39.

Winfree, T., Lynskey, D., & Maupin, J. (1999). Developing local police and federal law enforcement partnerships: GREAT as a case study of policy implementation. *Criminal Justice Review, 24*, 145–168.

Note: An earlier version of this article was presented at the annual meeting of American Society of Criminology Chicago, Illinois, 2002.

About the authors: *Pamela J. Schram* is an associate professor in the Department of Criminal Justice at California State University, San Bernardino. She received her Ph.D. in criminal justice from Michigan State University in 1996. Her research interest includes juveniles, with a focus on evaluating juvenile programs in San Bernardino and Riverside Counties as well as women in the criminal justice system, with an emphasis on women in prison. *Larry K. Gaines* currently is a professor and chair of the criminal justice department at California State University, San Bernardino. He received his doctorate in criminal justice from Sam Houston State University in 1975. His current research agenda centers on the evaluation of police tactics in terms of their effectiveness in reducing problems within the community policing paradigm. He is also researching the issue of racial profiling in a number of California cities.

Address correspondence to: Pamela J. Schram, Department of Criminal Justice, California State University, San Bernardino, California 92407.

Exercise for Article 28

Factual Questions

1. Is the purpose of this study to compare gang members who received the program with gang members who did not receive the program?

2. Did any of the participants in the programs commit violations serious enough for them to be sentenced to the California Youth Authority or some other form of out-of-home placement?

3. Did each program team include a social services practitioner?

4. Were the team members trained in how to collect and code the data for this evaluation?

5. Which group had a higher mean number of arrests during the program?

6. At the beginning of treatment, how many gang members indicated they had a drug problem? How many indicated they had a drug problem at the end of treatment?

Questions for Discussion

7. Are you convinced that the definition of "gangs" and definition of "gang membership" are important issues in this type of research? Explain. (See lines 76–136.)

8. In your opinion, is the MDT program described in sufficient detail given that journal articles tend to be relatively short? Explain. (See lines 144–351.)

9. Do you agree that a 12-month program would have been more desirable than the 6-month program? Explain. (See lines 346–348 and endnote number 6 near the end of the article.)

10. There was a significant racial/ethnic difference between the two comparison groups. In your opinion, is this problematic? Explain. (See lines 421–433 and Table 2.)

11. This evaluation did not take into consideration the extent of gang involvement. Is this an important issue? Explain. (See lines 667–671.)

12. Is the use of official arrest statistics an important issue? Explain. (See endnote number 3 near the end of the article.)

13. Based on this evaluation study, do you regard the MDT program as promising? Would you recommend funding to extend the program to additional jurisdictions? Explain.

Quality Ratings

Directions: Indicate your level of agreement with each of the following statements by circling a number from 5 for strongly agree (SA) to 1 for strongly disagree (SD). If you believe an item is not applicable to this research article, leave it blank. Be prepared to explain your ratings. When responding to criteria A and B below, keep in mind that brief titles and abstracts are conventional in published research.

A. The title of the article is appropriate.

SA   5   4   3   2   1   SD

B. The abstract provides an effective overview of the research article.

SA   5   4   3   2   1   SD

C. The introduction establishes the importance of the study.

SA   5   4   3   2   1   SD

D. The literature review establishes the context for the study.

SA   5   4   3   2   1   SD

E. The research purpose, question, or hypothesis is clearly stated.

SA   5   4   3   2   1   SD

F. The method of sampling is sound.

SA   5   4   3   2   1   SD

G. Relevant demographics (for example, age, gender, and ethnicity) are described.

SA   5   4   3   2   1   SD

H. Measurement procedures are adequate.

SA   5   4   3   2   1   SD

I. All procedures have been described in sufficient detail to permit a replication of the study.

SA   5   4   3   2   1   SD

J. The participants have been adequately protected from potential harm.

SA   5   4   3   2   1   SD

K. The results are clearly described.

SA   5   4   3   2   1   SD

L. The discussion/conclusion is appropriate.

SA   5   4   3   2   1   SD

M. Despite any flaws, the report is worthy of publication.

SA   5   4   3   2   1   SD

Article 29

Understanding Girls' Circle As an Intervention on Perceived Social Support, Body Image, Self-Efficacy, Locus of Control, and Self-Esteem

STEPHANIE STEESE
Dominican University of California

MAYA DOLLETTE
Dominican University of California

WILLIAM PHILLIPS
Dominican University of California

ELIZABETH HOSSFELD
Girls' Circle Association

GAIL MATTHEWS
Dominican University of California

GIOVANNA TAORMINA
Girls' Circle Association

ABSTRACT. The Girls' Circle is a support group for adolescent girls developed by Beth Hossfeld and Giovanna Taormina as a unique program that addresses the needs of girls by focusing on increasing connections, building empathic skills, and developing resiliency. The present study evaluates the effectiveness of the Girls' Circle intervention on improving social support, body image, locus of control, self-efficacy, and self-esteem. Sixty-three girls from nine support groups (comprising 5 to 15 girls each) across the United States completed the Multidimensional Scale of Perceived Social Support, the Body Parts Satisfaction Scale, the Nowicki-Strickland Personal Reaction Survey, Schwarzer's General Self-Efficacy Scale, and the Rosenberg Self-Esteem scale both before and after the 10-week Girls' Circle program. Results revealed a significant increase in social support, body image, and self-efficacy after completion of the program.

From *Adolescence, 41*, 55–74. Copyright © 2006 by Libra Publishers, Inc. Reprinted with permission.

Adolescent girls face numerous challenges during the transition from childhood to adulthood (Feldman & Eliot, 1990; Gunnar & Collins, 1988; Lerner & Foch, 1987). Threats to adolescent females' health and well-
5　being include suicide, substance abuse, sexually transmitted diseases, dieting, eating problems, and eating disorders (Millstein, Petersen, & Nightingale, 1993). Girls are three times more likely than boys to have experienced sexual abuse, a major pathway to delin-
10　quency (Office of Juvenile Justice Delinquency Prevention [OJJDP], 1998). Ten percent of girls between the ages of 15 and 19 become pregnant (Kaiser Family Foundation, 2003). Female adolescent peer relationships have been the source of numerous books and
15　studies in recent years. Delinquency cases involving girls increased by 83% between 1986 and 1997 (OJJDP). Depression remains disproportionately high among adolescent girls, with about a 2 to 1 ratio of girls to boys (Marcotte, Fortin, Potvin, & Papillon,
20　2002).

Girls' Circle

The Girls' Circle model, a structured support group for girls from 9 to 18 years of age, integrates relational theory, resiliency practices, and skills training in a specific format designed to increase positive connection,
25　personal and collective strengths, and competence. It aims to counteract social and interpersonal forces that impede girls' growth and development and has been utilized in a broad spectrum of settings with diverse populations and programs serving girls since 1994. The
30　model intends to respond to recommendations from national organizations, including the National Council on Research for Women (NCRW, 1998), the American Association of University Women (AAUW, 1991), the United Way of the Bay Area (2003), and the OJJDP
35　(1998) that have pointed to the need for gender-relevant programs that allow girls to voice their experiences, develop positive connections, and gain skills to pursue meaningful goals in education, careers, and relationships. While the programs in many youth-
40　serving organizations aim to support girls, few studies demonstrate the efficacy of a gender-specific model to support adolescent girls' development.

Theory

The Girls' Circle model is based upon the relational–cultural model of female psychology, identified
45　and developed by Miller (1991) and further refined in relation to adolescent girls by feminist and relational theorists and scholars (Brown & Gilligan, 1992; Ward, 2000; Jordan, 1991; Leadbeater & Way, 1996; and others). "Relational–Cultural Theory (RCT) suggests
50　that growth-fostering relationships are a central human necessity and disconnections are the source of psychological problems," according to the Jean Baker Miller Training Institute at Wellesley Stone Center, Wellesley Center for Women. The theory views a girl's connec-
55　tions with others as a central organizing feature in her psychological make-up. The quality of these connections determines her overall psychological health, self-

image, and relationships. Essential mechanisms of healthy connections include the capacity to voice experience honestly and to receive attentive, empathic listening. Brown and Gilligan (1992) state that "connection and responsive relationships are essential for psychological development" and suggest the critical need for girls to have the opportunity to experience authenticity within relationships with peers and adults, to counter the "crisis of connection" that characterizes adolescent female experience.

Within the relational–cultural theory, the Girls' Circle model aims to increase protective factors and reduce risk factors in adolescent girls, as defined by resiliency researchers such as Benard (2004). Hallmarks of the development of resiliency in youth are high expectations, caring and support, and meaningful participation within their communities. Positive identification with one's own cultural ethnic, or racial group increases resiliency traits as well (Benard, 2004). To this end, a key component of the model is the council-type format of one group member speaking at a time, with the expectation of attentive listening from other participants. This form of communication intends to increase empathy skills on the part of the listeners, as well as a mutual empathic understanding among the entire group. From the relational perspective, "the deepest sense of one's being is continuously formed in connection with others and is inextricably tied to relational movement. The primary feature, rather than structure marked by separateness and autonomy, is increasing empathic responsiveness in the context of interpersonal mutuality" (Jordan, 1997). Empathic connection is an integral aim of the Girls' Circle model, to increase girls' psychological health, including self-efficacy, self-esteem, locus of control, social support, and body image.

Self-Efficacy

A growing body of research indicates the powerful role self-efficacy plays in shaping individual behavior and the successful achievement of goals. "Self-efficacy refers to beliefs in one's capabilities to organize and execute the course of action required to manage prospective situations" (Bandura, 1995). In the research based on Bandura's social cognition theory, notions of one's personal competence are more important to academic achievement, for example, than actual ability (Pintrich & Schunk, 1996). Self-efficacy beliefs have been shown to be one indicator of adolescent development in family environments, school achievement, and peer or social self-efficacy (Bradley & Corwyn, 2001). A Study of European American and African American children aged 10 to 15 years sought to understand the role of self-efficacy in mediating and moderating the relation between home environment and well-being. Self-efficacy beliefs were found to be important influences in the home environment. Family self-efficacy beliefs were a factor in healthy adolescent development

and related to overall home environment experiences. For the European Americans, family self-efficacy beliefs were also related to achievement in school. For the African American children, there was a similar relationship between family self-efficacy beliefs and home environment, and less of a direct relationship in student achievement. The researchers accounted for this difference with the suggestion that efficacy beliefs and outcome expectations are both aspects of motivation to act, and that based on oppressive experiences, African American students may have less confidence in the rewards of their efforts in school, an institution associated with the dominant society.

Self-efficacy beliefs have also been shown to play a significant role in student achievement (Alfassi, 2003). One such study that demonstrated the instrumental role of self-efficacy in student achievement compared the instructional practices in two remedial high schools in Israel on their role in student achievement, one which applied a structured academic program and the other a conventional approach. The achievement scores of 37 students enrolled in the learner-centered structured academic program were compared to 15 students enrolled in the conventional remedial school. The study results showed significantly greater achievement by students in the structured approach and supported the idea that instructional designs which aim to increase student mastery will improve self-efficacy which, in turn, is a strong influence on achievement.

Another study sought to determine the degree to which each of the constructs of self-efficacy, self-concept, valuing school, and self-efficacy regarding self-regulation influences prediction of one's academic achievement. Participants were 529 students in a public middle school in the Northeast. Survey results confirmed the importance of positive self-efficacy beliefs in shaping predictive behavior among the students in academic as well as general well-being domains (Pajares, 2001).

Self-Esteem

Research on female's psychological development identifies adolescence as the most pivotal and vulnerable time for females (Kling, Hyde, Showers, & Boswell, 1999). At the same time, it is an especially important period for the formation of self-esteem. However, research has indicated that adolescent girls experience a "free-fall in self-esteem from which some will never recover" (Orenstein, 1994). For instance AAUW (1990) conducted a study on approximately 3,000 students that focused on attitudes toward the self, family, friends, and school. Results revealed that adolescent girls experience a rapid decline in self-esteem. Moreover, lower levels of self-esteem have been correlated with a wide range of negative outcomes, including higher rates of teenage pregnancy, alcohol and drug abuse, juvenile delinquency, suicide, depression, social anxiety, and alienation (Gurney, 1986). Self-esteem has

170 also been shown to be related to adolescents' body image dissatisfaction and dieting. Adolescents who report higher levels of body image dissatisfaction and dieting also report poorer self-esteem and are generally dissatisfied with other aspects of their lives (e.g., Folk, 175 Pederson, & Cullari, 1993; Kelly, Ricciardelli, & Clarke, 1999; Lawrence & Thelen, 1995; Mendelson & White, 1982; Mendelson, White, & Mendelson, 1996).

Body Image

Body image is a person's mental concept of his or her physical appearance, constructed from many differ- 180 ent influences. Female adolescents' body images are often distorted due to peer- and self-esteem (having a good opinion of one's self; self-complacency) influences. Negative body image can lead to eating disorders (Cash & Lavallee, 1997), depression, social- 185 evaluative anxiety, sexual difficulties, and poor self-esteem (Cash, 1990). Perception of one's physical appearance has been consistently recognized to be the number one factor in predicting self-esteem (Harter, 2000), as well as being associated with the onset of 190 adolescence and pubertal development (Fabian & Thompson, 1989; Shore & Porter, 1990). Current research indicates that girls as young as 8 to 9 years of age have negative views of being overweight and high levels of body image dissatisfaction (Hill, 1993; Koff 195 & Reirdan, 1991; Rolland, Farnhill, & Griffiths, 1997).

McCabe & Ricciardelli (2003) examined the perceived influence of parents, peers, and the media on body image and weight loss among adolescent boys and girls. The results indicated a consistency in the 200 perceived messages received from mother, father, best male friend, and best female friend in relation to body image and body change strategies for adolescents. Furnham, Badman, & Sneade (2002) studied 235 adolescents to determine whether girls who are dissatisfied 205 with their bodies have lower self-esteem. The study found that dissatisfaction with body image and weight was significantly correlated with low self-esteem. Similarly McCabe and Ricciardelli (2003) surveyed 507 adolescents aged 8 to 11 to examine the role of 210 gender, age, and body mass index in the development of self-esteem, body image concerns, and weight loss. The researchers found that children with poor self-esteem were more dissatisfied with their bodies. The authors suggested that self-esteem is more likely to 215 influence body image among girls than boys.

Locus of Control

Internal locus of control, the sense that one has influence over one's own experiences, has been widely researched in recent years. It has been identified as a key determinant of resilience (Benard, 2004). How- 220 ever, although relatively few studies have examined the relationship between age and locus of control beliefs, and little is known about the nature of locus of control changes in adolescent girls, Kulas (1996) investigated the development of locus of control in adolescence

225 over a three-year period. Participants included 84 seventh-graders (49 boys and 35 girls). The study found no significant changes among boys and girls in locus of control over the three years of the study and that adolescence is a period of relative stability of locus of con- 230 trol. The study also found that females demonstrated more external locus of control than did males. Furthermore, a longitudinal study on locus of control with adolescent males and females revealed gradual shifts toward greater internalized locus of control in later 235 years of high school (Chubb, Fertman, & Ross, 1997).

Perceived Social Support

Social support is defined as the experience or the perception of being cared for, valued, included, and/or guided by others, especially one's family, peers, and/or community members. Reciprocity and mutuality of 240 experience are also considered to be aspects of this construct, and the nature of social support is described as both a buffer against life stressors and an agent promoting health and wellness (Vaux, 1988). Social support from peers, teachers, and parents has been recog- 245 nized as a protective factor for children and teens (Benard, 2004). Studies have shown the increased risk of adolescent problems in the absence of or decreased levels of parental support, and the buffering effects of parental support on student stress (Quamma & Green- 250 berg, 1994).

Research on social support has shown it to be an important factor in predicting several positive outcomes in children and adolescents. In a study of 167 middle school students in a predominantly middle class 255 community, social support of parents, teachers, and peers were examined for their motivational influence on students' academic and prosocial goals. Perceived support from parents had predictive value related to academic goals, especially in early adolescence, while 260 peer-related support showed more of a significant role in later middle school years (Wentzel, 1998). Peer support influences adolescents' motivation for involvement in talent and sport activities (Patrick, Ryan, Alfeld-Liro, Eccles, & Fredericks, 1999). In a study of the 265 role of peers in the motivation of teens to stay involved in talent and sport activities, researchers found that when teens had positive peer interactions within the context of the extracurricular activities, they reported greater commitment to and motivation for these activi- 270 ties. Conversely, results indicated that teens whose activities did not include strong or positive peer relationships or teens whose activities were apart from their peer groups showed lower levels of commitment and motivation toward their talent and sport activities.

275 Studies have also shown the importance of support from teachers and close friends for adolescent girls (Kilpatrick-Demaray & Kerres-Malecki, 2003). Surveys of 1,688 students in grades 3 to 12 from the Midwest and eastern states indicated that girls rated the 280 importance of support from friends, teachers, and

classmates higher than did boys. Girls perceive higher levels of support, and they value social support more than boys, especially once they reach high school. These findings support the premise of relational–cultural theory as it relates to girls, that social connection is paramount to identity and health.

Numerous studies indicate that support groups, as stand-alone structures or as integrated components within schools and communities, are an effective setting in which to strengthen self-esteem and to improve body image and social connection (Waggoner, 1999; Conklin, 2002; Benard, 2004). Laszlo (2001), in research on the support group, Girls' Circle, set out to determine the effectiveness of a group intervention with adolescent girls relative to their level of self-esteem. Participants were enrolled in sixth and seventh grade, and each group consisted of six girls who met once a week for six weeks. Results indicated that participants' self-esteem improved overall from pretest to posttest. The adolescents in the support groups valued the group process, support, and curriculum of the class.

Hypotheses

The purpose of the present study was to learn if the gender-specific program, Girls' Circle, has a positive impact on self-efficacy, self-esteem, perceived body image, locus of control, and perceived social support among girls who participated in Girls' Circle programs. The hypothesis was that participation would have a positive impact on each of the aforementioned areas of psychological health.

Method

Participants

Sixty-three girls ranging in age from 10 to 17 years (Mean age = 13) were recruited to participate in nine separate Girls' Circle support group programs from across the United States and Canada. Each group consisted of 5 to 9 girls from various backgrounds. The total sample comprised 17% African American, 3% Asian or Pacific Islander, 51% Caucasian, 21% Hispanic, 3% Native American, and 5% Other.

Materials

Participants completed a battery of questionnaires assessing demographic variables: Self-Esteem, Locus of Control, Self-Efficacy, Body Image Satisfaction, and Social Support. Each of these scales is described below.

Self-Esteem. This variable was assessed using the Rosenberg Self-Esteem Scale (Rosenberg, 1965), a 10-item self-report instrument measuring the individual's feeling of self-worth.

Locus of Control. The 21-item Nowicki-Strickland Personal Reaction Survey (Nowicki & Strickland, 1972) measures the extent to which people believe that their lives are determined by external circumstances or their own behavior.

Self-Efficacy. Schwarzer's General Self-Efficacy Scale (Jerusalem & Schwarzer, 1992), a 10-item questionnaire, was administered to determine participants' attitudes regarding self-reliance.

Body Image Satisfaction. The Body Parts Satisfaction Scale-Revised (BPSS-R; Berscheid, Walster, & Bohrnsted, 1973), a 25-item questionnaire, was used to measure the degree to which participants feel comfortable with their own bodies.

Social Support. The Multidimensional Scale of Perceived Social Support (Zimet, Dahlem, Zimet, & Farley, 1998) is a 12-item questionnaire that evaluates participants' perception of the role that friends, family, and peers play in their lives. Also included in the battery were eight items used to collect demographic information.

Procedure

A pretest–posttest design was employed to evaluate the effectiveness of the Girls' Circle curriculum in nine separate classes. Prior to the beginning of class, the facilitators administered the pretest questionnaire packet containing the measures described above. Participants were given 45 min to complete the packet.

Curriculum. A 10-week curriculum was utilized for each group of girls. Groups met once a week for either 90 or 120 min per session. The curriculum addressed areas of girls' lives including friendship, self-image, body-image, relationships, assertiveness, and self-talk. Weekly themes were integrated into the Girls' Circle format, and verbal and creative activities focused on the theme for the week. For example, the theme for week one was "Friendships and Bonding," with objectives such as "to unite girls in their experience of getting to know one another, to explore the meaning of 'true' friendship; to learn from each other the key elements of healthy friendships; and to develop trust, bonding, and healthy friendships." Activities included creating group guidelines and dyad interviews. On week eight, the theme was "Body Image and Body Messages." Objectives were to explore messages girls encounter in everyday life through magazines, movies, and television; to critique the messages and their impact on girls' self-images; to empower girls to express their own messages or statements; and to raise awareness in terms of where these messages come from (i.e., family, friends, peers, culture); and to brainstorm healthy responses to these messages. Activities included Identifying Magazine Images, Exploration and Reflection, and "Pie of Influence" posters. After the curriculum was completed, participants once again completed the battery of questionnaires.

Results

The mean pretest and posttest scores for each variable appear in Table 1. It was hypothesized that posttest scores would be significantly greater than pretest scores for each variable, suggesting improvement on each of these measures. Statistical analyses incorporat-

ing the paired-samples *t* test revealed a significant increase in Body Image scores (Figure 1), Perceived Social Support (Figure 2), and levels of Self-Efficacy
390 (Figure 3). Results indicate that all three variables improved at the end of the 10-week curriculum. No such improvement occurred for measures of Self-Esteem (Figure 4) or Locus of Control (Figure 5). Pretest and posttest scores for these variables were found to be
395 statistically equivalent.

Table 1
Mean Scores and Standard Deviations for Each Dependent Variable

Variable	Pretest		Posttest	
	M	*SD*	*M*	*SD*
Body Image	107.11	22.58	113.11	24.73
Social Support	58.29	14.35	65.06	16.21
Self-Efficacy	27.42	5.00	30.55	4.65
Self-Esteem	22.94	2.58	23.16	3.08
Locus of Control	12.62	3.60	13.77	3.51

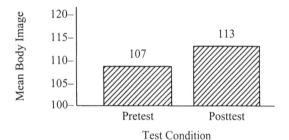

Figure 1. Mean pretest and posttest scores for Body Image $t(53) = -2.02$, $p < .05$.

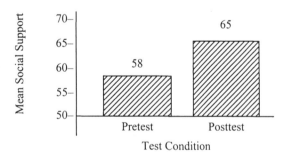

Figure 2. Mean pretest and posttest scores for Perceived Social Support $t(53) = -4.07$, $p < .05$.

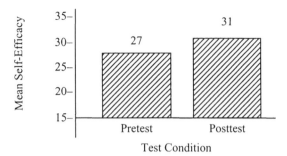

Figure 3. Mean pretest and posttest scores for Self-Efficacy $t(53) = -5.27$, $p < .05$.

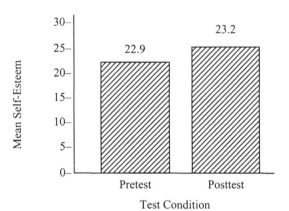

Figure 4. Mean pretest and posttest scores for Self-Esteem $t(53) = -.572$, $p > .05$.

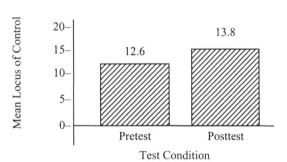

Figure 5. Mean pretest and posttest scores for Locus of Control $t(52) = -1.34$, $p > .05$.

Discussion

The aim of this study was to explore the effectiveness of the Girls' Circle model and curriculum in improving girls' self-esteem, self-efficacy, locus of control, perceived social support, and perceived body im-
400 age. Findings of significant increases in perceived social support, self-efficacy, and perceived body image support the hypothesis that the Girls' Circle model is effective as a gender-specific intervention. Results were not significant for self-esteem and locus of con-
405 trol. Each of these measures is discussed below.

Self-Efficacy

Girls' responses indicated significant changes in self-efficacy after participation in the program. The results on the Schwarzer Self-Efficacy scale, which has had solid, international and cross-cultural application
410 for two decades (Schwarzer & Scholz, 2000), indicates the positive impact of a circle experience on a girl's sense that she can do what she needs or desires to do to achieve her goals. The Girls' Circle curriculum attempts to promote safe spaces in which girls can take
415 risks and gain mastery through a variety of social-emotional and skill-building activities, and can challenge self-concepts. For example, one activity instructs participants to identify negative self-statements such as "I'm terrible at school" and to restate such statements
420 as positive ones, such as "I can pass my classes; I can ask for help if I need it."

Self-efficacy is also enhanced through positive ethnic identity (Benard, 2004; Rotheram, 1996). It is possible that the narrative and self-expressive aspects of
425 the curriculum increase girls' beliefs in their abilities and capacities, in part because they have experienced themselves as significant and effective members of their groups. These groups often reflect girls' varied ethnicities and engage them in reflection, recognition,
430 and expression of meaningful family and cultural experiences. One activity, for example, asks girls to write or draw and share seven personal representations of favorite family traditions, a family hero/heroine, a challenge the family survived, and a special belonging that
435 signifies one's culture. Increased positive identification and empathic interest from the group may be factors that promote self-efficacy. Since research has established a clear and important link between beliefs regarding one's abilities and outcomes in important do-
440 mains such as academics, home environment, and peer relationships, the positive improvement in self-efficacy beliefs demonstrated in this study suggests the potential value of the Girls' Circle model in the promotion and attainment of wellness activities for girls.

Body Image

445 These findings support data in previous research that link body image and social support, in which girls' self-perceptions are influenced by their peers and families. O'Dea and Abraham's (2000) results were consistent with previous research in regard to positive
450 changes in body image and intervention programs. They found significantly improved body satisfaction of the intervention students and changed aspects of their self-esteem. Also, social acceptance, physical appearance, and athletic ability became less important for the
455 intervention students and more important for the controls. Many of the control students significantly decreased their body weight, while the weight of the intervention students increased. Further, one year after the intervention, positive body image and attitude

460 changes were still present. These changes were a result of participation in the program.

One goal of the Girls' Circle model is to strengthen physical self-image. The model addresses girls' body image in particular aspects of the curriculum, in which
465 cultural, family, and peer messages about girls' bodies are identified, explored, and challenged. Also, during sessions, girls are welcome to express feelings and thoughts. Because a lack of recognition of emotions and physical sensations has been associated with risk
470 factors for eating disorders (Goleman, 1995), the Girls' Circle curriculum addresses feeling recognition in targeted activities related to body image, but also in numerous gender-relevant areas. This study supports research by Laszlo (2001), which showed that support
475 from peers increased positive body image. Support and intervention groups not associated with Girls' Circle also revealed improvement in body awareness, body anxiety, self-esteem, and self-worth (Rankin, 1974; O'Dea & Abraham, 2000).

480 Also, the curriculum includes facilitated discussions and activities that invite girls to express experiences in verbal or creative form. These discussions incorporate critical thinking strategies in which participants identify and question attitudes, norms, and prac-
485 tices, such as media techniques that influence their attitudes and behaviors. The intended outcome is for girls to recognize the influences shaping their perceptions, the impact of those perceptions, and the capacity for personal choice and decision making within such
490 aspects of their self-image. Such awareness and problem-solving skills development has been associated with "better psychological and social adjustment, lower levels of depression and anxiety, greater hope, better physical health, and better coping with adversity"
495 (Benard, 2004).

Perceived Social Support

The data revealed significant increases in perceived social support, supporting the hypothesis. This finding also supports earlier studies showing that belonging and connection increased through support group proc-
500 esses (Graczyk, 2000). This research suggests that prevention and intervention programs promoting social and emotional wellness in adolescents should focus on group success and the ability to develop and maintain supportive friendships. Other research has noted that
505 support and intervention groups should continue to promote positive messages with adolescents (Rosenbledt, 2003; Benard, 2004).

Empathic interactions are hallmarks of supportive relationships (Goleman, 1995). Resiliency research
510 maintains that children and youth who have supportive and caring relationships with at least one adult in their community are likely to succeed despite severe hardship (Benard, 2004). According to researchers (Miller, 1991; Jordan, 1997), the key ingredient in girls' con-
515 nections is mutual empathic interaction. In the Girls'

Circle model, girls voice experiences in verbal or creative form to an attentive group consisting of peers and one or two adult facilitators. These activities are conducive to group cohesion and bonding, and set into motion empathic reciprocity, increasing perception of social support.

Self-Esteem

This study did not reveal significant changes in self-esteem or locus of control for participants in the curriculum. The present self-esteem outcome was consistent with that of Royse (1998), who studied whether participation in Girl Scouts and the use of a scouting curriculum was beneficial for increasing the self-esteem of female adolescents. There was no noticeable improvement in self-esteem when the pretests and posttests were compared for the girls participating in troops or clubs. Similar findings were obtained by Marmorosh and Corazzini (1997), who examined the effectiveness of teaching group members how to use their group identity outside of the therapy group in order to enhance self-esteem. Their findings suggest that their intervention was effective among those who were longtime members of their groups.

Possible reasons for the absence of a self-esteem effect might include the question of whether 10 weeks is a sufficient time period to achieve measurable differences in global self-esteem, or whether the Rosenberg Self-Esteem Scale is an adequate measure of short-term changes. The Rosenberg measure may be confused by participant mood variables (Robertson & Simons, 1989). Further, the Rosenberg Scale is very general, though relatively simple to use. A tool that is specific to domains, and therefore likely to be more useful in analysis and recommendation, is the Harter Self-Perception Profile for Adolescents (Harter, 1998). This scale may be better suited for ascertaining specific areas of girls' perceived strengths as well as global self-worth. Additionally, the State Self-Esteem Scale (Linton & Marriott, 1995) may be better suited to assess short-term changes. One positive perspective on the relatively neutral outcome on self-esteem changes in this study may be that girls' self-esteem is buffered by participation in the program. This concept considers the results as bucking the downward trend shown in surveys about girls' self-esteem during the early and middle adolescent years (AAUW, 1991).

Locus of Control

Findings were consistent with other locus of control studies of adolescents, including Kulas (1996), which assessed changes in the development of locus of control over a 3-year period with 84 seventh-graders (49 boys and 35 girls) and found no significant changes for girls or boys. That study suggested that there is relative stability of locus of control during the adolescent years, wherever it falls on the scale. However, girls demonstrated more external locus of control than did boys. Changes in one's perception of control are likely to

take time, repeated experiences, and an integration of the meaning of one's perspective and its influence on outcomes. For girls and young women of color, a marginalized population in our culture, movement in the direction of internalization of locus of control may be a distinctly relevant measure of empowerment. Increases in the girls' internal locus of control were evident in the study, indicating gains in their awareness of personal power.

Conclusions

The present study provides quantitative data that show significant positive changes for girls in key areas of their development, their sense of belonging, their perception and acceptance of their own bodies, and their belief in their ability to accomplish meaningful tasks and goals in their lives. While this is the first study of the Girls' Circle model, it is important because it provides evidence for the effectiveness of providing a female-responsive circle format that serves girls' developmental needs. In future studies, we intend to investigate the impact of the Girls' Circle model on such variables as drug and alcohol use, delinquency, resiliency, and social relations. We also intend to explore different measures of these variables to accommodate the appropriate age of the girls represented.

References

Alfassi, M. (2003). Promoting the will and skill of students at academic risk: An evaluation of an instructional design geared to foster achievement, self-efficacy, and motivation. *Journal of Instructional Psychology, 30,* 28–40.

American Association of University Women. (1990). *Shortchanging girls, shortchanging America: Full data report.* Washington, DC: Author.

American Association of University Women. (1991). *Shortchanging girls, shortchanging America: Executive Summary.* AAUW Educational Foundation.

American Association of University Women. (1994). *Shortchanging girls, shortchanging America: Executive Summary.* AAUW Educational Foundation.

Bandura, A. (1995). Exercise of personal and collective efficacy in changing societies. In A. Bandura (Ed.), *Self-efficacy in changing societies* (pp. 1–45). New York, NY: Cambridge University Press.

Benard, B. (2004). *Resiliency: What we have learned.* San Francisco, CA: WestEd.

Berscheid, E., Walster, E., & Bohrnstedt, G. (1973). Body image and the happy American body: A survey report. *Psychology Today,* 119–131.

Bradley, R. H., & Corwyn, R. F. (2001). Home environment and behavioral development during early adolescence: The mediating and moderating roles of self-efficacy beliefs. *Merrill-Palmer Quarterly, 37,* 165–187.

Brown, L. M., & Gilligan, C. (1992). *Meeting at the crossroads.* New York: Ballantine Books.

Cash, T. F. (1990). The psychology of physical appearance: Aesthetics, attributes, and images. In T. F. Cash & T. Pruzinsky (Eds.), *Body images: Development, deviance, and change* (pp. 51–79). New York: Guilford.

Cash, T. F., & Lavallee, D. M. (1997). Cognitive-behavioral body image therapy: Extended evidence of the efficacy of a self-directed program. *Journal of Rational–Emotive and Cognitive-Behavior Therapy, 15,* 282–294.

Chubb, N., Fertman, C., & Ross, J. (1997). Adolescent self-esteem and locus of control: A longitudinal study of gender and age differences. *Adolescence, 32,* 113–129.

Conklin, D. L. (2002). *Feminist theory-based girls' group* (Doctoral dissertation, Chicago School of Professional Psychology). *Dissertation Abstracts International, 62,* 8-B.

Fabian, L. J., & Thompson, J. K. (1989). Body image and eating disturbance in young females. *International Journal of Eating Disorders, 8,* 63–74.

Feldman, S., & Elliot, G. (1990). *At the threshold: The developing adolescent.* Cambridge, MA: Harvard University Press.

Folk, L., Pederson, J., & Cullari, S. (1993). Body dissatisfaction and self-concept of third- and sixth-grade students. *Perceptual and Motor Skills, 76,* 547–553.

Furnham, A., Badmin, K., & Sneade, I. (2002). Body image dissatisfaction: Gender differences in eating attitudes, self-esteem and reasons for exercise. *The Journal of Psychology*, *136*, 581–596.

Goleman, D. (1995). Emotional intelligence: Why it can matter more than IQ. New York: Bantam Books.

Graczyk, P. A. (2000). Adolescent peer relationships and their association with emotional and physical wellness (Doctoral dissertation, Northern Illinois University). *Dissertation Abstracts International*, *60*, 12-B.

Gunnar, M., & Collins, W. A. (1988). *Development during transition to adolescence: Minnesota symposia on child psychology* (Vol. 21). Hillsdale, NJ: Erlbaum.

Gurney, P. W. (1986). Self-esteem in the classroom: Theoretical perspectives and assessment issues. *School Psychology International*, *7*, 199–209.

Harter, S. (1988). *Manual for the self-perception profile for adolescents*. Denver, CO: University of Denver.

Harter, S. (2000). Is self-esteem only skin deep? *Reclaiming Children and Youth*, *9*, 133.

Hill, A. (1993). Pre-adolescent dieting: Implications for eating disorders. *International Review of Psychiatry*, *5*, 87–100.

Jerusalem, M., & Schwartzer, R. (1992). Self-efficacy as a resource factor in stress appraisal processes. In R. Schwarzer (Ed.), *Self-efficacy: Thought control of action* (pp. 195–213). Washington, DC: Hemisphere.

Jordan, J. (1991). *Women's growth in connection: Writings from the Stone Center*. New York: Guilford.

Jordan, J. (Ed.). (1997). *Women's growth in diversity: More writings from the Stone Center*. New York: NY: Guilford Press.

Kaiser Family Foundation. (2003), *National survey of adolescents and young adults: Sexual health knowledge, attitudes and experiences*. Retrieved October 15, 2003, from http://www.kff.org

Kelly, C., Ricciardelli, L. A., & Clarke, J. D. (1999). Problem eating attitudes and behaviors in young children. *International Journal of Eating Disorders*, *25*, 281–286.

Kilpatrick-Demaray, M., & Kerres-Malecki, C. (2003). Importance ratings of socially supportive behaviors by children and adolescents. *School Psychology Review*, *32*, 108–131.

Kling, C. A., Hyde, J. S., Showers, C. J., & Buswell, B. N. (1999). Gender differences in self-esteem: A meta-analysis. *Psychological Bulletin*, *125*, 470–500.

Koff, E., & Reirdan, J. (1991). Perceptions of weight and attitudes towards eating in early adolescent girls. *Journal of Adolescent Health*, *12*, 307–312.

Kulas, H. (1993). Locus of control in adolescence: A longitudinal study. *Adolescence*, *31*, 721–729.

Laszlo, A. M. (2001). Effects of group Intervention on the self-esteem of sixth- and seventh-grade girls. *Dissertation Abstracts International Section B: The Sciences & Engineering*, *6*, 6140.

Lawrence, C. M., & Thelen, M. H. (1995). Body image, dieting and self-concept: Their relation in African-American and Caucasian children. *Journal of Clinical Child Psychology*, *24*, 41–48.

Leadbeater, B. J., & Way, N. (Eds.). (1996). *Urban girls: Resisting stereotypes, creating identities*. New York: New York University Press.

Lerner, R. M., & Foch, T. T. (1987). *Biological-psychosocial interactions in early adolescence: A lifespan perspective*. Hillsdale, NJ: Erlbaum.

Linton, K., &. Marriott, R. (1995). The State Self-Esteem Scale. *Personality and Individual Differences*, *21*, 85–90.

Marcotte, D., Forton, L., Potvin, P., & Papillon, M. (2002). Gender differences in depressive symptoms during adolescence: Role of gender-typed characteristics, self-esteem, body image, stressful life events, and pubertal status. *Journal of Emotional and Behavioral Disorders*, *10*, 29–42.

Marmarosh, C. L., & Corazzini, J. G. (1997). Putting the group in your pocket: Using collective identity to enhance personal and collective self-esteem. *Group Dynamics: Theory, Research, and Practice*, *1*, 65–74.

Mendelson, B. K., & White, D. R. (1982). Relation of body-esteem and self-esteem of obese and normal children. *Perceptual and Motor Skills*, *54*, 899–905.

Mendelson, B. K., White, D. R., & Mendelson, M. J. (1996). Self-esteem and body-esteem: Effects of gender, age, and weight. *Journal of Applied Developmental Psychology*, *17*, 321–346.

McCabe, M. P., & Ricciardelli, L. A. (2003). Body image and strategies to lose weight and increase muscle among boys and girls. *Health Psychology*, *22*, 39–46.

McCabe, M. P., & Ricciardelli, L. A. (2003). Sociocultural influences on body image and body changes among adolescent boys and girls. *The Journal of Social Psychology*, *143*, 5–26.

Miller, J. B. (1991). The development of women's sense of self. In J. Jordan et al., *Women's growth in connection: Writings from the Stone Center*. New York, NY: Guilford.

Millstein, S. G., Petersen, A. C., & Nightengale, E. O. (1993). *Promotion of health behavior in adolescence*. New York: Oxford University Press.

National Council on Research for Women. (1998). *The girls report: What we know & need to know about growing up female*. New York, NY.

Nowicki, S., & Strickland, B. R. (1973). A locus of control scale for children. *Journal of Consulting and Clinical Psychology*, *1*, 148–154.

O'Dea, J. A., & Abraham, S. (2000). Improving the body image, eating attitudes, and behaviors of young male and female adolescents: A new educational approach that focuses on self-esteem. *International Journal of Eating Disorders*, *28*, 43–57.

Office of Juvenile Justice Delinquency Prevention. *Guiding principles for promising female programming: An inventory of best practices*. October, 1998. Author.

Orenstein, P. (1994). *Schoolgirls: Young women, self-esteem, and the confidence gap*. New York: Anchor Books.

Pajares. F. (2001). Toward a positive psychology of academic motivation. *The Journal of Educational Research*, *95*, 27–35.

Patrick, H., Ryan, A. M., Alfred-Liro, C., Fredericks, J. A., Hruda, L. Z., & Eccles, J. S. (1999). Adolescents' commitment to developing talent: The role of peers in continuing motivation for sports and the arts. *Journal of Youth and Adolescence*, *28*, 741–763.

Phillips, L. (1998). National Council for Research on Women. *The girls' report: What we know and need to know about growing up female*. New York, NY.

Pintrich, P. R., & Schunk, D. H. (1996). *Motivation in education: Theory, research, and applications*. New Jersey: Prentice Hall.

Quamma, J. P., & Greenberg, M. T. (1994). Children's experience of life stress: The role of family social support and social problem-solving skills as protective factors. *Journal of Clinical Child Psychology*, *23*, 295–305.

Rankin, P. P. (1974). Looking at change in the area of body image and self-concept in adolescent females after exposure to two types of small group counseling experiences. (Doctoral Dissertation, University of Southern California.) *Dissertation Abstracts International*, *35*, 9-A.

Robertson, J. F., & Simons, R. L. (1989). Family factors, self-esteem and adolescent depression. *Journal of Marriage and the Family*, *51*, 125–138.

Rolland, K., Farnhill, D., & Griffiths, R. A. (1997). Body figure perceptions and eating attitudes among Australian school children aged 8 to 12 years. *International Journal of Eating Disorders*, *21*, 273–278.

Rosenberg, M. (1965). *Society and the adolescent self image*. Princeton, NJ: Princeton University Press.

Rosenbledt, N. S. (2003). The effects of a support group intervention on self-esteem, authenticity, and resiliency in early adolescent girls at high risk for school failure. (Doctoral Dissertation, University of San Francisco.) *Dissertation Abstracts International*, *63*, 12-B.

Rotheram, M. J. (1996). Personal and ethnic identity, values, and self-esteem among Black and Latino adolescent girls. In B. J. Leadbeater & H. Way (Eds.), *Urban girls: Resisting stereotypes, creating identities*, New York: New York University Press.

Royse, D. (1998). Scouting and Girl Scouts curriculum as interventions: Effects on adolescents' self-esteem. *Adolescence*, *33*, 159–168.

Schwarzer, R., & Scholz, U. (2000). *Cross-Cultural assessment of coping resources: The General Perceived Self-Efficacy Scale*. Paper presented at the First Asian Congress of Health Psychology: Health Psychology and Culture, Tokyo, Japan.

Shore, R. A., & Porter, J. E. (1990). Normative and reliability data for 11 to 18 year olds on the Eating Disorder Inventory. *International Journal of Eating Disorders*, *9*, 201–207.

United Way of the Bay Area. *Girls on the edge: A report on girls in the juvenile justice system (2003)*. San Francisco, CA: Author.

Vaux, A. (1988). *Social support: Theory, research, and intervention*. New York: England Praeger Publishers.

Waggoner, I. R. (1999). Cognitive-behavior therapy and cognitive therapy for body image awareness in sixth-grade females. (Doctoral Dissertation, Auburn University.) *Dissertation Abstracts International*, *59*, II-A.

Ward, J. V., (2000). *The skin we're in: Teaching our children to be emotionally strong, socially smart, and spiritually connected*. New York: Free Press.

Wellesley Centers for Women. (2001). Retrieved November 18, 2003, from http://www.wcwonline.org/index.html

Wentzel, K. R. (1998). Social relationships and motivation in middle school: The role of parents, teachers, and peers. *Journal of Educational Psychology*, *90*, 202–209.

Zimet, G. D., Dahlem, N. W., Zimet, S. G., & Farley, G. K. (1998). The Multidimensional Scale of Perceived Social Support. *Journal of Personality Assessment*, *52*, 30–41.

Acknowledgments: Special thanks to all the girls who participated in this study, their parents or guardians, the organizations and individual group facilitators; Lee Ann Bartolini, Dominican University of California; Norrine Russell; and all who collaborated to make this study possible.

About the authors: *Stephanie Steese, Maya Dollette*, and *William Phillips*, Department of Psychology, Dominican University of California. *Elizabeth Hossfeld*, Girls' Circle Association, Cotati, California. *Gail Matthews*, Department of Psychology, Dominican University of California. *Giovanna Taormina*, Girls' Circle Association, Cotati, California.

Address correspondence to: Reprint requests should be addressed to Giovanna Taormina, executive director, and Beth Hossfeld, associate director, Girls' Circle Association: A Project of The Tides Center, 458 Christensen Lane, Cotati, California 94931. Email: www.girlscircle.com

Exercise for Article 29

Factual Questions

1. According to Relational–Cultural Theory, what is "central human necessity"?

2. It was hypothesized that the Girls' Circle programs would have a positive impact in which five areas of psychological health?

3. What was the average age of the participants?

4. What was the pretest mean for self-esteem? What was the posttest mean?

5. Was the difference between the two means for Question 4 statistically significant?

6. What is the value of the probability associated with the difference between the means in Figure 5?

Questions for Discussion

7. The literature review is longer than the reviews in most of the other articles in this book. In your opinion, is this relatively long review a major strength of this research report? Explain. (See lines 1–309.)

8. Nine programs across the United States and Canada were examined in this evaluation. Is this an important strength? Explain. (See lines 310–317.)

9. A "pretest–posttest design" without a control group was used to evaluate the program. Would you recommend the use of control groups in future evaluations of this program? Explain. (See lines 348–350.)

10. In your opinion, is the Girls' Circle curriculum described in sufficient detail? Explain. (See lines 354–381.)

11. The means in Table 1 are repeated in Figures 1 through 5. Did you find the figures helpful even though they repeat the information in Table 1? Explain.

12. Do the data in this research article convince you that the Girls' Circle program is effective? Explain.

Quality Ratings

Directions: Indicate your level of agreement with each of the following statements by circling a number from 5 for strongly agree (SA) to 1 for strongly disagree (SD). If you believe an item is not applicable to this research article, leave it blank. Be prepared to explain your ratings. When responding to criteria A and B below, keep in mind that brief titles and abstracts are conventional in published research.

A. The title of the article is appropriate.

SA 5 4 3 2 1 SD

B. The abstract provides an effective overview of the research article.

SA 5 4 3 2 1 SD

C. The introduction establishes the importance of the study.

SA 5 4 3 2 1 SD

D. The literature review establishes the context for the study.

SA 5 4 3 2 1 SD

E. The research purpose, question, or hypothesis is clearly stated.

SA 5 4 3 2 1 SD

F. The method of sampling is sound.

SA 5 4 3 2 1 SD

G. Relevant demographics (for example, age, gender, and ethnicity) are described.

SA 5 4 3 2 1 SD

H. Measurement procedures are adequate.

SA 5 4 3 2 1 SD

I. All procedures have been described in sufficient detail to permit a replication of the study.

SA 5 4 3 2 1 SD

J. The participants have been adequately protected from potential harm.

SA 5 4 3 2 1 SD

K. The results are clearly described.

SA 5 4 3 2 1 SD

L. The discussion/conclusion is appropriate.

SA 5 4 3 2 1 SD

M. Despite any flaws, the report is worthy of publication.

SA 5 4 3 2 1 SD

Article 30

Temporal Stability of the Francis Scale of Attitude Toward Christianity Short-Form: Test–Retest Data over One Week

CHRISTOPHER ALAN LEWIS
University of Ulster at Magee College

SHARON MARY CRUISE
University of Ulster at Magee College

CONOR McGUCKIN
Dublin Business School of Arts

ABSTRACT. This study evaluated the test–retest reliability of the Francis Scale of Attitude toward Christianity short-form. Thirty-nine Northern Irish undergraduate students completed the measure on two occasions separated by one week. Stability across the two administrations was high, $r = .92$, and there was no significant change between Time 1 ($M = 25.2$, $SD = 5.4$) and Time 2 ($M = 25.7$, $SD = 6.2$). These data support the short-term test–retest reliability of the Francis Scale of Attitude toward Christianity short-form.

From *Psychological Reports*, 96, 266–268. Copyright © 2005 by Psychological Reports. Reprinted with permission.

Over the last 25 years, there have been more than 200 published studies examining the measurement, correlates, and consequences of variation in attitude toward Christianity among children, adolescents, and
5   adults (see Kay & Francis, 1996). At the centre of this work has been the 24-item Francis Scale of Attitude toward Christianity (Francis & Stubbs, 1987). Subsequently, Francis, Greer, and Gibson (1991) developed a 7-item short-form of the scale, intended to be a re-
10 placement for the full version when administration time is short. This short-form has demonstrated good psychometric properties (Francis, 1993), including high internal consistency (Lewis, 2001), a one-factor structure (Lewis, Shevlin, Lloyd, & Adamson, 1998), high
15 positive correlations with attitudinal and behavioural measures of religiosity (Maltby & Lewis, 1997), and is not affected by social desirability (Lewis, 1999, 2000).

To date no information on the test–retest reliability of this measure has been reported. Hill and Hood
20 (1999), in their review of measures in the psychology of religion, noted that "Test–retest reliabilities are not common in this area, despite their obvious value in identifying stable scores over time" (p. 7). Exceptions include data reported on the stability of the Duke Re-
25 ligion Index (Storch, Strawser, & Storch, 2004), the Religious Commitment Inventory–10 (Worthington, Wade, Hight, Ripley, McCullough, Berry, Schmitt, Berry, Bursley, & O'Connor, 2003), and the Systems of Belief Inventory (Holland, Kash, Passik, Gronert,

30 Sison, Lederberg, Russak, Baider, & Fox, 1998). The present aim was to evaluate the 1-wk. test–retest reliability of the Francis Scale of Attitude toward Christianity short-form among a sample of Northern Irish university students.

Method

Sample

35 Thirty-nine students (5 men and 34 women) whose mean age was 27.4 yr. ($SD = 10.0$), all in attendance at the University of Ulster at Magee College, Londonderry, Northern Ireland, and enrolled in a course in psychology, were employed as respondents.

Measure

40 The Francis Scale of Attitude toward Christianity short-form concerns attitude toward the Bible, prayer, church, God, and Jesus, a sample question being "I know that Jesus helps me" (Item 1). Items are scored on a 5-point scale with anchors of "agree strongly" (5)
45 through "uncertain" (3) and "disagree strongly" (1). Scores range from 7 to 35, higher scores indicating a more positive attitude toward Christianity. A satisfactory estimate of internal consistency has been reported in Northern Ireland among undergraduate students (.90;
50 Maltby & Lewis, 1997).

Procedure

The short-form was completed during class time on two occasions separated by a period of 1 wk. as part of a practical class. Participants recorded their names and age but were assured of confidentiality, and participa-
55 tion was voluntary. None of the class declined to participate, and no credit was given for completing the questionnaires on either occasion. The participants were not informed that the measure would be readministered.

Results

60 Satisfactory estimates of internal reliability (Cronbach, 1951) were found for the Francis Scale of Attitude toward Christianity short-form at both Time 1 (Cronbach alpha = .91) and Time 2 (Cronbach alpha = .93). Scores on the scale for Time 1 and Time 2 were

65 highly correlated ($r = .92$). No significant difference was found in the mean scores ($t_{38} = -2.43$, ns) between Time 1 (M = 25.2, SD = 5.4, range 14–35) and Time 2 ($M = 25.7$, $SD = 6.2$, range 12–35).

Discussion

The present data provide evidence for the test–
70 retest reliability over a 1-wk. period for the Francis Scale of Attitude toward Christianity short-form among a sample of Northern Irish university students. Furthermore, satisfactory values of internal reliability were also found, in line with previous research (e.g., Lewis,
75 2001). Although the generalizability of these findings is limited given the small sample, the selectivity of the sample (i.e., university students, mainly female, and the small duration of the intervening period between tests), the short-form does appear temporally stable.
80 These findings provide additional psychometric evidence which attests to the stability of the measure (Lewis & Maltby, 2000). Further research is required to examine the stability of the Francis Scale of Attitude toward Christianity short-form among large and more
85 representative samples and over longer testing periods.

References

Cronbach, L. J. (1951). Coefficient alpha and the internal structure of tests. *Psychometrika*, *16*, 297–334.

Francis, L. J. (1993). Reliability and validity of a short scale of attitude towards Christianity among adults. *Psychological Reports*, *72*, 615–618.

Francis, L. J., Greer, J. E., & Gibson, H. M. (1991). Reliability and validity of a short measure of attitude toward Christianity among secondary school pupils in England, Scotland, and Northern Ireland. *Collected Original Resources in Education*, *15*, Fiche 2, G09.

Francis, L. J., & Stubbs, M. T. (1987). Measuring attitudes towards Christianity: From childhood to adulthood. *Personality and Individual Differences*, *8*, 741–743.

Hill, P C., & Hood, R. W. (1999). *Measures of religiosity*. Birmingham, AL: Religious Education Press.

Holland, J. C., Kash, K. M., Passik, S., Gronert, M. K., Sison, A., Lederberg, M., Russak, S. M., Baider, L., & Fox, B. (1998). A brief spiritual beliefs inventory for use in quality of life research in life-threatening illness. *Psycho-oncology*, *7*, 460–469.

Kay, W. K., & Francis, L. J. (1996). *Drift from the churches: attitude toward Christianity during childhood and adolescence*. Cardiff, Wales: University. of Wales Press.

Lewis, C. A. (1999). Is the relationship between religiosity and personality "contaminated" by social desirability as assessed by the Lie Scale? A methodological reply to Michael W. Eysenck (1998). *Mental Health, Religion and Culture*, *2*, 105–114.

Lewis, C. A. (2000). The religiosity-psychoticism relationship and the two factors of social desirability: A response to Michael W. Eysenck (1999). *Mental Health, Religion and Culture*, *3*, 39–45.

Lewis, C. A. (2001). Cultural stereotype of the effects of religion on mental health. *British Journal of Medical Psychology*, *74*, 359–367.

Lewis, C. A., & Maltby, J. (2000). The Francis Scale of Attitude Toward Christianity (Adult Version: Short-Scale). In J. Maltby, C. A. Lewis, & A. Hill (Eds.), *Commissioned reviews of 250 psychological tests*, *1*, (pp. 301–306). Cardiff, Wales, UK: Edwin Mellen Press.

Lewis, C. A., Shevlin, M. E., Lloyd, N. S. V., & Adamson, G. (1998). The Francis Scale of Attitude Toward Christianity (short-scale): exploratory and confirmatory factor analysis among English students. *Journal of Social Behavior and Personality*, *13*, 167–175.

Maltby, J., & Lewis, C. A. (1997) The reliability and validity of a short scale of attitude towards Christianity among USA, English, Republic of Ireland, and Northern Ireland adults. *Personality and Individual Differences*, *22*, 649–654.

Storch, E. A., Strawser, M. S., & Storch, J. B. (2004). Two-week test–retest reliability of the Duke Religion Index. *Psychological Reports*, *94*, 993–994.

Worthington, E. L., Jr., Wade, N. G., Hight, T L., Ripley, J. S., McCullough, M. E., Berry, J. W., Schmitt, M. M., Berry, J. T., Bursley, K. H., & O'Connor, L. (2003). The Religious Commitment Inventory–10: development, refinement, and validation of a brief measure for research and counseling. *Journal of Counseling Psychology*, *50*, 84–96.

Address correspondence to: Dr. Christopher Alan Lewis, School of Psychology, University of Ulster at Magee College, Londonderry, Northern Ireland, UK, BT48 7JL. E-mail: ca.lewis@ ulster.ac.uk

Exercise for Article 30

Factual Questions

1. The 7-item short-form of the scale is intended to be a replacement for what?

2. Do "higher scores" *or* "lower scores" indicate a more positive attitude toward Christianity?

3. What is the value of Cronbach alpha (a measure of internal reliability) at Time 2 (i.e., the second administration)?

4. What is the value of the test–retest reliability coefficient?

5. Did the mean scores differ significantly from the first week to the second week?

Questions for Discussion

6. The researchers cite research that suggests that the Francis Scale is not affected by "social desirability." What is your understanding of the meaning of this term? (See lines 11–17.)

7. The researchers provide a sample question from the Francis Scale. How helpful is this to you in understanding what the scale measures? Explain. (See lines 42–43.)

8. Although participants recorded their names and age on the scale, they were assured of confidentiality. Is this important? Explain. (See lines 53–54.)

9. In your opinion, do the results reported in this study indicate that the Francis Scale has adequate test–retest reliability? Explain. (See lines 64–65.)

10. What is your understanding of the difference between "internal reliability" and "test–retest reliability"?

11. To what extent do you agree with the researchers that the generalizability of their findings is limited? (See lines 75–79.)

12. The researchers suggest that in future research it would be desirable to examine the stability of the scale "over longer testing periods." (See lines 82–85.) If your textbook addresses this issue, what time period(s) does it suggest as being suitable?

Quality Ratings

Directions: Indicate your level of agreement with each of the following statements by circling a number from 5 for strongly agree (SA) to 1 for strongly disagree (SD). If you believe an item is not applicable to this research article, leave it blank. Be prepared to explain your ratings. When responding to criteria A and B below, keep in mind that brief titles and abstracts are conventional in published research.

A. The title of the article is appropriate.

SA   5   4   3   2   1   SD

B. The abstract provides an effective overview of the research article.

SA   5   4   3   2   1   SD

C. The introduction establishes the importance of the study.

SA   5   4   3   2   1   SD

D. The literature review establishes the context for the study.

SA   5   4   3   2   1   SD

E. The research purpose, question, or hypothesis is clearly stated.

SA   5   4   3   2   1   SD

F. The method of sampling is sound.

SA   5   4   3   2   1   SD

G. Relevant demographics (for example, age, gender, and ethnicity) are described.

SA   5   4   3   2   1   SD

H. Measurement procedures are adequate.

SA   5   4   3   2   1   SD

I. All procedures have been described in sufficient detail to permit a replication of the study.

SA   5   4   3   2   1   SD

J. The participants have been adequately protected from potential harm.

SA   5   4   3   2   1   SD

K. The results are clearly described.

SA   5   4   3   2   1   SD

L. The discussion/conclusion is appropriate.

SA   5   4   3   2   1   SD

M. Despite any flaws, the report is worthy of publication.

SA   5   4   3   2   1   SD

Article 31

Criterion-Related Validity of the Marital Disaffection Scale As a Measure of Marital Estrangement

CLAUDIA FLOWERS
University of North Carolina, Charlotte

BRYAN E. ROBINSON
University of North Carolina, Charlotte

JANE J. CARROLL
University of North Carolina, Charlotte

ABSTRACT. The Marital Disaffection Scale was administered, along with measures of positive feelings toward spouse, problem-drinking behavior of spouse, workaholic behavior of spouse, and marital status, to 323 female members of the American Counseling Association. Scores on the Marital Disaffection Scale showed significant inverse correlations ($r = -.94$) with positive feelings toward spouse and ($r_{pb} = -.63$) with marital status. Scores on the Marital Disaffection Scale showed significant positive relationships ($r = .36$) with spouse's problem drinking behavior and ($r = .48$) with workaholic behavior of spouse. The results support the use of the Marital Disaffection Scale as a measure of emotional estrangement in marriage.

From *Psychological Reports*, 86, 1101–1103. Copyright © 2000 by Psychological Reports. Reprinted with permission.

The Marital Disaffection Scale (Kayser, 1996) is a 21-item inventory designed to measure the components of emotional estrangement in marriage by focusing on the experience of apathy and indifference, lack of car-
5 ing, and lack of attachments toward one's partner. Marital disaffection does not mean that a marriage will necessarily break down but simply is a description of the loss of love and affection by one partner for the other (Kayser, 1996). Scoring for each item was an-
10 chored by 1 (Not At All True) and 4 (Very True), and a total index of disaffection was the sum of points across all items—the higher the score the greater the disaffection. Kayser (1996) reported a correlation of .93 ($p < .001$) between the Marital Disaffection Scale and Sny-
15 der and Regts' scale of disaffection (1982). Scores on the Marital Disaffection Scale correlated inversely with general questions on marital happiness ($r = -.56$) and marital closeness ($r = -.86$). Cronbach coefficient alpha for the 21 items on the Marital Disaffection Scale was
20 .97.

The current study examined the concurrent validity of scores on the Marital Disaffection Scale by correlating Marital Disaffection Scale scores with measures of positive feelings toward spouse, problem-drinking be-
25 havior of spouse, and workaholic behavior of spouse.

Positive feelings toward spouse was assessed using the Positive Feelings Questionnaire (O'Leary, Fincham, & Turkewitz, 1983). The Problem Drinking Scale (Vaillant, 1980) assessed problem-drinking behavior of
30 spouse, and scores were hypothesized to be positively related to marital disaffection (Geiss & O'Leary, 1981). The Work Addiction Risk Test (Robinson, 1999) assessed workaholic behavior of spouse, and scores were hypothesized to have a positive relation-
35 ship (Robinson, 1998). The predictive validity of scores on the Marital Disaffection Scale was evaluated by correlating Marital Disaffection Scale scores with marital status (coded as 0 = divorced and 1 = married).

The four tests and a demographic form were mailed
40 to 1,000 randomly selected female members of the American Counseling Association. A total of 323 respondents returned and completed all the tests and demographic forms. The participants had a mean age of 47.9 yr. (SD = 10.4) ranging from 26 to 89 years. Most
45 participants were currently married (77.6%) and had been on the average 18.2 yr. (SD = 12.3). The means, standard deviations, ranges, and indexes of skewness for each of the four tests are reported in Table 1.

Table 1
Descriptive Statistics of Scores from Marital Disaffection Scale, Positive Feelings Questionnaire, Problem Drinking Scale, and Work Addiction Risk Test

Measures	M	SD	Range	Skewness
Marital Disaffection	36.86	15.75	20–81	1.12
Positive Feelings	94.33	24.07	18–119	−1.30
Problem Drinking	0.88	2.12	0–11	2.61
Work Addiction	52.79	12.35	28–94	0.51

Pearson product–moment correlation coefficients
50 were calculated between scores on the Marital Disaffection Scale and the Positive Feelings Questionnaire, the Problem Drinking Scale, and the Work Addiction Risk Test. A point-biserial correlation coefficient was calculated for scores on Marital Disaffection and mari-
55 tal status. Statistically significant correlations were found between scores on the Marital Disaffection Scale and all other measures. The Marital Disaffection Scale

had an inverse relationship with the Positive Feelings Questionnaire ($r = -.94$, $p < .001$) and marital status ($r_{pb} = -.63$, $p < .001$). Scores on the Marital Disaffection Scale had a positive association with those on the Problem Drinking Scale ($r = .36$, $p < .001$) and the Work Addiction Risk Test ($r = .48$, $p < .001$).

Hypothesized relationships of the scores on the Marital Disaffection Scale with other measures were supported in this study. The results further confirm the use of the Marital Disaffection Scale as a measure of emotional estrangement in marriage.

References

Geiss, S. K., & O'Leary, K. D. (1981). Therapist ratings of frequency and severity of marital problems: Implications for research. *Journal of Marital and Family Therapy, 7,* 515–520.

Kayser, K. (1996). The marital disaffection scale: An inventory for assessing emotional estrangement in marriage. *The American Journal of Family Therapy, 24,* 83–88.

O'Leary, K. D., Fincham, F., & Turkewitz, H. (1983). Assessment of positive feelings toward spouse. *Journal of Consulting and Clinical Psychology, 51,* 949–951.

Robinson, B. E. (1998). Spouses of workaholics: Clinical implications for psychotherapy. *Psychotherapy, 35,* 260–268.

Robinson, B. E. (1999). The work-addiction risk test: Development of a tentative measure of workaholism. *Perceptual and Motor Skills, 88,* 199–210.

Snyder, D. K., & Regts, J. M. (1982). Factor scales for assessing marital disharmony and disaffection. *Journal of Consulting and Clinical Psychology, 50,* 736–743.

Vaillant, G. E. (1980). Natural history of male psychological health: VIII. Antecedent of alcoholism and orality. *American Journal of Psychiatry, 137,* 181–186.

About the authors: Claudia Flowers is a member of the Department of Educational Administration, Research, and Technology. Bryan E. Robinson and Jane J. Carroll are members of the Department of Counseling, Special Education, and Child Development. All are at the University of North Carolina at Charlotte.

Address correspondence to: Claudia Flowers, Ph.D., Department of Educational Administration, Research and Technology, University of North Carolina at Charlotte, 9201 University City Blvd., Charlotte, NC 28223-0001.

Exercise for Article 31

Factual Questions

1. Does a high score on the Marital Disaffection Scale indicate a greater *or* lesser degree of disaffection?

2. The researchers state that they examined what type of validity for the Marital Disaffection Scale?

3. What percentage of the participants was currently married?

4. What was the average score on the Marital Disaffection Scale?

5. Which correlation coefficient reported in this article represents the strongest relationship?

6. What is the value of the correlation coefficient for the relationship between marital disaffection and problem drinking?

Questions for Discussion

7. Would you be interested in seeing sample items from the Marital Disaffection Scale? Why? Why not?

8. The response rate was 323 out of 1,000. In your opinion, does this limit the validity of the study? Explain. (See lines 41–43.)

9. Do you agree with the last sentence in this article? (See lines 66–68.)

10. This article is relatively short. In your opinion, does its shortness limit its usefulness and validity? Explain.

11. If you were going to conduct another study on this topic, what changes in the research methodology would you make, if any?

Quality Ratings

Directions: Indicate your level of agreement with each of the following statements by circling a number from 5 for strongly agree (SA) to 1 for strongly disagree (SD). If you believe an item is not applicable to this research article, leave it blank. Be prepared to explain your ratings. When responding to criteria A and B below, keep in mind that brief titles and abstracts are conventional in published research.

A. The title of the article is appropriate.

SA   5   4   3   2   1   SD

B. The abstract provides an effective overview of the research article.

SA   5   4   3   2   1   SD

C. The introduction establishes the importance of the study.

SA   5   4   3   2   1   SD

D. The literature review establishes the context for the study.

SA   5   4   3   2   1   SD

E. The research purpose, question, or hypothesis is clearly stated.

SA   5   4   3   2   1   SD

F. The method of sampling is sound.

SA   5   4   3   2   1   SD

G. Relevant demographics (for example, age, gender, and ethnicity) are described.

SA 5 4 3 2 1 SD

H. Measurement procedures are adequate.

SA 5 4 3 2 1 SD

I. All procedures have been described in sufficient detail to permit a replication of the study.

SA 5 4 3 2 1 SD

J. The participants have been adequately protected from potential harm.

SA 5 4 3 2 1 SD

K. The results are clearly described.

SA 5 4 3 2 1 SD

L. The discussion/conclusion is appropriate.

SA 5 4 3 2 1 SD

M. Despite any flaws, the report is worthy of publication.

SA 5 4 3 2 1 SD

Article 32

The Moral Justification Scale: Reliability and Validity of a New Measure of Care and Justice Orientations

LINDA S. GUMP
Psychological HealthCare

RICHARD C. BAKER
California School of
Professional Psychology

SAMUEL ROLL
University of New Mexico

ABSTRACT. Research increasingly suggests that there are limitations to Kohlberg's theory of moral development. Gilligan in particular has observed that Kohlberg's theory considers abstract principled reasoning as the highest level of moral judgment, and penalizes those who focus on the interpersonal ramifications of a moral decision. Gilligan calls these *justice* and *care* orientations. The present paper describes the development of the Moral Justification Scale, an objective measure of the two orientations. The scale consists of six vignettes, of which two are justice oriented, two are care oriented, and two are mixed, incorporating both orientations. Construct validity was evaluated by expert judges and, overall, was high. Cronbach's alpha was .75 for the Care subscale and .64 for the Justice subscale, indicating adequate internal consistency. Split-half reliabilities were as follows: Care, $r = .72$, $p < .01$, and Justice, $r = .60$, $p < .05$. Regarding test–retest reliability (approximately 2 weeks), $r = .61$, $p < .05$, for Care; $r = .69$, $p < .05$, for Justice. Neither subscale correlated significantly with the Marlowe-Crowne Social Desirability Scale. Thus, the Moral Justification Scale shows promise as an easily administered, objectively scored measure of Gilligan's constructs of care and justice.

From *Adolescence, 35*, 67–76. Copyright © 2000 by Libra Publishers, Inc. Reprinted with permission.

The Work of Kohlberg and Gilligan

Kohlberg (1981, 1985; Kohlberg & Kramer, 1969), using Piaget's theories of cognitive and moral development as a starting point, developed a model of moral development with six stages. Kohlberg's stages are grouped into three progressively higher levels: preconventional, conventional, and postconventional. People at the preconventional level (Stages 1 and 2), primarily children, conceive of rules and social expectations as external to the self. Moral decisions are made based on expectations of reward or punishment. At the conventional level (Stages 3 and 4), people subscribe to a morality of shared norms and values, centering on the needs of the individual and the rules and expectations of others. Interpersonal relationships and concern for others' opinions are crucial (Stage 3). At Stage 4, obeying society's laws becomes central. At the postconventional level (Stages 5 and 6), moral decision-making is based on principled reasoning. Stage 5 revolves around the utilitarian maxim, "the greatest good for the greatest number." At Stage 6, people make decisions based on universal principles of justice, liberty, and equality, even if these violate laws or social norms.

Critics of Kohlberg's model, most notably Gilligan (1982), have pointed out that his system is drawn from a Kantian philosophy that uses abstract principles of justice as the basis of advanced moral reasoning. This penalizes those who focus on the interpersonal ramifications of a moral decision. Gilligan (1981) has argued that Kohlberg's representation of women as fixated at Stage 3, which represents interpersonal morality, is flawed. Women's reasoning, according to Gilligan (1982), is contextual and deeply tied to relationships, and Kohlberg has undervalued the equally valid Aristotelian moral concerns voiced by women (Vasudev, 1988). Thus, the emphasis on justice as the embodiment of morality appears to have underestimated the impact that interpersonal connectedness can have on moral decision-making.

Gilligan set out to test the validity of a care perspective, with the assumption that it is morally equivalent to the justice construct. Gilligan's (1977) response to the apparent bias in Kohlberg's theory toward the male (justice) perspective included an alternative stage sequence for the development of females' moral reasoning. These stages are based on the degree of compassion and connection between self and others, manifested in the peace and harmony in relationships (Brabeck, 1983; Muuss, 1988).

Gilligan viewed women as progressing from initial selfishness (first level) to caring primarily for others (second level) and finally to an integration of concern for the needs of both self and others (third level). Her morality of responsibility emphasizes attachments, allows for both self-sacrifice and selfishness, and considers connections with others as primary, while Kohlberg's morality of justice emphasizes autonomy, rules, and legalities, and considers the individual as primary. Gilligan and Attanucci (1988) have stressed that neither orientation is superior; rather, care and justice are complementary.

Using measures designed to investigate more interpersonally oriented forms of moral reasoning, a number of studies (Gibbs, Arnold, & Burkhart; 1984; Gilligan & Attanucci, 1988; Lyons, 1983; Pratt, Golding, Hunter, & Sampson, 1988; Rothbart, Hanley, & Albert, 1986) have found gender differences, with males primarily focusing on issues of justice and females primarily focusing on interpersonal issues. However, other studies have not found significant differences (Crown & Heatherington, 1989; Friedman, Robinson, & Friedman, 1987; Galotti, 1989; Pratt, Golding, Hunter, & Sampson, 1988; Walker, 1989).

There may also be a degree of ethnocentrism in Kohlberg's theory. Miller and Bersoff (1992), for example, challenged Kohlberg's claim of universality in moral reasoning, having found that Americans focus on justice considerations, while Hindus in India emphasize interpersonal considerations in rendering a moral decision. Snarey (1985) likewise concluded that Kohlberg's model is specific to Western culture.

In short, there is reason to believe that Kohlberg's method of studying moral judgment has certain limitations. Other systems—most of which are based on interviews—are cumbersome, and require considerable expertise in administration and scoring. Thus, an easily administered, objectively scored measure of moral judgment, tapping both care and justice orientations, would have several advantages (e.g., it would have a greater chance of avoiding gender and cultural biases). The present paper describes such an instrument—the Moral Justification Scale—and provides data on reliability and validity.

Method

Participants

To recruit participants, sign-up sheets were posted at a large state university in Southern California. The study was described only as an investigation of how people make decisions, in order to provide general information while minimizing self-selection bias. Students received extra credit in psychology classes in return for their participation.

One hundred participants completed the research protocol. Since this was the first phase of research comparing Mexican Americans and Anglo Americans, certain inclusion criteria were employed. Using the Acculturation Rating Scale for Mexican Americans (Cuellar, Harris, & Jasso, 1980), Mexican Americans had to be classified as "very Mexican," "Mexican-oriented bicultural," or "syntonic bicultural," not "Anglo-oriented bicultural" or "very Anglicized."

The Anglo American group consisted of White, non-Hispanic individuals whose parents were not immigrants. All were European-origin "nonethnics," who Spindler and Spindler (1990) have referred to as the "referent ethniclass" (p. 33) of the United States, namely individuals of Anglo-Saxon or northern European Protestant descent, or who adhere to mainstream cultural practices.

The final sample consisted of 40 Mexican Americans and 40 Anglo Americans (20 females and 20 males in each group). Their ages ranged from 18 to 25 years ($M = 18.9$, $SD = 1.3$). A separate sample of 16 students (mean age = 29.1, $SD = 7.4$) was employed to investigate test–retest reliability.

Measures

Moral Justification Scale. The Moral Justification Scale (MJS; Gump, 1994), which is the focus of the present study, consists of six dilemmas presented in the form of vignettes. Two involve justice-oriented situations, two involve care-oriented situations, and two are mixed, combining both orientations. For example, the dilemma dealing with the possible breakup of a couple was classified as having a care orientation, as it primarily involves relational issues (i.e., responsiveness toward another person) rather than issues of individual rights and reciprocity between individuals. This is not to say that a justice mode of moral reasoning cannot be used, only that the essence of the dilemma is highly interpersonal. The other care vignette involves a dating dilemma. The justice dilemmas involve cheating on an exam and denting a car. The mixed dilemmas deal with the desire to shoplift to help a sibling and how to handle a friend's drug problem.

The six vignettes were written to be of interest and importance to college students. Furthermore, the names of all protagonists were common for both Anglo Americans and Mexican Americans (e.g., Ana, Michelle, and Tony). Each vignette can have either a male or female protagonist, allowing for counterbalancing. Participants respond to one care, one justice, and one mixed vignette with a male protagonist and one care, one justice, and one mixed vignette with a female protagonist.

After reading the vignette, participants are asked to take a moment to think about what the protagonist should do. They are presented with eight sentences that have been extracted from the vignette, four of which represent care concerns and four of which represent justice concerns. Each is followed by a 10-point scale, with anchors at 1 (not at all important) and 10 (very important); the participant is asked to indicate the importance of the item in making a judgment. An example of a care-oriented item is: "Tony was his closest friend, and Marcus didn't want to hurt him by telling the teacher and getting him into trouble." An example of a justice-oriented item is: "Julie glanced up at the sign on the wall which read: 'Shoplifting is illegal.' " A complete justice-oriented vignette, Denting the Car Dilemma (female version), follows.

Julie, a 16-year-old, is having difficulty making a decision. A few days ago, Julie's younger sister, Susanna, had a minor accident with their parents' car. Susanna only had her learner's permit and wasn't allowed to drive without her parents. She had taken the car out anyway and had driven around the neighborhood while her parents were away for the day. Upon her return, Susanna had accidentally dented the car a little by running into a telephone pole while attempting to park. Julie wasn't sure what she should do about this situation, but was seriously considering telling her parents that it was she who had caused the dent instead of Susanna in order to avoid a great deal of family fighting.

Having been in a lot of trouble recently, Susanna had strained her parents' relationship, as they frequently fought over what to do about her being bad. Julie didn't want to cause further strain on her parents' marriage by telling them about Susanna's latest blunder. On the other hand, she didn't want to have to lie about what happened either, as she felt that lying was wrong. Julie was also concerned about covering up for Susanna in this way. She always tried to set a good example for Susanna and didn't want Susanna to think that she could just break the rules whenever she pleased. Besides, Julie didn't want to damage her positive relationship with her parents—she'd worked hard on being close with them and didn't want to risk hurting them by losing their trust. She also worried about her relationship with Susanna. Julie and Susanna had stood up for each other equally in times of trouble in the past, especially when it came to getting in trouble with their parents.

Julie began to wonder what might happen if she told her parents the truth. She had always believed that her parents were too strict in certain areas, and thought that this would probably be one of those areas. More than likely, she thought, their punishment of Susanna would be quite severe, and she didn't want her little sister to have to suffer. If they thought that she had dented the car instead of Susanna, however, they would probably just laugh about it, as she had her driver's license but was just learning how to drive. Besides, Susanna kept it secret last year when Julie skipped school so that she could go to the beach with friends, and she felt she owed Susanna for this. But Julie also realized that the loss of self-respect she would experience might not be worth going along with the story she and Susanna had made up.

Please take a moment to think about what Julie should do, then turn the page and answer the questions.

If you were to make a decision, think about how important each of these statements would be. On a scale from 1 (not at all important) to 10 (very important), please circle the number [1 2 3 4 5 6 7 8 9 10] that indicates how important you think each of the following ideas was in making your decision.

1. Julie didn't want to cause further strain on her parents' marriage by telling them about Susanna's latest blunder.
2. Julie didn't want to have to lie about what happened, as she felt that lying was wrong.
3. Julie didn't want Susanna to think that she could just break the rules whenever she pleased.
4. Julie didn't want to damage her positive relationship with her parents—she'd worked hard on being close with them and didn't want to risk hurting them by losing their trust.
5. Julie and Susanna had stood up for each other equally in times of trouble in the past, especially when it came to getting in trouble with their parents.
6. More than likely, Julie thought, her parents' punishment of Susanna would be quite severe, and she didn't want her little sister to have to suffer.
7. Susanna kept it secret last year when Julie skipped school so that she could go to the beach with friends, and Julie felt she owed Susanna for this.
8. Julie realized that the loss of self-respect she would experience might not be worth going along with the story she and Susanna had made up.

The Care subscale score is based on responses to the four care items for the six vignettes. Scores across the 24 items are averaged, and thus range from 1 to 10. The Justice subscale is scored similarly.

Miller Social Intimacy Scale. The Miller Social Intimacy Scale (MSIS; Miller & Lefcourt, 1982) is a 17-item self-report inventory designed to assess the level of social intimacy experienced in marriage or friendships. Respondents are asked to rate, on a 10-point scale, their relationship with a spouse or closest friend. Responses are summed to produce a Total score, as well as scores for two subscales, Frequency and Intensity.

Cronbach alpha coefficients of .91 and .86 were reported by Miller and Lefcourt (1982). Test–retest reliability over a 1-month interval ($r = .84$, $p < .001$) and 2-month interval ($r = .96$, $p < .001$) reflected stability in scores over time (Miller & Lefcourt, 1982). Convergent validity was demonstrated using the UCLA Loneliness Scale (Russell, Peplau, & Ferguson, 1978), $r = -.65$, $p < .001$, and the Interpersonal Relationship Scale (Guerney, 1977), $r = .71$, $p < .001$.

Marlowe-Crowne Social Desirability Scale. The Marlowe-Crowne Social Desirability Scale (SDS; Crowne & Marlowe, 1960) was developed to control for participants who seek to present themselves in an exaggeratedly favorable or unfavorable light. It consists of 33 items, with true-or-false response categories. Crowne and Marlowe reported internal consistency of .88; the test–retest correlation after one month was .89. Construct validity was established through significant positive correlations with the L and K scales of the MMPI (Crowne & Marlowe, 1960).

Acculturation Rating Scale for Mexican Americans. The Acculturation Rating Scale for Mexican Americans (ARSMA; Cuellar, Harris & Jasso, 1980) is a self-report questionnaire designed to assess level of acculturation in both nonclinical and clinical populations. Each of the 20 items on the scale is assigned a value ranging from 1 (extremely Mexican oriented) to 5 (extremely Anglo oriented). The dimensions assessed are language familiarity and usage, ethnic pride and identity, ethnic interaction, cultural heritage, and generational proximity. Five groups of Mexican Americans are identified according to level of acculturation: very Mexican, Mexican-oriented bicultural, syntonic bicultural, Anglo-oriented bicultural, and very Anglicized.

A coefficient alpha of .88 was obtained for a nonclinical sample. Concurrent validity was demonstrated using the Behavioral Acculturation Scale (Szapocznik, Scopetta, Kurtines, & Aranalde, 1978), rho = .76, *p* < .001, and the Biculturalism Inventory (Ramirez, Cox, & Castaneda, 1977), rho = .81, *p* < .001.

Procedure

In a psychology laboratory on the college campus, participants signed a consent form and completed the MJS, MSIS, SDS, and ARSMA in groups of up to 14. Most took about one hour. Upon finishing, participants were debriefed.

Results

Validity of the Moral Justification Scale

To assess construct validity, the 48 MJS items (six vignettes, each with eight items) were rated by eight judges as to whether they represented the care or justice constructs. Judges were clinical psychologists who had taught graduate courses in ethics or developmental psychology, or doctoral candidates in clinical psychology who had taken courses in these areas. The judges were first provided with a brief summary of Gilligan's concepts of care and justice.

For 35 of the items, there was unanimous agreement by the eight judges that the care and justice constructs were accurately represented. There was agreement by seven of the judges for 10 items. The three items for which there was agreement by fewer than seven judges were not included in subsequent calculations of MJS scores.

Concurrent validity was assessed via comparison of Care subscale scores and Miller Social Intimacy Scale scores. The MSIS measures interpersonal intimacy and the Care subscale taps interpersonal considerations in moral judgment. While the underlying constructs overlap, they do so only moderately. Therefore, only a modest correlation was expected and, in fact, found (*r* = .22, *p* < .05).

Reliability of the Moral Justification Scale

Internal consistency (Cronbach, 1951), split-half reliability, and test–retest reliability were computed for a separate sample of 16 students. Internal consistency and split-half reliability were based on the first administration only, whereas test–retest reliability was calculated using both administrations.

Internal consistency. Cronbach's alpha was .75 for the Care subscale and .64 for the Justice subscale, indicating adequate internal consistency. Because of counterbalancing, it was possible to calculate Cronbach's alpha by sex of the protagonist in each vignette. Alpha

levels were expected to be lower than those for the full subscales and, in fact, ranged from .26 to .71.

It was also possible to calculate Cronbach's alpha based on dilemma content (care, justice, or mixed). Alphas ranged from .31 to .57, reflecting marginally acceptable reliability. Examining dilemma content (care, justice, or mixed) by sex of protagonist (male or female) by subscale (Care versus Justice) produced alphas ranging from −.84 to .47, with a mean of .12.

Split-half reliability. Split-half reliability of the Care and Justice subscales was also examined (exclusion of three items, as previously noted, prevented equal representation of dilemmas in each half). For the Care subscale, *r* = .72, *p* < .01 (correlation between halves was .91 using Kuder-Richardson Formula 20). For the Justice subscale, *r* = .60, *p* < .05 (.75 using Kuder-Richardson Formula 20).

Test–retest reliability. Approximately 2 weeks after the first administration, the MJS was readministered to the same 16 participants. Test–retest correlations for the Care subscale (*r* = .61, *p* < .05) and the justice subscale (*r* = .69, *p* < .05) indicated adequate reliability.

Social Desirability

To evaluate whether the 80 participants responded to the vignettes honestly, they were administered the Marlowe-Crowne Social Desirability Scale. The correlations between the SDS and the Care subscale (*r* = −.19) and the Justice subscale (*r* = −.17) were not significant. Thus, the MJS did not appear to be influenced by social desirability pressures.

Conclusion

The Moral Justification Scale may be a useful alternative to measures based on Kohlberg's system. For example, in clinical work with delinquent children, for whom the nature and style of moral reasoning are important issues, the MJS can be of special help. Those with the capacity to consider the needs and feelings of others (care-oriented) would be distinguished from those with more of a justice orientation. Separate interventions could then be designed and implemented.

Tracking the progress of different groups would itself be of interest, in order to determine whether outcomes differ. Further, with the current focus on values-related education, the MJS could be used to measure how various educational programs produce changes in care or justice orientations, or both.

In accord with the work of Gilligan (1982), Guisinger and Blatt (1994), and other theorists, cross-cultural studies should be undertaken with the MJS. In particular, it would be interesting to determine whether cultures under stress show declines in levels of moral reasoning.

References

Brabeck, M. (1983). Moral judgment: Theory and research on differences between males and females. *Developmental Review, 3*, 274–291.

Cronbach, L. J. (1951). Coefficient alpha and the internal structure of tests. *Psychometrika, 16*, 297–334.

Crown, J., & Heatherington, L. (1989). The cost of winning? The role of gender in moral reasoning and judgments about competitive athletic encounters. *Journal of Sport and Exercise Psychology, 11*, 281–289.

Crowne, D. P., & Marlowe, D. C. (1960). Marlowe-Crowne Social Desirability Scale. *Journal of Consulting Psychology, 24*, 349–354.

Cuellar, I., Harris, L. C., & Jasso, R. (1980). An acculturation scale for Mexican American normal and clinical populations. *Hispanic Journal of Behavioral Sciences, 2*, 199–217.

Friedman, W. J., Robinson, A. B., & Friedman, B. L. (1987). Sex differences in moral judgments? A test of Gilligan's theory. *Psychology of Women Quarterly, 11*, 37–46.

Galotti, K. M. (1989). Gender differences in self-reported moral reasoning: A review and new evidence. *Journal of Youth and Adolescence, 18*, 475–487.

Gibbs, J. C., Arnold, K. D., &. Burkhart, J. E. (1984). Sex differences in the expression of moral judgment. *Child Development, 55*, 1040–1043.

Gilligan, C. (1977). In a different voice: Women's conceptions of self and morality. *Harvard Educational Review, 47*, 481–517.

Gilligan, C. (1981). Moral development in college years. In A. Chickering (Ed.), *The modern American college* (pp. 139–157). San Francisco: Jossey-Bass.

Gilligan, C. (1982). *In a different voice: Psychological theory and women's development*. Cambridge, MA: Harvard University Press.

Gilligan, C., & Attanucci, J. (1988). Two moral orientations: Gender differences and similarities. *Merrill-Palmer Quarterly, 34*, 223–237.

Guerney, B. G. (1977). *Relationship enhancement*. San Francisco: Jossey-Bass.

Guisinger, S., & Blatt, S. J. (1994). Individuality and relatedness: Evolution of a fundamental dialectic. *American Psychologist, 49*, 104–111.

Gump, L. S. (1994). *The relationship of culture and gender to moral decision-making*. Unpublished doctoral dissertation, California School of Professional Psychology, San Diego, CA.

Kohlberg, L. (1976). Moral stages and moralization. In T. Lickona (Ed.), *Moral development and behavior* (pp. 31–53). New York: Holt, Rinehart and Winston.

Kohlberg, L. (1981). *The philosophy of moral development: Moral stages and the idea of justice* (*Vol. 1. Essays on moral development*). New York: Harper and Row.

Kohlberg, L. (1985). Resolving moral conflicts within the just community. In C. G. Harding (Ed.), *Moral dilemmas: Philosophical and psychological issues in the development of moral reasoning* (pp. 71–97). Chicago: Precedent Publishing.

Kohlberg, L., & Kramer, R. (1969). Continuities and discontinuities in childhood and adult moral development. *Human Development, 12*, 93–120.

Lyons, N. P. (1983). Two perspectives: On self, relationships, and morality. *Harvard Educational Review, 53*, 125–145.

Miller, J. G., & Bersoff, D. M. (1992). Culture and moral judgment: How are conflicts between justice and interpersonal responsibilities resolved? *Journal of Personality and Social Psychology, 62*, 541–554.

Miller, J. G., Bersoff, D. M., & Harwood, R. L. (1990). Perceptions of social responsibilities in India and in the United States: Moral imperatives or personal decisions? *Journal of Personality and Social Psychology, 58*, 33–47.

Miller, R. S., & Lefcourt, H. M. (1982). The assessment of social intimacy. *Journal of Personality Adjustment, 46*, 514–518.

Muuss, R. E. (1988). Carol Gilligan's theory of sex differences in the development of moral reasoning during adolescence. *Adolescence, 23*, 229–243.

Pratt, M. W., Golding, G., Hunter, W., & Sampson, R. (1988). Sex differences in adult moral orientations. *Journal of Personality, 56*, 373–391.

Ramirez, M., Cox, B., & Castaneda, A. (1977). *The psychodynamics of biculturalism*. (Study prepared for Organizational Research Programs, Office of Naval Research, Arlington, Virginia.) Santa Cruz, CA: Systems and Evaluations to Education.

Rothbart, M. K., Hanley, D., & Albert, M. (1986). Gender differences in moral reasoning. *Sex Roles, 15*, 645–653.

Russell, D., Peplau, L. A., & Ferguson, M. L. (1978). Developing a measure of loneliness. *Journal of Medicine, 60*, 910–921.

Snarey, J. R. (1985). Cross-cultural universality of social-moral development: A critical review of Kohlbergian research. *Psychological Bulletin, 97*, 202–232.

Spindler, G., & Spindler, L. (1990). *The American cultural dialogue and its transmission*. London: Palmer Press.

Szapocznik, J., Scopetta, M. A., Kurtines, W., & Aranalde, M. A. (1978). Theory and measurement of acculturation. *International Journal of Psychology, 12*, 113–120.

Vasudev, J. (1988). Sex differences in morality and moral orientation: A discussion of the Gilligan and Attanucci study. *Merrill-Palmer Quarterly, 34*, 239–244.

Walker, L. J. (1989). A longitudinal study of moral reasoning. *Child Development, 60*, 157–166.

Address correspondence to: Linda S. Gump, Ph.D., clinical psychologist, Psychological HealthCare, PLLC, 110 West Utica, Oswego, NY 13126.

Exercise for Article 32

Factual Questions

1. Have all previous researchers found gender differences when using more interpersonally oriented forms of moral reasoning?

2. The final sample consisted of how many students?

3. The Moral Justification Scale consists of how many vignettes?

4. The Marlowe-Crowne Social Desirability Scale was developed to control for participants who seek to do what?

5. The judges were in unanimous agreement on how many of the 48 items?

6. What was the value of the correlation coefficient for the relationship between Care subscale scores and Miller Social Intimacy Scale scores?

7. Was the relationship between the social desirability scores and the Care subscale scores significant?

Questions for Discussion

8. In order to recruit participants, do you think it was appropriate to describe the study as only "an investigation of how people make decisions"? Explain. (See lines 94–96.)

9. How important is the complete vignette in helping you understand this study? Would the report be just as strong if the vignette were omitted? Explain. (See lines 167–212.)

10. What do you think the researchers mean when they state that "participants were debriefed"? (See lines 302–303.)

11. How helpful is it to know the test–retest reliability of the MJS? Do you think it has adequate reliability? (See lines 356–360.)

12. Has this study convinced you that the MJS is reasonably valid? Explain.

Quality Ratings

Directions: Indicate your level of agreement with each of the following statements by circling a number from 5 for strongly agree (SA) to 1 for strongly disagree (SD). If you believe an item is not applicable to this research article, leave it blank. Be prepared to explain your ratings. When responding to criteria A and B below, keep in mind that brief titles and abstracts are conventional in published research.

A.   The title of the article is appropriate.

SA   5   4   3   2   1   SD

B.   The abstract provides an effective overview of the research article.

SA   5   4   3   2   1   SD

C.   The introduction establishes the importance of the study.

SA   5   4   3   2   1   SD

D.   The literature review establishes the context for the study.

SA   5   4   3   2   1   SD

E.   The research purpose, question, or hypothesis is clearly stated.

SA   5   4   3   2   1   SD

F.   The method of sampling is sound.

SA   5   4   3   2   1   SD

G.   Relevant demographics (for example, age, gender, and ethnicity) are described.

SA   5   4   3   2   1   SD

H.   Measurement procedures are adequate.

SA   5   4   3   2   1   SD

I.   All procedures have been described in sufficient detail to permit a replication of the study.

SA   5   4   3   2   1   SD

J.   The participants have been adequately protected from potential harm.

SA   5   4   3   2   1   SD

K.   The results are clearly described.

SA   5   4   3   2   1   SD

L.   The discussion/conclusion is appropriate.

SA   5   4   3   2   1   SD

M.   Despite any flaws, the report is worthy of publication.

SA   5   4   3   2   1   SD

Article 33

Diabetes Portrayals in North American Print Media: A Qualitative and Quantitative Analysis

MELANIE ROCK

University of Calgary, Alberta, and Université de Montréal, Quebec

Objectives. This study investigated how media coverage has portrayed diabetes as newsworthy.

Methods. The quantitative component involved tabulating diabetes coverage in two major Canadian newspapers, 1988–2001 and 1991–2001. The qualitative component focused on high-profile coverage in two major U.S. magazines and two major Canadian newspapers, 1998–2000.

Results. Although coverage did not consistently increase, the quantitative results suggest an emphasis on linking diabetes with heart disease and mortality to convey its seriousness. The qualitative component identified three main ways of portraying type 2 diabetes: as an insidious problem, as a problem associated with particular populations, and as a medical problem.

Conclusions. Overall, the results suggest that when communicating with journalists, researchers and advocates have stressed that diabetes maims and kills. Yet even when media coverage acknowledged societal forces and circumstances as causes, the proposed remedies did not always include or stress modifications to social contexts. Neither the societal causes of public health problems nor possible societal remedies automatically received attention from researchers or from journalists. Skilled advocacy is needed to put societal causes and solutions on public agendas.

From *American Journal of Public Health*, 95, 1832–1838. Copyright © 2005 by the American Public Health Association. Reprinted with permission.

Type 2 diabetes mellitus is a serious public health problem in developed countries and increasingly in developing countries too.[1] Yet only a handful of peer-reviewed articles have examined mass media coverage
5 of type 1 or type 2 diabetes.[2-5] This study examined how print media coverage portrayed diabetes as a newsworthy problem. The results suggest that public health advocacy needs to take into account the roles played by journalists but also by expert sources in in-
10 fluencing portrayals of health problems in the mass media and thereby influencing how members of the public understand health problems.

The premise underlying this mixed-method study is that discourses highlight some diseases, health risks,
15 and approaches to intervention—while obscuring others—by influencing how people think, express themselves, and act.[6-11] Problem framing can be understood as a social process that involves the selection of some aspects of a perceived reality and making them seem
20 more apparent or salient so as to promote particular definitions, causal interpretations, moral evaluations, or possible remedies.[12] This article's emphasis on media portrayals resonates with the "public arenas" model of how problems achieve social recognition.[13] Unlike the
25 "natural history" model of problem recognition, which emphasizes how bona fide harms achieve visibility, the public arenas model does not assume that objective harms become socially recognized problems. Instead, the public arenas model underscores that the mass me-
30 dia, public policy, scientific publications, and other discursive domains interact with one another to confer recognition or to obscure harm.

Methods

Quantitative Methods

The quantitative component aimed to establish the extent to which mass media coverage has portrayed
35 diabetes as problematic. To do so, the amount and select key features of diabetes coverage were tabulated longitudinally in two newspapers: *The Toronto Star* and *The Globe and Mail*. *The Toronto Star* is the largest-circulation newspaper in Canada, and *The Globe*
40 *and Mail* was the only newspaper distributed across Canada throughout the 1990s. LexisNexis was used to access the full-text electronic archives of *The Toronto Star* for all available years: 1988–2001. The data for *The Globe and Mail* were obtained from InfoGlobe for
45 all available years: 1991–2001.

The search term "diabet!" (the "!" denotes a wildcard search; in the case of "diabet!" items with the word "diabetic" and "diabetics" would be included, as well as those using the word "diabetes") was used to
50 identify references dealing with diabetes, and the search strategy "heart disease, heart attack, heart association, heart failure, cardiac OR cardiol!" was used to identify references dealing with heart disease.[2] Combining these two sets yielded the number of references

55 related to both diabetes and heart disease. The combined set was searched for mentions of death ("death, dead, dies, dying OR obit!"). To establish how often coverage focused attention on diabetes, rather than merely mentioning this condition, the search term
60 "diabet!" was used to retrieve items mentioning diabetes in obituaries, headlines, or lead paragraphs. All items found were tabulated.

Qualitative Methods

The qualitative component focused on identifying the framing devices[12] used in recent print media cover-
65 age of type 2 diabetes. First and foremost, the analysis examined how the print media portrayed type 2 diabetes as a problem by asking, "What is it about this condition that is made to seem problematic?" Related questions included, "Which dimensions and causes of
70 the problem are highlighted?" "Who or what is blamed?" and "What remedies are endorsed?"

Two large-circulation U.S. magazines (*Time* and *Newsweek*), *The Globe and Mail*, and *The Toronto Star* were monitored prospectively, 1998–2000. (Both *Time*
75 and *Newsweek* are sold on Canadian newsstands.) Only stories profiling type 2 diabetes in the first section of the newspaper or magazine cover stories were selected for analysis. To identify any items fitting these criteria that had been missed during prospective monitoring, I
80 searched the following databases: InfoGlobe (for *The Globe and Mail*), Canadian Newsstand (for the *Toronto Star*), and Business Source Premier (for *Newsweek* and *Time*).

Results

Quantitative Results

The number of *Globe and Mail* references mention-
85 ing diabetes increased nearly fivefold between 1991 and 2000 and then dropped off in 2001. Meanwhile, the number of articles mentioning diabetes in *The Toronto Star* did not increase overall from 1988 through 2001 but spiked dramatically in 1995, and again in 1998
90 (Figure 1). I hypothesized that these spikes might correlate to the publication in 1993 and 1995 of landmark clinical trial results showing that tight blood glucose control can curb the incidence of microvascular and macrovascular complications.[14,15] The University of
95 Toronto is home to Bernard Zinman, one of the investigators in these trials, so this international story would have a strong local "angle." Three articles published in 1993 that contained interviews with Zinman focused attention on these results, but searching the 1995 and
100 1998 diabetes coverage for mentions of Zinman did not retrieve any items.

The number of *Toronto Star* articles mentioning diabetes as well as heart disease and death spiked in 1995 and again in 1998 (Figure 2), and the number of
105 articles in *The Globe and Mail* mentioning both of these health problems increased most from 1991 through 2001 (Figure 3). The number of times that diabetes was mentioned in *Toronto Star* obituaries, head-

lines, and lead paragraphs did not increase overall from
110 1988 (75) through 2001 (55), but the number of times that diabetes appeared in *Globe and Mail* obituaries, headlines, and lead paragraphs more than tripled from 1991 (19) to 2001 (61).

Qualitative Results

In the time period studied, *The Globe and Mail*
115 published 14 items that met the inclusion criteria, *The Toronto Star* published nine items, *Newsweek* published two, and *Time* published none. All 25 articles that met the inclusion criteria were found to exhibit at least one of three frames, and six exhibited more than
120 one (Table 1).

Type 2 diabetes is an insidious problem. Each article in the sample that portrayed type 2 diabetes as an insidious problem provided at least one of the following two reasons: (1) modern comforts and conven-
125 iences contribute to this public health problem and (2) individual cases often escape detection for years; meanwhile, complications such as impaired vision, loss of sensation in the limbs, kidney damage, and heart disease often set in. These articles listed the following
130 as possible remedies for preventing complications or for reducing the incidence of type 2 diabetes (or both): intensive clinical treatment, lifestyle changes, improved disease surveillance, increased public awareness, and more public funding.

135 This frame was particularly prominent in two lengthy feature articles that appeared in 2000 and whose titles included the phrase *silent killer*. A September 4, 2000, *Newsweek* cover story (Table 1: NW2. For the remainder of the article, news and news maga-
140 zine articles will be followed by a bracketed referent to allow easy location in Table 1) bore the title "An American epidemic: Diabetes, the silent killer," whereas "Forgotten communities stalked by silent killer: Lost People" was the front-page headline of an
145 April 30, 2000, *Toronto Star* feature article (TS7). It is difficult to imagine that a contemporary report might bear a title like "Cancer: A serious disease," or "AIDS: A public health problem." But in 2000, the Centers for Disease Control and Prevention released "Diabetes: A
150 serious public health problem,"[16] which sparked the *Newsweek* cover story. Note that diabetes was called "serious" in the Centers for Disease Control and Prevention report title, and then *Newsweek* reframed it for a broader public as insidious or sinister. It is also useful
155 to compare the September 4, 2000, *Newsweek* "silent killer" cover story on type 2 diabetes (NW2) with an issue from a year earlier (September 27, 1999 [NW1]), whose cover featured the title, "Where health begins," placed over a photograph of a fetus. The subtitle for the
160 earlier cover story announced, "Obesity, cancer and heart attacks: How your odds are set in the womb." The lead paragraph of that story profiled a 73-year-old man who was diagnosed with type 2 diabetes as well as hypertension in his early 50s. Although diabetes figures

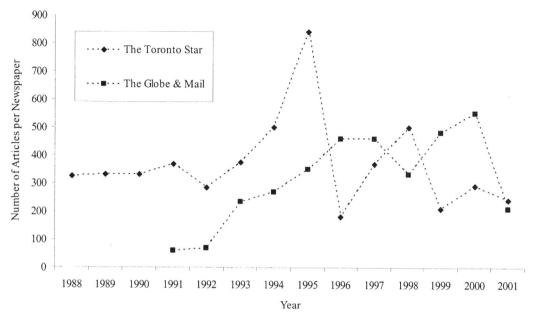

Figure 1. Mention of diabetes in Canadian newspapers.

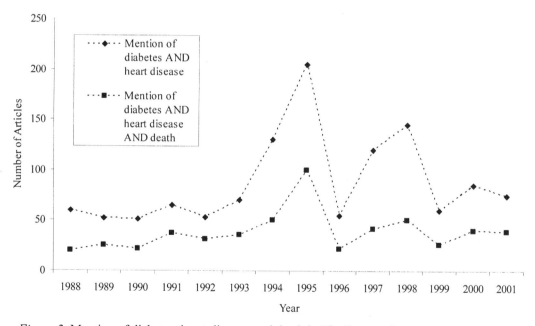

Figure 2. Mention of diabetes, heart disease, and death in *The Toronto Star*.

165   in the "typical case" mobilized in the lead paragraph to personify the lifelong impact of embryonic and fetal development, the editorial board apparently did not consider type 2 diabetes sufficiently dramatic for the cover page. But within a year, *Newsweek* dramatized
170   type 2 diabetes as a cover story by portraying it as an insidious problem whose human costs are unevenly distributed across different social groups and whose financial costs burden American society as a whole.

Type 2 diabetes is associated with certain groups.
175   This frame emphasized that type 2 diabetes and related complications are not randomly or evenly distributed. Articles deploying this frame emphasized one or more of the following: (1) type 2 diabetes is more prevalent in some groups than others; (2) type 2 diabetes has
180   spread to hitherto unaffected groups; (3) type 2 diabetes is more prevalent overall than it used to be across the United States or Canada; (4) type 2 diabetes incidence is expected to increase further; and (5) type 2

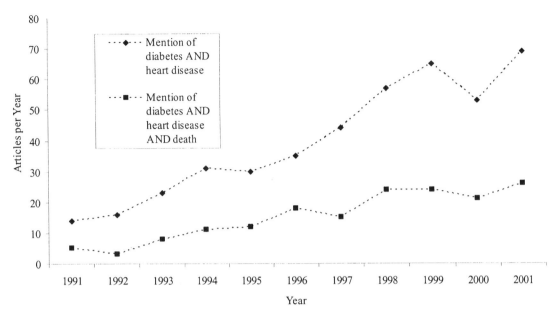

Figure 3. Mention of diabetes, heart disease, and death in *The Globe Mail*.

diabetes is costly—in human and financial terms. Articles using this frame portrayed modern lifestyles as the main cause. Proposed remedies included intensive clinical management, community-level interventions, lifestyle changes, increased public funding for health and social programs, improved disease surveillance, and further medical research. In articles rooting causation in the societal conditioning of lifestyle, the proposed remedies sometimes stressed informed individual choice (e.g., *The Toronto Star*, October 20, 1999 [TS4]).

This frame emerged as the most common in the sample. All the articles that portrayed type 2 diabetes as an insidious problem also used the group association frame. The disproportionate impact of type 2 diabetes on Aboriginal people across Canada was the most common topic. Other groups associated with type 2 diabetes in the sample included people older than 40 years (*The Toronto Star*, October 20, 1999 [TS4], and August 25, 2000 [TS5]), people of African or Latin American descent (*The Globe and Mail*, May 3, 2000 [GM13]; *The Toronto Star*, August 25, 2000 [TS5]; *Newsweek*; September 4, 2000 [NW2]) and—an alarming new development—youths (*The Globe and Mail*, June 28, 1999 [GM4]; *The Toronto Star*, August 25, 2000 [TS5]; *Newsweek*, September 4, 2000 [NW2]).

Type 2 diabetes is a medical problem. This frame presents type 2 diabetes as a problem requiring medical treatment rather than a problem stemming mainly from societal forces and circumstances. Portraying type 2 diabetes as a medical problem underscores that type 2 diabetes is truly a serious disease mainly because of its complications. For instance, one article in *The Toronto Star* (March 5, 1999 [TS2]) noted that "the disease remains a major factor in blindness, kidney disease and heart disease." The remedies to reduce complication among people who already have type 2 diabetes explicitly endorsed in this portrayal included pharmaceuticals (e.g., *The Globe and Mail*, March 26, 1998 [GM1]) or lifestyle changes (e.g., *The Globe and Mail*, September 11, 1998 [GM2]), and articles employing this frame all explicitly or implicitly endorsed further medical research.

One article featuring the insidious problem and associated group frames made clear reference to a competing medical problem frame in quoting an expert source as saying, "The question is: Is diabetes a problem of biology or a problem of sociology?" (*The Globe and Mail*, June 28, 1999 [GM4]). Yet the distinction between framing type 2 diabetes as a problem rooted in society or a medical problem could be subtle. Consider the article titled "Couch potatoes more likely to get diabetes" (*The Globe and Mail*, June 28, 1999 [GM5]). Although the article stressed that type 2 diabetes is common today because of sedentary lifestyles, it did not report on the social distribution of TV watching, physical activity, or type 2 diabetes, and it did not present lifestyle change as a process mediated by social norms and circumstances. By comparison, another article in the sample (*The Toronto Star*, October 20, 1999 [TS4]), reporting on a similar study led by the same investigator, framed type 2 diabetes as a problem associated with particular groups. It did so in two ways: by noting that type 2 diabetes is mainly found in people aged more than 40 years and by noting that the research focused on whether walking can reduce type 2 diabetes risk because walking is the most common form of physical activity among people middle-aged and older.

Table 1
Frames Deployed by Coverage Included in the Qualitative Analysis

Periodical	References	Insidious problem	Associated groups	Medical problem
		Frames		
The Globe and Mail	GM1. Diabetes drugs work together. *Globe and Mail*. March 26, 1998:A19.			√
	GM2. Fat cited as villain in diabetes. *Globe and Mail*. September 11, 1998: A19.			√
	GM3. Let's make a DNA deal. Sandy Lake has the third-highest diabetes rate in the world. The gene hunters pay to find out why. *Globe and Mail*. December 7, 1998:A1.		√	√
	GM4. "Adult" version of diabetes afflicting children. *Globe and Mail*. June 28, 1999:A8.		√	
	GM5. Couch potatoes more likely to get diabetes. *Globe and Mail*. June 28, 1999:A8.			√
	GM6. Diabetes outbreak hits Quebec Crees. *Globe and Mail*. May 5, 1999:A2.	√	√	
	GM7. Genetic link found to natives' diabetes. *Globe and Mail*. March 11, 1999:A10.		√	
	GM8. Genetic trait for diabetes uncovered. *Globe and Mail*. March 9, 1999:A11.		√	
	GM9. Ottawa to target diabetes. *Globe and Mail*. May 18, 1999:A5.		√	
	GM10. Ottawa to spend $115 million to fight diabetes. *Globe and Mail*. November 20, 1999:A12.	√	√	
	GM11. Pharmaceuticals: diabetes drug approved. *Globe and Mail*. October 14, 1999:A8.			√
	GM12. Research traces gene for obesity, diabetes. *Globe and Mail*. March 5, 1999:A12.			√
	GM13. Diabetes hits black women worst: study. *Globe and Mail*. May 3, 1999:A6.		√	
	GM14. Heart disease on increase for natives. Smoking, obesity and epidemic of diabetes in aboriginal community contributing. *Globe and Mail*. June 26, 2000:A2.		√	
The Toronto Star	TS1. Hot tub therapy helps diabetics, study suggests. *Toronto Star*. September 16, 1999:1.			√
	TS2. Mice tests offer hope in the war on diabetes; crucial enzyme discovery made by Montreal team. *Toronto Star*. March 5, 1999:1.			√
	TS3. Mutated gene behind diabetes rate; Ontario doctor finds why Ojibwa-Cree are at a much higher risk. *Toronto Star*. March 10, 1999:1.		√	
	TS4. Walking cuts risk of diabetes: research; Harvard study followed health of 70,000 women. *Toronto Star*. October 20, 1999:1.		√	
	TS5. Diabetes "epidemic" looming; no exercise, bad diet blamed for expected doubling of cases. *Toronto Star*. August 25, 2000:A02.	√	√	
	TS6. First nations need help to fight diabetes. *Toronto Star*. May 15, 2000:A19.		√	
	TS7. Forgotten communities stalked by silent killer: Lost People. *Toronto Star*. April 30, 2001:1.	√	√	
	TS8. The Lost People Natives' plight sparks outrage; readers react to *Star* series on reserve conditions. *Toronto Star*. May 1, 2000:A01.		√	
	TS9. Natives to get update on diabetes. *Toronto Star*. June 1, 2000:A23.		√	
Newsweek	NW1. Shaped by life in the womb. *Newsweek*; September 27, 1999:50–53.			√
	NW2. An American epidemic: diabetes, the silent killer. *Newsweek*. September 4, 2000:40–47.	√	√	

Discussion

As is common among studies of the popular press in public health,[17,18] previous studies of diabetes media coverage[2-5] assessed reporting accuracy. The evaluation of reporting accuracy presumes that there is a correct way for the media to convey health information to the public: Not only should accurate information be provided about diseases and health risks, but the allocation of coverage should reflect (presumably accurate) epidemiological survey data. Indeed, the contrasting conclusions reached in previous studies of diabetes mass media coverage—with two studies concluding that the coverage generally reflects mortality rates[2,5] and two studies concluding that coverage tends to distort its impact on mortality[3,4]—stem largely from differences in the epidemiological data used as the standard against which to evaluate reporting accuracy. Public health researchers and advocates certainly have an interest in ensuring that the health information transmitted to the public is accurate. But it is also important to understand why some health issues receive more attention than do others and to understand how these issues are defined as socially significant. In adopting a framing analysis, this study did not disregard accuracy, but it focused on meaning.

The status of the terms *diabetes* and *type 2 diabetes* differs when emphasizing meaning rather than content accuracy. When emphasizing content accuracy, the question is whether the terms are used correctly in describing health problems and risks. Emphasizing meaning presumes that such terms and their definitions constitute part of the framing process.[9,11,19] Naming is part of framing, and that brings into view some limitations and strengths of this study. Because the term *diabetes* is commonly used to refer to all types of diabetes mellitus, searching LexisNexis and InfoGlobe to tabulate references to diabetes likely retrieved references dealing with type 1 diabetes or type 2 diabetes, or both. Yet the qualitative results suggest that even with a detailed analysis of each and every instance of mass media coverage included in a study such as this, completely isolating type 2 diabetes coverage from type 1 diabetes coverage would be impossible because the high-profile newspaper items analyzed qualitatively for this study sometimes explicitly discussed how type 2 diabetes differs from type 1 diabetes (e.g., *Newsweek*, September 4, 2000 [NW2]).

Moreover, the qualitative results show that portraying type 2 diabetes as insidious or unevenly distributed, or both, brought into focus the societal nature of this health problem. Through these framing processes, the term *type 2 diabetes* acquired fresh significance beyond that connoted by the medical problem frame. Yet even when societal forces and circumstances were acknowledged as causes, the proposed remedies did not always include or stress social interventions, and that may reflect media interviews with expert sources: health professionals and researchers.[8] In other words, by conducting a framing analysis, this study highlights that mass media coverage reflects careful packaging, not only of facts but of interpretations. This study also underscores the role played by a journalist's expert sources in packaging interpretations and transmitting meaning.

When I adopted a framing analysis, I designed the qualitative and quantitative components to detect whether mass media coverage attended to links between diabetes and related complications, notably heart disease. In other words, the analysis sought to reveal whether these links were "framed in" or "framed out" in problem naming and definition. *The Toronto Star* and *The Globe and Mail* quantitative results each provide some support for increased emphasis on a link between diabetes and heart disease. The qualitative results, meanwhile, included several instances of heart disease and other complications being evoked to portray type 2 diabetes either as a serious medical problem or as a serious problem rooted in societal organization and norms. These results are particularly noteworthy because prevalence and mortality data often underestimate the overall impact of diabetes for two main reasons. First, about one-third of all type 2 diabetes cases in Canada and the United States remain undiagnosed and untreated.[20-23] Undiagnosed type 2 diabetes surely tends to hasten death, but other causes will be recorded, usually cardiovascular disease. In addition, surveys based on self-report data cannot capture undiagnosed cases. Second, even when diabetes is diagnosed, physicians often do not record diabetes on death certificates. Instead, the deaths of people diagnosed with diabetes are often attributed to cardiovascular disease.[24,25] Using frame analysis to investigate meaning rather than a conventional content analysis to assess reporting accuracy did not presume that available national or international statistics fully capture the impact of diabetes.[2-5]

Indeed, for the insidious problem frame, undiagnosed cases emerged as pivotal. Nevertheless, consistent with the current medical definition of diabetes, which pivots on hyperglycemia but not necessarily with how members of disadvantaged populations in particular develop and perceive hyperglycemia,[26] high-profile type 2 diabetes media coverage did not consider community mental health as a possible etiologic factor and intervention target. Overall, the qualitative and quantitative results suggest that when communicating with journalists, researchers and advocates have lobbied for greater recognition of diabetes by stressing that diabetes maims and kills.

The results therefore fit the public arenas model better than the natural history model of how health problems achieve media coverage and other forms of social recognition. Although the natural history model uses individualistic biological metaphors (birth, development, maturation, death) and often stresses correspondence with population trends,[2] the public arenas model argues that the definition and relative status of social problems never mirror objective harms, so this model proposes evolutionary metaphors (carrying capacity, competition, selection) to help explain why some problems and problem dimensions receive more recognition than others.[13] The key point is that newspapers and other public arenas have only limited space or time available, so public recognition is a scarce resource for which problems and their advocates compete—through social selection processes that often hinge on framing.[27,28] Although the present study suggests that the amount and emphasis of recent media coverage have taken into account the changing socioeconomic distribution of type 2 diabetes, neither increased prevalence nor the related impact on mortality has translated directly into media coverage; instead, garnering media coverage for public health issues always requires careful thought and organized effort.[27] Understanding how the mass media continually frame and reframe health-related phenomena can enhance public health's capacity to advocate for due attention to societal causes and possible societal solutions.

References

1. Screening for Type 2 Diabetes. Report of a World Health Organization and International Diabetes Federation Meeting. Geneva. Switzerland: World Health Organization: 2003. Available at: http://www.who.int/diabetes/publications/en/screening_mnc03.pdf. Accessed June 9, 2005.

2. Adelman RC, Verbrugge LM. Death makes news: The social impact of disease on newspaper coverage. *J Health Soc Behav*. 2000;4:347–367.

3. Frost K, Frank E, Maibach E. Relative risk in the news media: A quantification of misrepresentation. *Am J Public Health*. 1997;87:842–845.

4. Mercado-Martinez FJ, Robles-Silva L, Moreno-Leal N, Franco-Almazan C. Inconsistent journalism: The coverage of chronic diseases in the Mexican press. *J Health Community*. 2001;6:235–247.

5. Van der Wardt EM, Taal E, Rasker JJ, Wiegman O. Media coverage of chronic diseases in the Netherlands. *Semin Arthritis Rheum*. 1999;28:333–341.

6. Foucault M. *L'Ordre du discours*. Paris, France: Gallimard: 1970.

7. Foucault M. Governmentality. In: Burchell G, Gordon C, Miller P, eds. *The Foucault Effect: Studies in Governmentality With Two Lectures by and an interview With Michel Foucault*. Chicago, Ill: University of Chicago Press; 1991 [1978]:87–104.

8. Lloyd B, Hawe P. Solutions forgone? How health professionals frame the problem of postnatal depression. *Soc Sci Med*. 2003:57:1783–1795.
9. Rosenberg CE. Disease in history: Frames and framers. *Milbank Q*. 1989;67(suppl 1):1–15.
10. Sontag S. *Illness as Metaphor and AIDS and Its Metaphors*. New York, NY: Anchor Books: 1990 [1988].
11. Young A. The anthropologies of illness and sickness. *Annu Rev Anthropol*. 1982;11:257–285.
12. Entman RM. Framing: Toward clarification of a fractured paradigm. *J Community*. 1993;43(4):51–59.
13. Hiltgartner S, Bosk CL. The rise and fall of social problems: A public arenas model. *Am J Sociol*. 1988;84(1):53–78.
14. Diabetes Control and Complications Trial Research Group. Effects of intensive diabetes management on macrovascular events and risk factors in the Diabetes Control and Complications Trial. *Am J Cardiol*. 1995;75:894–903.
15. Diabetes Control and Complications Trial Research Group. Effects of intensive diabetes management on the development and progression of long-term complications in insulin-dependent diabetes mellitus. *N Engl J Med*. 1993;329:977–986.
16. Centers for Disease Control and Prevention. Diabetes Public Health Resource Web site Diabetes: A Serious Public Health Problem Available at: http//www.medhelp.org/NIHlib/GF-558.html. Accessed November 15, 2004.
17. Wenger L, Malone R, Bero L. The cigar revival and the popular press: A content analysis, 1987–1997. *Am J Public Health*. 2001;91:288–291.
18. Bartlett C, Sterne J, Egger M. What is newsworthy? Longitudinal study of the reporting of medical research in two British newspapers. *BMJ*. 2002;325:81–84.
19. Lock M. *Encounters With Aging: Myths of Menopause in Japan and North America*. Berkeley, Calif: University of California Press; 1993.
20. Harris MI, Eastman RC, Cowie CC, Flegal KM, Eberhardt MS. Comparison of diabetes diagnostic categories in the U.S. population according to the 1997 American Diabetes Association and 1980–1985 World Health Organization diagnostic criteria. *Diabetes Care*. 1997;20:1859–1862.
21. Harris MI. Undiagnosed NIDDM: Clinical and public health issues. *Diabetes Care*. 1993;16:642–652.
22. Meltzer S, Leiter L, Daneman D, et al. 1998 Clinical practice guidelines for the management of diabetes in Canada. *CMAJ*. 1998;159(suppl 8):S1–S29.
23. Leiter LA, Barr A, Belanger A, et al. Diabetes Screening in Canada (DIASCAN) Study: Prevalence of undiagnosed diabetes and glucose intolerance in family physician offices. *Diabetes Care*. 2001;24:1038–1043.
24. Balkau B, Papal L. Certification of cause of death in French diabetic patients. *J Epidemiol Community Health*. 1992;46(1):63–65.
25. Tan M-H, Wornell C. Diabetes mellitus in Canada. *Diabetes Res Clin Pract*. 1991;14:S3–S8.
26. Rock M. Sweet blood and social suffering: Rethinking cause–effect relationships in diabetes. distress and duress. *Med Anthropol*. 2003;22(2):131–174.
27. Finnegan JR Jr., Viswanath K, Hertog J. Mass media, secular trends, and the future of cardiovascular disease health promotion: An interpretive analysis. *Prev Med*. Dec 1999;29(6 pt 2):S50–S58.
28. Randolph W, Viswanath K. Lessons learned from public health mass media campaigns: Marketing health in a crowded media world. *Annu Rev Public Health*. 2004;25:419–437.

Acknowledgments: This study was made possible by a doctoral fellowship from the Social Sciences and Humanities Research Council of Canada (award 753-91-0166), a postdoctoral fellowship jointly funded by the Canadian Health Services Research Foundation and the Canadian Institutes of Health Research (award PDA-0800-05), and a research grant from the Groupe de recherche interdisciplinaire en santé (Interdisciplinary Health Research Group) at the Université de Montréal. Jean-Michel Billette assisted with collecting and organizing the quantitative data. Drs. Jennifer Godley, Penelope Hawe, Pascale Lehoux, Lindsay McLaren, and Louise Potvin provided helpful feedback on previous versions. Dr. Mary E. Northridge and three anonymous reviewers also provided helpful feedback while this paper was under review with the Journal. No protocol approval was needed for this study.

About the author: Melanie Rock, Ph.D., MSW, is with the Department of Community Health Sciences, the Faculty of Social Work, and the Department of Anthropology at the University of Calgary, Alberta, and the Université de Montréal, Quebec.

Address correspondence to: Melanie Rock, University of Calgary, Department of Community Health Sciences, Health Sciences Centre, 3330 Hospital Drive NW, Calgary, AB, Canada T2N 4N1. E-Mail: mrock@ucalgary.ca

Exercise for Article 33

Factual Questions

1. Which newspaper is the largest circulation newspaper in Canada?

2. In the quantitative methods, the research searched in three areas for mention of diabetes. One of the areas was in obituaries. What were the other two?

3. For the qualitative methods, did the researcher select stories appearing in all sections of the newspapers? Explain.

4. Which "frame" emerged as the most common?

5. In the Discussion section, the researcher states that portraying diabetes as insidious or unevenly distributed brings what into focus?

6. The research states that while the natural history model uses individualistic biological metaphors, the public arenas model proposes what type of metaphors?

Questions for Discussion

7. In your opinion, is it important to know the search terms used to locate the articles used in this research? Explain. (See lines 46–62.)

8. The material in Figure 1 is summarized in lines 84–90. In your opinion, how important is the figure? Would the article be as effective without it? Explain.

9. To what extent does the information in Table 1 add to your understanding of the results of this study? Explain.

10. Do you think the quantitative *or* qualitative results are more interesting? Are they equally interesting? Explain. (See lines 84–252.)

11. Would you recommend replication of this study using samples of other newspapers and magazines? Explain.

12. This article illustrates how documents (e.g., newspapers) can be analyzed to obtain information. Does this article convince you that the analysis of documents is an important scientific method? Explain.

Quality Ratings

Directions: Indicate your level of agreement with each of the following statements by circling a number from 5 for strongly agree (SA) to 1 for strongly disagree (SD). If you believe an item is not applicable to this research article, leave it blank. Be prepared to explain your ratings. When responding to criteria A and B below, keep in mind that brief titles and abstracts are conventional in published research.

A.   The title of the article is appropriate.

SA   5   4   3   2   1   SD

B.   The abstract provides an effective overview of the research article.

SA   5   4   3   2   1   SD

C.   The introduction establishes the importance of the study.

SA   5   4   3   2   1   SD

D.   The literature review establishes the context for the study.

SA   5   4   3   2   1   SD

E.   The research purpose, question, or hypothesis is clearly stated.

SA   5   4   3   2   1   SD

F.   The method of sampling is sound.

SA   5   4   3   2   1   SD

G.   Relevant demographics (for example, age, gender, and ethnicity) are described.

SA   5   4   3   2   1   SD

H.   Measurement procedures are adequate.

SA   5   4   3   2   1   SD

I.   All procedures have been described in sufficient detail to permit a replication of the study.

SA   5   4   3   2   1   SD

J.   The participants have been adequately protected from potential harm.

SA   5   4   3   2   1   SD

K.   The results are clearly described.

SA   5   4   3   2   1   SD

L.   The discussion/conclusion is appropriate.

SA   5   4   3   2   1   SD

M.   Despite any flaws, the report is worthy of publication.

SA   5   4   3   2   1   SD

Article 34

Poverty As We Know It:
Media Portrayals of the Poor

ROSALEE A. CLAWSON
Purdue University

RAKUYA TRICE
Indiana University

From *Public Opinion Quarterly*, *64*, 53–64. Copyright © 2000 by the American Association for Public Opinion Research. All rights reserved. Reprinted with permission.

Introduction

On the campaign trail during the 1992 presidential election, Bill Clinton's stump speech included a pledge to "end welfare as we know it" to the delight of most audiences. Two years later during the 1994 congres-
5 sional election, one of the most popular planks of the Republicans' Contract with America was the "Personal Responsibility Act," which called for a major overhaul of the welfare system. The election of this Republican Congress initiated a great deal of legislative activity
10 and presidential maneuvering on the issue of welfare reform. The culmination of those efforts occurred in August 1996 when President Clinton signed into law sweeping welfare reform legislation. By ending the federal guarantee of support for the poor and turning
15 control of welfare programs over to the states, this legislation reversed 6 decades of social policy and begot a new era of welfare politics. Throughout this period of intense political activity, the media focused a significant amount of attention on poverty and welfare re-
20 form.

In this research, we analyze media portrayals of the poor during this time when welfare reform was high on the nation's agenda. We investigate whether the media perpetuate inaccurate and stereotypical images of the
25 poor. Specifically, we examine the photographs that accompany stories on poverty in five U.S. news magazines between January 1, 1993, and December 31, 1998.

Portrayals of the Poor

In a study of news magazines between 1988 and
30 1992, Gilens (1996a) investigated the accuracy of the media in their portrayals of the poor. Gilens (1996a) found that poverty was disproportionately portrayed as a "Black" problem. Blacks make up less than one-third of the poor, but the media would lead citizens to be-
35 lieve that two out of every three poor people are Black. Moreover, Gilens (1996a) found that the "deserving" poor, especially the Black deserving poor, were under-

represented in news magazines. For example, the Black elderly poor and Black working poor were rarely por-
40 trayed. In addition, Gilens examined media depictions of the poor between 1950 and 1992 and found that Blacks were "comparatively absent from media coverage of poverty during times of heightened sympathy for the poor" (1999, p. 132). In this research, we pick
45 up where Gilens left off by analyzing media portrayals of the demographics of poverty between 1993 and 1998.

In addition, we extend Gilens's work by investigating whether common stereotypical traits or behaviors
50 associated with the poor are portrayed in the media. In our society, citizens believe poor people have many undesirable qualities that violate mainstream American ideals. For example, many citizens say people are poor due to their own "lack of effort" and "loose morals and
55 drunkenness" (Kluegel & Smith, 1986, p. 79). A majority of Americans believe that "most people who receive welfare benefits are taking advantage of the system" (Ladd, 1993, p. 86). Another piece of conventional wisdom is that poor mothers on public assistance
60 have additional babies to receive greater welfare benefits. People also believe that poor families are much larger than middle-class families (Sidel, 1996).

Several media studies have found such stereotypical representations of poverty (Golding & Middleton,
65 1982; Martindale, 1996). The media often describe the underclass in behavioral terms as criminals, alcoholics, and drug addicts, and the underclass is linked with pathological behavior in urban areas (Gans, 1995). Parisi's (1998) in-depth analysis of a *Washington Post*
70 series on poverty demonstrated that the media perpetuate stereotypes of the poor as lazy, sexually irresponsible, and criminally deviant. Coughlin (1989) discussed the media's emphasis on "welfare queens"—a phrase that invokes images of poor women living the high life
75 by defrauding and taking advantage of the welfare system. These studies focused on how the poor were described in the text of news stories; in this study, we analyze whether stereotypical traits of the poor are presented in magazine photographs.
80 Why is it important to study the visual images surrounding the issue of poverty? The visual representa-

Table 1
Representations of Poverty by Magazine, 1993–1998

	Business Week	Newsweek	New York Times Magazine	Time	U.S. News & World Report	Total
Number of stories	18	13	8	13	22	74
Number of pictures	21	24	18	30	56	149
Number of poor people	40	64	35	78	140	357

Table 2
The Percent of True Poor and the Percent of Magazine Poor by Race, 1993–1998

	Whites	African Americans	Hispanics	Asian Americans
True poor	45	27	24	4
Magazine poor	33[***]	49[***]	19[*]	0[**]
Poor in *Newsweek*, *Time*, and *U.S. News & World Report*	33[***]	45[***]	22	0[**]

Source: *March Current Population Survey* (U.S. Bureau of the Census, 1996).

Note. We conducted difference of proportion tests in which the proportion observed in the magazine is compared to the true proportion as reported by the Current Population Survey for each racial category (Blalock, 1979). A statistically significant result indicates that the magazine portrayal of a particular racial group is not representative of the true poor. Due to rounding, the percentages may sum to more than 100%. The sample size is 347 for the analysis based on all five magazines. The sample size is 272 for the analysis based on *Newsweek*, *Time*, and *U.S. News & World Report*.

[*]$p < .05$; [**]$p < .01$; [***]$p < .001$.

tion of a political issue is an integral part of the definition of that issue.[1] Visual images (along with metaphors, exemplars, and catchphrases) define and illus-
85 trate particular issue frames (Gamson & Lasch, 1983). For example, Nelson and Kinder (1996) demonstrate that visual frames have a significant impact on public attitudes toward affirmative action. People and events that appear in photographs accompanying news stories
90 are not simply indicative of isolated individuals and occurrences; rather, the photographs are symbolic of "the whole mosaic" (Epstein, 1973, p. 5). The pictures provide texture, drama, and detail, and they illustrate the implicit, the latent, the "taken for granted," and the
95 "goes without saying." Furthermore, scholars should pay attention to visual images because journalists and editors perceive them to be a central part of a news story. In his classic study of how journalists select stories, Gans argues that magazine "editors consider still
100 pictures as important as text" (1979, p. 159).

Research Design

In this research, we test the hypothesis that the media portray poor people inaccurately and stereotypically. The data were collected by examining every story on the topics of poverty, welfare, and the poor
105 between January 1, 1993, and December 31, 1998, in five news magazines: *Business Week*, *Newsweek*, *New York Times Magazine*, *Time*, and *U.S. News & World Report*.[2] We used the *Reader's Guide to Periodical Literature* to locate the stories and to identify other
110 cross-referenced topics (e.g., income inequality). Seventy-four stories were identified as relevant for a total of 149 pictures of 357 poor people.[3] See Table 1 for the

distribution of stories, pictures, and people by magazine.
115 The photographs were analyzed in two ways. First, we scrutinized each picture as a whole. For those pictures that included a mother with children, we noted the size and race of the family. Second, we examined the demographic characteristics of each poor individual
120 in the pictures. For coding race, we departed from Gilens's coding procedure. Gilens (1996a, 1999) coded whether the poor person was Black, non-Black, or undeterminable. In contrast, we used a more detailed classification scheme and coded whether the poor person
125 was White, Black, Hispanic, Asian American, or undeterminable.
We coded each person's gender (male or female), age (young: under 18; middle-aged: 18–64; or old: 65 and over), residence (urban or rural), and work status
130 (working/job training or not working).[4] We also analyzed whether each individual was depicted in stereotypical ways, such as pregnant, engaging in criminal behavior, taking or selling drugs, drinking alcohol, smoking cigarettes, or wearing expensive clothing or
135 jewelry.[5] For many of our variables, we were able to compare the portrayal of poverty in news magazines to the reality of poverty as measured by the Current Population Survey (CPS) conducted by the U.S. Census Bureau or as reported by the U.S. House of Representa-
140 tives Committee on Ways and Means.[6]

Research Findings

Many citizens greatly overestimate the number of Black people among the poor (Gilens, 1996a). Do news magazines perpetuate and reinforce that belief? According to the 1996 CPS, African Americans make up

145 27% of the poor, but these five magazines would lead citizens to believe that Blacks are 49% of the poor ($p <$ .001; see Table 2). Whites, on the other hand, are depicted as 33% of the poor, when they really make up 45% of those in poverty ($p <$ .001). There were no

150 magazine portrayals of Asian Americans in poverty, and Hispanics were underrepresented by 5%.

This underrepresentation of poor Hispanics and Asian Americans may be part of a larger phenomenon in which these groups are ignored by the media in general.

155 For example, Hispanics and Asian Americans are rarely found in mass media advertising (Bowen & Schmid, 1997; Wilkes & Valencia, 1989). Similarly, Dixon (1998) documented the invisibility of Hispanics in local news; however, there is evidence that in par-

160 ticular regions, Hispanics are represented in accordance with their proportion in the population (Greenberg & Brand, 1998; Turk et al., 1989). Unlike Blacks, Asian Americans are associated with intelligence, not welfare dependency (Gilbert & Hixon, 1991; Gilens, 1999).

165 Thus, their absence may reflect a positive stereotype, but a stereotype nonetheless. Clearly these comments regarding Hispanics and Asian Americans are speculative. Further research is needed on media representations of these two groups.

170 Focusing on just the three magazines Gilens included in his study (i.e., *Newsweek, Time,* and *U.S. News & World Report*), Whites make up 33%, Blacks make up 45%, and Hispanics are 22% of the magazine poor (see Table 2). In comparison, Gilens (1996a)

175 found that 62% of the poor were African American in these magazines between 1988 and 1992. Although at first glance our statistics may suggest that the magazines have become less likely to put a Black face on poverty, we hesitate to draw that conclusion given the

180 coding difference mentioned earlier. Recall that Gilens coded whether the poor person was Black, non-Black, or undeterminable. Since Gilens (1996a) reports a higher percentage of poor people for which race was not identified (12% compared to our 4%), it seems

185 likely that many of the poor people we coded as Hispanic, Gilens would have coded as undeterminable. If we treat Hispanics in that fashion and therefore exclude them from our analysis, Blacks make up 58% of the poor and Whites make up 42%—figures that mirror

190 Gilens's data quite closely. Regardless of the exact proportion, it is clear these news magazines continue to race code the issue of poverty.[7]

Since we are examining portrayals of the poor during a period of intense debate over welfare reform,

195 perhaps the racial characteristics of the magazine poor mirror welfare recipients more closely than they represent poor people in general. The House Ways and Means Committee provides the racial breakdown for parents on Aid to Families with Dependent Children

200 (AFDC). Therefore, in Table 3 we compare the racial composition of AFDC parents to the magazine portrayal of poor adults. Indeed, the portrayal of poor

Whites and Hispanics matches more closely the true racial characteristics of welfare recipients; however,

205 Blacks are still heavily overrepresented (48%) among the magazine poor. Moreover, Blacks make up 52% of the poor adults who are portrayed in stories that focus specifically on welfare (rather than on poverty in general).

Table 3
The Percent of AFDC Parents and the Percent of Magazine Adult Poor by Race, 1993–1998

	Whites	African Americans	Hispanics	Native Americans, Asian Americans, and Other
AFDC parents	36	37	21	7
Magazine adult poor	34	48**	18	0***

Source: *Overview of Entitlement Programs* (U.S. House of Representatives, Committee on Ways and Means, 1998).

Note. N = 159

**$p < .01$; ***$p < .001$.

210 Gilens (1996a, 1999) found that Blacks were even more prominent in stories on poverty topics that were not very popular with the public. Between 1993 and 1998, there were several stories on unpopular issues, such as welfare reform and pregnancy, public housing,

215 and welfare and the cycle of dependency.[8] We examined the proportion of Blacks among the poor in these stories and found that it jumped to 63%, whereas Whites made up only 19% and Hispanics were 18%. In contrast, Blacks were associated less often with sympa-

220 thetic topics. In stories on welfare reform and children, welfare recipients and day care, and job training, 46% of the poor were Black, while 32% were White and 22% were Hispanic.[9] We also analyzed two stories that focused on various "myths" surrounding welfare re-

225 form. Ironically, 16 of the 22 poor people depicted in these two stories were Black.

The news magazines exaggerated the feminization of poverty by about 14%. According to the CPS, 62% of the adult poor are women, whereas 76% of the

230 magazine poor are women ($N = 161$).[10] Again, though, since most of these stories discuss poverty specifically in the context of welfare reform, it is important to compare the magazine poor to people on welfare. The vast majority of adult AFDC recipients are female, so the

235 predominance of women among the poor is fairly accurate (U.S. House of Representatives, Committee on Ways and Means, 1998).

In terms of the age of the poor people, we found that children were overrepresented among the maga-

240 zine poor (see Table 4).[11] Children are usually thought of as a fairly deserving group of poor people (Cook & Barrett, 1992); however, the large proportion of Black children among the magazine poor may undermine that belief. In Iyengar's (1990) experimental research on

245 attributions of responsibility for poverty, subjects indicated that Black children should take responsibility for their own plight, whereas White children were not expected to solve their own problems.

In contrast, the elderly, who are the most sympa-
250 thetic group of poor people, were rarely portrayed. Most people believe the elderly really need their benefits and that they use them wisely (Cook & Barrett, 1992). Iyengar (1990) found that people thought society should aid (both Black and White) poor elderly
255 widows. This sympathetic group makes up 9% of the true poor, but only 4% of the magazine poor (see Table 4).

We also examined whether poor people were portrayed in urban or rural settings. The magazine depic-
260 tions implied that poverty is almost completely an urban problem. Ninety-six percent of the poor were shown in urban areas.[12] According to the CPS, most poor people (77%) do reside in metropolitan areas; however, the magazine portrayals greatly exaggerate
265 the true proportion ($p < .001$).[13] According to Gans (1995), the urban underclass is often linked with various pathologies and antisocial behavior. Thus, this emphasis on the urban poor does not promote a positive image of those in poverty.

Table 4
The Percent of True Poor and the Percent of Magazine Poor by Age, 1993–1998

	Under 18	18–64	65 and over
True poor	40	51	9
Magazine poor	53[***]	43[**]	4[**]

Source: *March Current Population Survey* (U.S. Bureau of the Census, 1996).

Note. N = 347.

[**]$p < .01$; [***]$p < .001$.

270 The media leave the impression that most poor people do not work: only 30% of poor adults were shown working or participating in job training programs ($N = 198$). In reality, 50% of the poor work in full- or part-time jobs, according to the CPS ($p < .001$).[14] When we
275 focus solely on those stories that specifically discuss welfare, 35% of the poor are shown either working or in job training. According to the House Ways and Means Committee, 23% of AFDC recipients worked or participated in education or job training programs in
280 1995. These photographs reflect the emphasis of many contemporary welfare reformers, liberal and conservative, on "workfare" rather than welfare. Since many citizens support work requirements for welfare recipients (Weaver, Shapiro, & Jacobs, 1995), these images
285 are positive ones. Not surprisingly, Whites were more likely to be shown in these pictures than Blacks.

Next, we analyzed the extent to which the news magazines relied on stereotypical traits in their depictions of the poor. We examined whether the media per-
290 petuate the notion that women on welfare have lots of

children. When a mother was portrayed with her children in these magazines, the average family size was 2.80. This is virtually identical to the figure of 2.78 reported by the House Ways and Means Committee for
295 the average AFDC family size in 1996. In the magazines, the representation of poor women and their children differed by race. The average family size for Whites was 2.44, whereas the average size for Blacks was 3.05 and 2.92 for Hispanics. Although these dif-
300 ferences are not statistically significant, the direction suggests that citizens received a less flattering view of poor minority families. The Ways and Means Committee does not report the true figure by race; however, the U.S. Bureau of the Census (1995) provides data on the
305 average number of children ever had (rather than the average number of children currently receiving benefits) by AFDC mothers by race.[15] These data show that Black AFDC women have only slightly (and nonsignificantly) more children than White AFDC women.
310 Hispanic AFDC mothers, on the other hand, do have more children than non-Hispanic AFDC women.

To our surprise, the media did not overly emphasize other stereotypical characteristics associated with the poor. Of the 357 people coded, only three were shown
315 engaging in criminal behavior, and another three were shown with drugs. No alcoholics were presented, and only one person was smoking a cigarette. However, of those seven stereotypical portrayals, only the person smoking was White—the others were either Black or
320 Hispanic. Only one poor woman was pregnant, so the media were not providing images suggesting that poor women simply have babies to obtain larger welfare checks. Again, though, this stereotypical portrayal is of a Hispanic woman. We also examined whether the
325 media presented images consistent with the "welfare queen" stereotype. We felt that poor people who were shown wearing expensive jewelry or clothing would fit this stereotype. Thirty-nine individuals were shown with flashy jewelry or fancy clothes; Blacks and His-
330 panics were somewhat more likely to be portrayed this way than Whites.

In sum, the magazines often portrayed an inaccurate picture of the demographic characteristics of poor people. These magazines overrepresented the Black, urban,
335 and nonworking poor. Blacks were especially prominent in stories on unpopular poverty topics, and Black women were portrayed with the most children. Other stereotypical traits linked with poor people were not common in the magazine portrayals. Nevertheless, in
340 those instances when the media depicted poor people with stereotypical characteristics, they tended to be Black or Hispanic. The most sympathetic group of poor people, the elderly, was underrepresented among the magazine poor. The media were most accurate in mir-
345 roring the predominance of women among welfare recipients.

Discussion

These portrayals of poverty are important because they have an impact on public opinion. A variety of experimental research demonstrates that negative images of Blacks influence public opinion (Gilliam et al., 1996; Iyengar, 1990; Johnson et al., 1997; Mendelberg, 1997; Peffley, Shields, & Williams, 1996). Furthermore, White citizens' stereotypical beliefs about Blacks decrease their support for welfare (Gilens, 1995, 1996b).

In turn, public opinion has an impact on public policy (Page & Shapiro, 1983). Thus, if attitudes on poverty-related issues are driven by inaccurate and stereotypical portrayals of the poor, then the policies favored by the public (and political elites) may not adequately address the true problems of poverty. Furthermore, these inaccurate portrayals of the racial characteristics of the poor may prime the White public to favor political candidates who make racially coded arguments a linchpin of their campaign strategies. When these candidates are elected, they favor welfare (and other) policies that are in keeping with their racialized rhetoric.

It is possible that the text of these stories on poverty contains data describing the true demographic characteristics of the poor. It is unclear what impact a story that dispels stereotypes in its text but perpetuates stereotypes in its photographs would have on public opinion. Graber's research on television suggests that audiovisual themes are more memorable than verbal information (Graber, 1990, 1991). Although news magazines are a very different medium from television, it is certainly possible that magazine photos capture the audience's attention in the same way as television visuals. Psychological research suggests that vivid images of particular cases are more memorable and influential than dry statistical data (Fischhoff & Bar-Hillel, 1984). Indeed, Hamill, Wilson, and Nisbett's (1980) experimental research shows that a vivid, detailed description of a poor woman on welfare has a larger impact on subjects' opinions about welfare recipients than statistical information about women on welfare.

Gilens (1996a, 1999) investigated several explanations for why Blacks are overrepresented among the poor and concluded that, at least in part, it is due to journalists' stereotypes. Gilens's research received considerable attention from media elites, including being the lead topic of discussion on CNN's *Reliable Sources* on August 24, 1997. Unfortunately, our data illustrate that journalists and editors have continued the practice of race coding the issue of poverty even after it was brought to their attention.

We must also point out that this race coding of poverty in news magazines is not an isolated incident; rather, the racial bias reported here is a widespread phenomenon. For example, Clawson and Kegler (in press) conducted a comparable analysis on the portrayal of poverty in introductory textbooks on American government and found that Blacks were dispropor-tionately represented. In addition, several scholars have documented the negative images of Blacks in news coverage of crime (Delgado, 1994; Dixon, 1998; Entman, 1990, 1992, 1994; Johnson, 1987). And it does not end there: Whether it is children's programs, "reality-based" programs, sitcoms, or advertising, Blacks are often portrayed in a stereotypical fashion (Graves, 1996; Humphrey & Schuman, 1984; Oliver, 1994; Poindexter & Stroman, 1981). These images are pervasive in our society.

Conclusion

In conclusion, Blacks were disproportionately portrayed among magazine portrayals of the poor between 1993 and 1998. Blacks were especially overrepresented in negative stories on poverty and in those instances when the poor were presented with stereotypical traits. In addition, the "deserving" poor were underrepresented in the magazines. Overall, the photographic images of poor people in these five news magazines do not capture the reality of poverty; instead, they provide a stereotypical and inaccurate picture of poverty which results in negative beliefs about the poor, antipathy toward Blacks, and a lack of support for welfare programs.

References

Blalock, Hubert M., Jr. 1979. *Social Statistics*. 2d ed. New York: McGraw-Hill.

Bowen, Lawrence, and Jill Schmid. 1997. "Minority Presence and Portrayal in Mainstream Magazine Advertising: An Update." *Journalism and Mass Communication Quarterly* 74(1):134–46.

Clawson, Rosalee A., and Elizabeth R. Kegler. In press. "The 'Race Coding' of Poverty in American Government Textbooks." *Howard Journal of Communications.*

Cook, Fay Lomax, and Edith Barrett. 1992. *Support for the American Welfare State*. New York: Columbia University Press.

Coughlin, Richard M. 1989. "Welfare Myths and Stereotypes." In *Reforming Welfare: Lessons, Limits, and Choices*, ed. Richard M. Coughlin. Albuquerque: University of New Mexico.

Delgado, Richard. 1994. "Rodrigo's Eighth Chronicle: Black Crime, White Fears—on the Social Construction of Threat." *Virginia Law Review* 80:503–48.

Dixon, Travis L. 1998. "Race and Crime on Local Television News." Paper presented at the annual meeting of the National Communication Association, New York.

Entman, Robert M. 1990. "Modern Racism and the Images of Blacks in Local Television News." *Critical Studies in Mass Communication* 7:332–45.

1992. "Blacks in the News: Television, Modern Racism and Cultural Change." *Journalism Quarterly* 69(2):341–61.

1994. "Representation and Reality in the Portrayal of Blacks on Network Television News." *Journalism Quarterly* 71(3):509–20.

1995. "Television, Democratic Theory and the Visual Construction of Poverty." *Research in Political Sociology* 7:139–59.

Epstein, Edward Jay. 1973. *News from Nowhere*. New York: Random House.

Fischhoff, Baruch B., and Maya Bar-Hillel. 1984. "Diagnosticity and the Base Rate Effect." *Memory and Cognition* 12:402–10.

Gamson, William A., and Kathryn E. Lasch. 1983. "The Political Culture of Social Welfare Policy." In *Evaluating the Welfare State*, ed. Shimon E. Spiro and Ephraim Yuchtman-Yaar. New York: Academic Press.

Gans, Herbert J. 1979. *Deciding What's News*. New York: Pantheon Books.

1995. *The War against the Poor*. New York: Basic Books.

Gilbert, Daniel T., and J. Gregory Hixon. 1991. "The Trouble of Thinking: Activation and Application of Stereotypic Beliefs." *Journal of Personality and Social Psychology* 60(4):509–17.

Gilens, Martin. 1995. "Racial Attitudes and Oppositions to Welfare." *Journal of Politics* 57(4):994–1014.

1996a. "Race and Poverty in America." *Public Opinion Quarterly* 60(4):515–41.

1996b. "'Race Coding' and White Opposition to Welfare." *American Political Science Review* 90(3):593–604.

1999. *Why Americans Hate Welfare*. Chicago: University of Chicago Press.

Gilliam, Franklin D., Jr., Shanto Iyengar, Adam Simon, and Oliver Wright. 1996. "Crime in Black and White." *Harvard International Journal of Press/Politics* 1(3):6–23.

Golding, Peter, and Sue Middleton. 1982. *Images of Welfare.* Oxford: Martin Robertson.

Graber, Doris A. 1990. "Seeing Is Remembering: How Visuals Contribute to Learning from Television News." *Journal of Communication* 40:134–55.

1991. "What You See Is What You Get." Paper presented at the annual meeting of the American Political Science Association, Washington, DC.

Graves, Sherryl Browne. 1996. "Diversity on Television." In *Tuning In to Young Viewers*, ed. Tannis M. MacBeth. Thousand Oaks, CA: Sage Publications.

Greenberg, Bradley S., and Jeffrey E. Brand. 1998. "U.S. Minorities and the News." In *Cultural Diversity and the U.S. Media*, ed. Yahya R. Kamalipour and Theres Carilli. Albany, NY: SUNY Press.

Hamill, Ruth, Timothy DeCamp Wilson, and Richard E. Nisbett. 1980. "Insensitivity to Sample Bias: Generalizing from Atypical Cases." *Journal of Personality and Social Psychology* 39:578–89.

Humphrey, Ronald, and Howard Schuman. 1984. "The Portrayal of Blacks in Magazine Advertisements: 1950–1982." *Public Opinion Quarterly* 48:551–63.

Iyengar, Shanto. 1990. "Framing Responsibility for Political Issues: The Case of Poverty." *Political Behavior* 12(1):19–40.

Johnson, James D., Mike S. Adams, William Hall, and Leslie Ashburn. 1997. "Race, Media, and Violence: Differential Racial Effects of Exposure to Violent News Stories." *Basic and Applied Social Psychology* 19(1):81–90.

Johnson, Kirk A. 1987. "Black and White in Boston." *Columbia Journalism Review* 26 (May/June): 50–52.

Kluegel, James R., and Eliot R. Smith. 1986. *Beliefs about Inequality.* New York: Aldine de Gruyter.

Ladd, Everett Carll, ed. 1993. "Public Opinion and Demographic Report: Reforming Welfare." *Public Perspective* 4(6):86–87.

Martindale, Carolyn. 1996. "Newspaper Stereotypes of African Americans." In *Images That Injure*, ed. Paul Martin Lester. Westport, CT: Praeger.

Mendelberg, Tali. 1997. "Executing Hortons." *Public Opinion Quarterly* 61(1):134–57.

Nelson, Thomas E., and Donald R. Kinder. 1996. "Issue Frames and Group-Centrism in American Public Opinion." *Journal of Politics* 58(4):1055–78.

Oliver, Mary Beth. 1994. "Portrayals of Crime, Race, and Aggression in 'Reality-Based' Police Shows: A Content Analysis." *Journal of Broadcasting and Electronic Media* 38(2):179–92.

Page, Benjamin I., and Robert Y. Shapiro. 1983. "Effects of Public Opinion on Policy." *American Political Science Review* 77:175–90.

Parisi, Peter. 1998. "A Sort of Compassion: The *Washington Post* Explains the 'Crisis' in Urban America." *Howard Journal of Communications* 9:187–203.

Peffley, Mark, Todd Shields, and Bruce Williams. 1996. "The Intersection of Race and Crime in Television News Stories: An Experimental Study." *Political Communication* 13:309–27.

Poindexter, Paula M., and Carolyn A. Stroman. 1981. "Blacks and Television: A Review of the Research Literature." *Journal of Broadcasting* 25:103–22.

Sidel, Ruth. 1996. *Keeping Women and Children Last.* New York: Penguin Books.

Turk, Judy VanSlyke, Jim Richstad, Robert L. Bryson, Jr., and Sammye M. Johnson. 1989. "Hispanic Americans in the News in Two Southwestern Cities." *Journalism Quarterly* 66(1):107–13.

U.S. Bureau of the Census. 1995. "Statistical Brief: Mothers Who Receive AFDC Payments—Fertility and Socioeconomic Characteristics." *Census Bureau Web Page.* http://www.census.gov

1996. "March Current Population Survey." *Census Bureau Web Page.* http://www.census.gov/ftp/pub/income/histpov

U.S. House of Representatives, Committee on Ways and Means. 1998. *Overview of Entitlement Programs.* Washington, DC: U.S. Government Printing Office.

Weaver, R. Kent, Robert Y. Shapiro, and Lawrence R. Jacobs. 1995. "The Polls—Trends: Welfare." *Public Opinion Quarterly* 59(4):606–27.

Wilkes, Robert E., and Humberto Valencia. 1989. "Hispanics and Blacks in Television Commercials." *Journal of Advertising* 18(1):19–25.

Acknowledgments: We would like to thank the Purdue University MARC/AIM Summer Research Program for providing summer support for Rakuya Trice, the Purdue Research Foundation for providing a Summer Faculty Grant for Rosalee Clawson, and the Purdue University Library Scholars Grant Program. We greatly appreciate the efforts of Jill Clawson and Chris Salisbury, who were instrumental in obtaining information from the Census Bureau Web site. We would also like to thank the editor and anonymous reviewers for their helpful comments.

Endnotes

[1] See Entman (1995) for a discussion of how poverty is implicitly linked to other issues such as crime, drugs, and gangs through visual images on television news.

[2] Taken as a whole, these five magazines have a circulation of over 12 million: *Business Week* reaches 1,000,000 people; the *New York Times Magazine* has a circulation of 1,650,179; *Newsweek* has an audience of 3,100,000; *U.S. News & World Report* has a distribution of 2,351,313; and *Time* has the largest readership with 4,083,105 subscribers.

[3] There were several stories on poverty we did not include in our sample because: (1) the story did not include any pictures; (2) the story was an editorial or opinion column that only included a picture of the author; (3) the story was found to be irrelevant to our research topic (e.g., one story was cross-listed as income inequality and poor, but actually focused on Democratic and Republican party efforts to win working-class votes); (4) the pictures in the story did not pertain to contemporary poverty in the United States; (5) the story itself was missing from its bound volume ($n = 6$); or (6) the story was in a magazine that was at the binders ($n = 1$).

[4] A "Do Not Know" category was included for these variables.

[5] To ensure the integrity of our data, we conducted a test of intercoder reliability. A second person, who was unaware of the hypotheses, coded a subset of our sample of photographs. Across the variables of interest, there was an average intercoder reliability of .90.

[6] Although we are analyzing media portrayals of poverty between 1993 and 1998, for ease of presentation we use CPS data from March 1996 or Ways and Means Committee data from 1996 to establish the true characteristics of the poor. The 1996 data represent a reasonable midpoint. Moreover, the relevant numbers do not vary much across the time period of interest; in no instance would the minor fluctuations change the substantive or statistical interpretation of our results.

[7] Unfortunately, we faced a trade-off between providing a more detailed analysis of the racial portrayal of the poor and making exact comparisons with Gilens's research.

[8] These stories on unpopular issues included 75 poor individuals.

[9] These stories on sympathetic topics included 100 poor individuals.

[10] There was no race by gender interaction.

[11] There was no race by age interaction.

[12] Please note these statistics are based on a reduced sample size ($N = 205$), because many (43%) of the poor individuals were coded as "Don't Know" for their residency. In many cases it was difficult to ascertain whether the setting was a rural or urban one, so we decided to err on the conservative side and code only the unambiguous settings.

[13] There was no race by residence interaction.

[14] The data on the working poor from the Current Population Survey include people who are 16 and over, whereas the data on the magazine working poor include people who are 13 and over.

[15] These data are from the Survey of Income and Program Participation conducted between June and September of 1993 (U.S. Bureau of the Census, 1995).

Exercise for Article 34

Factual Questions

1. According to the researchers, the visual representation of a political issue is an "integral" part of what?

2. A person was coded as being "young" if he or she appeared to be what age?

3. According to the 1996 CPS, African Americans make up what percentage of the poor?

4. For Hispanics, was the difference between the percentage of "True Poor" and "Magazine Poor" statistically significant?

5. According to the researchers, who constitutes the most sympathetic group of poor people?

6. When mothers were portrayed with their children in the magazines (without regard to race), was there a substantial difference between the average family size in the magazines and the figure cited by Congress? Explain.

Questions for Discussion

7. The five magazines are listed in lines 106–109. Would you be interested in knowing the basis for their selection (i.e., how and why they were selected)?

8. Each person in a photograph was coded as either being White, Black, Hispanic, Asian American, or undeterminable. In addition, they were coded for other characteristics such as their age. In your opinion, might it be difficult to make some of these judgments? Explain. (See Endnote 5 at the end of the article.)

9. Does it surprise you that the researchers found it difficult to ascertain whether the setting in a photograph was rural or urban? Explain. (See Endnote 12.)

10. In Endnote 3, the researchers note that some stories on poverty were omitted for a variety of reasons. In your opinion, could these omissions have affected the validity of the study? Explain.

11. The researchers mentioned that they were surprised by some of the findings. Were you surprised by any of them? (See lines 312–331.) Explain.

Quality Ratings

Directions: Indicate your level of agreement with each of the following statements by circling a number from 5 for strongly agree (SA) to 1 for strongly disagree (SD). If you believe an item is not applicable to this research article, leave it blank. Be prepared to explain your ratings. When responding to criteria A and B below, keep in mind that brief titles and abstracts are conventional in published research.

A. The title of the article is appropriate.

SA   5   4   3   2   1   SD

B. The abstract provides an effective overview of the research article.

SA   5   4   3   2   1   SD

C. The introduction establishes the importance of the study.

SA   5   4   3   2   1   SD

D. The literature review establishes the context for the study.

SA   5   4   3   2   1   SD

E. The research purpose, question, or hypothesis is clearly stated.

SA   5   4   3   2   1   SD

F. The method of sampling is sound.

SA   5   4   3   2   1   SD

G. Relevant demographics (for example, age, gender, and ethnicity) are described.

SA   5   4   3   2   1   SD

H. Measurement procedures are adequate.

SA   5   4   3   2   1   SD

I. All procedures have been described in sufficient detail to permit a replication of the study.

SA   5   4   3   2   1   SD

J. The participants have been adequately protected from potential harm.

SA   5   4   3   2   1   SD

K. The results are clearly described.

SA   5   4   3   2   1   SD

L. The discussion/conclusion is appropriate.

SA   5   4   3   2   1   SD

M. Despite any flaws, the report is worthy of publication.

SA   5   4   3   2   1   SD

Article 35

Contributions to Family and Household Activities by the Husbands of Midlife Professional Women

JUDITH R. GORDON
Boston College

KAREN S. WHELAN-BERRY
Utah Valley State College

ABSTRACT. This article presents an exploratory study that furthers our understanding of the functioning of two-career couples at midlife and, in particular, our understanding of the husband's contributions to family and household activities. More specifically, it addresses the following questions regarding dual-career couples: (a) Whose career has precedence? (b) What is the nature of the husband's contributions to the family and household? and (c) What types of support result? This study is part of a larger research project that focuses on the professional and personal lives of a group of midlife professional women who were married, had children, and had enduring careers. The results presented here describe the women's perceptions of support (or lack of support) provided by their spouses in their family and household. It discusses the implications of such support for family functioning and for the ability of midlife women to pursue full-time careers.

From *Journal of Family Issues*, 26, 899–923. Copyright © 2005 by Sage Publications. Reprinted with permission.

Recent research has suggested that between one-third and one-half of women in top executive and professional positions at midlife do not have children. They remain childless as a result of a "creeping 'non-choice'" because they cannot successfully combine employment and family responsibilities and still rise to high-level positions (Hewlett, 2002). Although organizations have instituted family-friendly programs as one way of supporting women employees, most of these programs address concerns of women early in their careers. Husbands are another potential source of support for midlife professional women; in fact, such support has been shown to result in greater well-being for the women (Cutrona & Russell, 1990; Greenglass, 1993). Although research has recognized the contributions of men in two-career families, their involvement has been studied primarily for families with young children (Barnett & Rivers, 1996; Deutsch, 1999; Deutsch, Lussier, & Servis, 1993; Ehrensraft, 1987; Gilbert, 1993). Are these contributions the same for the families of midlife professional women? As more women have moved into higher positions at midlife, have the contributions of their spouses changed?

The study reported here examines the contributions of husbands of midlife women in helping them balance employment and family demands. More specifically, it addresses the following questions: (a) Whose career has precedence? (b) What is the nature of the husband's contributions to the family and household? and (c) What types of support result?

A great deal has been written about women who work outside the home and the special challenges women with children face in balancing employment and family. During the past 20 years most of this work has focused on women in early career stages, although some of the more recent research has examined women at midlife (e.g., Apter, 1995; Borysenko, 1996; Gordon & Whelan, 1998; James & Liewkowicz, 1997; Levinson, 1996; J. Marshall, 1994). We have been particularly interested in studying professional women at midlife who are married, have children, but also have had enduring careers because they have likely experienced the potential conflict between employment and family. Because they have had enduring careers, they most likely have established a workable division of responsibilities with their husbands and have found ways to either overcome or minimize this conflict.

Women who reached midlife in the mid-1980s to early 1990s were among the first who attempted to work full-time throughout their adult lives while still marrying and having children without significant time away from the workforce as a result of childbearing. As pioneers, they faced special challenges in dealing with employment and home in ways that professional men had never considered. Some of these professional women achieved a degree of success previously unknown for women who were married and had children. This particular group of women, one that has been able to meld the responsibilities of employment and family, provides insight into the broader array of challenges women who work outside the home face and the ways their partners help or hinder their balancing act.

This article describes a group of midlife professional women with enduring careers and their perceptions of the role their husbands played in sustaining and
supporting their careers. As an exploratory study, it
attempts to delineate the participation by the husbands
of professional midlife women in the family and
household arena. Although these contributions represent only part of the potential support that husbands
can provide (e.g., they can also offer emotional or financial support), they represent areas that appear to be
important for balancing employment and family. Subsequent research examines other areas of support.

We first present some background about the functioning of two-career families. Next we describe the
research method, including data collection, analysis
procedures, and an overview of the sample. Then we
consider the results of the analysis, looking specifically
at the midlife women's perceptions of their husband's
involvement and support in employment and family
domains. Finally, we discuss the implications of the
results, as well as limitations to the study and directions for future research.

Background

As the baby boomers reach midlife and beyond,
they have swelled the ranks of workers between the
ages of 40 and 50 years. For example, the percentage
of the labor force between the ages of 35 and 54 years
increased from 42% in 1990 to 47% in 2004 (U.S. Bureau of Labor Statistics, 2004). The number of women
between the ages of 35 and 44 years was 16.6 million
in 2004, as compared to 11.7 million in 1985 (U.S.
Bureau of Labor Statistics, 2004). Understanding the
issues faced by these workers at midlife and beyond
can facilitate the development of appropriate policies
and practices.

Although some research has addressed the issues of
midlife workers (A. Kruger, 1994; Levinson, 1978;
O'Connor & Wolfe, 1991) and now midlife women
(Apter, 1995; Gordon & Whelan, 1998; Grambs, 1989;
L. Jacobson, 1995; Levinson, 1996; J. Marshall, 1995),
little of this work has looked at women with enduring
careers at midlife and similarly at the roles their
spouses play in their lives. Women at midlife typically
have established their careers and home and family life
(Gordon & Whelan, 1998; Reid & Willis, 1999; White,
1995). They often have school-age or young-adult
children, although they can still have preschool children at home. Other published data from this study of
married midlife women with enduring professional
careers and families (Gordon & Whelan, 1998) indicated that these women had needs for renewed work-
family balance, more personal time, and continued
achievement, accomplishment, and perceived value to
the organization. They also perceived a need for assistance in preparing for the next decade's challenges,
which included good mothering, especially of adolescents; building their career path and continuing to ad-

vance in their organization; maintaining balance in
their lives; developing career competencies; and dealing with their aging parents. Most of these women developed personal coping strategies as ways of meeting
these needs. Yet Gordon and Whelan's (1998) study
did not address the role that husbands played in the
midlife of these professional women. As the number of
dual-career couples continues to increase and the workforce continues to age, a significant number of dual-
career couples at midlife and beyond will continue to
face the challenge of balancing employment and family
responsibilities.

Support Provided by Wives and Husbands in Two-Career Families

Prior research indicates that many women significantly support their husband's careers. Women provide
support by taking primary responsibility for family and
household (Beck, 1998; Bonney, Kelley, & Levant,
1999; P. Kruger, 1998; Manke, Seery, Crouter, &
McHale, 1994; Shelton & John, 1993). Historically,
employed women have done a greater share of family
work than their husbands (Biernat & Wortman, 1991;
Coverman, 1989). Even when women jointly own family companies with their husbands, they have assumed
more family and household responsibilities (Marshack,
1994). Wives have also been viewed as partners in
their husband's careers. Recruitment for executive positions, for example, has often included the husband
and wife in interviews and on-site visits, even investigating the wife's character, personality, and marital
relations (Murray, 1986). Women with careers may
relinquish them or reduce their career advancement as
a result of their spouse's career moves, thus becoming
the trailing spouse.

Women have rarely experienced the same type of
support from their spouse, even if they have equal or
primary careers, although husbands contributed more
to household labor in a younger cohort of spouses
(Pleck, 1997; Robinson & Godbey, 1997; Rogers &
Amato, 2000). A study, for example, indicated that
husbands' participation in childcare increases as mothers have extended work hours (Bonney et al., 1999).
Traditionally, however, men have worked outside the
home and women worked inside the home. Employed
women merely added job-related responsibilities to
their home responsibilities (Potuchek, 1997). In large
part, this lack of support results from the competing
career obligations that the husbands have because their
participation in dual-career families has personal and
professional consequences (Rosin, 1990). The amount
and sharing of household, childcare, and family work
evolves, increasing and decreasing, as children and
parents age or are ill. At midlife, women and men may
find themselves sandwiched between generational responsibilities, placing additional burdens on them.

Outcomes in Two-Career Couples

Satisfaction with the division of household labor influences marital happiness (Suitor, 1991). A larger percentage of wives than husbands restructured their work for family reasons (Karambayya & Reilly, 1992). Even though the men were equally involved with their families, they did not restructure their employment as much as the women to meet family obligations, instead making so-called special arrangements instead of more consistent adjustments. Some men felt stuck in what has been called the "daddy trap" (Hammonds & Palmer, 1998), where they face significant work demands that conflict with their (and their wife's) desire for them to be equal participants in dealing with family and household responsibilities (Hertz, 1999). Women were more satisfied when their husbands shared the chores they had traditionally performed rather than spent more time performing household chores in general (Benin & Agostinelli, 1988). Clearly, the intertwining of their careers and lives can create problems for the advancement of one member of the couple if relocation is required (Cohen, 1994; Taylor & Lounsbury, 1988). Yet their relationship and support for each other can overcome some of these negative outcomes (Gilbert, 1985, 1993). Special cases exist when husband and wife work in the same business, altering and increasing the requirements for support (Marshack, 1994). Decision making and responsibilities in these careers are not equal, with women primarily responsible for the home arena and husbands for the work arena (Marshack, 1994; Ponthieu & Caudill, 1993; Wicker & Burley, 1991).

In addition to the impact of the actual attitudes and behaviors on the wives' outcomes, the wives' perceptions can also influence their attitudes and behaviors. Wives' perceptions of their husbands' attitudes toward the wives working influenced the wives' attitudes about their own work (Spitze & Waite, 1981). The impact of perceptions is further illustrated in a study where perceptions of unfairness in household chores and spending money were significantly related to husbands' and wives' assessment of marital quality (Blair, 1993). Perceptions of equity play a key role in marital satisfaction and quality (Gager, 1998; Gilbert, 1993).

Summary and Unanswered Questions

As more women have entered the workforce, their husbands have contributed to the family by helping with household and child care tasks. Most of the research so far has focused on men and women at early career stages with young children. Husbands' contributions to two-career families have been chronicled in numerous studies, although most have not specifically considered the nature of participation in couples at midlife (Aldous, Mulligan, & Bjarnasin, 1998; Barnett & Baruch, 1987; Barnett & Rivers, 1996; Deutsch, 1999; Gilbert, 1993). This stage of career and life offers new complexities and poses special challenges that make understanding the role of husbands important. Does one person's career take precedence, or does true equality exist in the careers of husbands and wives at midlife? What happens at midcareer to career precedence and sharing of home and family responsibilities, for example, when both partners are highly successful in their careers? Furthermore, what do these pioneering women have to say about their husbands' contributions to family life? To what extent do the husbands share in the work of the family? What happens when the husband and wife have career aspirations that call for spending significant time on job-related activities and also have children who require attention?

The current exploratory study attempted to take a first step in addressing these unanswered questions by looking at the husbands' involvement in employment and family in midlife dual-career couples. We focus on three questions (a) Whose career has precedence? (b) What is the nature of the husbands' contributions to the family and household? and (c) What types of support result? In the current study, we report the results in the women's voice as a way of better identifying, describing, and understanding the subtleties, complexities, and common issues of the families of midlife professional women.

Method

We used a qualitative methodology in the current exploratory study because it provides a richness of data that helps identify key themes that can form the basis of subsequent quantitative studies (Denzin & Lincoln, 1998; C. Marshall & Rossman, 1999; Strauss & Corbin, 1990). We interviewed 36 professional women between the ages of 36 and 50 years. These women were part of a pioneering group who combined marriage and parenting with enduring and relatively uninterrupted full-time work throughout their adult lives. They are an unusual group because of the degree of their career accomplishments—each woman had attained significant professional stature; the sample included top business executives, well-regarded physicians, partners in major legal firms, and successful self-employed consultants and businesswomen. Their husbands were equally accomplished, holding high-level business, not-for-profit, legal, and medical positions. Most of the women and men in the sample were at the pinnacle of demanding careers that required large amounts of time and energy and gave no indication of diminishing in importance during the next 10 years.

Data Collection and Analysis

Although the current study was part of a larger one that involved an extensive interview protocol, the results of the current study were based primarily on the women's responses to the following questions, which allowed us to delineate the contributions made by the husbands of the midlife professional women: "What role has your husband played in helping you manage family and career?" "How do you interface with your husband's career and vice versa?" We also coded comments about the woman's spouse in other parts of the interview, which included questions about the nature of their employment and family responsibilities, the way they manage these responsibilities now and in the past, their key challenges, the major issues they faced at various times in their lives, the nature of the transition between life stages, the impact and contributions of their organization in handling their employment and family responsibilities, and their satisfaction with their job, career, and life.

We used a nonrandom sample of Boston-area professionals; securing a random sample or a complete sample of the population would have been desirable but was unrealistic because of difficulty in locating married, professional women with children and enduring careers. The first author contacted a small group of women who could help identify women in professional-level jobs who had worked full-time throughout their adult lives, were married, and had at least one child. The women identified in this way were contacted by telephone and asked to participate in the current study. All but two of the women contacted agreed to be interviewed; these two women declined to participate, not because of lack of interest, but because of significant time demands on their lives at that time. The women who participated were then asked to suggest additional women. This snowball technique resulted in a convenience sample, which is appropriate for an exploratory study. The interviews lasted between 1 and 3 hours and were audiotaped. The first author conducted all interviews to ensure relative consistency in their content.

Each interview was transcribed. We analyzed the transcripts using the qualitative analysis approach suggested by Miles and Huberman (1994) as follows. We created a data set with the responses to questions that related directly to the husband, household and family management, and career interfaces between the husband's and wife's career. We then searched the full interview transcript and included any interviewee comments that related to the spouses of the women interviewed. We first coded the responses according to the broad, thematic areas of the interview questions related to spouse, for example, the role the husband played in helping manage family and career and the nature of the two careers. During this coding, we focused on and identified the themes that related to the involvement of the spouses in helping the women handle career and family responsibilities, although the larger research project addressed multiple themes and issues. Next, we reviewed each transcript to identify any additional thematic areas not yet specified and to ensure that all relevant themes were identified. For this article, we focused on career precedence and the husband's contribution to family and household. A second coder then coded the nature of career precedence and the husband's contribution to family and household based on comments about the husband previously extracted from the interviews. The interrater agreement

(Miles & Huberman, 1994) between the two coders initially was 83% for career precedence and 69% for husband's contributions. When the second coder read the entire transcript of the interviews of the women where coding differences existed, and after discussing discrepancies between the two sets of codes and trying to reconcile them, the agreement rose to 97% and 81%, respectively. In cases where no agreement could be reached, the codings by the first coder are reported in this article.

Sample

The women in the sample were all White, and the majority were between the ages of 40 and 45 years, although younger and older women were included in the sample to capture the breadth of experiences at midlife. The length of their marriage varied from fewer than 5 years to more than 20 years, with most of the women having marriages of 15 to 20 years, followed in frequency by 11 to 15 and 6 to 10 years, respectively. Some women had been divorced previously; however, all were married at the time of the interview. More than one-half of the sample had two children, and one-third had only one child; having three or more children was less common. These children ranged in age from preschool to adult. Table 1 provides more specific information about the sample.

Table 1
Age, Marital Status, and Children of the Women in the Sample (N =36)

	Number of women
Age of the women (*M*)	(41)
36 to 39 years	8
40 to 45 years	26
46 to 50 years	2
Length of marriage (*M*)	(15)
0 to 5 years	1
6 to 10 years	8
11 to 15 years	10
15 to 20 years	12
More than 20 years	5
Number of children (*M*)	(2)
1	12
2	20
3 or more	4
Age of youngest child	
Preschool	9
Elementary school	20
Secondary school	6
College or older	1
Age of oldest child	
Preschool	4
Elementary school	19
Secondary school	5
College or older	8

The women in our sample were quite successful and worked in an array of professions, as shown in the left-hand column of Table 2. Many held high-level positions in major Boston-area organizations; they

Table 2
Occupations of the Women and Their Husbands (N = 36)

Woman's occupation	Number of women with this occupation	Woman's description of husband's occupation			
Account manager	1	Self-employed			
Attorney	3	Attorney (2)	Bank executive		
Bank executive	4	Consultant	Development officer	Higher education executive	High technology manager
Chief financial officer	1	Psychologist			
Consultant	3	Administrative judge	Consultant	Medical researcher	
Development officer[a]	1	N/A			
Film producer	2	Media executive	Television reporter		
Financial manager	1	Attorney			
Human resource manager[a]	5	Development director	Executive chef	Human resource manager	Psychoanalyst N/A
Information systems manager	2	Attorney	Professor		
Investment banker	1	Consultant			
Physician	4	Physician (4)			
Professor	1	Hotel administrator			
Psychologist	1	Hospital administrator			
Real estate developer	1	Real estate developer			
Senior administrator	2	Attorney	Politician		
Social worker	1	Physician			
Systems engineer	1	Architect			
Systems planning manager	1	Physician			

[a]The data from the interviews of one of the women with this occupation did not include the husband's occupation, shown in the table as N/A.

were partners in law firms, well-regarded physicians, top human resources executives, senior vice presidents in financial services organizations, and top managers in the nonprofit sector. The husbands of these women also held professional-level positions, as shown in Table 2; the right-hand column lists the professions of the husband of each woman with the specified occupation. One-fourth held the same type of job as their wives; for example, the sample included couples who were attorneys, physicians, media-related professionals, or human resources managers. This sample was unusual because in most of the couples the husband and wife had achieved a high, relatively equal level of success in their careers.

Results

We present the results as they answer our three research questions. First, we analyze whose career has precedence. Next, we present the data regarding the husband's contribution to the family and household. Finally, we combine these data into a typology of four types of husbands to describe the overall type of support they offer.

Career Precedence

Career precedence was reflected either in whose career was the primary focus of career decisions or in who assumed the burden of balancing employment and family. The women in the current study described whose career took precedence in one of three ways: their husband's, their own, or equal.

Husband's career had precedence. The husband's career took precedence for 22% of the couples. The women explained this precedence as occurring for four reasons. First, the salaries associated with the two careers may have resulted in the husband's career having precedence. A social worker reported, for example, that her husband's career took precedence because he made a higher salary: "I still did most of the daytime stuff, I mean, that was an economic reality." Second, decisions about job location, such as whether the wife trailed the husband in job relocations, reflected the type of career precedence. A husband's career took precedence, for example, because job mobility for the wife was easier. Third, the husband may have had ego needs, such as providing security for his family or having status or power, that were met by his having the dominant career. The wife in a physician couple noted this motivation:

> His career is skyrocketing and all that, and I've come to realize that that's important to him. Because of his needs and deprivations and so on as a child [his career] is something he just had to keep working at until he feels comfortable.

Finally, this traditional attitude toward career precedence may be a function of many men's socialization to expect to be the family's breadwinner.

One attorney noted this influence when she described her husband's career having precedence:

> Oh, definitely if there has to be any give it seems to be mine.... Men have a fascinating way of forgetting that they had to be home at six.... I think they just naturally assume they're primo. I think women are by nature more accommodating.

Wife's career had precedence. For a slightly smaller percentage of couples, 19%, the wife's career had precedence. For these couples, only two of the factors—salary and job mobility—seemed to play a major role in the decision. For a human resources manager, for example, her higher salary resulted in her career having precedence. She believed that her husband also felt comfortable limiting his career achievement:

It just sort of happened gradually because of my advancement. It wasn't a choice, do you take this promotion or not? And the fact that he also was someone who has a lot of interests around the home, is very interested in the computer, and is project oriented. [He] didn't feel like he had to prove himself professionally. And we just felt for the total family, this was the best thing to do.

A physician described the lesser mobility of her career because of job vacancies or the special nature of her work: "In many ways, he has a more common and saleable job…. So when we've talked about moving, it's always been with an eye to what academic jobs are out there for me that he could find a job around."

The careers had equal precedence. The largest group of the women interviewed, 58%, either stated or implied that the two careers held equal precedence, as captured in one attorney's comment about her husband, also an attorney: "Every time I go to give up mine, he says he'll retire too." Yet the equality is not without some tension and trade-offs. As one physician noted, "We're even. If anything, I got to be an associate professor a year ahead…[however,] I would have left several times for good job offers, but [my husband] does not want to leave Boston." A human resource manager commented,

We both sacrifice somewhat in our career. My husband is an executive chef, and in that business if you're really going to get ahead, you have to be willing to put in the 60, 70, 80 hours per week. You have to be willing to relocate with some of the bigger chains or work in Boston and make the long commute, put in the hours. He has sacrificed that to help maintain the family life at home. So in that respect he sacrificed, and I have sacrificed also.

Another woman described the trade-offs in her family:

Now I'm reaching another sort of crossroads where I'm feeling maybe the business isn't really going to bring in enough money in the next few years to pay all those bills easily. The other dilemma is that my husband has been working at his job for so many years…and he's got a great job but he's also in midlife crisis. I mean, he doesn't want to do that forever. And I'm feeling a bit more pressure to pull a little more weight so he can slack off a little and try something new in a couple of years. So there's always a dilemma, there's always a trade-off. You know, things change.

Trade-offs have a lot to do with managing the logistics of the two careers. They also relate to personal issues about growing older, accomplishing desired goals, and an equal commitment to ensuring that family needs are met. It is a dynamic process, with adjustments occurring continuously.

Contributions to Family and Household

No midlife woman did all of the family and child care herself. Most husbands made some contributions to the family and household activities, although some contributions were extremely limited. The husbands' contributions ranged from doing a small part, to sharing relatively equally, to the husbands having primary responsibility. Our thematic analysis indicated that many of the husbands played specific supportive roles, as well as offered general support. This support helped the wife handle the challenges created by the requirements of a professional career and a demanding family. For example, an information systems manager noted that "I think having a supportive husband and a supportive daughter have always been important." A business executive noted,

I think that [my husband] has always been real supportive around my career and very supportive around the intellectual challenges that I find associated with my work. Not that it doesn't create stress, when there's not enough clean underwear, but I think that's [support's] the key.

Without this basic type of support, managing employment and family likely would be even more stressful for the midlife women.

Although most families purchased extensive child care and household services (depending, of course, on the ages of their children), significant responsibilities for managing and implementing family-related activities remained. Of the wives, 42% explicitly characterized their husband's involvement using the language of "managing" and "doing." In the remainder of the cases, this distinction was based on women's description of the tasks and responsibilities performed by themselves and their husbands. *Managing* refers to the planning, coordinating, and initiating of all household and family-related activities. The person or persons who manage carry the emotional burden or psychological responsibility for making sure that the household runs smoothly and that children receive appropriate care. The manager often initiates and delegates various family and household activities to other family members or paid caregivers or household service providers. One woman, for example, described herself as the "domestic coordinator" of her family. Another noted about her husband, "On a day-to-day basis, he does more of the planning part of it."

Doing refers to the carrying out, performing, or implementing of a sequence of household activities. Typically these activities occur in response to initiatives or requests by the person who manages the household and family-related activities. The same person can manage and do, or one person can manage while the other person does the family and household work. Often the women describe their husbands as helping in the household. As one woman noted, "He

Table 3
Types of Support Provided by Husbands (N = 36)

		Managing	
		Low	High
Doing	Low	Uninvolved (*n* = 5)	Coordinator (*n* = 3)
		The *au pair* does it…. Oh, he couldn't plan [household responsibilities] if his life depended on it…. We have to send somebody to do the grocery shopping…. The major need is for carpooling, baseball. I mean [the nanny] doesn't really take care of the kids.	[Husband] probably [makes greater contributions]. It's changing. Right now, it's about 60–40, but until recently, it's probably been 90–10…. [My husband] always has the higher percentage. He would do drop off and pick up. He would do teacher conferences. He would do whatever.
	High	Helpmate (*n* = 18)	Egalitarian (*n* = 10)
		[He's] a great husband. He'll do anything I ask him to do. He doesn't necessarily think of things on his own. And there were a number of years when that bothered me, but then I realized that…I ought to be thankful that he does these things, and all I have to do is say, "Would you do this?" and he says, "Sure, fine."	But he was always very good about [my traveling] on short notice. He certainly did more than half, pitching in, running errands, and taking kids to the doctor and making sure that there was food in the house and that kind of thing…. It's always been shared. I think I did more of some things than he did all along, even when my career was maybe even busier than his.

545 couldn't plan it if his life depended on it." Another woman described doing as follows: "Sometimes you just have to ask him. He knows the basics. He cooks, he cleans, he grocery shops, he does errands. It's just part of the routine. He's there to help out."

Categories of Support

550 Based on the wives' perceptions as expressed during our interviews, we identified the extent to which husbands manage or do most activities regarding family and household as high or low. We characterized (not counted) the content of the wives' comments to 555 determine the level of each type of support by their husbands. We categorized a husband as high on managing if the wife reported that he consistently and of his own initiative performed numerous tasks related to the planning, coordinating, and initiating of activities; 560 we categorized a husband as low on managing if the wife described him as rarely performing such activities. Similarly, we categorized a husband as high on doing if his wife described him as implementing household-related activities, typically after she specified that they 565 needed to be done; we categorized a husband as low on doing if he rarely performed any household-related activities.

This results in four possible combinations. Table 3 illustrates the combinations and offers an example of a 570 woman's comments about husbands who fall into each category. We have chosen descriptive names—uninvolved, helpmate, egalitarian, and coordinator—to reflect the underlying approach of these husbands to the sharing of household and family responsibilities. 575 The labels are intended solely to differentiate about possibilities rather than definitively characterize each husband.

Uninvolved husbands. Of the husbands, 14% were low on managing and doing household and family activities and so were perceived as making very limited 580 contributions in these areas. Some men lack the time because of extensive career commitments. As one physician commented, "If I ever had any question about where my focus would be, knowing that he's so busy means that somebody has to be home running the 585 show."

Other men remain uninvolved because they believe that they can completely enjoy their family in less time than their wives need. Still, others have retained a view, often based on early socialization, that women 590 should assume primary responsibilities for their family and household. These husbands can serve as a source of security by providing the financial backing that allows their wife the freedom to work at any career, regardless of its compensation: "His doing all of the 595 things he's doing gives us a lot of security." The husband can also give his wife the opportunity to opt out of working because the family does not need her salary to maintain its standard of living: "My husband refers 600 to it as 'women have this net.' They can always say 'I'll just stop working.'"

Helpmate husbands. One-half of the husbands are low on managing and high on doing. They help with family and household either by doing the chores men 605 typically do or by willingly doing whatever their wives ask them to do. One woman described her husband's contribution as follows:

I went and I did laundry, and I had a laundry basket, and I carried it and put it at the foot of the stairs. And all the 610 clothes were folded and the laundry basket sat there for a day. And so the next day I put a second laundry basket next to it. And the next day I had like three laundry baskets sitting at the bottom of the stairs. Everybody stepped over them. The kids took out what they needed. After the third or fourth day, I said to [my husband], "Could you take these upstairs?" "Oh, sure dear. No problem."…. I probably do more than he does…but I probably could get him to do more by asking him to do more.

Helpmate husbands can also serve as a personal lifeline. In this role, the husband acts as a stabilizing force by being a calm center or reminding his wife about the importance of her personal health and well-being:

My husband, who has just been the most consistent center of my life, [is] a very calm, tranquil being that I've kind of run around for 20 years. I think that to the extent that that has been a center of my life, it's been a quiet center, and it's been an extremely important one in that we've always kind of figured out how to get things done together.

In some families, the wives preferred to retain responsibility for, control of, and psychological oversight of the family and child care. Perhaps because many of the women care more about the details of home life, they spend more energy than their husbands in this regard. As one senior executive noted,

I probably have always done more of that [managing the household]. I think that's pretty classic, too. And that's by choice…I can't stand a messy house. So if nobody else in the house is going to do it, I'm going to do it. And I feel guilty if my kids don't have sort of a square meal at the end of the day…. But I clearly impose on myself a level of responsibility that's ridiculous.

Even if husbands share child care, the couple may take a more traditional approach to household management, resulting in the husbands acting as helpmates rather than truly egalitarian:

I'd say [we divide up] the child care responsibilities 50-50. With the running of the house and making decisions for the house and all that kind of thing, 90/10, with me taking 90% and him taking 10%. Because no matter what I do, no matter how many agreements we make, no matter how we sit down and write it down on paper, after 3 weeks it just goes back to me taking responsibility for it. It doesn't get done. He says that, although he thinks that he is very liberated and that he thinks I have every much a right to a career as he does, when it comes right down to it, he thinks he has old-fashioned values about who is going to be in charge of the house and he just won't help with it.

Helpmate husbands can also act as team players, playing the role of facilitator or partner. One woman noted, "He's a facilitator because when he's home he's a 50-50 participant." Another commented,

He's been very, very much a partner. He really encouraged me to take advantage of the work opportunities [to be self-employed] and convinced me that whatever support I needed at home to make that work out would be, we'd make it.

Egalitarian husbands. Of the husbands, 28% shared responsibilities for managing and doing family and household responsibilities relatively equally. As one woman commented, "Absolutely [he still does half]. More if I can get him to." Such sharing results in more positive balance between employment and family responsibilities, although the negotiations involved in allocating responsibilities and ensuring that either the husband or wife has the so-called big picture can sometimes be associated with more stress and reduced life satisfaction in the short run.

Our strategy has been that I do mornings and my husband does the evenings and afternoon type thing. So whatever I do workwise, I am always going to be late for work [in comparison to other employees] in the morning…. We use chores actually as trade-offs because I hate to clean the bathroom; he hates to iron. So this Sunday I ironed 10 shirts so he's cleaned the bathroom; I had to sort of learn to not want the housework done as I would do it, but just, you know, done.

Although a number of the women say that their husbands share the responsibilities relatively equally, the men do not assume quite as much responsibility for organizing or managing as their wives. If they straddle the helpmate and egalitarian categories, they likely spend more time in doing than managing family and household activities than the typical helpmate. Yet a number of the wives justify this less-than-equal contribution by acknowledging that their husbands do more than most husbands do. This seems particularly the case in household work as opposed to childcare.

Coordinator husbands. Of the husbands, 8% were perceived to have the primary responsibility for managing the family and household responsibilities and rely on their wives' help in doing the related activities. This type of activity by the husband as manager and wife as doer is analogous to the helpmate type; however, the roles are reversed. The coordinator husbands may make it possible for some women to work at all and for others to have high-level, high-profile, extremely demanding careers. As one woman noted,

But over the years…because of what was happening in my career in terms of advancement and because he had flexibility…we decided that we didn't need more money. We needed more time, and we needed to have some semblance of sanity in our life. He has continued to cut back…. Realistically, I could never have done this if my husband had a career that required him to be gone from 7:00 in the morning till 7:00 at night or traveling.

One woman described her husband's attitude in assuming the coordinator role that she should "do what you need to do." Another husband felt that he was missing important times with his children, so he changed his priorities and schedule to take responsibility for them.

Coordinator husbands can serve as the family manager, such as by organizing family activities. One woman described her husband's role: "[My husband]

organizes field trips for us all the time, which we joke about, [calling him] Mr. Field Trip." It is also possible for the husband to take charge of all household and family activities. The wife of one husband who had this role estimated that she had only 10% of the responsibility in the household or family.

Discussion

Families with both spouses employed are the major pattern in the United States (Elloy & Flynn, 1998); however, most of the research attention has been paid to young couples early in their careers. By midlife, such couples have likely established workable patterns of sharing responsibilities. The current study was a first step in documenting the nature of this pattern and, more specifically, the husband's contribution to the family and household in which the wife held a high-level professional job. This article presented preliminary results regarding the career precedence of spouses in the families of midlife professional women, the contributions to family and household by husbands in those families, and the pattern of overall support offered by the husbands to the midlife women. In this section, we discuss the results in each of these areas.

Career Precedence

Our results suggest that equal career precedence is more common than either the husband's or the wife's career having precedence. Yet even when the wives report equal career precedence, creating truly equal careers often requires trade-offs and sacrifices from one or both partners that may be extremely difficult, often testing their commitment to their careers and sometimes to their families. In almost all cases, precedence is economically driven; however, equal economic contributions do not necessarily translate into equal precedence because other factors, such as logistics, early socialization, or personal ego needs may moderate the impact of the economic contributions. At the same time, organizations need to better appreciate the movement toward greater equality in career precedence. For example, managers are more likely to assume that female employees who are mothers would handle any household or family emergencies that occur (Hammonds & Palmer, 1998). Such assumptions may be inaccurate and negatively affect the wife's career advancement, increase stress for male employees who have assumed such responsibilities, or undermine the arrangements made by spouses for handling the challenges posed by the interaction of employment and family.

We captured these couples at one time in their careers. Over time, shifts in career precedence to ensure a sense of open fairness in the marriage occurred for many couples, as either the husband or wife wished to change his or her level of involvement with family or as job opportunities opened or closed. This dynamic, somewhat free-form texture reflects the value partners placed on ensuring their husband's or wife's happiness

and fulfillment. The couples continually renegotiated priorities as a way of making the family situation work and the partners feel happy and successful.

Contributions to Family and Household

Not unexpectedly, the contributions by husbands of midlife women vary significantly. When we categorized the contributions as managing and doing, we noted that some midlife professional women characterized their husbands as contributing in neither, one, or both ways. Regardless of their relative contributions, men still spend more time doing than managing in the household. This pattern of contribution continues to put the psychological burden on women, causing them to face the necessity of either acting as so-called superwomen or finding other ways of handling the overload at work or home. Because of their relatively high income, many of the professional women we interviewed bought household services as a way of handling this potential conflict, a solution available only to those women or families with sufficient discretionary income. Still, the nature of the husband's contribution likely has a psychological impact and hence consequences for the life satisfaction, career commitment, and job satisfaction of the midlife professional women (and their husbands).

Some husbands may complement or substitute for their performance of household or family responsibilities by providing support in other ways. For example, some act as career advisors to their working wives. As sounding boards, the husbands may offer advice about career-related issues that range from decisions about returning to work after a maternity leave to how to handle specific personnel problems. In this role, they might also serve as mentors or role models in which they demonstrate desirable professional behavior.

A number of the women described their relationships with their husbands as ones of "independence and dependence." The analysis we presented about husband's contributions highlights this tension. By midlife, however, the couples have developed the mechanisms, such as hiring household staff, alternating whose job requirements receive priority, or developing responsive scheduling patterns, for resolving conflicting demands.

Support Provided by the Husbands

We presented the beginnings of a four-cell typology of support provided by the husbands of midlife professional women. Such a typology highlights the critical role that husbands play in supporting the individual work–life balance of professional midlife women. The typology provides a way for husbands and wives to consider all the tasks necessary to support effective, functional home and family life. Such intentional consideration may provide a more satisfactory division of these responsibilities and related work than a division based on family-of-origin patterns or traditional gender roles and responsibilities.

Where the husband falls in the typology could provide insight into the amount and type of support needed from the husband's and the wife's employer. For example, the woman with a helpmate may need less flexibility and more referral services; the woman with a coordinator husband may need the reverse. This highlights the need for use of benefits to be equally accepted for men and women. Until recently, it was more acceptable for women than men to take advantage of various benefits, such as leave following the birth of a child or flextime to attend children's activities.

Just as career precedence and contributions to household and family may change during an individual's life span, so may a husband's place in the typology. Although a husband may act as a helpmate early in his and his wife's career, later he may shift to a coordinator as the demands of his work lessen and his wife's increase. Organizations, too, must be flexible in responding to such changes. They must offer an array of benefits so that professional women and their spouses can tailor their choices to their specific needs.

Limitations and Future Research

Although the current study has taken a first step in trying to understand the contributions and support that the husbands of midlife professional women provide, future research should involve a larger study that would verify our results. The work on career precedence could be extended, such as by measuring career precedence on a 100% scale, where husbands and wives are asked to divide the percentage according to the contribution of each spouse. How career precedence changes during the course of the marriage would also provide interesting insights into husbands' support in dual-career families. Future research might also involve obtaining data about career precedence and family and household contributions from the husbands and comparing the two sets of perceptions. In addition, the typology proposed here should be tested and expanded to describe the wife's role as perceived by the husband and the relationship as perceived by the husband and wife.

Future research should also test specific hypotheses about the impact of perceived or actual behaviors and attitudes on both spouses' job, family, life satisfaction, employment and family balance, and stress. Additional research should compare perceptions to actual attitudes and behavior to determine which has the greater impact on these outcomes. Replicating this research with younger and older workers will also provide insight into whether this support is a unique midlife phenomenon or a general set of behaviors and attitudes in dual-career couples. This research should also be extended to different racial and ethnic groups, occupational categories, and geographical locations. In addition, the role of children in performing household chores and supporting their parents' careers should be considered.

Conclusion

Personal, relationship, and societal factors affect the way partners combine occupational and family roles (Gilbert, 1988, 1993). The extent of the husbands' contributions depends on factors such as the husbands' egos, the relative salaries of the spouses, their job mobility, the flexibility of their work situations, and the early socialization of husband and wife regarding the appropriate roles for each spouse. The current study suggested that wives' perceptions of their husbands' attitudes and behaviors about employment and family are important. It represents a next step in understanding the complex dynamics of dual-career families at midlife. The midlife professional women whom we interviewed were almost uniformly enthusiastic about the support they received from their husbands. This support facilitated their management of employment and family obligations. Although the nature of support varied, knowing that their husbands valued them and their careers helped them deal with the challenges of balancing the many facets of their lives.

References

Aldous, J., Mulligan, G. M., & Bjarnasin, R. (1998). Fathering over time: What makes the difference? *Journal of Marriage and the Family, 60,* 809–820.

Apter, T. (1995). *Secret paths: Women in the new midlife.* New York: Norton.

Barnett, R. C., & Baruch, G. K. (1987). Determinants of fathers' participation in the family work. *Journal of Marriage and the Family, 49,* 29–40.

Barnett, R. C., & Rivers, C. (1996). *She works/he works: How two-income families are happier, healthier, and better-off.* San Francisco: Harper San-Francisco.

Beck, B. (1998). Women and work: At the double. *Economist, 348,* S12–S16.

Benin, M. H., & Agostinelli, J. (1988). Husbands' and wives' satisfaction with the division of labor. *Journal of Marriage and the Family, 50,* 349–361.

Biernat, M., & Wortman, C. (1991). Sharing of home responsibilities between professionally employed women and their husbands. *Journal of Personality and Social Psychology, 60,* 844–860.

Blair, S. L. (1993). Employment, family, and perceptions of marital quality among husbands and wives. *Journal of Family Issues, 14,* 189–212.

Bonney, J. F., Kelley, M. L., & Levant, R. F. (1999). A model of fathers' behavioral involvement in child care in dual-earner families. *Journal of Family Psychology, 13,* 401–415.

Borysenko, J. (1996). *A woman's book of life: The biology, psychology, and spirituality of the feminine life cycle.* New York: Riverhead Books.

Cohen, C. E. (1994). The trailing-spouse dilemma. *Working Woman, 19,* 69–70.

Coverman, S. (1989). Women's work is never done: The division of domestic labor. In J. Freeman (Ed.), *Women: A feminist perspective* (pp. 356–368). Palo Alto, CA: Mayfield.

Cutrona, C., & Russell, D. (1990). Type of social support and specific stress: Toward a theory of optimal matching. In B. Sarason, I. Sarason, & G. Pierce (Eds.), *Social support: An Interactional View* (pp. 319–366). New York: John Wiley.

Denzin, N. K., & Lincoln, Y. S. (1998). Introduction: Entering the field of qualitative research. In N. K. Denzin & Y. S. Lincoln (Eds.), *Strategies of qualitative inquiry* (pp. 1–17). Thousand Oaks, CA: Sage.

Deutsch, F. M. (1999). *Halving it all: How equally shared parenting works.* Cambridge, MA: Harvard University Press.

Deutsch, F. M., Lussier, J. B., & Servis, L. J. (1993). Husbands at home: Predictors of paternal participation in childcare and housework. *Journal of Personality and Social Psychology, 65,* 1154–1166.

Ehrensraft, D. (1987). *Parenting together: Men and women sharing the care of children.* New York: Free Press.

Elloy, D. F., & Flynn, W. R. (1998). Job involvement and organization commitment among dual-income and single-income families: A multiple-site study. *Journal of Social Psychology, 138,* 93–101.

Gager, C. T. (1998). The role of valued outcomes, justifications, and comparison referents in perceptions of fairness among dual-earner couples. *Journal of Family Issues, 19,* 622–648.

Gilbert, L. A. (1985). *Men in dual-career families: Current realities and future prospects.* Hillsdale, NJ: Lawrence Erlbaum.

Gilbert, L. A. (1988). *Sharing it all: The rewards and struggles of two-career families.* New York: Plenum.

Gilbert, L. A. (1993). *Two careers/one family: The promise of gender equality.* Newbury Park, CA: Sage.

Gordon, J. R., & Whelan, K. S. (1998). Successful professional women in midlife: How organizations can more effectively understand and respond to the challenges. *Academy of Management Executive, 12,* 8–24.

Grambs, J. D. (1989). *Women over forty: Visions and realities.* New York: Springer.

Greenglass, E. R. (1993). Social support and coping of employed women. In B. C. Long & S. E. Kahn (Eds.), *Women, work and copying: A multidisciplinary approach to workplace stress* (pp. 215–239). Montreal, Canada: McGill-Queen's University Press.

Hammonds, K. H., & Palmer, A. T. (1998, September 21). The daddy trap. *Business Week, 3596,* 56–60.

Hertz, R. (1999). Working to place family at the center of life: Dual-earner and single-parent strategies. *Annals of the American Academy of Political and Social Science, 562,* 16–31.

Hewlett, S. A. (2002). Executive women and the myth of having it all. *Harvard Business Review, 80,* 66–72.

Jacobson, J. M. (1995). *Midlife women: Contemporary issues.* Boston: Jones and Bartlett.

James, J. B., & Liewkowicz, C. (1997). Themes of power and affiliation across time. In M. E. Lachman & J. B. James (Eds.), *Multiple paths of mid life development* (pp. 109–144). Chicago: University of Chicago Press.

Karambayya, R., & Reilly, A. H. (1992). Dual earner couples: Attitudes and actions in restructuring work for family. *Journal of Organizational Behavior, 13,* 585–601.

Kruger, A. (1994). The midlife transition: Crisis or chimera? *Psychological Reports, 75,* 1299–1305.

Kruger, P. (1998). The good news about working couples. *Parenting, 12,* 69.

Levinson, D. J. (1978). *The seasons of a man's life.* New York: Knopf.

Levinson, D. J. (1996). *The seasons of a woman's life.* New York: Knopf.

Manke, B., Seery, B. L., Crouter, A.C., & McHale, S.M. (1994). The three corners of domestic labor: Mothers, fathers, and children's weekday and weekend housework. *Journal of Marriage and the Family, 56,* 657–668.

Marshack, K. J. (1994). Copreneurs and dual-career couples: Are they different? *Entrepreneurship Theory and Practice, 19,* 49–69.

Marshall, C., & Rossman, G. B. (1999). *Designing qualitative research* (3rd ed.). Thousand Oaks, CA: Sage.

Marshall, J. (1994). Why women leave senior management jobs. In M. Tanton (Ed.), *Women in management: A developing presence* (pp. 185–201). London: Routledge.

Marshall, J. (1995). Working at senior management and board levels: Some of the issues for women. *Women in Management Review, 10,* 21–25.

Miles, M. B., & Huberman, A. M. (1994). *Qualitative data analysis.* Thousand Oaks, CA: Sage.

Murray, T. J. (1986). Checking out the new corporate wife. *Dun's Business Month, 128,* 50–51.

O'Connor, D., & Wolfe, D. M. (1991). From crisis to growth at midlife: Changes in personal paradigm. *Journal of Organizational Behavior, 12,* 323–340.

Pleck, J. (1997). Paternal involvement: Levels, sources, and consequences. In M. E. Lamb (Ed.), *The role of the father in child development* (3rd ed., pp. 66–103). New York: John Wiley.

Ponthieu, L., & Caudill, H. (1993). Who's the boss? Responsibility and decision making in copreneurial ventures. *Family Business Review, 6,* 3–17.

Potuchek, J. L. (1997). *Who supports the family? Gender and breadwinning in dual-earner marriages.* Stanford, CA: Stanford University Press.

Reid, J. D., & Willis, S. L. (1999). Middle age: New thoughts, new directions. In S. L. Willis & J. D. Reid (Eds.), *Life in the middle: Psychological and social development in middle age* (pp. 276–280). San Diego, CA: Academic Press.

Robinson, J. P., & Godbey, G. (1997). *Time for life: The surprising ways Americans use their time.* State College: Pennsylvania State University Press.

Rogers, S. J., & Amato, P. R. (2000). Have changes in gender relations affected marital quality? *Social Forces, 79,* 731–754.

Rosin, H. M. (1990). Consequences for men of dual career marriages: Implications for organizations. *Journal of Managerial Psychology, 5,* 3–8.

Shelton, B. A., & John, D. (1993). Does marital status make a difference? Housework among married and cohabitating men and women. *Journal of Family Issues, 14,* 401–423.

Spitze, G. D., & Waite, L. J. (1981). Wives' employment: The role of husbands' perceived attitudes. *Journal of Marriage and the Family, 45,* 117–124.

Strauss, A., & Corbin, J. (1990). *Basics of qualitative research: Grounded theory procedures and techniques.* Newbury Park, CA: Sage.

Suitor, J. J. (1991). Marital quality and satisfaction with the division of household labor across the family life cycle. *Journal of Marriage and the Family, 53,* 221–230.

Taylor, A. S., & Lounsbury, J. W. (1988). Dual-career couples and geographic transfer: Executives' reactions to commuter marriage and attitude toward the move. *Human Relations, 41,* 407–424.

U.S. Bureau of Labor Statistics. (2004). *Employment status of the population by sex and age.* Available at www.bls.gov/cps/home.htm

White, B. (1995). The career development of successful women. *Women in Management Review, 10,* 4–15.

Wicker, A., & Burley, K. (1991). Close coupling in work–family relationships: Making and implementing decisions in a new family business and at home. *Human Relations, 44,* 77–92.

Acknowledgment: We thank Mary Dunn and Peter Rivard for their assistance with the data analysis for this article.

Exercise for Article 35

Factual Questions

1. The researchers state that they are "particularly interested in studying professional women at mid-life who are married, have children, but also have had enduring careers." What reason do they give for this interest?

2. The results of this study are based primarily on the women's responses to two questions. What is the first question?

3. The researchers indicate that securing a random sample would have been desirable but was unrealistic for what reason?

4. Why were all interviews conducted by only one of the authors (i.e., researchers)?

5. According to the researchers, why were younger and older women included in the sample?

6. What was the mean (average) age of the women in the sample?

7. In their conclusion, do the researchers conclude that the women were enthusiastic about the support they received from their husbands?

Questions for Discussion

8. The researchers provide "Background" for this study in lines 85–251. How helpful is this background in establishing the context for this study? Would the report of the study be as effective without the background material? Explain.

9. The researchers indicate that this study is an "exploratory study." Do you agree with this characterization? If yes, what could be done in future studies on this topic to make them more definitive? (See lines 66, 240, 253, and 310–311.)

10. In your opinion, is the process of coding the participants' responses described in sufficient detail? (See lines 315–351.)

11. The researchers describe interrater reliability in lines 337–351. In your opinion, how important is this information? Would it be a weakness of the report if this information were not given? Explain.

12. The women in this study had diverse occupations. Is this a strength of this study? Explain. (See Table 2.)

13. How helpful are the direct quotations of the words of the women in this study in helping you understand the results? Are there a sufficient number of quotations? Are there too many? Explain. (See lines 403–733.)

14. The researchers make suggestions for future research in lines 859–892. Do some of these seem more important than others? Explain.

Quality Ratings

Directions: Indicate your level of agreement with each of the following statements by circling a number from 5 for strongly agree (SA) to 1 for strongly disagree (SD). If you believe an item is not applicable to this research article, leave it blank. Be prepared to explain your ratings. When responding to criteria A and B below, keep in mind that brief titles and abstracts are conventional in published research.

A. The title of the article is appropriate.

SA   5   4   3   2   1   SD

B. The abstract provides an effective overview of the research article.

SA   5   4   3   2   1   SD

C. The introduction establishes the importance of the study.

SA   5   4   3   2   1   SD

D. The literature review establishes the context for the study.

SA   5   4   3   2   1   SD

E. The research purpose, question, or hypothesis is clearly stated.

SA   5   4   3   2   1   SD

F. The method of sampling is sound.

SA   5   4   3   2   1   SD

G. Relevant demographics (for example, age, gender, and ethnicity) are described.

SA   5   4   3   2   1   SD

H. Measurement procedures are adequate.

SA   5   4   3   2   1   SD

I. All procedures have been described in sufficient detail to permit a replication of the study.

SA   5   4   3   2   1   SD

J. The participants have been adequately protected from potential harm.

SA   5   4   3   2   1   SD

K. The results are clearly described.

SA   5   4   3   2   1   SD

L. The discussion/conclusion is appropriate.

SA   5   4   3   2   1   SD

M. Despite any flaws, the report is worthy of publication.

SA   5   4   3   2   1   SD

Article 36

Exploring Young Adults' Perspectives
on Communication with Aunts

LAURA L. ELLINGSON
Santa Clara University

PATRICIA J. SOTIRIN
Michigan Technological University

ABSTRACT. Women are typically studied as daughters, sisters, mothers, or grandmothers. However, many, if not most, women are also aunts. In this study, we offer a preliminary exploration of the meaning of aunts as familial figures. We collected 70 nieces' and nephews' written accounts of their aunts. Thematic analysis of these accounts revealed nine themes, which were divided into two categories. The first category represented the role of the aunt as a teacher, role model, confidante, savvy peer, and second mother. The second category represented the practices of aunting: gifts/treats, maintaining family connections, encouragement, and nonengagement. Our analysis illuminates important aspects of aunts in family schema and kin keeping.

From *Journal of Social and Personal Relationships*, 23, 483–501.

Despite the tremendous proliferation in family forms, the popular image associated with "the family" is still overwhelmingly a heterosexual nuclear family with a husband, wife, and children (Garey & Hansen,
5   1998). Many family communication researchers, particularly feminists, are committed to honoring a plurality of family forms and relationships, for both ideological and pragmatic reasons because families that deviate from the idealized nuclear norm outnumber supposedly
10   normative families (Coontz, 2000). Kinship resources are important to many families, yet these resources have been understudied by family researchers (Johnson, 2000). Anecdotal evidence of the significance of kin exists, but modern studies demonstrate a decline
15   both in families' involvement with, and scholarly interest in, kinship ties (Johnson, 2000). We know little about the relationship between aunts and their nieces/nephews. Aunts are not nuclear family members, but neither are they obscure, distant relations.
20   They are typically a sibling from a parent's immediate family of origin. Traeder and Bennett (1998), in their popular tribute, claim that aunts are a crucial resource for maintaining and enriching family and community life, and provide anecdotal evidence of the importance
25   of aunts in family relations in family stories and everyday conversation.

Women are typically studied by family communication researchers as daughters, sisters, mothers, or grandmothers. Yet many, if not most, women in these
30   roles are also aunts. In this study, we explore the meaning of aunts as extended kin. We contend that the meanings of aunting have been ignored in favor of framing motherhood as women's essential role (e.g., O'Reilly & Abbey, 2000; Peington, 2004). As feminist
35   researchers, we seek not to idealize aunts or to essentialize them within a single, fixed identity. Instead, we intend to recognize the complexities of the roles aunts may play in their nieces' and nephews' lives. Our goal is to uncover patterns among nieces' and nephews'
40   experiences of relating to their aunts. We frame our thematic analysis by first offering a theoretical perspective on family communication and reviewing literature on kinship and kin keeping.

Theoretical Perspective

The traditional nuclear family model of family
45   communication is "losing its ecological validity" due to the proliferation of alternative family forms in modern society (Koerner & Fitzpatrick, 2002, p. 71). Koerner and Fitzpatrick suggest that theories of family communication "increasingly define family as a group of inti-
50   mates who generate a sense of home and group identity and who experience a shared history and a shared future" (p. 71). Transactional definitions are useful because they expand the boundaries of the family and therefore better reflect the tremendous variation in how
55   families define themselves (Noller & Fitzpatrick, 1993). Jorgenson (1989) positions the family "as a system of relations that comes about as individuals define those relations in their everyday communication with another" (p. 28). Boundaries between households in
60   extended kin networks are porous and negotiable, rather than fixed or rule bound (Wellman, 1998). Hence, extended families may be understood as constituted through their communication as they mutually negotiate relationship norms. Our intention in this
65   study was to delineate the organized knowledge structures, or schemas, that nieces and nephews have for aunts. Koerner and Fitzpatrick (2002) proposed a theory of family communication that identified a hierarchy of relational schemas used by family members to inter-

70 pret their communication with other family members. Relational schemas consist of declarative and procedural knowledge and interpersonal scripts. Such schemas include information and beliefs concerning: "Intimacy, individuality, affection, external factors, conver-
75 sation orientation, and conformity orientation" (p. 88). Individuals cognitively process interactions with other family members by drawing upon relationship-specific schemas first (e.g., a sister's relationship to her younger brother). If a schema does not provide the in-
80 formation or insights necessary to interpret or address the family member's behavior or to form an appropriate response, the person then draws upon more general family relationship schemas. If family relationship schemas also prove insufficient, then an individual
85 family member draws upon general social schemas regarding relationships for information. It follows, then, that when nieces and nephews communicate with aunts and with others about aunts, they both rely on and construct schemas for who aunts are and how they
90 behave. These schemas develop through communication and, in turn, influence subsequent communication. Because knowledge contained in family relationship schemas influences family communication, it is imperative to understand such knowledge (Koerner &
95 Fitzpatrick, 2002).

Researchers suggested that the concept of family scripts also is helpful in exploring understanding of kinship roles and relationships. Family scripts "are mental representations that guide the role performance
100 of family members within and across contexts" (Stack & Burton, 1998, p. 408). In extended kin relationships, "kin-scripts" designate who is obligated or entitled within a particular network to perform types of kin-work tasks, when such tasks should be performed (kin-
105 time), and how the process of assigning kin-work should be handled (kin-scription) (Stack & Burton, 1998). We posit that underlying their extended family's kin-scripts, people have relationship schemas regarding the norms and expectations of aunts, as well as rela-
110 tionship-specific schema for particular aunts. Moreover, there are social level messages in the dominant U.S. culture about what it means to be or have an aunt (Sotirin & Ellingson, in press). Hence, perceived cultural norms will influence aunts' and nieces'/nephews'
115 schema for family communication (Koerner & Fitzpatrick, 2002).

Aunts and Kinship

Kinship and Kin Keeping

Garey and Hansen (1998) define kinship as a "system of rights and responsibilities between particular categories of people...'kinship' refers not only to bio-
120 logical or legal connections between people but also to particular positions in a network of relationships" (p. xviii). Cultures vary in the norms for determining who counts as kin, in the rights and responsibilities accorded to various types of kin, and in the degree to

125 which kinship association is voluntary (Wellman, 1998). Kinship networks may also change over time (Garey & Hansen, 1998). Aunts are part of the extended kinship network. Aunts can be either "consanguineal" kin (related biologically) or "affinal" (related
130 through marriage). In some families "fictive" kin are created by inducting people not biologically related into a network of kinship, such as calling one's mother's best friend "aunt" (Stack, 1974).

Researchers have demonstrated that women are the
135 primary "kin keepers" in extended families (Dill, 1998). This suggests the importance of aunts in establishing and maintaining relational bonds with nieces and nephews (Arliss, 1994) and implies that kin keeping is likely part of relationship-type schemas for aunts.
140 Kin keeping has been traditionally associated with feminine roles and remains largely the province of women, despite changing gender roles (Garey & Hansen, 1998). Feminist scholars rendered visible the unpaid work of women—including kin keeping—and
145 acknowledged its importance within a capitalist society that values only paid labor (di Leonardo, 1998). Moreover, feminists have reclaimed women's focus on kin networks as potential sources of personal satisfaction, empowerment, and, at times, vital material and emo-
150 tional resources (Gerstel & Gallagher, 1993). Juggled beside paid employment, housework, and child care, *kin work* involves "the collective labor expected of family centered networks across households and within them" (Stack & Burton, 1998, p. 408). Kin work in-
155 cludes such activities as child and dependent care, wage and nonwage labor, and relationship-maintaining communication, and tasks such as "visits, letters, telephone calls, presents, and cards to kin; the organization of holiday gatherings; the creation and maintenance of
160 quasi-kin relations" (di Leonardo, 1998, p. 420). Leach and Braithwaite (1996) found that kin keeping communication has five primary outcomes: providing information, facilitating rituals, providing assistance, maintaining family relationships, and continuing a previous kin
165 keeper's work.

Kin keepers are most likely to be mothers, aunts, or grandmothers (Leach & Braithwaite, 1996); and of course, mothers and grandmothers are also likely to be aunts within kinship networks. Many kinship studies
170 discuss mothers, grandmothers, and sisters without considering aunting. Rather, kin work is framed in terms of sisterhood or motherhood (e.g., di Leonardo, 1998). Thus the experience and meaning of an aunt's role is implied more than specified in research. Re-
175 search on communication among adult siblings and their spouses implicitly addresses communication with aunts when they focus on women's roles and sister relations (e.g., Cicirelli & Nussbaum, 1989). Given that sibling relationships among parents affect children's
180 perceptions of their relatives, aunts who are emotionally close to a child's parents are likely to be perceived as more integral in the child's experiences of family

life. At the same time, Troll (1985, as cited in Arliss, 1994) points out that conflicts among adult siblings obligate husbands and wives to distance themselves from their siblings, and such "family feuds" negatively impact relationships within the extended family including aunts, nieces, and nephews. Further, adult sisters who may have gone separate ways often become closer as they begin to follow parallel paths in life (marriage, children), providing material and emotional support for each other and renewing familial bonds (Arliss, 1994). Cicirelli and Nussbaum (1989) suggest that the association of women with feminine nurturing and expressiveness leads family members to turn to their sisters for support and aid as adults. This observation implies both the likelihood that aunts will be closer to their nieces and nephews if aunts and mothers find themselves on parallel life paths and that aunts may provide emotional and material support not only for their sisters and other adult family members but for their nieces and nephews as well. Sisters may work to make their respective children close to each other as cousins (di Leonardo, 1998).

Moreover, aunting schemas are likely to reflect other culturally significant female figures. The significance of "othermothers" (Collins, 2000) and "godmothers" in Black, Latino, and Native American child-rearing practices has been recognized and even celebrated and promoted as a model for White, mainstream American culture (see Clinton, 1996). Godmothers also are particularly important in Catholic communities (e.g., Italian-Americans, see di Leonardo, 1984; Mexican-Americans, see Falicov & Karrer, 1980), whose members choose godparents for their child as a crucial aspect of religious and cultural practice (Sault, 2001). Of course, "othermothers" and "godmothers" may or may not overlap the aunt, so despite the increased, often feminist-inspired, attention to such practices, there is not an explicit focus on aunts and aunting per se in this research. So although we may know where aunts are and that they are important within extended family configurations, we do not know much about how they communicatively enact those locations.

One topic in family communication where aunts are explicitly identified are studies of extended family configurations. Studies of extended family roles and practices generally focus on the following three themes: the extended family as a historically, racially, or ethnically identified familial form (the African American urban family, the traditional Latino family, or the immigrant Asian family; e.g., Stack, 1974); mapping extended family configurations (e.g., Galvin, Bylund, & Brommel, 2003) or family histories (e.g., Halsted, 1993); and the extended family as threatened by contemporary patterns of mobility, divorce, and nonfamilial commitments and identifications (Stone, 2000). These themes overshadow the particular communication characteristics and functions (as they constitute relationship-type schemas) of aunt–niece/nephew relationships.

Other types of kinship studies in which aunts appear are kinship foster care, kinship networks for immigrants, and family histories, all of which constitute kin keeping and thus are likely to be reflected in students' relationship schema for aunts. Studies of kinship foster care show that aunts are second only to grandmothers in numbers of kin who function voluntarily (although increasingly regulated and, in some states, compensated) as foster caregivers for children removed from their parents' custody (Davidson, 1997; Thorton, 1991). Research also explores the importance of kinship networks for new immigrants needing financial and social support. For instance, aunts featured prominently in the accounts of Mexican migrant women as they relocated, found work, and established households (Bastida, 2001). Finally, aunts often figure prominently in family stories (Wilmot, 1995), perhaps because family culture and lore are preserved and promulgated primarily by women (Stone, 2000). Stone holds that family stories define the family, providing rules for its enactment, identities for its members, and a shared memory and view of family and the world. For example, women report learning "commonplace" wisdom about relating to men from older women relatives, including aunts (Romberger, 1986).

Our goal in this project is to follow up on the allusions to the aunt in family scholarship by describing nieces' and nephews' family relational schemas for aunts. If kinship is constituted through communication rather than through biological and legal ties (Koerner & Fitzpatrick, 2002), then exploring how aunts are constructed in nieces' and nephews' communication is a good starting point for understanding the meaning of aunts in families. Further, this inquiry may shed light on the issue of choice and voluntary association with extended kin of various types: "Because the American kinship networks are flexible in their expectations, personal preferences can play a key role" in how the meaning of kin ties is negotiated (Johnson, 2000, p. 626). To these ends, we posed our research question: How do nieces and nephews describe communication with their aunts?

Method

Participants

Participants in this study were 70 undergraduate students enrolled in communication courses in a private university in the western U.S., a public university in the northern U.S., Midwest, and a public university in the southeast U.S. Our sample ranged in age from 18 to 27, with the vast majority being between 20 and 22 years of age (median age = 21, M = 21.07). Most participants self-identified as European American or White (n = 51), 4 as Latino/a, 4 as African American, 7 as Asian American, and 1 each as: from Kurdistan, biracial African American and White, Guyanese East Indian, and Ecuadorian Romanian. Most participants (n = 52) were female and 18 were male.

Data Collection and Analysis

Students in four courses were offered extra credit points to write a brief (typed) narrative in response to the statement, "Please describe communicating with one or more of your aunts." We consciously left the parameters of the response open by phrasing the prompt broadly. Participants were also asked to provide their age, sex, and ethnic/racial group. Responses were written outside of class over a 1- to 2-week span and returned to the course instructor.

We collected 70 responses that ranged in length from less than one double-spaced page to four pages, with an average of about two pages (154 pages of data). We used Owen's (1984) criteria for inductively deriving themes in our qualitative data: repetition, recurrence, and forcefulness. Repetition exists when the precise word or phrase is present across the data. Recurrence is present when different wording is used to express similar ideas. The third criterion, forcefulness, includes nonverbal cues that stress words or phrases (e.g., underlining, bolding, or italicizing text, one or more exclamation points, or all-caps for a word or phrase).

Thematic analysis began with the two authors independently reading the narrative data. We noted key words that repeated, recurrent ideas, and forceful words and phrases. We then independently inductively grouped repeated, recurrent, and forceful phrases into a set of preliminary themes. At that point, we discussed our themes and continually refined our inductive categorization until we were confident that our themes were coherent, inclusive, and saturated in data (Fitch, 1994). Finally, because our sample was predominantly female and European American, the first author inspected the responses from males and people of color and reviewed them to determine whether all themes were present and whether other critical ideas emerged within this subset of the data. After careful consideration, we judged that the male responses and person of color responses did not vary collectively from the larger sample, and there were no differences that could be attributed to gender or race. There was as much variation within these groups as there was between groups.

Results

We derived nine content themes from the data and divided them into two groups. The first group of themes focused on aunting roles, such as teacher, role model, confidante, savvy peer, and second mother. The second group focused on aunting practices, such as gifts/treats, maintaining family connections, encouragement, and nonengagement. We contend that these roles and practices collectively reflect nieces' and nephews' relationship-type schema for aunts.

Aunting Roles

Teacher. Participants indicated that their aunts taught them many skills. Aunts taught their niece/nephew everything from how to ride a bike, knit, and cook special meals, to running a successful business and the meaning of religion. Nieces/nephews depicted learning from an aunt as fun, particularly in comparison to school and to learning from parents. An Asian American woman wrote: "The reason why [my aunt] and I became more communicative was because she'd show me how to bake cakes and cookies. And I loved cooking, so this was a fun and good thing for us both." At times, an aunt may teach an appreciation or understanding of something rather than a specific skill or technique, for example, a European American male student reported, "[My aunt] got me started being a fan of Duke basketball, which I still am today." Or it may be appreciation of a serious topic, such as religious faith. As one European American woman student explained: "When I was confused about the Lord and my beliefs, [my aunt] took the time to explain things to me, and why faith is important." Other nieces/nephews described their aunts as preparing them for life by guiding them to become competent adults. One European American woman noted that her aunts "have helped me with a million lessons…. They have taken me college hunting, apartment searching, as well as [on] trips across the country so I could learn and live and see what this big world was made of." We understand teaching as conscious efforts by aunts to instill skills or attitudes in a niece/nephew. The next theme, role model, places more emphasis on nieces'/nephews' agency.

Role model. Aunts function as role models to their nieces/nephews when they serve as examples of how to be in the world. Participants reported that they looked to their aunts as models of proper behavior, religious devotion, wives, mothers, and successful career women. Aunts may embody appropriate or ideal actions, roles, and identities for their nieces and nephews. One European American woman wrote:

> She has been one of my greatest role models. Her work has taken her to many exciting places, and she is now the CEO of a nonprofit charity that offers services to families and children. She has accomplished so much in her life…and she has set a great example for women.

Clearly, this niece will benefit from her aunt's example when she begins her career. Aunts also provide role models for how to be aunts, of course. A European American woman explains how her aunt inspired her to be a good aunt to her niece. In this case, her sister "asked me to be [niece's] godmother…I am going to be the best aunt to that little girl. I hope that I can be as good an aunt to her as [my aunt] was to me." This niece considers her aunt to embody the standard for aunting that the niece wants to reach. The participant's sister's designation of her as a godmother adds a sense of formality and responsibility to the aunt role.

Several participants also noted that aunts can serve as negative role models, reinforcing to nieces/nephews what they do not want to be. One European American woman poignantly explained that she did not want to be like one of her aunts in whom there was

> just always something missing—like she lacked a spirit, or vitality, that I seek in others. My uncle is hilarious—we get along great...but I think he kind of pushes her around. Not literally, but it is very clear who wears the pants in that relationship. I guess I always knew that, even when young, and I have always preferred strong, independent women.

This niece perceives her aunt's submissiveness to a dominating husband as a barrier to her connection with her aunt. The niece does not indicate disapproval of her uncle's behavior, and instead frames her lack of closeness with her aunt as due to her aunt's personality. While we found her placement of blame problematic, clearly the niece believes her aunt has nonetheless served a vital role in her life. That is, watching her aunt's life inspired the niece to think about the kind of woman she wants to be and the type of relationships she wants to have. Another European American woman explains how her aunt went from being a positive to a negative role model: "My aunt was my idol. As a young girl...she represented everything I thought a woman should: Beauty and femininity. In my eyes—she was perfect...[Now] I truly have lost all respect for [her]...." As an adult, this niece understood that feminine behavior she found charming in her aunt as a small child—obsessive attention to hairstyling, makeup, and other beauty regimes at the expense of being fiscally responsible, holding down a job, or maintaining healthy relationships—was irresponsible and reflected consistently poor judgment by her aunt. Clearly, aunts were powerful figures—both positive and negative—to nieces and nephews.

Confidante/advisor. Many participants reported that the aunts with whom they were closest were those to whom they could talk easily, who listened carefully and sympathetically, and were trustworthy. One European American man was confident of his aunt's willingness to listen: "I know that if I ever need advice or financial help or just wanted someone to talk to for fun, my aunt would be absolutely thrilled that I chose her to call." These aunts functioned as important confidantes and sources of good advice. The terms "nonjudgmental" and "open minded" were repeated. The aunt functioned as a safe person to turn to when a mistake had been made or a tough decision needed to be faced, and advice was needed.

A key component of this theme is that nieces/nephews discussed with their aunts topics that they felt they could not approach with their parents. Participants reported that aunts were not as closely tied to them as were their parents, and that this differing relational dynamic enabled aunts to help the niece/nephew without the emotional upheaval expected from their parents. In this sense, the aunt's third-party perspective enabled them to become ideal confidantes. The aunt knew both the niece/nephew and the parent, and hence was in a good position to understand the nature of the problem, the personalities involved, and what steps would best address the problem. This "third-party" perspective was articulated by a European American man who offered an analysis of why he could confide in his aunt:

> I have one small theory on why I'm so close to my aunt. She wasn't immediate family, so when I was introduced to her when I was 11 or so...I got to choose just how much I wanted to accept my aunt. It sort of took the family part out of the equation...I don't trust a lot of people, and I don't really have that many close friends...I mention this because what I share with my aunt is really special.

Likewise, another European American man explained that with his aunt, "Its [sic] almost like talking to a long-distance friend, your [sic] not afraid to really tell them anything because they are not present in your life, yet you still feel comfortable with them when they are around."

Sometimes the problem actually involved one or more parents. "When there is a huge family fight between my mother and I, I would call [my aunt]," explained one Asian American man. Other times, the issues involved sensitive topics. One European American woman explained: "If I need someone to talk to about taboo issues that my mom would slip into cardiac arrest over, I call [my aunt]." Confidante aunts can also be trusted to have integrity. A Latina described her aunt: "I can trust her with my problems— that she'll be empathetic, loving, kind, nonjudgmental...not only will she be wonderful at providing wisdom...she'll also call it like she sees it, whether she thinks I'll like hearing it or not." For this niece, her aunt's willingness to express an unpopular opinion was taken as a sign of her aunt's love and respect for her. While not all aunts fulfilled the role of confidante and advisor, aunts considered by nieces/nephews to be "favorite," "the best," or "the aunt I am closest to" shared this role.

Savvy peer. This theme involves references to an aunt who is closer in age to the respondent than other relatives. This youngest aunt is often the "coolest." That is, the aunt who is closest in age to her nieces/nephews is most often the one who was described as being able to identify with the niece/nephew, being the most fun, giving the best gifts, and being the most able to understand the experiences of the niece/nephew. Age was frequently mentioned as the primary reason why the aunt shared many common interests. A European American man described the nature of his conversations with his young aunt: "[My aunt] is quite a bit younger than my mother is and it seems like our conversations are more about the 'cooler' stuff in my life...she understands the vernacular of kids in their early 20s." For this nephew, his aunt speaks a language that his mother is unable or unwilling to speak. He perceived that he was comprehensible to his aunt because of her biological age. For a Guyanese/East Indian niece, her favorite aunt is much like herself:

525 The reason why I think my aunt is the coolest, is because she is not old fashion[ed] at all: she is outgoing, loves shopping, likes to be in style with the young girls and she fits in well. I also like that she has a lot of energy to keep up with me, we would often go out on Friday and Satur-
530 day night every week, and we don't get home until 5 a.m.

The ability to share common activities brings nieces/nephews closer to younger aunts. Of course, commonalities could also bring nieces and nephews together with older aunts, but participants' descriptions
535 strongly associated age similarity of an aunt with shared views and interests. An Asian American woman contrasted aunts who "are very old and very traditional and so they do not understand some of the things I do" to the youngest of her mother's sisters who "dresses
540 very fashionably and loves to party...I refer to her as my cool aunt who loves to have fun." Such aunts are seen as more like slightly older peers than like parents, and that perception appears to be critical to nieces'/nephews' views of their aunts. Aunts who were
545 kind and nurturing but who did not understand youth culture fit into the next theme, second mother.

Second mother. Participants described their nurturing aunts as a "second mother" and "like another mother to me," and described themselves as like an
550 aunt's child: "I'm her other daughter." A Kurdistan man stated that he often stayed at his aunts' homes where his aunts "were parents to me." An African American male said of one aunt, "I believe she looks at me as another son of her own," and of another aunt,
555 "We spent so much time together that she developed a 'mother's sense' (the sense that a mom 'just knows') and helped me through those tough times." Sometimes the second mother title was literal: the aunt had been instrumental in raising the niece/nephew. For example,
560 one European American woman related that her mother had been an unwed mother and was expected to give up her baby. A week before giving birth, her mother went to her sister's home to stay with her. She says of her mother's sisters: "My mom's sisters are my closest
565 aunts. They had a hand in raising me. They were my second mothers." Other aunts provided childcare for young nieces/nephews. A European American woman recalled that her aunt regularly provided childcare: "[My aunt] is my Godmother, and in a lot of ways, my
570 mother. She took very good care of me when I was a little girl and my mom was at work."

For other nieces/nephews, aunts provided a temporary home in times of trouble during their teen years. A Latina described her aunt's kindness in inviting her
575 niece to live with her "for a short period in high school when I wasn't getting along with my parents.... This was an important time in our relationship...a whole lot of bonding went on." This aunt allowed breathing room for her niece and the niece's parents until their differ-

580 ences could be resolved. For those months, she served as a mother to her niece. An Asian American niece has lived with her aunt throughout high school and college: "She acts on behalf of my mother who lives overseas; she is my guardian.... Basically, I treat her like another
585 mother." One European American male reported that he turned to his aunt for comfort during college:

I am closest to her because she was there for me when I first went away to college. I was homesick and she would pick me up and I would stay weekends at her house....
590 *Every* time I go to her house she makes a gourmet meal.... Whenever I go over to her house that room is "my room," and I love it, I feel like I have a home away from home.

In some ways, the second mother has an easier role
595 than the mother. As one European American woman succinctly put it: "To me, an aunt is like a mom, only they don't have to enforce the rules. They just give you guidance and direction but never have to punish you, so they always stay on your good side." Like the confi-
600 dante, the second mother has the benefit of a third-party perspective. From her position outside the parent–child relationship, she is able to nurture without having to be responsible for many parents' duties, particularly discipline.

Aunting Practices
605 Having explored the roles aunts play in their nieces'/nephews' lives, we now turn to specific practices that emerged in our data as central to participants' perceptions of aunts.

Gifts/treats. Nieces/nephews reported that gifts of-
610 fered tangible evidence of the quality of their relationships with aunts. Participants considered the receiving of holiday and birthday gifts that were appropriate to their age and interests to be signs of a caring aunt. Spontaneous gift giving and/or taking them for special
615 meals, trips, movies, or other activities that parents did not provide often were especially valued. Sometimes, the treat involves special foods; a Latina enthusiastically stated: "Every time I go to visit, she cooks for me—anything I want. She spoils me rotten!" An Asian
620 American male shared this memory of his aunt: "My greatest memory of [my aunt] was when I was still a little boy was when we went to [a local] park.... We would all bike around the park and then go to the museum." Other aunts allowed indulgences that parents
625 presumably did not. One European American female stated that her favorite aunt "often took us out to the movies or out to dinner...and shopping for toys. We went to Lake Tahoe every summer together. She would cook for us every night and let us eat junk food on the
630 beach."

Allowing such tame but "naughty" behavior was seen as a sign of affection and indulgence. Other aunts were prized because they indicated their understanding of a child's point of view, as in this example from a
635 European American man: "I remember going to a fam-

ily Christmas party and [aunt] was so cool, she was the only relative that got my brother and I completely separate gifts." As a little boy, having his own gift was meaningful, and the aunt who provided separate gifts was "cool" because she understood her nephews' desires. Conversely, receiving no gifts or gifts that reflected a lack of understanding of the niece's or nephew's personality (e.g., a doll given to a 16-year-old) were seen as signs of an aunt not caring enough to find out what the child likes.

Maintaining family connections. Aunts were key hubs in the networks of extended family kin. We were intrigued by the fact that virtually all participants—with no prompting—volunteered explanations of how their aunts were related to them through their mother's or father's family and the aunt's position in that family (e.g., younger or older than the participant's parent). For example, one European American man explained that he would discuss "my mother's sister…[my aunt] is the second oldest child in a family of seven. [My aunt] has two female children." Locating the aunt within the constellation of relationships was critical to understanding the relationship to the aunt. That is, as a nonnuclear family member, the aunt had to be accounted for. This is in contrast to participants' mentioning of their parents or siblings, who evidently needed no such kinship contextualization before they could be described.

Family gatherings also helped to maintain relationships. Nieces/nephews described family celebrations (e.g., Christmas, birthdays, Thanksgiving) as primary times for seeing aunts, particularly those who did not live nearby. The sharing of family rituals influenced the relationships of some nieces/nephews to their aunts. A Latina explained: "Tia [Spanish for 'aunt'] is the aunt that I know the best. Our family spent numerous holidays with her family." For others, family gatherings were the only occasions in which they interacted with aunts. Another Latina said of her mother's sister, "While all the other siblings moved on…[my aunt] stayed behind to take care of my grandparents…. I get to see her most because…when I go [to] visit my grandparents, [my aunt] is there." An Asian American woman explained how a family gathering provided her with an opportunity to converse with an aunt: "I went to a family gathering for my grandma's birthday. This was the first one I had gone to in a few years…. I got to talk to my aunt again and amazingly, we had a great conversation." Aunts were often strongly associated with family gatherings, whether as primary organizers of such events or as key participants. One Asian American woman explained that in Hawaii, women in the community, such as neighbors and parents' friends, are addressed as "aunty." She describes one aunty who has been her neighbor "since the day I was brought home from the hospital" as instrumental to organizing gatherings:

[My aunty] maintains very close relationships with all the kids in the cul-de-sac and is known as the "Party Coordinator." Ever since I can remember, Aunty has planned the neighborhood parties for Christmas, Easter, and summer…. So, if someone asked me how many people were in my family, I would not be able to give them an exact number because my family extends beyond my Mom and Dad, it consists of other special people…and aunties like my Aunty [name].

Finally, an African American woman told of attending her great-grandmother's 90th birthday party in a distant state and assumed she was invited to stay with her aunt. Upon her arrival, "I realized that my grandmother and uncle were staying with my great-grandparents, and I had just invited myself to [my aunt's] home…. She just laughed and said it was ok because I'm young and I'm family." Thus, family connections are facilitated by aunts whose presence, cooperation, and (often) hospitality fosters interaction and ritual celebrations among extended kin.

Encouragement. Participants described the aunts they liked as those who were very encouraging to them in school, sports, work, and other activities. Aunts' verbal encouragement appeared to significantly and positively influence nieces'/nephews' self-esteem. Sometimes this encouragement was a sense of being cherished. A Latina participant described her affectionate aunt: "My aunt is also demonstrative with her love for me. Not only does she make herself available when I need her but she lets me know how much she cares with her tender hugs and kisses." An African American nephew characterized aunts as increasing his self-worth: "I think that is the great thing about aunts: They make you feel good about yourself." A European American woman reported how much her aunt increased her self-confidence. She explained: "[My aunt] made me feel like queen of the world. I remember when she gave birth to my cousin Katie. I was only 8 and she let me hold her." By trusting in her niece to behave competently, this aunt demonstrated her faith in her young niece and made her feel special.

At the same time as making nieces/nephews feel good about themselves, aunts provide encouragement to do and be more. An African American man explained that: "My aunts love to 'push' all of their nephews and nieces toward success by any means necessary…. They are also big advocates of higher education. They have pushed my whole life." This participant attributed his educational success in part to his aunts' "pushing," and he valued their role in his success. Likewise, an African American woman explained that "when no one [in] the family thought I should leave home and got [sic] to college, [my aunt] supported the idea of me leaving and recommended it…. She [talked] with the rest of [my] family," and eventually the aunt persuaded her niece's parents to support her plan to attend college. Participants felt inspired by their aunts' belief in them and appreciated their efforts to encourage them in their goals.

Nonengagement. Perhaps one of the most intriguing findings was the unapologetic way in which nieces/nephews expressed a lack of closeness with some aunts. While examples of nonengagement were numerous, participants rarely stated that they perceived the lack of closeness as regrettable or problematic. We propose that this is an important difference between aunting and mothering: in the dominant U.S. culture, reporting that one is not close to one's mother would seem to require some explanation, and perhaps be accompanied by an expression of regret, sadness, or anger. No such feelings are needed for lack of closeness to an aunt. For example, a European American woman stated: "I'm not as close to [my aunts] as I am with my friends or cousins. They just kind of exist as relatives." A Latina described her communication with an aunt as fairly impersonal: "We tend to discuss more general, 'safe' topics rather than anything deeply personal…because I don't feel all that close to her." An Asian American woman reported that "I am not particularly close to any of my aunts, and do not look forward to talking to them. When I do, it is mostly for practical reasons or to be sociable…. This is not because I have a bad relationship with them, but that tends to be how [it is]."

The lack of closeness is just something to be accepted and not worried over. The matter-of-fact attitude toward lack of closeness with some aunts was explained as due to lack of proximity that precluded frequent interaction. A European American man's explanation is representative: "As I was growing up I did not get many opportunities to see her, as I [was]…raised in [another state]. So as a result of this distance, my relationship with [aunt] is not a very close one." Living close to an aunt did not necessarily entail great emotional attachment. However, more frequent interactions with their aunts did seem to relate to perceptions of them as meaningful figures in participants' lives. While geographic distance recurred, no other consistent or cohesive reason was given for not being close to an aunt. Nieces and nephews listed personality traits they disliked, unfortunate events, and family patterns that led to or perpetuated nonengagement, but such justifications were diverse, and we found no pattern among them.

Discussion

The themes reported here illustrate the roles (teacher, role model, confidante, savvy peer, and second mother) and practices (gifts/treats, family gatherings, encouragement, and nonengagement) of aunts as perceived by their nieces and nephews. Participants described how communication (or the lack thereof) with aunts is integral to their self-development and has significant impacts on their relationships and their lives. While the relationship-specific schemas (Koerner & Fitzpatrick's first level of cognitive processing) necessarily varied among the nieces and nephews and the relationships with each of their aunts, central characteristics of a relationship-type schema (second level of Koerner & Fitzpatrick's model) emerged. Taken together, the themes in our data point to four core aspects of a relational schema for aunts.

First, aunts are defined within the kin network but outside of the nuclear family. The biological, marital, and/or fictive relationships that create both connection and "third-party" perspectives for aunts and their nieces/nephews are part of what made aunts powerful in their lives. That is, whether an aunt was wonderful, weird, dull, absent, or unpleasant, her position as nonparent and nonsibling is an integral part of her identity *as an aunt.* Occupying a niche outside the nuclear family enables the aunt to avoid the deep identification, responsibility, and vulnerability of the parent–child bond that (ideally) leads both to closeness and to children's need to rebel to establish their own identity. Perceived vulnerability is a critical factor in an individual's decisions over what information to disclose to others (Petronio, 2002). Thus, it follows that nieces and nephews are likely to feel less vulnerable with aunts than with parents.

Aunts usually are free from the burden of imposing everyday rules, and nieces and nephews need not separate themselves from their aunt in order to establish their independence. Hence, aunts may make ideal confidantes for nieces and nephews who do not wish to discuss sensitive issues with their parents, and fun and indulgent time spent with aunts does not threaten a child's sense of having a stable and secure home. Likewise, lack of attention from an aunt generally is unlikely to wound a child, certainly not to the degree that rejection by a parent would, and a niece's or nephew's choice to not engage with a particular aunt was generally not problematic. Thus to be structurally apart from the nuclear family was to enjoy a greater degree of flexibility in determining the relationship-specific schema for each aunt-niece/nephew relationship. Multiple ways of enacting roles and practices fit within the boundaries of aunt schemas. Unlike motherhood, the successful performance of which generally is circumscribed within the boundaries of a full-time nurturer of children (e.g., Rich, 1977; Trebilcot, 1984), the aunt can be successful as an aunt in a multiplicity of ways. Enacting the role of nurturer (second mother) is acceptable, but so is visiting just once a year, mailing cards or gifts without regular visits, briefly interacting at family gatherings, or engaging in a fun, peer relationship.

Second, the benefits of the relationship are almost entirely unidirectional, focusing on the aunt as fulfilling the needs and desires of the niece or nephew, with no implicit or explicit reciprocity. Nieces and nephews told of learning skills from their aunts but not teaching their aunts, confiding in their aunts but not of being confidantes for them, receiving gifts and encouragement from aunts, but not of giving to them, and so on. From college-age nieces' and nephews' perspective, the role of aunt is that of a giver rather than a receiver of care and support. This phenomenon is likely related to the age difference between nieces and nephews who participated in this study and their aunts; reciprocity may increase over time as nieces and nephews leave college, assume adult responsibilities (e.g., full-time work), and grow older.

Third, the aunt relationship-type schema included passing on of a wide range of knowledge from aunts to nieces and nephews. This knowledge included specific skills, religious beliefs, family lore and traditions, and broader knowledge of the world. Knowledge was transmitted through direct instruction and interpersonal conversations, but also more diffusely through role modeling, such as when nieces/nephews sought to emulate aunts' career paths.

Fourth, when the previous two conditions were met (i.e., aunts focused on the nieces'/nephews' needs, knowledge was passed on), the communication involved in the aunt–niece/nephew relationship fostered (and in turn was fostered by) a sense of closeness to the aunt. The word "close" was invoked again and again to describe participants' feelings toward their aunts. Many emphasized that a close relationship was maintained despite geographical distance, busy schedules, and other obstacles. Aunts with whom the niece or nephew was not engaged (whether by conscious choice or circumstances) were labeled "not close" relationships and accepted as such. The nonengagement of (some) aunts in their nieces' and nephews' lives should not be dismissed as a failure or an unacknowledged kinship tie. Limited, infrequent, or even no contact between aunts, nieces, and nephews is not necessarily negative or a violation of the aunt schema. Nieces and nephews stated their lack of involvement matter of factly, expressing no discomfort about revealing the lack of a close tie with a given aunt.

We posit that these four aspects constitute an exploratory relationship-type schema that may be useful in understanding how nieces and nephews engage in cognitive processing regarding interactions with (and about) their aunts (Koerner & Fitzpatrick, 2002). While there is variation among our participants, there were also several prominent themes that suggest that U.S. culture reflects some shared commonalities in the understandings of and enactment of aunting.

Limitations

This study was limited in several ways. Our participants included a convenience sample of undergraduate students. Families whose members are enrolled in college may have different expectations for aunts than those whose members have not attended college, particularly poor and immigrant communities. Also, the age range of participants reflects one life stage: young adulthood. In some ways, this is an ideal group to study, for whom childhood was recent enough to be easily recalled and for whom going to college made shifts in familial relationships and roles more immediate and evident. However, future research should explore niece/nephew perspectives on aunts across the lifespan. Our findings also reflect predominantly European Americans and females. Clearly, more research is required to locate potential gender and ethnic/racial group understandings of aunts. Finally, the study focused on communication with aunts solely from the perspective of nieces and nephews. Of course, aunts' perspectives must be incorporated into our understanding of aunting in order to construct a more complex rendering of these roles and relationships. Ideally, matched pairs of aunts and nieces or nephews could shed light on how the perceptions of aunts reflect and/or vary from those of their nieces/nephews.

Implications and Conclusion

Several implications of our findings are relevant to research on communication within family and kin networks. First, aunts embody a great deal of flexibility in their enactment of acceptable roles and practices, and we recognize and celebrate flexibility within this gendered construct. Despite changing social gender roles, women's roles in the home and family too often are circumscribed within narrow parameters of appropriate (feminine) behavior (e.g., Coontz, 2000; Wood, 2002). Aunts, nieces, and nephews are making choices of how to communicate together, and we suggest that the range of behavior reported here reflects openness to privileging the needs and desires of each niece/nephew and aunt dyad over those of a perceived social standard. While most of the communication and behavior reported here is hardly radical or unusual, the ability for nieces and aunts to choose a variety of ways of interacting with a variety of aunts reflects a truly transactional definition of a family relationship constituted in interaction rather than dictated by legal or biological ties (Noller & Fitzpatrick, 1993). Such a pseudo-aunt model of flexibility could be instructive or even inspirational to those adapting to new family forms, such as blended families (e.g., Braithwaite, Olson, Golish, Soukup, & Turman, 2001).

Our study also contributes to studies of extended families and kinship. Aunts' kin-keeping work reported here is consistent with previous studies' findings that many women put significant effort into kin keeping (e.g., Dill, 1998). It also suggests that while the recent trend away from studying extended kin may reflect declining interest in maintaining kinship relationships, that also may not be the case. Johnson (2000) proposed that studies that find declining instances of kin keeping may suffer from methodological flaws that focus on sustained interaction and thus fail to consider contemporary means of maintaining close ties over large geographical distances and within increased nuclear family mobility. Our findings support that critique, as our participants clearly recognized and valued aunts' kin-keeping work and participation in rituals, gatherings, and long-distance communication.

980 Our third implication concerns the lack of reciprocity of nieces/nephews toward meeting aunts' needs or desires. We believe that the almost complete lack of reciprocity reported is a function of the age of our participants. As college students, they appear to have not 985 yet assumed the role expectations of adults, and remain self-focused, as is characteristic of children. Preliminary data analysis of interviews with aunts, nieces, and nephews indicates that at least some adult nieces and nephews feel an obligation and/or take pleasure in ma-990 terially and emotionally giving to their aunts (Sotirin & Ellingson, 2006). Some research has shown cultural differences in this area of kinship; in African American families, for example, nieces and nephews were considered by their elderly aunts and uncles to be impor-995 tant family members and the latter reported receiving assistance from them, while elderly Whites reported no expectations of assistance from siblings' children (Johnson & Barer, 1995). Clearly, more research is needed on how aunt–niece/nephew relationships 1000 change over time.

Finally, we note that none of the participants mentioned popular culture images of aunts. Given Koerner and Fitzpatrick's (2002) position that cultural messages about relationships influence the formation and main-1005 tenance of family relationship schemas, we anticipated that nieces and nephews might compare their aunts to popular figures, perhaps claiming that an aunt was cruel like *Harry Potter's* Aunt Petunia or very kind and maternal, like *Andy Griffith's* Aunt Bea. Such was not 1010 the case, indicating that at least in this exploratory study nieces and nephews made no conscious associations between their own experiences with aunts and those in the media. Future research should seek to determine what, if any, relationships exist between rela-1015 tionship-type schemas for aunts and cultural messages about aunts.

Our findings support the value of inquiry into aunts, family relationship schemas, and kin keeping. While the practices and functions of family communication 1020 and kinship may be changing, extended family such as aunts remain vital aspects of many people's lives. As Gerstel and Gallagher (1993) suggest, "contemporary extended family does not simply persist. Someone expends a great deal of time and energy to maintain it" 1025 (p. 598). That many aunts, nieces, and nephews are expending time and energy with each other is significant to our scholarly understanding of contemporary extended family networks and certainly warrants further study.

References

Arliss, L. P. (1994). *Contemporary family communication: Meanings and messages*. New York: St. Martin's Press.

Bastida, E. (2001). Kinship ties of Mexican migrant women on the United States/Mexico border. *Journal of Comparative Family Studies, 32*, 549–569.

Braithwaite, D. O., Olson, L. N., Golish, T. D., Soukup, C., & Turman, P. (2001). "Becoming a family": Developmental processes represented in blended family discourse. *Journal of Applied Communication Research, 29*, 221–247.

Cicirelli, V., & Nussbaum, J. (1989). Relationships with siblings in later life. In J. Nussbaum (Ed.), *Life-span communication: Normative processes* (pp. 283–299). Hillsdale, NJ: Lawrence Erlbaum.

Clinton, H. (1996). *It takes a village: And other lessons children teach us*. New York: Simon & Schuster.

Collins, P. H. (2000). *Black feminist thought: Knowledge, consciousness and the politics of empowerment*. New York: Routledge.

Coontz, S. (2000). *The way we never were: American families and the nostalgia trap* (revised ed.). New York: Basic Books.

Davidson, B. (1997). Service needs of relative caregivers: A qualitative analysis. *Families in Society, 78*, 502–510.

di Leonardo, M. (1984). *The varieties of ethnic experience: Kinship, class, and gender among California Italian-Americans*. Ithaca, NY: Cornell University Press.

di Leonardo, M. (1998). The female world of cards and holidays: Women, families, and the work of kinship. In K. V. Hansen & A. I. Garey (Eds.), *Families in the U.S.: Kinship and domestic politics*. Philadelphia: Temple University Press.

Dill, B. T. (1998). Fictive kin, paper sons, compadrazgo: Women of color and the struggle for family survival. In K. V. Hansen & A. I. Garey, (Eds.), *Families in the U.S.: Kinship and domestic politics* (pp. 431–445). Philadelphia, PA: Temple University Press.

Falicov, C. J., & Karrer, B. M. (1980). Cultural variations in the family life cycle: The Mexican-American family. In E. A. Carter & M. McGoldrick (Eds.), *The family life cycle: A framework for family therapy* (pp. 383–425). New York: Gardner Press.

Fitch, K. L. (1994). Criteria for evidence in qualitative research. *Western Journal of Communication, 58*, 32–38.

Fitzpatrick, M. A., & Vangelisti, A. L. (Eds.). (1995). *Explaining family interactions*. Thousand Oaks, CA: Sage Publications.

Galvin, K. M., Bylund, C. L., & Brommel, B. J. (2003). *Family communication: Cohesion and change*. Boston, MA: Allyn & Bacon.

Galvin, P. J., & Cooper, P. J. (2000). *Making connections: Readings in relational communication*. Los Angeles: Roxbury.

Garey, A. I., & Hansen, K. V. (1998). Introduction: Analyzing families with a feminist sociological imagination. In K. V. Hansen & A. I. Garey (Eds.), *Families in the U.S.: Kinship and domestic politics* (pp. xv–xxi). Philadelphia, PA: Temple University Press.

Gerstel, N., & Gallagher, S. K. (1993). Kin keeping and distress: Gender, recipients of care, and work–family conflict. *Journal of Marriage and the Family, 55*, 598–607.

Halsted, I. (1993). *The aunts*. Boston, MA: Sharksmouth Press.

Hansen, K. V., & Garey, A. I. (1998). *Families in the U. S.: Kinship and domestic politics*. Philadelphia, PA: Temple University Press.

Johnson, C. L. (2000). Perspectives on American kinship in the later 1990s. *Journal of Marriage and the Family, 62*, 623–639.

Johnson, C. L., & Barer, B. M. (1995). Childlessness in late life: Comparisons by race. *Journal of Cross Cultural Gerontology, 9*, 289–306.

Jorgenson, J. (1989). Where is the "family" in family communication?: Exploring families' self-definitions. *Journal of Applied Communication Research, 17*, 27–41.

Koerner, A. F., & Fitzpatrick, M. A. (2002). Toward a theory of family communication. *Communication Theory, 12*, 70–91.

Leach, M. S., & Braithwaite, D. O. (1996). A binding tie: Supportive communication of family kin keepers. *Journal of Applied Communication Research, 24*, 200–216.

Noller, P., & Fitzpatrick, M. A. (1993). *Communication in family relationships*. Englewood Cliffs, NJ: Prentice Hall.

O'Reilly, A., & Abbey, S. (Eds.). (2000). *Mothers and daughters*. Lanham, MD: Rowman & Littlefield.

Owen, W. F. (1984). Interpretive themes in relational communication. *Quarterly Journal of Speech, 70*, 274–287.

Peington, B. A. (2004). The communicative management of connection and autonomy in African American and European American mother-daughter relationships. *Journal of Family Communication, 4*, 3–34.

Petronio, S. (2002). *The boundaries of privacy: Dialectics of disclosure*. New York: SUNY Press.

Rich, A. (1977). *Of woman born: Motherhood as experience and institution*. New York: Bantam Books.

Romberger, B. V. (1986). "Aunt Sophie always said....": Oral histories of the commonplaces women learned about relating to men. *American Behavioral Scientist, 29*, 342–367.

Rosenthal, C. S. (1985). Kin keeping in the familial division of labor. *Journal of Marriage and the Family, 47*, 965–974.

Sault, N. L. (2001). Godparenthood ties among Zapotec women and the effects of Protestant conversion. In J. W. Dow & A. R. Sandstrom (Eds.), *Holy saints and fiery preachers: The anthropology of Protestantism in Mexico and Central America* (pp. 117–146). Westport, CT: Praeger.

Sotirin, P., & Ellingson, L. L. (2006). The "other" woman in family life: Aunt/niece/nephew communication. In K. Floyd & M. Morman (Eds.), *Under-studied family relationships* (pp. 81–99). Thousand Oaks, CA: Sage Publications.

Sotirin, P., & Ellingson, L. L. (in press). Rearticulating the aunt in popular culture. *Cultural Studies.*

Stack, C. (1974). *All our kin.* New York: BasicBooks.

Stack, C. B., & Burton, L. M. (1998). Kinscripts. In K. V. Hansen & A. I. Garey (Eds.), *Families in the U.S.: Kinship and domestic politics* (pp. 405–415). Philadelphia, PA: Temple University Press.

Stone, L. (2000). *Kinship and gender: An introduction.* Boulder, CO: Westview Press.

Thorton, J. (1991). Permanency planning for children in kinship foster homes. *Child Welfare, 5,* 593–601.

Traeder, T., & Bennett, J. (1998). *Aunties: Our older, cooler, wiser friends.* Berkeley, CA: Wildcat Canyon Press.

Trebilcot, J. (Ed.). (1984). *Mothering: Essays in feminist theory.* Lanham, MD: Rowman & Littlefield.

Troll, L. E. (1985). *Early and middle adulthood.* Pacific Grove, CA: Brooks/Cole.

Wellman, B. (1998). The place of kinfolk in personal community networks. In K. V. Hansen & A. I. Garey (Eds.), *Families in the U.S.: Kinship and domestic politics* (pp. 231–239). Philadelphia, PA: Temple University Press.

Wilmot, W. (1995). The relational perspective. In *The relational communication reader* (pp. 1–12). New York: McGraw-Hill.

Wood, J. T. (2002). "What's a family, anyway?" In J. Stewart (Ed.), *Bridges not walls: A book about interpersonal communication* (pp. 375–383). New York: McGraw-Hill.

Address correspondence to: Laura L. Ellingson, Communication Department, Santa Clara University, Santa Clara, CA 95053. E-mail: lellingson@scu.edu

Exercise for Article 36

Factual Questions

1. According to the literature review, how is the term "kinship" defined?

2. What is the research question posed by the researchers?

3. What was the median age of the participants?

4. Of the 70 participants, how many were female?

5. In analyzing the data, the researchers used Owen's (1984) criteria. What were the criteria?

6. What is a key component of the theme of "confidante/advisor"?

Questions for Discussion

7. The researchers refer to themselves as "feminist researchers." Speculate on the meaning of this term. (See lines 34–35.)

8. The sample was heterogeneous in terms of racial and ethnic background. If you had conducted this study would you have used a heterogeneous sample or a homogeneous one (e.g., only European

Americans)? (See lines 289–294, 327–337, and 926–929.)

9. Is it important to know that the researchers *independently* read and *independently* grouped responses into themes? Explain. (See lines 318–323.)

10. The researchers used a "convenience sample." What is your understanding of the meaning of this term? Could the fact that it was a convenience sample affect the validity of the results? Explain. (See lines 913–915.)

11. What is your opinion on the researchers' suggestion for using matched pairs of aunts and nieces or nephews in future research on this topic? (See lines 934–937.)

12. If you had planned this study, would you have opted to use qualitative *or* quantitative methodology (*or* both)? Explain.

Quality Ratings

Directions: Indicate your level of agreement with each of the following statements by circling a number from 5 for strongly agree (SA) to 1 for strongly disagree (SD). If you believe an item is not applicable to this research article, leave it blank. Be prepared to explain your ratings. When responding to criteria A and B below, keep in mind that brief titles and abstracts are conventional in published research.

A. The title of the article is appropriate.

  SA   5   4   3   2   1   SD

B. The abstract provides an effective overview of the research article.

  SA   5   4   3   2   1   SD

C. The introduction establishes the importance of the study.

  SA   5   4   3   2   1   SD

D. The literature review establishes the context for the study.

  SA   5   4   3   2   1   SD

E. The research purpose, question, or hypothesis is clearly stated.

  SA   5   4   3   2   1   SD

F. The method of sampling is sound.

  SA   5   4   3   2   1   SD

G. Relevant demographics (for example, age, gender, and ethnicity) are described.

  SA   5   4   3   2   1   SD

H. Measurement procedures are adequate.

      SA   5   4   3   2   1   SD

I. All procedures have been described in sufficient detail to permit a replication of the study.

      SA   5   4   3   2   1   SD

J. The participants have been adequately protected from potential harm.

      SA   5   4   3   2   1   SD

K. The results are clearly described.

      SA   5   4   3   2   1   SD

L. The discussion/conclusion is appropriate.

      SA   5   4   3   2   1   SD

M. Despite any flaws, the report is worthy of publication.

      SA   5   4   3   2   1   SD

Article 37

The Voices of Black and White Rural Battered Women in Domestic Violence Shelters

APRIL L. FEW

Virginia Polytechnic Institute and State University

ABSTRACT. Very little research has examined the experiences of black and white rural battered women. In this exploratory study of 88 participants, 30 rural battered women who sought assistance from domestic violence shelters in southwest Virginia were interviewed. Black and white rural women's experiences in the shelters, helpseeking, and perceived social support during and after their stay in the shelter were compared. Future research directions and suggestions to improve services are presented.

From *Family Relations, 54*, 488–500. Copyright © 2005 by the National Council on Family Relations. Reprinted with permission.

Background and Significance: Rurality and Domestic Violence

According to the U.S. Census Bureau (2000), more than 24% of U.S. residents live in rural areas. However, despite an increasing body of research on domestic violence, few research studies focus on domestic
5 violence in rural settings (Van Hightower, Gorton, & DeMoss, 2000). Much of the research on battered women is conducted with samples from urban and college populations, rendering the experiences of rural battered women practically invisible (Van Hightower
10 & Gorton, 2002; Van Hightower, Gorton, & DeMoss, 2000; Websdale, 1995, 1998). This lack of attention to domestic violence in rural communities may result, in part, from existing perceptions and myths about the "idyllic, tranquil, and nonviolent life in rural communi-
15 ties" (Krishnan, Hilbert, & Pase, 2001, p. 2). Yet research debunks this myth and has consistently found that domestic violence is as prevalent in rural areas as it is in urban areas (Websdale, 1995).

Scholarship on domestic violence in rural areas is
20 necessary as there is some evidence that women in rural contexts face unique barriers in terms of accessing help. Beliefs and values are elements of the rural culture that impact women's experience with violence as well as their helpseeking practices. For example,
25 domestic violence research in rural Kentucky (Websdale, 1995, 1998) and rural Appalachia (Gagne, 1992) indicates that residents of rural communities generally hold patriarchal views of the family, tradi-

tional sex-role ideologies, strong religious values, and
30 conventional beliefs about privacy. These beliefs, rules, and values, in turn, promote gender inequality, failure to report incidents to police, and potentially undermine intervention when it does occur (Websdale, 1998; Wendt, Taylor, & Kennedy, 2002).

35 In addition to challenges in rural life with regard to values and beliefs that make it difficult for rural battered women to seek help, rural battered women also often face logistic barriers. Rural residence is an isolating factor that can reduce access to domestic violence
40 services and contribute to the perpetuation of battering (Van Hightower et al., 2000). Physical isolation can allow battering to go on without neighbors being aware of the violence, and access to services can be challenging in rural areas where shelters may be located many
45 miles away from the battered wife who seeks services.

The overall inattention given to domestic violence in rural settings extends to minority women. This is a particularly glaring omission, given that blacks are the largest minority group (i.e., 4.1 million) living in rural
50 areas, and rural counties with high concentrations of blacks frequently are characterized by a greater degree of economic disadvantage, higher rates of family violence, and lower availability of and access to community services than white rural counties (Whitener, Jen,
55 & Kassel, 2004).

For black women in rural communities, racial status in and of itself can be an isolating factor contributing to their victimization and further compromising intervention. For example, McNair and Neville (1996) sug-
60 gested that institutional racism and blacks' historical distrust of social services and mental health facilities were reasons for blacks' underuse of the domestic violence shelters. In addition, Wilson, Cobb, and Dolan (1987) found that rural black women were often un-
65 aware that domestic violence shelters even existed in their community. They conducted a study to assess a domestic violence shelter's success in reaching black clients in rural Virginia communities. They surveyed black workshop participants and found that 70% of the
70 respondents reported that they did not know about the existence of a local domestic violence shelter, yet 95%

reported either having experienced or knowing some-one who had experienced domestic violence.

The Importance of Domestic Violence Shelters

Research indicates that shelters are beneficial for many women and shelter stays dramatically reduce the likelihood of new violence (Berk, Newton, & Berk, 1986; Davis & Srinivasan, 1995; Roberts & Lewis, 2000). Battered women have also credited shelters for helping them secure employment, further their educa-tion, and lead healthier lives (Brown, Reedy, Fountain, Johnson, & Dichiser, 2000; Gordon, 1996). Shelter staff is credited for providing a safe environment, ef-fectively manning crisis telephone lines, maintaining emotional ties to and community resources for former residents, and training other professionals who service battered women (Davis, Hagan, & Early, 1994; John-son, Crowley, & Sigler, 1992; Tutty, Weaver, & Roth-ery, 1999).

For many women and their children, shelters pro-vide a reprieve from the violence in their lives. Domes-tic violence shelters seem to be a primary resource for women seeking safety from violent intimate partners (Tutty et al., 1999), yet very few studies examine the efficacy of domestic violence shelters in assisting rural battered women to make the transition back into their communities and families (Van Hightower & Gorton, 2002; Websdale, 1998). Further, as previously noted, very little is known about black battered women in rural communities who seek shelter. There is some evidence that abused black women may seek help more frequently from their social support networks (i.e., family and friends) before seeking help from police or shelters (Few & Bell-Scott, 2002; West, 2003). Thus, it seems that the nuances of rural social life are linked to the underuse of shelters (Websdale, 1995, 1998). There is also concern that for black rural women, racism can be an additional isolating factor contributing to this underuse (McNair & Neville, 1996). In their effort to increase the participation of black clients in domestic violence shelters, Wilson et al. (1987) reported that culturally specific training and community volunteers were key in bridging the gap between shelters and black communities. Respondents described the shelter staff and community volunteers as credible transmitters of information about alternatives to domestic violence and positive role models because they shared similar (e.g., racial/ethnic, rurality) background and personal experiences. These studies highlight how race/ethnicity matters in the rural context in terms of accessibility to community resources and personal empowerment.

Study Purpose: Using a Feminist Lens

Feminist scholars have underlined the importance of linking the personal with the political in research and advocacy (Jackson, 1998; Young, 1997). From a feminist perspective, the choices made by abused women are political acts, and their personal narratives are political testimonies. Both Harding (1987) and Thompson (1992) have suggested that feminist re-search is done for women and "acknowledges women as active agents in their own lives, even if not within the conditions of their own making" (Thompson, p. 6). Harding also asserted that our research questions need to come out of women's experiences; thus, using the experiences of women within research should allow women to understand themselves and provide them with the explanations and insights that they need to become more self-empowered.

Feminist theory is particularly applicable to the pre-sent study because it emphasizes how structural and cultural contexts inform the social construction of gen-der and advocate for policies and programs that are responsive to women's needs and interests (Thompson & Walker, 1995). A feminist framework informs our understanding of the rural context in which abused women have to negotiate and the barriers to receiving help that are inherent in such a context. Further, femi-nism contextualizes women's helpseeking and shelter experiences. Helpseeking can be viewed as a dimen-sion of coping used to deal with personal and emo-tional crises, buffering the negative effects of traumatic life events (Kaukinen, 2002). It may include talking to family, friends, police, and shelter hotlines to process a crisis.

One aim of the present study was to learn more about how women seek help, reflect back on their ex-periences, and generate ideas that can help abused women facing similar challenges to transition more successfully out of the shelter. A second aim of the present study was to explore "shelter culture" in greater depth. Shelter culture encompasses the extent to which shelter staff followed standard operating procedures and helped the women feel safe, and also includes cul-tural differences that might have emerged and caused conflict among the staff and residents. For example, I wondered if rural ethnic women felt isolated in the shelter because other ethnic women were not present in the shelter, if resource materials offered reflected eth-nic women and their social networks, or if ethnic women experienced overt or covert racism by staff or other residents. I was also curious as to whether ethnic women had difficulty negotiating the politics of inter-sectionality (i.e., race, class, gender, region, age) while existing in a vulnerable state—healing from the vio-lence in their lives. In this descriptive study, a forum is provided for women to share their interpretations of experiences in shelters and in their communities and to provide suggestions to improve shelter services for future patrons. It is in this sense, by sharing parts of their lives, that study participants are indeed activists.

Research Questions

The present study explores domestic violence and shelter culture through descriptions of black and white rural women's helpseeking practices and experiences in shelters in hopes of assisting human service provid-

ers in constructing and augmenting intervention programs to better accommodate the needs of diverse,
185 rural, battered women. Through a feminist lens, the personal narratives of 30 women were interpreted to discern similarities and differences in two contexts—outside and within the shelter environment.

The following research questions guided the study:

190   1. Are there differences in how black and white battered rural women seek and receive help from their social networks and community?
    2. How do battered rural women describe their experiences in domestic violence shelters?
195   3. What are battered rural women's perceptions of the efficacy of shelter staff and services?

Method

Procedures

Eighteen shelters in southwest Virginia were contacted to request their assistance with this project. Fourteen of 18 domestic violence shelters agreed to
200 participate and to have caseworkers or other staff personnel solicit current and former residents to participate in our project.

Interview procedures. Shelter caseworkers were given a brief description of the study and instructions
205 to read to women who might be interested in participating in this study. The caseworkers notified the research team when women agreed to be interviewed and scheduled the interviews with the women to take place at the shelter. In this way, the caseworkers were able to
210 control our access to women and any disruption to the daily routines of staff and residents. Thirty women were interviewed for at least 2 hr. A semistructured list of questions guided the interview. The questions addressed helpseeking behaviors, experiences in the shel-
215 ter environment, and suggestions to improve the efficacy of shelters in assisting the women to transition back into the community and their families.

The research team, which consisted of the author and trained graduate students, interviewed women only
220 after they signed a consent form and completed a survey that assessed the types of violence the women received from their abusive partners, social support they received, coping (included helpseeking) strategies used, and their shelter experiences. This particular pa-
225 per focuses only on women's interview narratives and the qualitative findings regarding helpseeking strategies and shelter experiences. For the safety of the researchers and the women, all but one of the interviews were held in a private room at the shelter (we inter-
230 viewed one woman who was bedridden at her home). Shelter staff were not present in the room during interviews. Most of the women preferred to be interviewed alone. However, in keeping with a feminist epistemology that was responsive to the needs of our participants
235 (e.g., Ramazanoglu & Holland, 2002), we also interviewed women in three focus groups that were composed of three or four women. The women interviewed

in groups tended to have transportation issues, mandated appointments, or work that would prevent par-
240 ticipation longer than 2 hr. The same interview protocol was followed for the focus groups. We limited the size of focus groups with the intention of facilitating the transcription process and being respectful of time constraints of the women. The women reported com-
245 fort in being interviewed in groups because the experience was similar in format to their resident support groups.

The interview protocol consisted of questions that asked the participants to recall (a) their family of ori-
250 gin, current family, and intimate partner histories; (b) substance abuse or mental health histories; (c) incidences of intimate partner violence; (d) helpseeking strategies; (e) community response; (f) shelter experiences; (g) and their own suggestions for how shelters
255 could improve their transition back into the community. Examples of questions are "How did you make the decision to go to the shelter?" "From whom did you seek help while you were in the relationship with your partner?" "What things hindered your decision to go to
260 the shelter?" "What things do you think the shelter could do that would help you adjust (get back on your feet) once you leave the shelter?"

All women who completed an interview received a stipend of $20.00. Directly after each interview, the
265 researcher's reactions to the dynamics of participant–researcher interactions and salient issues were audiotaped and later integrated into the researcher's journal. Each interview was transcribed by students in the office of the author and reviewed by the author for accu-
270 racy.

We asked participants to complete the survey before the interview so that they could begin thinking about helpseeking, shelter culture, and messages family and friends communicated to them about shelters be-
275 fore participating in the interview.

Study Design and Qualitative Data Analysis

The overall approach of the study was exploratory and qualitative. As mentioned above, a survey was administered to residents and former residents of 14 shelters during a 16-month time period in order to
280 compare the shelter experiences and helpseeking strategies of black and white rural women. Women were solicited and identified by shelter staff to participate, and those women would often recommend other residents to participate while we were at the interview
285 site. Interviewing ceased upon saturation (i.e., nothing really new was being introduced in response to the interview questions) (Glaser & Strauss, 1967). The strengths of qualitative research are derived from its inductive approach, its focus on specific context and
290 people, and its emphasis on personal narratives (Maxwell, 1996). Although the emphasis on context limits generalization, a major goal of quantitative research, the qualitative approach provides thick, rich descrip-

tions of the participant's interpretations of the phenomenon being studied in specific contexts or social settings (Janesick, 1994).

With the greater acceptance of postmodern research methods, personal narratives are now seen as a valid means of knowledge production (Reissman, 1993). Narratives are integral to understanding culture because culture is constituted through the "ensemble of stories we tell about ourselves" (Plummer, 1995, p. 5). Whether it is in the community, marketplace, or home, culture shapes how individuals interpret their world and talk about their "places" in it (Berg, 1998; Fraser, 2004).

The present study appropriately utilizes personal narrative, via interview, as cultural representation in an attempt to understand the context of woman abuse within rural culture and shelter life. Indeed, methodologists note the importance of telling and listening to stories through narrative interviews as a means of understanding culture and experience (Narayan & George, 2001). Additionally, interviews are critical tools for "the developing of new frameworks and theories based on women's lives and women's formulations" (Anderson & Jack, 1991, p. 18). By entering into dialogue with others, narrative interviewers may unearth hidden or subordinated ideas (Borland, 1991). Thus, the findings produced may lead to the development of new theories that relate more with people's lives (Hyden, 1994).

Interviews were analyzed using a form of modified analytic induction (Gilgun, 1995; Patton, 2002). Inductive, rather than deductive, reasoning is involved, allowing for modification of concepts and relationships between concepts to occur throughout the process of doing research, with the goal of most accurately representing the reality of the situation. There are basically six steps to analytic induction. These are:

1. A research topic is defined in a tentative manner.
2. A hypothesis is developed about it.
3. A single instance is considered to determine if the hypothesis is confirmed.
4. If the hypothesis fails to be confirmed, either themes are redefined or the hypothesis is revised so as to include the instance examined.
5. Additional cases are examined and, if the new hypothesis is repeatedly confirmed, some degree of certainty about the hypothesis results.
6. Each negative case requires that the hypothesis be reformulated until there are no exceptions to identified themes.

Analyses are tentative and provisional throughout the study and only become comprehensive once the data are completely collected.

A list of markers to sensitize us to indicators of helpseeking and shelter experiences (featuring our preselected concepts) was developed from a review of the literature. Each transcript was read four times and coded independently by the research team using NVivo qualitative software. Interview transcripts, interviewer notes, coding lists, and entries from the author's journal were triangulated in order to identify and confirm inconsistencies, salient issues, and patterns. Participant's statements for inconsistencies, contradictions, and omissions were scrutinized by a line-by-line process in NVivo. Independent coding allowed for the isolation of subcategories and the reintegration or creation of density in the data by focusing on relationships between categories (Strauss, 1987). If, for example, participants' narratives about their experiences were incongruent with markers identified in the literature, we would have made a revision of the major categories.

Findings

Participants

The interview sample. Ten black women and 20 white women agreed to be interviewed at their local shelters. Eight of the 10 black women interviewed came from a town with a higher black population than many counties in southwest Virginia (U.S. Census Bureau, 2000). With the exception of one, all participants' income fell under $10,000. Only one of the women had a bachelor's degree. The majority of women ($n = 26$, $M = 2.16$, $SD = 1.17$) had at least one child. Eight women were married, 13 women were divorced or in the process of divorcing, and 9 women were never-married cohabitants.

Women's Ways of Helpseeking

Only 5 of 30 women interviewed ($n = 3$ black, $n = 2$ white) reported that they had prior knowledge that a shelter existed in their community at the time of deciding to leave their abusive partners. Women sought community assistance in leaving their abusive partners mainly from the police, family, friends, and from a doctor in the emergency room. Many of the women were sidetracked from seeking help from the local shelter by abusive partners feeding them misinformation about who used shelters and what shelter life would be like.

The police. The majority of white women interviewed ($n = 12$) reported that the police recommended the local shelter to them after responding to their domestic violence calls. In contrast, only 2 black women reported being told about a local shelter at the time of police response. Several black and white women reported that they did not initially telephone the police themselves for help. As one woman stated, "I was ashamed. Who wants to admit your ass is being kicked by your husband?" Rather, it seemed that for those women who were not surrounded by extended kin, unrelated neighbors were most likely to call the police.

Some women found that the police could be helpful in providing a temporary respite from their abusive partners. Half of the women ($n = 15$), all white, reported using the police to threaten their partner. None of the black women reported that the police could be

405 used as a vehicle for temporary safety or as a kind of "weapon" against their abusive partner.

It was not surprising that black and white women did discuss how geographic isolation may have contributed to poor police response. For instance, Char-
410 lotte, a 26-year-old white woman, talked about how the geographic isolation gave her a feeling that her community had a lawless quality:

> [My town] is way out. It's maddening to me. It's out far enough so that the law doesn't bother you. I can tell a
415 dozen people driving around with no license, drunk half the time and fighting with each other—men, women. There's no patrolling. There's nothing…. Help comes too late or not at all.

White women were more likely than black women
420 to live outside city limits. However, black women reported feeling isolated in predominantly black neighborhoods because those areas were not regularly policed.

When speaking of the police as a source for help,
425 most of the women, black and white, reported that the perpetrator was either told to "walk away" or was arrested at the scene but later released after the women failed to file charges. Only 8 women spoke in positive terms about the police. Three white women mentioned
430 that they were given brochures about domestic violence and a local shelter by the police. Two women's stories particularly emphasized their negative experiences with the police. Tamara, a 48-year-old, bedridden white woman whose ex-husband was a police officer, shared:

435 > None of the police round here are any good. They all abusers themselves like my ex-husband. There's no use in calling them because nobody takes those calls seriously. Especially when the call is made from the house of one of their own.

440 Yvette, a 43-year-old black woman, shared her harrowing experience of waiting for police response:

> I was beaten until my head swoll the size of a watermelon. I was unrecognizable. I knew I was gonna die. The Devil blinked and I was able to get to a phone. I di-
445 aled 911…. I left the phone off the hook so they had everything on tape from the last 20, 30 minutes, and they stayed outside of my mobile home for 20 minutes…. This man only got a knife, and they had to wait until four, five carloads of police to come…. And that's when I lost trust
450 in the police department because I almost died. My own child couldn't recognize me. And they were just sitting out there. Now I see that they're ready to solve a murder case. Yeah, but not a domestic violence thing.

Yvette stated that the police finally arrested the
455 abusive partner after she managed to crawl out of the mobile home herself. She also believed that poor police response to abused black rural women was a common thing in her area. Black women in her focus group all nodded their heads in agreement. Black women talked
460 about feeling like victims of racial discrimination by white police officers. White participants in the study more commonly discussed gender discrimination when

describing their perceptions of sexist attitudes on the part of police officers.

465 *Support from family and friends.* Black women were more likely than white women to report that family and friends were more helpful than the police. Black women were also more likely to learn of local shelters through family and friends than through the
470 police. Nine of the 10 black participants in the study reported that family members were likely to provide temporary shelter before recommending that they go to the police station for more help. Only 5 white women reported that family and friends were primary sources
475 of help. For the most part, white women were more likely to be geographically separated from their families and surrounded by the extended kin of the abusive partner. The majority of white women reported being estranged from their own families because either their
480 families did not like the abusive partner or the women had previously left their families of origin to escape family violence (e.g., incest, physical and psychological abuse) or multigenerational alcoholism. Many white women spoke of being ostracized by the com-
485 munity if they left their abusive partners. Lauren, a 24-year-old white woman reported:

> The Bible says we's supposed to stay together and for a long time. I had no place else to go. His kin surrounded me in the hollow. I would run to them when he beat me
490 and they acted like nothin' was wrong. People in church knew I was being beaten. No one said a thing but for us to stay together. Stay. I felt if I left, I'd be letting everybody down.

Those women who described themselves as reli-
495 gious seemed to have difficulty leaving a marital partner. Leaving was a difficult decision because they were raised to believe that marriages were supposed to last forever. Some thought that leaving their marital partners was "almost sacrilegious" and that their actions of
500 breaking up the family would be viewed that way by their close-knit communities. It is not surprising that some of the more religious women, particularly white women, felt isolated even within their church communities.

Misled by Partners

505 Women in the study were asked about their initial thoughts regarding domestic violence shelters as a primary help seeking strategy. Many of the women reported feeling a little anxious about using a shelter because of the stories they were told about shelters. Nine
510 white women and 1 black woman stated that they were misled, usually by their abusive partners, family members, and in-laws, about what to expect in the environment and the kind of women who resided in domestic violence shelters. For instance, Katie, a 26-year-old
515 white woman said:

> My husband just told me lies. He knew I wasn't well-educated and stuff…. He said that you wouldn't have

520 your privacy. They'd be constantly going through your things. They could walk right in on you through the night. They'd rape me and my daughter. He would tell me these things to keep me with him. I understand that now.

525 Joan, a 37-year-old white woman, told a similar story of how her partner kept her from seeking help from a shelter: "When my boyfriend found out that I was coming here, he said 'the women that stay there are whores and there are men…men hang out over there at the park waiting for [the women] to come out.'"

530 Like Katie and Joan, all of the women interviewed reported that they did not know exactly what to expect when they first entered the shelter. Black women were more likely to state that shelters were not discussed by family and that domestic violence was considered "un-535 suitable conversation" or "dirty laundry." For these black women, the shelter was "the last resort" as long as there was family present and willing to get involved.

The Shelter Experience

Interviews revealed five main themes about partici-540 pants' shelter experiences: (a) the shelter was a safe haven from intimate violence; (b) racial or cultural differences were not significant detractors from a satisfactory experience; (c) shelter residents and staff became a new family in this stressful time; (d) shelter 545 residents experienced a positive, supportive relationship with shelter staff; and (e) shelter residents were highly satisfied with shelter service efficacy.

A safe haven. The women were asked to talk about their experience in the shelter. White women reported 550 staying at the shelter longer and requesting extensions more often than black women. All but two women stated that they immediately felt safe once they entered the shelter. One middle-aged white woman revealed, "They showed me my room and once my head hit the pillow, I slept hard and long for the first time in years." 555 All of the women felt that the shelter was a safe haven for themselves and their children. Four of 10 black women reported noticing the absence of ethnic staff and feeling somewhat isolated. These four women were located in counties where the black population 560 was less than 5% (U.S. Census Bureau, 2000). These four women spoke of the racism that they and other blacks experienced outside the shelter. They came to the shelter very mindful about their minority status in their communities. These four black women stated that 565 overall they were more concerned about the racial attitudes of the staff rather than their fellow residents. The black women watched the staff to see whether racism would be a factor in receiving the best assistance and resources available during this vulnerable time. They 570 developed relationships with white residents that did not directly confront issues of ethnicity or race or the more complex systems of intersecting multiple oppressions. Despite the potential for ethnic women's cultural

575 isolation, narrative material suggested that black women still felt like they were a part of the group on the basis that all residents were survivors of male violence and were most likely poor. Conversations between black and white women in the hallways and support group meetings focused on abuse and transitioning 580 out of that experience. The other six black women interviewed were in the only shelter in southwest Virginia, where all staff and residents were black and did not report cultural isolation.

585 Once arriving in the shelter, the majority of participants (17 white women and five black women) reported in the interviews that they trusted other women in the shelter. For instance, Rhonda, a 38-year-old black woman, stated, "I trust the women that are here. Basically, what it all comes down to is each has a 590 unique, original story, but the rope that ties us all together…we've been bound by abuse."

Cultural differences muted by violence. Rhonda's attitude reflected the sisterhood that black and white rural women reported feeling in the shelters that of-595 fered them a safe haven from the violence in their lives. It seemed that the common experience of domestic violence and shelter life united the women. Yet racial differences, although muted by their shared experiences, were an issue. For example, in mandatory sup-600 port group meetings, black women revealed that they did not discuss with white women how it felt to be abused by black men or challenges they may have faced with different social services. However, in speaking with the author, a black researcher, black women 605 reported that they believed racism in their interactions with community resources employees may have contributed to their receiving fewer services or less information than their white counterparts. Black study participants avoided talking about these types of chal-610 lenges because they believed that fellow white residents "just wouldn't understand" racism or what they perceived as differential treatment by an occasional shelter staff member or resident. Still, it is important to note that, although black women seemed less likely to 615 "culturally identify" with others (i.e., perceived themselves as sharing a common history of racial and institutional discrimination or common religious background) in the shelter, they were not less likely to feel comfortable in the shelter environment or among most 620 white staff.

My new family. The majority of women reported that they felt that for the time they were there in the shelter, the other residents were their family. When they were asked if racial discrimination was felt by 625 anyone, black women reported that they did not feel racially discriminated against by the other women or the staff. One 32-year-old black woman laughed when she answered our question: "We're all just the same here. We see past the skin color and the bruises." Ruth, 630 a 25-year-old white woman who only had an eighth-grade education and was in the process of getting a divorce, said that the other women were a comfort to her: "Yes, I trust the women here…they knowed the Lord, and we had a lot in common, so it was like a little, happy family…what I always dreamed a family would be like."

The women expressed a bond in the shelter because they all had a common experience: abuse. The result of this bond was the formation of a kind of temporary family and contained "fictive kin network."

For instance, many of the older women revealed that they took on a caretaking role over younger women and children in the shelter. Two particular women, 1 black and 1 white, both older than 40 years of age, were proud to list their caretaking activities in their shelter. They reported that they prepared meals, taught younger women how to prepare certain meals, acted as emotional counselors to younger women, made younger women complete their chores, and actively took care of other women's children. "We keep each other in line whenever we feel crazy." Barbara, a 48-year-old black woman, felt such "motherly responsibility" to abused women that after she made the transition back into the community, she has returned to the shelter as a volunteer and activist.

Relationship with shelter staff. The women were asked about their interactions with the shelter staff. All of the women, with the exception of 1 white woman, positively evaluated the emotional support and extensive caregiving given by staff members. Pamela, a middle-aged black woman, shared her observation of the staff's emotional support and accessibility: "They spoil us really. If you need somebody to talk to, somebody will make time. Some ladies like myself come in here and do have very low self-esteem."

Pamela's comments were echoed by the majority of the women in the shelter. None of the women felt that the staff were ever too busy to help them process their abusive experience. In fact, only 1 participant, Terry (a 40-year-old white woman), complained that she felt her confidence by shelter staff had been violated. In this case, the participant learned that a staff member gossiped about her with a social services employee, a close friend of the staff member.

Shelter efficacy. The last research question asked women to specifically discuss which shelter services were the most useful to them. We prompted them by querying, "What is this shelter doing really well for you and other women?" All but Terry reported that the staff performed their responsibilities effectively with "all their heart and soul," and, with the exception of Terry, all the women in the study reported that staff helped them recognize their inner strength and build up their self-esteem. For example, Mary, a 45-year-old white woman, outlined the many services that the shelter provided her and her family:

I took advantage of every service that was offered to me. They helped me find a job and a lawyer…. Actually a week and a half after I moved in here, I got my kids back.

She got somebody to go to court with me. I came here with no clothes. She took care of that for me. Helped me to get an apartment. They helped me to get a welfare check and food stamps. Every program the shelter had, I took full advantage. When I got here, I wanted for nothing.

Like Mary, the majority of women praised staff members in their roles as primary liaisons and advocates for dealing with social services, the workforce, housing, and the legal system. The women also emphasized the importance of taking full responsibility for actively pursuing opportunities that shelter staff provided them. No one framed these opportunities as "easy handouts" but saw them as "opportunities for real change."

Finally, the women talked about the staff monitoring their attendance at drug and alcohol rehabilitation programs and psychiatric services. One white woman, 32-year-old Betty, stated, "I'm in AA because if I stop going, I won't qualify for an extension if I need it. I'm sober because these women [staff] make sure I'm there and they support me all the way." All but one white woman, Terry, felt empowered that the staff quickly arranged for these wellness services and incorporated some issues related to addiction or depression into group counseling sessions. Overall, these rural battered women found the shelters to be safe and supportive.

Discussion

The results from this study are supported by two bodies of literature—research on rural abused women and on domestic violence among black couples and families. Using qualitative methods, a picture of the experiences of black and white women in domestic violence shelters in rural communities was constructed. Narrative material revealed interesting similarities and differences found between white and black rural women.

White and black rural women experienced different interactions with law-enforcement officers that have important implications with regard to helpseeking behaviors within the context of domestic violence. Study findings provide confirmation of previous research on barriers to seeking help from the police as a result of a violent incident at the hands of an intimate partner. Similar to other research (e.g., U.S. Department of Justice, 1998), both white and black women in this study reported being too ashamed to call the police. Important differences also emerged with regard to how forthcoming shelter information was from the police for victims. It seemed that white women were better informed than black women in terms of the availability and use of shelters, and this is likely due in part to police apparently discussing shelters more often with white participants than with minority women. Even so, the extent of shelter information given to any woman in the study, white or black, was "thin." For example, although several police officers reportedly did tell the participants about the shelter, only 2 participants reported that police officers gave them written material about the shelter. Further, less than a third of the women spoke enthusiastically or in positive terms about their experience with the police.

Both white and black women felt discriminated against by police, although the nature of the discrimination differed in that black women talked about feelings of racial discrimination by white police officers and white women mostly discussed sexist attitudes of some police officers. It is interesting that some white participants saw the police as a potential resource, even threatening their batterers with calling the police. Although it appears that the police certainly could have done a better job overall, the fact that white battered women could consider the police as a potential resource, whereas black battered women did not seem to consider the police as a resource, is perhaps a result of white privilege. This difference between the experiences of black and white battered women suggests how privilege mediates the experience of gender and geographic location for rural battered women. Also, it is possible that black women were likely not to see the police as a resource because of the traditionally hostile relationship law enforcement has had with black communities (Richie, 1996). This finding supports our earlier suggestion that racism can be an additional isolating factor.

These findings suggest that more training needs to be offered to rural police officers dealing with domestic violence. Ongoing training of police officers should be conducted to address gender and cultural sensitivity relative to racial/ethnic minorities. Policy should provide law-enforcement officers with a structured format for addressing domestic violence cases, including the expectation that written material about community services for domestic violence victims be delivered to all possible victims of domestic violence. Community policing, a philosophy that includes all efforts of the police to achieve the goal of a closer relationship with the public, may also help victims see the police and criminal justice system as supportive (Robinson & Chandek, 2000).

There were also differences in how black and white survivors experienced shelters. All of the black women revealed being ashamed of being in a shelter and that within their families, discussion about shelters was considered airing "dirty laundry." This attitude may reflect the internalization of the Superwoman stereotype of black women. Few (1999) has noted that for some black women who internalize the Superwoman myth, "disclosure to and helpseeking from those outside of the abusive relationship may be perceived as a sign of vulnerability and weakness" (p. 70). Similarly, Asbury (1987) observed that black women may be more reluctant to call attention to the abuse because they feel they should be able to find the strength to handle their own relationship problems. The findings in

this study seem to confirm black women's reluctance to discuss help seeking, and shelter assistance was not deemed as appropriate conversation among family or friends.

Black women also described experiencing the shelter culture differently, and several felt that the lack of racial diversity in the shelter sometimes affected what they would share with others. The remaining black women were in a shelter in a predominantly black community; they talked about having access to black shelter staff and other resources (e.g., counselors), pointing to the importance of black shelter staff and community volunteers as credible role models because of shared background and personal experiences (e.g., Wilson et al., 1987). Indeed, Collins (1991) has written about the positive effects of black community "other-mothers" who take part in caring for vulnerable groups within the community. Despite differences between black and white participants that may center around race, it is important to recognize that the majority of black participants emphasized bonding within the shelter based on the common experience of victimization.

Perhaps one of the reasons that white women strongly identified with and trusted other shelter residents is because the shelter residents were, in a sense, a new social support network to combat isolation. White women in this study particularly highlighted the impact of geographic and social isolation on their ability to seek help, whereas black women seemed to rely on social support of family outside the shelter as a means to provide a reprieve from an abusive partner. Scott and Black (1999) discussed the importance of kinship networks for black women as obligatory resources that are basic to the economic, emotional, and community survival among black poor and near-poor. blacks have survived crises and violence by the strength of family ties. Compared to white women, fellow shelter residents were not the major source of emotional support for black women. Thus, isolation and an inability to access shelters may, in fact, have more profound implications for white women, given their heavier reliance on such services for assistance and emotional support.

The issue of isolation seems to be of great significance with respect to domestic violence and women's victimization. Both Gagne (1992) and Websdale (1995) note that rural women are more likely to be isolated from health care, social services, transportation, housing, educational opportunities, and child care. Geographic, social, and economic isolation amplified the extent of control by abusive partners and was the major constraint that all of the women had to negotiate effectively in order to walk in the door of a shelter. In this study, white women were more likely to be surrounded by their partner's kinship network, and thus their social support networks were quite limited as they were often defined by their abusive partners' affiliation. White women also told more stories of marrying early to escape the "normalcy" of family of origin violence and openly talked about multigenerational substance abuse fueling family violence.

In contrast, all of the black women lived close to their own extended family and had alternate venues of social support. Black families, although not as likely to suggest a domestic violence shelter as a primary option for leaving abusive relationships, were more likely to offer their homes as temporary sanctuary. Consequently, the duration of shelter stay was often shorter for black women. Black women did not have to rely on transitional housing solely because there were relatives in the area to take them in once they left the shelter. However, this finding should not be misinterpreted to suggest that shelters are not an important service for abused black rural women. In fact, studies suggest that black women are satisfied with their shelter stay (Thomas, 2000) and report a high quality of life at follow-up (Sullivan & Rumptz, 1994). These findings may suggest that black rural women bring into the shelter potential resources such as a stronger or existing social support system that can be tapped into by the women and shelter staff for child care, housing, and employment, or to assist the survivor in relocation plans. Since white rural women were more likely to be in need of reconnecting or building new social support systems that are independent of their abusive partners, transitional housing and extended shelter stays may be more pertinent to or instrumental to their success in leaving abusive relationships and making the transition from the shelter back into the community.

The significance of social support networks for women in transition cannot be overlooked. Tan, Basta, Sullivan, and Davidson (1995) examined the importance of social support networks and their connection to self-esteem and psychological well-being among 141 participants. They found that 79% of shelter residents identified social support as one of the areas they would most like to work on after leaving the shelter. Within 10 weeks after shelter exit, 41% of the women reported working on increasing their social support networks. Further, abused women who had closer ties to family and friends were more likely to be pleased with their lives and less depressed.

Implications for Practice

It should be noted that, overall, the women were satisfied with the services offered by the shelters. Both black and white rural women reported that shelter staff did a good job of caring for residents with sincerity and honesty, creating a safe, structured environment, and providing assistance with resources such as legal aid and social services. However, participants did make suggestions as to how shelters could improve their services for rural battered women. Feminist research centers on the everyday experiences of participants with the intention of learning how coproduced knowledge in the research process can inform personal, institutional, or social change (DeReus, Few, & Blume, 2005). In this study, the participants became "advocates" who provided practical suggestions to help women who would come to the shelter after they had long left.

1. *Provide greater visibility of services.* All of the women suggested that shelters located in rural communities needed greater visibility. They suggested placing more pamphlets in faith-based organizations, grocery stores, and places women frequent the most (e.g., beauty parlors, women's restrooms). The results of this study indicated that the majority of women (especially black women) did not know that a local domestic violence shelter existed in their community. Clearly, greater collaboration with local law enforcement is needed because the police are important liaisons between shelters and victims of domestic violence. Shelters were "invisible" to many black women because the police simply did not appear to discuss shelters as a viable reprieve from domestic violence to black women. Community outreach on the part of shelter staff may achieve stronger collaborations. For example, shelter staff may be able to incorporate law-enforcement, community, and legislative representatives into workshops or training sessions to create mutually beneficial relationships aimed at providing services to rural women.

2. *Include employment training.* Women expressed a need for state and local job bulletins to be accessible or posted in the shelters. They suggested that computers and computer training be made available in shelters to search for jobs and to improve clerical skills to increase their probability of getting higher-paid jobs. A need for a separate phone service or line with which they could communicate with possible employers quickly was requested. In sum, these women realized that part of what kept them in abusive homes was a lack of employment opportunities.

3. *Offer shelter exit aftercare.* Women felt they needed to be in touch with shelter staff and resources for longer than 90 days to get their lives back on track. Some women felt that once they left the shelter, they were "cast away." Their suggestion was that shelters have transitional housing with longer stay periods.

4. *Consider inspirational resources.* Black and Appalachian women specifically requested more interaction with the faith-based organizations and space to nurture their spirituality. The majority of white women and all black women were primarily raised participating in rural faith-based organizations. They identified spirituality as one of the main coping strategies that allowed them to reconnect to themselves positively and to have hope for a better future. Although researchers have identified the church and fundamentalism in rural

975 regions as institutional foundations of rural patriarchy (Navin, Stockum, & Campbell-Ruggaard, 1993), it is important to note that these women recommended working on their spiritual selves rather than focusing on religious passages that re-
980 quired the submission of women to men. Additionally, faith-based organizations may be particularly important sources of support for black women (Eugene, 1995).

5. *Diversify shelter staff.* Black women specifically
985 requested that more racial/ethnic women be recruited as shelter directors and staff to create a more diverse shelter culture. Only black women suggested that a staff person with foreign language proficiency be on call for rural migrant
990 women. It is noteworthy that the majority of black women were less likely to believe that they could say what they felt in the shelter environment and wished they had access to black resources. Black community leaders and othermothers could work
995 in collaboration with shelters to depathologize shelters and other health services.

Conclusion

Black and white rural women in this exploratory study experienced domestic violence differently in terms of helpseeking access, behaviors, and social sup-
1000 port, but shared many commonalities once they were in the shelter environment. Our findings invite researchers and practitioners to consider the recommendations proposed by women who have lived and are living in transition from the shelter back into their communities and
1005 families. Longitudinal studies with rural women, especially black women, who have sought assistance from battered women's shelters are needed to further track the barriers or successes of transitioning from the shelter.

References

Anderson, K., & Jack, D. C. (1991). Learning to listen: Interview techniques and analyses. In S. Berger Gluck & D. Patai (Eds.), *Women's words: The feminist practice of oral history* (pp. 11–26). New York: Routledge.

Asbury, J. (1987). African-American women in violent relationships: An exploration of cultural differences. In R. Hampton (Ed.), *Violence in the black family: Correlates and consequences* (pp. 89–119). Lexington, MA: Lexington Books.

Berg, B. (1998). *Qualitative research methods for the social sciences.* Boston: Allyn & Bacon.

Berk, R. A., Newton, P. J., & Berk, S. F. (1986). What a difference a day makes: An empirical study of the impact of shelters for battered women. *Journal of Marriage and the Family, 48,* 481–490.

Borland, K. (1991). "That's not what I said": Interpretive conflict in oral narrative research. In S. Berger Gluck & D. Patai (Eds.), *Women's words: The feminist practice of oral history* (pp. 63–76). New York: Routledge.

Brown, C., Reedy, D., Fountain, J., Johnson, A., & Dichiser, T. (2000). Battered women's career decision-making self-efficacy: Further insights and contributing factors. *Journal of Career Assessment, 8,* 251–265.

Collins, P. H. (1991). *Black feminist thought: Knowledge, consciousness, and the politics of empowerment.* New York: Routledge.

Davis. L. V., Hagan. J. L., & Early, T. J. (1994). Social services for battered women: Are they adequate, accessible, and appropriate? *Social Work, 39,* 695–704.

Davis, L. V., & Srinivasan, M. (1995). Listening to the voices of battered women: What helps them escape violence? *Affilia, 10,* 49–69.

DeReus, L., Few, A. L., & Blume, L. B. (2005). Multicultural and critical race feminisms: Theorizing families in the third wave. In V. L. Bergtson, A. C. Acock, K. R. Allen, P. Dilworth-Anderson, & D. M. Klein (Eds.), *Source-*

book of family theory and research (pp. 447–468). Thousand Oaks. CA: Sage.

Eugene, T. M. (1995). There is a balm in Gilead: Black women and the Black Church as agents of a therapeutic community. *Women & Therapy, 16,* 55–71.

Few, A. L. (1999). The (un)making of martyrs: Black mothers, daughters, and intimate violence. *Journal for the Association of Research on Mothering, 1,* 68–75.

Few, A. L., & Bell-Scott. P. (2002). Grounding our feet and hearts: Black women's coping strategies and the decision to leave. *Women & Therapy, 25,* 59–77.

Fraser, H. (2004). Doing narrative research: Analyzing personal stories line by line. *Qualitative Social Work, 3,* 179–201.

Gagne, P. L. (1992). Appalachian women: Violence and social control. *Journal of Contemporary Ethnography, 20,* 387–415.

Gilgun, J. F. (1995). We shared something special: The moral discourse of incest perpetrators. *Journal of Marriage and the Family, 51,* 265–281.

Gordon, J. S. (1996). Community services for abused women: A review of perceived usefulness and efficacy. *Journal of Family Violence, 11,* 315–329.

Glaser, B. G., & Strauss, A. L. (1967). *The discovery of grounded theory: Strategies for qualitative research.* Hawthorne, NY: Aldine deGruyer.

Harding, S. (Ed.). (1987). *Feminism and methodology.* Bloomington: Indiana University Press.

Hyden, M. (1994). Women battering as a marital act: Interviewing and analysis in context. In C. K. Riessman (Ed.), *Qualitative studies in social work research* (pp. 95–112). Thousand Oaks, CA: Sage.

Jackson, S. (1998). Telling stories: Memory, narrative, and experience in feminist research and theory. In K. Henwood, C. Griffin, & A. Phoenix (Eds.), *Standpoints and differences: Essays in the practice of feminist psychology* (pp. 45–64). London: Sage.

Janesick, V. (1994). Dance of qualitative research design: Metaphor, methodology, and meaning. In L Denzin & Y. Lincoln (Eds.), Handbook of qualitative research (pp. 209–219). Newbury Park, CA: Sage.

Johnson, I., Crowley, J., & Sigler, R. (1992). Agency response to domestic violence: Services provided to battered women. In E. Viano (Ed.), *Intimate violence: Interdisciplinary perspectives* (pp. 191–202). Washington, DC: Hemisphere.

Kaukinen, C. (2002). The help-seeking decisions of violent crime victims: An examination of the direct and conditional effects of gender and the victim–offender relationship. *Journal of Interpersonal Violence, 17,* 432–456.

Krishnan, S. P., Hilbert, J. C., & Pase, M. (2001). An examination of intimate partner violence in rural communities: Results from a hospital emergency department study from Southwest United States. *Family and Community Health, 24,* 1–16.

Maxwell, J. (1996). *Qualitative research design: An interactive approach.* Thousand Oaks, CA: Sage.

McNair, L., & Neville, H. (1996). African American women survivors of sexual assault: The intersection of race and class. *Women & Therapy, 18,* 107–118.

Narayan, K., & George, K. (2001). Personal and folk narrative as cultural representation. In J. Gubrium & J. Holstein (Eds.), *Handbook of interview research: Context & method* (pp. 815–831). Thousand Oaks, CA: Sage.

Navin, S., Stockum, R., & Campbell-Ruggaard, J. (1993). Battered women in rural America. *Journal of Humanistic Education and Development, 32,* 9–16.

Patton, M. Q. (2002). *Qualitative research and evaluation methods* (3rd ed.). Thousand Oaks, CA: Sage.

Plummer, K. (1995). *Telling sexual stories: Power, change, and social worlds.* London: Routledge.

Ramazanoglu, C., & Holland, J. (2002). *Feminist methodology: Challenges and choices.* London: Sage.

Reissman, C. (1993). *Narrative analysis.* Newbury Park, CA: Sage.

Richie, B. (1996). *Compelled to crime: The gender entrapment of battered black women.* New York: Routledge.

Roberts, A. R., & Lewis, S. J. (2000). Giving them shelter: National organizational survey of shelters for battered women and their children. *Journal of Community Psychology, 28,* 669–681.

Robinson, A. L., & Chandek, M. S. (2000). Philosophy into practice? Community policing units and domestic violence victim participation. *Policing: An International Journal of Police Strategies and Management, 23,* 280–302.

Scott, J. W., & Black, A. (1999). Deep structures of African American family life: Female and male kin networks. In R. Staples (Ed.), *The black family* (pp. 232–240). New York: Wadsworth.

Strauss, A. (1987). *Qualitative analysis far social scientists.* Cambridge. NY: Cambridge University Press.

Sullivan, C., & Rumptz, M. (1994). Adjustment and needs of African American women who utilize a domestic violence shelter. *Violence and Victims, 9,* 275–285.

Tan, C., Basta. J., Sullivan. C. M., & Davidson, W. S. (1995). The role of social support in the lives of women exiting domestic violence shelters: An experimental study. *Journal of Interpersonal Violence, 10,* 437–451.

Thomas, E. K. (2000). Domestic violence in African American and Asian American communities: A comparative analysis of two racial/ethnic minority cultures and implications for mental health service provision for women of color. *Psychology: A Journal of Human Behavior, 37,* 32–43.

Thompson, L. (1992). Feminist methodology for family studies. *Journal of Marriage and the Family, 54,* 3–18.

Thompson, L., & Walker, A. (1995). The place of feminism in family studies. *Journal of Marriage and the Family, 57,* 847–856.

Tutty, L. M., Weaver, G., & Rothery, M. A. (1999). Resident's views of efficacy of shelter services for assaulted women. *Violence Against Women, 5,* 898–925.

U.S. Census Bureau. (2000). *American fact finder database.* Retrieved March 2, 2005, from http://factfinder.census.gov/

U.S. Department of Justice. (1998). *Violence by intimates: Analysis of data on crimes by current or former spouses, boyfriends, and girlfriends.* Washington, DC: Bureau of Justice Statistics.

Van Hightower, N. R., & Gorton, J. (2002). A case study of community-based responses to rural woman battering. *Violence Against Women, 8,* 845–872.

Van Hightower, N. R., Gorton, J., & DeMoss, C. L. (2000). Predictive models of domestic violence and fear of intimate partners among immigrant and seasonal farm worker women. *Journal of Family Violence, 15,* 137–154.

Websdale, N. (1998). Rural woman abuse: The voices of Kentucky women. *Violence Against Women, 1,* 309–338.

Websdale, N. (1998). *Rural woman battering and the justice system: An ethnography.* Thousand Oaks. CA: Sage.

Wendt, S., Taylor, J., & Kennedy, M. (2002). Rural domestic violence: Moving towards feminist poststructural understandings. *Rural Social Work, 2,* 25–35.

West, C. M. (Ed.). (2003). *Violence in the lives of black women.* New York: Haworth.

Whitener, L., Jen, J., & Kassel, K. (2004. February). *Programs and partnership in a dynamic rural America.* U.S. Department of Agriculture, Economic Research Service. Retrieved November 8, 2004, from http://www.ers.usda.gov/Amberwaves/February04

Wilson, M. N., Cobb, D. D., & Dolan, R. T. (1987). Raising the awareness of wife battering in rural black areas of central Virginia: A community outreach approach. In R. L. Hampton (Ed.). Violence in the black family: Correlates and consequences (pp. 121–131). Lexington. MA: Lexington Books.

Young, I. M. (1997). *Intersecting voices: Dilemmas of gender, political philosophy, and policy.* Princeton, NJ: Princeton University Press.

Acknowledgments: I wish to acknowledge Dr. Sandra Stith for her review of previous drafts; the Support Program for Innovative Research Strategies (ASPIRES), which is sponsored by the Office of the Provost; and the Office of the Vice President for Research at Virginia Polytechnic Institute and State University for funding this research. I also humbly thank the participating domestic violence shelters in southwest Virginia for their generous assistance.

About the author: April L. Few is an assistant professor in the Department of Human Development, Virginia Polytechnic Institute and State University, 401-A Wallace Hall, Blacksburg, VA 24061. E-mail: alfew@vt.edu

Exercise for Article 37

Factual Questions

1. The researcher states two "aims" of the study. What is the second aim?

2. How many women were interviewed?

3. What was done for the safety of the researchers and the women?

4. Were all the participants interviewed in private one-on-one interviews? Explain.

5. How many of the black women came from a single town?

6. How many of the women spoke in positive terms about the police?

Questions for Discussion

7. In your opinion, is it important to know that this study was conducted through a "feminist lens"? Explain. (See lines 121–196.)

8. Is it important to know that the participants were drawn from 14 different shelters? Explain. (See lines 199–202.)

9. While the researcher indicates that 30 women were interviewed, she does not state how many women were approached but declined to be interviewed. Would you be interested in knowing the number who declined? Why? Why not?

10. The researcher states that this research was "exploratory." Do you agree with this characterization of the research? Explain. (See lines 276–277 and 997–998.)

11. In your opinion, does the researcher make a strong argument for using qualitative research to explore the research problem? (See lines 287–322.)

12. In your opinion, is the method of analysis described in sufficient detail? (See lines 323–364.)

13. If you had planned a study on this topic, would you have used interviews (as in this study) or structured questionnaires? Explain.

Quality Ratings

Directions: Indicate your level of agreement with each of the following statements by circling a number from 5 for strongly agree (SA) to 1 for strongly disagree (SD). If you believe an item is not applicable to this research article, leave it blank. Be prepared to explain your ratings. When responding to criteria A and B below, keep in mind that brief titles and abstracts are conventional in published research.

A. The title of the article is appropriate.

SA   5   4   3   2   1   SD

B. The abstract provides an effective overview of the research article.

SA   5   4   3   2   1   SD

C. The introduction establishes the importance of the study.

SA   5   4   3   2   1   SD

D. The literature review establishes the context for the study.

SA   5   4   3   2   1   SD

E. The research purpose, question, or hypothesis is clearly stated.

SA   5   4   3   2   1   SD

F. The method of sampling is sound.

SA   5   4   3   2   1   SD

G. Relevant demographics (for example, age, gender, and ethnicity) are described.

SA   5   4   3   2   1   SD

H. Measurement procedures are adequate.

SA   5   4   3   2   1   SD

I. All procedures have been described in sufficient detail to permit a replication of the study.

SA   5   4   3   2   1   SD

J. The participants have been adequately protected from potential harm.

SA   5   4   3   2   1   SD

K. The results are clearly described.

SA   5   4   3   2   1   SD

L. The discussion/conclusion is appropriate.

SA   5   4   3   2   1   SD

M. Despite any flaws, the report is worthy of publication.

SA   5   4   3   2   1   SD

Article 38

Generational Differences and Similarities Among Puerto Rican and Mexican Mothers' Experiences with Familial Ethnic Socialization

ADRIANA J. UMAÑA-TAYLOR
Arizona State University

ANI YAZEDJIAN
Texas State University

ABSTRACT. We used focus group methodology to explore differences and similarities in the process of familial ethnic socialization among first- and second-generation Mexican and Puerto Rican mothers ($N = 75$). Across all groups, mothers communicated the importance and purposefulness of familial ethnic socialization practices that took place in their homes. A number of similarities emerged across national origin and generational groups, indicating that there were numerous shared experiences that did not change with greater time in the U.S. and did not vary by national origin. Nevertheless, origin groups were also discovered. Findings are discussed within the context of Bronfenbrenner's ecological theory and an acculturative framework.

From *Journal of Social and Personal Relationships*, *23*, 445–464.

The United States population is undergoing a rapid demographic shift, with Latinos contributing greatly to this change. Given high fertility rates and high levels of continuing immigration, Latinos represent the largest ethnic minority group in the U.S., outnumbering both Black and Asian populations (U.S. Census Bureau, 2004). Despite this rapid growth, current theoretical and empirical knowledge regarding the experiences of Latino youth and families in the United States is relatively limited. Nevertheless, existing work suggests that Latino parents play a critical role in the important developmental process of ethnic identity formation (Knight, Bernal, Garza, Cota, & Ocampo, 1993; Umaña-Taylor & Fine, 2004). Although parents' ethnic socialization has emerged as a significant factor that predicts healthy ethnic identity formation, we have limited knowledge concerning parents' experiences in this process.

Furthermore, many studies continue to treat Latinos as a homogenous population and do not account for the variation that exists among them (Umaña-Taylor & Fine, 2001). Latinos in the U.S. represent over 20 distinct national origins, with Mexicans and Puerto Ricans being the two largest groups. The varied histories of Latino national origin groups distinguish them from each other on a number of significant demographic variables (Baca Zinn & Wells, 2000). The two largest Latino groups, for example, differ with regard to immigration status (i.e., Puerto Ricans are U.S. citizens by birth, whereas Mexicans must apply for entry into the U.S.), are concentrated in different regions of the U.S. (i.e., 55% of Mexicans live in the West, while 61% of Puerto Ricans live in the Northeast [Guzman, 2001]), and differ significantly with regard to household composition (i.e., 31% of Mexican households vs. 17% of Puerto Rican households contain five or more people [Ramirez & de la Cruz, 2002]). These demographic differences can differentially affect family life and therefore provide an important context within which to examine the family experiences of Latino groups (Baca Zinn & Wells, 2000). As such, the current study examined generational differences in parental practices and experiences regarding familial ethnic socialization among Mexican and Puerto Rican parents.

Guiding Theoretical Frameworks

Although the current study was primarily of an exploratory nature, two theoretical frameworks (i.e., ecological and acculturation) guided our interpretation of the results. Bronfenbrenner's (1989) ecological theory suggests that processes and outcomes of human development are a joint function of individuals and the environments in which their lives are embedded. Furthermore, ecological theory posits that proximal (e.g., family) and distal (e.g., societal ideologies) settings influence human development. Given that familial ethnic socialization is a process that involves adolescents, their families, and society, ecological theory fittingly provides a framework from which to understand the interface of immediate settings and broader social contexts. Thus, we used ecological theory as a framework from which to understand the interconnectedness of mothers' and adolescents' lives as well as to understand how familial experiences were informed by broader social contexts, such as children's schools, neighborhoods, and societal ideologies.

65 　While ecological theory provides an understanding of how individuals' lives are influenced by (and influence) their environments, an acculturation framework helps us to understand how experiences within cultural groups may vary based on individuals' degree of ad-
70 herence to mainstream and native cultures. Past theoretical work on acculturation asserted that in the process of adapting to the ways of the dominant culture, individuals will lose their identification with their ethnic group; however, current empirical and theoretical
75 work indicates that such dichotomous thinking is no longer relevant in today's increasingly heterogeneous society (Cortes, Rogler, & Malgady, 1994). Individuals are clearly demonstrating that they can maintain strong ties with their ethnic group, while also becoming adept
80 at surviving in the dominant culture (Rosenthal, Whittle, & Bell, 1989; Saylor & Aries, 1999). Furthermore, research reveals that while immigrants do bring with them a series of cultural patterns and traditions, which have a strong influence on family functioning and indi-
85 vidual behavior, the nature of these cultural patterns may change in the process of adaptation to the new culture (Foner, 1997; Garcia Coll, Meyer, & Brillon, 1995). The redefined culture becomes a hybrid of the native culture in order to allow ethnic group members
90 the opportunity to continue to maintain the ethnic experience within the broader framework of the dominant culture. Thus, ethnicity is redefined and is experienced in a new way in response to the circumstances that immigrants encounter in their new culture. Accord-
95 ingly, we were interested in exploring how the process of familial ethnic socialization remained unchanged across generational cohorts, as well as possible adaptations that emerged over time as families adapted to U.S. culture.

Familial Ethnic Socialization

100 　Familial ethnic socialization has been defined as the degree to which family members (e.g., grandparents, parents, siblings, and other kin) expose, discuss, and possibly directly teach children about their ethnic background. Although children gain information about
105 their ethnicity from various sources (e.g., peers, media, etc.), scholars agree that the family plays a central role in this process (Harrison, Wilson, Pine, Chan, & Buriel, 1995; Knight, Bernal, et al., 1993; Phinney & Rosenthal, 1992). On a broader level, Erikson (1968)
110 also discusses familial influences on identity, suggesting that individuals define themselves partly through their relationships and interactions with family members. In line with these ideas, and consistent with an ecological framework, theoretical models of ethnic
115 identity formation (e.g., Knight, Bernal et al., 1993; Umaña-Taylor & Fine, 2004) present familial ethnic socialization as a central construct.

　Although familial ethnic socialization has been considered a central component in theoretical models
120 of ethnic identity, little empirical work has been con-

ducted on this construct. In studies that have explored familial ethnic socialization, it has been described as both covert and overt (see Umaña-Taylor & Fine, 2004). With covert familial ethnic socialization, par-
125 ents are not intentionally trying to teach their children about ethnicity but may be inadvertently doing so with their choice of decor and everyday activities (e.g., decorating the home with objects from their native country). Overt familial ethnic socialization refers to
130 family members purposefully and directly attempting to teach adolescents about their ethnicity (e.g., buying books about the native country and requiring adolescents to read them). Research with ethnic minority parents indicates that families report a need to pass on
135 their ethnic culture via language (Sridhar, 1988), beliefs, and customs (Dasgupta, 1998). Furthermore, scholars suggest that a major goal of socialization for ethnic minority families is to foster a positive orientation toward one's ethnic group and promote bicultural-
140 ism (Harrison et al., 1995). Thus, whether ethnic socialization is occurring in an overt or covert manner, it appears to be an important parenting goal for ethnic minority families.

　Ethnic socialization appears to have beneficial out-
145 comes for ethnic minority youth. Research conducted with children and adolescents suggests that familial ethnic socialization has positive implications for ethnic identity development. A study of Mexican-origin adolescents found that familial ethnic socialization was
150 positively related to ethnic identity achievement. That is, the more adolescents reported that their families were socializing them about their ethnicity, the higher their reports of exploration, commitment, and affirmation regarding their ethnic identity (Umaña-Taylor &
155 Fine, 2004). This same relationship was found in other studies conducted with Asian, Black, and Latino adolescents (Phinney & Nakayama, 1991; Umaña-Taylor, Bhanot, & Shin, 2006). Furthermore, research conducted with Mexican-origin children has found a simi-
160 lar relationship, in that mothers who reported teaching their children about their ethnic culture tended to have children who were more ethnically identified (Knight, Cota, & Bernal, 1993; Knight, Bernal et al., 1993).

　Although families appear to be an important me-
165 dium through which adolescents learn about their cultural background, researchers have not directly explored the ways in which parents transmit their culture to their children, nor have they examined parents' beliefs regarding the factors that assist them in the proc-
170 ess of ethnic socialization. Because previous research indicates that familial ethnic socialization is strongly related to Latino adolescents' ethnic identity, and ethnic identity is positively associated with adolescents' self-esteem (Umaña-Taylor, Diversi, & Fine, 2002), it
175 is critical to understand how Latino parents are negotiating this process.

Familial ethnic socialization and generational status. An important variable that may be associated

180 with variation in familial ethnic socialization practices is generational status. Research reveals that while immigrants do bring with them a series of cultural patterns and traditions, these may change in the process of adaptation to the new culture. These changes may in turn have a significant influence on both family func-
185 tioning and individual behavior (Foner, 1997).

The relation between language loss and generational status has been well documented by Portes and Schauffler (1994) who showed that knowledge of and fluency in the native tongue often disappear by the
190 third generation. Similarly, Alba (1990) found that greater separation from the immigrant generation corresponds with a decline of salient ethnic markers, such as language, which serve to maintain boundaries between the majority group and the ethnic group. Finally,
195 researchers also found that generational status was related to individuals' ethnic identification, such that knowledge of and adherence to ethnic values, and engagement in ethnic behaviors tended to diminish with greater removal from the immigrant generation (Lay &
200 Verkuyten, 1999; Rosenthal & Feldman, 1992). Thus, it is plausible that as families gain more experience in mainstream culture and perhaps become more acculturated, the ways in which they teach their children about ethnic group membership may also change over
205 time.

Research also reveals that value systems change both as ecological contexts change and as individuals move into new ecological niches. As a result, even within ethnic groups, values can vary due to length of
210 exposure to another culture (Roosa, Dumka, Gonzales, & Knight, 2002). For example, Sabogal, Marin, Otero-Sabogal, Marin, and Perez-Stable (1987) examined changes in three dimensions of familism among Latinos and Whites. When compared with second-
215 generation respondents, first-generation and foreign-born respondents differed on two of the three dimensions of familism. This suggests that adherence to practices and values varies by generational status. Given that values appear to change within a specified popula-
220 tion as a result of generational status, it is plausible that not only the content but also the process of the transmission of culture may change from one generation to the next. This idea is consistent with research reporting a negative relationship between generation and familial
225 ethnic socialization among Mexican-origin adolescents; that is, adolescents who reported fewer family members born in the U.S. tended to report high levels of familial ethnic socialization (Umaña-Taylor & Fine, 2004). Thus, it is critical to explore not only the proc-
230 ess of familial ethnic socialization, but also the factors by which it varies across families.

Familial ethnic socialization and national origin. Another potential source of variation to consider is families' national origin. Unfortunately, variation in
235 familial ethnic socialization practices among Latino national-origin groups has not received scholarly atten-

tion. The limited research that exists focuses on parent socialization strategies, in general, and emphasizes the focus on familism among Mexican-origin families
240 (Baca Zinn & Wells, 2000; Buriel & DeMent, 1997) and respect for elders among Puerto Rican families (Garcia-Preto, 1996b; Gonzales-Ramos, Zayas, & Cohen, 1998). One important difference between Puerto Rican and Mexican families, which may con-
245 tribute to variability in familial ethnic socialization, is the facility with which families can travel to the country of origin. In fact, the facility of migration between the island and the mainland has been shown to exert a strong influence on family life by facilitating the links
250 that families maintain to Puerto Rican culture (Garcia-Preto, 1996a). In contrast, migration between Mexico and the U.S. is more complicated, as individuals must obtain visas to travel between countries. The current study explored this potential source of variability by
255 examining the individual experiences of these two groups.

Goals of the Present Study

Few studies have explored the ethnic socialization practices of either foreign-born or U.S.-born Latino parents, and knowledge is further limited with regard to
260 possible variations in familial ethnic socialization that exist within ethnic groups. Although our purpose was exploratory, the following research questions guided our inquiry: (a) Are families socializing their children about ethnicity? (b) If so, how is this socialization oc-
265 curring? (c) What resources and/or barriers are families encountering, if any, to ethnic socialization? (d) What are the commonalities among Mexican and Puerto Rican mothers with regard to the process of ethnic socialization? (e) Is familial ethnic socialization similar
270 and/or different for Mexico-born mothers versus their U.S.-born counterparts? (f) Is familial ethnic socialization similar and/or different for Puerto Rico-born mothers versus their mainland-born counterparts?

Method

Participants

Participants included 75 mothers who were of
275 Puerto Rican ($n = 39$) or Mexican ($n = 36$) descent, had a child between the ages of 10 and 20, and lived within the city limits of one large midwestern city. Twelve focus groups were conducted, with group composition determined by mothers' country of origin and genera-
280 tional status. Generational status was assigned based on the location where mothers were born and/or raised (i.e., Puerto Rico, Mexico, or U.S. mainland). For example, a mother who was born in the U.S. (mainland) but taken to Puerto Rico as an infant and raised in
285 Puerto Rico participated in the focus group with mothers who were born in Puerto Rico; for ease of presentation, these mothers are referred to as Puerto Rico born. In the entire sample, mothers' ages ranged from 26 to 66 ($M = 38.13$, $SD = 7.15$), and educational levels
290 ranged from no formal schooling to a masters degree.

A detailed description of each focus group is available from the first author.

Procedure

To facilitate recruitment, we developed relationships with county organizations (e.g., recreational centers, organizations serving Latino populations, neighborhood associations, and consulates). The first author visited these locations with members of the research team and actively recruited mothers for participation. Based on mothers' availability, focus group dates were set and participants were given several reminder calls. We provided participants with a $5 gift certificate to a local store for each referral that resulted in active participation.

We conducted separate focus groups for Puerto Rico-born mothers, mainland-born Puerto Rican mothers, Mexico-born mothers, and U.S.-born Mexican mothers. Thus, our study involved four cases with multiple examples within each case (Miles & Huberman, 1994). Focus groups lasted between 90 and 120 minutes, were conducted in participants' language of preference, and were audiotaped. All mothers who were born outside the U.S. preferred Spanish and all U.S.-born mothers preferred English. Thus, groups with Mexico-born and Puerto Rico-born mothers were all conducted in Spanish and focus groups with U.S. (mainland)-born mothers were conducted in English. Focus groups took place in a recreational center that was near participants' homes and on a bus route. Complimentary transportation, onsite childcare, and refreshments were provided. Furthermore, mothers received a $20 gift certificate to a local store for their participation.

Focus groups were conducted with moderators and note takers fluent in both Spanish and English. After brief introductions, the moderator explained the purpose of the project and began the focus group by stating, "Some people believe that teaching their children about their ethnic background is very important, while others feel that this is not so important and that there are other things that are more important. We are here to find out your ideas about this topic. There is no right or wrong answer; we would just like to hear your thoughts on this issue."

Design

Given the limited research on ethnic socialization practices, we felt it necessary to first understand the process by which parents teach children about their ethnic backgrounds. We attempted to eliminate our presuppositions regarding the process of ethnic socialization by adopting an emic, or insider, approach. Our aim was to gather rich data from mothers describing *their* views on ethnic socialization (Rubin & Rubin, 1995).

We chose focus group methodology because of its usefulness when researchers may be unfamiliar with issues specific to a particular context or population

(Patton, 1990). Specifically, we adopted a "bottom-up" approach, which enabled us to understand the practices, attitudes, and values within the framework of Latina mothers' national culture of origin (Zayas & Rojas-Flores, 2002). While we wanted to allow mothers' experiences to be clearly heard through the interviews, our stance as researchers who view socialization from an ecological perspective led us to establish basic parameters for the study. Thus, focus group moderators followed a semistructured protocol in which parents were asked about both proximal and distal sources of socialization. Specifically, three general areas were introduced in all focus groups: (1) the ways in which families socialized their children about ethnicity, (2) the ways in which children learned about ethnicity outside the home, and (3) the resources and/or barriers that facilitated/hindered the process of socialization. The same protocol was followed for all focus groups, and moderators were trained to probe until mothers could provide no more examples for the particular topic under discussion. Nevertheless, we did not presume that mothers engaged in ethnic socialization and therefore began each focus group with a question regarding whether or not mothers socialized their children regarding their ethnicity.

Results

Preparing the Data

Because our data were analyzed by Spanish-speaking *and* non-Spanish-speaking researchers, tapes were transcribed and also translated for meaning. Interviews conducted in Spanish were transcribed and translated by one staff member and checked for accuracy by a second staff member. For focus groups with Mexican-origin parents, a Mexican-origin research team member was always involved in at least one of the steps above; this was also the case for focus groups with Puerto Rican mothers.

Analyzing the Data

Given the exploratory nature of the study, data analysis was guided by Hill, Thompson, and Williams's (1997) Consensual Qualitative Research (CQR) approach. This study collected data using a uniform protocol in order to ensure the consistency of responses. Further, this study incorporated a team of individuals to arrive at consensus in coding judgments. Finally, data were compared across the four cases to determine whether themes were relevant.

The first author and a research team worked together in analyzing the transcripts. After discussion of the guiding questions of the study, all team members independently read one transcript and developed codes. Coding discrepancies were then discussed until consensus was reached regarding the best representation of the data. Individual team members then coded a second focus group, creating new codes as necessary. The research then discussed the second focus group and, again, the process of coding via consensus ensued. We repeated this process until all focus groups were coded.

The authors reexamined the coding sheets to determine the most salient codes. To formulate categories or themes, both authors independently summarized the core idea of each code for each focus group (Hill et al., 1997). The themes discussed below were deemed typical because mothers in all focus groups in a particular case (e.g., island-born Puerto Rican mothers) described them as a component of ethnic socialization. We begin our discussion with the similarities that transcended national origin and generational status. We follow that with similarities by generational status and conclude with an exploration of within-group differences and similarities.

Similarities Across All Groups

Nine themes were applicable across all groups regarding how familial ethnic socialization took place. First, when asked how they taught their children about their culture, mothers often emphasized the importance of *traveling to their country of origin*. Although Puerto Rico is a territory of the U.S., for ease of discussion we refer to Puerto Rico as a "country of origin." Dolores (all names presented are pseudonyms), a U.S.-born Mexican mother, said, "You can always talk to your kids about it, but it's not the same as being there and actually seeing it." Thus, parents indicated that their children experienced a connection to the culture by visiting the native country that was more valuable than anything that parents could provide in the U.S. Parents felt that visiting their country of origin exposed children to a way of life that was absent in the U.S. For immigrant parents, there was an additional component of having children experience first-hand some of the same things parents had experienced when they were growing up. Mothers indicated that visiting the country of origin enriched children's understanding of their heritage and promoted a degree of internalization that could not be achieved through discussion alone.

A second mechanism involved *books, videos, and the Internet*. These tools facilitated parents' efforts to expose children to their cultures. One immigrant Mexican mother explained, "And, like, one can teach the history of Mexican[s]. Buy yourself a book of the history of Mexico and, well, help them read it. Then they can understand what each date signifies, why it is being celebrated, because it could be the Battle of Puebla, the Mexican Independence.... I believe that one has to teach the history."

Third, parents in all groups mentioned the importance of *food as a mechanism* to expose their children to their background. For example, Ana, a mainland-born Puerto Rican mother expressed the importance of daily rice and beans, while Raquel, a Mexico-born mother, discussed the availability of traditional foods in the U.S. All mothers discussed traditional food as a part of daily life, interwoven throughout their daily routines.

Beyond specific practices and behaviors, a fourth commonality among mothers involved a more abstract discussion of instilling a sense of ethnic identification in their children. There was a general sentiment that *instilling their roots* would facilitate cultural transmission to future generations. For example, Elsa, a mainland-born Puerto Rican stated,

I think every kid should know where you're coming from, their parents are coming from. I mean, it's nice to know where you come from...from your ancestors and sometimes, you get a good sense and a strong sense from where your, you know, you've been, where your parents come from. So that way, you can teach your children also.

There appeared to be a hope that if parents taught their children about their heritage, they would be equipped to continue this with their own children.

Fifth, children also learned about their respective cultures from their *extended family* (particularly grandparents). A number of U.S.-born mothers stated that their children were able to speak Spanish because their children's grandparents were around to expose them to the native language. Similarly, a Puerto Rico-born mother stated, "Taking them to their grandparents to have them talk to them [children], because sometimes the grandparents know more than we do." Thus, because of their life experiences, grandparents appeared to supplement mothers' efforts by providing a more direct link to the homeland.

Mothers reported that children often raised *questions* about ethnicity covering a range of topics including group history, traditions, ways of celebrating holidays, and ways of life in the country of origin. Broadly, questions appeared from children's experiences in their immediate environments. Mothers shared instances where children asked questions because of something they saw on Spanish television, or when a family member was cooking a traditional meal using a plantain leaf, or during a visit to the island. Parents appeared to use children's questions to initiate a dialogue about culture. One mother explained, "Well, I won't actually just tell my Ashley, 'come on let's sit down and talk about Puerto Rico', no, it just happens. There's something in, all over, my house that will explain about Puerto Rico, so if she asks me, 'where did this come from?' then we'll get down into the questions" [another mother agrees].

Mothers discussed the importance of the Spanish language. *Teaching children how to speak Spanish* served a dual purpose: first, passing on the language skills themselves, and second, as a method of passing on the ethnic culture. In addition, teaching the native language allowed parents to reinforce their children's unique identities and distinguish them from the dominant culture. Mothers across all groups discussed the importance of being fluent in *both* English and Spanish and the benefits one gained in the workplace as a result of being bilingual. The following conversation illustrates this sentiment:

515 *Patricia*: Especially nowadays, you know you need that, that Spanish to get a good job. So you, so they need to know it.

Yolanda: Yeah, and it's very important. As a matter of fact, you have a lot of different people going to school to
520 learn Spanish [many agree]. Yeah, so that's very important and here at home we can teach it to them without having to pay for it.

Many mothers felt that teaching English wasn't a concern. Generally, mothers indicated that they could as-
525 sume that their children would learn English, but not Spanish, through their school and community environments.

In addition to maintaining culture via language, mothers also continued their respective native *tradi-*
530 *tions* in the U.S. Mothers described that these traditions brought their children closer to the culture and, in some cases, children valued the traditions because they represented their native culture. As described by one Mexican U.S.-born mother, "I mean, we went through
535 this whole...she [daughter] just had a quinceañera [traditional Mexican 15th birthday party for girls]...a little while ago, and it was very important to her. And, I think it was because, not because it was a party, or because she was gonna dress up. For her, it was because
540 this was a Mexican tradition." Although mothers introduced children to familial traditions, children elicited the continuation of these practices. In addition, how traditions were practiced changed over time as they adapted to the U.S.

545 Although these eight themes all pertain to aspects of active familial ethnic socialization, mothers also mentioned that the process was facilitated via the *school curriculum.* For example, Mexico-born mothers mentioned that the curriculum exposed their children to
550 Mexican culture via textbooks and homework assignments that required them to research Mexican culture (e.g., *Cinco de Mayo,* Day of the Dead, and Day of the *Puebla* Battle). Similarly, Puerto Rico-born mothers mentioned that they specifically chose their children's
555 schools based on whether dual language or bilingual programs were available. As Estella put it, "That is why we have our children here, because here in this school they speak both English and Spanish."

Differences by Generational Status

Our analysis revealed differences by generational
560 status. Specifically, foreign-born mothers reported three themes that were not reported by their U.S.-born counterparts. The first theme unique to the experiences of Mexico- and Puerto Rico-born mothers involved the importance of instilling in their children a sense of
565 *pride in being Latino* generally, and Mexican or Puerto Rican specifically. For example, one mother stated, "I think that more than anything instilling in them the

pride of being...of being Hispanic, of being Mexican...the respect, the family, to feel proud of, of being,
570 of being Mexican. Because unfortunately racism exists here and, well, we like to prepare them a little." Both Mexico- and Puerto Rico-born mothers mentioned the importance of instilling this sense of pride as a buffer for potential encounters with racism.

575 Another difference across generational status was the notion that traditional *religious foods* were an important component of celebrating religious holidays and provided an opportunity for mothers to socialize their children. For example, Mexico-born mothers dis-
580 cussed the importance of the Christmas *posadas* (a reenactment of Mary and Joseph's search for shelter to await the birth of Christ, which culminates in a celebration at a community member's home) and how it was important to carry on this tradition in the U.S. Further-
585 more, they went into detail about the special meals that were prepared during this occasion. Generally, mothers discussed with their children the traditional ways of celebrating Christmas in their country of origin, and those conversations often revolved around the tradi-
590 tional meals that were served.

Foreign-born mothers also introduced the importance of instilling in their children the value of *respect*, not only toward elders, but toward humankind. As one mother stated, "I think that since they are young, one
595 has to teach them the respect for people, and for one [i.e., herself], and for themselves." Thus, there was a common sentiment across foreign-born groups that children should be taught to respect people, in general. Furthermore, mothers implied that this value was a
600 unique representation of their culture.

Analysis of Mexican-Origin Mothers

Similarities by generation. Mexican-origin mothers shared one common theme across generations: the idea that identity transcends birthplace or place of residence. Their discussions emphasized the idea that their
605 children's identity as Mexican would not change regardless of place of residence or birth. For example, the statements below illustrate this sentiment:

Tina: Because he is never going to stop being Mexican no matter where he is, or where he was born.

610 *Cecilia*: He is Mexican, despite that they can give him a legal citizenship, yes, he can be a resident...but his parents are Mexican and he has to...follow.

Differences by generational status. There were also differences in the process of ethnic socialization that
615 emerged between Mexican mothers born in Mexico and those born in the U.S. Specifically, seven themes emerged in the focus groups of Mexico-born mothers, which did not emerge in the focus groups of Mexican mothers born in the U.S. In contrast, one theme
620 emerged in the focus groups of U.S.-born mothers but did not emerge in the focus groups of Mexico-born mothers. Finally, while teaching cultural differences emerged in the groups of both U.S.-born and Mexico-

born mothers, the types of cultural differences that
625 were discussed were different.

First, Mexico-born mothers often discussed *family get-togethers* as a method of socializing their children about their Mexican heritage. Specifically, events such as birthdays, baptisms, Christmas, and New Year's
630 were critical to the process of familial ethnic socialization. In these events, family members could pass on their heritage and their traditions. Yet it was not necessarily through the activities that children learned, but through the family unity that the gatherings provided.
635 Furthermore, family gatherings were mentioned as an important aspect of Mexican culture that should be continued throughout generations.

Mothers also socialized their children about their Mexican heritage by *exposing them to Mexican music,*
640 *dances, and traditional costumes.* Specifically, Mexico-born mothers indicated that music symbolized culture and that by teaching their children how to distinguish the music and dances from various regions, they were teaching them about the Mexican culture.

645 Mexico-born mothers also explained that part of the process of ethnic socialization involved *instilling* the value of a *strong* work ethic. For many mothers, this idea was discussed in the context of discriminatory experiences or the lower status that they felt that Mexi-
650 cans, in general, experienced. The following statement illustrates this idea: "But we are never at the top, we are always at the bottom. We are always the worst. And I think that I sometimes talk to my son about that, that there are a lot of negative things out there about us,
655 and that we should try to excel, that we should try to show them that we are not what they show we are."

Mexico-born mothers also emphasized the role of *religion* in the process of familial ethnic socialization. They discussed the value of teaching their children
660 about God and taking them to church. In fact, mothers seemed in agreement that religion was not separate from culture.

When asked where and how their children learned about their culture from outside the home, Mexico-
665 born mothers indicated that community museums provided an opportunity to teach their children about their Mexican heritage. As Tina explained, "once a month, ah, we go to the, the museum where there is everything about…we usually go as a family…where there is eve-
670 rything about Mexico…. And who better [to explain] than us who truly know or who studied a little bit of that."

Watching *Spanish television* or listening to *Spanish radio stations* were other important ways in which
675 children of Mexico-born mothers learned about their background. Specifically, Mexico-born mothers discussed the value of having their children learn about the culture and maintain the Spanish language by watching Spanish television.

680 Finally, Mexico-born mothers discussed how their children learned about their ethnic culture by attending

celebrations, festivals, and dances in their schools. This was not discussed by U.S.-born Mexican mothers, although, as described earlier, all Mexican-origin
685 groups discussed the school curriculum as a facilitator of the process of familial ethnic socialization.

One theme that emerged among U.S.-born mothers but did not emerge among Mexico-born mothers involved using home decor as an opportunity for ethnic
690 socialization. Specifically, they discussed decorating their homes with objects such as pottery, posters, and Mexican flags, which taught their children about their background.

Interestingly, while *teaching cultural differences*
695 emerged in the focus groups of both U.S.-born and Mexico-born mothers, the types of cultural differences that were discussed were very different for the two groups. Both U.S.- and Mexico-born Mexican mothers discussed teaching their children cultural differences as
700 a method of exposing them to their ethnic background. For U.S.-born mothers, however, the focus was on teaching children about diversity in general. For example, mothers discussed teaching their children about the diversity in customs and language that exists within
705 cultures. On the other hand, Mexico-born mothers emphasized the importance of teaching their children the specific differences between U.S. and Mexican cultures. These discussions usually emerged from their children's interest in doing something that their friends
710 were doing, and something that Mexico-born parents felt was inappropriate. Ricarda's statement nicely illustrates the sentiment expressed by various mothers:

> For example, my daughter says to me, "Mom, can I go with my friend?" I say to her, "yes." She says, "what is
715 my curfew?" I say to her, "seven in the evening." She says, "that is too early." I tell her, "no," I say, "you have to obey the rules and you can…." For example, we are Mexicans, our culture is Mexican and, for example, we have to emphasize that they understand that. They are not
720 Americans. They ask why I am not very liberal. They say I am very strict. I tell them that we are here in the United States, but I want for them to have the Mexican customs. Like I was raised.

Analysis of Puerto Rican Mothers

Similarities across generations. Four themes appeared salient in the narratives of all Puerto Rican
725 mothers. First, mothers discussed regularly *getting together with family members* and spending time with one another as a part of their culture. They viewed this as an integral practice for maintaining family unity and
730 described the ways in which their children were socialized regarding this value. Two island-born mothers discussed how holidays provided opportunities for families to get together:

> Zoraida: Yes, but every holiday, well, one, the family
735 gets together and everyone, everyone brings something. But all traditional food.

Veronica: Yeah, that's something already in us as Hispanics. Like, it already is a given that we have to get together and....

740   *Nancy*: ...and celebrate.

Mothers often *reminisced* by comparing childhood
experiences in Puerto Rico with their children's experiences growing up in the United States. Specifically,
island-born mothers like Stella used their own child-
745   hood experiences in Puerto Rico as a way of reminding
their children of their ethnic roots saying, "And it's a
dialogue all the time in, or how we, remember, 'Oh, oh,
ok, look, this is done in Puerto Rico.' In other words,
we bring, bring up 'in Puerto Rico, we do that', 'Oh,
750   yes, look, I learned this in Puerto Rico'." While island-
born mothers discussed their own childhood experiences, mainland-born mothers relayed stories of others'
experiences in Puerto Rico. Although whose stories
were being recounted varied by generational status,
755   both groups of mothers discussed instances of contrasting life in Puerto Rico with life in the U.S.

In addition to reminiscing, mothers in both groups
also discussed how *music and dancing* were ways of
getting their children interested in their ethnic heritage.
760   Ethnic music and dances provided mothers with opportunities to talk to their children about their ethnic heritage because these were topics in which their children
were already interested. Mothers capitalized on their
children's interest and used it as a starting point for
765   explaining Puerto Rican culture. What was unique to
this discussion of music and dance was that it was cited
as something that children learned about both in the
family and in the community. Beyond what happened
in their homes, mothers stated that children also
770   learned about their culture through community events
such as parades, dances, and concerts. Although the
communities provided these events, mothers often discussed instances where they attended the events with
their children. Their statements illustrated a tacit un-
775   derstanding regarding the interplay between community and familial ethnic socialization. Although mothers were lucky to live in an area where such events
were readily available, if they did not choose to attend
with their children, these events would probably no
780   longer occur.

Finally, mothers discussed the importance of teaching their children how to *prepare traditional meals*.
Similar to their sentiments regarding teaching Spanish,
a number of mothers stressed that if they did not teach
785   these skills, their children would have no way of learning about traditional Puerto Rican cuisine. The following exchange illustrates this point:

Lisa: And the thing is, if we don't teach it to our kids,
you're not going to find books on it. There ain't no books
790   on it. So we have to make sure, that we teach *our* kids,
when our kids grow up, they teach *their* kids and it keeps
going.

Mary: It continues throughout the generations.

Blanca: Put it this way, you know what, you don't learn
795   that from books...it's like you learn it from watching
your parents cooking it.

Thus, while there are obvious practical benefits to
teaching children how to cook, mothers' discussions
also conveyed the importance of food as a connection
800   to the ethnic culture.

Differences by generational status. Although both
generations of Puerto Rican mothers shared similar
views regarding ethnic socialization, one theme appeared unique to the experiences of island-born moth-
805   ers. While both generations of mothers agreed on the
importance of fluency in Spanish, island-born mothers
also discussed the importance of rhetoric. For example,
Stella's statement illustrates the responsibility she felt
about ensuring not only that her children could speak
810   Spanish, but also were able to write it properly:

Ah, when I taught my daughter, it's repetition. One
doesn't say "..." one repeats. Repeating a lot so that they
can and they catch it more easily because they already
come with, they have their, they are descendants of....
815   Yeah, but repetition. Afterwards, there's writing. Because
writing is very important, because yes, they probably
know how to speak it but sometimes they don't know
how to write it, and it's very important to me that we sit
down to teach them how to write it.

Discussion

820   Our study aimed to discern how Mexican and
Puerto Rican-origin mothers were socializing their adolescent children about ethnicity. Across all groups,
mothers communicated the importance and purposefulness of familial ethnic socialization practices that took
825   place in their homes. A number of these practices did
not change with greater time in the U.S. For example,
mothers in all groups emphasized the importance of
exposing their children to their country of origin and
utilizing extended family as a resource to facilitate eth-
830   nic socialization. The narratives also support previous
findings with Latinos suggesting that parents try to
instill a sense of one's ethnic roots by exposing children to the culture, history, and heritage (Hughes,
2003). The prevalence of this finding suggests that
835   ethnic socialization is a normative component of child
rearing and undercuts national origin or generational
status (Garcia Coll et al., 1995; Hughes, 2003). Perhaps
parents recognized that although group membership
would not change, the connection to the culture might
840   lose its meaningfulness from one generation to the
next.

Another factor discussed across all groups was the
importance of teaching the Spanish language. These
findings support Padilla's (1999) argument that the
845   native language is a tool that allows individuals to
transmit information about the culture from one generation to the next. Mothers' reported fears about the
loss of the native tongue are not unfounded. Portes and
Schauffler's (1994) study of Latino youth in southern

243

850 Florida revealed that Spanish language use was greater among second-generation youth in a city with a larger Latino population than in one with a more diverse population. The mothers' statements indicate that they recognize the influence of the community on their chil-
855 dren's language proficiency.

Finally, although the family is viewed as the earliest and most influential context for ethnic socialization (Phinney & Rosenthal, 1992), our findings also supported the idea that children's ethnic socialization is a
860 product of the interactions among family, school, and community (e.g., Phinney, 1996). Mothers viewed schools as participating in the ethnic socialization process of their *specific* ethnic origin (e.g., Puerto Rican), as opposed to a panethnic (e.g., Latino) culture.
865 This may be a result of Latino segregation in the city where data were gathered: Puerto Ricans are found predominantly in the northern part of the city, while Mexicans are found predominantly in the south-central part of the city. Given that backdrop, it is easier to un-
870 derstand how parents can find schools that focus on their specific Latino population.

An analysis of similarities by generation provided support for the influence of acculturation on socialization behaviors. Regardless of national origin, foreign-
875 born mothers' statements reflected an awareness of their immigrant (or immigrant-like) status in society that are absent in U.S.-born mothers' statements. First, foreign-born mothers focused on ethnic practices and their authenticity as they were performed in the U.S.
880 For example, they were able to discuss, from firsthand experience, practices of religious celebrations, which appeared to revolve around traditional meals. This is consistent with previous research that finds that religion is a central component of cultural identity and
885 serves as a bridge between the family and the community (Maldonado, 2000; Garcia Coll et al., 1995).

Second, mothers' discussions of values also appeared to serve as a mechanism for preparing their children for stigmatization, an experience that previous
890 research found to be common among Latino groups (Garcia Coll et al., 1995). Regardless of what factors (e.g., discrimination) prompt these discussions, previous research has identified instilling ethnic pride as important among Latinos (Hughes, 2003; Phinney &
895 Chavira, 1995). Finally, mothers' statements regarding the importance of showing respect to *all* individuals support previous research indicating that Asians and Latinos report placing a higher value on respecting others in general and authority figures in particular
900 than do those of European origin (Fuligni, 1998; Fuligni, Tseng, & Lam, 1999; Garcia Coll et al., 1995; Garcia-Preto, 1996a; Harwood, 1992). In addition, Fuligni's (1998) findings with adolescent populations suggested generational differences in that those born
905 and raised in the U.S. were more likely to maintain beliefs and values consistent with the norms of U.S. society. The fact that we did not hear similar discus-

sions among U.S.-born mothers may be a reflection of the acculturation process occurring within the family
910 system, a finding documented in previous work (Rodriguez, Ramirez, & Korman, 1999).

Our findings indicate a number of differences by generation in the narratives of Mexican-origin mothers. These differences in practices could be a reflection of
915 the effects of chronosystem and macrosystem influences on family life. Specifically, as U.S. society becomes more diverse, parents have increased opportunities to expose their children to their ethnic heritage. Given that we found a number of differences by gen-
920 erational status, our findings appear consistent with an acculturation framework, which suggests that families discontinue certain practices as a result of their adaptation to the host culture. The redefined traditions reflect the transactional nature of the acculturative process
925 whereby the interactions between parents, children, and community contribute to the evolution of cultural traditions in both meaning and practice (Foner, 1997; Martinez, 1986). Thus, it is possible that U.S.-born mothers' biculturalism leads them to acknowledge greater
930 complexities in their own group identification, which in turn is reflected in their discussions with their children (Rodriguez et al., 1999).

Puerto Rican mothers revealed more agreement than difference. Specifically, mothers' narratives
935 stressed the importance of connectedness between family members, reflecting the sociocentric (interconnected) orientation of Puerto Rican culture (Harwood, 1992). For example, Harwood, Schoelmerich, Schulze, and Gonzalez (1999) found that when compared to
940 White mothers, Puerto Rican mothers tended to emphasize values and behaviors that reinforced their children's obligations and connections to others.

Our findings regarding the importance of family get-togethers also support this interconnected orienta-
945 tion. These gatherings served the purpose of instilling a cultural value of family unity (Garcia-Preto, 1996b) and allowed mothers to convey their culture to their children by maintaining practices that were common on the island. Given that these gatherings were discussed
950 across generational groups may imply that, in contrast to Mexican mothers, such a practice, with all else that may go along with it (e.g., food), may be more feasible for Puerto Rican mothers because of the close proximity to the island.
955 In addition to differences by generational status, a salient difference that emerged when comparing the experiences of Mexican and Puerto Rican mothers was that Puerto Ricans were more similar across generational groups than were Mexicans. That is, Puerto Ri-
960 can mothers cited similar practices associated with ethnic socialization regardless of whether they were born on the island or the mainland, whereas greater variation existed in the themes raised by Mexican-origin mothers based on their place of birth. The rela-
965 tionship between the country of origin and the U.S.

likely plays a significant role in the practices and behaviors that families maintain after migrating to the U.S. For Puerto Ricans, families can travel with ease between the U.S. and the island because Puerto Rico is a territory of the U.S., and those born on the island automatically gain U.S. citizenship. For Mexican-origin families, on the other hand, travel is encumbered by federal policies that restrict movement between the two countries. These regulations at the macrosystem level may be influencing familial ethnic socialization (i.e., the microsystem level); thus, the differences that are found between generations among Mexicans but not Puerto Ricans may be a result of the differing governmental policies. Nevertheless, it appears that there are more similarities in the process of ethnic socialization between these national origin groups than there are differences, and differences that do exist may be attributed to generational status.

Strengths and Limitations

This study represents an important first step in understanding familial ethnic socialization as experienced by Latino mothers. Our work moves beyond past research that sought to understand minority parents' experiences using a comparative framework, whereby their practices are interpreted according to the traditional paradigm of the dominant population. Further, few studies have explored ethnic socialization practices of either foreign-born or U.S.-born Latino parents. Our study allowed the mothers' voices to be heard through the data that enabled us to highlight unique experiences by both national origin and generational status.

Given the exploratory nature of our study, there remain questions about generalizability. We examined only two national origin groups and therefore our findings do not represent the vast diversity that exists among Latinos with regard to national origin. Further, given our recruitment strategies, our findings do not represent the views of those who are not at least minimally involved in the community. It is possible that mothers who maintain involvement in their community are more likely to consider and value issues surrounding the process of familial ethnic socialization.

One of the strengths of qualitative research is that it allows for the collection of rich and detailed data. For example, the differences in themes between Puerto Rican and Mexican mothers suggest the importance of viewing the acculturative process as an experience unique to specific ethnic groups rather than a uniform process occurring within broad ethnic categories. Our findings are consistent with the claim that heterogeneity can be found both within and between cultural groups (Garcia Coll et al., 1995). Thus, our findings can serve as a foundation with which to develop a more comprehensive understanding of the impact of the acculturative process and the complex interface between ecological systems on socialization practices.

Directions for Future Research

Future studies should explore the experiences of other cultural groups, explore nonfamilial socialization agents, and investigate how ecological factors influence adolescents' conceptions and understanding of their ethnicity. For instance, immediate environmental factors (e.g., representation of ethnic group in one's neighborhood) may influence salience of ethnicity. Furthermore, the impact of macroecological factors (i.e., broader and more distal influences such as SES and race relations) should be examined as they can have a considerable impact on adolescents' and families' experiences.

It is also important to decipher whether differences between foreign-born and U.S.-born mothers are related to the acculturation process or are a function of life experiences. For example, due to their relatively recent arrival in the US, immigrant mothers may have greater familiarity with the cultural practices from the country of origin, which can lead to more diverse strategies than are available to their U.S.-born counterparts. This is not because the U.S.-born are any less attached to or engaged in their native culture but because they cannot draw from the recent experiences.

Finally, our findings underscore the need for future studies to incorporate a more comprehensive and multifaceted theoretical framework when studying familial processes among ethnic groups. For example, we saw the influence of acculturation in how mothers taught their children the Spanish language; however, we also saw the relevance of ecological theory, as mothers relied heavily on their communities to supplement their efforts. As future studies are conceptualized, there should be an increased emphasis on the unique role that these perspectives provide as well as attention to their interactive influence on relational practices and outcomes.

References

Alba, R. D. (1990). *Ethnic identity: The transformation of white America.* New Haven, Yale University Press.

Baca Zinn, M., & Wells, B. (2000). Diversity within Latino families: New lessons for family social science. In D. H. Demo, K. R. Allen, & M. A. Fine (Eds.), *Handbook of family diversity* (pp. 252–273). Oxford: Oxford University Press.

Bronfenbrenner, U. (1989). Ecological systems theory. *Annals of Child Development, 6,* 187–249.

Buriel, R., & DeMent, T. (1997). Immigration and sociocultural changes in Mexican, Chinese, and Vietnamese American families. In A. Booth, A. C. Crouter, & Landale (Eds.), *Immigration and the family: Research policy on U.S. immigrants* (pp. 165–200). Mahwah, NJ: Erlbaum.

Cortes, D. E., Rogler, L. H., & Malgady, R. G. (1994). Biculturality among Puerto Rican adults in the United States. *American Journal of Community Psychology, 22,* 707–721.

Dasgupta, S. D. (1998). Gender roles and cultural continuity in the Asian Indian immigrant community in the U.S. *Sex Roles: A Journal of Research, 38,* 953–974.

Erikson, E. H. (1968). *Identity: Youth and crisis.* New York: W. W. Norton and Company.

Foner, N. (1997). The immigrant family: Cultural legacies and cultural changes. *International Migration Review, 31,* 961–974.

Fuligni, A. J. (1998). Authority, autonomy, and parent-adolescent conflict and cohesion: A study of adolescents from Mexican, Chinese, Filipino, and European backgrounds. *Developmental Psychology, 34,* 782–792.

Fuligni, A. J., Tseng, V., & Lam, M. (1999) Attitudes toward family obligations among American adolescents with Asian, Latin American, and European backgrounds. *Child Development, 70,* 1030–1044.

Garcia Coll, C. T., Meyer, E. C., & Brillon, L. (1995). Ethnic and minority parenting. In M. H. Bornstein (Ed.), *Handbook of parenting* (pp. 189–209). Mahwah, NJ: Erlbaum.

Garcia-Preto, N. (1996a). Latino families: An overview. In M. McGoldrick, J. Giordano, & J. K. Pearce (Eds.), *Ethnicity and family therapy* (pp. 141–154). New York: Guilford.

Garcia-Preto, N. (1996b). Puerto Rican families. In M. McGoldrick, J. Giordano, & J. K. Pearce (Eds.), *Ethnicity and family therapy* (pp. 183–189). New York: Guilford.

Gonzalez-Ramos, G., Zayas, L. H., & Cohen, E. V. (1998). Child-rearing values of low-income, urban Puerto Rican mothers of preschool children. *Professional Psychology: Research and Practice, 29,* 377–382.

Guzman, B. (2001). The Hispanic population: Census 2000 Brief. *Current Population Reports,* C2KBR/01-3. Washington, DC: U.S. Census Bureau.

Harrison, A. O., Wilson, M. N., Pine, C. J., Chan, S. Q., & Buriel, R. (1995). Family ecologies of ethnic minority children. In N. R. Goldberger & J. B. Veroff (Eds.), *The culture and psychology reader* (pp. 292–320). New York: New York University Press.

Harwood, R. L. (1992). The influence of culturally derived values on Anglo and Puerto Rican mothers' perceptions of attachment behavior. *Child Development, 63,* 822–839.

Harwood, R. L., Schoelmerich, A., Schulze, P. A., & Gonzalez, Z. (1999). Cultural differences in maternal beliefs and behaviors: A study of middle-class Anglo and Puerto Rican mother-infant pairs in four everyday situations. *Child Development, 70,* 1005–1016.

Hill, C. E., Thompson, B. J., & Williams, E. N. (1997). A guide to conducting consensual qualitative research. *Counseling Psychologist, 25,* 517–72.

Hughes, D. (2003). Correlates of African American and Latino parents' messages to children about ethnicity and race: A comparative study of racial socialization. *American Journal of Community Psychology, 31,* 15–33.

Knight, G. P., Bernal, M. E. Garza, C. A., Cota, M. K., & Ocampo, K. A. (1993). Family socialization and the ethnic identity of Mexican-American children. *Journal of Cross-Cultural Psychology, 24,* 99–114.

Knight, G. P., Cota, M. K., & Bernal, M. E. (1993). The socialization of cooperative, competitive, and individualistic preferences among Mexican American children: The mediating role of ethnic identity. *Hispanic Journal of Behavioral Sciences, 15,* 291–309.

Lay, C., & Verkuyten, M. (1999). Ethnic identity and its relation to personal self esteem: A comparison of Canadian-born and foreign-born Chinese adolescents. *The Journal of Social Psychology, 139,* 288–299.

Maldonado, D., Jr. (2000). The changing religious practice of Hispanics. In P. S. J. Cafferty & D. W. Engstrom (Eds.), *An agenda for the 21st century: Hispanics in the United States* (pp. 97–121). New Brunswick, NJ: Transaction.

Martinez, M. A. (1986). Family socialization among Mexican Americans. *Human Development, 29,* 264–279.

Miles, M., & Huberman, M. A. (1994) *Qualitative data analysis.* Thousand Oaks, CA: Sage Publications.

Morgan, D. L. (1997). *Focus groups as qualitative research.* Thousand Oaks, CA: Sage Publications.

Padilla, A. (1999). Psychology. In J. A. Fishman (Ed.), *Handbook of language and ethnic identity* (pp. 109–121). New York: Oxford University Press.

Patton, M. Q. (1990). *Qualitative evaluation and research methods.* Newbury Park, CA: Sage Publications.

Phinney, J. S. (1996). Understanding ethnic diversity: The role of ethnic identity. *American Behavioral Scientist, 40,* 143–152.

Phinney, J. S., & Chavira, V. (1995). Parental ethnic socialization and adolescent coping with problems related to ethnicity. *Journal of Research on Adolescence, 5,* 31–53.

Phinney, J. S., & Nakayama, S. (1991, April). Parental influences on ethnic identity formation in adolescents. Paper presented at the Biennial Meeting of the Society for Research in Child Development, Seattle, WA.

Phinney, J. S., & Rosenthal, D. A. (1992). Ethnic identity in adolescence: Process, context, and outcome. In G. R. Adams, T. P. Gullota, & R. Montemayor (Eds.), *Adolescent identity formation* (pp. 145–172). Newbury Park, CA: Sage Publications.

Portes, A., & Schauffter, R. (1994). Language and the second generation: Bilingualism yesterday and today. *International Migration Review, 28,* 640–661.

Ramirez, R. R., & de la Cruz, G. P. (2002). The Hispanic population in the United States: March 2002. *Current Population Reports,* 520–545. Washington, DC: U.S. Census Bureau.

Rodriguez, N., Ramirez III, M., & Korman, M. (1999). The transmission of family values across generations of Mexican, Mexican American, and Anglo American families: Implications for mental health. In R. H. Sheets et al. (Eds.), *Racial and ethnic identity in school practices: Aspects of human development* (pp. 7–28). Mahwah, NJ: Erlbaum.

Roosa, M. W., Dumka, L. E., Gonzales, N. A., & Knight, G. P. (2002). Cultural/ethnic issues and the prevention scientist in the 21st century. *Prevention and Treatment, 5,* Article 5.

Rosenthal, D. A., & Feldman, S. S. (1992). The nature and stability of ethnic identity in Chinese youth. *Journal of Cross-Cultural Psychology, 23,* 214–227.

Rosenthal, D., Whittle, J., & Bell, R. (1989). The dynamic nature of ethnic identity among Greek-Australian adolescents. *Journal of Social Psychology, 129,* 249–258.

Rubin, H. J., & Rubin, I. S. (1995). *Qualitative interviewing: The art of hearing data.* Thousand Oaks, CA: Sage Publications.

Sabogal, F., Marin, G., Otero-Sabogal, R., Marin, B. V., & Perez-Stable, E. J. (1987). Hispanic familism and acculturation: What changes and what doesn't. *Hispanic Journal of Behavioral Sciences, 9,* 397–412.

Saylor, E. S., & Aries, E. (1999). Ethnic identity and change in social context. *The Journal of Social Psychology, 139,* 549–566.

Sridhar, K. K. (1988). Language maintenance and language shift among Asian-Indians: Kannadigas in the New York area. *International Journal of Sociology of Language, 69,* 73–87.

Umaña-Taylor, A. J., Bhanot, R., & Shin, N. (2006). Ethnic identity formation during adolescence: The critical role of families. *Journal of Family Issues, 27,* 390–414.

Umaña-Taylor, A. J., Diversi, M., & Fine, M. A. (2002). Ethnic identity and self-esteem among Latino adolescents: Making distinctions among the Latino populations. *Journal of Adolescent Research, 17,* 303–327.

Umaña-Taylor, A. J., & Fine, M. A. (2001). Methodological implications of grouping Latino adolescents into one collective ethnic group. *Hispanic Journal of Behavioral Sciences, 23,* 347–362.

Umaña-Taylor, A. J., & Fine, M. A. (2004). Examining a model of ethnic identity development among Mexican-origin adolescents living in the U.S. *Hispanic Journal of Behavioral Sciences, 26,* 36–59.

U.S. Census Bureau. (2004). 2004 Fact Sheet for U.S. Retrieved December 1, 2005, from http://factfinder.census.gov/servlet/ACSSAFFFacts

Zayas, L. H., & Rojas-Flores, L. (2002). Learning from Latino parents: Combining etic and emic approaches to designing interventions. In J. M. Contreras, K. A. Kerns, & A. M. Neal-Barnett (Eds.), *Latino children and families in the United States* (pp. 233–249). Westport, CT: Greenwood/Praeger.

Acknowledgments: The authors would like to thank Jennifer Hardesty for her comments on a previous version of this article. Stanley O. Gaines, Jr., was the action editor on this article.

Address correspondence to: Adriana J. Umaña-Taylor, Arizona State University, Department of Family and Human Development, P.O. Box 872502, Tempe, AZ 85287-2502. E-mail: adriana.umana-taylor@asu.edu

Exercise for Article 38

Factual Questions

1. According to the literature review, does *current* theoretical work on acculturation indicate that in the process of adapting to the ways of the dominant culture, individuals will lose their identification with their ethnic group?

2. How is "familial ethnic socialization" defined?

3. The researchers state how many research questions?

4. To facilitate recruitment, the researchers developed relationships with what?

5. Did the researchers *independently* summarize the core idea of each code?

6. In the Results section, the researchers indicate that nine themes were applicable across all groups. What is the first theme the researchers discuss?

Questions for Discussion

7. The researchers used a sample that was heterogeneous in age (ranging from 26 years to 66 years old). If you had planned this study, would you have used a sample this heterogeneous in age? Explain. (See lines 288–289.)

8. In your opinion, did the researchers use a convenience sample? Explain. (See lines 293–303 and 1000–1006.)

9. The researchers show the exact words used to introduce the purpose of the research project to the focus groups. How helpful is it to know these words? (See lines 324–333.)

10. The researchers present quotations from participants in the Results section. How helpful are these quotations in helping you understand the results of this study? Could the presentation of the results be improved by adding more quotations? By reducing the number of quotations? Explain. (See lines 371–819.)

11. The Results section in lines 371–819 and the Discussion section in lines 820–1056 are longer than corresponding sections in most of the articles in this book. Is the length of these sections a strength of this research report? Explain.

12. If you had planned this research, would you have opted to use a qualitative approach or a quantitative approach? Explain.

Quality Ratings

Directions: Indicate your level of agreement with each of the following statements by circling a number from 5 for strongly agree (SA) to 1 for strongly disagree (SD). If you believe an item is not applicable to this research article, leave it blank. Be prepared to explain your ratings. When responding to criteria A and B below, keep in mind that brief titles and abstracts are conventional in published research.

A. The title of the article is appropriate.

SA   5   4   3   2   1   SD

B. The abstract provides an effective overview of the research article.

SA   5   4   3   2   1   SD

C. The introduction establishes the importance of the study.

SA   5   4   3   2   1   SD

D. The literature review establishes the context for the study.

SA   5   4   3   2   1   SD

E. The research purpose, question, or hypothesis is clearly stated.

SA   5   4   3   2   1   SD

F. The method of sampling is sound.

SA   5   4   3   2   1   SD

G. Relevant demographics (for example, age, gender, and ethnicity) are described.

SA   5   4   3   2   1   SD

H. Measurement procedures are adequate.

SA   5   4   3   2   1   SD

I. All procedures have been described in sufficient detail to permit a replication of the study.

SA   5   4   3   2   1   SD

J. The participants have been adequately protected from potential harm.

SA   5   4   3   2   1   SD

K. The results are clearly described.

SA   5   4   3   2   1   SD

L. The discussion/conclusion is appropriate.

SA   5   4   3   2   1   SD

M. Despite any flaws, the report is worthy of publication.

SA   5   4   3   2   1   SD

Article 39

Help-Seeking Behaviors and Depression among African American Adolescent Boys

MICHAEL A. LINDSEY
University of Maryland

WYNNE S. KORR
University of Illinois

MARINA BROITMAN
National Institute of Mental Health

LEE BONE
Johns Hopkins University

ALAN GREEN
Johns Hopkins University

PHILIP J. LEAF
Johns Hopkins University

ABSTRACT. This study examined the help-seeking behaviors of depressed, African American adolescents. Qualitative interviews were conducted with 18 urban, African American boys, ages 14 to 18, who were recruited from community-based mental health centers and after-school programs for youths. Interviews covered sociodemographic information, questions regarding depressive symptomatology, and open-ended questions derived from the Network-Episode Model—including knowledge, attitudes and behaviors related to problem recognition, help seeking, and perceptions of mental health services. Most often adolescents discussed their problems with their family and often received divergent messages about problem resolution; absent informal network resolution of their problems, professional help would be sought, and those receiving treatment were more likely to get support from friends but were less likely to tell friends that they were actually receiving care. Implications for social work research and practice are discussed.

From *Social Work, 51*, 49–58. Copyright © 2006 by the National Association of Social Workers. Reprinted with permission.

Childhood depression is a serious public health concern for families, schools, social workers, and other mental health practitioners. Annual estimates in the general population indicate that 8.3% of adolescents
5 suffer from depression (Birmaher et al., 1996). Although research indicates that depression is highly amenable to treatment (Petersen et al., 1993), the *Surgeon General's Report on Mental Health* (U.S. Department of Health and Human Services [HHS], 2001)
10 indicated that few children and adolescents with a depressive disorder receive care.

African American adolescents who reside in urban, high-risk communities may be among the most underserved populations. African American adolescents ex-
15 perience depression more than adolescents from other racial and ethnic groups (Garrison, Jackson, Marsteller, McKeown, & Addy, 1990; Roberts, Roberts, & Chen, 1997; Wu et al., 1999). Because African American adolescents are more likely than other groups to live in
20 low-income households, they may be at particularly high risk of depression. Depression among African American adolescent boys, in particular, has been linked to having fewer perceived future opportunities (Hawkins, Hawkins, Sabatino, & Ley, 1998); low
25 neighborhood social capital and kinship social support (Stevenson, 1998); and violent behavior in African American adolescent boys living in an urban, high-risk setting (DuRant, Getts, Cadenhead, Emans, & Woods, 1995). Furthermore, African American adolescents
30 may experience barriers to identifying and using effective treatments.

Although African American adolescent boys have been recognized as a group having multiple needs, few of these discussions address their mental health needs.
35 High rates of substance abuse, academic failure (i.e., dropout rates), and high arrest and incarceration rates are problems disproportionately experienced by urban African American adolescent boys (Gibbs, 1990; Hutchinson, 1996; Majors & Billson, 1992). Unrecognized
40 and untreated mental illness may underlie these problems. Although researchers have recognized that few African American children and adolescents in need of mental health services receive them (Angold et al., 2002; HHS, 2001), there has been little discussion of
45 the attitudes and beliefs of the youths, their families, and their peers that might contribute to their underutilization of mental health services.

It is unlikely that access to services will increase unless we achieve a better understanding of how these
50 youths view their symptoms and service options and how their networks influence these views. For example, studies indicate African American adolescents and adults are less likely than white adolescents and adults to acknowledge the need for mental health services and
55 to be skeptical of using mental health services, especially when they believe they may be stigmatized by their social networks because of their service use (McKay, Nudelman, McCadam, & Gonzales, 1996; Richardson, 2001). African American adolescents and
60 their families are therefore likely to have many negative perceptions (and experiences) of mental health

care that reduce the likelihood of their seeking care even when it is available.

Social networks (peers and families) play an impor-
65 tant role regarding help-seeking behaviors and re-
sponses to ill health (Pescosolido & Boyer, 1999; Pescosolido, Wright, Alegria, & Vera, 1998; Rogler & Cortes, 1993). Studies regarding access to care indicate that pathways to care are shaped by the type of prob-
70 lem experienced, as well as the social support provided by network members (Bussing et al., 2003; Pescosolido, Gardner, & Lubell, 1998). Social net-works may attempt to provide care or are used as a resource for identifying pathways to formal help,
75 sometimes coercing the affected individual into care (Pescosolido, Gardner, & Lubell; Pescosolido & Boyer). Social networks also monitor the care received and provide assistance with maintenance of care (i.e., offer transportation to care, give appointment remind-
80 ers), or network members may perpetuate stigma re-garding formal service use.

Earlier studies examining the use of mental health services have tended to ignore the social processes re-lated to seeking care and advice (Pescosolido, 1991),
85 but these processes may be particularly cogent in con-sidering service seeking among African American ado-lescent boys. A majority of African American adults use informal help sources exclusively or in combina-tion with professional help in response to psychological
90 distress (Chatters, Taylor, & Neighbors, 1989). These processes are particularly important to consider when discussing adolescents, because adolescents turn first to family members and friends when experiencing a men-tal health problem (Boldero & Fallon, 1995; Offer,
95 Howard, Schonert, & Ostrov, 1991; Saunders, Resnick, Hobermann, & Blum, 1994).

It is important to improve access to care for African American adolescent boys in mental health treatment. Therefore, the purpose of this study was to explore the
100 help-seeking behaviors and mental health attitudes of depressed African American adolescent boys. To better control for variability in disorder type, the study fo-cused on depression in youths. To better understand the factors that facilitate or hinder entrée into treatment,
105 participants included both youths receiving mental health services and youths not in treatment. Findings from this study can inform social work practitioners and other mental health providers in their efforts to facilitate this group's use of services through better
110 understanding of the role that network members play in facilitating or inhibiting service use; and increase the number of services perceived as acceptable and effec-tive to this underserved group through the design of more culturally appropriate interventions and engage-
115 ment strategies.

Method

Participants and Data Collection

Eighteen respondents ages 14 to 18 who were al-ready participating in a broader study titled "Social Network Influences on African American Adolescents'
120 Mental Health Service Use" (Lindsey, 2002) were re-cruited for this study. Participants (n = 10) were re-cruited from community-based mental health treatment centers and a mental health practitioner in private prac-tice and from community-based, nonclinical programs
125 for high-risk youths (i.e., a violence prevention pro-gram, truancy abatement center, and homeless shelter) (n = 8). In each setting, all potential participants were individually approached by a therapist or program staff member who explained the study and assessed their
130 participation interest. Flyers were posted in each re-cruitment site describing the study. Informed consent for participation was obtained from parents or guardi-ans, and informed assent was obtained from partici-pants.

Participants in this study were selected on the basis
135 of elevated depressive symptoms as assessed by the Center for Epidemiologic Studies Depression Scale (CES-D) (Radloff, 1977). Of the 69 who participated in the original study, 18 met this criterion and agreed to participate. This study received Institutional Review
140 Board (IRB) approval at the University of Pittsburgh (IRB Approval: #001132).

Data were collected through a semi-structured in-terview schedule. Questions were derived from the Network-Episode Model (NEM) (Pescosolido, 1991);
145 in particular, the NEM concept network content (i.e., degree of support, attitudes, and beliefs toward mental illness and mental health care). In addition to network content, questions were derived from the literature on help-seeking behaviors among adolescents (i.e., help-
150 seeking pathways engaged in by youths), as well as the literature on mental health service utilization among African Americans. (See Table 1 for examples of the questions and follow-up probes used in the protocol.) Most of the interviews were conducted in the respon-
155 dents' homes and a few in community sites: mental health centers or community-based organizations. All interviews were conducted in private areas and lasted between 45 min and 1 hr and 45 min.

The interview covered processes and help-seeking
160 patterns, network influences, and attitudes toward men-tal health care and race or ethnicity of the provider. The first author and a trained research assistant conducted the interviews. Participants were encouraged to talk at length about their help-seeking behaviors in relation to
165 their depressive symptoms, with detailed accounts re-garding the ways their network influenced their behav-iors. They were also asked how they conceptualized and defined mental health and associated emotional and psychological struggles (described in the protocol
170 as "feeling sad or hurt inside").

Interviews were tape-recorded, transcribed, and analyzed using inductive coding techniques (Miles & Huberman, 1994). Three readers, including the first author and two research assistants, independently re-

Table 1
Sample Interview Questions and Follow-Up Probes Regarding the Help-Seeking Behaviors among African American Adolescent Boys

Question	Probe
When you start feeling like something makes you feel sad or hurt inside, what do you do?	How did you know that you needed to talk with somebody?
	Was there anyone who helped you to recognize or identify the feelings that you were having?
	Whom did you turn to first for help?
	Are there other things you tried to do to help you feel better beyond talking with other people?
	How did these other things work?
If you felt you just couldn't handle things going on in your life, where would you prefer to go for help? Why?	(If therapist/counselor not mentioned) Why wouldn't you go to a therapist/counselor?
	What would your friends think if you went to a therapist/counselor?
	What about your family?

175 viewed and coded transcripts to identify patterns and themes emerging from the data. After the review and designation of codes, the readers convened consensus sessions to determine the categories and subcategories of themes. A final coding matrix was developed by the
180 first author to indicate the category and subcategory of themes, a definition clarifying the meaning for each category and subcategory, and corresponding sample quotes that best captured the theme.

Findings

Themes emerged in the following areas: type of
185 problems experienced, descriptions of help-seeking behaviors, dealing with emotional pain, influence of the social network on help seeking, and perceptions of mental illness and mental health care. Within these themes, differences emerged between respondents in
190 treatment for their depressive symptoms and those not in treatment (see Table 2).

Influences of Social Network on Experiences of Depression

Family members played an important role as sources for help and support as the respondents discussed how they actively sought out family members
195 for help when dealing with depressive symptoms—that is, feeling sad or hurt inside. In many cases, respondents from both groups reported that their mother was the family member they talked to most frequently:

When problems are too bad where I just can't, I can't like
200 stop them, I can't do nothing, can't control it or nothing. I try to go out and play, but for some reason it pops back up in my head, and I can't get it out so I go to her [referring to his mother]. (*Participant not in treatment.*)

(*Referring to what prompts him to talk to his mother.*)
205 Like, I mean if something happened like with me or my friends that we couldn't handle as friends, we couldn't handle as minors, but something that my mother should know…. I mean I'm thankful that I have an understanding mom and all that. (*Participant in treatment.*)

210 Family members were equally important for both groups regarding advice or counsel received when feeling sad or hurt inside. However, those in treatment typically received advice and counsel from friends as well, whereas those not in treatment typically sought
215 the advice and counsel of only their family members.

As a way to deal with feeling sad or hurt inside, some respondents talked about how they would spend time alone or isolate themselves before or in place of talking with someone in their network:

220 Just deal with it. There's nothing—I mean it's just life. I go through. I mean, I don't know. I don't seek no help. I don't talk to nobody or nothing. I just go on with whatever I'm doing. (*Participant in treatment.*)

I try to go within myself, so I pretty much get the an-
225 swers. It's like a self-conscious. (*Participant in treatment.*)

Adolescent boys in treatment typically identified their emotional and psychological struggles on their own, first, with eventual assistance from family mem-
230 bers:

I just feel it…. It's a certain, it's a certain rush that you get sometimes. Nothing like on a football field or anything, but just your heart's racing, and I think that's the best sign of you knowing when to talk to someone. Even
235 if you say you don't have the courage or you say you don't want to, but deep down you really do because the only way to really solve anything is to talk to someone. (*Participant in treatment.*)

Engagement in religious or spiritual activities was
240 not a common response to feeling sad or hurt inside among this sample. This finding was striking given the historical role of spirituality and religion as a source for coping, support, and healing among African Americans. Only two of the 18 respondents, one from each
245 group, reported that they currently engaged in activities such as praying or going to church.

Table 2
Emerging Themes Regarding Help Seeking and Depression among African American Adolescent Boys, by Treatment Status

Area	In treatment ($n = 10$)	Not in treatment ($n = 8$)
Problems experienced	Interpersonal conflict among peers	Family strain
	Problems at school (behavioral or academic)	
Behaviors when dealing with a problem	Talks to family and friends	Talks to family only
	Isolation	
People helping to identify the problem (other than family)	Self	No one
	Teacher or other school personnel	
Preference for help	Family first, then professionals	Family only

Influences of Social Network on Help Seeking and Service Use

Network's Influence on Receipt of Formal Services.
The respondents who were in treatment ($n = 10$) were asked to address questions regarding the process by which they were initially referred to formal mental health treatment. Five of the 10 respondents reported that they were referred to treatment by their school when teachers noted a decrease in functioning (academically and behaviorally) and parents or guardians agreed that professional help should be sought for these problems:

> They [teachers and school officials] were like, maybe what you should do is and they were feeding her [mother]—and it's like more than one teacher saying it…. And they're like maybe you should do this. And then she put me in the program up at [outpatient treatment facility].

> It was a recommendation…. It was a recommendation, yeah, from a lady at school…to my mother. And they had said, you know, try this out. They thought I had ADHD, they thought I was bipolar and all this stuff, but they couldn't put their finger on it. There was nothing that they could do to figure out exactly what was wrong with me.

Four of the 10 reported that a parent suggested or referred them for treatment:

> My mom, yeah. Because she thought I had, you know, problems, issues or whatever. She just got me a counselor.

A parent's suggestion, however, should be distinguished here from a parental mandate. Several respondents (3 of 10) reported that a parent mandated formal mental health treatment, and they disagreed with this mandate:

> She's making me [go to a MH professional]. If I had a choice or my say so, all this wouldn't be going on because I'm cool. I don't feel there's nothing wrong. I don't need no help. She asked me if I did. I laughed at her like, "What? Yeah, right."

Network Members' Thoughts about Respondent's Use of Formal Services. When asked whether family or friends would be supportive of their use of mental health services, respondents from both groups said that their family would support their use of formal mental health treatment:

> They've [family] always been very supportive…. Even though a lot of them aren't really around me, aren't really that close to me. There's still enough love to go around. And with that, it makes it easier to come here [to treatment] instead of just being alone and coming here…. That [if family was not supportive] would definitely affect my mood at least. Maybe not necessarily coming here, but confidence-wise, it would definitely be a lot lower than what it is right now. (*Participant in treatment.*)

In contrast to those respondents not in treatment who reported that their family would support their use of mental health services, some from this group said that their family would not support their use of formal services. This finding should be further viewed in light of the problem the not-in-treatment group typically reported experiencing: family strain (problems related to family relations). Two respondents not in treatment reported that their family would want to handle problems regarding family relations among themselves without seeking professional help:

> Because they feel as though why [should I] go to a counselor when I could come to them?

> I think my mom would probably ask me why I didn't come to her first or something like that. "What's wrong with you?" She'd probably get mad. I don't know. But it's like, why didn't I come to her first and talk to her about it instead of me going to a therapist.

Respondents not in treatment also said that they would not talk to friends about their problems typically because their friends would not be supportive of their receipt of formal mental health services. In contrast, many respondents in treatment would talk to their friends when dealing with depressive symptoms. However, they would not tell their friends they were receiving mental health treatment—fearing that friends would laugh, joke, or tease them:

> They'd probably think—they might joke around and say like, it's bad for me, you know, like I'm crazy or some-

330   thing, so I would like keep it to my family and myself. (*Respondent in treatment.*)

Attitudes toward Mental Health Care and Professionals

Respondents from both groups were asked to share their thoughts and perceptions regarding why it is diffi-cult for mental health treatment providers to engage 335 African American adolescent boys in mental health services. The respondents talked about the issue of stigma as a barrier associated with mental health ser-vice use. In particular, shame, embarrassment, and ex-clusion emerged from the interviews as themes regard-340 ing the influences of the network on mental health ser-vice use:

Because their friends might sometimes think like they're crazy and stuff like that. Wouldn't want to hang around them. And they'll just sit there and make up more ex-345 cuses to stay away from them. It [mental health treat-ment] would draw all that person's friends away from him too. Then that person would just be, like, down in the dumps. (*Respondent in treatment.*)

Respondents from both groups said that many Afri-350 can American adolescent boys sought to handle their problems on their own or had too much pride to go to formal mental health treatment:

And I guess a lot of them would think, well, I don't need it. I'm this. I'm from here. I can do this. I can do that. So 355 they would…they have a certain feeling where they think they could get through it alone when they really couldn't. (*Respondent in treatment.*)

(*Referring to pride.*) Like I'm not, you know, I'm too good to go to a counselor. Like I don't think I'm very 360 sick or I don't think nothing's wrong with me. I act nor-mal. I'm normal. You know, different things like that. False sense of themselves. (*Respondent not in treatment.*)

Furthermore, respondents shared their perceptions that talking to a mental health professional, for some 365 African American adolescent boys, meant that they would have to express their emotions associated with feeling sad or hurt inside, and that the expression of emotions was viewed as a sign of weakness among this population:

370   Like they weren't manly enough. Like little girls. (*Re-spondent in treatment.*)

(*Asking for help.*) …means that you're gay. That's what it means. That's how they [African American adolescent boys] interpret it. It means—well, I mean you go down 375 the line. If you ask for help, or if you cry, or if you look emotional, if you feel depressed, that means you're soft. If you're soft, then you're gay and you're not hard and not tough…. You can't let anybody know that you're soft. I swear it's like being in jail. (*Respondent in treat-*380 *ment.*)

These comments reflect a certain machismo related to what may be defined among this population as a lack of strength when expressing emotions (i.e., crying) or asking for help. Similarly, use of the vernacular "gay"

385 among this group is part of a machismo culture that ascribed being weak or lacking strength to being femi-nine and further serves as an impediment to acknowl-edging the need for help and engaging in healthy forms of emotional expression.

390   When asked whether race of the provider affected mental health service utilization among African American adolescent boys, respondents said:

They [African American adolescent boys] don't think that they [white professionals] can understand what 395 they're coming from. (*Respondent in treatment.*)

And I mean it might be one of the…it might be a race is-sue because some—I think that there are some black peo-ple who close themselves off from white people. And, you know, in the mental health field, there is a majority 400 of white people, I think. (*Respondent in treatment.*)

Although the majority of the respondents said that race mattered, a few indicated that race of the provider was not as important; rather, what was important was how the provider treated them and how well the pro-405 vider engaged them. One respondent said:

I can't say it [race of the provider] would make a differ-ence at all because it's about getting help. It's about hav-ing someone that's there for you to understand what you're going through and to give you advice, to give you 410 encouragement, to help you sort out things that you're going through. So with me, white or black doesn't really make a difference. What matters is that we're trustworthy of each other. (*Respondent in treatment.*)

Discussion

The adolescent boys in this study were generally 415 similar to those in broader studies of nonclinical popu-lations (see Boldero & Fallon, 1995; Snell, 2002) in terms of seeking help first from family and at other times from friends and peers. In particular, peers ap-pear to have a powerful influence on this group regard-420 ing the admission of emotional or psychological prob-lems, as well as the acknowledgment of the receipt of formal mental health services. Those who were in treatment said that they received emotional support from their friends, and that they were able to talk to 425 friends about their problems. However, additional analyses of this group revealed that most were reluctant to tell their friends that they were going to formal men-tal health services, fearing that friends would poke fun at them.

430   These contrasting findings reflect the importance of distinguishing between individually felt stigma (i.e., negative beliefs or perceptions of service use emanat-ing from within the individual) and network-induced stigma (i.e., negative beliefs or perceptions articulated 435 by friends regarding the affected individual's service use) when developing interventions and strategies to combat stigma related to service use for this group. Findings regarding the influence of peer networks also reflect the seemingly reasoned calculation about 440 friends by respondents in this study, such as when to

talk to them, what to share with them, and how supportive friends would be regarding the problem they are facing.

This study gives a detailed description of the pathways to help seeking for African American adolescent boys with depressive symptoms, in particular, the roles of family, schools, and social agencies. For respondents receiving mental health care, identification of their mental health problems was more likely to come from family members and school personnel. Although respondents in mental health treatment reported that they initially tried to solve their problems on their own, family members and school personnel still played an active role in confirming their depressive symptoms and facilitating their access to mental health services. It is worth noting that the majority of the respondents who were receiving mental health services reported that the types of problems they experienced concerned issues associated with the school environment (that is, academic achievement or behavioral problems). This finding highlights the important role teachers and other school personnel (such as school social workers) play in the assessment of mental health problems and making referrals to treatment.

Challenges for Social Work

Adolescent boys with high levels of depressive symptoms who are not in treatment, however, may pose a special challenge. Respondents who were not in treatment in this study reported that the problems they most often experienced concerned strained family relations. However, family members often counseled them against going to a professional for help regarding these emotional problems.

The predicament of the subgroup of respondents in this study who were experiencing high levels of depressive symptoms but were not in mental health treatment raises concern. At the time of the interview, each respondent was involved in community-based programs targeting high-risk youths, including a youth employment program, a violence prevention program, a truancy abatement program, and a homeless shelter. However, no one in these settings engaged them about their emotional and psychological struggles by attending to their needs or referring them to care. Although it is important that social work practitioners and other mental health professionals target the development of strategies to address the attitudes of youths toward mental illness and treatment, the situation for this subgroup of youths also reveals that those involved with serving them need to be more sensitive to their mental health needs. These professionals could provide assistance to youths by being referral agents and sources of personal support.

For this high-risk group, religious congregations and affiliated organizations that address contemporary youth problems from a spiritual perspective may serve as an alternative to seeking formal professional help

when dealing with mental health problems. However, unlike earlier literature (e.g., Varon & Riley, 1999) that documented the importance of spirituality and the church in the lives of African Americans, problem solving through prayer or seeking support from the church did not play a significant role in the lives of respondents in this study. This finding could be misleading and illustrates the need for more empirical research to examine the extent to which the general population of African American adolescent boys seeks help from lay and ministry counselors and other adult spiritual figures.

Functional impairment as a result of experiencing depressive symptoms may clarify the issue of why two subgroups of youths with similar depressive symptom scores have disparate treatment trajectories. Based on the self-report of problems experienced between the two subgroups, respondents in treatment said that their problems related to interpersonal conflict and problems at school—behavioral or academic, whereas respondents not in treatment said that their problems related to family strain. Depressive symptoms and associated problems seemed to be recognized or identified by network members when there was an accompanying issue related to functionality. Thus, the perceptions of network members regarding what constitutes impairment needs to be understood as a potential facilitator or barrier to formal mental health treatment.

Limitations of the Study

Because this study focused on depressive symptoms as an indicator of mental health need, we cannot determine how other mental health problems, for example, behavioral disorders (such as conduct disorder and ADHD), in addition to depressive disorders might differentially or concomitantly affect service referral or service use.

Confirmatory and comparative analyses from the perspective of actual network members would have been desirable, but limitations of time and funding dictated that this study be restricted to the adolescents' perceptions of their social network's influences on mental health services use or nonuse. Although the findings are based on the perspectives of a subgroup of African American adolescent boys, this study laid the groundwork for a more extensive investigation of these issues in follow-up studies and for the design of an outreach and an engagement strategy for depressed African American adolescents.

Implications for Practice

Findings from this study have important implications regarding the recognition and identification of depressive symptoms among African American adolescent boys. Strategies to improve the identification and recognition of depressive symptoms among members of this group are needed, especially in schools and other community-based organizations. Social workers and mental health services providers might be looking for depressive symptom expression that fits the *Diagnostic and Statistical Manual of Mental Disorders* (DSM-IV-TR) criteria (American Psychiatric Association, 2000) and may miss the more subtle forms of expression unique to this group. Social workers and mental health service providers need to work collaboratively with community-based organizations serving this group. For example, social workers may provide training and education to staff regarding the signs and symptoms of depression, target strategies that attempt to ameliorate the perceived stigma among this group and those in their network, and develop intervention models that better engage families by incorporating them into the treatment process throughout the course of care. Better identification of mental health problems (i.e., depression) by social network members and those who provide treatment needs to become a targeted education strategy.

Quite often, professional help is a source of mental health care of last resort. There are multiple barriers regarding the help-seeking behaviors among adolescents enrolled in community-based programs, including stigma associated with mental illness, machismo and pride, and families and adolescents who believe that depression can be resolved without professional help. Therefore, it is necessary to reframe help seeking as a positive, proactive behavior among African American adolescent boys and their families.

Implications for Research

Future research needs to address the role of family and peers in the help-seeking process. Interventions that are effective for African American youths are particularly needed because social and family networks are not likely to be active users of mental health services, except when these are initiated through school. Survey research is needed to determine the extent to which the attitudes shown by youths in the single community studied are consistent across the country and the extent to which these attitudes are similar to or different from those of youths from other racial and ethnic groups. Particular attention should be given to determining the extent to which parents, especially mothers, and peers may inhibit help-seeking among this group. Once a better understanding of the network members' role in inhibiting the help-seeking process is ascertained, strategies for removing these barriers can be developed.

Studies examining the impact of referral type (mandated versus choice) on perceptions and use of mental health services have been done with adults (Pescosolido, Gardner, & Lubell, 1998). However, future research needs to examine this issue among adolescents of color, as well as the extent to which parent and child disagreement regarding problem identification and definition negatively affect the engagement process and utilization of mental health services.

Finally, findings from this study indicate that race of the provider was seen as an important issue among some respondents, particularly the belief that providers who were not African American would be unable to effectively treat this population. Thus, future research regarding the mental health treatment experiences of this group is necessary to determine how provider characteristics (i.e., race and gender) affect engagement and mental health treatment.

References

American Psychiatric Association. (2000). *Diagnostic and statistical manual of mental disorders (text revision)* (DSM-IV-TR). Washington, DC: American Psychiatric Press.

Angold, A., Erkanli, A., Farmer, E. M. Z., Fairbank, J. A., Burns, B. J., Keeler, G., & Costello, E. J. (2002). Psychiatric disorder, impairment, and service use in rural African American and white youth. *Archives of General Psychiatry, 59*, 893–901.

Birmaher, B., Ryan, N. D., Williamson, D. E., Brent, D. A., Kaufman, J., Dahl, R. E., Perel, J., & Nelson, B. (1996). Childhood and adolescent depression: A review of the past 10 years. Part I. *Journal of the American Academy of Child & Adolescent Psychiatry, 35*, 1427–1439.

Boldero, J., & Fallon, B. (1995). Adolescent help-seeking: What do they get help for and from whom? *Journal of Adolescence, 18*, 193–209.

Bussing, R., Zima, B. T., Gary, F. A., Mason, D. M., Leon, C. E., Sinha, K., & Garvan, C. W. (2003). Social networks, caregiver strain, and utilization of mental health services among elementary school students at high risk for ADHD. *Journal of the American Academy of Child & Adolescent Psychiatry, 42*, 842–850.

Chatters, L., Taylor, R., & Neighbors, H. (1989). Size of informal helper network mobilized during a serious personal problem among black Americans. *Journal of Marriage and the Family, 51*, 667–676.

DuRant, R. H., Getts, A., Cadenhead, C., Emans, S. J., & Woods, E. R. (1995). Exposure to violence and victimization and depression, hopelessness, and purpose in life among adolescents living in and around public housing. *Developmental and Behavioral Pediatrics, 16*, 233–237.

Garrison, C., Jackson, K., Marsteller, F., McKeown, R., & Addy, C. (1990). A longitudinal study of depressive symptomotology in young adolescents. *Journal of the American Academy of Child & Adolescent Psychiatry, 29*, 581–585.

Gibbs, J. (1990). Mental health issues of black adolescents: Implications for policy and practice. In A. Stiffman & L. Davis (Eds.), *Ethnic issues in adolescent mental health* (pp. 21–52). Newbury Park, CA: Sage Publications.

Hawkins, W., Hawkins, M., Sabatino, C., & Ley, S. (1998). Relationship of perceived future opportunity to depressive symptomotology of inner-city African-American adolescents. *Children and Adolescent Services, 20*, 757–764.

Hutchinson, E. (1996). *The assassination of the black male image.* Los Angeles: Middle Passage Press.

Lindsey, M. (2002). *Social network influences on African-American adolescents' mental health service use.* Unpublished doctoral dissertation, University of Pittsburgh.

Majors, R., & Billson, J. (1992). *Cool pose—The dilemmas of black manhood in America.* New York: Lexington Books.

McKay, M., Nudelman, R., McCadam, K., & Gonzales, J. (1996). Involving inner-city families in mental health services: First interview engagement skills. *Research on Social Work Practice, 6*, 462–472.

Miles, M., & Huberman, A. (1994). *Qualitative data analysis: An expanded source book* (2nd ed.). Thousand Oaks, CA: Sage Publications.

Offer, D., Howard, K., Schonert, K., & Ostrov, E. (1991). To whom do adolescents turn for help? Differences between disturbed and nondisturbed adolescents. *Journal of the American Academy of Child & Adolescent Psychiatry, 30*, 623–630.

Pescosolido, B. (1991). Illness careers and network ties: A conceptual model of utilization and compliance. *Advances in Medical Sociology, 2*, 161–184.

Pescosolido, B., & Boyer, C. (1999). How do people come to use mental health services? Current knowledge and changing perspectives. In A. Horwitz & T. Scheid (Eds.), *A handbook for the study of mental health: Social contexts, theories, and systems* (pp. 392–411). New York: Cambridge University Press.

Pescosolido, B., Garner, C., & Lubell, K. (1998). How people get into mental health services: Stories of choice, coercion, and "muddling through" from "first timers." *Social Science and Medicine, 46*, 275–286.

Pescosolido, B., Wright, E., Alegria, M., & Vera, M. (1998). Social networks and patterns of use among the poor with mental health problems in Puerto Rico. *Medical Care, 36*, 1057–1072.

Petersen, A. C., Compas, B. E., Brooks-Gunn, J., Stemmler, M., Ey, S., & Grant, K. (1993). Depression in adolescence. *American Psychologist, 48*, 155–168.

Radloff, L. S. (1977). The CES-D Scale: A self-report depression scale for research in the general population. *Applied Psychological Measurement, 1,* 385–401.

Richardson, L. (2001). Seeking and obtaining mental health services: What do parents expect? *Archives of Psychiatric Nursing, 15,* 223–231.

Roberts, R., Roberts, C., & Chen, R. (1997). Ethnocultural differences in prevalence of adolescent depression. *American Journal of Community Psychology, 25,* 95–110.

Rogler, L., & Cortes, D. (1993). Help-seeking pathways: A unifying concept in mental health care. *American Journal of Psychiatry, 150,* 554–561.

Saunders, S., Resnick, M., Hobermann, H., & Blum, R. (1994). Formal help-seeking behavior of adolescents identifying themselves as having mental health problems. *Journal of the American Academy of Child and Adolescent Psychiatry, 33,* 718–728.

Snell, C. (2002). Help-seeking and risk-taking behavior among black street youth; Implications for HIV/AIDS prevention and social policy. *Journal of Health and Social Policy, 16,* 21–32.

Stevenson, H. (1998). Raising safe villages: Cultural–ecological factors that influence the emotional adjustment of adolescents. *Journal of Black Psychology, 24,* 44–59.

U.S. Department of Health and Human Services. (2001). *Mental health: Culture, race, and ethnicity—A supplement to mental health: A report of the surgeon general.* Rockville, MD: Author.

Varon, S., & Riley, A. (1999). Relationship between maternal church attendance and adolescent mental health and social functioning. *Psychiatric Services, 50,* 799–805.

Wu, P., Hoven, C., Bird, H., Moore, R., Cohen, P., Alegria, M., Dulcan, M., Goodman, S., Horwitz, S., Lichtman, J., Narrow, W., Rae, D., Regier, D., & Roper, M. (1999). Depressive and disruptive disorders and mental health service utilization in children and adolescents. *Journal of the American Academy of Child & Adolescent Psychiatry, 38,* 1081–1090.

Acknowledgments: This study was funded by the National Institute of Mental Health through a dissertation grant (1 RO3 MH63593-01), the W. K. Kellogg Foundation (Community Health Scholars Program), Michael A. Lindsey, Ph.D., principal investigator; as well as the Grants for National Academic Centers of Excellence on Youth Violence Prevention (R49/CCR318627-01), Philip J. Leaf, Ph.D., principal investigator. An earlier version of this article was presented at the meeting of the Society for Social Work and Research, January 2004, New Orleans.

About the authors: *Michael A. Lindsey,* Ph.D., MSW, MPH, is assistant professor, School of Social Work, University of Maryland, 525 West Redwood Street, Baltimore, MD 21201 (e-mail: mlindsey@ssw.umaryland.edu). *Wynne S. Korr,* Ph.D., is dean and professor, School of Social Work, University of Illinois, Urbana-Champaign. *Marina Broitman,* Ph.D., is scientific review administrator, Division of Extramural Affairs, National Institute of Mental Health, Bethesda, MD. *Lee Bone,* MPH, RN, is associate public health professor, Bloomberg School of Public Health, Johns Hopkins University; *Alan Green,* Ph.D., is assistant professor, School of Counseling and Professional Services, Johns Hopkins University; and *Philip J. Leaf,* Ph.D., is professor; Bloomberg School of Public Health, Johns Hopkins University.

Exercise for Article 39

Factual Questions

1. What is the explicitly stated purpose of this research?

2. What is the total number of participants in this study?

3. What is the name of the scale used to assess depressive symptoms?

4. In determining the categories and subcategories of themes, did the researchers convene to arrive at a consensus?

5. Which group ("those in treatment" *or* "those not in treatment") typically sought the advice and counsel of only their family members?

6. Do the researchers explicitly discuss the limitations of their study?

Questions for Discussion

7. Is it important to know that the researchers obtained informed consent? Explain. (See lines 130–133.)

8. Is it important to know where the interviews were conducted? Explain. (See lines 154–158.)

9. In your opinion, are there advantages to tape-recording the interviews? Are there disadvantages? Explain. (See lines 171–173.)

10. The researchers state that three readers independently reviewed and coded transcripts. Is it important to know that this was done independently? Explain. (See lines 173–176.)

11. To what extent did the sample questions in Table 1 help you understand this research?

12. In your opinion, are the suggestions for future research important? Explain. (See lines 580–615.)

13. If you had planned a study on this topic, would you have planned a qualitative study (as the authors of this article did) *or* a quantitative study (e.g., a survey with closed-ended questions)? Explain.

Quality Ratings

Directions: Indicate your level of agreement with each of the following statements by circling a number from 5 for strongly agree (SA) to 1 for strongly disagree (SD). If you believe an item is not applicable to this research article, leave it blank. Be prepared to explain your ratings. When responding to criteria A and B below, keep in mind that brief titles and abstracts are conventional in published research.

A. The title of the article is appropriate.

SA   5   4   3   2   1   SD

B. The abstract provides an effective overview of the research article.

SA   5   4   3   2   1   SD

C. The introduction establishes the importance of the study.

SA   5   4   3   2   1   SD

D. The literature review establishes the context for the study.

SA   5   4   3   2   1   SD

E. The research purpose, question, or hypothesis is clearly stated.

SA   5   4   3   2   1   SD

F. The method of sampling is sound.

SA   5   4   3   2   1   SD

G. Relevant demographics (for example, age, gender, and ethnicity) are described.

SA   5   4   3   2   1   SD

H. Measurement procedures are adequate.

SA   5   4   3   2   1   SD

I. All procedures have been described in sufficient detail to permit a replication of the study.

SA   5   4   3   2   1   SD

J. The participants have been adequately protected from potential harm.

SA   5   4   3   2   1   SD

K. The results are clearly described.

SA   5   4   3   2   1   SD

L. The discussion/conclusion is appropriate.

SA   5   4   3   2   1   SD

M. Despite any flaws, the report is worthy of publication.

SA   5   4   3   2   1   SD

Article 40

Risk Taking As Developmentally Appropriate Experimentation for College Students

JODI DWORKIN
University of Minnesota

ABSTRACT. Researchers have suggested that experimentation may be a necessary, constructive component of identity formation. However, these researchers have also noted the paradox of risk taking; an individual may experience both positive and negative precursors and consequences of risk taking. The present investigation used qualitative methods to explore the personal meaning of experimentation behaviors and of this paradox to college students. A stratified sample of 12 community college students (6 female) and 20 university students (10 female) was interviewed. Data were analyzed using grounded theory methods. Students described a deliberate and functional process of experimenting with a variety of risk behaviors. This included articulating the ways in which the college culture promotes participation in risk behaviors as developmentally appropriate experimentation.

From *Journal of Adolescent Research*, 20, 219–241. Copyright © 2005 by Sage Publications. Reprinted with permission.

The concept of risks as opportunities for adolescents can be traced back to the work of G. Stanley Hall (1904). Hall argued that parents and educators should exert limited control over adolescents, thereby enabling
5   their experimentation. However, this perspective has not received serious attention until recently (Lightfoot, 1997). From this perspective, it has been suggested that risk behaviors are deliberate and goal directed, the product of subjectively rational decisions. In fact,
10 scholars have posited that adolescents actively choose and shape their environment and actively seek out risks because of the potential for challenge and excitement (Chassin, 1997; Lightfoot, 1997). It has further been argued that experimentation serves developmentally
15 appropriate functions (Baumrind, 1985; Jessor & Jessor, 1977; Maggs, Almeida, & Galambos, 1995; Silbereisen, Noack, & Reitzle, 1987), such as facilitating peer interactions, teaching youth to negotiate behaviors that become legal post-adolescence, and facilitating
20 identity achievement. This perspective challenges the traditional assumption that adolescents are merely victims of antisocial peer influences (Chassin, 1997) and presents risk behaviors as experimentation behaviors that afford youth positive developmental opportunities.

25 However, researchers have also noted the paradox of risk taking; an individual may experience both positive and negative precursors and consequences of risk taking (Maggs et al., 1995; Maggs & Hurrelmann, 1998). The present investigation used qualitative meth-
30 ods to explore the personal meaning of experimentation behaviors and of this paradox to emerging adults in college. Emerging adults are in a transitional period between adolescence and young adulthood, actively experimenting to figure out who they are (Arnett,
35 2000). College students are often immersed in an anti-academic culture of athletics, campus parties, drinking, fraternities and sororities, and dating (Sperber, 2000). Thus, emerging adults in college are an ideal population to ask about their experiences.

Literature Review

40 During college, the majority of individuals participate in at least one behavior that adults would consider dangerous and health compromising. Specifically, rates of participation with most substance use, alcohol use, and unprotected sexual activity have been found to
45 peak during emerging adulthood (Johnston, O'Malley, & Bachman, 2003). In addition, college students are more likely to be binge drinkers than their same-age noncollege counterparts. However, in high school, college-bound seniors are less likely to report heavy
50 drinking than noncollege-bound youth. This suggests that emerging adults in college "catch up to and pass" their noncollege peers (Johnston et al., 2003, p. 21). This is not surprising given that college students are in a life stage characterized by risk and testing their limits
55 to find out who they are, living in a relatively unregulated environment surrounded by same-age peers (Arnett, 2000). Fortunately, the majority of these emerging adults are not subject to drastic consequences (Arnett, 1991). Still, there is tremendous concern among par-
60 ents and educators regarding how to protect emerging adults from these outcomes. Parents and educators strive to help emerging adults make responsible decisions about potentially risky behaviors and to reduce the number of tragedies resulting from poor decisions.
65 In a study of college students, Parsons, Siegel, and Cousins (1997) found that the perceived benefits of an outcome were more predictive of participation in risky

behaviors than students' assessment of the perceived risks. Emerging adults seeking out these benefits might 70 be described as sensation seeking (Zuckerman, 1990). Individuals high on the sensation-seeking personality trait desire sensory stimulation. College students high in sensation seeking, immersed in the college culture, are likely to be seduced by the excitement and intensity 75 of risk behaviors (Horvath & Zuckerman, 1993). And the college culture abounds with opportunities for risk. Unfortunately, the line at which experimentation behaviors become dangerous is often blurred. It is a challenge to determine the point at which developmentally 80 beneficial behaviors become dangerous (Irwin, 1993).

Experimentation behaviors are not inherently dangerous or problematic; rather, negative outcomes occur under certain conditions. It is unlikely that a behavior will be either entirely problematic or conventional. It is 85 possible to engage in both groups of behaviors simultaneously. College students may participate to a greater or lesser degree in a problem behavior and may do so independently of, or in addition to, engaging in more conventional behavior (Jessor & Jessor, 1977). For 90 example, all alcohol use is not the same. There is a difference between having a few sips of beer and getting drunk four times a week. There is a difference between having alcohol during a holiday dinner with family and drinking with friends. There is a difference 95 between drinking and drinking that is followed by driving. Behavior is the product of the interaction between a person and his or her environment. Therefore, to fully understand college student behavior, the influence of both these factors must be examined simultaneously 100 (Jessor, 1987).

To begin to explore this, Shedler and Block (1990) categorized a sample of young people into three groups based on their level of substance use. They defined frequent users as youth who used marijuana frequently 105 and had tried at least one other drug. Abstainers were defined as youth who had never tried drugs. Experimenters were defined as youth who used marijuana no more than once a month and who had tried no more than one other drug. Their data revealed that beginning 110 in childhood, experimenters demonstrated the most positive outcomes. Frequent users were described as undercontrolled, and these youth reported being more alienated, distressed, and having less impulse control than experimenters. Abstainers were described as over-115 controlled and unnecessarily delaying gratification. These youth reported feeling more anxious, emotionally constricted, and having poorer social skills than experimenters.

Maggs and colleagues (e.g., Maggs et al., 1995; 120 Maggs & Hurrelmann, 1998; Schulenberg, Maggs, & Hurrelmann, 1997) have consistently found that young people who experiment, in a controlled way, with risk behaviors, show the most positive developmental outcomes. For instance, substance use has been found to 125 facilitate peer relationships for adolescents. Research

has concluded that adolescents who experiment with substances show higher levels of peer acceptance and involvement, compared with young people participating in more delinquent, antisocial behavior who have 130 fewer and less satisfying peer relationships (Maggs et al., 1995; Maggs & Hurrelmann, 1998).

The finding that participation in risk behaviors often accompanies positive developmental outcomes, in combination with high rates of participation in certain 135 risk-taking behaviors, such as alcohol use, supports the contention that a certain level of risk taking is normative for young people (Baumrind, 1985; Schulenberg et al., 1997; Shedler & Block, 1990). Consequently, to fully understand risk during emerging adulthood, we 140 must recognize and consider both risks and opportunities. The present study builds on this perspective by exploring emerging adults' perspectives of risk behaviors.

Present Investigation

145   College creates an experience that encourages a period of experimentation that is longer than experienced by previous generations and perhaps longer than experienced by emerging adults who do not attend college full-time immediately following high school. As a 150 result, college students are at risk for crossing the unclear boundary between healthy experimentation and dangerous risk taking by participating in behaviors such as binge drinking and unprotected sexual activity. Sperber (2000) even argues that colleges advertise an 155 uninhibited collegiate subculture centered around leisure to attract students, and this culture "demands beer" (p. 192).

The present study is designed to explore the process of experimentation from the viewpoint of the ex-160 perimenters and to work toward a better understanding of experimentation behaviors. The following questions are addressed:

1. In what ways do emerging adults view risk behavior as a form of developmentally appropriate ex-165 perimentation?
2. How does the college culture promote risk as experimentation?
3. How does experimentation reflect what is going on developmentally during emerging adulthood?
170   4. What are the implications of these findings for research and for outreach?

The present investigation used in-depth interviews. In-depth interviewing provides access to a clearer understanding of why people act as they do by working 175 toward an appreciation of the meaning they give to their behaviors (Jones, 1985). Interviews address an individual's subjective experience of a preanalyzed situation in an attempt to draw out his or her definitions of the situation. Allowing emerging adults to describe 180 their experiences, in depth, using their own words, provides the best understanding of their construction of

their experiences with experimentation (Jones, 1985).
Interviews help formulate new hypotheses that will
support the systematic examination of experimentation
185 behaviors in the future (Merton, Fiske, & Kendall,
1990).

Method

To obtain a more holistic view of experimentation,
I used a dual interpretive methodology. First, a phenomenological perspective guided data collection and
190 analysis (van Manen, 1984) to provide access to the
meanings that individuals assign to the process of experimentation (Morse, 1994). Second, grounded theory
(Glaser & Strauss, 1967) provided a method for building a theory of experimentation usable by scholars
195 (Morse, 1994), without being limited by preconceived
notions of risk taking (Glaser, 1978).

Participants

A stratified sample of 32 college students was interviewed for this research (see Table 1). The sample
was stratified across institution, gender, age, and ethnic
200 group. Twenty students were recruited from a large
midwestern university, and 12 students were recruited
from a midwestern community college. Incorporating
student experiences at different types of institutions
allows for a sample and an experience more representa-
205 tive of college students. At the time of the study, all
participants were full-time students. To assist with
stratification, students were recruited through student
organizations on each campus, including cultural, ethnic, arts, academic, and athletic organizations.

Table 1
Participants

Demographics	Community College (*n* = 12)	University (*n* = 20)
Age		
18 years	2	1
19 years	4	5
20 years	3	4
21 years	2	7
22 years	1	3
Gender		
Female	6	10
Male	6	10
Ethnicity		
Latino	0	6
African American	3	6
White	8	8
Asian (not U.S. born)	1	0
Hometown		
Urban	2	8
Suburban	4	7
Rural	6	5
Family Structure		
Two-parent family	7	14
Single-parent family	4	5
Grandparents	1	1

Note. Cells = *n*

210   To recruit university students, an electronic mail
message was forwarded to at least 1,500 students who
were involved in registered student organizations. Students who had already participated recruited a few students through word of mouth. Interested participants
215 were asked to contact me directly to learn more about
the study and arrange a time for an interview. Because
of the large number of university students who volunteered to participate, I was able to select the students I
chose to interview. Interested students were sent an
220 electronic mail message requesting their gender, age,
academic year, ethnicity, and when they would be
available for an interview. University students were
then selected for interviews based on gender, academic
year, and ethnicity. Every student I contacted to par-
225 ticipate in an interview participated. The lower response rate at the community college did not allow me
to be as selective.

To recruit students at the community college, I contacted the director of student life who provided me with
230 a list of student organizations. Because of the limited
number of organizations, an electronic mail message
describing the study was sent to the 15 faculty advisors
who were responsible for active student organizations.
Six advisors responded to my initial electronic mail.
235 Phone calls were then made to the advisors who did not
respond. As a result of this effort, three advisors agreed
to forward an electronic mail message to group members. The electronic mail message described the study
and requested that interested students contact me di-
240 rectly to learn more about the study and arrange a time
for an interview. Two advisors agreed to allow me to
speak to their groups. In the groups, I handed out fliers
and had interested students provide contact information. The sixth advisor was responsible for an inactive
245 organization. She agreed to mention the study to students with whom she still had contact. Approximately
100 students were contacted either via electronic mail
or in person about the study. Again, a few participants
were recruited through word of mouth, by students who
250 had already participated, and by the director of student
life. With the exception of one, all students whom I
contacted to participate in an interview participated.

There was much diversity among the community
college students whom I interviewed, which reflects
255 the diversity of community college students. The majority of students whom I spoke with were planning on
transferring to a 4-year college. One student attended a
state university and only attended classes at the community college in the summer. Three students were
260 attending the community college because they had academic trouble at a 4-year university and decided they
wanted to remain in college. One of these students was
planning on returning to the university to graduate.

Data Collection

Students were interviewed individually, face to
265 face. Interviews were in-depth and semistructured.

259

Questions were developed from a thorough review of the literature to explore the meaning of risk taking and experimentation to college students (see the Appendix at the end of this article for the core interview questions relevant to the present analyses). Interviews lasted between 50 and 90 minutes and were audiotaped. They were held at a time that was convenient for the student, either on the university campus or on the community college campus. Following the interview, participants completed a brief background questionnaire and a checklist assessing how frequently they participated in a variety of experimentation behaviors. Students received $10 for their participation.

The first five interviews were conducted to pilot the interview protocol and are included in the data analysis. This allowed me to generate additional questions, eliminate questions, and adjust the order of the questions as needed. However, it should be noted that adaptations were made throughout the process of data collection to continuously adapt the interview and obtain the most complete data. This modification process is consistent with grounded theory methods (Strauss & Corbin, 1990).

Throughout data collection, I maintained a journal. Immediately following each interview, I recorded nonverbal expressions, emerging themes, interpretations, details of the interview, and conversations that were not recorded (Taylor & Bogdan, 1998). This information was treated as data and analyzed accordingly.

Data Analysis

The present investigation relied on the constant comparative method of interpretive analysis. This method of analysis encourages systematic generation of theory through inductive coding and analysis (Glaser & Strauss, 1967).

These data were analyzed under the assumption that the data provided by participants correspond to their actual experiences and to the meanings they apply to these experiences. In addition, interpretation of the data included distinguishing between solicited and unsolicited statements and considering how my background affected the direction of the interview and influenced the data (Taylor & Bogdan, 1998).

Consistent with the constant comparative method of interpretive analysis, data analysis consisted of seven steps, using three levels of coding. First, I transcribed the interviews verbatim, noting salient features such as long pauses and laughter (Riessman, 1993). To preserve participant confidentiality, the interviews were transcribed using pseudonyms and eliminating any identifying information. To ensure accuracy, I then carefully checked the transcripts against the tapes. The second step was to read the transcripts many times, looking for themes, patterns, and concepts. Each interview was summarized. Third, the interview data were sorted by the eliciting empirical interview question (see the Appendix for the interview questions). Fourth, to categorize and sort the interview data, the data were coded into conceptual categories within empirical questions. This was the first level of coding (Charmaz, 1988; Taylor & Bogdan, 1998). Every event and idea of a given phenomenon was named. Data were then grouped around phenomena, or categorized, thereby reducing the number of units of analysis (Strauss & Corbin, 1990). For example, in one set of analyses, data were grouped around the type of activity the student described.

Fifth, I performed axial coding, the second level of coding. Axial coding is a more intense form of coding centered on a specific phenomenon or category. It is used to identify the properties of the already identified categories, thereby providing more specificity. I labeled specific events and experiences within each phenomenon, thereby generating subcategories (Strauss, 1987). Analyses were conducted both within and between categories and within and between subcategories. For instance, grouping data by activity allowed for analyses both within and between social activities that did and did not involve substance use. I was then able to identify shared experiences between individuals and those experiences that were unique (Patton, 1990; Taylor & Bogdan, 1998).

Sixth, I performed selective coding, the third level of coding. To gain even more specificity, I coded those subcategories that were significantly tied to the core category and that facilitated an understanding of this category (Strauss, 1987). Finally, I identified the cases that did not fit the model as a way to either discount part of the model or for suggesting additional relationships (Strauss & Corbin, 1990; Taylor & Bogdan, 1998).

Following grounded theory procedures, after the data were coded, I diagrammed the relationships between constructs (Strauss & Corbin, 1990). Diagrams allowed me to visually depict the relationships between concepts and move from coding to defining the emerging concepts. After data analysis was complete, I went back to the literature to improve my understanding of the findings, not to support, discount, or provide additional data but to help explain the findings, and put them in a context (Strauss & Corbin, 1990).

The relationships that emerged from students' descriptions of their experiences and that were diagrammed are described in the following sections. These relationships are exemplified by direct quotes from students (Ryan & Bernard, 2000). Consistent with this process, the results and discussion are presented as one section.

Results and Discussion

Although risk taking has been explored extensively (Bell & Bell, 1993; Jessor & Jessor, 1977), researchers have yet to give as much attention to experimentation and include the emerging adult perspective in this definition. First, the relationship between experimentation and risk taking from the perspective of emerging adults will be explored. Next, I will consider the ways in which the college culture promotes emerging adult experimentation. Third, the ways in which experimentation is developmentally appropriate for college students will be considered. Finally, there will be a discussion of the implications of these findings for research and outreach.

Relationship Between Experimentation and Risk Taking

Experimentation. Students described experimentation as an active process of figuring out who they are and what they are capable of through making intentional and deliberate decisions. For instance, Alexis said, "you have to experiment to find out who you are, and what you like. It's like as little as trying new foods to whether or not you want to sleep around." These emerging adults described a process of experimentation consistent with the process of decision making about risky behavior described by Furby and Beyth-Marom (1992). They described being motivated to experiment by a desire to test their limits, both their personal limits and the limits of the behavior.

Emerging adults described experimenting with a variety of different behaviors. Many students described starting to question the religious beliefs their parents raised them with and having the opportunity in college to experiment with other religions through coursework. Next, students described meeting new people, more specifically meeting people different from them. For instance, a few students mentioned that dating someone of a different race was a form of experimentation. Through experimentation, they could learn about others and have their stereotypes debunked, not only stereotypes based on race or ethnicity but also on sexual orientation, or stereotypes based on whether someone grew up in a city or on a farm. Students also talked about experimenting with taking different classes and with extracurricular activities, such as joining a new club or trying a new sport.

In addition, the overwhelming majority of students mentioned substance use, alcohol use, or sexual activity. Ben described experimenting with alcohol: "I think it's important for people to test alcohol out. You know part of that is you're gonna get sick sometimes but hopefully that's in the beginning stages and you learn from that."

Risk taking. Students defined risk taking as intentional and functional behavior. They described a deliberate process of trial and error, taking a chance, or a risk, to see what would happen. Many of these emerging adults were unclear about whether the risk was the behavior, and, as such, certain behaviors were inherently risky, or whether the risk was the outcome, and a behavior could not be defined as risk taking until after experiencing the outcome. Nearly every student described risk taking based on the outcome. For instance,

Gabriel, a substance user, believed drugs were not inherently risky and noted that whether an individual views them as risky is dependent on the outcome.

> If people value their body as a temple, then taking drugs is a risk because you're harming your body. If you see your body as just a vessel that you're in then it's not really risky, then it's just experimentation, how much can you do to this vessel before it collapses.

Consequently, whether emerging adults choose to take a risk is based on their understanding of the potential outcomes, their assessment of the probability of the outcomes, the personal value of the outcomes, and whether they see themselves as vulnerable to experiencing the outcomes, regardless of the probability that each will actually occur. This is consistent with past research (Beyth-Marom & Fischhoff, 1997; Fischhoff, Lichtenstein, Slovic, Derby, & Keeney, 1981; Furby & Beyth-Marom, 1992). Individuals are willing to risk different things and see themselves as more or less vulnerable to actually experiencing those outcomes. As Jacob said, "The risk is defined by what you view as acceptable."

Consistent with this, when asked to identify behaviors they viewed as risk taking, there was a huge range in students' responses. The most frequently mentioned behaviors were applying for a job, drinking to excess, drunk driving, drag racing, unprotected sexual activity, stealing, and certain drugs, with only three to six out of 32 emerging adults mentioning each.

Risk taking as a form of experimentation. After considering experimentation and risk taking independently, students were asked to discuss the relationship between the two. Students offered three possible relationships: experimentation and risk taking are the same, experimentation and risk taking are opposite ends of one continuum, and experimentation and risk taking are two separate constructs. When describing the first scenario, which was only endorsed by four students, students discussed that there are many similarities between experimentation and risk taking. Perhaps most important, both are functional and intentional behaviors. For instance, emerging adults described a similar process for assessing the outcome of experimentation and risk-taking behaviors. Dalila described her impressions of the similarities between experimentation and risk taking.

> With experimenting you're trying to see if it's gonna work or not, and that's what you're doing with risk taking. And they both do have side effects....I think they go hand in hand because when you take a risk or when you experiment, you're gonna find out a solution that's good or bad.

In the second scenario, in which experimentation and risk taking are opposite ends of one continuum, which again was only supported by four students, the intensity of the behavior determines whether a behavior is experimentation or risk taking. Although unable to

261

490 identify the point at which behaviors become dangerous, students were clear that an acceptable risk reaches
a threshold at which point it becomes dangerous. For
instance, Amanda said,

> I think there's a point to where you're experimenting,
495 > like...if it's your first time drinking...I think that that's
> when you're experimenting, but after awhile it just be-
> comes risk taking...you know whether you like it....I think
> there is a point to where it kind of switches over...you're
> just plain taking a risk.

500 In this example, casual drinking might be experimentation, whereas habitual drinking would be risk taking.

The final relationship, that experimentation and risk
taking are unique constructs, earned the most endorse-
ment from students. This relationship suggests that a
505 behavior could be experimentation, it could be risk
taking, or it could be both. Therefore, although they are
two unique constructs, they are not mutually exclusive
categories. Gabriel explained this well when he said,

> You can experiment with something and it can also be a
510 > risk, just as you can take a risk which might be an ex-
> periment. But you can also do an experiment that has no
> risk to it, and you can also take risks that aren't experi-
> ments. So I mean, I think they're sort of interrelated, but
> they don't have to be.

515 When discussing experimentation and risk taking as
two separate constructs, emerging adults distinguished
between them in two ways. They described a public
distinction and a personal distinction. The public distinction lies in other's perceptions, particularly the per-
520 ceptions of parents and other adult authority figures, of
what emerging adults do and the connotation of the
language used by the general public to describe emerging adult behavior. From this perspective, risk-taking
behaviors are most often functionally irrelevant. The
525 personal distinction, or how emerging adults understand their experimentation, will be highlighted here.

The primary distinction between experimentation
and risk taking articulated by emerging adults was in
the process. Experimentation was described as a learn-
530 ing process, a process designed to achieve a goal. Risk
taking was more likely to be spontaneous and motivated by a desire to be challenged. Participants described risk taking as inherently more dangerous.

Students also described the personal distinction as
535 being influenced by their knowledge and preparation
before participating in a given behavior, including
whether they were aware of the potential consequences
and whether they took precautions to avoid a negative
outcome. With experimentation, emerging adults de-
540 scribed being more prepared and taking precautions to
avoid undesirable outcomes. They described risk taking
as less likely to be planned. And some emerging adults
explained that whether a behavior was experimentation
or risk taking was determined simply by their personal
545 values and how they felt about the behavior.

In these descriptions, students explained that there
is something about college that is conducive to and
encourages, or perhaps even facilitates, experimentation in a way that other contexts do not. To gain a bet-
550 ter understanding of this, students were asked to describe "what is it about college that encourages experimentation." In their explanations, students sponta-
neously produced the phrase *college culture*. They
were then asked to describe the college culture.

College Culture

555 Students' descriptions of the college culture were
consistent with the image of college portrayed in the
media and described by Sperber (2000): students struggling academically, all night parties that include drinking alcohol, promiscuous sex, and drug use. For exam-
560 ple, Paul said, "I hear college student, I think, alright
this guy drinks every weekend, keeps a 2.5 maybe."
And many emerging adults described entering college
with the expectation that their experiences were going
to be consistent with this image. Stacey, a community
565 college student, described her expectations: "You're
supposed to drink, and you're supposed to listen to
Dave Mathews Band....It's just the rule when you're in
college." Students described the college culture as providing them with the free time and opportunity to ex-
570 periment with what it meant to be independent from
their parents, including questioning the things their
parents had always told them. Alexis described this
experience:

> You have adolescents, and they're all trying to figure out
575 > who they are, and they're all saying, well my parents said
> this was wrong, well really is it? Everything comes into
> question. Is it really wrong to smoke pot? Is it really
> wrong to sleep around? Is it really wrong to swear?

Community college students who were still living
580 at home described maintaining much more contact with
their families and, therefore, being more influenced by
their parents' beliefs or at least feeling obligated to
respect their parents' beliefs while they were still living
with them.

585 Both university and community college students
explained that many things contribute to college students' high rates of participation in risk behaviors, such
as drinking alcohol, using substances, and sexual activity. Emerging adults said that participation in risk be-
590 haviors and the development of a college culture was
most influenced by independence and living away from
their parents, or at least spending significantly more
time away from their parents. Most students reported
having few real world responsibilities. For example,
595 most said they were not financially independent from
their parents, thus, they did not have to worry about
budgeting their money between leisure activities, such
as buying alcohol and paying their bills. Emerging
adults described college as an environment in which
600 they were responsible for making their own decisions,
relatively unburdened by real world responsibilities,

surrounded by other young people making the same decisions. For example, Jacob, a university student said,

605 There's a carefree attitude experiencing college...my friends and I refer to as the safety bubble of school, you can do whatever you want. You can get up at 8 in the morning and drink for a football game, you're not an al-coholic, you're a party animal. But if you do that in the
610 real world, then you'll go to treatment.

Most students expressed this same sentiment, that there were few or no consequences to their behaviors. This is consistent with past research, which has found that the majority of young people do not experience
615 negative consequences as a result of participating in risky behaviors (Arnett, 1991).

Another important contributor to the development of the college culture described by these young people was the college environment. They defined the college
620 environment to include the opportunities for experi-mentation that were available and the array of new ex-periences, people, and ideas to which students were exposed. Alexis, a community college student, de-scribed how she felt the college environment contrib-
625 uted to the college culture.

You stick 36,000 students who are basically between the ages of 18 and 25 together, without parents...they're on their own for the first time, they're all going to school...when you shove all of these people in a small
630 area, I think it's gonna develop a culture of its own, and I think that would be the weekend ritual of getting dressed up and going out and getting blitzed [drunk] or going dancing or finding a guy to sleep with. Not everybody does it, but a lot of people do. It's kind of more accept-
635 able.

As highlighted by Alexis, college students are sur-rounded by opportunity, with plenty of free time to act on those opportunities. This represents one extreme of how students described their experiences.

640 At the other extreme, students described adamantly opposing the stereotypical college culture and working hard to not behave in ways consistent with that image. The group of emerging adults in the middle described behaving with moderation, refusing to accept the col-
645 lege culture without experiencing it for themselves. They described a process of negotiating the image of the college student and figuring out how that fit into their developing sense of self. For example, Jacob, a university student, said,

650 The first thing I saw was a frat house, with girls in bikinis and guys throwing beer cans at cars, and I was like, this place is gonna be awesome. That was my idea of school then....All these beautiful girls who are just willing to have sex on a drop of a dime....I opted to change that
655 rather quickly. I didn't find it to be as rewarding as most people think....It kind of lured me away from the stereo-typical idea of fun, kinda made hanging out and relaxing with a smaller group of people who you really value as your friends...much more important.

660 Negotiating where they fit into the college culture might be seen as one part of the larger process of find-ing their niche in society. For instance, Amina said, "I think the whole time in college it's just about learning about yourself and then learning about things that are
665 interesting to you, just exploring the different parts of your identity or interests."

Moratorium and the college culture. Emerging adults' descriptions of the college culture suggest that although they believed that they would be actively ex-
670 perimenting throughout their lives to constantly refine who they are, rates of experimentation are particularly high throughout college. For instance, Stacey said,

Right now, you're just kinda in between. You're about to be on your own, where you have to decide everything for
675 yourself. I think before I make those decisions without anything to back me up, I think right now is a good time to kind of figure all that stuff out before I get more into a job and a family and things like that.

This period of active exploration described by stu-
680 dents is consistent with Erikson's (1959, 1965, 1968) description of the period of moratorium, a period char-acterized by change and transition during which indi-viduals search for their niche in society. Moratorium is characterized by experimentation and learning about
685 oneself to move closer to a stable identity. In morato-rium, young people experiment with many different things that facilitate learning about self, including learning their limits; learning how things affect them; learning about others; learning about society and social
690 norms; learning facts, skills, and information; and gain-ing experiences to use for future reference (Erikson, 1959; Grotevant, 1992).

Emerging adulthood, characterized as a period of moratorium for many young people, may be the most
695 intense time of life. Young people have survived the dependence associated with adolescence, but having not yet earned all of the responsibilities of adulthood (Arnett, 2000). During this transition, young people approach the adult world and work toward accepting an
700 introductory adult identity, making commitments to interpersonal relationships and occupational undertak-ings, and identifying a value system that is consistent with both self and society (Hauser & Greene, 1991).

When asked whether they felt they were "in a pe-
705 riod of active exploration to figure out who you are," overwhelmingly, students reported they were. In the interview, 25 students said they were definitely in a period of active exploration, four students said "sort of," two students said they were not exploring but their
710 responses suggested otherwise, and one student was not asked because he had to end the interview early to keep a prior commitment. In the interview, all students described extremely high rates of trying new things, evidence they were actively involved in this process of
715 exploration. In the questionnaire, 77% of all emerging adults reported having changed peer groups, 91%

joined or quit an activity, 75% began or ended an intimate relationship, and 81% changed fashion, at least once in the past year, indications of being in moratorium.

This group of emerging adults attributed their high rates of experimentation to two primary transitions: the transition out of high school and into college and the transition to greater independence. What they described as most meaningful about the transition from high school to college was that it was a transition to a new environment. Data revealed that the intensity of this experience varied by whether they moved away from home, how far they moved, and how different the new location was. These emerging adults explained that a new environment provided access to many new opportunities, experiences, behaviors, ideas, options, and people who provided access to many of these opportunities. Because the majority of the community college students were still living at home or in their hometown, they described having access to different experiences than university students. They had access to fewer extracurricular activities, but to a student body that was more diverse in terms of age and life stage. This group of community college students described being more committed to their education than the university students and was more certain about their career goals.

The second major transition described was increased independence. The development of independence was greatly affected by the factors just described. Regardless of whether students continued to live at home or moved away, they described spending significantly more time away from their parents and, thus, felt they had more responsibility for making their own decisions.

Emerging adults' descriptions of being in moratorium and actively working to figure out who they are serves as further support for the contention that experimentation is intentional and functional behavior, which is developmentally appropriate for college students.

Implications

This study focused on the ways emerging adults in college view risk behavior as a form of developmentally appropriate experimentation, providing many implications for research and for outreach.

Implications for Research

These data provide a foundation for future research in numerous ways. First, these students did not identify themselves as risk takers. They identified themselves as experimenters. This suggests that it may be more effective to talk with emerging adults about experimentation rather than a continued focus on risk taking. However, the use of the word experimentation may have confounded the process of data collection. The word experimentation connotes a systematic scientific process. Consequently, some students may have been defining the word *experimentation* rather than describing how they viewed their experiences with experimentation.

Second, students made a distinction between behavioral extremes, suggesting that consistent with the findings of other researchers, emerging adults do not view their activities as inherently risky (Graber & Brooks-Gunn, 1995; Jessor, 1987).

Third, college students' descriptions suggest that research needs to study a variety of behaviors to identify healthy experimentation behaviors that are functionally equivalent to dangerous risk taking behaviors and would therefore help emerging adults avoid negative consequences from risk behaviors (Silbereisen et al., 1987; Silbereisen & Reitzle, 1991). Research needs to work toward identifying the point in the process of experimentation at which participation in these behaviors becomes dangerous, the point at which the potential for negative outcomes greatly increases, and the point at which participation in dangerous behaviors becomes habitual.

Implications for Outreach

The challenge of outreach becomes evident very quickly when talking with college students about experimentation and risk taking. These students defined behaviors as dangerous based on the outcome. If a behavior cannot be identified as dangerous until after a negative outcome has been experienced, how can prevention efforts aimed at identifying and avoiding dangerous risk taking be successful? Although there is still a tremendous amount of research to be conducted, these data are critical for a new approach to outreach.

Outreach efforts that have focused on prevention and intervention typically target the minority of youth who are inexperienced risk takers or experimenters and the minority of youth experiencing real crisis. However, there is a large, often neglected number of youth in a middle group, a group described as experimenters (Shedler & Block, 1990) who experiment with a variety of behaviors and often demonstrate optimal outcomes but could experience crisis. Identifying the process of experimentation and the functions that experimentation behaviors serve, outreach efforts can begin to target experimenters and work to redirect youth behaviors, provide youth with alternatives to dangerous behavior, encourage youth to take precautions when participating in potentially dangerous behaviors, and prevent youth from experiencing real crisis.

Preventing participation in dangerous risk taking might also be achieved by promoting positive behaviors. Rather than trying to directly prevent youth substance use, an alternative approach would be to promote social activities that do not involve substances but fulfill the same needs of young people and thereby eliminate the need for substances, what others have referred to as functionally equivalent behaviors (Silbereisen & Reitzle, 1991). Jason, a heavy drug user, said,

> I think they're [drugs] important because it has added beneficial aspect, but if I had to do without and was said, okay you just have to party without drugs and without alcohol, that wouldn't be a big deal because...it's not really a focus, it's just something we do.

Thus, outreach efforts might be directed toward strengthening and promoting healthy experimentation and risk taking and responsible decision making rather than only working to prevent youth participation in dangerous risk taking. Students supported this. Josh, who had been a heavy substance and alcohol user, described changing his activities:

> I still take risks. I just changed it. I do more [rock] climbing and stuff like that....I always like that sense of danger a little bit, that risk to take, but I just do it in other ways.

Limitations and Future Directions

Although the present investigation begins to elucidate the process of experimentation for emerging adults in college, this study is limited. First, these students represent volunteers from one large public university and one community college, both in the same midwestern town. It is also cautioned that these results not be generalized to the experiences of emerging adults who do not attend college, the "forgotten half" ("The Forgotten Half," 1988), or to younger youth. Second, although the sample was relatively diverse in terms of gender and race and ethnicity, the small sample size does not allow for analyses within or between groups. Future research should explore experimentation from the perspective of different populations and should explore gender, racial and ethnic, and socioeconomic differences in young people's experiences with both healthy experimentation and dangerous risk taking. Quantitative measures are needed to survey much larger samples of young people to better understand their experiences with experimentation and risk taking. Third, although most students were describing behaviors that they were still participating in, hindsight self-report may have distorted their understanding of their experiences. Future research might work to capture young people's experiences when they are in the moment, so to speak.

Conclusion

The concept of experimentation as distinct from risk taking was salient for nearly every student interviewed. Although researchers (e.g., Baumrind, 1985; Jessor & Jessor, 1977; Maggs et al., 1995) have suggested a definition of experimentation as functional and intentional, the present results contribute the emerging adult perspective to this definition. Students were able to articulate the relationship between experimentation and risk taking and distinguish between functional experimentation and dangerous risk taking. They situated experimentation in the college culture, an environment

resulting from increased independence and spending less time with their parents.

Overwhelmingly, this group of emerging adults described their experiments as successful, even the decisions that might have had an undesirable outcome. The majority agreed that "I wouldn't change anything ...because it's a learning experience." With each behavior providing emerging adults with opportunities for learning and growth, perhaps emerging adults need to experiment with a variety of behaviors to gain the full array of skills necessary for adult life. Mark said, "I think if you want to learn a really good lesson, the best way to learn it is by experiencing it and knowing first-hand that I can't do that or else such and such will happen." Students' ability to articulate their process of experimentation is extremely valuable, and their words have many implications for research and for outreach.

Appendix–Partial Interview Guide

Today, I would like to hear about your experiences of trying things as you work to figure out who you are. This might include clothes, activities, alcohol, drugs, driving, art, poetry, friendships, intimate relationships, sexuality and anything else, whether it is legal or illegal. I want this to be a casual conversation, and I want to hear your opinions and your stories. My goal is to develop a more realistic definition and understanding of young adults' experiences.

1. What new behaviors have you tried since starting college?
2. How do you think you have changed since starting college?
3. How would you describe yourself?
4. What sorts of things do you do to help you figure out who you are?

A. I would like to start off by talking specifically about your experiences with these behaviors. (I will go through the following questions for one or two of the behaviors identified above. In the first few interviews, I will ask which behavior they would like to talk about. As I conduct more interviews, I may choose which behaviors we discuss to ensure a diversity of behaviors.)

1. What are the different reasons that you do [the behavior]?
2. What, if anything, is dangerous or risky about this?
3. What, if anything, is safe or positive about this?
4. How likely are these outcomes?
5. How important are the risks to you?
6. How important are the positive things to you?
7. What do you learn about yourself from this experience?
8. What do you learn about others from this experience?
9. How does it help you grow as a person?
10. How does it help you develop your sense of self?
11. How do you feel about yourself when you do it?

12. How do you feel about yourself afterwards?

13. Would you make the same decision again? Why or why not?

14. Would you recommend this behavior to someone 940 else? Why or why not?

15. What do you tell people about it?

16. What would your parents or guardians think about it?

17. How does being X (gender, race or ethnicity, social 945 class, religion) influence what you do or how you feel about it?

B. Application

1. How do you decide if a behavior is too dangerous or too risky?

950 2. How do your friends or peers make this distinction?

C. I'm interested in how you define experimentation and risk taking.

1. How do you define experimentation?

955 2. What things do people do that count as experimenting?

3. How do you define risk taking?

4. What things do people do that count as risk taking?

5. Do the reasons you would experiment differ from 960 the reasons you might take risks?

6. Can you give some specific examples?

7. Talk about the similarities and differences between risk taking and experimentation.

8. How does being X (gender, race or ethnicity, social 965 class, religion) influence how you think about experimentation or risk taking?

Moratorium

1. Some people believe that college students are in a period of active experimentation as they work to 970 figure out who they are. Tell me about how this does or does not describe you right now.

2. What is it about college that allows you to do that?

References

Arnett, J. (1991). Still crazy after all these years: Reckless behavior among young adults aged 23–27. *Personality and Individual Differences, 12,* 1305–1313.

Arnett, J. J. (2000). Emerging adulthood: A theory of development from the late teens through the twenties. *American Psychologist, 55,* 469–480.

Baumrind, D. (1985). Familial antecedents of adolescent drug use: A developmental perspective. *National Institute on Drug Abuse: Research Monograph Series, 56,* 13–44.

Bell, N. J., & Bell, R. W. (1993). *Adolescent risk taking.* Newbury Park, CA: Sage.

Beyth-Marom, R., & Fischhoff, B. (1997). Adolescents' decisions about risks: A cognitive perspective. In J. Schulenberg, J. L. Maggs, & K. Hurrelmann (Eds.), *Health risks and developmental transitions during adolescence* (pp. 110–135). Cambridge, UK: Cambridge University Press.

Charmaz, K. (1988). The grounded theory method: An explication and interpretation. In R. M. Emerson (Ed.), *Contemporary field research: A collection of readings* (pp. 109–126). Prospect Heights, IL: Waveland.

Chassin, L. (1997). Foreword. In J. Schulenberg, J. L. Maggs, & K. Hurrelmann (Eds.), *Health risks and developmental transitions during adolescence* (pp. xiii–xvi). Cambridge, UK: Cambridge University Press.

Erikson, E. H. (1959). Identity and the life cycle. *Psychological Issues, 1*(1, Monograph 1).

Erikson, E. H. (1965). Youth: Fidelity and diversity. In E. H. Erikson (Ed.), *The challenge of youth* (pp. 1–28). Garden City, NY: Anchor.

Erikson, E. H. (1968). *Identity: Youth and crisis.* New York: Norton.

Fischhoff, B., Lichtenstein, S., Slovic, P., Derby, S. L., & Keeney, R. L. (1981). *Acceptable risk.* New York: Cambridge University Press.

The forgotten half: Pathways to success for American's youth and young families. (1988). Washington, DC: Youth and America's Future.

Furby, L., & Beyth-Marom, R. (1992). Risk taking in adolescence: A decision-making perspective. *Developmental Review, 12,* 1–44.

Glaser, B. G. (1978). *Theoretical sensitivity: Advances in the methodology of grounded theory.* Mill Valley, CA: Sociology Press.

Glaser, B. G., & Strauss, A. L. (1967). *The discovery of grounded theory: Strategies for qualitative research.* Chicago: Aldine.

Graber, J. A., & Brooks-Gunn, J. (1995). Models of development: Understanding risk in adolescence. *Suicide and Life-Threatening Behavior, 25,* 18–25.

Grotevant, H. D. (1992). Assigned and chosen identity components: A process perspective on their integration. In G. R. Adams, T. P. Gullotta, & R. Montemayor (Eds.), *Adolescent identity formation* (pp. 73–90). Newbury Park, CA: Sage.

Hall, G. S. (1904). *Adolescence: Its psychology and its relations to physiology, anthropology, sociology, sex, crime, religion, and education.* New York: Appleton-Century-Crofts.

Hauser, S. T., & Greene, W. M. (1991). Passages from late adolescence to early adulthood. In S. I. Greenspan, & G. H. Pollock (Eds.), *The course of life: Vol. 4. Adolescence* (pp. 377–405). Madison, CT: International Universities Press.

Horvath, P., & Zuckerman, M. (1993). Sensation seeking, risk appraisal, and risky behavior. *Personality & Individual Differences, 14,* 41–52.

Irwin, C. (1993). Adolescence and risk taking: How are they related? In N. J. Bell & R.W. Bell (Eds.), *Adolescent risk taking* (pp. 7–28). Newbury Park, CA: Sage.

Jessor, R. (1987). Problem-behavior theory, psychosocial development, and adolescent problem drinking. *British Journal of Addiction, 82,* 331–342.

Jessor, R., & Jessor, S. L. (1977). *Problem behavior and psychosocial development: A longitudinal study of youth.* New York: Academic Press.

Johnston, L. D., O'Malley, P. M., & Bachman, J. G. (2003). *Monitoring the Future: National survey results on drug use, 1975–2002. Volume II: College students and adults ages 19–40* (NIH Publication No. 03-5376). Bethesda, MD: National Institute on Drug Abuse.

Jones, S. (1985). Depth interviewing. In R. Walker (Ed.), *Applied qualitative research* (pp. 45–55). Aldershot, UK: Gower.

Lightfoot, C. (1997). *The culture of adolescent risk-taking.* New York: Guilford.

Maggs, J. L., Almeida, D. M., & Galambos, N. L. (1995). Risky business: The paradoxical meaning of problem behavior for young adolescents. *Journal of Early Adolescence, 15,* 344–362.

Maggs, J. L., & Hurrelmann, K. (1998). Do substance use and delinquency have differential associations with adolescents' peer relations? *International Journal of Behavioral Development, 22,* 367–388.

Merton, R. K., Fiske, M., & Kendall, P. L. (1990). *The focused interview: A manual of problems and procedures* (2nd ed.). New York: Free Press.

Morse, J. M. (1994). Designing funded qualitative research. In N. K. Denzin & Y. S. Lincoln (Eds.), *Handbook of qualitative research* (pp. 220–235). Thousand Oaks, CA: Sage.

Parsons, J. T., Siegel, A.W., & Cousins, J. H. (1997). Late adolescent risk-taking: Effects of perceived benefits and perceived risks on behavioral intentions and behavioral change. *Journal of Adolescence, 20,* 381–392.

Patton, M. Q. (1990). *Qualitative evaluation and research methods* (2nd ed.). Newbury Park, CA: Sage.

Riessman, C. K. (1993). *Narrative analysis* (Vol. 30). Newbury Park, CA: Sage.

Ryan, G.W., & Bernard, H. R. (2000). Data management and analysis methods. In N. K. Denzin & Y. S. Lincoln (Eds.), *Handbook of qualitative research* (2nd ed., pp. 769–802). Thousand Oaks, CA: Sage.

Schulenberg, J., Maggs, J. L., & Hurrelmann, K. (Eds.). (1997). *Health risks and developmental transitions during adolescence.* Cambridge, UK: Cambridge University Press.

Shedler, J., & Block, J. (1990). Adolescent drug use and psychological health: A longitudinal inquiry. *American Psychologist, 45,* 612–630.

Silbereisen, R. K., Noack, P., & Reitzle, M. (1987). Developmental perspectives on problem behavior and prevention in adolescence. In K. Hurrelmann, F. Kaufmann, & F. Losel (Eds.), *Social intervention: Potential and constraints* (pp. 205–218). New York: de Gruyter.

Silbereisen, R. K., & Reitzle, M. (1991). On the constructive role of problem behavior in adolescence: Further evidence on alcohol use. In L. P. Lipsitt & L. L. Mitnick (Eds.), *Self-regulatory behavior and risk taking: Causes and consequences* (pp. 199–217). Norwood, NJ: Ablex.

Sperber, M. (2000). *Beer and circus: How big-time college sports is crippling undergraduate education.* New York: Henry Holt.

Strauss, A. L. (1987). *Qualitative analysis for social scientists.* New York: Cambridge University Press.

Strauss, A. L., & Corbin, J. (1990). *Basics of qualitative research: Grounded theory procedures and techniques.* Newbury Park, CA: Sage.

Taylor, S. J., & Bogdan, R. (1998). *Introduction to qualitative research methods: A guidebook and resources* (3rd ed.). New York: John Wiley.

van Manen, M. (1984). Practicing phenomenological writing. *Phenomenology and Pedagogy, 2*, 36–69.

Zuckerman, M. (1990). The psychophysiology of sensation seeking. *Journal of Personality, 58*, 313–345.

About the author: Jodi Dworkin earned her Ph.D. in 2002 in human development and family studies from the University of Illinois, Urbana-Champaign. She is currently an assistant professor and extension specialist at the University of Minnesota in the Department of Family Social Science. Her research interests include promoting positive family development, normative adolescent development, adolescent and emerging-adult risk behavior, and parenting.

Address correspondence to: Jodi Dworkin, Department of Family Social Science, 1985 Buford Ave., 290 McNeal Hall, University of Minnesota, St. Paul, MN 55108. E-mail: jdworkin@che.umn.edu

Exercise for Article 40

Factual Questions

1. How many students participated in this study?

2. How many of the students in this study were Latino?

3. To recruit university students, an electronic mail message was forwarded to at least 1,500 students who were involved in what?

4. Did all the community college students the researcher contacted agree to participate? If not, how many did not?

5. In this study, a checklist was used to assess what?

6. According to the researcher, what word might have confounded the process of data collection because it connotes a systematic scientific process?

Questions for Discussion

7. In your opinion, has the researcher provided a convincing argument for the use of in-depth interviews for this study? (See lines 172–186.)

8. In your opinion, to what extent is the use of both community college students and university students a strength of this study? Explain. (See lines 202–205.)

9. In your opinion, are there advantages to audiotaping interviews? Are there disadvantages? Explain. (See lines 270–271 and 310–316.)

10. Before reading this article, how familiar were you with the constant comparative method of qualitative data analysis? To what extent did the descrip-

tion of the data analysis in lines 308–372 in this article improve your understanding of this type of data analysis? Explain.

11. In the results section of qualitative research articles, it is common to provide quotations in the word of the participants. To what extent do the quotations in the results section of this article help you understand the results? In your opinion, would the report of results in this article be as effective without the quotations? Explain. (See lines 373–756.)

12. It is common for the results sections of research reports on qualitative research to be longer than the results sections in reports on quantitative research. In your opinion, could the results section of this article have been shortened without losing important information? Explain. (See lines 373–756.)

13. The researcher describes three limitations of her research in lines 844–869. Do you think that all three are equally important? Is one more important than the others? Explain.

Quality Ratings

Directions: Indicate your level of agreement with each of the following statements by circling a number from 5 for strongly agree (SA) to 1 for strongly disagree (SD). If you believe an item is not applicable to this research article, leave it blank. Be prepared to explain your ratings. When responding to criteria A and B below, keep in mind that brief titles and abstracts are conventional in published research.

A. The title of the article is appropriate.

SA   5   4   3   2   1   SD

B. The abstract provides an effective overview of the research article.

SA   5   4   3   2   1   SD

C. The introduction establishes the importance of the study.

SA   5   4   3   2   1   SD

D. The literature review establishes the context for the study.

SA   5   4   3   2   1   SD

E. The research purpose, question, or hypothesis is clearly stated.

SA   5   4   3   2   1   SD

F. The method of sampling is sound.

SA   5   4   3   2   1   SD

G. Relevant demographics (for example, age, gender, and ethnicity) are described.

SA   5   4   3   2   1   SD

H. Measurement procedures are adequate.

SA   5   4   3   2   1   SD

I. All procedures have been described in sufficient detail to permit a replication of the study.

SA   5   4   3   2   1   SD

J. The participants have been adequately protected from potential harm.

SA   5   4   3   2   1   SD

K. The results are clearly described.

SA   5   4   3   2   1   SD

L. The discussion/conclusion is appropriate.

SA   5   4   3   2   1   SD

M. Despite any flaws, the report is worthy of publication.

SA   5   4   3   2   1   SD

Article 41

Conflicting Bureaucracies, Conflicted Work: Dilemmas in Case Management for Homeless People with Mental Illness

LINDA E. FRANCIS
State University of New York at Stony Brook

ABSTRACT. This ethnographic study finds a case management agency torn between the rules of two conflicting bureaucracies. Funded by a federal grant, the agency is administered by the county, and the regulations of the two systems turn out to be incompatible. This conflict creates dilemmas in providing services to clients: meeting eligibility criteria for services from the federal grant meant the clients did not meet the eligibility criteria for many county services. Agency staff reacted to this dilemma by bending rules, finding loopholes, and investing extra time and emotional labor in each client. The role-conflict engendered by bureaucratic disjunction creates frustration, resentment, and burnout within the agency.

From *Journal of Sociology and Social Welfare*, *XXVII*, 97–112. Copyright © 2000 by Journal of Sociology and Social Welfare. Reprinted with permission.

Case Management in the Mental Health System

Prior to deinstitutionalization, institutions provided all needed services under one roof, including food, shelter, clothing, medical care, and psychiatric treatment. By contrast, outside of the institution, these ser-
5   vices were fragmented and spread across the medical and social service systems (Grob, 1994). For persons with mental illness, such services were difficult to access. Even with symptoms under control with medication, many patients lacked the skills necessary to nego-
10 tiate these complex service systems, leaving many with no services at all (Freedman & Moran, 1984).

In 1977, the National Institute of Mental Health began the Community Support Program in an attempt to coordinate these diverse services in ways that were not
15 covered under the 1963 Community Mental Health Centers Act. This program created a federal and state partnership to develop community support programs. The program sought to increase the availability of housing, income support, psychiatric treatment, medi-
20 cal treatment, and other services by encouraging states to change their own mental health systems. Though the Community Support Program later refocused on evaluation, in its inception we see the roots of intensive case management programs for persons with severe
25 mental illness (Grob, 1994).

Over the past decade, case management has become one of the most widely used methods to deliver services to persons with severe mental illness. At the most basic level, the role of the case manager is to determine
30 the needs of clients, connect them to services, and help to ensure a reasonable quality of life in the community. Case managers in intensive service agencies provide services at a much higher level, including teaching skills of daily living, arranging transportation, and pro-
35 viding services outside traditional locations and hours. The tasks of case managers vary widely depending on the environment in which they work, with some located in agencies that provide most services in-house, and others drawing primarily on resources in the commu-
40 nity (Robinson & Toff-Bergman, 1990). The common denominator is that case managers serve as liaison, advocate, and resource for persons with mental illness and their families (Rog, 1988).

Most of the research on case management for peo-
45 ple with severe mental illness has focused on measuring client outcomes as a determinant of efficacy, usually in terms of keeping people out of the hospital and living as independently as possible. However, the results of these studies are difficult to interpret because
50 the definitions of case management and the conditions under which case managers practice are variable (Solomon, 1992; Rubin, 1992; Chamberlain & Rapp, 1991). As a result, it is impossible to determine if cross-sectional client outcome variables are even
55 measuring the same things (Solomon, 1992; Spicer et al., 1994).

Addressing problems such as this is one of the greatest strengths of ethnography. Through naturalistic observation and unstructured interviews, the researcher
60 can illuminate the contents of the "black box" of interventions (Corbin & Strass, 1990) and determine what is really happening in the course of service delivery. The initial intent of this study was just that: to illuminate the crucial activities of case management and clarify
65 what those activities accomplish in the eyes of the

workers. However, as is often the case with qualitative research, the questions proved more complicated than anticipated. This case study demonstrates the extremely influential nature of the social work context, that is, the resources, bureaucratic rules, and politics of social systems in which the agency is embedded. The agency in this study was forced into a "Catch-22" situation, in which the rules regulating its operation prevented it from delivering the services it was being funded to provide. This vulnerability to vagaries of local conditions may give us a clue to why case management services are not only so difficult to measure, but frequently difficult to provide.

Despite the growing importance of case management, few have done ethnographic research of this part of the mental health care system. The experiences of people in other parts of health care have been well documented, some in extremely well-known studies. In *Asylums,* Goffman (1961) examines life in the mental hospital. In *Life in the Ward,* Coser (1959) tells the story of both patients and staff in a nonpsychiatric hospital, while Becker et al. (1961) in *Boys in White* do the same for physicians-in-training in medical school. Estroff (1981), in *Making It Crazy,* brings to light the lives of clients of one of the first Assertive Community Treatment Programs. More recently, Hopper (1998) and Liebow (1993) have brought to life the once invisible experiences of homeless people, many of whom suffer mental illness.

Despite the contributions of each of these studies, none of them truly explores the delivery of *social* services in mental health. With the decline of the psychiatric institution, such services have become cornerstones of the community mental health system. Case management, with its growing role in this system, offers an ideal point of entry to study how mental health service delivery occurs. A qualitative approach allows for an assessment of this process without the imposition of preconceived hypotheses. That is, the providers themselves have the opportunity to tell the story of their own experiences on case management teams. As will become evident in the pages to follow, this allows the participants in the study to provide not only the answers, but the questions as well.

The research questions for this study developed in two stages. Initially I sought to uncover in more detail some of the crucial components of the social services intervention that is case management. However, the issues which emerged in the course of the fieldwork proved to be more interesting than the original question. The results reported in this paper thus address two concerns: 1) what activities constitute intensive case management, and 2) how does the system environment affect their implementation? The data presented in the following pages give at least one possible answer to the second question, and indirectly, to the first research question as well.

Data

Ethnography of an Intensive Case Management Agency

The Research Site. The research site for this study is an agency providing intensive case management services to homeless persons who suffer from mental disorder and substance abuse. This agency, called REACH (a pseudonym), is located in a moderately large city in the southeastern U.S. and is funded by a federal grant as part of an ongoing multisite national demonstration project. The purpose of the demonstration was to investigate means of integrating and defragmenting community mental health service systems. Despite federal funding, however, the administration of REACH was under the jurisdiction of the county community mental health system.

The organization and mission of REACH were nontraditional. The agency was made up of two teams of service providers rather than autonomous case managers. Each client was assigned to a team, rather than a single case manager, and worked with all members of each team. In addition, both teams were familiar with each others' clients. Morning staff meetings each day reviewed all new material, problems, or achievements, so that all staff of the agency were updated and capable of handling emergencies for any client of REACH. All staff members (teams and administration) shared revolving 24-hour on-call support duties.

The REACH teams had not only case managers, but consumer-staff members and nurses. At the time of the research, there was one consumer-staff person on each team, both with histories of addiction and homelessness or near homelessness. Ideally, each team was supposed to have five members, including a nurse on each team, but due to a budget freeze by the county, the teams were working only partially staffed, each with three members plus one shared nurse.

The mission of the agency was very client-directed, with active follow-ups of clients, an emphasis on client choice, and a requirement that clients be included in all formal discussions of their cases. Meetings with clients took place *in vivo,* that is, where the client was. This frequently required appointments at the clients' residences, on park benches, or at the local drop-in center, wherever the client was able to be. Clients who missed appointments were sought and rescheduled. Emphasis was on keeping clients in services, despite the formidable obstacles to achieving continuity with an inherently transient population. To maintain this intensive level of service, caseloads were very small, about 50 clients per team, or roughly 15 clients per team member.

Data Collection. As a study of process, this project was done ethnographically, with data coming primarily from participant observation of case management work and unstructured interviews with the team members. This includes an inventory and description of the daily activities that constitute case management for service recipients. Over a 5-month period, I attended staff meetings, participated in daily agency activities, and accompanied every team member on at least 2 days

180 when they provided services out of the office. I had opportunities to see my participants working both with clients in a variety of settings, and with staff from other parts of the social services system. On an average day, I arrived in time for the morning staff meeting and re-

185 view of clients. I then accompanied the team I was "shadowing" that week into their team room for their team meeting. I spent the rest of the day with a single team member, who would explain paperwork, relate phone calls, and take me along on visits to clients.

190 Over the course of the study, I also conducted detailed individual unstructured interviews with all 10 staff members in the agency to gather insight into their views on the different constraints and resources under which staff members and teams operate. These staff

195 members constitute the 10 participants in this study, including 6 team members, a nurse, an outreach worker, the project manager, and the project director. In total, the data comprise 5 months of field notes, 10 interviews, and program documents. As with many

200 case studies, the sample size for this study is quite small due to the limited size of the agency; however, the detail and length of data collection lend credibility to the results. These data were transcribed as text onto a computer, and qualitatively coded and analyzed using

205 HyperResearch, a text analysis program.

Results

The Contradictions of the Case Management Role

I originally entered the field with a general question: *What is case management, and what, in their own eyes, do case managers do?* I soon found this question to be inadequate. My respondents all gave answers

210 couched in terms of what they would like to do as managers, what they intended to do, or what they were supposed to do by the terms of the agency's federal grant funding. However, nearly all then wanted to tell me in the next breath why it was very difficult to do the

215 activities they had just described to me. Indeed, they spent much more time telling me why they were not able to provide the services they wanted to or felt they were supposed to than they did telling me about what they did do. That is, what they really wanted to talk

220 about was their frustration.

This frustration has become the topic that has emerged from this analysis, and the main subject of this paper. My main question here is: *Why is it so difficult in this agency to deliver their intensive case man-*

225 *agement services to homeless persons with mental illness, and what are the consequences of this difficulty?* Such a question is tightly tied to the immediate circumstances of this particular agency, and as such appears to have little generalizability. However, the broader im-

230 plications of structural and bureaucratic conflict have repercussions for social workers throughout the field of human services.

REACH was a federally funded project that had been inserted into an already functioning county sys-

235 tem. This position of being juxtaposed between two systems created tensions from the day the agency opened its doors, and interfered with the agency's ability to serve their clients. REACH was designed and federally funded to develop nontraditional approaches

240 to engaging a difficult population, but they were stymied by more traditional expectations and structures at the local level. REACH staff often found themselves torn between the rules of the two systems—federal and county—and the needs of the clients. That is, they

245 could not meet all three points simultaneously.

An example of this was that the agency was funded by their grant to provide services for homeless people with mental illness, especially those with substance abuse problems as well. To provide these services,

250 REACH was supposed to draw on local resources. Homeless services in the county wanted only clients whose mental illness had been stabilized and who did not abuse substances. Yet the mental health treatment available to stabilize clients through Community Men-

255 tal Health Services assumed that the client had not only transportation, but an address and phone number—in other words, that they be housed. And many substance abuse services frequently had mental illness as an exclusion criterion from their residential programs, or

260 required that clients have housing and transportation to attend their outpatient programs. In other words, in order to get housing, you had to be already treated, but in order to get treated, you had to have housing. Thus, the county system had services set up for people who

265 were homeless *or* mentally ill *or* substance abusers, but not all three. So, the federal grant regulations and the county system in practice often had mutually exclusive targets: eligibility for the grant sometimes created automatic ineligibility for many county services. As

270 one case manager protested, they were often caught between the two government bureaucracies with which they had to deal:

The way [our program] is set up, we're caught in not just one bureaucracy but two. So it's like [we were funded

275 with] the understanding was that [we] were going to be able to do some creative things. But when we attempted the creativity, the county system was like: oh, no, you can't do that.... And then we also have [federal] guidelines and their bureaucracy and criteria and you run

280 against some things with them. So in between here we are, and it's like we're being squished. And what's happening is that the client is getting lost in all this.

As a result, there was a pervasive sense among the case managers that neither of the two systems were

285 really concerned about whether their clients were actually getting any help.

This feeling was repeatedly reinforced by the contradictions between system rules and client needs. For instance, the eligibility criteria for many services ex-

290 cluded the very people most in need of the service. One

concern was that a grant that had been allocated to the county to provide housing for homeless people stipulated that clients be homeless when they applied, and that they remained homeless until they received the housing certificate. However, the process of sending an application through county bureaucracy often took 3 or 4 months. The case managers were simply not willing to leave their clients with no housing that long just so they would stay eligible for a particular source of housing. After all, housing was only the first step in a long road to improvement. According to one team member:

> We can't just leave them out there on the streets with wolves and not place them somewhere safe.... So while we're trying to get them to move forward, I've crossed the boundaries to the [housing] status now, and so I've jeopardized their housing. And so now I'm going to have to come up with another strategy on how I'm going to find you housing because you're not eligible for the certificate anymore.

A diagnosis of substance abuse could complicate matters even more by reducing the already small number of housing options available to the clients. Another team member described these difficulties:

> I set up two interviews for [supported housing]. But you have to have 6 mos. clean time.... Some of these people are not going to meet these criteria. I mean, you can have the ideal drunk, and you can say stop drinking and he's going to get better. It doesn't work that way. Things don't fit like that.

Often, the case managers resort to bending, or even breaking, the rules in order to do their jobs: that is, to provide services to their clients.

> The way everything's set up doesn't make sense. You can't do this because this person doesn't meet this criteria, so you almost have to make it fit. Be flexible and break some rules...you have to look at it and say, this didn't happen exactly like this, but if he's eligible for this, and then we start getting picky about things and find little loopholes and stuff. Sometimes the system doesn't work.

This working around the rules holds even for the federal requirements of REACH. For example, many of their clients suffer from severe addictions to the point that this problem overshadows everything else, even their mental illness. Indeed, this sometimes seems to be the norm for homeless people with severe mental illness, at least among the REACH participants. But substance abuse—or even related personality disorders—could not be their primary diagnosis, due to the eligibility criteria of the grant. So rather than disqualify someone in need of their help, they would find a way to make that person eligible.

> Interviewer: I'm thinking of this morning, when the assistant director said to the psychiatrist 'We need a different diagnosis in order to make him eligible.'

> Respondent: Yes, like I'm doing the medical records, and a lot of the people have substance abuse diagnoses. Well,

this program is set up for homeless, severely and persistently mentally ill people.... These people have mental illness, but we cannot put it as the substance abuse is what we're treating. We've got to put it that we're treating major depression, or something. And really...we are, even though they do need the substance abuse treatment too. [So] these people, either you change their diagnoses, or they don't meet the criteria. I mean, it's not like they don't have a mental illness, but the substance abuse is something that's coming up front more so than the mental illness. The system says, 'We want it this way,' we'll get it this way.

So, agency staff are often torn between their clients and the system. If they are unable to "make it fit," they lose clients and the ability to provide for their needs. Such an outcome goes against their mission and their funding. As a result, the agency is caught in sort of a case management "Catch-22" between system rules and client needs.

> You do feel powerless, because you promise to support someone who is mentally ill and who's without a home, and that's a big task. Because...there's always administrative stuff that you have to adhere to; it's like, you really don't have any power. It's like a hierarchy, it's the administrators, it's [our agency] and it's the participants. And they look at you as the one with the power, and it's like, but I really don't have power. And they don't understand that. All they see is one system.

Another team member:

> [But] what's going to happen is, if you tell them "I can help you," and then as it turns out you can only help them for three months, you know, they're going to be like, "You're not meeting my needs."

The result is that the agency has difficulty keeping clients. With clients who are extremely hard to engage, and who can disappear if they feel no need to be visible, the lack of means to keep them engaged adds aggravation to the frustration the REACH teams already experience. To forestall client drop-outs, team members invest themselves personally through persuasion and emotional labor (Hochschild, 1983) to keep each client on board while the case managers struggle with the system. Such conditions are unsurprisingly a cause of burnout.

> I don't think that there are many elected representatives that will understand that Shawn going to an ice hockey game with friends from the Drop In Center is a better place for him to be than where he was. And the fact that he was there is going to make a difference, and it was money well spent. We don't know how to quantify those stories...and it's because [they're all unique and individual]. And we cherish individuality, and it's part of what our nation calls our own, but it's also something that we don't know how to support.

The service providers in this study were torn between three disjunctive sets of expectations: the rules of the two systems, and the needs of their clients. They try to find a workable compromise and frequently do not succeed. One of the three sets is often left unmet. This is a constant source of frustration for the team members, especially when it is the client who loses out.

Discussion

410 The present research is a case study of a single agency located in a single county mental health system, which raises questions about its generalizability to social services. What can we learn from the case managers of REACH? While on the surface this analysis only illuminates the personal agonies of the workers in one

415 agency, the results have broader theoretical and practical implications. In terms of my first research question on the activities of case management, we see that case managers engage in more than the concrete services identified in the literature, they invest emotional labor

420 as well. The stress literature identifies both of these activities as forms of social support, instrumental and socioemotional (Thoits, 1986). Instrumental support includes all the basic services considered part of case management: money, food, shelter, clothes, transporta-

425 tion, medical care, etc. Socioemotional support, on the other hand, includes more invisible aid in the form of talking about problems, listening, encouraging, and applauding success.

The staff in this study most likely provided more

430 socioemotional support than most workers in their position, as they used it as a means of making up for shortcomings in the instrumental support they had to offer. Nonetheless, most social service providers engage in this as a sort of "invisible service" to their cli-

435 ents. Empathy, rapport, and understanding are overtly part of social work training, and are highly valued skills in the profession. Their influence appears even in the accomplishment of more instrumental tasks. For instance, the staff at REACH did not merely link their

440 clients to other services, but negotiated barriers to services in a politically charged system. In addition, like all case managers, they were perpetually engaged in trying to tailor a general system to the unique needs of individual clients. Such efforts entail diplomacy, sensi-

445 tivity, and rapport, all of which have sizable emotional components. Intensive case management, then, entails service linkage, advocacy, *and* socioemotional support as crucial elements of service delivery.

Regarding my second research question, the results

450 on the difficulty of delivering services illustrate possible consequences of bureaucratic conflict for any agency straddling two or more systems. Weber lists as the first characteristic of a bureaucracy that "[t]here is the principle of fixed and official jurisdictional areas,

455 which are generally ordered by rules, that is, by laws or administrative regulations" (Gerth & Mills, 1946). These rules and areas circumscribe the duties and powers of those working within the bureaucracy, maintaining and supporting its authority. As Weber points out,

460 in a well-ordered bureaucracy, these duties are routinized and well regulated, and conflict seldom arises.

Yet, in this study, we see an example of two routinized bureaucracies coming into conflict within a single agency. As a result, duties are no longer clear-cut

465 and powers even less so. Merton (1957, 1967) captures this dilemma nicely in his conception of role-conflict within a role-set. The case manager holds a social position—a role—within a social system, that is, the system of county mental health. To the degree that the

470 case manager has incongruent expectations between the roles defined by each bureaucracy, the role occupant, the case manager, is conflicted.

Such a situation illustrates rather well a partial answer to a question raised by Merton himself:

475 The assumed structural basis for potential disturbance of a role-set gives rise to a double question: Which social mechanisms, if any, operate to counteract the theoretically assumed instability of role-sets, and, correlatively, under which circumstances do these social mechanisms

480 fail to operate, with resulting inefficiency, confusion, and conflict?

This study provides a partial answer; the overlap of bureaucracies, institutions, or social systems, more generally, sets up conditions under which expectations

485 collide, and role-sets become unstable.

Such a notion adds a new dimension to existing work on the difficulty of providing services to persons with severe mental illness. Previous research has focused on barriers to service delivery (e.g., as described

490 by Boyer, 1987; Rog, 1988; and Morrissey et al., 1986), such as fragmentation in the system, or noncompliance and lack of resources among the service population. The case managers in this study did not see their frustration in that light, however. To them, the

495 source of the frustration was their perception of being caught between disparate federal and county systems. In particular, the case managers experienced a sense of being bound in a web of bureaucratic contradictions, such that their own service system was itself prevent-

500 ing them from providing services. Under the rules of these two systems, they had contradictory work expectations. In other words, the case managers experienced this conflict between two bureaucracies as conflict within their occupational role.

505 According to Merton's (1957) theory of the "role-set," each position in the social structure has not just one associated role, but a set of roles reflecting the various obligations vis-à-vis relevant others. His own example of a teacher has one set of expectations re-

510 garding interactions with students, and entirely another set regarding her interactions with the school principal or superintendent. This is roughly comparable to a case manager who has three sets of role-expectations, one with each of two funding agencies, and one with cli-

515 ents. To the degree that these expectations are mutually incompatible, the case manager experiences conflict between roles within a set, what Merton calls role conflict. Thus, role-set theory provides a vocabulary for discussing the process whereby the structural becomes

520 personal, and the external conflict of systems becomes internalized.

Stryker (1980) describes how external conflict can have psychological and emotional effects through our roles. According to Stryker, roles are the materials we 525 use to identify who we are. Engaging in actions that are in keeping with our role-identities reinforces our sense of self. Expanding on Stryker's work, Heise (1978, 1987) argues that if conflicts within established roles endure and cannot be argued away, these conflicts will 530 lead to change in the role-identity. If the conflicts consist of negative or disempowering information, the change in the role-identity will be negative as well. By this argument, the role conflict experienced by the case managers may have been more than frustrating, it may 535 have been threatening to their sense of self. By preventing the case managers from doing what they wanted to do, the systemic contradiction could potentially prevent them from being who they want to be. That is, by constraining their actions, the systems also 540 prevented them from enacting their chosen occupational role-identities in a positive way (Stryker, 1980). This bred a range of discontents, including anger, defensiveness, bitterness, powerlessness, and apathy. If frustration was the short-term result of contradiction, 545 its long-term consequence was occupational demoralization among the very people striving to ameliorate the despair of others.

Such a conflict between bureaucracies is hardly unusual in the social services. Indeed, multiple funding 550 sources and overlapping bureaucracies may be more the norm than the exception. If this is the case, then the role conflict illuminated in this study may be widespread indeed. While such conflict may not consistently reach the same proportions as in this case— 555 indeed, exacerbating factors were rife in this site—the conflict appears quite likely to exist.

The lesson for program planners and policymakers, then, is this: bureaucratic disjunctions may well be played out in occupational role conflict for program staff. Burnout is 560 not merely personal, it is structural as well. When designing new programs, a hostile or conflicted system can make the most well-planned program go awry. To limit such disjunctions, planners must take into account flaws in the existing system and degrees to which the existing 565 system may not match with the program to be implemented.

Conclusion

This agency's untenable position between two systems obviously makes a difference in the effectiveness of its services. The fact that the agency's targets are, by 570 definition, extremely difficult clients to serve is a contributing factor to the dilemma as well. REACH found itself torn between the rules and resources of two conflicting bureaucracies. This conflict created dilemmas in providing services to clients: Meeting eligibility 575 criteria for services from the federation grant meant the clients did not meet the eligibility criteria for many county services. REACH staff reacted to this dilemma by bending rules, finding loopholes, and investing extra time and emotional labor in each client. Despite this, it 580 remained very hard to provide desired services to their clients, and many slipped away. Aware of the bureaucratic conflict, but unable to find recourse for their dilemmas, the REACH staff grew frustrated, angry, and resentful of the county system.

Epilogue

585 The agency's untenable situation between two incompatible bureaucracies was, as evident in this paper, inherently unstable. It, combined with budgetary complications in the system, led to increasing resentment between the county and REACH. Toward the end of 590 my fieldwork, the county abruptly took advantage of a quiet offer from the state to take over administration of the program. REACH staff arrived at work one day to find a letter informing them that they were suddenly state, rather than county, employees. Despite the shock 595 and consternation produced by the change, it turned out to be an improvement for all concerned. A few months after my departure from the field, REACH had moved into its new role at the outreach and community service arm of the local State Psychiatric Hospital. Oddly 600 enough, despite the expected greater ideological conflict between an in-patient hospital and an intensive community support program, the combination worked. The reduction in bureaucratic conflict (largely due to the fact that the state had few pre-existing community 605 service regulations to conflict with those of REACH) seemed to more than compensate for the surface disparities. REACH continued in this position through the end of its federal funding, obtaining stability that it had been unable to achieve when dealing with the county, 610 its apparent systemic peer.

References

Becker, Howard S., B. Geers, E. Hughes, and A. Strauss. 1961. *Boys in White: Student Culture in Medical School.* Chicago: University of Chicago Press.

Boyer, Carol A. 1987. "Obstacles in Urban Housing Policy for the Chronically Mentally Ill," pp. 71–81 in David Mechanic (Ed.), *Improving Mental Health Services: What the Social Sciences Can Tell Us.*

Chamberlain, R., MSW, and C. A. Rapp, Ph.D. 1991. "A Decade of Case Management: A Methodological Review of Outcome Research." *Community Mental Health Journal*, 27, 3:171–188.

Corbin, Juliet, and Anselm Strass. 1990. *The Basics of Qualitative Research.* Thousand Oaks, CA: Sage.

Coser, Rose Laub. 1962. *Life in the Ward.* East Lansing: Michigan State University Press.

Estroff, Sue E. 1981. *Making It Crazy: An Ethnography of Psychiatric Clients in an American Community.* Berkeley: University of California Press.

Freedman, Ruth I., and Ann Moran. 1984. *Wanderers in a Promised Land: The Chronically Mentally Ill and Deinstitutionalization.* Supplement of *Medical Care*, Vol. 22, No. 12.

Gerth, H. H., and C. Wright Mills, eds. 1946. *From Mar Weber: Essays in Sociology.* New York: Oxford University Press.

Goffman, Erving. 1961. *Asylums: Essays on the Social Situation of Mental Patients and Other Inmates.* New York: Anchor.

Goffman, Erving. 1974. *Asylums: Essays on the Social Situation of Mental Patients and Other Inmates.* Garden City, N.Y: Anchor.

Grob, Gerald N. 1994. *The Mad Among Us: A History of the Care of America's Mentally Ill.* NY: Free Press.

Heise, David R. 1979. *Understanding Events: Affect and the Construction of Social Action.* New York: Cambridge.

------- 1987. "Affect Control Theory: Concepts and Model." *Journal of Mathematical Sociology*, 13:1–33.

Hochschild, Arlie. 1983. *The Managed Heart: Commercialization of Human Feeling.* Berkeley: University of California Press.

Hopper, Kim. 1998. "Housing the Homeless." *Social Policy*: Spring, 1998.

Jencks, Christopher. 1994. "Housing the Homeless." *The New York Review,* May 12.

Liebow, Elliot. 1993. *Tell Them Who I Am: The Lives of Homeless Women.* New York: Free Press.

Merton, Robert K. 1967. *On Theoretical Sociology.* NY: The Free Press.

Merton, Robert K. 1957. "The Role-Set: Problems in Sociological Theory." *The British Journal of Sociology.* Volume VIII, June.

Morrissey, Joseph P., Kostas Guinis, Susan Barrow, Elmer L. Struening, and Steven E. Katz. 1986. "Organizational Barriers to Serving the Mentally Ill Homeless," pp. 93–108 in Billy E. Jones (Ed.), *Treating the Homeless: Urban Psychiatry's Challenge.*

Morse, Janice M. (ed.) 1994. *Critical Issues on Qualitative Research Methods.* Newbury Park: Sage.

Rog, Debra J. 1988. "Engaging Homeless Persons with Mental Illness into Treatment." Publication #PE-0501 of the National Mental Health Association. Prepared for the Division of Education and Service Systems Liaison of the National Institute of Mental Health.

Rubin, Allen. 1992. "Is Case Management Effective for People with Serious Mental Illness? A Research Review." *Health and Social Work,* 17, 2:138–150.

Solomon, Phyllis. 1992. "The Efficacy of Case Management Services for Severely Mentally Disabled Clients." *Community Mental Health Journal,* 28, 3:163–180.

Spicer, Paul, Mark Willenbring, Frank Miller, and Elgie Raymond. 1994. "Ethnographic Evaluation of Case Management for Homeless Alcoholics." *Practicing Anthropology,* 16, 4:23–26.

Strauss, Anselm, and Juliet Corbin. 1990. *Basics of Qualitative Research: Grounded Theory Procedures and Techniques.* Newbury Park: Sage.

Thoits, Peggy. 1986. "Social support as coping assistance." *Journal of Consulting and Clinical Psychology.* 54:416–423.

Exercise for Article 41

Factual Questions

1. What was the "initial intent" of this study?

2. REACH was under the jurisdiction of what level of government?

3. What was the size of the caseloads in this program?

4. On an average day, what would the researcher do after the morning staff meeting (including review of clients) and attending the team meeting?

5. According to the researcher, what lends credibility to the results despite the small sample size?

6. To provide services to homeless people with mental illness and substance abuse problems, the agency was supposed to draw on what?

Questions for Discussion

7. In the Contents of this book, this study is classified as an example of qualitative research. Do you agree with this classification? Explain.

8. If you were conducting a study on this topic, would you select a qualitative or quantitative approach? Explain.

9. The researcher uses the term "participant observation." What do you think this term means? (See lines 171–174.)

10. Do you think the generalizability of the results of this study is limited? Explain. (See lines 227–232 and 409–416.)

Quality Ratings

Directions: Indicate your level of agreement with each of the following statements by circling a number from 5 for strongly agree (SA) to 1 for strongly disagree (SD). If you believe an item is not applicable to this research article, leave it blank. Be prepared to explain your ratings. When responding to criteria A and B below, keep in mind that brief titles and abstracts are conventional in published research.

A. The title of the article is appropriate.

   SA   5   4   3   2   1   SD

B. The abstract provides an effective overview of the research article.

   SA   5   4   3   2   1   SD

C. The introduction establishes the importance of the study.

   SA   5   4   3   2   1   SD

D. The literature review establishes the context for the study.

   SA   5   4   3   2   1   SD

E. The research purpose, question, or hypothesis is clearly stated.

   SA   5   4   3   2   1   SD

F. The method of sampling is sound.

   SA   5   4   3   2   1   SD

G. Relevant demographics (for example, age, gender, and ethnicity) are described.

   SA   5   4   3   2   1   SD

H. Measurement procedures are adequate.

   SA   5   4   3   2   1   SD

I. All procedures have been described in sufficient detail to permit a replication of the study.

   SA   5   4   3   2   1   SD

J. The participants have been adequately protected from potential harm.

   SA   5   4   3   2   1   SD

K. The results are clearly described.

SA   5   4   3   2   1   SD

L. The discussion/conclusion is appropriate.

SA   5   4   3   2   1   SD

M. Despite any flaws, the report is worthy of publication.

SA   5   4   3   2   1   SD

Article 42

Unretired and Better Than Ever:
Older Adults As Foster Parents for Children

DONALD H. GOUGHLER
Family Services of Western Pennsylvania

ANNETTE C. TRUNZO
Family Services of Western Pennsylvania

ABSTRACT. The authors explore issues concerning employing older adults as foster parents for children. A survey of agencies in the United States suggests that agencies that utilize older adults as foster parents experience benefits, including elders' abilities to impart life experience and to offer a high degree of tolerance and time flexibility. Older foster parents, when surveyed, reported that fostering benefited them, citing pleasures they derived and defining contributions gained to their own welfare. The authors recommend strategies for agencies to recruit older adults as foster parents as well as public consciousness-raising efforts that promote the value gained by society and the older adults when they choose second careers in child care.

From *Families in Society: The Journal of Contemporary Social Services*, 86, 393–400. Copyright © 2005 by Children and Families. Reprinted with permission.

Foster parents are a vital part of the child welfare system and are asked to fulfill all the role responsibilities of natural parents. Each year, family foster care is being provided to an estimated 542,000 children who have been abused or neglected (Adoption and Foster Care Analysis and Reporting System [AFCARS], 2003.). Two significant factors contribute to the challenge of foster care placement for social service agencies. On one hand, continuing high numbers of children are entering the child welfare system whereas, on the other hand, the number of available foster care homes is declining. Although the total number of licensed family foster homes in the United States is not known, 38 states reported a total of 133,503 homes on the last day of 1998 (Child Welfare League of America [CWLA], 2000). When compared with the number of children in out-of-home placement, it becomes clear that the number of foster homes has been insufficient to accommodate the demand. Of the children in out-of-home care, 19% were cared for in a group home or institutional placement, with the remaining children primarily being cared for in a nonrelative foster home or relative placement (AFCARS, 2003). Unfortunately, the lack of foster homes sometimes leads child welfare agencies to place the child in a more restrictive level of care than needed.

Foster Care: The Literature

Changes in Foster Care Service Arena

Shifts arose in the foster care system with the passage of the Adoption Assistance and Child Welfare Act of 1980, an amendment to the Social Security Act of 1935. This law emphasized family reunification and permanency planning for children who are in out-of-home placement (Pecora, Whittaker, Maluccio, & Barth, 2000), and with the inception of this law, the population of children in foster care was reduced by nearly one-half (CWLA, 2002). However, with the rate of co-occurring mental health disorders and substance abuse in the adult population estimated to have ranged from 29% to 59% in 1978 (Regier et al., 1990), alcohol and drug abuse issues in the birth parents were factors for out-of-home placement in nearly 75% of all children entering care (Child Welfare Partnership, 1999). In spite of the decrease of the number of children in out-of-home care as a result of this legislation, the number of children who are not living with their parents has grown, requiring more foster home families. Between 1986 and 1995, there was a 44% increase in children in out-of-home placements in the United States (Child Welfare Partnership, 1999). In addition to the number of children involved in the child welfare system, there were, and continue to be, many children who are being cared for by grandparents or other relatives not placed through formal mechanisms. There are approximately 6 million children living in the United States who are being cared for in a household headed by a grandparent or other relative who is not a birth parent (Brown, 2003).

Adoption was renewed as a viable option for a child to achieve permanency with the passage of the Adoption and Safe Families Act of 1997. The foster parents who were already caring for the child in their home were often looked upon as the first option to achieving permanency. When they adopted children, these foster parents typically left the resource pool of foster care providers, leaving a shortage of experienced and capable foster families for many agencies. In addition, changes in economics and social customs over the past several decades have exacerbated the shortage. Throughout earlier generations in American history

when there was a different economic climate, two-
70 parent households could afford one wage earner and a
parent at home. On the contrary, most modern households need two wage earners. In addition, with the rise
of single-parent-headed households over recent years,
the pool of families with time to assume the role of
75 foster parent has decreased.

The Role of Older Adults in Foster Care

   Traditionally, older adults have served a vital role
in the lives of children, whether as grandparents or
community members. In the field of foster care, older
adults could become a major resource in providing the
80 necessary stable homes for the child who is in need of a
temporary home. Older adults bring with them a perspective on life and life experiences that makes them
uniquely suitable for the task of foster parents. They
have been recognized in a volunteer capacity as being
85 more flexible and spontaneous in their interactions with
others and for their ability to contribute to a program's
services (Strom & Strom, 1999). At the voluntary level,
they have demonstrated notable capacities to provide
care for children in such national programs as the Fos-
90 ter Grandparent Program. Older foster parents may also
be more committed to providing foster care services
once involved with an agency. In a study of predictors
of foster parents' satisfaction, older foster mothers
tended to be more satisfied in their role as foster par-
95 ents and more content in continuing to be foster parents
than younger foster mothers (Denby, Rindfleisch, &
Bean, 1999).

   Benefits derived from continued work or volunteer
experience for the older adult have been demonstrated
100 in the literature. In Dulin and Hill (2003), altruistic
activity in older adults was predictive of positive affect.
The older adult worker who engaged in providing services to others reported better psychological functioning than their nonaltruistic cohorts. In a large sample of
105 members of a church, those who engaged in altruistic
social behaviors experienced higher levels of mental
health functioning than those who did not engage in
these activities (Schwartz, Meisenhelder, Ma, & Reed,
2003). Other findings suggest that older adults who
110 participated in community service work derived benefits of positive social integration and the activity served
as a buffer against stress (Piliavin, 2003). Older adults
who participated in The Foster Grandparent Program
reported less depression, more social support, and en-
115 hanced life satisfaction than did adults who were not
foster grandparents (Sweeney, 2000).

Older Americans

Changes in the Older Population

   In 1965, the United States Congress passed the
Older Americans Act, which established a strong policy of support for ten important social objectives that
120 addressed concerns of older people. Among those objectives was the declaration that "older people should
have the opportunity for employment with no discrimi-

natory practices because of age" (Older Americans Act
of 1965). At the time when the act was passed, a rela-
125 tively small proportion (9.2%) of the United States
population was 65 years of age or older (U.S. Department of Commerce, Bureau of the Census, 1960, Table
45). At the same time, an unusually high proportion of
Americans (39%) were younger than 20 and were fill-
130 ing schools and colleges at unprecedented rates (U.S.
Department of Commerce, Bureau of the Census, 1960,
Table 45). American society built new structures and
developed new resources based on the ascendancy of
that group of young people, the so-called baby boom
135 generation.

   Today, 40 years after the passage of the Older
Americans Act, the first born of the baby boom generation are nearly 60 years old, now number 77 million
people, and soon will become the subjects of this legis-
140 lation. In some ways, these new elders will represent
importantly different demographic characteristics from
their grandparents of the mid-1960s. For one, they constitute a larger proportion of the total population than
the earlier older generation (12.4% as compared with
145 9.2%), and by 2040, this group will peak at 19.5% of
the population (Hobbs & Damon, 2004). They also
differ from their grandparents because they can expect
to live longer, experience better health, are better educated, and have more retirement income.

150 Panek (1997) notes that the current aging generation will be expected to remain in the workforce longer
for a variety of reasons, including increased longevity.
This group has experienced improvements in health
and life expectancy, which could allow them to remain
155 active in the work force until older ages (Johnson,
2004). In the area of education, the American population as a whole, as well as older adults specifically, has
a higher level of educational achievement than was the
case 40 years ago. Only 6.5% of the older adults of
160 1965 had graduated from college (U.S. Department of
Commerce, Bureau of the Census, 1960, Table 173), as
compared with 10.0% of persons who were 65 in 2002
(U.S. Department of Commerce, Bureau of the Census,
2002). Although economic security is still an important
165 concern for older adults, they are better off than their
cohorts of the past. In contrast to the older adults of the
1960s, today's elders have benefited from the development of Medicare and the increases in Social Security and enjoy a stronger base of retirement income
170 than their predecessors had. The Social Security program has been key to bringing the poverty rate among
the elderly down from 28% in 1967 to about 12% today (Zimmerman, 2000).

Potential for Future Worker Shortages

   In fact, economic advances represented by Social
175 Security and pension advances have significantly improved the retirement prospective, and some believe
that employer and government pensions and health
plans will prompt them to leave the labor force and

stay out, causing shortages in the labor force (Penner, Perun, & Steuerle, 2003). This trend has already been recognized in Europe and is the subject of major employment policy research and planning (Employment Task Force of the European Union, 2003). Dychtwald, Erickson, and Morison (2004) observed,

While the ranks of the youngest workers (16–24) are growing at 15% this decade, the 25- to 34-year-old segment is growing at just half that, and the workforce population between ages 35 and 44, which are the prime executive development years, is actually declining. (p. 1)

Much has been written about the impact this retired generation will impose on the economy. Some draw the conclusion that as the income provided by this retired generation recedes, some level of continued work by them is needed to contribute to the support of American society (Ekerdt, 2004; Kleyman, 2003; Penner et al., 2003; Steuerle & Carasso, 2001). The Older Americans Act of 1965 recognized that work might continue to retain a role in the lives of older adults. Although the Act focused on community service employment, administration of this employment program over the years has featured an effort to develop unsubsidized employment across all sectors of the economy.

Self-Actualization Through Work

Another reason to encourage able and willing elders to continue to work is that work is a positive lifestyle option for many. Gradual retirement via part-time jobs or new careers can be compatible with better health and self-actualization (Dahlherg, 2004; Dychtwald et al., 2004). Older adults in the 21st century are now and will continue to be more educated and physically and mentally active; these factors will have significant implications for both the quality and quantity of older adults as a labor force in the coming years (Besl & Kale, 1996; McManus, 2004). Many of these individuals will seek to continue working in endeavors that provide self-actualization as a primary benefit even if financial rewards are more limited. In recent research by the American Association for Retired Persons, 2,000 preretirees confirmed that for them, retirement work will need to "keep you mentally active" (80%), "make you feel useful" (74%), and "provide fun and enjoyment" (73%) (Brown, 2003).

Resource for Social Services

Social service agencies are among those employers that need to consider the attractive characteristics of these new elders in terms of future staffing needs. Agencies should evaluate the potential of older workers to be employed in those categories of jobs that currently present agencies with a recruitment challenge, as well as those categories expected to challenge recruitment in the future. The focus should be on retaining people beyond normal retirement or proactively developing strategies to recruit older adults into some of these jobs. Agencies need to examine myths about the capacity of older adults to perform effectively in specific social service job categories.

The field of child foster care is an example of a social service area in which older adults in the 21st century may seek and find a rewarding experience that offers them a direct opportunity to contribute to the social good. This field is also being challenged to recruit a workforce in the 21st century.

Method

Participants and Procedures

In gathering background information for this article, we were interested in the experiences of foster care agencies and older adults who are foster parents, so we drew a stratified random sample of foster care agencies from the Alliance for Children and Families and the Foster Family Treatment Association membership lists. The original sample size contained 132 agencies, with 66 agencies coming from states with the highest percentage of older adult residents (13.8% to 17.6% of older adults in the population) and the remaining 66 agencies dispersed across the United States. Of the 132 agencies surveyed, 44 returned the questionnaire (33%). In these agencies, there were a total of 2,387 foster families with 261 individuals who were identified as being aged 60 or older. The agency foster care programs varied in size from two foster families to 443 families, with the average agency having 55 foster families.

We also distributed 261 surveys to older foster parents who were identified by the agencies, and from these, we received 67 (26%) responses. The average age of these respondents was 64, with 22% being male and 78% female; 68% were married, and the responding foster parents had provided an average of 23 years of foster care services. The minimum time of providing services in this population was 6 months and the maximum time was 36 years.

All potential participants were sent a letter explaining the purpose of the study to encourage their participation. Respondents were asked to complete a one-page questionnaire and return the completed questionnaire in a self-addressed, stamped envelope. In addition to the agency surveys, a foster parent questionnaire was supplied for the older adults serving as foster parents. Agencies that were sent the agency surveys were asked to distribute the foster parent surveys to their foster parents who were 60 and older. Overall, the questionnaires were mailed and collected over a period of 8 weeks.

Measures

The agency questionnaire contained 10 questions relating to the foster care program. Specifically, we were interested in the number of older adults who were employed as foster parents, any recruitment efforts they utilized to enroll older adults, and their perception of challenges and benefits in utilizing older adults as foster parents. The foster parent questionnaire had 4 questions about providing foster care services that were rated on a 5-point scale, with 5 being the highest positive response. In addition, there was an open-ended question regarding the foster parents' "favorite thing" about being a foster parent; there were also two satisfaction questions and demographic information questions.

Findings

Of the agencies responding, 32% acknowledged a concern or challenge related to the prospect of using older adults as foster parents. The identified challenges tended to be centered on concerns over the foster parent's health or physical capabilities (43%) and negative personality characteristics such as "being set in own ways" (35%). The agencies reported 58% positive responses in the question of benefits associated in having an older adult as a foster parent. Many of the respondents (48%) identified the older adult's experience and wisdom as a benefit for the children and program. Other responses cited the older adult's time and flexibility afforded by being retired as a positive aspect (13%); others noted favorable characteristics such as patience, understanding, and tolerance (15%); and others felt that the older foster parents provided more stability and dependability (10%). Another beneficial element that was noted was the tendency of birth families to relate differently to older foster parents, feeling less challenged by a foster parent who is in the age range of a grandparent (8%; see Table 1). Only two of the agencies had age requirements not allowing people older than 65 to serve as foster parents, whereas most of the agencies had requirements that a foster parent had to be at least 21 years of age. Only three agencies specifically focused on recruiting older adults as foster parents.

Table 1
Challenges and Benefits of Older Adults as Foster Parents

		N	%
Challenges (*N* = 23)	Health/lifespan issues	10	43
	Negative characteristics	8	35
	Technology use/ documentation	2	9
	Need for more support/ training	2	9
	Other	1	4
Benefits (*N* = 52)	Experience/wisdom	25	48
	Patience/tolerance	8	15
	Flexibility with time schedules	7	13
	Stability/dependability	5	10
	Decreased role confusion	4	8
	Other	3	6

The foster parents responded quite positively concerning their feelings about providing foster care services. Such questions as, "How much do you like providing foster care?" yielded a 4.71 rating, and "How often are your main interests and pleasures in life con-

nected with doing foster care?" yielded a rating of 4.08. Foster parents felt very strongly that providing foster care was valuable (4.82), and they were very satisfied with doing foster care (4.37; see Table 2).

Table 2
Mean Score for Foster Parent Survey

	N	M	SD
1. How much do you like providing foster care?	65	4.71	.46
2. How often do you feel satisfied with doing foster care?	65	4.37	.57
3. How often are your main interests and pleasures in life connected with doing foster care?	63	4.08	.75
4. How often do you feel it is valuable to provide foster care?	65	4.82	.39

In determining a foster parent's perceptions about being a foster parent, respondents indicated several categories of responses. Many identified an altruistic desire or pleasure in seeing changes or growth in the child (44%), and the pursuit of providing care and love to a child emerged as being almost equally important (33%; see Table 3).

Table 3
Foster Parents' Favorite Things About Providing Foster Care (N = 57)

	N	%
Changes/growth in child	25	44
Providing/caring for child	19	33
Companionship	7	12
Challenge	3	5
Other	3	5

Qualitative Research: Foster Parent Interviews

Survey data were augmented by qualitative interviews of 12 foster parents. The interviews were conducted in person with older foster parents from the foster care program at Family Services of Western Pennsylvania. All foster parents 55 years of age or older from the agency were telephoned by an agency researcher who asked whether an interview could be arranged. Of the 16 foster parents who met this criterion, 12 agreed to be interviewed. All interviews were conducted by a master's-level clinician in the respondent's home, with one interview in an agency office; all interviews occurred between September 24 and October 11, 2004. In homes where there was a spouse, both foster parents were invited to participate in the interview. The interviews were approximately 60 to 90 minutes in length and involved an exploration of the foster parents' experiences, including their perceptions of the benefits and difficulties in providing foster care to children. Several areas related to foster care were discussed, such as why they became foster parents, what they find valuable about being foster parents, struggles or difficulties they experience, and the supports and resources they have used to manage the diffi-

360 culies. All interviews were tape-recorded and transcribed for analysis, and two independent raters reviewed transcripts of the interviews to determine common themes.

Qualitative Findings

365 An analysis of the transcripts identified four topical areas relevant to a foster parent's experience: (a) motivation to be a foster provider, (b) values in the provision of foster care services, (c) struggles or difficulties in providing foster care, and (d) issues of resources and supports. Examples of typical reactions in each of these 370 areas are presented.

Motivation to Be Foster Parents

In discussing the motivation for providing foster care, foster parents tended to express their desire and delight in being around children and wanting to help them. Other times, it was noted that providing foster 375 care involved dealing with the empty nest syndrome or addressing deeper self-actualization needs or fulfilling religious ones. Most of the foster parents were able to recall a specific time in their lives when they were motivated to decide to become a foster parent. What ap-380 peared to be the motivating factor appeared also to sustain these foster parents to continue to provide care.

Enjoyment of children. Mrs. T is a 76-year-old married Caucasian woman who has been providing foster care services for 11 years with her husband, who is 79 385 years old. This couple talked about their love for children and enjoying a home filled with children.

> When my own youngest child, who is now 34, started school I wanted foster care then. We do nothing and we go nowhere. I liked kids all my life. I had my neighbor's
390 kids over all the time. I think I should have children in the house.

Another foster parent, twice-widowed Mrs. B, Caucasian, 63, who started providing foster care at the age of 55, said, "I never enjoyed or found anything more 395 rewarding than having those kids."

Mrs. H, a widowed African American woman of 57, said, "I became a foster parent because I love kids; I got gangs of grandkids, but I just love kids. I'd rather be in a house full of kids than adults." A single African 400 American woman of 66 who has been providing foster care for 4 years said, "I love kids. I never had none. I figured maybe this is my job to help kids in need, and I enjoy doing it."

Religious reasons. Another foster parent, a 79-year-405 old Caucasian widowed woman, Mrs. S, was motivated by a deal she had made with God when she was going through a medical crisis with her daughter and herself:

> I thought I was pregnant in my 40s and I was tickled to death. I went to the doctor and I wasn't pregnant.... They
410 told me that I had leukemia and I had approximately 9 months to live. My daughter came down with spinal meningitis. They kept her in isolation...I screamed. I didn't pray. I screamed at God above and told him he couldn't do that, take my crippled child and take me. The doctor

415 told me that I couldn't bargain with God. I told him I am not making a bargain. I am telling him that if he doesn't take my kid, I will do anything for his children. I will take care of his children. Dr. Young didn't understand, but my husband did. Kate [her daughter] came out OK
420 with no severe problems. Our church had a foster mother, and she told me to go down to this agency. I went down and I became a foster mother.

Another foster parent, Mrs. C, African American, divorced, 70, phrased it like this, "It is because that is 425 why God has me here. That is the mission that he put me on this earth to do." Mr. and Mrs. D, 68 and 72, Caucasian, said, "It is a wonderful ministry of love. You cannot be a selfish person and do this because if you are, there is no place. So your life, half the time, is 430 put on the back burner."

Value of Providing Foster Care

The foster parents interviewed identified similar values in providing foster care to those of the foster parents who responded to the questionnaire. Typical responses centered on the desire to make a difference 435 in a child's life and to care for children. Other responses also indicated that the foster parent benefited from the foster care relationship. To some respondents, being a foster parent gives them purpose and adds meaning to their lives.

440 *Contributions to others.* A married couple in their 70s stated the importance of giving something to the child. The wife said, "I think if I can save one child, one is better than none at all. If everybody could just save one of these little kids, that makes a difference." 445 The husband added that it was valuable to "give them something that their own family couldn't give them, which may be love and affection."

A 79-year-old African American foster mother viewed her service of foster care as an opportunity for 450 teaching children. She said, "I teach the kids these things so it will stick with them for the rest of their life. I plant seeds."

Contributions to self. A foster mother (age 79) said, "I am not alone in this big house. It gives me some-455 thing to do. I have to get up in the morning whether I want to or not." A 70-year-old divorced African American woman said, "[Being a foster parent] helped me a lot because it kept me busy after my mother passed. The children...helped keep my mind off of my 460 mother passing. It helped me to keep myself busy." Another single foster mother (age 79, African American) said, "Yes, because I don't want to just sit here and do nothing, worry about just me and get old by myself."

Struggles or Difficulties of Providing Foster Care

465 The foster parents consistently talked about having difficulties with saying goodbye to the children whom they have cared for when it is time to return them to their birth families. They also noted the difficulties in their relationships with the birth parents; they struggled

470 with the birth parents over parenting issues. They also struggled to manage the child's torn feelings of loyalty between the foster parent and the birth parent.

Conflict with birth parents. Widowed foster mother Mrs. C (age 74) said, "The mothers sometimes can be
475 difficult. I got some mothers that have really been a headache. They are mad at the system. They are upset with the foster parent. They blame us that we have their children."

Child's feelings. Ms. MJ (age 67) said,

480 They [the children] can be rebellious because they want to be with their mother. It is a struggle to let them know that I am here to help them and give them support and love till they can go back to their mother.

An African American widowed woman of 67 said,

485 It is hard. It is hard. It is hard on them. It is harder on them than you because you are the adult. But the kids, it is a shame that they have to leave, pushed and moved around like that; it is not fair. They are depending all on an adult until they can depend on themselves.

490 A widowed Mrs. S identified the struggle for a child: "But can you imagine the torn morale in this kid—the love for her mother and still the love and respect for the foster mother that raised her."

Factors Contributing to Success

The foster parents spoke about the importance of
495 having support and resources available to them from the agency and the community. They appeared willing to acknowledge that they cannot do the work of foster care without assistance from others. It is apparent that when the foster care agency provides the day-to-day
500 assistance for the foster parents, they are appreciative and are able to fulfill their roles. When the children have special needs, assistance from professionals, whether it is from mental health or physical health providers, is necessary to assist these families. Friends and
505 family members also appear to play an important role in providing the social support needed to carry out this challenging work.

Mrs. W, a widowed woman of 71, said, "I have a friend who told me that if I get to the point I obviously
510 need a break, she will watch the kids for me." She went on to explain that she also utilizes the respite services of the agency when she needs a longer break from the "work." Mrs. G stated that she also utilized respite services after an operation when she "just couldn't keep
515 up with them [the children]." Mr. and Mrs. D said, "We left one church and joined another church, which was loving and accepting. This is an absolute must because if you do not have this support, you cannot go out in public."

520 Ms. M, a single African American woman of 67, said,

Oh, I have phone numbers of whom to call. CYF [Children, Youth and Families]...tells me where to go and what to do, and usually they help me to go. Well, CYF

525 and Family Services helps me a whole lot; at least they show me the way to go.

She noted the following about when she cared for a child with behavioral health needs: "The therapist was with him in school during the day, and then he came to
530 the house every evening for 2 hours. So really, I am learning from them; this is teaching me, too."

Discussion

Older adults can be an important resource for social service agencies by working as foster parents. Their experience and life perspective appear to be advanta-
535 geous qualities for any foster care agency. As many older adults are retired, they may have more time available to devote themselves to the care of children, which is an asset because available time is necessary in completing the many tasks associated with child care,
540 such as attending doctor appointments, enrolling for school, and attending court hearings. Whereas working foster parents often struggle when a new child comes into their home for emergency placement in the middle of the night when there is little time to secure babysit-
545 ting so that they can attend work the following day, a retired adult does not have to grapple with that situation.

The contributions of older adults working as foster parents appear not only to have a beneficial effect for
550 the foster care program but also to enhance the elder's own sense of well-being. It is understood in the literature that older adults who seek work after retirement do so to contribute their experience in a meaningful way and to feel valued. These individuals may seek em-
555 ployment that provides self-actualization as a primary benefit and not for financial rewards. An older adult who provides foster care appears to experience similar benefits of self-actualization.

Older adults serving as foster parents also make an
560 important contribution to society as a whole. An altruistic goal to give of oneself for the benefit of another is a higher level human experience. Individuals whose work enables them to give profoundly to children who have been neglected or abused find an avenue for
565 achieving this goal. The value of the contribution made by the foster parent is beyond any monetary compensation.

Limitations

The ability to generalize the results of this study is limited due to the relatively small agency sample size
570 ($N = 44$) and foster parent sample size ($N = 67$), yielding a relatively modest response rate to the total number of surveys mailed (33% and 26%, respectively). The study was conducted on a very small budget that did not include the possibility of an incentive to either
575 the agency or the foster parents for their participation. The study was limited to only those foster care agencies and foster parents who responded to the request to participate. These factors limit the generalizability and

interpretation of the findings. The possibility that the
580 limited results could be attributed to chance cannot be
ruled out and thus would need replication before inter-
pretative value can be given. The qualitative study,
though yielding a response rate of 75%, also has limited generalizability as the population of foster parents
585 was from Western Pennsylvania and connected with a
single provider agency.

Recommendations for Practice

The United States currently has the largest older
population in its history; this population possesses
great potential to continue to contribute to the eco-
590 nomic and social wealth of the nation and the better-
ment of conditions for fellow citizens. At the same
time, the United States needs older adults' continued
contribution. In the social arena, child foster care offers
a sterling opportunity for older people to pass the best
595 of their experience to a new generation that needs
someone to care for them. To capitalize on this resource, foster care agencies need to consider several
recommendations relating to recruitment of older
adults as foster parents and tailoring supports for them,
600 as well as boosting public awareness of productive
aging alternatives.

Recruitment. First, foster care agencies should look
at marketing directly to the older population to provide
the additional foster care homes that society requires.
605 An important target would be associations where educated and skilled older adults may have natural connections, such as retired nurse or teacher associations. It
would also be beneficial to acknowledge directly the
benefits the agency and the older person may experi-
610 ence by forming the foster care relationship. Other
marketing tools should depict older adults serving in
the capacity of foster parents, and current older foster
parents can be utilized directly in recruiting efforts.

Tailored training and support. For older adults who
615 decide to become foster parents, foster care agencies
may need to provide additional support to help them
cope with the stress of caring for young children and to
deal with the demands placed on them by the placing
agency. Training that acknowledges their unique per-
620 spectives on parenting should be provided and should
include additional lessons on how to manage the complex details of foster parenting. If they are on a limited
income and the small stipend that is provided for foster
care services causes difficulty, they may face chal-
625 lenges in managing economics. They also may need to
utilize respite services more often as they take time to
attend to their own medical or health situations if additional family support is not available. This additional
support may also increase the odds that an experienced
630 foster parent who enters older life may continue being
a foster parent.

Productive aging options. Finally, public information sources need to publicize more comprehensive
options for healthy aging. Since the time when the

635 Older Americans Act (1965) was adopted, a great
amount of attention to preretirement education programs has developed in the United States. In addition,
the popular media frequently feature information related to planning for retirement. Typically, these pro-
640 grams emphasize the rich potential of leisure activities
to fill the retirement years and are based on the notion
that older adults want to withdraw from work and relax. Although this is often true, some older adults, for
various reasons, would like to continue to work, and
645 some of these would like to enter a second or different
type of career. Because this larger, new generation of
older adults is so well prepared to continue their contribution to society, it behooves planners of preretirement programs and providers of information on aging
650 in the present and future to make a greater effort to
incorporate information on new careers.

References

Adoption and Safe Families Act, 105 U.S.C.§89. (1997).
Adoption Assistance and Child Welfare Act, 96 U.S.C.§272. (1980).
Adoption and Foster Care Analysis and Reporting System. (2003). *The AF-CARS Report: Preliminary FY 2001 Estimates as of March 2003 (8).* Re-trieved on October 10, 2004, from http://www.acf.hhs.gov/programs/cb/publications/afcars/report8.htm
Besl, J. R., & Kale, B. D. (1996, June). Older workers in the 21st century: Active and educated, a case study. *Monthly Labor Review, 119,* 18–28.
Brown, K. (2003). *Staying ahead of the curve 2003: The AARP working in retirement study.* Retrieved April 20, 2005, from http://www.aarp.org/research/reference/publicopinions/aresearch-import-417.html
Child Welfare League of America. (2000). Licensed homes and facilities, 1998. Retrieved March 13, 2001, from http://ndas.cwla.org/data_stats/access/predefined/Report.asp?ReportID=49
Child Welfare League of America. (2002). *Research Roundup: Family Reuni-fication.* Retrieved March 14, 2003 from http://www.cwla.org/programs/r2p/rrnews0203.pdf
Child Welfare Partnership. (1999). *Cohort IV report. An examination of longer-term foster care in Oregon between 1995–1997.* Retrieved August 2, 2004, from www.cwp.pdx.edu/assets/Long_Term_Cohort_IV_Report.pdf
Dahlberg, S. (2004, February). The new elderhood. *Training, 141,* 46–47.
Denby, R., Rindfleisch, N., & Bean, G. (1999). Predictors of foster parents' satisfaction and intent to continue to foster. *Child Abuse & Neglect, 23,* 287–303.
Dulin, P. L., & Hill, R. D. (2003). Relationships between altruistic activity and positive and negative affect among low-income older adult service provid-ers. *Aging & Mental Health, 7,* 294–299.
Dychtwald, K., Erickson, T., & Morison, B. (2004, March). It's time to retire retirement. *Harvard Business Review, 82,* 1.
Ekerdt, D. J. (2004). Born to retire: The foreshortened life course. *The Geron-tologist, 44,* 3–9.
Employment Task Force of the European Union. (2003). *Jobs, jobs, jobs: Creating more employment in Europe.* Retrieved April 20, 2005, from http://europa.eu.int/comm/employment_social/employment_strategy/pdf/etf_en.pdf
Hobbs, F. B., & Damon, B. L. (2004). *65+ in the United States.* Retrieved on September 24, 2004, from http://www.census.gov/prod/1/pop/p23-190/p23-190.html
Johnson, R. W. (2004, July). Trends in job demands among older workers. *Monthly Labor Review, 127,* 48–56.
Kleyman, P. (2003, July/August). Phased retirement will ease many into active older years [Electronic version]. *Aging Today: The Bimonthly Newspaper of the American Society for Aging,* 1.
Panek, P. E. (1997). The older worker. In A. D. Fisk & W. A. Rogers (Eds.), *Handbook of human factors and the older adult* (pp. 363–387). New York: Academic.
Pecora, P. J., Whittaker, J. K., Maluccio, A. N., & Barth, R. P. (2000). *The child welfare challenge.* New York: Aldine de Gruyter.
Penner, R. G., Perun, P., & Steuerle, C. E. (2003). *Letting older workers work.* Retrieved April 20, 2005, from http://www.urban.org/url.cfm?ID=310861
Piliavin, J. A. (2003). Doing well by doing good: Benefits for the benefactor. In C. L. M. Keyes & J. Haidt (Eds.), *Flourishing: Positive psychology and the life well lived* (pp. 227–247). Washington, DC: American Psychological Association.
Regier, D. A., Farmer, M. E., Rae, D. S., Locke, B. Z., Keith, S. J., Judd, L. L., & Goodwin, F. K. (1990). Comorbidity of mental disorders with alcohol and

other drugs: Results from the Epidemiologic Catchment Area (ECA) Study. *JAMA, 264*, 2511–2518.

Schwartz, C., Meisenhelder, J. B., Ma, Y., & Reed, G. (2003). Altruistic social interest behaviors are associated with better mental health. *Psychosomatic Medicine, 65*, 778–785.

Social Security Act, 42 U.S.C.§1320. (1935).

Steuerle, C. E., & Carasso, A. (2001). *A prediction: Older workers will work more in the future*. Retrieved April 20, 2005, from http://www.urban.org/url.cfm?ID=310258

Strom, R., & Strom, S. (1999). Establishing school volunteer programs. *Child and Youth Services, 20*, 177–188.

Sweeney, A. R. (2000). An evaluation of the foster grandparent program in Fresno, California. Dissertation abstracts international: Section BL the Sciences and Engineering. Vol 61 (1-B), July 2000, 550.

University of Michigan, Institute for Social Research. (2004). *Boomers unexpected ethos: Work until we drop?* Retrieved from http://www.umich.edu/news/index.html?Releases/2004/Jul04/r071504c

U.S. Department of Commerce, Bureau of the Census. (1960). *1960 Census of the population: Vol. 1. Characteristics of the population*. Washington, DC: U.S. Bureau of the Census.

U.S. Department of Commerce, Bureau of the Census. (2002). *Current population Survey*. Retrieved on September 24, 2004, from http://www.census.gov/population/socdemo/age/ppl-167/tab01.txt

Zimmerman, S. L. (2000). A family policy agenda to enhance families' transactional interdependencies over the life span. *Families in Society, 81*, 557–575.

About the authors: *Donald H. Goughler*, MSW, is chief executive officer, Family Services of Western Pennsylvania, and part-time faculty member at the University of Pittsburgh, School of Social Work, where he teaches courses in management. *Annette C. Trunzo*, MSW, is director of research and program evaluation, Family Services of Western Pennsylvania.

Address correspondence to: Donald H. Goughler at goughlerd@fswp.org or Family Services of Western Pennsylvania, 3230 William Pitt Way, Pittsburgh, PA 15238-1361.

Exercise for Article 42

Factual Questions

1. What percentage of the 261 surveys that were distributed to older foster parents were returned to the researchers?

2. What did the researchers do to encourage participation?

3. The researchers used an open-ended question regarding what?

4. How many of the responding agencies specifically focused on recruiting older adults?

5. How many of the 16 foster parents who were contacted by telephone agreed to be interviewed?

6. The mean (*M*) for the first question in Table 2 is 4.71. In light of the measure used, is this a high value?

Questions for Discussion

7. The literature review in this article is longer than the literature reviews in most of the other articles in this book. In your opinion, is this relatively long review a special strength of this article? Explain. (See lines 27–240.)

8. The researchers state that they drew a "stratified random sample." What is your understanding of the meaning of this term? (See lines 243–244.)

9. Of the 132 agencies surveyed, 33% returned the questionnaire. Is this an important weakness of this research? Why? Why not? (See lines 251–253.)

10. The results shown in Table 1 are described in lines 296–314. How helpful is the table in helping you understand these results?

11. The qualitative part of this research was based on interviews. The participants who were interviewed were from one foster care program. In your opinion, does this limit the generalizability of the results? (See lines 337–341.)

12. The researchers present quantitative findings in lines 294–336 and qualitative findings in lines 364–531. In your opinion, are both types of findings equally informative? Is one type more informative than the other? Explain.

13. Unlike most of the other articles in this book, this article is based on both quantitative and qualitative research. Do you believe that this is a strength of this article? Explain.

Quality Ratings

Directions: Indicate your level of agreement with each of the following statements by circling a number from 5 for strongly agree (SA) to 1 for strongly disagree (SD). If you believe an item is not applicable to this research article, leave it blank. Be prepared to explain your ratings. When responding to criteria A and B below, keep in mind that brief titles and abstracts are conventional in published research.

A. The title of the article is appropriate.

SA 5 4 3 2 1 SD

B. The abstract provides an effective overview of the research article.

SA 5 4 3 2 1 SD

C. The introduction establishes the importance of the study.

SA 5 4 3 2 1 SD

D. The literature review establishes the context for the study.

     SA   5   4   3   2   1   SD

E. The research purpose, question, or hypothesis is clearly stated.

     SA   5   4   3   2   1   SD

F. The method of sampling is sound.

     SA   5   4   3   2   1   SD

G. Relevant demographics (for example, age, gender, and ethnicity) are described.

     SA   5   4   3   2   1   SD

H. Measurement procedures are adequate.

     SA   5   4   3   2   1   SD

I. All procedures have been described in sufficient detail to permit a replication of the study.

     SA   5   4   3   2   1   SD

J. The participants have been adequately protected from potential harm.

     SA   5   4   3   2   1   SD

K. The results are clearly described.

     SA   5   4   3   2   1   SD

L. The discussion/conclusion is appropriate.

     SA   5   4   3   2   1   SD

M. Despite any flaws, the report is worthy of publication.

     SA   5   4   3   2   1   SD

Article 43

High Hopes in a Grim World: Emerging Adults' Views of Their Futures and "Generation X"

JEFFREY JENSEN ARNETT
University of Maryland

ABSTRACT. Views of the future were explored among emerging adults (aged 21 through 28). In general, they viewed their personal futures optimistically and believed their lives would be as good or better than their parents' lives in aspects such as financial well-being, career achievements, personal relationships, and overall quality of life. Interview responses indicated that many participants emphasized personal relationships, especially marriage, as the foundation of their future happiness. However, regarding the future of their generation as a whole, they were pessimistic. A majority of them agreed with the "Generation X" characterization of their generation as cynical and pessimistic. Reasons for this cynicism and pessimism were diverse and included economic prospects as well as societal problems such as crime and environmental destruction. Nevertheless, the participants tended to believe they would succeed in their personal pursuit of happiness even amidst the difficult conditions facing their generation and the world.

From *Youth & Society*, 31, 267–286. Copyright © 2000 by Sage Publications, Inc. All rights reserved. Reprinted with permission.

Dramatic demographic changes have taken place during the past 30 years for young people in their late teens and 20s in American society. As recently as 1970, the median age of marriage was 21 for females
5 and 23 for males; by 1996, it had risen to 25 for females and 27 for males (U.S. Bureau of the Census, 1997). Age of first childbirth followed a similar pattern. Also during this time, the proportion of young people obtaining higher education after high school
10 rose steeply from 48% in 1970 to 60% by 1993 (Arnett & Taber, 1994; Schulenberg, Bachman, Johnston, & O'Malley, 1995). Similar changes have taken place in other industrialized countries (Noble, Cover, & Yanagishita, 1996).
15 In effect, a new period of life has opened up between adolescence and adulthood as a normative experience for young people in industrialized societies. The late teens and early 20s are no longer a period in which the typical pattern is to enter and settle into
20 long-term adult roles. On the contrary, it is a period of life characterized for many young people by a high degree of change, experimentation, and instability (Rindfuss, 1991) as they explore a variety of possibilities in love, work, and worldviews (Arnett, 1998, in
25 press; Arnett, Ramos, & Jensen, in press). The period was originally termed "youth" by Keniston (1971), but because of certain inadequacies in the term *youth*, it has more recently been called *emerging adulthood* (see Arnett, 1998, in press; Arnett & Taber, 1994). Emerg-
30 ing adulthood is conceptualized as beginning with the end of secondary education, usually age 18 in American society, and ending in the mid- to late 20s for most people as the experimentation of the period is succeeded by more enduring life choices (Arnett, 1998, in
35 press).

Emerging adulthood is distinct demographically and subjectively from adolescence (roughly from ages 10 through 17) and young adulthood (roughly from age 30 to the early 40s). Emerging adulthood is distinct
40 demographically because it is a period characterized by an exceptionally high level of demographic change and diversity. For example, residential mobility peaks in the mid-20s, and the 20s are also years of frequent change and transition in occupation, educational status,
45 and personal relationships (Rindfuss, 1991). Emerging adulthood is also distinct subjectively. The majority of adolescents do not believe they have reached adulthood, and the majority of people aged 30 and older believe they have, but most people in their 20s see
50 themselves as somewhere in between adolescence and adulthood: The majority answer "in some respects yes, in some respects no" when asked whether they feel they have reached adulthood (Arnett, 1997, 2000).

Despite the fact that a period of emerging adult-
55 hood has become normative in American society, little research has focused on development during the 20s. Although studies of college students are abundant in social science research, research on young people who do not attend college and on young people beyond col-
60 lege age is scarce (William T. Grant Foundation Commission on Work, Family, & Citizenship, 1988). Keniston's (1971) conception of youth did not generate research attention to the period, and the concept of

emerging adulthood has only been articulated very
65 recently (Arnett, 1998, in press; Arnett & Taber, 1994).
One exception to this neglect is the long tradition of
sociological and demographic research on the timing of
transition events such as marriage and parenthood (e.g.,
Hogan & Astone, 1986; Marini, 1984; Rindfuss, 1991).
70 Other than this area, however, there is little research on
this age period (Jessor, Donovan, & Costa, 1991).

In lieu of scholarly attention, a great deal of public
attention has focused on this period in the past decade
in works of fiction and in journalistic accounts. These
75 works have tended to depict young people in their 20s
as pessimistic and uncertain as they approach the
threshold of adulthood. Most notably, Coupland's
(1991) novel *Generation X* portrayed three rootless
young people in their mid- to late 20s and their reluc-
80 tance to make the role transitions associated with the
transition to adulthood (e.g., marriage, a long-term
occupation). The novel generated a remarkable amount
of attention and commentary, and "Generation X"
quickly became familiar as a term applied to the cur-
85 rent generation of young people in their late teens and
20s.

Journalists have devoted considerable attention to
Generation X. In journalistic accounts, Generation X
has been described as materialistic, pessimistic, and
90 cynical (Giles, 1994; Hornblower, 1997; Kinsley,
1994). Young people in their 20s are often depicted as
daunted by the mixed economic prospects that face
them in the workplace, by the personal debt they have
accumulated by the time they leave higher education,
95 and by the national debt that has been left to them by
previous generations (Roper Organization, 1993). At
the same time, they are depicted as ambitious and eager
to pursue their financial, occupational, and personal
goals (Hornblower, 1997).
100 Most of the information used by journalists in de-
picting Generation X in this way comes from polling
data and marketing research, especially by
Yankelovich Partners and the Roper Organization. For
example, in a 1996 poll, Yankelovich Partners found
105 that 64% of young people aged 18 to 24 agreed that
"material things, like what I drive and the house I live
in, are really important to me" (Hornblower, 1997, p.
65). About one-half believed that they would be better
off financially than their parents. Nearly all—96%—
110 agreed, "I am very sure that someday I will get to
where I want to be in life" (p. 62). In a 1992 poll, the
Roper Organization found 18- to 29-year-olds to have
higher material aspirations than 18- to 29-year-olds
polled by the organization in 1978 (Roper Organiza-
115 tion, 1993). Fifty-nine percent aspired to have a lot of
money (compared with 50% in 1978), 42% aspired to
have a second car (28% in 1978), and 41% aspired to
have a vacation home (25% in 1978). Sixty-nine percent included a job that pays a lot more than average as
120 part of their definition of "the good life" (58% in
1978). However, an equal percentage included an in-

teresting job as part of their definition. Many of the
poll results on the views of emerging adults concern
economic issues, partly because these are believed to
125 be issues that are especially salient to young people as
they enter the workforce, but also because the objective
of pollsters such as Yankelovich Partners and the
Roper Organization is to inform their corporate clients
about the economic characteristics of their potential
130 customers.

This study is an exploration of views of the future
among emerging adults, including not only economic
issues but also their views of their prospects in terms of
career achievements, personal relationships, and over-
135 all quality of life. Views of the future are an important
topic with respect to emerging adults because for many
of them, the nature and quality of their adult lives remain to be constructed. It is a time when, for many
young people, few major life decisions have been set-
140 tled and a wide range of options remains possible. For
this reason, questions about the future are especially
relevant to their lives.

In addition to questions about their own futures,
participants in the study were asked what they per-
145 ceived to be the view of the future held by young people more generally. Specifically, they were asked
whether they agreed with the depiction of their generation as pessimistic and cynical as reflected in the term
Generation X. This question was asked in order to
150 compare it with the questions on their personal futures
to get a sense of how they compared their own view of
the future with the view of the future held by their generation. It was also asked to explore the validity of
popular ideas about Generation X.

Method

Participants
155 The participants were 140 persons aged 21 to 28
years. General characteristics of the sample are shown
in Table 1. The sample was evenly divided between
21- to 24-year-olds (50%) and 25- to 28-year-olds
(50%) and between males and females. Close to half of
160 the participants were married, and about one-fourth had
had at least one child. Two-thirds of the participants
were employed full-time, and one-fourth part-time;
28% were in school full-time, and 8% were enrolled
part-time. "Some college" was the modal level of edu-
165 cation, indicated by 52% of the participants. There was
a broad range of variability in the social class of the
participants' families of origin, as indicated by father's
and mother's education.

Procedure
The data presented here were collected as part of a
170 larger study on emerging adults in their 20s. The study
took place in a medium-sized city in the Midwest. Potential participants were identified through enrollment
lists from the two local high schools for the previous 3
to 10 years. All persons on the enrollment lists who had
175 current addresses in the area that could be identified

through phone book listings or by contacting their parents were sent a letter describing the study and then contacted by phone. Of the persons contacted, 72% agreed to participate in the study. Data collection took
180　place in the author's office or the participant's home, depending on the participant's preference. The study was conducted during 1994 and 1995.

Measures

　　The study included an interview and a questionnaire. Questionnaire items that pertained to partici-
185　pants' views of the future were as follows:

> Overall, do you think the quality of your life is likely to be better or worse than your parents' has been?
>
> Overall, do you think your financial well-being in adulthood is likely to be better or worse than your parents' has
190　been?
>
> Overall, do you think your career achievements are likely to be better or worse than your parents' have been?
>
> Overall, do you think your personal relationships in adulthood are likely to be better or worse than your par-
195　ents' have been?

　　For each of these questions, participants could answer "better," "worse," or "about the same."

　　From the interview, two questions were of interest for this article. One was similar to one of the items on
200　the questionnaire and concerned participants' personal futures: "Do you think your life, overall, is likely to be better or worse than your parents' lives have been?" The second concerned their perceptions of their generation's views of the future: "Some people have called
205　your generation *Generation X* and said that one of the distinctive characteristics of your generation is that you tend to be cynical and pessimistic about the future. Do you think this is true of your generation?" This question was added after the study had begun and was an-
210　swered by 76 of the participants.

Results and Discussion

　　The results and the discussion are integrated in this section. This approach was taken because it was believed that the qualitative interview results, in particular, were better suited to discussion commentary at the
215　time they were presented rather than in a separate section. With respect to the statistics on the quantitative data, analyses were conducted using chi-square tests. The four questionnaire items about participants' personal futures and the coded Generation X question
220　from the interview were analyzed in relation to age (21 to 24 vs. 25 to 28), gender, marital status, parenthood (no children vs. one or more children), father's education, mother's education, and parental divorce. These are all variables that could conceivably be related to
225　emerging adults' views of the future. Only analyses that were statistically significant are discussed below.

　　With respect to the qualitative data, for the interview question on overall quality of life in comparison to parents' lives, there was a nearly identical question
230　on the questionnaire, so the interview data were used only for illustration of certain themes underlying their responses to the questionnaire item. For the interview question about Generation X, responses were coded into three categories: agree, disagree, and ambiguous or
235　uncodable. Responses were coded by the author, and 30% of the responses were coded by a second coder, a colleague of the author who was not otherwise involved in the study. The rate of agreement was more than 90%. The author then identified themes within
240　participants' responses to the interview question and selected quotes for illustrating those themes.

Table 1
Background Characteristics of the Sample

Characteristic	%
Gender	
Male	53
Female	47
Employment	
Full	67
Part	24
None	9
Ethnicity	
White	94
Black	5
Other	1
Marital status	
Married	60
Single	40
Current educational status	
In school full-time	28
In school part-time	8
Not in school	65
Number of children	
None	73
One	14
Two or more	13
Mother's education	
Less than high school degree	8
High school degree	23
Some college	23
College degree	27
Some graduate school or graduate school degree	19
Father's education	
Less than high school degree	8
High school degree	24
Some college	15
College degree	24
Some graduate school or graduate school degree	30

Views of Their Personal Futures

　　The questionnaire results indicated that overwhelmingly, the emerging adults believed their lives would be as good or better than their parents' lives had been (see
245　Table 2). This was true for overall quality of life, $\chi^2(2, N = 138) = 41.2$, $p < .001$, as well as for the specific areas of financial well-being, $\chi^2(2, N = 139) = 11.1$, $p < .01$; career achievements, $\chi^2(2, N = 139) = 30.3$, $p < .001$; and personal relationships, $\chi^2(2, N = 139) = 62.6$,
250　$p < .001$. A majority believed that their overall quality of life (52%) and their personal relationships (58%) would be better than their parents' had been, 45% believed that their financial well-being would be better

than their parents' had been, and 47% believed that their career achievements would be better. The finding that slightly less than half believed their financial well-being would be better than their parents was nearly identical to the results of a similar question in a national poll in 1996 by Yankelovich Partners (Hornblower, 1997).

Table 2
Emerging Adults' Comparisons of Their Future Lives in Relation to Their Parents' Lives (in Percentages)

	Worse	Same	Better
Overall quality of life	9	39	52
Financial well-being	22	34	45
Career achievements	12	42	47
Personal relationships	4	39	58

Further insights into the meaning of their responses on the questionnaire were provided in their interview responses to the question, "Do you think your life, overall, is likely to be better or worse than your parents' lives have been?" Several themes emerged in the interviews. One theme was that when emerging adults indicated that they expected their lives were going to be the same as their parents' lives, this was typically a highly optimistic response because it was the response of emerging adults who viewed their parents' lives in highly favorable terms. In other words, "the same as parents" meant a happy and successful life. For example, a 24-year-old woman responded:

I would be very, very content if it was the same. I definitely don't want it to be worse, that's for sure. And I don't know if it could be any better. They have a great life.

Similarly, a 24-year-old man answered:

I think it will be about the same, actually. I want it to be. I think they've been a great example. I think they're wonderful people and they've given a lot to this world.

A second theme in the interviews was that financial well-being was secondary to other aspects of their hopes for the future, especially for emerging adults whose parents had been financially successful. For example, a 27-year-old man who was a singer in a rock band and whose father had been a biology professor indicated that he would probably not make as much money as his father but that it did not matter in terms of his future happiness:

I have meager needs. The things that I'm looking for in life aren't going to come with a bunch of money and a big house...I don't think I'll make as much money as him, but I don't need as much either.

A 25-year-old man believed the overall quality of his life would be better in comparison to that of his father, who was a successful and wealthy physician:

As I view it, yes, my quality of life will be better. I don't think my dad's happy. He thinks he's happy, but he's on a grind. He's on a rat race. The good side is he's in a pro-

fession that helps people.... But personally, all these career things that have to be done, I don't know. I think I'm able to step back, so I think I'll be able to be more happy, and that translates into a higher quality of life. I won't be anywhere as wealthy as they will; I've accepted that.... That's the whole point of most fathers' lives is to make their son's life better, and we're reaping the benefit of that. I'm able to choose not to be rich because I know what it's like. I know I can live without it.

However, this view depended to some extent on the economic status of the parents. Those whose parents were not as wealthy tended to place more value on the attainment of financial security, and were more likely to see their future lives as better financially and occupationally. In the quantitative analyses, those whose fathers' education was relatively lower were more likely to believe that their lives would be better than their parents' lives financially, $\chi^2(8, N = 118) = 28.20$, $p < .001$; in terms of career achievements, $\chi^2(8, N = 118) = 30.28$, $p < .001$; and overall, $\chi^2(8, N = 118) = 30.21$, $p < .001$. (A similar pattern was found with respect to mother's education.) For example, this 25-year-old woman saw her and her husband's financial success as part of a sequence of generational progress:

[My parents] both came from hard childhoods and they made a lot of their life. And I think their lives were better than their parents' lives, and I think it can only get better. I mean, they've brought us up to a stage higher than what they were, and I think that I can bring myself up higher than the stage that they were. I think with [my husband] and I both having all this education, we would be having jobs that will put us in a little higher bracket than them. So financially, I think we'll be a little better off.

Overall, however, the results of the interviews suggest that poll results indicating that emerging adults are materialistic and prize financial well-being may be misleading. It appears that although they like having material things and would prefer to be well-off financially, for many of them, that goal is secondary to their enjoyment of their work and to their more general pursuit of happiness. Similar results have been found in other studies of American's views of work (Colby, Sippola, & Phelps, in press; Jensen, 1998).

It should be added that the views of this sample on their financial futures may be different from the views of emerging adults from other parts of American society. The emerging adults in this study were predominantly White (94%), and the majority of them had at least one parent with a college degree. Would views of their personal futures be different, more pessimistic, among emerging adults who were from lower social classes and/or who were members of ethnic minorities? Perhaps. It is interesting to note that in this study, those from relatively low socioeconomic backgrounds were more optimistic than others about their personal futures (in relation to their parents' lives). Similar results were reported in a recent study of college students' views of their futures (Eskilson & Wiley, 1999).

It is possible that there are relations between social class and ethnicity in emerging adults' views of the future. Studies of young African Americans have shown that those from lower social classes are more optimistic about their prospects of succeeding in American society than those from the middle class, because those in the middle class are more likely to have had direct experience with racism from Whites as a result of having more daily contact with them (Hochschild, 1996). However, this study cannot speak to the experience of emerging adults in ethnic minorities except to suggest that their views of the future would be an intriguing topic for further investigation.

A third theme in the interviews was the preeminence of personal relationships as a basis for happiness. Of the four questions on the questionnaire comparing their future lives with their parents' lives, the emerging adults were most likely to think their lives would be better than their parents' lives in terms of personal relationships. (Binomial tests showed that only for the question on personal relationships were emerging adults more likely to answer "better" than "the same," $p < .05$.) In response to the interview question as well, this theme was prominent. Personal relationships, especially the marriage relationship, were seen as the ultimate source of happiness by many of them.

This was especially true for those who had come from a family in which the parents had divorced or had had frequent conflicts. They emphatically believed that their own marriages would be better. Samuel Johnson is often quoted as having said, "Remarriage is the triumph of hope over experience." For this generation of emerging adults, even a first marriage often represents such a triumph. On the questionnaire, participants whose parents had divorced were more likely than participants from nondivorced families to believe their personal relationships would be better than their parents' had been, $\chi^2(2, N = 137) = 9.90, p < .01$. It was only with respect to personal relationships—and not with respect to financial well-being, career achievements, or their overall lives—that participants from divorced families were more likely than those from nondivorced families to believe their lives would be better than their parents' lives.

This view was also evident in interview responses. For example, a 24-year-old woman asserted: "I think [my life is] going to be better [than my parents']. I don't foresee a divorce in my future." Similarly, a 26-year-old man said he thought his life would be

better.... I don't think about it so much financially. I think about it more from a personal standpoint. The fact that they got divorced, I consider that as not being successful and therefore I obviously hope that does not happen to me. So in that respect, I expect it to be better.

A 29-year-old man responded:

Mentally, it will be better.... I ain't going to divorce Chris. She'd have to kill me to get rid of me, you know,

because she's a one of a kind woman, you know. I've never met anybody like her. Like I said, I can just see us staying together just like this, always getting along.

A 26-year-old woman hoped to succeed in this respect where her friends had failed:

I think it's going to be better. I'm hoping to have a marriage that lasts forever. I know too many of my friends who have gotten married and gotten divorced already, and I don't want that to happen. I want to be one of those people that are married for 60 years or something.

In sum, the emerging adults in this study viewed their personal futures with high hopes. With few exceptions, they expected their lives to be as good or better than their parents' lives. When they talked about their occupational futures, they emphasized the importance of finding personal satisfaction in their work rather than seeking jobs that would provide financial well-being first and foremost. Personal relationships, especially marriage, were viewed by them as the most important component of their future happiness, and the majority of them believed that they would be more successful in this respect than their parents had been.

Views of Generation X

Overall, the questionnaire results in combination with the interview results indicated a considerable amount of optimism among the participants with respect to their personal lives. However, they tended to see their generation's prospects in much more pessimistic terms. The question was, "Some people have called your generation 'Generation X' and said that one of the distinctive characteristics of your generation is that you tend to be cynical and pessimistic about the future. Do you think this is true of your generation, or not?" Of the participants, 59% agreed with the characterization of their generation as cynical and pessimistic, whereas 22% disagreed (the other 19% gave ambiguous or uncodable responses). The difference in the proportion of "agree" and "disagree" responses was significant in a binomial test ($p < .001$). Chi-square analyses indicated that there were no differences among participants in their responses to this question with respect to age, gender, marital status, parenthood status, father's education, mother's education, parental divorce, or their responses to any of the four questions concerning their views of their personal futures.

The reasons many of them viewed their generation as cynical and pessimistic were varied, but common responses included limited economic opportunities and increased awareness of societal problems such as crime and environmental destruction. Although most of them viewed their personal financial and career prospects as bright (as we have seen), many of the participants viewed their generation's economic prospects as bleak. A 23-year-old woman stated,

I think we're kind of, in some ways, the lost generation. We all were brought up to think, "You finish high school, you go to college, you get a degree, and you go out to work," just like our parents did. Then when we get to college, we realize we don't know what we want, and we still don't know. We graduate with a degree we didn't want. I would say probably 7 out of 10 of my friends do that right now; they've already had their degrees and have jobs totally unrelated to their field.

A 27-year-old man had a similar view and gave it a political lineage:

I guess it comes from growing up during the 70s with Watergate and all the problems with Carter. Then you start college and you've got Reagan who's slashing everything in education, and you just kind of think, "Well, they're trying to do everything they can just to knock us down a little bit, to keep the haves and the have nots further apart," and it seems a lot now that you've got people with college degrees that work in McDonald's, you know. There's nowhere to go when you get out of school because all the jobs are already taken.

These views support the perspective of Cote and Allahar (1994), who attacked *credentialism*, the increased requirement for educational degrees simply for the sake of the credential, although the material learned in the course of obtaining the degree often has little relationship to the skills necessary for the jobs young people end up taking. Cote and Allahar (1994) also argued that more higher education graduates are produced than the economy demands, so that many graduates—in their analysis, close to half—end up underemployed after graduation with jobs that require lower levels of skill than their education has provided them.

A second common theme of pessimism was increased awareness of problems such as crime and the destruction of the environment. For example, a 28-year-old woman saw a variety of formidable problems in the world around her:

There's so many things going on in the world that are so horrible now that haven't always been going on.... Things from the ozone layer, to overcrowding, to natural disasters, to AIDS and hunger and poverty, all those things.

With respect to these sorts of problems too, the participants could see the world as grim even when they viewed their own lives optimistically. Another 28-year-old woman explicitly contrasted the conditions of her own life with the conditions of the world as a whole:

I feel like I work very hard to be positive about what I have firm control over, and that's my life and how I lead my life and how I behave toward people around me. But I have a lot of concerns about society as a whole. I mean, I guess you could say that I am, deep down, pessimistic about events happening in the world.... Crime and guns scare me to death.... I've always been careful, but I've never had an edge of fear on me, and I think I have that now. And that makes me real pessimistic that society has come to that and especially makes me scared about the idea of ever having a family of my own, because if it's like this now, what will it be 10 or 20 years from now in terms of trying to raise a family?

Similarly, this 24-year-old man hoped to preserve his prospects and those of his family in the face of difficult conditions in the world:

I think the nation as a whole is really headed for some tough stuff.... Just picking up the paper or watching the news, it kind of gets you down on the future, you know. You hear about all these kids with their guns in school.... It doesn't leave you with too much hope, but I try not to get down about it.... I mean, it's going to affect everybody, all this stuff that's going on, but I think if I raise my kids the way that I was raised, in what I believe is the truth, then I think they'll have an advantage over the other kids.

However, participants sometimes stated that it was not so much that societal problems had actually become worse but that awareness of the problems had increased in their generation due to pervasive media coverage. A 24-year-old man found his optimism difficult to sustain in the face of the media:

I try to be pretty optimistic about things, but then I like to watch the news too, and sometimes you have to be pessimistic about some of that stuff you see. It's like it's never going to change, you know.

This view was echoed by a 24-year-old woman:

It seems like the world just isn't as safe a place anymore. There's more violence on TV, and everywhere you go, it's there. People are more on guard much of the time.

The views of this 25-year-old man were similar:

Overpopulation...crime, and all that stuff. Just the way governments are; just everything.... It's a big mess. And I think, just through media and stuff, it's in your face so much that I think that adds to it. I mean, I threw my TV out; I don't even watch TV.... I just try to deal with my little circle right in town here, and I'm having the time of my life, to tell you the truth.... As far as being happy, it doesn't take a lot to make me happy, but as far as the whole world picture goes, it's a lot more crazy.

These comments provide support for the cultivation hypothesis (Gerbner, Gross, Morgan, & Signorelli, 1994), which has proposed that television distorts the way people view the condition of the society around them. A variety of studies have demonstrated an aspect of the cultivation hypothesis known as the "Mean World Syndrome," which states that people who watch relatively large amounts of television are more likely than others to see the world as dangerous, violent, and crime ridden. This has been found to be true for both children (Singer, Singer, & Rapaczynski, 1984) and adults (Gerbner, Gross, Morgan, & Signorelli, 1980, 1986). The comments shown above indicate that in the views of some emerging adults, watching television contributes to a perception of the world as dangerous and filled with problems. However, it should be added that this was a theme that came up in response to a question that was not specifically about media or television. It would take further, more systematic investigation of this issue to determine how widespread this view is among emerging adults and to assess the contribution of television to their pessimism in relation to other factors.

There were also emerging adults who agreed that many in their generation were cynical and pessimistic, but who dissented from this view themselves, sometimes quite vehemently. As one 21-year-old man stated,

> I recycle as much as the next guy, but I really don't see the world as just becoming covered with garbage or the ozone layer disappearing. I really think it may have been exaggerated. It just seems like a lot of my generation just likes to whine about the horrible world that they were left by the generation before, but I think the generation before had to worry about nuclear war and stuff like that a lot more than my generation does now. I think if anything the world's gotten better in the past 50 years than it had been before.

Some of those who dissented also believed implicitly in the cultivation hypothesis. For example, this 24-year-old man stated,

> I think we're bombarded with a sense of helplessness. If it's not homosexuality, it's the great whales or the ozone layer.... [The media] just bombard us with negatives. Violence, crime, everything. Guns, drugs, disease. [But the truth is that] we are not in trouble.... Life is not in the balance. We're all not going to fall off the face of the earth tomorrow like we would be made to believe. I think a lot of people my age buy into everything the media says.... Our generation was raised by the television. We weren't raised by our parents in a lot of instances.... I don't think that anybody realizes how affected they are.

Furthermore, although a majority of participants agreed with the Generation X description of their generation as cynical and pessimistic, a substantial proportion (22%) disagreed with this view, not just as applied to themselves but as applied to their generation as a whole. For example, this 28-year-old woman stated,

> No. Not at all, because I think maybe the generation before us was pessimistic and that's why we're now having to be more optimistic and set our sights a little differently. This is the recycling generation, this is the plan-for-our-future generation.

Overall, however, participants agreed that their generation sees the world pessimistically and has good reason to see it that way.

Summary and Conclusion

Emerging adulthood is a time when, for many young people, questions about the future are paramount. Of course, ruminating about the future is part of the human condition, and people of all ages speculate about what their lives may be like one year, five years, and many years into the future. However, questions about the future are especially salient for emerging adults because for many of them, major decisions in love, work, and worldviews have yet to be made (Arnett, in press). Even for those who have made these decisions and entered adult roles, as most of them have by their late 20s, the majority of their adult lives lie ahead of them, and the fate of their early aspirations has yet to be determined.

The results of this study show a sharp distinction between how they view their personal futures and how they view their generation's perspective on the future. The study provides some support for the Generation X view that there is a cynical and pessimistic generational identity among young Americans currently in their 20s. Many young people do believe that their generation is cynical and pessimistic. They hear this view articulated by their peers and in the media, and many of them share this view themselves. They realize that a college degree is by no means a guarantee of finding a satisfying, fulfilling occupation. They worry about crime and a variety of other societal problems, and they wonder if they will be able to protect their children from being harmed by those problems. Some of them believe that the media inflate the extent of the problems in American society and resent the way they believe the media "bombard us" with news about the problems. But they feel there is no escape from the bombardment and, ultimately, no escape from living with the fear that those problems may one day harm them and those close to them.

Even amidst what they see as a grim world, however, most emerging adults maintain high hopes for their personal futures. A large proportion of them believe that their lives will be better than their parents' lives have been, in a variety of respects. Even when they believe the quality of their lives is likely to be the same as their parents' lives, this tends to be an optimistic response because it is often stated by emerging adults who see their parents' lives in a favorable light. Having a life like their parents' lives means having a life of personal success and happiness.

Where their parents have succeeded in life, they generally believe they will do just as well. Where their parents have failed, especially for those with parents whose marriages have failed, they believe they will do better. None of them believe that their own marriages will be among some 60% of first marriages forecasted to end in divorce. Financially too, they are optimistic, even if they have grown up in a family of relatively low socioeconomic status. In fact, in this study, social class background was inversely related to their views of their personal futures: those from relatively low social class backgrounds were even more confident than those from relatively high social class backgrounds that their lives would be better than their parents, financially as well as in other respects.

The optimism of these emerging adults is, in part, a reflection of the optimistic bias that exists for most people in most aspects of life (Weinstein & Klein, 1996). In general, people of all ages tend to believe that unpleasant events are more likely to happen to other people than to themselves. However, this view is per-

haps especially easy to sustain in emerging adulthood when so many things about their lives remain to be determined and when so many possibilities have yet to
700 harden into accomplished facts. Although their views of their futures may be optimistic and may not accurately reflect the futures in store for them, their optimism arguably serves an important psychological function. The belief that they will ultimately prevail in their
705 personal pursuit of happiness, that their personal success is not only possible but inevitable, allows them to proceed with confidence through a world they regard as fraught with peril.

References

Arnett, J. J. (1997). Young people's conceptions of the transition to adulthood. *Youth & Society, 29*, 1–23.

Arnett, J. J. (1998). Learning to stand alone: The contemporary American transition to adulthood in cultural and historical context. *Human Development, 41*, 295–315.

Arnett, J. J. (2000). *Conceptions of the transition to adulthood from adolescence through midlife.* Manuscript submitted for publication.

Arnett, J. J. (in press). Emerging adulthood: A theory of development from the late teens to the late twenties. *American Psychologist.*

Arnett, J. J., Ramos, K. D., & Jensen, L. A. (in press). Ideological views in emerging adulthood: Balancing autonomy and community. *Journal of Adult Development.*

Arnett, J., & Taber, S. (1994). Adolescence terminable and interminable: When does adolescence end? *Journal of Youth & Adolescence, 23*, 517–537.

Colby, A., Sippola, L., & Phelps, E. (1999). Social responsibility and paid work in contemporary life. In A. Rossi (Ed.), *Caring and doing for others: Social responsibility in the domains of family, work, and community.* Chicago: University of Chicago Press.

Cote, J. E., & Allahar, A. L. (1994). *Generation on hold: Coming of age in the late twentieth century.* New York: New York University Press.

Coupland, D. (1991). *Generation X.* New York: St. Martin's.

Eskilson, A., & Wiley, M. G. (1999). Solving for the X: Aspirations and expectations of college students. *Journal of Youth & Adolescence, 28*, 51–70.

Gerbner, G., Gross, L., Morgan, M., & Signorelli, N. (1980). The "mainstreaming" of America: Violence profile no. 11. *Journal of Communication, 30*, 10–29.

Gerbner, G., Gross, L., Morgan, M., & Signorelli, N. (1986). The dynamics of the cultivation process. In J. Bryant & D. Zillman (Eds.), *Perspectives on media effects* (pp. 17–48). Hillsdale, NJ: Lawrence Erlbaum.

Gerbner, G., Gross, L., Morgan, M., & Signorelli, N. (1994). *Television violence profile no. 16.* Philadelphia: Annenberg School for Communication.

Giles, J. (1994, June 6). Generalizations X. *Newsweek*, pp. 64–72.

Hochschild, J. L. (1996). *Facing up to the American dream: Race, class, and the soul of the nation.* Princeton, NJ: Princeton University Press.

Hogan, D. P., & Astone, N. M. (1986). The transition to adulthood. *Annual Review of Sociology, 12*, 109–130.

Hornblower, M. (1997, June 9). Great Xpectations. *Time*, pp. 58–68.

Jensen, L. (1998). *The culture war and the American dream: Family and work.* Manuscript submitted for publication.

Jessor, R., Donovan, J. E., & Costa, F. M. (1991). *Beyond adolescence: Problem behavior and young adult development.* New York: Cambridge University Press.

Keniston, K. (1971). *Youth and dissent: The rise of a new opposition.* Orlando, FL: Harcourt Brace.

Kinsley, M. (1994, March 21). Back from the future. *The New Republic*, p. 6.

Marini, M. M. (1984). The order of events in the transition to adulthood. *Social Forces, 63*, 229–244.

Noble, J., Cover, J., & Yanagishita, M. (1996). *The world's youth.* Washington, DC: Population Reference Bureau.

Rindfuss, R. R. (1991). The young adult years: Diversity, structural change, and fertility. *Demography, 28*, 493–512.

Roper Organization. (1993, July). Twentysomething Americans. *The Public Pulse, 8*(7), 1–3.

Schulenberg, J., Bachman, J. G., Johnston, L. D., & O'Malley, P. M. (1995). American adolescents' views on family and work: Historical trends from 1976–1992. In P. Noack, M. Hofer, & J. Youniss (Eds.), *Psychological responses to social change: Human development in changing environments* (pp. 37–66). New York: de Gruyter.

Singer, D. G., Singer, J. L., & Rapaczynski, W. (1984). Family patterns and television viewing as predictors of children's beliefs and aggression. *Journal of Communication, 34*, 73–89.

U.S. Bureau of the Census (1997). *Statistical abstracts of the United States: 1997.* Washington, DC: Author.

Weinstein, N., & Klein, W. M. (1996). Unrealistic optimism: Present and future. *Journal of Social and Clinical Psychology, 15*, 1–8.

William T. Grant Foundation Commission on Work, Family, & Citizenship. (1988, February). *The forgotten half: Non-college-bound youth in America.* Washington, DC: William T. Grant Foundation.

Note: Jeffrey Jensen Arnett is a visiting associate professor in the Department of Human Development at the University of Maryland. His research interests include risk behavior and media use in adolescence and a wide variety of topics in emerging adulthood. He is the author of *Metalheads: Heavy Metal Music and Adolescent Alienation*, published in 1996 by Westview Press. Recent publications include "Adolescent Storm and Stress, Reconsidered," in the *American Psychologist.*

Exercise for Article 43

Factual Questions

1. "Emerging adulthood" is conceptualized as beginning with the end of what?

2. What was the age range of the participants in this study?

3. The second interview question (about Generation X tending to be cynical and pessimistic) was answered by how many participants?

4. What was the percentage rate of agreement for the coding by the researcher and the second coder?

5. Whites constituted what percentage of the sample?

6. What does the "cultivation hypothesis" propose?

7. The "optimistic bias" suggests that people of all ages tend to believe what?

Questions for Discussion

8. Of the persons contacted, 72% agreed to participate in the study. In your opinion, is this an adequate response rate? Explain. (See lines 178–179.)

9. The researcher used both a questionnaire and an interview. Does this make the study more interesting than if he had used only one of these methods to collect data? Explain.

10. Comment on the adequacy of the questions the researcher asked. Would you add any questions? Delete any? Modify any? Explain. (See lines 183–210.)

11. To what population(s), if any, would you be willing to generalize the results of this study?

12. If you were to conduct another study on the same topic, what changes in the research methodology, if any, would you make?

Quality Ratings

Directions: Indicate your level of agreement with each of the following statements by circling a number from 5 for strongly agree (SA) to 1 for strongly disagree (SD). If you believe an item is not applicable to this research article, leave it blank. Be prepared to explain your ratings. When responding to criteria A and B below, keep in mind that brief titles and abstracts are conventional in published research.

A. The title of the article is appropriate.

SA   5   4   3   2   1   SD

B. The abstract provides an effective overview of the research article.

SA   5   4   3   2   1   SD

C. The introduction establishes the importance of the study.

SA   5   4   3   2   1   SD

D. The literature review establishes the context for the study.

SA   5   4   3   2   1   SD

E. The research purpose, question, or hypothesis is clearly stated.

SA   5   4   3   2   1   SD

F. The method of sampling is sound.

SA   5   4   3   2   1   SD

G. Relevant demographics (for example, age, gender, and ethnicity) are described.

SA   5   4   3   2   1   SD

H. Measurement procedures are adequate.

SA   5   4   3   2   1   SD

I. All procedures have been described in sufficient detail to permit a replication of the study.

SA   5   4   3   2   1   SD

J. The participants have been adequately protected from potential harm.

SA   5   4   3   2   1   SD

K. The results are clearly described.

SA   5   4   3   2   1   SD

L. The discussion/conclusion is appropriate.

SA   5   4   3   2   1   SD

M. Despite any flaws, the report is worthy of publication.

SA   5   4   3   2   1   SD

Article 44

A Congregation of One:
Individualized Religious Beliefs
Among Emerging Adults

JEFFREY JENSEN ARNETT
University of Maryland

LENE ARNETT JENSEN
University of Maryland

ABSTRACT. Religious beliefs and practices were examined among 140 emerging adults aged 21 to 28, using quantitative and qualitative methods. There was great diversity in the importance they ascribed to religion, in their attendance at religious services, and in the content of their religious beliefs. Overall, their beliefs fell into four roughly even categories—agnostic/atheist, deist, liberal Christian, and conservative Christian—but there was also considerable diversity within each category. In combination, the quantitative and qualitative results showed that the participants' beliefs were highly individualized, that there was little relationship between childhood religious socialization and current religious attendance or beliefs, and that the participants were often skeptical of religious institutions. The results reflect the individualism of American society as well as the focus in emerging adulthood on forming one's own beliefs.

From *Journal of Adolescent Research*, *17*, 451–467. Copyright © 2002 by Sage Publications. Reprinted with permission.

It is well established that the late teens and early 20s are ages of relatively low religious participation in American society. Even many young people who attended religious services frequently as children and
5 adolescents fall off in their religious participation in their late teens and 20s (Gallup & Castelli, 1989; Gallup & Lindsay, 1999; Hoge, Dinges, Johnson, & Gonzales, 1998a, 1998b; Hoge, Johnson, & Luidens, 1993). Most young people leave home after high
10 school (Goldscheider & Goldscheider, 1999), and the change of residence often breaks the tie to the religious institution they had attended while growing up (Hoge et al., 1993). Leaving home also removes the encouragement and perhaps the coercion of parents to attend
15 religious services.

Other reasons for the drop in religious participation in the late teens and early 20s include becoming busy with other activities, doubting previously held beliefs, and simply losing interest in being involved in a reli-
20 gious institution (Hoge et al., 1998a, 1998b). However, religious participation tends to rise in the late 20s, as young people marry, have children, settle down per-
sonally and geographically, and express an increased spiritual need for religious involvement (Gallup & Cas-
25 telli, 1989; Hoge, et al., 1998a, 1998b; Hoge et al., 1993; Stolzenberg, Blair-Loy, & Waite, 1995; Wilson & Sandomirsky, 1991).

Most studies on the religiosity of young people in their late teens and 20s have focused on the issue of
30 why their religious participation tends to fall and then rise again. Here, we focus more directly on the religious beliefs and attitudes of young people in their 20s. What are their religious beliefs? How important a part does religion play in their lives? To what extent is their
35 childhood religious socialization related to their current beliefs? How do they view religious institutions?

The conceptual framework used here for understanding young people's religious beliefs is the theory of *emerging adulthood*. Emerging adulthood has been
40 proposed as a term for the new period that has opened up in the life course of people in industrialized societies during the past half-century, bridging adolescence and young adulthood (Arnett, 1998, 2000a, 2000b). During recent decades, the median ages of marriage
45 and first birth in the United States have risen to unprecedented levels, into the late 20s (Arnett, 2000b). Similarly, rates of participation in higher education after secondary school have steadily increased so that by now, more than two-thirds of young Americans
50 obtain at least some higher education (Bianchi & Spain, 1996). As a consequence of these changes, the late teens and early 20s are no longer a period of intensive preparation for and entry into stable and enduring adult roles but are more typically a period of exploring
55 various life possibilities while postponing role transitions into the middle to late 20s (Arnett, 1998, 2000a, 2000b).

Exploration is central to development during emerging adulthood. The explorations described dec-
60 ades ago by Erikson (1950, 1968) and Marcia (1966) as part of identity formation in adolescence now extend well into the 20s for most young people in industrialized societies. In areas such as love, work, and ideology, many emerging adults explore diverse possibili-

65 ties. The focus during emerging adulthood tends to be on self-development and on becoming independent and self-sufficient (Arnett, 1998). Part of this process, in the view of most emerging adults, is forming a distinctive set of beliefs about religious issues. Several studies
70 have indicated that deciding on one's own beliefs and values is one of the criteria young people view as most important to becoming an adult (Arnett, 1997, 1998; Greene, Wheatley, & Aldava, 1992).

Emerging adulthood is a period of the life course
75 when the focus tends to be on self-development and self-sufficiency; in addition, today's emerging adults are coming of age in an especially individualistic period in American society (Alwin, 1988; Bellah, Madsen, Sullivan, Swidler, & Tipton, 1985; Jensen,
80 1995). In the course of the 20th century, the qualities American parents most desired to teach their children changed from obedience and respect for others to independence and self-esteem (Alwin, 1988). With regard to religious beliefs in particular, surveys indicate that a
85 strong majority of Americans agree that individuals should form their religious beliefs independently of religious institutions (Gallup & Castelli, 1989).

Few studies have yet explored the content of emerging adults' religious beliefs, but one recent theo-
90 retical exposition was presented by Beaudoin (1998). Beaudoin theorized that the themes of the religiosity of "Generation X" include skepticism about the value of religious institutions and an emphasis on personal experience rather than religious authorities as a source of
95 religious beliefs. Beaudoin also emphasized the tentative, ambiguous quality of young people's religious beliefs. He interpreted this as reflecting the shifting, unfixed nature of young people's identities and their preference during their late teens and 20s to remain
100 open to changing their beliefs rather than arriving on a fixed set of beliefs.

Roof (1993) has made similar observations about the baby boom generation. According to Roof, many boomers regard personal experience and self-discovery
105 as more important to their religious faith than religious institutions and customs. In Roof's view, boomers mix and match ideas from a variety of sources and traditions to create new, individualized faiths. More generally, Hervieu-Leger (1993) argued that religious tradi-
110 tions have become "symbolic toolboxes" (p. 141) from which individuals can draw without accepting as a whole the worldview that was historically part of the religion.

In this study, the goal was to examine the content of
115 emerging adults' religious beliefs. There were three hypotheses. Based on previous studies and on the nature of emerging adulthood as a time of focusing on self-development and self-sufficiency, we expected emerging adults to emphasize forming their own be-
120 liefs independently of their parents' beliefs. Specifically, we expected emerging adults' religious beliefs to be highly diverse and individualized as they drew from

a variety of cultural sources in the course of constructing their beliefs. We also expected to find only a weak
125 relationship between childhood religious socialization and religious beliefs in emerging adulthood because emerging adults would be intent on deciding on their own beliefs. Furthermore, we expected emerging adults to have only a tenuous tie to religious institutions, even
130 when they had been raised in a specific religious tradition, because institutional membership would be viewed as a compromise of their individuality.

Method

Participants

The participants were 140 persons aged 21 to 28. General characteristics of the sample are shown in Ta-
135 ble 1. Close to half of the participants were married, and about one-fourth had at least one child. Two-thirds of the participants were employed full-time, and one-fourth were employed part-time. A total of 28% were in school full-time, and 8% were part-time students.
140 "Some college" was the modal level of education, indicated by 52% of the participants. There was a broad range of variability in the social class of the participants' families of origin, as indicated by fathers' and mothers' education.

Table 1
Background Characteristics of the Sample

Characteristic	%
Gender	
Male	53
Female	47
Ethnicity	
White	94
Black	5
Other	1
Current educational status	
In school full time	28
In school part time	8
Not in school	65
Mothers' education	
Less than high school degree	8
High school degree	23
Some college	23
College degree	27
Some graduate school or graduate degree	19
Fathers' education	
Less than high school degree	8
High school degree	24
Some college	15
College degree	24
Some graduate school or graduate degree	30
Employment	
Full	67
Part	24
None	9
Marital status	
Married	60
Single	40
Number of children	
None	73
One	14
Two or more	13

Note. Some categories do not add up to 100% due to rounding figures.

Table 2
Religiosity of Emerging Adults

Question	%
How often do you attend religious services?	
About 3 to 4 times a month	19
About 1 to 2 times a month	10
Once every few months	20
About 1 to 2 times a year or less	50
How important is it to you to attend religious services?	
Very important	16
Quite important	11
Somewhat important	24
Not at all important	50
How important to you are your religious beliefs?	
Very important	30
Quite important	22
Somewhat important	30
Not at all important	18
How important is religious faith in your daily life?	
Very important	27
Quite important	20
Somewhat important	21
Not at all important	32
How certain are you about your religious beliefs?	
Very certain	38
Quite certain	33
Somewhat certain	21
Not at all certain	8
To what extent do you believe that God or some higher power watches over you and guides your life?	
Strongly believe this	52
Somewhat believe this	22
Somewhat skeptical of this	16
Definitely do not believe this	10
Were you brought up to believe any particular set of religious beliefs, or did your parents more or less leave it up to you?	
High exposure	64
Moderate exposure	13
Low exposure	23
What are your religious or spiritual beliefs now, if any?	
Agnostic/atheist	24
Deist	29
Liberal Christian	26
Conservative Christian	22

Note. The first six questions in the table are from the questionnaire. The final two questions are coded questions from the interview. Some categories do not add up to 100% due to rounding of figures.

Procedure

145   The data presented here were collected as part of a larger study on emerging adults in their 20s. The study took place in a medium-sized city in the Midwest. Potential participants were identified through enrollment lists from the two local high schools for the previous 3
150   to 10 years. All persons on the enrollment lists who had a current local address that could be identified through phone book listings or through contacting their parents were sent a letter describing the study, then contacted by phone. Of the persons contacted, 72% agreed to
155   participate in the study. Data collection took place in the first author's office or the participant's home, depending on the participant's preference. Interviews

were conducted by the first author and two research assistants.

Measures

160   The study included an interview and a questionnaire. Six items on the questionnaire pertained to religion and concerned religious attendance, the importance ascribed to religion, the certainty of the participant's beliefs, and belief in God (see Table 2). Two questions
165   in the interview pertained specifically to participants' childhood exposure to religion and participants' current religious beliefs (see Table 2).

Coding categories for each interview question were developed from reading through the interviews and
170   identifying common themes. The two authors inde-

pendently coded all participants' responses to the two interview questions. Rate of agreement was more than 80% for each question. Discrepancies were resolved through discussion.

175 The full text of the interview question on childhood exposure to religious socialization was "Were you brought up to believe any particular set of religious beliefs, or did your parents more or less leave it up to you?" The categories for the coding of this interview
180 question were:

Low exposure: Parents rarely or never took children to church; religion clearly was not important to them.

Moderate exposure: Parents made some effort to
185 take children to church and expose them to religious ideas but not on a regular basis; and/or parents did not attend themselves; and/or religion did not seem very important to parents. Parents may have taken children to church now and then in a
190 perfunctory way.

High exposure: Parents took children to church on a regular and fairly frequent basis and clearly regarded religion as important.

The full text of the question on current religious be-
195 liefs was "What are your religious or spiritual beliefs now, if any?" The categories for the coding of this question were:

Agnostic/atheist: Person explicitly rejects any belief in religion or declares that he or she is unsure about
200 own beliefs, and/or says it is not possible to know anything about God.

Deist: Person declares a general belief in God or "spirituality," but only in a general sense and not in the context of any religious tradition. Person may
205 refer to self as "Christian," but beliefs do not reflect traditional Christian dogma and may even explicitly reject parts of the Christian dogma (e.g., that Jesus was the son of God). Person may also reject organized religion generally and may include idiosyn-
210 cratic personal elements drawn from various sources, such as Eastern religions, witchcraft, and popular culture.

Liberal Christian: Person describes self as Christian (or as adherent of particular denomination; e.g.,
215 Methodist, Lutheran, Catholic). However, person may express skepticism about the institution of the church and/or about some aspects of Christian dogma, such as the idea that Christianity is the only true faith. Person may express favorable or at least
220 tolerant view of other (non-Christian) faiths.

Conservative Christian: Person expresses belief in traditional Christian dogma, for example, that Jesus is the son of God and the only way to salvation. Person may mention being saved or refer to after-

225 life of heaven and hell. Person may mention that Christianity is the only true faith.

Only one participant in the study had a Jewish background, and his response was coded as "deist."

Results

The three hypotheses of the study were that emerg-
230 ing adults' religious beliefs would be highly individualized, that childhood religious socialization would be only weakly related to religious beliefs in emerging adulthood, and that emerging adults would be skeptical of religious institutions. These three hypotheses will be
235 used as the framework for describing the results, combining quantitative and qualitative data. First, the overall patterns of the quantitative analyses will be presented.

Quantitative Analyses

Age, gender, marital status, parenthood status, edu-
240 cational attainment, mother's education, and father's education were analyzed in relation to each of the religious variables shown in Table 2. Chi-square tests were used for the analyses involving gender, marital status (married vs. unmarried), and parenthood status (no
245 children vs. one or more children). Bivariate correlations were used for the analyses involving age, educational attainment, mother's education, and father's education.

Age and educational attainment were unrelated to
250 any of the religious variables. In the analyses by gender, women were more likely than men to indicate that it is important to them to attend religious services, $\chi^2(1, 118) = 8.70$, $p < .05$; and more likely to indicate that religious faith was important in their daily lives, $\chi^2(1,
255 94) = 11.98$, $p < .01$. Women were also more likely to be liberal Christians and less likely to be agnostics/atheists, $\chi^2(1, 130) = 10.43$, $p < .05$. With regard to marital status, married persons were more likely to be conservative Christians, and single persons were more
260 likely to be deists, $\chi^2(3, 122) = 11.79$, $p < .01$. Married persons were also more likely than single persons to attend religious services, $\chi^2(3, 116) = 11.34$, $p < .05$; to indicate that it is important to them to attend religious services, $\chi^2(3, 116) = 8.52$, $p < .05$; and to indicate that
265 religious beliefs are important to them, $\chi^2(3, 136) = 11.10$, $p < .05$.

Parenthood status also was related to the religious variables. Parents were more likely than nonparents to be religiously conservative and less likely to be agnos-
270 tics or deists, $\chi^2(3, 125) = 16.64$, $p < .001$. Parents were also more likely than nonparents to attend religious services, $\chi^2(3, 119) = 11.00$, $p < .05$; to indicate that it is important to them to attend religious services, $\chi^2(3, 119) = 11.34$, $p < .05$; to indicate that religious beliefs
275 are important to them, $\chi^2(3, 136)$, $p < .05$; to indicate that religious beliefs are important in their daily lives, $\chi^2(3, 94) = 9.58$, $p < .05$; and to believe that God or

some higher power watches over them and guides their lives, $\chi^2(3, 119) = 15.67$, $p < .01$.

280   Mother's education was inversely related to several religious variables, with persons with mothers who had relatively lower education being more likely to indicate that religious beliefs are important to them ($r = -.22$, $p < .05$); that religious beliefs are important in their daily

285 lives ($r = -.24$, $p < .05$); and that they believe God or some higher power watches over them and guides their lives ($r = -.21$, $p < .05$). Similarly, fathers' education was inversely related to participants believing it is important to attend religious services ($r = -.22$, $p < .05$);

290 to indicating that religious beliefs are important to them ($r = -.22$, $p < .05$); and to believing that God or some higher power watches over them and guides their lives ($r = -.21$, $p < .05$).

Emerging Adults' Beliefs Are Highly Individualized

    The emerging adults in this study were highly di-
295 verse in their religious beliefs and practices, as shown in Table 2. Half reported rarely or never attending religious services, but the other half attended occasionally or regularly, with about one-fifth attending 3 to 4 times per month. Half reported that it was not at all important
300 to them to attend religious services, whereas, for the other half, the importance of attendance varied from "somewhat important" to "very important." Participants also varied widely in their views of the importance of their religious beliefs, the importance of reli-
305 gious faith in their daily lives, and their belief in God. In the classification of their current beliefs—the coded responses to the question "What are your religious or spiritual beliefs now, if any?"—participants were spread more or less evenly among the four categories:
310 agnostic/atheist, deist, liberal Christian, and conservative Christian (Table 2).

    The quantitative results indicated that emerging adults' religious views are highly diverse, and the qualitative results provided numerous examples of this
315 diversity. In their responses to the question about their current religious or spiritual beliefs, emerging adults often combined concepts and practices from different religious and nonreligious traditions in unique, highly individualized ways.

320   One reason their beliefs were highly individualized was that the emerging adults expressed a high value on thinking for themselves with regard to religious questions and on forming a unique set of religious beliefs rather than accepting a readymade dogma. For exam-
325 ple, Will described himself as a Christian, but he also said he believed that,

> you don't have to be one religion. Take a look at all of them; see if there is something in them you like—almost like an á la carte belief system. I think all religions have
330 > things that are good about them.

    Josie said "I was raised Catholic...and I guess if I had to consider myself anything, I would consider myself Catholic," but she also said,

335 > I don't have any really strong beliefs because I believe that whatever you feel, it's personal.... Everybody has their own idea of God and what God is, and because you go to a church doesn't define it any better because you still have your own personal beliefs of how you feel about it and what's acceptable for you and what's right
340 > for you personally.

    In forming their individualized beliefs, emerging adults often combined Christian beliefs with Eastern ideas such as reincarnation or with ideas taken from popular culture. Julie's father was a minister in a Dis-
345 ciples of Christ church, and she went to church every Sunday growing up, but at age 23, her beliefs had become a pastiche of New Age, Eastern, and Christian notions.

350 > A lot of my beliefs border on what would be labeled as witchcraft. I believe that objects can capture energy and hold it...I do believe it's possible to communicate with people who have died...I do believe in reincarnation...I believe I've had past lives...I am what I would label a "guardian angel," and there are certain people that I'm
355 > supposed to help out.

    Joseph invoked ideas from *Star Wars*, which he combined with ideas from a variety of religions. He said his parents "put me through a Catholic Sunday school; I was baptized and stuff." Now his beliefs are
360 eclectic.

> I've read some Joseph Campbell, and just the theory that all these religions, Mohammed and Buddha and Jesus, all the patterns there are very similar.... And I believe that there's a spirit, an energy. Not necessarily a guy or some-
365 > thing like that, but maybe just a power force. Like in *Star Wars*—the Force. The thing that makes it possible to live.

Childhood Religious Socialization Has Limited Effects

    Nearly two-thirds of participants were coded as having had high exposure to religious socialization; the coding was based on their response to the interview
370 question about whether their parents had brought them up to believe any particular set of religious beliefs (Table 2). In χ^2 tests, childhood religious socialization was analyzed in relation to current religious attendance (the questionnaire item) and religious views (the coded in-
375 terview question and the five questionnaire items on religious views). There was no relationship between childhood religious socialization and current religious attendance or between childhood religious socialization and any of the six items on religious views.

380   Although it may seem odd that childhood religious socialization did not significantly predict religious attendance or beliefs in emerging adulthood, it is easier to understand after examining the qualitative results. These results suggest that the lack of association be-
385 tween their childhood religious beliefs and their current beliefs was a reflection of their individualism and of their resolve to think for themselves and form their own beliefs.

    For example, Jack said he was a "full-blown Catho-
390 lic" as a child, but when he was 17 years old,

299

I just flat told Mom I wasn't going to go any more. It was a waste of time. I didn't like it. I went because I was under Mom and Dad's rules. I did what they said to do, went to Sunday school and stuff like that. [But] I can go to church all you want, and I'm still going to believe what I believe. You're not going to change me.

The typical pattern was attending church throughout childhood but stopping as soon as parental encouragement or coercion eased, usually during adolescence. Mike said,

I had my "perfect attendance" pins for the Methodist Sunday school up until the day I was confirmed, and then they said it was up to me whether or not I go to church, and I haven't been back since.... I guess I would still consider myself Methodist, but in all honesty, I'd probably have to say that I'm agnostic.

Theresa said,

I made a deal with my mom in high school that if I got confirmed I would never have to go to church again. And she said okay, so after I was confirmed I didn't have to get up on Sunday mornings any more, and I didn't have to fight with her about "I don't want to go to church."

Of course, not all parents' attempts at religious socialization had come to naught. Ryan was raised in a family where "our faith was certainly present in the home," and said that "I still believe in the principles and doctrines taught by our church." Sharon said, "I was brought up Presbyterian, and I belong to the same church I've gone to since I was a child." But generally, emerging adults had formed their own beliefs independently of the religious socialization provided by their parents, and overall there was no correlation between childhood religious socialization and current beliefs.

Some of those whose religious participation had waned after high school saw their unchurched status as temporary, to be resumed after they had children. Bill was among those who viewed religion as something he had no interest in now but wanted his children to be exposed to.

Growing up, we went to church every Sunday. I don't go to church every Sunday now, just because the weekends now, to me, are a time to relax and I sleep late. [But] I will come around. I firmly believe that a religion should be a part of a kid's growing up.

For the one-fourth of persons in the study who had children, parenthood had already inspired some of them to resume church attendance. As noted in the quantitative analyses, parents were more likely than nonparents to attend religious services and were more religious in other respects as well. For example, Sharon and her husband had recently begun attending church with their 4-year-old daughter because "we both decided that we better start going because we have a child now, and we need to give her some type of feeling of church." Some parents viewed religious socialization as part of their children's moral socialization. Tom said

he and his wife planned to begin attending with their young daughters because "I think religion has a lot to do with ethics and morals and values.... I think it has a lot to do with teaching them right from wrong."

Emerging Adults Are Skeptical of Religious Institutions

Religious beliefs were more likely than attendance at religious services to be important to emerging adults. Although 50% indicated that it was "not at all important" to them to attend religious services, only 18% indicated that their religious beliefs were "not at all important" to them (Table 2). Also, 47% reported that religious faith was "quite" or "very" important in their daily lives, compared to 27% for whom attendance at religious services was "quite" or "very" important.

In the qualitative results, many emerging adults expressed skepticism about the value of religious institutions. Ryan said,

I don't think that organized religion as a whole is a good thing, I really don't...I just think that having an organized religion is like having a gang. It's your beliefs against their beliefs, and whoever is left standing at the end is the one whose beliefs are the best.

Sometimes their rejection of religious institutions was based on negative experiences. Tracy had unpleasant memories of her church experiences in childhood. "I remember going to church [as a child] and being bored, and seeing everybody around me being bored." By emerging adulthood, she had rejected the Catholicism of her youth because of

the guilt. I got so sick of feeling guilty all the time. And, oh God, "lust is so awful." I really feel like there are things that are natural to us, because yes, we are human, but we also still have animal tendencies, and you can't guilt those out of people. And I decided that, yes, I did have an animal in me and I wasn't going to guilt my animal any more because it made me unhappy. So I gave up being Catholic.

Another reason for emerging adults' skepticism about religious institutions was that they tended to view participation in any institution as a compromise of their individuality. As Gabe said, "I'm just not real big on the church thing. I think that's a manmade thing. I don't need anyone telling me what's right or wrong. I know what's right and wrong." Similarly, Curtis viewed clerical exhortations as a threat to his individual autonomy:

I believe in God; I just don't necessarily believe in an organized religion.... Jesus was probably an actual thing, but I don't think you have to go to church to worship God and his teachings. I think God is in here, in how you feel, and not what somebody at the pulpit's telling you God is.

Many expressed the view that they could be religious or spiritual on their own without institutional membership. In Jerry's view,

Just being outside is more spiritual to me than going in and sitting in a church with a bunch of people and somebody preaching from the Bible. I think it's almost more religious and more spiritual for me to go out in the woods by myself or go fishing.

Similarly, Jean observed,

I'm the kind of person that feels that you don't have to go to church to be religious. I mean, that's just something that you do for yourself. It's not necessary to be in a certain place to be religious.

Discussion

What do emerging adults in American society believe about religious issues? "Whatever they choose for themselves" might be a concise summary of the study presented here. The salient impression of the results is that emerging adults form their beliefs independently with little influence from their parents or religious institutions. Consequently, their beliefs are extremely diverse as they form unique combinations of beliefs from various religious traditions as well as other sources, including popular culture. It is not just that religious traditions have become "symbolic toolboxes" (Hervieu-Leger, 1993, p. 141) from which young people can draw freely, but that these traditions are only one source among many from which young people construct their religious beliefs.

Overall, their beliefs fell more or less evenly into four categories: agnostic/atheist, deist, liberal Christian, and conservative Christian. Within these categories, there was also considerable diversity. The diversity of religious beliefs among the emerging adults in this study reflects the fact that they have grown up in a pluralistic society. No matter what religious socialization they have received in their families, they have also been exposed to diverse influences from friends, schools, and popular culture. Out of these diverse materials, they construct their own beliefs by the time they reach emerging adulthood. Often, the beliefs they form bear little or no resemblance to what their parents believed and taught them to believe (Hoge, Dinges et al., 1998b; Hoge, Johnson et al., 1993).

Perhaps it should not be so surprising that there is little relationship between childhood religious socialization and religious beliefs in emerging adulthood. As young people grow beyond childhood into adolescence and emerging adulthood, the strength of family socialization wanes while the influence of socialization sources outside the family increases (Arnett, 1995; Larson, Richards, Moneta, Holmbeck, & Duckett, 1996). Because young people view it as both their right and their responsibility to form their beliefs and values independently of their parents (Arnett, 1997, 1998), they pick and choose from the ideas they discover as they go along and combine them to form their own unique, individualized set of beliefs, "an à la carte belief system."

Emerging adults view their independence from their parents' beliefs as a good and necessary thing. In their view, simply to accept what their parents have taught them about religion and carry on the same religious tradition as their parents would represent a kind of failure, an abdication of their responsibility to think for themselves, become independent from their parents, and decide on their own beliefs. Quite consciously and deliberately, they seek to form a set of beliefs about religious questions that will be distinctly their own. Forming one's own beliefs and values is part of the process of identity formation in an individualistic culture and part of the process of becoming an adult (Arnett, 1998; Erikson, 1950, 1968).

An emphasis on individualism also underlies their rejection of religious institutions. Just as it would be wrong in their eyes for them to accept wholesale the beliefs of their parents, so many of them view participation in religious institutions as an intolerable compromise of their individuality. Participating in a religious institution inherently means subscribing to a common set of beliefs, declaring that you hold certain beliefs that other members of the institution also hold. To the majority of emerging adults, this is anathema. They prefer to think of their beliefs as unique, the product of their own individual questioning and exploring (Beaudoin, 1998).

Will they return to religious institutions as they grow beyond emerging adulthood? Other studies have indicated that young people often return to religious participation once they marry and have children (Gallup & Castelli, 1989; Hoge, Dinges et al., 1998a, 1998b; Hoge, Johnson et al., 1993; Stolzenberg et al., 1995; Wilson & Sandomirsky, 1991). In the present study, too, being married and having children were both related to higher likelihood of religious participation. Thus, it appears that for some members of the current cohort of young people, as in previous cohorts, their departure from religious participation is temporary, to be resumed once they enter adult roles of marriage and parenthood. However, like the baby boomers before them, they may retain the individualism of their beliefs even as they (and their children) return to religious institutions (Roof, 1993).

Even for emerging adults who are not currently involved in religious institutions, it is not as if they are uninterested in religious issues. On the contrary, their responses in the interviews show that they have given religious issues much thought. Also, their responses to the questionnaire items indicated that religious beliefs are important to many for whom religious participation is not. However, for the most part, they have concluded that at this time of their lives their beliefs are best observed not through regular participation in a religious institution with other like-minded believers, but by themselves, in the privacy of their own hearts and minds, in a congregation of one.

References

Alwin, D. F. (1988). From obedience to autonomy: Changes in traits desired in children, 1924–1978. *Public Opinion Quarterly, 52,* 33–52.

Arnett, J. J. (1995). Broad and narrow socialization: The family in the context of a cultural theory. *Journal of Marriage and the Family, 57*, 617–628.

Arnett, J. J. (1997). Young people's conceptions of the transition to adulthood. *Youth & Society, 29*, 1–23.

Arnett, J. J. (1998). Learning to stand alone: The contemporary American transition to adulthood in cultural and historical context. *Human Development, 41*, 295–315.

Arnett, J. J. (2000a). High hopes in a grim world: Emerging adults' views of their futures and of "Generation X." *Youth & Society, 31*, 267–286.

Arnett, J. J. (2000b). Emerging adulthood: A theory of development from the late teens through the twenties. *American Psychologist, 55*, 469–480.

Beaudoin, T. M. (1998). *Virtual faith: The irreverent spiritual quest of Generation X.* San Francisco: Jossey-Bass.

Bellah, R. N., Madsen, R., Sullivan, W. M., Swidler, A., & Tipton, S. M. (1985). *Habits of the heart: Individualism and commitment in American life.* New York: Harper & Row.

Bianchi, S. M., & Spain, D. (1996). Women, work, and family in America. *Population Bulletin, 51*, 1–48.

Erikson, E. (1950). *Childhood and society.* New York: Norton.

Erikson, E. (1968). *Identity: Youth and crisis.* New York: Norton.

Gallup, G., Jr., & Castelli, J. (1989). *The people's religion: American faith in the '90s.* New York: Macmillan.

Gallup, G., Jr., & Lindsay, D, M. (1999). *Surveying the religious landscape: Trends in U.S. beliefs.* Harrisburg, PA: Morehouse.

Goldscheider, F., & Goldscheider, C. (1999). *The changing transition to adulthood: Leaving and returning home.* Thousand Oaks, CA: Sage.

Greene, A. L., Wheatley, S, M., & Aldava, J. F., IV. (1992). Stages on life's way: Adolescents' implicit theories of the life course. *Journal of Adolescent Research, 7*, 364–381.

Hervieu-Leger, D. (1993). Present-day emotional renewals: The end of secularization or the end of religion? In W. H. Swatos (Ed.), *A future for religion? New paradigms for social analysis.* Thousand Oaks, CA: Sage.

Hoge, D., Dinges, W., Johnson, M., & Gonzales, J. (1998a, November). *Religious beliefs and practices of American young adult Catholics.* Paper presented at the annual meeting of the Religious Research Association, Montreal, Canada.

Hoge, D., Dinges, W., Johnson, M., & Gonzales, J. (1998b, November). *Young adult Catholics: Family and religious history and institutional identity.* Paper presented at the annual meeting of the Religious Research Association, Montreal, Canada.

Hoge, D., Johnson, B., & Luidens, D. A. (1993). Determinants of church involvement of young adults who grew up in Presbyterian churches. *Journal of the Scientific Study of Religion, 32*, 242–255.

Jensen, L. A. (1995). Habits of the Heart revisited: Autonomy, community and divinity in adults' moral language. *Qualitative Sociology, 18*, 71–86.

Larson, R. W., Richards, M. H., Moneta, G., Holmbeck, G., & Duckett, E. (1996). Changes in adolescents' daily interactions with their families from ages 10 to 18: Disengagement and transformation. *Developmental Psychology, 32*, 744–754.

Marcia, J. (1966). Development and validation of ego identity status. *Journal of Personality and Social Psychology, 3*, 551–558.

Roof, W. C. (1993). *A generation of seekers.* New York: HarperCollins.

Stolzenberg, R. M., Blair-Loy, M., & Waite, L. J. (1995). Religious participation in early adulthood: Age and family life cycle effects on church membership. *American Sociological Review, 60*, 84–103.

Wilson, J., & Sandomirsky, S. (1991). Religious affiliation and the family. *Sociological Forum, 6*, 289–309.

About the authors: Jeffrey Jensen Arnett is affiliated with the Department of Human Development at the University of Maryland. He is the author of a book on heavy metal fans, *Metalheads: Heavy Metal Music and Adolescent Alienation* (1996, Westview Press), and the textbook *Adolescence and Emerging Adulthood: A Cultural Approach* (2001, Prentice Hall). He is the chair of the Special Interest Group on Emerging Adulthood (www.s-r-a.org/easig.html) sponsored by the Society for Research on Adolescence.

Exercise for Article 44

Factual Questions

1. The researchers state that most studies on the religiosity of young people in their late teens and 20s have focused on what issue?

2. The researchers examined how many hypotheses?

3. What percentage of the participants was male?

4. Data collection took place where?

5. Were women *or* men more likely to indicate that it is important to them to attend religious services?

6. The researchers found that fathers' education was inversely related to participants believing that it is important to attend religious services. What is the value of *r* that is reported for this finding?

Questions for Discussion

7. Of the persons contacted, 72% agreed to participate in the study. Could the fact that this is less than 100% have had an effect on the results of this study? Explain. (See lines 154–155.)

8. The researchers provided all of the questions they used in full. Did having the questions help you understand the study? Explain. (See lines 160–167 and Table 2.)

9. The researchers state that "Perhaps it should not be so surprising that there is little relationship between childhood religious socialization and religious beliefs in emerging adulthood." (See lines 536–538.) To what extent do you agree with the statement? Explain.

10. In your opinion, was one approach (i.e., quantitative *or* qualitative) better suited for testing the hypotheses?

11. If you were conducting a follow-up study on this topic and could choose only one approach (i.e., quantitative *or* qualitative), which one would you choose?

Quality Ratings

Directions: Indicate your level of agreement with each of the following statements by circling a number from 5 for strongly agree (SA) to 1 for strongly disagree (SD). If you believe an item is not applicable to this research article, leave it blank. Be prepared to explain your ratings. When responding to criteria A and B below, keep in mind that brief titles and abstracts are conventional in published research.

A. The title of the article is appropriate.

SA   5   4   3   2   1   SD

B. The abstract provides an effective overview of the research article.

SA   5   4   3   2   1   SD

C. The introduction establishes the importance of the study.

SA   5   4   3   2   1   SD

D. The literature review establishes the context for the study.

SA   5   4   3   2   1   SD

E. The research purpose, question, or hypothesis is clearly stated.

SA   5   4   3   2   1   SD

F. The method of sampling is sound.

SA   5   4   3   2   1   SD

G. Relevant demographics (for example, age, gender, and ethnicity) are described.

SA   5   4   3   2   1   SD

H. Measurement procedures are adequate.

SA   5   4   3   2   1   SD

I. All procedures have been described in sufficient detail to permit a replication of the study.

SA   5   4   3   2   1   SD

J. The participants have been adequately protected from potential harm.

SA   5   4   3   2   1   SD

K. The results are clearly described.

SA   5   4   3   2   1   SD

L. The discussion/conclusion is appropriate.

SA   5   4   3   2   1   SD

M. Despite any flaws, the report is worthy of publication.

SA   5   4   3   2   1   SD

Article 45

Project D.A.R.E. Outcome
Effectiveness Revisited

STEVEN L. WEST
Virginia Commonwealth University

KERI K. O'NEAL
University of North Carolina, Chapel Hill

OBJECTIVES. We provide an updated meta-analysis on the effectiveness of Project D.A.R.E. in preventing alcohol, tobacco, and illicit drug use among school-aged youths.

METHODS. We used meta-analytic techniques to create an overall effect size for D.A.R.E. outcome evaluations reported in scientific journals.

RESULTS. The overall weighted effect size for the included D.A.R.E. studies was extremely small (correlation coefficient = 0.011; Cohen's d = 0.023; 95% confidence interval = –0.04, 0.08) and nonsignificant (z = 0.73, NS).

CONCLUSIONS. Our study supports previous findings indicating that D.A.R.E. is ineffective.

From *American Journal of Public Health*, *94*, 1027–1029. Copyright © 2004 by American Journal of Public Health. Reprinted with permission.

In the United States, Project D.A.R.E. (Drug Abuse Resistance Education) is one of the most widely used substance abuse prevention programs targeted at school-aged youths. In recent years, D.A.R.E. has been the country's largest single school-based prevention program in terms of federal expenditures, with an average of three-quarters of a billion dollars spent on its provision annually.[1] Although its effectiveness in preventing substance use has been called into question, its application in our nation's schools remains very extensive.[2-6]

Given the recent increases in alcohol and other drug use among high school and college students,[7] the continued use of D.A.R.E. and similar programs seems likely. In a meta-analysis examining the effectiveness of D.A.R.E., Ennett et al.[3] noted negligible yet positive effect sizes (ranging from 0.00 to 0.11) when outcomes occurring immediately after program completion were considered. However, this analysis involved 2 major limitations. First, Ennett et al. included research from nonpeer-reviewed sources, including annual reports produced for agencies associated with the provision of D.A.R.E. services. While such an inclusion does not necessarily represent a serious methodological flaw, use of such sources has been called into question.[8]

Second, Ennett and colleagues included only studies in which postintervention assessment was conducted immediately at program termination. As noted by Lynam et al.,[6] the developmental trajectories of drug experimentation and use vary over time. Thus, if individuals are assessed during periods in which rates of experimentation and use are naturally high, any positive effects that could be found at times of lower experimentation will be deflated. Likewise, assessments made during periods in which experimentation and use are slight will exaggerate the overall effect of the intervention.

Ideally, problems such as those just described could be solved by the use of large-scale longitudinal studies involving extensive follow-up over a period of years. There have been several longer-term follow-ups, but the cost of such efforts may limit the number of longitudinal studies that can be conducted. In the present analysis, we attempted to overcome this difficulty by including a wider range of follow-up reports, from immediate posttests to 10-year postintervention assessments, in an updated meta-analysis of all currently available research articles reporting an outcome evaluation of Project D.A.R.E.

Methods

We conducted computer searches of the *ERIC*, *MEDLINE*, and *PsycINFO* databases in late fall 2002 to obtain articles for the present study. In addition, we reviewed the reference lists of the acquired articles for other potential sources. We initially reviewed roughly 40 articles from these efforts; 11 studies appearing in the literature from 1991 to 2002 met our 3 inclusion criteria, which were as follows:

1. The research was reported in a peer-reviewed journal; reports from dissertations/theses, books, and unpublished manuscripts were not included. We selected this criterion in an attempt to ensure inclusion of only those studies with rigorous methodologies. As noted, a previous meta-analysis of Project D.A.R.E. included research from nonreviewed sources, a fact that critics have suggested may have added error to the reported findings.[8]

2. The research included a control or comparison group (i.e., the research must have involved an experimental or quasi-experimental design).

Table 1
Primary Articles Included in the Meta-Analysis

Study (year)	Sample	r	d	95% confidence interval
Ringwalt et al. (1991)[18]	5th and 6th graders (*n* = 1270; 52% female/48% male; 50% African American/40% Anglo/10% other), posttested immediately	0.025	0.056	−0.06, 0.16
Becker et al. (1992)[19]	5th graders (*n* = 2878), posttested immediately	−0.058	−0.117	−0.19, −0.04
Harmon (1993)[20]	5th graders (*n* = 708), posttested immediately	0.015	0.030	−0.12, 0.18
Ennett et al. (1994)[21]	7th and 8th graders (*n* = 1334; 54% Anglo/22% African American/9% Hispanic/15% other), 2 years post-D.A.R.E.	0.000	0.000[a]	−0.11, 0.11
Rosenbaum et al. (1994)[22]	6th and 7th graders (*n* = 1584; 49.7% female/50.3% male; 49.9% Anglo/24.7% African American/8.9% Hispanic/16.5% other), 1 year post-D.A.R.E.	0.000	0.000[a]	−0.10, 0.10
Wysong et al. (1994)[23]	12th graders (*n* = 619), 5 years post-D.A.R.E.	0.000	0.000[a]	−0.16, 0.16
Dukes et al. (1996)[24]	9th graders (*n* = 849), 3 years post-D.A.R.E.	0.035	0.072	−0.06, 0.21
Zagumny & Thompson (1997)[25]	6th graders (*n* = 395; 48% female/52% male), 4–5 years post-D.A.R.E.	0.184	0.376	0.07, 0.68
Lynam et al. (1999)[6]	6th graders (*n* = 1002; 57% female/43% male; 75.1% Anglo/20.4% African American/0.5% other), 10 years post-D.A.R.E.	0.000	0.000[a]	−0.15, 0.15
Thombs (2000)[26]	5th through 10th graders (*n* = 630; 90.4% Anglo/5.5% African American/4.1% other), posttested at least 1 to 6 years post-D.A.R.E.	0.025	0.038	−0.15, 0.23
Ahmed et al. (2002)[14]	5th and 6th graders (*n* = 236; 50% female/50% male/69% Anglo/24% African American/7% other), posttested immediately	0.198	0.405	0.01, 0.80

Note. r = correlation coefficient; *d* = difference in the means of the treatment and control conditions divided by the pooled standard deviation. Negative signs for *r* and *d* indicate greater effectiveness of control/comparison group.
[a]Assumed effect size.

3. The research included both preintervention and postintervention assessments of at least 1 of 3 key variables: alcohol use, illicit drug use, and tobacco use. We chose to include only those effect sizes that concerned actual substance use behaviors, since the true test of a substance use prevention effort is its impact on actual rates of use.

Using these criteria, we refined the original list of studies to 11 studies (Table 1). We calculated effect sizes using the procedures outlined by Rosenthal.[9] Meta-analysis results are commonly presented in the form of either a correlation coefficient (*r*) or the difference in the means of the treatment and control conditions divided by the pooled standard deviation (Cohen's *d*).[10] Since both are ratings of effect size, they can readily be converted to one another, and, if not provided in the original analyses, they can be calculated via F, *t*, and χ^2 statistics as well as means and standard deviations.[9]

We calculated both estimations for the individual included studies and for the overall analysis. As discussed by Amato and Keith,[11] tests of significance used in meta-analyses require that effect sizes be independent; therefore, if 2 or more effect sizes were generated within the same outcome category, we used the mean effect size. We also used the procedure for weighting effect sizes suggested by Shadish and Haddock[12] to ensure that all effect sizes were in the form of a common metric. In addition, we calculated 95% confidence intervals (CIs) for each study and for the overall analysis.

Results

The average weighted effect size (*r*) for all studies was 0.011 (*d* = 0.023; 95% CI = −0.04, 0.08), indicating marginally better outcomes for individuals participating in D.A.R.E. relative to participants in control conditions. The fact that the associated CI included a negative value indicates that the average effect size was not significantly greater than zero at *p* < .05. According to the guidelines developed by Cohen,[13] both of the effect sizes obtained were below the level normally considered small. Four of the included studies noted no effect of D.A.R.E. relative to control conditions, and 1 study noted that D.A.R.E. was less effective than the control condition.

Furthermore, the 6 reports indicating that D.A.R.E. had more positive effects were for the most part small (Figure 1). The largest effect size was found in a report in which the only outcome examined was smoking. Finally, we conducted a test of cumulative significance to determine whether differences existed between D.A.R.E. participants and non-D.A.R.E. participants. This test produced nonsignificant results (*z* = 0.73, NS).

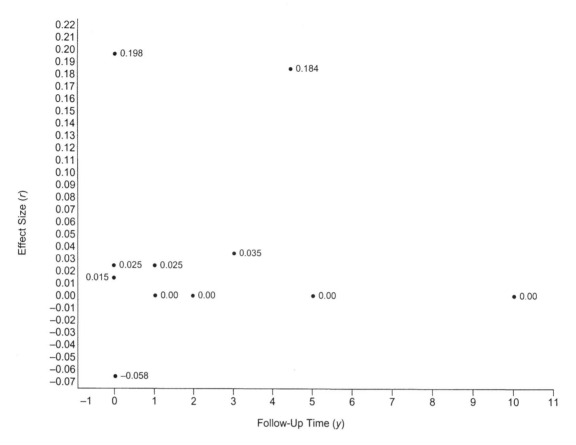

Figure 1. Plot of effect sizes, by follow-up time.

Discussion

Our results confirm the findings of a previous meta-analysis[3] indicating that Project D.A.R.E. is ineffective. This is not surprising, given the substantial information developed over the past decade to that effect. Critics of the present analysis might argue that, despite the magnitude of our findings, the direction of the effect of D.A.R.E. was generally positive. While this is the case, it should be emphasized that the effects we found did not differ significantly from the variation one would expect by chance. According to Cohen's guidelines,[13] the effect size we obtained would have needed to be 20 times larger to be considered even small. Given the tremendous expenditures in time and money involved with D.A.R.E., it would appear that continued efforts should focus on other techniques and programs that might produce more substantial effects.

Our findings also indicate that D.A.R.E. was minimally effective during the follow-up periods that would place its participants in the very age groups targeted. Indeed, no noticeable effects could be discerned in nearly half of the reports, including the study involving the longest follow-up period. This is an important consideration for those involved in program planning and development.

As noted earlier, progression in regard to experimentation and use varies over time. Use of alcohol and other drugs reaches a peak during adolescence or young adulthood and decreases steadily thereafter.[7,15] Such a developmental path would be expected of all individuals, regardless of their exposure to a prevention effort. Ideally, individuals enrolled in a program such as D.A.R.E. would report limited or no use during their adolescent and young adult years. The fact that half of the included studies reported no beneficial effect of D.A.R.E. beyond what would be expected by chance casts serious doubt on its utility.

One shortcoming of our analysis should be noted. In many of the studies we included, individual students were the unit of analysis in calculating effects. As noted by Rosenbaum and Hanson,[16] this practice tends to lead to overestimates of program effectiveness, since the true unit of analysis is the schools in which the students are "nested." Because our meta-analysis was limited to the types of data and related information available from the original articles, the potential for such inflation of program effectiveness exists. However, the overall effect sizes calculated here were small and nonsignificant, and thus it is unlikely that inclusion of studies making this error had a significant impact on the current findings.

An additional caveat is that all of the studies included in this analysis represent evaluations of what is commonly referred to as the "old D.A.R.E.": programs generally based on the original formulations of the D.A.R.E. model. In response to the many critiques of

the program, the D.A.R.E. prevention model was substantially revamped in 2001, thanks in part to a $13.6
180 million grant provided by the Robert Wood Johnson
Foundation.[17] The revisions to the model have since
given rise to programs working under the "new
D.A.R.E." paradigm. However, at the time of the writing of this article we were unable to find any major
185 evaluation of the new D.A.R.E. model in the research
literature, and the effectiveness of such efforts has yet
to be determined.

References

1. McNeal RB, Hanson WB. An examination of strategies for gaining convergent validity in natural experiments: D.A.R.E. as an illustrative case
study. *Eval Rev.* 1995:19:141–158.
2. Donnermeyer J, Wurschmidt T. Educators' perceptions of the D.A.R.E.
program. *J Drug Educ.* 1997;27:259–276.
3. Ennett ST, Tobler NS, Ringwalt CL, Flewelling RL. How effective is
Drug Abuse Resistance Education? A meta-analysis of Project D.A.R.E.
outcome evaluations. *Am J Public Health.* 1994;84:1394–1401.
4. Hanson WB. Pilot test results comparing the All Stars Program with
seventh-grade D.A.R.E.: Program integrity and mediating variable
analysis. *Subst Use Misuse.* 1996;31:1359–1377.
5. Hanson WB, McNeal RB. How D.A.R.E. works: An examination of
program effects on mediating variables. *Health Educ Behav.*
1997;24:165–176.
6. Lynam DR, Milich R, Zimmerman R, et al. Project D.A.R.E: No effects
at 10-year follow-up. *J Consult Clin Psychol.* 1999;67:590–593.
7. Johnston LD, O'Malley PM, Bachman JG. *National Survey Results on
Drug Use From the Monitoring the Future Study, 1975–1998. Volume 1:
Secondary School Students.* Rockville, Md: National Institute on Drug
Abuse; 1999. NIH publication 99–4660.
8. Gorman DM. The effectiveness of D.A.R.E. and other drug use prevention programs. *Am J Public Health.* 1995;85:873.
9. Rosenthal R. *Meta-Analytic Procedures for Social Research.* 2nd ed.
Thousand Oaks, Calif: Sage Publications; 1991.
10. DasEiden R, Reifman A. Effects of Brazelton demonstrations on later
parenting: A meta-analysis. *J Pediatr Psychol.* 1996;21:857–868.
11. Amato PH, Keith B. Parental divorce and well-being of children: A
meta-analysis. *Psychol Bull.* 1991;110:26–46.
12. Shadish WR, Haddock CK. Combining estimates of effect size. In: Cooper H, Hedges LV, eds. *The Handbook of Research Synthesis.* New
York. NY: Russell Sage Foundation; 1994:261–281.
13. Cohen J. *Statistical Power Analysis for the Behavioral Sciences.* 2nd ed.
Hillsdale, NJ: Lawrence Erlbaum Associates; 1998.
14. Ahmed NU, Ahmed NS, Bennett CR, Hinds JE. Impact of a drug abuse
resistance education (D.A.R.E.) program in preventing the initiation of
cigarette smoking in fifth- and sixth-grade students. *J Natl Med Assoc.*
2002;94:249–256.
15. Shedler J, Block J. Adolescent drug use and psychological health: A
longitudinal inquiry. *Am Psychol.* 1990;45:612–630.
16. Rosenbaum DP, Hanson GS. Assessing the effects of a school-based
drug education: A six-year multilevel analysis of Project D.A.R.E. *J Res
Crime Delinquency.* 1998;35:381–412.
17. Improving and evaluating the D.A.R.E. school-based substance abuse
prevention curriculum. Available at: http://www.rwjf.org/programs/
grantDetail.jsp?id=040371. Accessed January 8, 2003.
18. Ringwalt C, Ennett ST, Holt KD. An outcome evaluation of Project
D.A.R.E. (Drug Abuse Resistance Education). *Health Educ Res.*
1991;6:327–337.
19. Becker HK, Agopian MW, Yeh S. Impact evaluation of drug abuse resistance education (D.A.R.E.). *J Drug Educ.* 1992;22:283–291.
20. Harmon MA. Reducing the risk of drug involvement among early adolescents: An evaluation of drug abuse resistance education (D.A.R.E.).
Eval Rev. 1993;17:221–239.
21. Ennett ST, Rosenbaum DP, Flewelling RL, Bieler GS, Ringwalt CL,
Bailey SL. Long-term evaluation of drug abuse resistance education.
Addict Behav. 1994;19:113–125.
22. Rosenbaum DP, Flewelling RL, Bailey SL, Ringwalt CL, Wilkinson DL.
Cops in the classroom: A longitudinal evaluation of drug abuse resistance education (D.A.R.E.). *J Res Crime Delinquency.* 1994;31:3–31.
23. Wysong E, Aniskiewicz R, Wright D. Truth and D.A.R.E.: Tracking
drug education to graduation and as symbolic politics. *Soc Probl.*
1994;41:448–472.
24. Dukes RL, Ulllman JB, Stein JA. Three-year follow-up of drug abuse
resistance education (D.A.R.E.). *Eval Rev.* 1996;20:49–66.
25. Zagumny MJ, Thompson MK. Does D.A.R.E. work? An evaluation in
rural Tennessee. *J Alcohol Drug Educ.* 1997;42:32–41.
26. Thombs DL. A retrospective study of D.A.R.E.: Substantive effects not
detected in undergraduates. *J Alcohol Drug Educ.* 2000;46:27–40.

Acknowledgments: Portions of this research were presented at the
Eighth Annual Meeting of the Society for Prevention Research,
Montreal, Quebec, Canada, June 2000.

About the authors: *Steven L. West* is with the Department of Rehabilitation Counseling, Virginia Commonwealth University, Richmond. *Keri K. O'Neal* is with the Center for Developmental Science,
University of North Carolina, Chapel Hill. Drs. West and O'Neal
contributed equally to all aspects of study design, data analysis, and
the writing of this article. No protocol approval was needed for this
study.

Address correspondence to: Steven L. West, Ph.D., Virginia Commonwealth University, Department of Rehabilitation Counseling,
1112 East Clay St., Box 980330, Richmond, VA 23298-0330.
E-mail: slwest2@vcu.edu

Exercise for Article 45

Factual Questions

1. To identify the articles for this meta-analysis, the
researchers conducted computer searches of which
three databases?

2. Which study had the largest effect size (r)? (Identify it by the name of the author and year of publication.) What was the value of r in this study?

3. What was the average weighted effect size (r) for
all studies included in this meta-analysis?

4. The study with the largest effect size examined
only one outcome. What was the outcome?

5. According to Figure 1, the study with the longest
follow-up time had what effect size?

6. Were the researchers able to find any major
evaluations of the *new* D.A.R.E. paradigm?

Questions for Discussion

7. The researchers do not describe the D.A.R.E. program components. In your opinion, would it have
been desirable for them to do so? Explain.

8. What is your opinion of the researchers' decision
to include only research reported in peer-reviewed
journals? (See lines 58–66.)

9. What is your opinion of the researchers' decision
to include only evaluations that included a control
or comparison group? (See lines 67–69.)

10. Does it surprise you that the study by Becker et al. in Table 1 has negative effect sizes? Explain.

11. In Table 1, 95% confidence intervals are reported. What is your understanding of the meaning of these intervals?

12. What is your opinion on the researchers' suggestion in lines 134–138? Is your opinion based on the data in this meta-analysis? Explain.

Quality Ratings

Directions: Indicate your level of agreement with each of the following statements by circling a number from 5 for strongly agree (SA) to 1 for strongly disagree (SD). If you believe an item is not applicable to this research article, leave it blank. Be prepared to explain your ratings. When responding to criteria A and B below, keep in mind that brief titles and abstracts are conventional in published research.

A. The title of the article is appropriate.

    SA   5   4   3   2   1   SD

B. The abstract provides an effective overview of the research article.

    SA   5   4   3   2   1   SD

C. The introduction establishes the importance of the study.

    SA   5   4   3   2   1   SD

D. The literature review establishes the context for the study.

    SA   5   4   3   2   1   SD

E. The research purpose, question, or hypothesis is clearly stated.

    SA   5   4   3   2   1   SD

F. The method of sampling is sound.

    SA   5   4   3   2   1   SD

G. Relevant demographics (for example, age, gender, and ethnicity) are described.

    SA   5   4   3   2   1   SD

H. Measurement procedures are adequate.

    SA   5   4   3   2   1   SD

I. All procedures have been described in sufficient detail to permit a replication of the study.

    SA   5   4   3   2   1   SD

J. The participants have been adequately protected from potential harm.

    SA   5   4   3   2   1   SD

K. The results are clearly described.

    SA   5   4   3   2   1   SD

L. The discussion/conclusion is appropriate.

    SA   5   4   3   2   1   SD

M. Despite any flaws, the report is worthy of publication.

    SA   5   4   3   2   1   SD

Appendix A

Reading Research Reports: A Brief Introduction

DAVID A. SCHROEDER   DAVID E. JOHNSON   THOMAS D. JENSEN

To many students, the prospect of reading a research report in a professional journal elicits so much fear that no information is, in fact, transmitted. Such apprehension on the part of the reader is not necessary, and we
5 hope that this article will help students understand more clearly what such reports are all about and will teach them how to use these resources more effectively. Let us assure you that there is nothing mystical or magical about research reports, although they may be somewhat
10 more technical and precise in style, more intimidating in vocabulary, and more likely to refer to specific sources of information than are everyday mass media sources. However, once you get beyond these intimidating features, you will find that the vast majority of research
15 reports do a good job of guiding you through a project and informing you of important points of which you should be aware.

A scientific research report has but one purpose: to communicate to others the results of one's scientific
20 investigations. To ensure that readers will be able to appreciate fully the import and implications of the research, the author of the report will make every effort to describe the project so comprehensively that even a naïve reader will be able to follow the logic as he or she
25 traces the author's thinking through the project.

A standardized format has been developed by editors and authors to facilitate effective communication. The format is subject to some modification, according to the specific needs and goals of a particular author for
30 a particular article, but, in general, most articles possess a number of features in common. We will briefly discuss the six major sections of research articles and the purpose of each. We hope that this selection will help you take full advantage of the subsequent articles and to
35 appreciate their content as informed "consumers" of social psychological research.

Heading

The heading of an article consists of the title, the name of the author or authors, and their institutional affiliations. Typically, the title provides a brief descrip-
40 tion of the primary independent and dependent variables that have been investigated in the study. This information should help you begin to categorize the study into some implicit organizational framework that will help you keep track of the social psychological material. For
45 example, if the title includes the word *persuasion*, you should immediately recognize that the article will be related to the attitude-change literature, and you should prepare yourself to identify the similarities and differences between the present study and the previous litera-
50 ture.

The names of the authors may also be important to you for at least two reasons. First, it is quite common for social psychologists to use the names of authors as a shorthand notation in referring among themselves to
55 critical articles. Rather than asking, "Have you read 'Videotape and the attribution process: Reversing actors' and observers' points of view'?," it is much easier to say, "Have you read the Storms (1973) article?" In addition, this strategy gives the author(s) credit for the
60 material contained in the article. Second, you will find that most researchers actively pursue programs of research that are specific to a particular area of interest. For example, you will eventually be able to recognize that an article written by Albert Bandura is likely to be
65 about social learning processes, while an article by Leonard Berkowitz is probably going to discuss aggression and violence. Once you begin to identify the major researchers in each area, you will find that you will be able to go beyond the information presented within an
70 article and understand not only how a piece of research fits into a well-defined body of literature but also how it may be related to other less obvious topics.

Abstract

The Abstract is a short (often less than 150 words) preview of the contents of the article. The Abstract
75 should be totally self-contained and intelligible without any reference to the article proper. It should briefly convey a statement of the problem explored, the methods used, the major results of the study, and the conclusions reached. The Abstract helps to set the stage and to pre-
80 pare you for the article itself. Just as the title helps you place the article in a particular area of investigation, the Abstract helps pinpoint the exact question or questions to be addressed in the study.

Introduction

The Introduction provides the foundation for the

85 study itself and therefore for the remainder of the article. Thus, it serves several critical functions for the reader. First, it provides a context for the article and the study by discussing past literature that is relevant to and has implications for the present research. Second, it per-

90 mits a thorough discussion of the rationale for the research that was conducted and a full description of the independent and dependent variables that were employed. Third, it allows the hypotheses that were tested to be stated explicitly, and the arguments on which these

95 predictions were based to be elucidated. Each of these functions will be considered in detail.

The literature review that is typically the initial portion of the Introduction is not intended to provide a comprehensive restatement of all the published articles

100 that are tangentially relevant to the present research. Normally, a selective review is presented—one that carefully sets up the rationale of the study and identifies deficiencies in our understanding of the phenomena being investigated. In taking this approach, the author is

105 attempting to provide insights into the thought processes that preceded the actual conducting of the study. Usually, the literature review will begin by discussing rather broad conceptual issues (e.g., major theories, recognized areas of investigation) and will then gradually narrow its

110 focus to more specific concerns (e.g., specific findings from previous research, methods that have been employed). It may be helpful to think of the Introduction as a funnel, gradually drawing one's attention to a central point that represents the critical feature of the article.

115 Following the review of the past literature, the author typically presents the rationale for his or her own research. A research study may have one of several goals as its primary aim: (1) It may be designed to answer a question specifically raised by the previous lit-

120 erature but left unanswered. (2) It may attempt to correct methodological flaws that have plagued previous research and threaten the validity of the conclusions reached. (3) It may seek to reconcile conflicting findings that have been reported in the literature, typically

125 by identifying and/or eliminating confounding variables by exerting greater experimental control. (4) It may be designed to assess the validity of a scientific theory by testing one or more hypotheses that have been deduced or derived from that theory. (5) It may begin a novel

130 line of research that has not been previously pursued or discussed in the literature. Research pursuing any of these five goals may yield significant contributions to a particular field of inquiry.

After providing the rationale for the study, the au-

135 thor properly continues to narrow the focus of the article from broad conceptual issues to the particular variables that are to be employed in the study. Ideally, in experimental studies, the author clearly identifies the independent and dependent variables to be used; in correla-

140 tional studies, the predictor and criterion variables are specified. For those readers who do not have an extensive background in research methodology, a brief ex-

planation of experimental and correlational studies may be in order.

145 *Experimental studies.* An experimental study is designed to identify cause–effect relationships between independent variables that the experimenter systematically manipulates and the dependent variable that is used to measure the behavior of interest. In such a

150 study, the researcher controls the situation to eliminate or neutralize the effects of all extraneous factors that may affect the behavior of interest in order to assess more precisely the impact of the independent variables alone. In most instances, only the tightly controlled ex-

155 perimental method permits valid inferences of cause–effect relationships to be made.

Correlational studies. In some circumstances, the researcher cannot exert the degree of control over the situation that is necessary for a true experimental study.

160 Rather than giving up the project, the researcher may explore alternative methods that may still permit an assessment of his or her hypotheses and predictions. One such alternative is the correlational approach. In a correlational study, the researcher specifies a set of

165 measures that should be related conceptually to the display of a target behavior. The measure that is used to assess the target behavior is called the criterion variable; the measure from which the researcher expects to be able to make predictions about the criterion variable is

170 called the predictor variable. Correlational studies permit the researcher to assess the degree of relationship between the predictor variable(s) and the criterion variable(s), but inferences of cause-and-effect cannot be validly made because the effects of extraneous variables

175 have not been adequately controlled. Correlational studies are most frequently used in naturalistic or applied situations in which researchers must either tolerate the lack of control and do the best they can under the circumstances or give up any hope of testing their hy-

180 potheses.

After the discussion of these critical components of the study, the author explicitly states the exact predictions that the study is designed to test. The previous material should have set the stage sufficiently well for

185 you as a reader to anticipate what these hypotheses will be, but it is incumbent on the author to present them nonetheless. The wording of the hypotheses may vary, some authors preferring to state the predictions in conceptual terms (e.g., "The arousal of cognitive disso-

190 nance due to counterattitudinal advocacy is expected to lead to greater attitude change than the presentation of an attitude-consistent argument.") and others preferring to state their predictions in terms of the actual operationalizations that they employed (e.g., "Subjects who

195 received a \$1 incentive to say that an objectively boring task was fun are expected to subsequently evaluate the task as being more enjoyable than subjects who were offered a \$20 incentive to say that the task was interesting.").

200   In reading a research report, it is imperative that you pay attention to the relationship between the initial literature review, the rationale for the study, and the statement of the hypotheses. In a well-conceived and well-designed investigation, each section will flow logi-
205   cally from the preceding one; the internal consistency of the author's arguments will make for smooth transitions as the presentation advances. If there appear to be discontinuities or inconsistencies throughout the author's presentation, it would be wise to take a more critical
210   view of the study—particularly if the predictions do not seem to follow logically from the earlier material. In such cases, the author may be trying to present as a prediction a description of the findings that were unexpectedly uncovered when the study was being conducted.
215   Although there is nothing wrong with reporting unexpected findings in a journal article, the author should be honest enough to identify them as what they really are. As a reader, you should have much more confidence in the reliability of predictions that obtain than you do in
220   data that can be described by postdictions only.

Method

To this point, the author has dealt with the study in relatively abstract terms, and has given little attention to the actual procedures used in conducting it. In the Method section, the author at last describes the opera-
225   tionalizations and procedures that were employed in the investigation. There are at least two reasons for the detailed presentation of this information. First, such a presentation allows interested readers to reconstruct the methodology used, so that a replication of the study can
230   be undertaken. By conducting a replication using different subject populations and slightly different operationalizations of the same conceptual variables, more information can be gained about the validity of the conclusions that the original investigator reached. Second,
235   even if a replication is not conducted, the careful description of the method used will permit you to evaluate the adequacy of the procedures employed.

The Method section typically comprises two or more subsections, each of which has a specific function to
240   fulfill. Almost without exception, the Method section begins with a subject subsection, consisting of a complete description of the subjects who participated in the study.[1] The number of subjects should be indicated, and there should be a summary of important demographic
245   information (e.g., numbers of male and female subjects, age) so that you can know to what populations the findings can be reasonably generalized. Sampling techniques that were used to recruit subjects and incentives used to induce volunteering should also be clearly speci-
250   fied. To the extent that subject characteristics are of primary importance to the goals of the research, greater

detail is presented in this subsection, and more attention should be directed to it.

A procedures subsection is also almost always in-
255   cluded in the Method section. This subsection presents a detailed account of the subjects' experiences in the experiment. Although other formats may also be effective, the most common presentation style is to describe the subjects' activities in chronological order. A thorough
260   description of all questionnaires administered or tasks completed is given, as well as any other features that might be reasonably expected to affect the behavior of the subjects in the study.

After the procedures have been discussed, a full de-
265   scription of the independent variables in an experimental study, or predictor variables in a correlational study, is typically provided. Verbatim description of each of the different levels of each independent variable is presented, and similar detail is used to describe each pre-
270   dictor variable. This information may be included either in the procedures subsection or, if the description of these variables is quite lengthy, in a separate subsection.

After thoroughly describing these variables, the author usually describes the dependent variables in an
275   experimental study, and the criterion variables in a correlational study. The description of the dependent and/or criterion variables also requires a verbatim specification of the exact operationalizations that were employed. When appropriate and available, information about the
280   reliability and validity of these measures is also presented. In addition, if the investigator has included any questions that were intended to allow the effectiveness of the independent variable manipulation to be assessed, these manipulation checks are described at this point.
285   All of this information may be incorporated in the procedures subsection or in a separate subsection.

After you have read the Method section, there should be no question about what has been done to the subjects who participated in the study. You should try to
290   evaluate how representative the methods that were used were of the conceptual variables discussed in the Introduction. Manipulation checks may help to allay one's concerns, but poorly conceived manipulation checks are of little or no value. Therefore, it is important for you as
295   a reader to remember that you are ultimately responsible for the critical evaluation of any research report.

Results

Once the full methodology of the study has been described for the reader, the author proceeds to report the results of the statistical analyses that were conducted on
300   the data. The Results section is probably the most intimidating section for students to read, and often the most difficult section for researchers to write. You are typically confronted with terminology and analytical techniques with which you are at best unfamiliar, or at
305   worst totally ignorant. There is no reason for you to feel bad about this state of affairs; as a neophyte in the world of research, you cannot expect mastery of all phases of

---

[1] *Editor's note*: Many researchers prefer the terms *participants* or *respondents* to the term *subjects.*

310 research from the start. Even experienced researchers are often exposed to statistical techniques with which they are unfamiliar, requiring them either to learn the techniques or to rely on others to assess the appropriateness of the procedure. For the student researcher, a little experience and a conscientious effort to learn the basics will lead to mastery of the statistical skills necessary.

315   The author's task is similarly difficult. He or she is attempting to present the findings of the study in a straightforward and easily understood manner, but the presentation of statistical findings does not always lend itself readily to this task. The author must decide

320 whether to present the results strictly within the text of the article or to use tables, graphs, and figures to help convey the information effectively. Although the implications of the data may be clear to the researcher, trying to present the data clearly and concisely so that the

325 reader will also be able to discern the implications is not necessarily assured. In addition, the author is obligated to present all the significant results obtained in the statistical analyses, not just the results that support the hypotheses being tested. Although this may clutter the

330 presentation and detract from the simplicity of the interpretation, it must be remembered that the researcher's primary goal is to seek the truth, not to espouse a particular point of view that may not be supported by the data.

Discussion

335   The Discussion section is the part of the manuscript in which the author offers an evaluation and interpretation of the findings of the study, particularly as they relate to the hypotheses that were proposed in the Introduction. Typically, the author will begin this section

340 with a brief review of the major findings of the study and a clear statement of whether the data were consistent or inconsistent with the hypotheses. The discussion will then address any discrepancies between the predictions and the data, trying to resolve these inconsisten-

345 cies and offering plausible reasons for their occurrence. In general, the first portion of the Discussion is devoted to an evaluation of the hypotheses that were originally set forward in the Introduction, given the data that were obtained in the research.

350   The Discussion may be seen as the inverse of the Introduction, paralleling the issues raised in that section in the opposite order of presentation. Therefore, after discussing the relationship of the data with the hypotheses, the author often attempts to integrate the new findings

355 into the body of research that provided the background for the study. Just as this literature initially provided the context within which you can understand the rationale for the study, it subsequently provides the context within which the data can be understood and inter-

360 preted. The author's responsibility at this point is to help you recognize the potential import of the research, without relying on hype or gimmicks to make the point.

The Discussion continues to expand in terms of the breadth of ideas discussed until it reaches the broad,

365 conceptual issues that are addressed by the superordinate theoretical work that originally stimulated the past research literature. If a particular piece of research is to make a significant contribution to the field, its findings must either clarify some past discrepancy in the litera-

370 ture, identify boundary conditions for the applicability of the critical theoretical work, reconcile differences of opinion among the researchers in the field, or otherwise contribute to a more complete understanding of the mechanisms and mediators of important social phenom-

375 ena.

Once the author has reached the goals that are common to most journal articles, attention may be turned to less rigorous ideas. Depending on a particular journal's editorial policy and the availability of additional space,

380 the author may finish the article with a brief section about possible applications of the present work, implications for future work in the area, and with some restraint, speculations about what lies ahead for the line of research. Scientists tend to have relatively little toler-

385 ance for conclusions without foundation and off-the-cuff comments made without full consideration. Therefore, authors must be careful not to overstep the bounds of propriety in making speculations about the future. But such exercises can be useful and can serve a

390 heuristic function for other researchers if the notions stated are well conceived.

Finally, particularly if the article has been relatively long or complex, the author may decide to end it with a short Conclusion. The Conclusion usually simply re-

395 states the major arguments that have been made throughout the article, reminding the reader one last time of the value of the work.

As we suggested earlier, not all articles will follow the format exactly. Some latitude is allowed to accom-

400 modate the particular needs of the author and the quirks of the research being described. Given that the goal is effective communication of information, it would not be reasonable for the format to dictate what could and could not be included in a manuscript. We hope that this

405 introduction will help to demystify research articles and provide you with some insights into what an author is trying to accomplish at various points in the report. Let us end with a word of encouragement: Your enjoyment of social psychology will be enhanced by your fuller

410 appreciation of the sources of the information to which you are being exposed, and, to the extent that you are able to read and understand these original sources for yourself, your appreciation of this work will be maximized.

Reference

Storms, M. D. (1973). Videotape and the attribution process: Reversing actors' and observers' points of view. *Journal of Personality and Social Psychology, 27*, 165–175.

Exercise for Appendix A

Factual Questions

1. What four elements should the Abstract convey?

2. Which part of a report provides the "foundation" for the study and the remainder of the article?

3. Normally, should the literature review be selective *or* comprehensive?

4. If there is a research hypothesis, should it be explicitly stated in the Introduction?

5. Are experimental *or* correlational studies better for making inferences about cause-and-effect?

6. What is a *criterion variable* in a correlational study?

7. Which part of a report describes the operationalizations and procedures employed in the study?

8. The Method section usually begins with a description of what?

9. According to the authors, what is probably the most intimidating section of a research report for students?

10. Should experienced researchers expect to find statistical techniques with which they are unfamiliar when they read research reports?

11. How should the Discussion section of a research report typically begin?

12. Which part of a report usually simply restates the major arguments that have been made throughout the article?

Notes:

Notes:

Notes:

Notes:

Notes:

Notes:

Notes: